WRISTWATCH ANNUAL

2015

THE CATALOG

of

PRODUCERS, PRICES, MODELS,

and

SPECIFICATIONS

BY PETER BRAUN

ABBEVILLE PRESS PUBLISHERS

New York   London

Senator Perpetual Calendar

www.glashuette-original.com

Senator Perpetual Calendar. Precision and art united in a true classic. This superb achievement in the art of making mechanical watches has excited connoisseurs for many years now. Our watchmakers have ensured that this enthusiasm will continue through the year 2100.

Contents

A

A. Lange & Söhne..........................46
Alpina...52
Aquadive.......................................54
Anonimo..56
Aristo...57
Armin Strom..................................58
Arnold & Son 60
ArtyA..62
Audemars Piguet..........................64
Azimuth...70

B

Ball Watch Co. 72
Baume & Mercier 76
Bell & Ross 78
Ernst Benz...................................148
Benzinger.......................................80
Blancpain.......................................82
Borgward..87
Bovet..88
Breguet...90
Breitling..94
Bremont..98
BRM..100
Carl F. Bucherer...........................106
Bulgari..102

C

Carl F. Bucherer...........................106
Cartier...110
Chanel...116
Chopard...117
Christiaan van der Klaauw 122
Christophe Claret 123
Chronoswiss.................................124
Corum...128
Cuervo y Sobrinos 131
Cvstos 132

D

D. Dornblüth & Sohn....................134
Davosa..135
De Bethune...................................137
de Grisogono 138
DeWitt...139
Dodane 1857................................141
Doxa..142
Roger Dubuis................................296

E

Eberhard & Co..............................144
Edox..146
Epos..147
Ernst Benz....................................148
Erwin Sattler.................................150
Eterna 151

F

Fortis...154
Franck Muller 156
François-Paul Journe....................158
Frédérique Constant.....................160

G

Genesis...162
Girard-Perregaux 164
Glashütte Original 168
Graham..174
Greubel Forsey 176

H

H. Moser & Cie. 178
Habring² 180
Hamilton 182
Hanhart...184
Harry Winston...............................186
Hautlence 188
Hermès..190
Hublot..192

I

Itay Noy...196
IWC..198

J

Jaeger-LeCoultre..........................204
Jaquet Droz...................................210
Jeanrichard...................................212
Romain Jerome 306
Jörg Schauer.................................213
François-Paul Journe....................158
Urban Jürgensen & Sønner 336
Juvenia..214

K

Kobold...216
Kudoke..218

L

Maurice Lacroix............................228
A. Lange & Söhne...........................46
Linde Werdelin 219
Longines 220
Louis Moinet.................................223
Louis Vuitton.................................224

M

Maîtres du Temps 226
Maurice Lacroix............................228
MB&F 232
Meccaniche Veloci 233
MeisterSinger 234
Richard Mille 294
Milus 236
Mk II 238
Louis Moinet.................................223
Montana Watch Co. 239
Montblanc.....................................240
H. Moser & Cie. 178
Mühle-Glashütte...........................244
Franck Muller 156

N

Ulysse Nardin 332
Nienaber Bünde...........................246
Thomas Ninchritz 323
Nivrel..247
Nomos...248
Itay Noy...196

O

Omega 252
Oris 258

P

Panerai..262
Parmigiani.....................................266
Patek Philippe 270
Paul Picot......................................278
Perrelet 280
Peter Speake-Marin 282
Piaget..284
Porsche Design 288

R

Rado 290
RGM 292
Richard Mille 294
Roger Dubuis................................296
Rolex 300
Romain Jerome 306

S

Erwin Sattler.................................150
Jörg Schauer.................................213
Schaumburg Watch......................308
Seiko 310
Sinn..312
Peter Speake-Marin 282
Stowa 316
Armin Strom...................................58

T

TAG Heuer.....................................318
Temption 322
Thomas Ninchritz 323
Tissot...324
Towson Watch Co. 326
Tudor 328
Tutima 330

U

Ulysse Nardin 332
Urban Jürgensen & Sønner 336
Urwerk...337
UTS..338

V

Vacheron Constantin 340
Christiaan van der Klaauw 122
Victorinox Swiss Army 346
Vogard...348
Vostok-Europe..............................349
Louis Vuitton.................................224
Vulcain 351

W

Wempe 352
Harry Winston...............................186

Z

Zeitwinkel......................................354
Zenith 355

Movement manufacturers

Concepto 360
ETA 361
Sellita 366
Soprod...368

Editorial

Letter to the Reader........................6
Independent Watchmaking............12
Closely Watched Watches 22
Watch Tech:
Revolution in the Balance 32
The Chronograph
Challenge in Time..........................36
Chronographs:
Technical Insights
and Technicalities..........................42
Watch Your Watch 374
Glossary...376
Masthead.......................................384

TO BREAK THE RULES,
YOU MUST FIRST MASTER
THEM.

THE ROYAL OAK CONCEPT SERIES CONTINUES TO PUSH THE
BOUNDARIES OF AUDEMARS PIGUET SAVOIR-FAIRE. THIS
CONCEPT GMT TOURBILLON, WITH DUAL TIME FUNCTION,
FEATURES WHITE CERAMIC BEZEL, CROWN, PUSHER AND
BRIDGE. NINE TIMES HARDER THAN STEEL, CERAMIC IS
EXCEPTIONALLY DIFFICULT TO WORK, YET HERE IT IS FINELY
BRUSHED AND POLISHED AS IF IT WERE PRECIOUS METAL.

THE COMPLEX FORM OF THE CASE IS MILLED FROM A SOLID
BLOCK OF TITANIUM. THE INDIVIDUAL FACETS ARE THEN
MICRO SAND BLASTED TO ACHIEVE THE DISTINCTIVE MATT
GRAINING. AUDACIOUS STYLING, PEERLESS CRAFTSMANSHIP.

ROYAL OAK
CONCEPT GMT
TOURBILLON
IN TITANIUM,
WHITE CERAMIC BEZEL.

AUDEMARS PIGUET
Le Brassus

AUDEMARS PIGUET BOUTIQUES. 646.375.0807
NEW YORK: 65 EAST 57TH STREET, NY. 888.214.6858
BAL HARBOUR: BAL HARBOUR SHOPS, FL. 866.595.9700
AUDEMARSPIGUET.COM

Dear Reader

O ne of the goals of *Wristwatch Annual* is to deliver a snapshot of the trends in mechanical watches. It would be tempting to simply report to you "different year, more of the same," but that would not do justice to the very real dynamism of an industry that continues to expand and evolve.

The Federation of the Swiss Watch Industry recorded growth of over 3 percent in April 2014, and expectations are for a prosperous year. The sustained revenue of the past years has driven companies to increase production capacities by building new facilities and hiring more personnel. Some of this expansion is a natural outcome of Swatch's ETA announcing it would restrict its formerly indiscriminate sale of movements to anyone who wanted to make a watch. The late Nicolas Hayek Senior, sire of the Swatch Group, may well have been right when he forecast that this would lead to a reindustrialization of the watch world. Brands that are too small to build their own movements are becoming good customers of the other firms, such as La Joux-Perret, Sellita, Soprod, Concepto, and Technotime.

This boom has maintained momentum and reached a symbiotic equilibrium between design and engineering.

One of the more notable aesthetic trends falls under the rubric of retro-vintage-classic. For brands with deep roots, this has obviously involved digging around the archives and dusting off old models (see Tudor, for example). Others with less history have had to be creative, while still others have always come up with timepieces our great-grandfathers would have found perfectly acceptable.

This horological redux fits well with the post-recession Age of Reason and the staggering rise of the Asian markets, notably China. Having abandoned their slightly irritating sycophancy vis-à-vis the Middle Kingdom, many brands set out to educate young Chinese consumers by supplying beautiful, classical pieces with discreet complications (Moser's Endeavours are an excellent example).

The other burgeoning trend is color. More and more timepieces are being spruced up with hands, bezels, or subsidiary dials in strong reds, blues, greens, yellows . . . Timepieces are increasingly offered with boldly colorful straps in traditional leather, rubber, or silicon. Modern materials are important as they often give the new hues greater vibrancy (see Omega's bright orange ceramic bezel).

Finally, the industry has taken to heart that the sartorial appetite of women extends to watches. The girlish pieces with big roundish numerals and soft edges have their place, but so do robust mechanical watches with complications, with or without precious

THE WEMPE CHRONOMETERWERKE
GLASHÜTTE I/SA – TOURBILLON

PRECISION – MADE IN GERMANY

 The world's only officially certified Chronometer Tourbillon, handcrafted in Glashütte, the German center for fine watchmaking. Tested in accordance with the DIN standard, with twin-barrel movement, 40 hour power reserve in platinum. Limited to 25 pieces worldwide.

WEMPE

EXQUISITE TIMEPIECES & JEWELRY
ESTABLISHED 1878

700 FIFTH AVENUE & 55TH STREET · NEW YORK · 212.397.9000
Hamburg Berlin Munich Dusseldorf Frankfurt London Madrid Paris Vienna Beijing
OPEN SUNDAYS 12 TO 5

stones. Look at the female wrists at Baselworld or the SIHH, what do you see?

In sum, there is energy and creativity brewing in an industry that is consolidating into groups and looking to its tradition of excellence and the *métiers d'art* (enameling, guilloché, marquetry, and so forth) for inspiration. This entropy, as it were, may be reaching a critical level, however, at which point the aesthetics could switch from refreshing to contrived and then fail to satisfy consumers. In addition, the world economy is still very unsteady, not the best playing field for an emotional industry like luxury goods. Or has Swatch, with its extremely simple Sistem51, once again thrown a monkey wrench into the machinery? Food for thought, perhaps.

This is the backdrop for this year's *Wristwatch Annual*, in which you will find the big, the beautiful, the brilliant, the bashful, the trenders, the trendees, the trendsetters, and those who chart a very individual course, from the majestic output of Greubel and Forsey to the richly minimalistic Nomos. The excellent developments among American brands are also documented in the work of RGM, Kobold, and Towson, among others.

In the editorial pages, the peripatetic Elizabeth Doerr tours the independents for us (page 12), while I report on serendipitous encounters with professionals and dreamers who are inventing special timepieces (page 22). In this edition we'll also explore technical or historical aspects of watchmaking to give a better knowledge of the industry and understanding of the product. So in addition to the Glossary and the Dos and Don'ts at the end of the book, you will find an article by Watchonista.com's editor in chief Joël Grandjean on silicon (page 32) and how it went from substitute material in balances to key player, as in the Girard-Perregaux Constant Escapement L.M. and the new Ulysse Nardin Anchor Escapement. Another article (page 36) under the heading Watch Insights explores the chronograph through the insights of a group of writers, including watchmaker Bill Yao (Mk II), Joël Grandjean, and myself.

Finally, there are many people to thank. First, thanks go to Peter Braun, for his preparation of the German edition, and Ashley Benning, for proofing the copy quickly and expertly, catching errors and tightening rambling thoughts. And my deepest gratitude goes to all the people at the brands who take the time to check prices and information while respecting our editorial independence. Any comments or suggestions are welcome, as they will help us improve the book next year.

As always, bear in mind that the prices given in these pages are subject to change.

Enjoy reading.

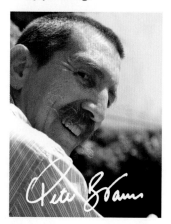

Peter Braun   Marton Radkai

This year's Wristwatch Annual *cover showcases the stainless steel*

Saxon One Chronograph *from the "Made in Glashütte" collection by Tutima. This automatic is driven by the Tutima Caliber 521 and features hours, minutes, subsidiary seconds, and date. The chronograph, activated by two discreet pushers, has a sweep minute hand and a 12- and 24-hour totalizer. The case has a screw-in crown, is water-resistant to 20 atm, and comes with a reptile skin strap.*

/RITUALS
OF TIME/

Salthora
The new jumping hour
from MeisterSinger

—

www.meistersinger.net

MeisterSinger
MeisterSinger

Bell & Ross

TIME INSTRUMENTS

Independent Watchmaking

Elizabeth Doerr

The independents are coming on stronger every year now, both in terms of inventiveness and sheer numbers. More young mavericks are popping out of the woodwork all the time, and the experienced master watchmakers keep honing their considerable skills with each passing year.

Take Ressence. Though not "old" by any stretch of the imagination—founder **Benoît Mintiens** is just forty-two—this Belgian super-independent only gets better with his maturing experience in the world of horology. Neither watchmaker nor engineer, Mintiens nevertheless ingeniously conceived and completed the technical drafts for the complicated module needed to make his original "platform" time display function. Last year's Type 3 Le Scaphandrier was simply ingenious.

He used his experiences from the Type 3, ZeroSeries and SeriesOne models, to come up with the **Type 1**, which is practically an evolution incorporating the best of all worlds. From the outside, it looks very similar to his previous timepieces. On the inside, however, much has changed, mostly to benefit production processes and later care and servicing. In addition, the crown has disappeared to be replaced with wind-

ing and setting via the back bezel. This lends the timepiece a much more organic look and provides Mintiens with the satisfaction of knowing that the 42 mm titanium timepiece is exactly what he wanted it to be.

The Type 3 was honored by the 2013 Grand Prix d'Horlogerie de Genève with the Horological Revelation Prize.

A BEAUTIFUL CASE FOR TECHNOLOGY

Another winner of the 2013 Grand Prix d'Horlogerie de Genève was Le Sentier-based **Romain Gauthier**, who picked up the Men's Complication Watch Prize for the Logical One, while AHCI member **Kari Voutilainen** took home the prize for the best men's watch for the V-8R.

In 2014 Gauthier extended his edgy line with the artful **Logical One Secret**, which fuses technology and craftsmanship. A hinged red gold cover hides the gorgeous mechanics of the intelligent chain-and-fusée mechanism providing constant force to the movement. This cover is not only practical, but beautifully illustrates the art of gem setting. A total of 181 invis-

Horological firebrand Benoît Mintiens continues seeking an ultramodern aesthetic and technical solutions for his unique watches: Type 1 wows again.

ibly set, baguette-cut diamonds amounting to 6.9 carats add brilliance to the cover, case, and strap lugs. This microcosm of details is housed in a 43 mm red gold case, whose button winds the watch.

Magical, mysterious, and complex: Romain Gauthier's Logical One Secret opens onto complex mechanical vistas.

Japan meets Voutilainen in the flowery Oukamon.

A lot less is a lot more, proven by Vincent Calabrese's Régulus.

Voutilainen continues to extend his highly limited line of lacquer-dialed timepieces. Joining forces with the **Unryuan** studio in Japan, Voutilainen uses one-of-a-kind dials to top off his equally fascinating horological art. The dial, just like the manually wound movement containing Voutilainen's own escapement, takes months to complete. The latest in the line is a timepiece called **Oukamon**, which sees both teams of artisans contributing their traditional crafts to make a functional object of exceptional beauty. Inspired by the look of cherry blossoms, this limited series of twenty-five unique pieces are housed in a 37 mm white gold case.

CREATIVE CLUB

While on the subject of the AHCI, the association has been very busy again this year, with a host of new horological projects completed.

Cofounder **Vincent Calabrese** led the way with two original products, the first of which is simultaneously an homage to one of the most creative clockmakers in recent history, Jean Kazès. Calabrese, acting as both custodian and collaborator, carries on Kazès's work with "mechanical sculptures," this year with the Explorer, a small-series, mechanical, steel-and-brass, key-wound clock with an eight-day

power reserve that displays the hours and minutes.

Calabrese also produced a new wristwatch celebrating his own history. The **Régulus** is a purist rendition of a tourbillon that fascinates the eye in its 36 mm case of beveled sapphire crystal, which contains a minimalist, hand-wound movement in either 18 kt white or yellow gold as the future owner desires.

Like Benoît Mintiens discussed earlier, Zurich-based AHCI member **Marc Jenni** also makes a timepiece that is outfitted with a clever turning ring that eliminates the need for a crown. In 2014 he introduced new versions of the **Prologue WDT** boasting silver and copper-colored dials, thereby extending his current collection of 44 mm automatic timepieces with a few new beauties.

Marc Jenni leaves the crown and moves onto the dial with his Prologue WDT collection.

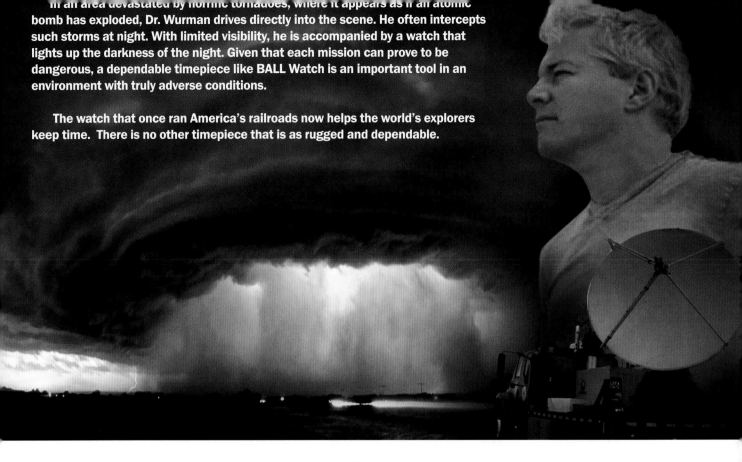

In an area devastated by horrific tornadoes, where it appears as if an atomic bomb has exploded, Dr. Wurman drives directly into the scene. He often intercepts such storms at night. With limited visibility, he is accompanied by a watch that lights up the darkness of the night. Given that each mission can prove to be dangerous, a dependable timepiece like BALL Watch is an important tool in an environment with truly adverse conditions.

The watch that once ran America's railroads now helps the world's explorers keep time. There is no other timepiece that is as rugged and dependable.

"Let there be light."

Dr. Josh Wurman
- Meteorologist and Creator of the Doppler Radar on Wheels

Chronograph with accumulated measurement up to 12 hours

Telemeter

Aluminium top bezel

5,000Gs shock resistance

Self-powered micro gas lights on hands and dial that glow for up to 25 years

100m water resistance

Sapphire crystal case back

Fireman Storm Chaser Pro
Automatic - 42mm

BALL
OFFICIAL RR STANDARD
Since 1891

Since 1891, accuracy under adverse conditions

BALL Watch USA   **www.ballwatch.com**

Functionality galore: the Tourbillon Astronomique by Martin Braun takes the wearer to the stars and back.

REACHING THE STARS

Antoine Martin's founder, master watch-maker **Martin Braun**, celebrates a milestone birthday with a masterpiece of a watch: the **Tourbillon Astronomique**. After successfully creating a reliable *manufacture* movement to serve as the base, he combined it with a plethora of astronomical complications and a beautiful tourbillon. The functions as seen on the front of the watch include a display of sunrise and sunset customized to the wearer's geographical location, a display of zodiac and season, the date, the equation of time, and a retrograde moon with a moon phase display and day/night indication. On the back there are three further displays: power reserve, declination (in degrees and graphically), and polar shadow line.

This sounds terribly complicated, and indeed it is. Braun, however, was adamant about producing a very user-friendly timepiece. So, the sunrise/sunset, zodiac, season, equation of time, and display of declination are all set via the crown. Only the date and moon phase need to be adjusted using a corrector recessed into the 46 mm rose gold case.

SAXON BALANCE

Marco Lang and his boutique brand Lang & Heyne rest in the cradle of Saxon watch-making in Dresden. Thus, the owner and master watchmaker follows certain horological traditions that reflect this special status. His latest oeuvre, **Augustus I**, is therefore typically named for the Saxon prince-elector whose love of art and mechanics laid the cornerstone for Dresden's world-famous museum collections. This new watch, inspired by an invention of Dutch aficionado John Twaalfhoven, was originally conceived as a one-off creation, but went on to become the most complicated and expensive model in the regular collection. No more than three can be manufactured per year. The hand-wound Caliber VII contains more than 340 exquisitely finished components, including those comprising the "calculator" that performs this watch's special function: indicating a specific event (such as a birthday) through several windows showing the name, age (two digits), and specific date including month and year. Housed in a 44 mm rose gold case, it is fully customizable.

Classic and noble, Marco Lang's Augustus I honors Saxony's greatest monarch and remembers birthdays.

The spirit of exploration cannot be confined. It goes where no man has dared to go before, to redefine the frontiers of achievement. The pioneer heads where his inner compass points him. He takes the road less traveled, to scale new heights of endurance and endeavor.

The watch that once ran America's railroads now helps the world's explorers keep time, from the top of the world to the bottom of the sea. There is no other timepiece that is as rugged and dependable.

"Let there be light."

Anti-reflective
sapphire crystal

5,000Gs
Shock resistance

4,800A/m
Anti-magnetic

Self-powered micro
gas lights on hands
and dial that glow
for up to 25 years

100m/330ft
water resistance

Engineer II Marvelight
Automatic - 40mm

BALL
OFFICIAL RR STANDARD
Since 1891

Since 1891, accuracy under adverse conditions

BALL Watch USA   www.ballwatch.com

Andreas Strehler's Sauterelle à Lune Perpétuelle displays the moon's rising and setting for almost fifteen million years.

Time and its many symbols animate Konstantin Chaykin's Carpe Diem.

LUNATIC FRINGE

Andreas Strehler presented a new watch at Baselworld that extends his attractive Sauterelle line: the **Sauterelle à Lune Perpétuelle.** It boasts deadbeat seconds and constant force using a *remontoir d'égalité*—which assures that the escape wheel receives the same amount of energy once per second, making for a much more accurate wristwatch. But it features another even more remarkable element: the world's most accurate moon phase. In fact, it will only need correcting every 14,189.538 years, to be precise. He chose the name Sauterelle (French for grasshopper) because of the movements the *remontoir* makes.

OF MYTHS AND LEGENDS

Russian watchmaker **Konstantin Chaykin** produced the insanely deep **Carpe Diem** watch this year. Its idea is to depict the abstract concept of time using classic metaphors from the books, music, and art that are traditionally accepted by scholars as the most influential in shaping Western culture. The symbols included in the design of this particular timepiece are inspired by the works of German Renaissance painter Bartholomäus Bruyn the Elder, Dutch Golden Age painter Pieter Claesz, and Ukrainian painter Heorhiy Narbut. The main character on the Carpe Diem dial is the Greek god Chronos (also known as Father Time). The technical innovation here is a patented mechanism that creates the illusion of sand flowing through an hourglass. The motion of the sand serves as the minute indicator. It also displays the day of the week using the appropriate astrological sign. The Carpe Diem is limited to just five pieces.

Chaykin, as usual, has created a very clever, extremely thoughtful timepiece that is both mechanically innovative and artfully meaningful. And while it is not exclusively the domain of the AHCI and other independent watchmakers to produce such thought-provoking, aesthetically pleasing masterpieces, these creative mavericks are surely on the cutting edge of what is possible in these areas of horology.

Elizabeth Doerr is a freelance journalist specializing in watches and was senior editor of Wristwatch Annual *until the 2010 edition. She is now the editor in chief of* Quill & Pad, *an online magazine that "keeps a watch on time." http://quillandpad.com*

Cellini Jewelers

Why do we love watches?

For some, it's a physical attraction to the look and feel. For others, it's an intellectual fascination with the machinery of time. Whether you appreciate a well-designed dial, a beautifully constructed movement, or both, Cellini Jewelers understands your passion. That's why its Manhattan boutiques offer one of the most extensive selections of timepieces from the world's best watchmakers.

That incredible depth is what separates Cellini, and allows it to create an unparalleled experience for aficionados. Between its stores in the Hotel Waldorf-Astoria and on Madison Avenue, Cellini has the ability to satisfy nearly every request, says Leon Adams, founder and president of Cellini. "It's rare that someone asks for a watch that we don't have," he says. "People value the immediacy of being able to find what they want, when they want it."

What the company does best, perhaps, is use the range of its collection to help someone find the right watch. "If you like a particular style — chronographs, ultra-thins, anything — we can line up different models from various brands so you can see what options are out there. Then you can judge for yourself how a watch looks and feels on your wrist."

Cellini added Arnold & Son to its collection this year, including the limited edition DSTB. The acronym refers to the watch's signature complication, a true beat seconds hand. Unlike a sweep seconds, the hand stops completely before advancing.

DEEP ROOTS

Over the years, Cellini has earned a reputation for being the place to see—not just the best-known brands—but also the most-promising watch companies. The impressive list of brands that found an early home in America at Cellini includes: A. Lange & Söhne, Arnold & Son, De Bethune, Franck Muller, Greubel Forsey, HYT, Jean Dunand, Ludovic Ballouard, Maîtres du Temps, Parmigiani Fleurier and Richard Mille. Today, Cellini is widely regarded as the tastemaker to watch among collectors and brands alike.

Cellini maintains its status as a pacesetter this year with the addition of Arnold & Son to its collection. Over the past few years, the brand has rapidly developed a series of impressive calibers inspired by the inventions of John Arnold, the influential English watchmaker who made timepieces for King George III and later specialized in highly accurate marine chronometers. Shortly after Arnold's death in 1799, Abraham-Louis Breguet paid his friend and fellow watchmaker an amazing compliment by mounting his first tourbillon into one of Arnold's chronometers. To celebrate the brand's 250th anniversary in 2014, Arnold & Son unveiled several impressive watches, including the DSTB, which showcases a deadbeat seconds mechanism on the dial.

NATURAL BEAUTY

But even so, Cellini is known for more than just watches. It is also ranked among the finest jewelers in New York City, charming visitors from around the world for 35 years with its unrivaled selection, sublime quality and impeccable service.

Whether you seek understated, overwhelming, or something in between, the extraordinary scope of its collection opens up a world of possibilities. For those who favor a particular gem, Cellini covers the full spectrum with

Opal bracelet accented with tanzanites, emeralds, and diamonds, set in 18-karat white gold.

diamonds in all shapes, sizes and colors, as well as lush emeralds, mysterious alexandrites, lustrous South Sea and Tahitian pearls, plus Burmese rubies and Kashmir sapphires, two rare gemstones legendary for their dramatic hues.

The jewelry settings used to show off these natural wonders are equally varied and range from elegant designs made to transcend time, to styles that evoke a modern point of view. You may also commission a custom jewelry creation to realize a personalized design.

Whether you desire jewelry or watches, Cellini's friendly experts will be there to offer honest advice and provide impeccable service before, during and after a purchase.

Cellini is an authorized retailer for A. Lange & Söhne, Arnold & Son, Audemars Piguet, Bell & Ross, Bulgari, Cartier, Chopard, De Bethune, Franck Muller, Girard-Perregaux, Giuliano Mazzuoli, Greubel Forsey, H. Moser & Cie., Hublot, HYT, IWC, Jaeger-LeCoultre, Jean Dunand, Ludovic Ballouard, Maîtres du Temps, Parmigiani Fleurier, Piaget, Richard Mille, Roger Dubuis, Ulysse Nardin, Vacheron Constantin, and Zenith.

Cellini's boutique on Madison Avenue was established in 1987 at the epicenter of the world's most elite shopping district.

STORE LOCATIONS

Hotel Waldorf-Astoria
301 Park Avenue at 50th Street
New York, NY 10022
212-751-9824

509 Madison Avenue at 53rd Street
New York, NY 10022
212-888-0505

800-CELLINI
www.CelliniJewelers.com

Closely Watched Watches

Marton Radkai

As any extroverted industry, the world of fine watchmaking is populated by remarkable personalities. Some are courageous, entrepreneurial, visionary; many are just happy-go-lucky; and a few are profoundly idealistic. Their product, to use a bland word, is often unique and difficult to pigeonhole. The following pages are therefore devoted to a selection of these individuals and the watches they have created.

THE NAME ON THE FACE

The seal of approval "Swiss-made" is a gateway to good things, say the marketing moguls. Strictly speaking, however, it is a misnomer when applied to watches. The horological hotbed of the country can be narrowed down to French-speaking Switzerland, with the exception of some parts of the adjacent canton of Bern with large Francophone populations. Yes, Geneva—which some Swiss consider to be just barely Swiss—looms large, but when it comes to finding the cradle of the industry, almost all point to the Jura mountains.

The most important hub without a doubt is La Chaux-de-Fonds. The old town was destroyed by fire in 1794, and the new town was rebuilt along the best lines for natural lighting, a boon to the watchmaking industry. This particularly impressive combination of form and function earned La Chaux-de-Fonds and neighboring Le Locle a place on the UNESCO World Heritage list. So why has that trundling, hyphenated name never appeared on a watch dial?

The answer to that question is now moot thanks to Julien Fleury, a young *chaudefonnier* with strong convictions. He went to art school and learned graphic design, trained as a jeweler, and one day decided to put together a watch honoring his hometown—one assembled locally using local components and local suppliers. The result is a timepiece that essentially pushes all the right technical and aesthetic buttons for a debut piece appropriately called Exploration: a 44.5 mm steel case (titanium and gold also available) made up of several components and black ceramic inserts, definitely sporty, but not on steroids. The coolness is in the details—the satin-brushed surfaces, contrasting polished beveling, open-worked hands, markers that shorten on the left to make way for the sub-dials. For complications, he chose a power reserve indicator—the two spring barrels of the customized Technotime automatic movement can drive the watch for up to 120 hours—and a retrograde date hand that takes up about one-third of the dial.

His town is honored twice: La Chaux-de-Fonds appears on the flange between 1 and 3 o'clock. And the brand name of duManège refers to an old riding school built in 1855 that later provided families with low-cost housing and became an architectural ideal of community living.

The DM-Exploration, a promising debut watch, chic outside, technical inside.

Technotime's bespoke movement offers five days' worth of power reserve from two spring barrels.

Lastly, thanks to a subscription system for the steel version, buyers can pick up the watch at half the retail price (about $5,500).

For more information, visit www.dumanege.ch.

Julien Fleury and his DM-Exploration, the first watch explicitly La-Chaux-de-Fonds-made.

Watch Country

La Chaux-de-Fonds is in the heart of watch country. To the southwest is Le Locle, where you will find Zenith, Greubel Forsey, Christophe Claret, and many others. To the northeast, in the canton of Jura, lie the Franches Montagnes (Free Mountains), sheltering every type of watch component supplier imaginable, from the box makers, to *guillocheurs*, and of course more brands (Maurice Lacroix, Richard Mille, Paul Picot, to name a few). The "Free Mountains" were thus named because in 1380, the bishop of Basel promoted settlement in this harsh region by offering hardy volunteers tax-free living as long as they occupied an area above 1,000 meters.

The typical watchmaker's farm: the sundial ended up on the case back of the Rudis Sylva Harmonious Oscillator (insert).

Few people are more enthusiastic about this region than Jacky Epitaux, the powerhouse behind the exclusive Rudis Sylva brand. When working on a project, he will find outstanding craftspeople in neighboring farmhouses, which traditionally have additional windows cut into the southern façade to let natural light in. He leveraged that talent and inventiveness for his large Harmonious Oscillator watch, which bears a copy of the sundial that still adorns his uncle's house. It is inscribed with the words *Ultima Forsan*, meaning in Latin: "Maybe the last," one of the ultimate consequences of time's inexorable advance.

Epitaux's SIHH presence each January in Geneva is unique in the industry. Instead of the über-chic presentations, he lands in the city with the butcher from Les Bois, the pastry chef from Saignelégier, a brewer whose alchemy has made it into the *New York Times* . . . all to honor the earthbound quality of the *jurassiens*, farmers who have made high-end watches while living frugal, tough lives.

It's a region to discover, with friendly people, a wonderful breed of horse—the Franche Montagnes, a workhorse with a touch of frisky Arab in the genes—and lots of watch air to breathe. To pay homage to the famous Jura "peasant-watchmaker," Epitaux and a group of investors opened a restaurant and hotel at Le Boéchet. Besides tasting local specialties, visitors will find a small museum in the basement with objects, photos, and a video documenting the lives of the hardy local folk. There are tools of their trade, photos of the men and women of the region, the snowed-in trains, the "ladders of death" used by smugglers to carry components back and forth across the canyon-like Doubs River that separates Switzerland from France. A horological hike in the region is an important part of the package.

The Espace Paysan Horloger in Le Boéchet is accessible by train or car. The restaurant and museum are open Wednesday to Monday. *Website: www.paysan-horloger.ch*

Cottage industry: the Boillat family at work in the window of their farm.

The museum at the Espace Paysan Horloger provides insight into the life and work of the exceptional Jura watchmakers and farmers.

BIENNOISERIES

The other major horological hub *not* mentioned on dials (anymore) is Biel/Bienne. This slightly tattered, bilingual industrial city at the foot of the Jura in the canton of Bern is home to none other than Swatch, Omega, Perrelet, Milus, and many others. Patrik Mürner is not a watchmaker. He studied philosophy, literature, and theater and then got into antiques. A few years ago, the city's horological spirit finally caught up with him when a number of his clients encouraged him to pursue the idea of launching a brand.

Beginner's luck: the pieces fell into place rapidly. He purchased the name of the defunct Union Horlogère Bienne-Genève, along with its venerable logo featuring the trademarked Swiss cross. Mostly forgotten today, the Union was originally an important alliance of companies founded in 1883 and that existed until World War II. Its brands included, among others, Alpina, Dugena, and even the American Gruen. Mürner also found offices on "rue de L'Union," opposite the former premises of the original company.

What was missing was a workshop in Geneva, since any mention of Geneva on a dial is only allowed to brands with production facilities in the "city at the end of the lake." As it happened, Magma Concept S.A. in the industrial suburb of Plan-les-Ouates was searching for an investor. The company manufactures prototypes and movements—modified Valjoux movements, in fact, the most effective ETA caliber. Within a short period, Mürner had not only a brand, but one that was almost vertically integrated from the start.

Union Horlogère came out with three basic models all in retro style. The dials are symmetrical and easy to read, with Arabic numerals in a large self-confident perspective font. The first is a three-hander in a delicately crafted case. It comes with various dials, though the warm chocolate one in a harmonizing pink gold case perhaps best recreates the prewar atmosphere. The second model is a chronograph in a case of gold or Argentium, a silver alloy that does not oxidize. Finally, for lovers of complications, there is a pretty moon phase with the moon in mother-of-pearl and diamond-studded stars. A version was also made with a silver dial and discreetly engraved numerals.

The team at the revived Union Horlogère Bienne-Genève discusses strategy.

Besides creating a watch in tune with today's retro trend, the Union Horlogère Bienne-Genève has also revived the tradition of the family-run business, which bodes well for the future. Mürner's father Paul is a committed associate; his mother Suzanne does the accounting; and his sister Nadine, a professional pianist, composed the music for the company film.

For more information, visit www.unionhorlogere.ch.

The old HQ, a reminder of the alliance's glory days.

The Union's first chronograph, a bicompax with classic chocolate dial and an in-house movement.

Manufacture Royale has its own movements, and the Androgyne shows them off well.

UNANSWERED QUESTIONS

Would you like to wear the Sydney Opera House on your wrist? The question is absurd, of course, but why not? At any rate, the creator of the Opera by Manufacture Royale must have thought that when he decided to amplify the sound of a minute repeater by adding a folding shell that looks a little like the one gracing the Sydney skyline.

This peculiar watch is the main talking piece of this company, whose origins go back to Voltaire, the great French philosopher, liberal thinker, and enlightened business wizard—one of Europe's ten richest commoners. It was his way to create jobs and sell high-end timepieces to his royal friends and acquaintances.

After over two centuries of dreamless sleep, the brand was revived as a family affair owned and operated by Gérard Gouten, Marc Guten, David Gouten, and Alexis Gouten, all highly experienced watch executives. The brand is located in Vallorbe, a modest little township at the foot of the Jura. Their claim to fame is having the most affordable tourbillons on the market,

so they actually put one in each of three collections. The 1770, in homage to the initial foundation of the *manufacture*, has an uncluttered dial in a simple, round, 43 mm case, with the tourbillon a little cockily positioned at 7 o'clock. By contrast, the Androgyne collection exhibits the technological wizardry of the rejuvenated brand with virtually no dial, so the wearer can gaze admiringly at the wheelworks and bridges inside. It boasts a silicon escapement and traditional *côtes de Genève* on the main plate. The case, which comes in various metals, is a complex construction with hinges and crossbars and a screwed-down bezel that enhances the techno look. It has enough space too for a generous display of sapphires, diamonds, tsavorites, or rubies. Finally, there is the Opera mentioned above, whose 50 mm case can unfold. It is made up of sixty different parts—probably a record in *haute horlogerie*.

All Manufacture Royale watches are equipped with an in-house movement that delivers 108 hours of power reserve.

For more information, visit www.manufacture-royale.com.

Unique concept for amplifying a minute repeater, inspired by the Sydney Opera House.

It's a tire, it's a bolt, it's steampunk, it's disco, it's Stéphane Greco's vision for Les Temps Modernes.

LET THERE BE LIGHT

Behind every great watch stands a great supplier. Rhodior is such a great supplier. Its client list reads like a *Who's Who* of the luxury watch world, from DeWitt to de Grisogono, by way of Rolex. The little workshop in the horological and industrial Geneva suburb of Plan-les-Ouates specializes in finishing. In this case that covers treating and enhancing metal surfaces by galvanoplasty, rhodium-plating, luminescence, coloring metals in chemical baths; in short, all those touches that can turn plain mechanics into beautiful mechanics.

Founder Stéphane Greco calls himself a chemist, to summarize his training. While working for one major brand, he dreamed up what may well be the ultimate steampunk watch, one that glorifies the most symbolic component of the old industrial era: the bolt. They can be made in vari-

ous metals, brushed, plated, polished, PVD-coated, whatever is needed to make the wearer feel that he or she is inside the Machine. The hands of his Temps Modernes series are screwdrivers or wrenches, of course, and they are driven by a solid ETA movement. To add a comic touch, they come with a rubber strap decorated with car tire treads.

But Greco is restless and a very visual person. Among his many friends and acquaintances, he spotted a target group that was not being addressed by the industry: nighthawks, those people who wander about after sundown, going from disco to disco, club to club, or other UV-lit haunts. So Greco found a special fluorescent ink on the market and invented a process to fix it into the dials. It was a very expensive product, but with a free sample, he managed to get started. During the day these

watches just tell the time. But give them a dose of ultraviolet light, and they suddenly display complex and filigree decoration, or even a skull or two, all in bright colors.

The year was about 2001. One day he received a visit from four serious gentlemen, representatives from the European Central Bank. They had come to inform him that he could no longer use that terrific ink, because it had become a key security feature for the new euro banknotes. He argued that he had gotten it first and that his business depended on it. After some discussions, they finally allowed him to make one purchase of the ink. "I scratched together as much money as I could and bought enough for several generations of watches," he says with a grin. He keeps it in a very safe place, of course.

For more information, visit www.rhodior.com.

BREMONT

CHRONOMETERS

ALT1-C/CR

Born in the air, defined in the cockpit, assembled in England.
Bremont mechanical chronometers are made by professionals to exacting standards... for the rest of us.

EXQUISITE
TIMEPIECES

THE SOUL OF DISCRETION

You will rarely find quartz-driven watches in the pages of *Wristwatch Annual*. Mondaine's famous Swiss Railways Watch may be one of the few exceptions. Designed by the engineer Hans Hilfiker in the 1940s, the clock in Swiss train stations that served as inspiration is pure Bauhaus. The clock dial, with stringent rectangular hour and minute hands on a plain white surface and the red seconds hand tipped with the signalman's disk, is eminently legible. Turning this clock into a wristwatch, and then into a wall clock, desk clock, and decorative element on saucers, aprons, and elsewhere, was a stroke of genius by André and Ronnie Bernheim, the co-CEOs of Mondaine Ltd. It was an icon even before conception. The pure features exude deep Swiss values of precision, understatement, punctuality.

The Railways Watch has been around since 1986, and so the Bernheims decided it was time to produce a successor, something, again, deeply Swiss. They summoned a cross section of Swiss professionals and brainstormed. Oddly, the solution had been staring everyone in the face. Really everyone, around the planet. In fact, every New Yorker using the subway sees it as well. Hundreds of brands use it for their communications: the Helvetica font.

Fonts are actually one of Switzerland's lesser known exports. Helvetica was created by the graphic artist Max Miedinger and Haas Type Foundry business manager

André and Ronnie Bernheim, co-CEOs of Mondaine Ltd., putting the Helvetica into Swiss watchmaking.

Eduard Hoffmann. Their goal was to design a typeface that was, among other things, "well conceived, discreet enough and tempered, matter-of-fact, soft and flowing, with harmonious and logically structured forms," according to an old Haas flyer.

The Bernheims put designer Martin Drechsel in charge of transferring these qualities to the newborn watch. The Mondaine Helvetica, to be released in the fall of 2014, is the embodiment of unobtrusiveness, just like its model. A close look reveals a few dissonant touches that create an attractive tension. The date aperture, for instance, was moved off center to fit in with the lettering on the dial. In hom-

age to both the font and the first watch of the family, the Helvetica "1," with its notorious curved bar, was cleverly used to shape the lugs. As for the Mondaine logo, which is always in Futura, it is etched into the sapphire crystal to avoid mixing fonts on a single surface.

The watch was presented at Baselworld 2014. True to type, the No. 1 collection comes in three sizes, light (33 mm), regular (40 mm), and bold (43 mm). Can one make an icon or are they made by the market? Deconstructing the Helvetica in the future may well answer that question.

For more information, visit
www.mondaine.ch.

From Swiss railway stations, to wrists around the world: the iconic Swiss Railways Watch by Mondaine.

The new Helvetica by Mondaine, post-Bauhaus minimalism in the service of beauty.

AIRMAN, the pilot's pilot watch

AIRMAN AIRFIGHTER REF. 3921
AUTOMATIC CHRONOGRAPH, 46MM, 20 ATM

GLYCINE

SINCE 1914

Watch Tech: Revolution in the Balance

Joël A. Grandjean

IMAGE SOURCE: SIGATEC SILICON MICROPARTS

While watchmakers tend to look for rarer and more precious elements for their products, the one that is beginning to sweep through the industry is silicon. This grayish metalloid has certain outstanding properties for watches: It requires no lubrication, it does not fatigue, it is abundant. But silicon also represents a new challenge to both the designers and engineers... and the purists.

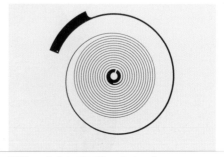

Philippe Pellaton's silicon hairspring, a quantum leap in watches: antimagnetic by nature, never fatigues.

The odd and brilliant idea of manufacturing silicon springs is associated with a young English watchmaker named Anthony Randall. This graduate from the technical college at La Chaux-de-Fonds studied with one of the industry greats: Jean-Claude Nicolet, known as the "last of the great *orologeurs*," a kind of multitasking watchmaker. Then, in the late winter of 2002, a few initial experiments with twenty-five silicon springs were carried out by Philippe Pellaton of the department of restoration at the International Museum of Horology in La Chaux-de-Fonds, which at the time was under the directorship of Ludwig Oechslin. The movements employed were the Unitas 6445, 18,000 vph. In his report, Pellaton concludes: "The results speak for themselves, we do not need to insist on further sampling."

Oechslin, a watchmaker, inventor, and astronomer in the old style, had already linked up with the brand Ulysse Nardin through the patronage of the late Rolf Schnyder and come up with the first ever silicon escapement. That was in 2001. The watch was the Freak, and it raised

eyebrows for its technical daring, its materials, and its off-the-perch design.

More research and development were needed, however, and that demanded some serious financing. So three heavyweights decided to step up to the plate: Patek Philippe, the Swatch Group, and Rolex. Their joint project, which was headed by the CSEM (Swiss Center for Electronics and Microtechnology) in Neuchâtel, held no guarantee of success. The deal was for each of the participants to keep the results secret; yet they had the right to make use of those results.

Of the collaborators, it was Patek Philippe that let off the first salvo from its Advanced Research department, which in 2005 came up with the Silinvar escape wheel requiring no lubrication, followed in 2006 by the Spiromax balance spring. In 2008 came the Pulsomax, and finally in 2011, to round off the collection, the GyromaxSi appeared, a balance that combined gold on a special silicon frame. In each case the specific properties of silicon, such as no need for lubrication, were able to improve certain aspects of the watch's functioning. Swatch Group also started

The Unitas 6445, first movement to receive a silicon hairspring.

Ulysse Nardin dared to go the silicon way with the ultramodern Freak.

introducing silicon components into its movements, notably at Omega and then Tissot, which even won a chronometry contest.

The other horological behemoth, Rolex, took a little more time to get its silicon heart in place. But when it did so, it was in the manner of a very big market test. For the first time ever, in 2014, the brand introduced the Oyster Perpetual Datejust Pearlmaster in a 34 mm case run by Caliber 2236 fitted with the Syloxi hairspring. This innovative little heart boasts no fewer than five patents, four of which are Rolex's own and the last affecting the material itself. The caliber—which has COSC certification—will later be used for men's models.

Detail of the silicon mechanism in Girard-Perregaux's Constant Escapement L.M.

SEEDS OF DOUBT

State-of-the-art technology goes down a different pipe in watchmaking than in other industries because "tradition" is the key term in the revival of mechanical watchmaking. Quartz was the enemy, and there are some troubling similarities between silicon and quartz. It is the main component in the microprocessors that run digital systems, like that in the Casio G-Shock for instance. As with quartz, the manufacturing of silicon pieces is highly standardized. Moreover, perhaps ironically, when a silicon movement is well regulated, it is extremely precise, which accounts for the victory of Technotime, Chopard, and Tissot at the 2011 chronometry ranking. All three participating models were equipped with silicon hairsprings. The other technology that offers outstanding precision and a heart of silicon is quartz, of course.

Generally speaking, purists believe that the best illustration of good manufacturing and tradition is to be found at Patek Philippe. It's doubtful whether they welcome the thought of modern materials coming to dilute the Great Tradition, even if it be the 5550P Advanced Research.

And so silicon has given rise to something of a debate among points of view that range from the doomsaying of traditional watchmaking to the neophiliac adoption of evolution. Naturally, many insiders are making their voices heard online—one boisterous discussion can be seen at www.watchonista.com/silicium.

SNAPPY FUTURE

All the talk will not stop the engineers, visionaries, and designers from further exploring the opportunities offered by this banal metalloid. Some of its properties make it ideal as a replacement for existing movement parts, notably the fact that it does not require lubrication—an age-old headache for watchmakers. But there is more: Silicon does not fatigue like metal. This permanent elasticity made it perfect for use in springs and the choice material in two recent innovations that touch the core of the movement. The first is Girard-Perregaux's Constant Escapement, dreamed up by Nicolas Déhon while he was absentmindedly snapping a train ticket held under tension between his thumb and third finger. The new GP movement features a blade that gathers the energy from the mainspring and snaps it out in even bursts. This guarantees that the force of the mainspring never changes as it unwinds.

Snapping silicon blades are also at the heart of a second innovation: a complex and clever new concept from Ulysse Nardin again following seven years of research and development. The new Anchor Escapement has the pallet arms suspended inside a circular silicon frame by two blades set at right angles to each other. These pick up the energy from each semi-oscillation and release it by snapping back and forth. No arbor means less friction and less energy loss. It's a tiny little assembly, but it could make a very big difference someday.

Joël Grandjean is one of the leading experts on the watch industry and a professional horological journalist. He edits and writes for a number of major publications in the industry, notably the webzine Watchonista.com.

Girard-Perregaux's Constant Escapement L.M. uses a snapping silicon blade to even out the mainspring's output.

Above: the silicon frame holding the pallet arms of Ulysse Nardin's new Anchor Escapement (below). Even force is guaranteed by silicon's properties.

The Chronograph: Challenge in Time

Marton Radkai and Joël A. Grandjean

On March 21, 2013, the Observatory in Neuchâtel dismantled the story of the first chronograph. Jean-Marie Schaller, CEO of the brand Louis Moinet, had all the historic proof and experts on hand to show that the watchmaker Louis Moinet was the real inventor of the chronograph and not, as had been thought until then, Nicolas Mathieu Rieussec. This technically and aesthetically outstanding horological piece was signed by him and dated 1816, and that sent a minor shock wave through the industry

TICKER TINKERERS

No great invention comes about in a total vacuum, of course. Before learning how to stop seconds, watchmakers had to actually make them go. Mariners, doctors, and even the average owner all had use for a ticking hand: the first to position himself in distant seas, the next to take the pulse of a patient, and all of them to actually *see* that the watch was working. This demand led to a separate seconds mechanism being introduced in 1776 by one Jean Moïse Pouzait (1743–1793) from the Société des Arts in Geneva.

Now that the seconds were visible, attempts were made to stop them so that a certain amount of time could be tracked and measured. The watchmakers sat at their drawing boards to no avail: stopping seconds often ended up halting the whole movement. Research was especially intense in England, where horseracing was all the rage. Interestingly, sports in general were to foster ever more precise time measurement later on, especially as the twentieth century got underway. But the mechanics had to be in place first.

Louis Moinet's compteur de tierces *is now considered the world's first chronograph.*

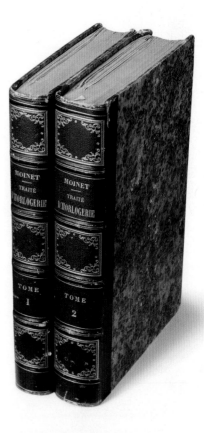

Louis Moinet, artist, astronomer, and watchmaker, published a seminal treatise on his craft.

LOUIS MOINET'S DEVICE

Louis Moinet—born in Bourges in 1768, died in Paris 1853—was an artist, astronomer, inventor, and master watchmaker, who rubbed elbows with the greatest watchmakers of his time. He was also a professor of art and president of the Chronometry Society of Paris, among other things.

The object by Moinet that turned up so recently is the first actual chronograph ever built. His term for the object, however, was *compteur de tierces*, and he did not set out to invent a chronograph. His revolutionary concept was the very high frequency of 30 hertz, which is 216,000 vph. This is a remarkable feat considering most wristwatches today operate in the 18,000–28,800 range. So the *compteur de tierces* became the world's most precise tool to measure time, six times more precise than the reference back then.

The piece itself is an authentic tool and therefore almost simplistic compared to the elaborate clocks Moinet is known for. The large sweep chrono hand races around the large railway track. Inside this circle are three subdials that give the timepiece a real face (screaming "Oh!"): top left are the minutes, top right the seconds, and below, the hours.

At the top of the case are two pushers. The central one starts the mechanism. To stop, the user has to remove his or her thumb. A small hole was drilled through the pusher and sleeve for a pin to hold down the pusher for longer measurements. The button on the left of the pusher activates a long lever that resets the chronograph by pressing on a bar under the escape wheel, which, in turn, directly drives the sweep *tierce* hand. In fact, the mechanism inside is almost rudimentary, with a cylinder escapement and a chain-and-fusée *remontoir* system. The escapement was simplified to allow for the extremely high frequency of the timepiece.

Moinet had the reputation of being a modest man, even though he was considered one of the greatest watchmakers of all times. Today, 247 years after his birth, his star shines bright. And that is a good thing, because during his lifetime, he never bothered with self-promotion. On the contrary, according to a certain Delmas, his vice president at the Chronometry Society, he was "precise, lucid, patient, informing the neophyte through encouragement, offering advice without being vain, spreading his wisdom liberally, without ulterior motive."

Simple but effective movement: note the fusée and chain in the foreground, and the levers to start, stop, and reset.

The components making up the compteur de tierces.

Moinet's invention (see box) was something of an exception. He did not intend to build a chronograph as such. This painter, sculptor, professor, engineer, astronomer, and watchmaker just wanted to construct an instrument that would help him track the stars and planets more accurately, and for that he needed to count one-sixtieth of a second, the so-called *tierces* in French, an old pre-decimalization term, hence the name *compteur de tierces*. The fact that he had invented something special may have passed him by entirely. His little chronograph does look very modest next to his elaborate empire table clocks, and as far as anyone can tell, it had no impact on the future evolution of the chronograph.

And so the honor of the first official chronograph went to Nicolas Mathieu Rieussec by default. In 1822, he offered

YOUR TIME IS NOW.

MAKE A STATEMENT WITH
EVERY SECOND.

Pontos S
The best-selling Super Sport Chronograph.
Diver rated water resistant (660ft) and
antimagnetic to aerospace specifications.
43mm surgical steel case with patented inner rotating
bezel on bracelet and colored Nato strap. Now.

MAURICE 𝖒 LACROIX
Manufacture Horlogère Suisse

Call 1-855-248-2840 or email usi@mlxusa.com

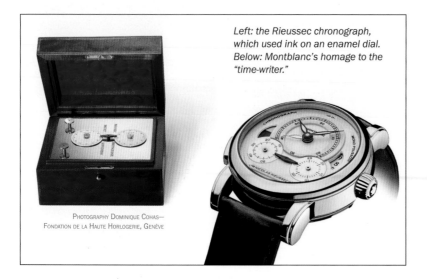

Left: the Rieussec chronograph, which used ink on an enamel dial. Below: Montblanc's homage to the "time-writer."

PHOTOGRAPHY DOMINIQUE COHAS—
FONDATION DE LA HAUTE HORLOGERIE, GENÉVE

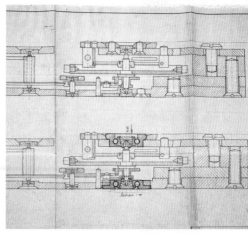

Cross section of a Hanhart chronograph showing the crowded insides of the watch.

Louis XVIII, king of France and a horse-racing fan, a curious instrument that deposited drops of ink on an enamel dial to mark time. The gadget was called—this *is* a first—a chronograph, or time writer.

Rieussec's invention was clever, but it was not inside a pocket watch yet. In the 1830s, Austrian Joseph Thaddeus Winnerl was the first to construct a mechanism that allowed the chrono hand to be stopped and then started again and catching up the paused time (*rattrapante*), which implies having a mechanical memory. Winnerl even made a double chronograph at one point.

Adolphe Nicole is the one credited with the flyback system in 1844, which allows the user to take a measurement and start another immediately after. The function had many real applications during races, for aviators, even for artillery officers.

The next century saw a plethora of technical improvements to the chronograph. Various mechanisms using single pushers or the traditional two (start/stop and reset) were invented and then improved. Pushers, cams, wheelworks . . . nothing was left untouched in the slow but inexorable drive to perfect this mechanism. Peripheral improvements were made as well, such as water-resistant chronographs. This process hasn't stopped yet. For instance, Ball Watch introduced a patented slide chronograph button this year.

GRAND FINALE
Two relatively recent major innovations bear mentioning. The first is the clever addition of a tachymeter scale onto the flange (1958, Breitling). Indeed, knowing time and distance allows one to quickly compute speed. The second is more important: the combination of a chronograph with an automatic movement, deemed an insurmountable challenge owing to the height of the two modules. Achieving that goal was sort of a moon landing, but in 1969, ironically, after decades of research, three were unveiled: the Movado-Zenith El Primero coproduction in January; the Breitling-Heuer Caliber 11 coproduction in March; and finally, the Seiko Caliber 6139A, which was already on the market in June.

All this happened without anyone knowing about Moinet's *compteur de tierces*. It begs the question: If a chronograph is invented and no one knows it, does it exist? Now we know.

TAG Heuer's 1916 Mikrograph, the best stopwatch of its day.

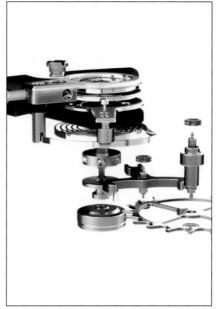

The modern Mikrotimer high-frequency escapement by TAG Heuer.

The legendary Zenith El Primero, combining an automatic with a chrono module in one case.

Vintage Hanhart chronographs:
the column wheel is visible near 12 o'clock.

Chronographs: Technical Insights and Technicalities

Bill Yao and Andy Tempalski

Chronographs have evolved considerably since their inception from a simple heart-shaped cam introduced in 1862 that allows chronographs to be reset to zero to complex operations on individual parts on contemporary Richard Mille chronos or TAG Heuer's linear second displays.

Essentially, however, chronographs fall into two main categories. There is the cam-activated chronograph and the column wheel–activated chronograph. The "column" part of the wheel refers to the shape, somewhat like a slice of an ancient column. Its purpose is to translate the orders received from the chronograph levers. Each category can then be subdivided by clutch mechanism, that

is, the system used to stop and start the machine. The two types are the vertical clutch and horizontal clutch. The clutch system describes how the power is relayed from the movement to the chronograph complication.

There are many reasons why the mechanical chronograph retains its place as one of the most admired complications. The number of components and asymmetrical parts required make it challenging to manufacture even today. A reason that the column wheel chronograph is more traditional is that this symmetrical part was easier to shape before CNC machining and higher precision modern equipment made the cam system more efficient to manufacture.

WHO'S BEST

It is a widely held belief among collectors that the column wheel chronograph is the higher quality design, although in truth both are comparable. Quality in this situation is defined by the smoothness and accuracy with which the chronograph starts and stops. These qualities are actually dependent on the clutch system and not the actuation system. The vertical clutch is not necessarily better but, generally speaking, does have the advantage of engaging faster and more smoothly. From a practical perspective the cam-operated chronograph is actually the more advanced design, easier to manufacture and service. The column wheel chronograph is more aesthetically pleasing, while

Our watches are made for moments like this.

KOBOLD
Embrace Adventure

its relative difficulty to manufacture has granted it a certain degree of exclusivity.

While there are many ways to differentiate chronographs, the general view is that an integrated chronograph is better than a modular one. An integrated chronograph is one where the entire movement was designed as a chronograph from the very beginning. The modular chronograph uses a separate detachable module that was designed to be installed on top of an existing movement. Integrated chronographs are superior primarily because all of the parts were conceived to work together from the beginning as a chronograph. From a watchmaker's perspective they are also easier to service and require fewer specialized tools and less training to maintain. Materials used also have a contribution, as nontraditional materials such as rubber and plastic do not have the longevity that traditional materials possess. Note as well, that high-end models even have two separate escapements for their chronographs, which avoids loss of power from a single balance spring.

Bill Yao is president of Mk II in Wayne, Pennsylvania. His company specializes in customizing and modernizing retired watch designs (www.mkiiwatches.com). Andrew Tempalski is a professional watchmaker currently employed at Mk II.

Chrono dial definitions: Hanhart (right) with a bicompax arrangement of two totalizers. Below the Milus Zetios has three totalizers in a tricompax arrangement. The Maurice Lacroix Pontos features the Valjoux layout, with space on the right of the dial.

YOUR CHRONOGRAPH QUESTIONS ANSWERED

You own a chronograph, or you intend to buy one. Here are some responses to the most commonly asked questions. If you need to know more, you may find a great deal on the Internet.

Is it better to run a chronograph when not used regularly?

This question arises from the idea that to keep the oils distributed in the movement it needs to run occasionally, like a car engine. In modern watchmaking, there have been advances in lubricants and surface treatments that enable the oils to stay where they are placed, and it is not necessary to run the movement for the sake of keeping the parts properly lubricated. Running the movement for this purpose only adds wear and does not increase the longevity of the movement. The idea that a watch is analogous to a car is actually misleading largely because, unlike a parked car, there is not a lot of force being applied to a watch when in a static position.

When a chronograph is serviced, what parts need to be replaced most often?

This depends primarily on the caliber and design. Each movement has its own pros and cons. The wear points and design limitations differ from one movement to the next.

Does the service interval for a chrono differ from a standard watch?

If you do not experience a disruption in performance, the service interval for modern watches is the same for both: five years. Regular servicing as well as general care and caution are the best ways to minimize higher service bills.

The chronograph is a very intricate mechanism and needs specific care when serviced. There are many problems that can occur simply because a watch was serviced by an unqualified individual. When searching for a qualified watchmaker, CW21, SAWTA, and WOSTEP represent the gold standards in U.S. certifications. For those outside the United States, WOSTEP is recognized the world over.

Does it cost more to service a chronograph?

As one would guess, it does cost more because it takes more time and is made up of more components.

SOME CHRONOGRAPH TERMS

Accuracy: The oscillations of the balance spring (measured in vibrations per hour or hertz, for example) determine the "breakdown" of the seconds, hence where the chrono hand can stop inside a second. A chrono running at 28,800 vph can show 1/8th of a second, at 18,000 vph 1/5th of a second. Zenith's El Primero runs at 36,000 vph for 1/10th of a second. Moinet's *compteur de tierces* ran at 216,000 vph for 1/60th of a second. TAG Heuer, the chronograph specialists, achieved 1/100th of a second with the Mikrograph and even 1/1,000th of a second with the Mikrotimer.

Chronograph: Essentially a watch with an integrated stopwatch actuated with a single button, standard two, or with a slider.

Flyback: For fast measurements, the flyback system allows for an instant reset and restart.

Foudroyante: A sweep second or chronograph hand that revolves around the dial once a second (flashing seconds). The advantage is accuracy when reading the results (see above).

Split-second or rattrapante: A chronograph with two hands and a mechanism that allows one of the hands to be stopped, while the other continues. This permits multiple measurements.

Stopwatch: Instrument to measure time by a start/stop and reset button.

IMAGE SOURCE: TAG HEUER.

Lange Uhren GmbH
Ferdinand-A.-Lange-Platz 1
D-01768 Glashütte
Germany

Tel.:
01149-35053-44-0

Fax:
01149-35053-44-5999

E-Mail:
info@lange-soehne.com

Website:
www.lange-soehne.com

Founded:
1990

Number of employees:
500 employees, almost half of whom are
watchmakers

U.S. distributor:
A. Lange & Söhne
645 Fifth Avenue
New York, NY 10022
800-408-8147

Most important collections/price range:
Lange 1 / $32,400 to $341,900; Saxonia
/ $18,600 to $58,400; 1815 / $22,500
to $213,000; Richard Lange / $30,300 to
$223,600; Zeitwerk / $68,900 to $117,500

A. Lange & Söhne

On December 7, 1990, on the exact day 145 years after the firm was founded by his great-grandfather Ferdinand Adolph Lange, Walter Lange re-registered the brand A. Lange & Söhne in its old hometown of Glashütte. Ferdinand Adolph had originally launched the company as a way to provide work to the local population. And shortly after German reunification in 1990, that is exactly what Glashütte needed as well.

The company quickly regained its outstanding reputation as a robust innovator and manufacturer of classically beautiful watches. A. Lange & Söhne uses only mechanical, manually wound *manufacture* calibers or automatic winders finished according to the highest Glashütte standards. The movements are decorated and assembled by hand with the fine adjustment done in five positions. The typical three-quarter plate and all the structural parts of the movement are made of undecorated German silver; the balance cock is engraved freehand. The movements combine equal parts traditional elements and patented innovations, like the Lange large date, the SAX-O-MAT with an automatic "zero reset" for the seconds hand, or the patented constant force escapement (Lange 31, Lange Zeitwerk). Of the company's fifty calibers, thirty are currently in production, and two-thirds of those have their own balance spring.

The highlight of the new models is the Richard Lange Terraluna, whose most interesting display is on the back. It features the synodic moon cycle of the Northern Hemisphere. The moon travels around the earth—which is actually flat here—and is illuminated by the sun—the balance. On the dial side the perpetual calendar features the characteristic large date, weekday, and month, as well as a small leap year display. The time is indicated with three scales, because the hours, minutes, and seconds each have their own individual sector.

Richard Lange Perpetual Calendar "Terraluna"

Reference number: 180.032
Movement: manually wound, Lange Caliber L096.1; ø 37.3 mm, height 11.1 mm; 80 jewels; 21,600 vph; three-quarter plate, double spring barrel, constant force escapement with intermediate winding spring, screw balance, 336-hour power reserve
Functions: hours (off-center), minutes, subsidiary seconds; power reserve indicator; perpetual calendar with large date, weekday, month, leap year, orbital moon phase with day/night display on case back
Case: pink gold, ø 45.5 mm, height 16.5 mm; sapphire crystal; transparent case back; water-resistant to 3 atm
Price: $215,100

Richard Lange

Reference number: 232.025
Movement: manually wound, Lange Caliber L041.2; ø 30.6 mm, height 6 mm; 26 jewels; 21,600 vph; hand-engraved balance cock, 2 screw-mounted gold chatons, finished and assembled by hand; in-house balance spring with patent-pending anchoring clip; 38-hour power reserve
Functions: hours, minutes, sweep seconds
Case: platinum, ø 40.5 mm, height 10.5 mm; sapphire crystal; transparent case back; water-resistant to 3 atm
Band: reptile skin, buckle
Price: $44,600
Variations: pink gold ($30,300); as "Pour le Mérite"; limited to 200 pieces ($113,500)

Richard Lange Tourbillon "Pour le Mérite"

Reference number: 760.032
Movement: manually wound, Lange Caliber L072.1; ø 33.6 mm, height 7.6 mm; 32 jewels including diamond endstone; 21,600 vph; chain and fusée drive; 1-minute tourbillon; hand-engraved balance cock
Functions: hours (off-center), minutes, subsidiary seconds (on tourbillon cage)
Case: pink gold, ø 41.9 mm, height 12.2 mm; sapphire crystal; transparent case back; water-resistant to 3 atm
Band: reptile skin, buckle
Remarks: hour dial retracts to reveal full tourbillon once hour hand has passed
Price: $223,600

1815 Tourbillon
Reference number: 730.032
Movement: manually wound, Lange Caliber L102.1;
ø 32.6 mm, height 6.6 mm; 20 jewels; 21,600 vph;
1-minute tourbillon; 3 screw-mounted gold chatons, 1
diamond endstone; screw balance, balance stop with
zero reset hand setting mechanism; hand-engraved
balance cock; 72-hour power reserve
Functions: hours, minutes, subsidiary seconds
Case: pink gold, ø 39.5 mm, height 11.1 mm; sapphire
crystal; transparent case back; water-resistant to 3 atm
Band: reptile skin, folding clasp
Price: $153,700
Variations: platinum ($178,300; limited to 100
pieces)

1815 Rattrapante Perpetual Calendar
Reference number: 421.025
Movement: manually wound, Lange Caliber L101.1;
ø 32.6 mm, height 9.1 mm; 43 jewels; 21,600 vph; 4
screw-mounted gold chatons, hand-engraved balance
cock, screw balance, swan-neck fine adjustment;
42-hour power reserve
Functions: hours, minutes, subsidiary seconds; power
reserve; split-seconds chronograph; perpetual calendar
with date, weekday, month, moon phase, leap year
Case: platinum, ø 41.9 mm, height 14.7 mm; sapphire
crystal, transparent case back; water-resistant to 3 atm
Band: reptile skin, folding clasp
Price: $213,000
Variations: pink gold ($189,000)

1815
Reference number: 235.021
Movement: manually wound, Lange Caliber L051.1;
ø 30.6 mm, height 4.6 mm; 23 jewels; 21,600
vph; 5 screwed-down gold chatons, hand-engraved
balance cock, finished and assembled by hand;
55-hour power reserve
Functions: hours, minutes, subsidiary seconds
Case: yellow gold, ø 38.5 mm, height 8.8 mm;
sapphire crystal; transparent case back; water-
resistant to 3 atm
Band: reptile skin, buckle
Price: $21,600
Variations: white gold ($22,800); platinum
($34,800)

1815 Chronograph
Reference number: 402.032
Movement: manually wound, Lange Caliber L951.5;
ø 30.6 mm, height 6.1 mm; 34 jewels; 18,000 vph;
hand-engraved balance cock, 4 screw-mounted
gold chatons; 60-hour power reserve
Functions: hours, minutes, subsidiary seconds;
flyback chronograph
Case: pink gold, ø 39.5 mm, height 10.8 mm;
sapphire crystal; transparent case back; water-
resistant to 3 atm
Band: reptile skin, buckle
Price: $47,000
Variations: white gold ($48,200)

Datograph UP/DOWN
Reference number: 405.035
Movement: manually wound, Lange Caliber L951.6;
ø 30.6 mm, height 7.9 mm; 46 jewels; 18,000
vph; 4 screwed-down gold chatons; 60-hour power
reserve
Functions: hours, minutes, subsidiary seconds;
flyback chronograph with precisely jumping minute
counter; large date; power reserve indicator
Case: platinum, ø 41 mm, height 13.1 mm; sapphire
crystal; transparent case back; water-resistant to
3 atm
Band: reptile skin, buckle
Price: $87,400

Datograph Perpetual
Reference number: 410.032
Movement: manually wound, Lange Caliber L952.1;
ø 32 mm, height 8 mm; 45 jewels; 18,000 vph;
column wheel control of chronograph functions; 4
screw-mounted gold chatons
Functions: hours, minutes, subsidiary seconds;
additional 24-hour display; day/night indicator;
flyback chronograph; perpetual calendar with
month, weekday, month, moon phase, leap year
Case: pink gold, ø 41 mm, height 13.5 mm;
sapphire crystal; transparent case back; water-
resistant to 3 atm
Band: reptile skin, buckle
Price: $127,700

Grand Lange 1 Moon Phase

Reference number: 139.032
Movement: manually wound, Lange Caliber L095.3; ø 34.1 mm, height 4.7 mm; 45 jewels; 21,600 vph; three-quarter, hand-engraved balance cocks, 7 screw-mounted gold chatons, screw balance, swan-neck fine adjustment; 72-hour power reserve
Functions: hours, minutes, subsidiary seconds; power reserve indicator; large date, moon phase
Case: pink gold, ø 41 mm, height 9.2 mm; sapphire crystal; transparent case back; water-resistant to 3 atm
Band: reptile skin, buckle
Price: $47,800
Variations: yellow gold ($47,800); platinum ($62,600)

Lange 1 Tourbillon Perpetual Calendar

Reference number: 720.032
Movement: automatic, Lange Caliber L082.1; ø 34.1 mm, height 7.8 mm; 68 jewels; 21,600 vph; 1-minute tourbillon on back; 4 gold chatons, 1 diamond endstone, hand-engraved cocks, rotor with gold weight; 50-hour power reserve
Functions: hours, minutes, subsidiary seconds; day/night indicator; perpetual calendar with large date, weekday, month, moon phase, leap year
Case: pink gold, ø 41.9 mm, height 12.2 mm; sapphire crystal; exhibition case; water-resistant to 3 atm
Band: reptile skin, buckle
Price: $332,500
Variations: platinum ($341,900; limited to 100 pieces)

Lange 1

Reference number: 101.032
Movement: manually wound, Lange Caliber L901.0; ø 30.4 mm, height 5.9 mm; 53 jewels; 21,600 vph; hand-engraved balance cock, finished and assembled by hand; double spring barrel; 72-hour power reserve
Functions: hours, minutes, subsidiary seconds; large date; power reserve indicator
Case: pink gold, ø 38.5 mm, height 10 mm; sapphire crystal; transparent case back; water-resistant to 3 atm
Band: reptile skin, buckle
Price: $32,400
Variations: yellow gold ($32,400); white gold ($33,600); platinum ($46,700)

Grand Lange 1

Reference number: 117.028
Movement: manually wound, Lange Caliber L095.1; ø 34.1 mm, height 4.7 mm; 42 jewels; 21,600 vph; 7 screwed-mounted gold chatons, hand-engraved balance cock; 72-hour power reserve
Functions: hours, minutes, subsidiary seconds; power reserve indicator; large date
Case: white gold, ø 40.9 mm, height 8.8 mm; sapphire crystal; transparent case back; water-resistant to 3 atm
Band: reptile skin, buckle
Price: $40,500
Variations: yellow gold ($39,300); pink gold ($39,300); platinum ($53,200); as "Lumen" in platinum ($53,200)

Lange 1 Daymatic

Reference number: 320.032
Movement: automatic, Lange Caliber L021.1; ø 31.6 mm, height 6.1 mm; 67 jewels; 21,600 vph; hand-engraved balance cock, 7 screwed-mounted gold chatons, central rotor with platinum weight; 50-hour power reserve
Functions: hours, minutes, subsidiary seconds; large date; weekday (retrograde)
Case: pink gold, ø 39.5 mm, height 10.4 mm; sapphire crystal; transparent case back; water-resistant to 3 atm
Band: reptile skin, buckle
Price: $40,400
Variations: yellow gold ($40,400); platinum ($54,700)

Lange 1 Timezone

Reference number: 116.039
Movement: manually wound, Lange Caliber L031.1; ø 34.1 mm, height 6.65 mm; 54 jewels; 21,600 vph; hand-engraved balance cock, 4 screw-mounted gold chatons; 72-hour power reserve; home time and zone time with day/night indicator, pusher-driven bezel with city names
Functions: hours, minutes, subsidiary seconds; 2nd time zone; large date; power reserve indicator; day/night indicator for both time zones
Case: white gold, ø 41.9 mm, height 11 mm; sapphire crystal; transparent case back
Band: reptile skin, buckle
Price: $50,100
Variations: pink gold ($47,700); platinum ($61,800)

Lange Zeitwerk

Reference number: 140.029
Movement: manually wound, Lange Caliber L043.1; ø 33.6 mm, height 9.3 mm; 66 jewels; 18,000 vph; hand-engraved balance cock; 2 screw-mounted gold chatons; continuous drive through constant force escapement; 36-hour power reserve
Functions: hours and minutes (digital, jumping), subsidiary seconds; power reserve indicator
Case: white gold, ø 41.9 mm, height 12.6 mm; sapphire crystal; transparent case back; water-resistant to 3 atm
Band: reptile skin, buckle
Price: $70,100
Variations: pink gold ($68,900)

Lange Zeitwerk Striking Time

Reference number: 145.032
Movement: manually wound, Lange Caliber L043.2; ø 33.6 mm, height 10 mm; 78 jewels; 18,000 vph; hand-engraved balance cock; 3 screw-mounted gold chatons; continuous drive through constant force escapement; acoustic signal on hour/quarter hour; 36-hour power reserve
Functions: hours and minutes (digital, jumping), subsidiary seconds; power reserve indicator
Case: pink gold, ø 44.2 mm, height 13.1 mm; sapphire crystal; transparent case back; water-resistant to 3 atm
Band: reptile skin, buckle
Price: $117,500
Variations: white gold ($107,900)

Langematik Perpetual

Reference number: 310.025
Movement: automatic, Lange Caliber L922.1; SAX-O-MAT; ø 30.4 mm, height 5.7 mm; 43 jewels; 21,600 vph; hand-engraved balance cock; rotor with gold/platinum oscillating weight; hand-setting mechanism with zero reset; main pusher for synchronous correction of all calendar functions, plus 3 individual pushers; 46-hour power reserve
Functions: hours, minutes, subsidiary seconds; added 24-hour display; perpetual calendar with large date, weekday, month, moon phase, leap year
Case: platinum, ø 38.5 mm, height 10.2 mm; sapphire crystal; transparent case back; water-resistant to 3 atm
Band: reptile skin, buckle
Price: $91,800

Saxonia Annual Calendar

Reference number: 330.032
Movement: automatic, Lange Caliber L085.1; SAX-O-MAT; ø 30.4 mm, height 5.4 mm; 43 jewels; 21,600 vph; hand-engraved balance cock; integrated three-quarter rotor with gold/platinum oscillating weight, reversing and reduction gears with 4 ball bearings; hand-setting mechanism with zero reset; 46-hour power reserve
Functions: hours, minutes, subsidiary seconds; full calendar with large date, weekday, month, moon phase
Case: pink gold, ø 38.5 mm, height 9.8 mm; sapphire crystal, transparent case back; water-resistant to 3 atm
Band: reptile skin, buckle
Price: $58,400
Variations: white gold ($46,500); platinum ($58,400)

Saxonia Thin

Reference number: 211.026
Movement: manually wound, Lange Caliber L093.1; ø 28 mm, height 2.9 mm; 21 jewels; 21,600 vph; hand-engraved balance cock, 3 screw-mounted gold chatons; 72-hour power reserve
Functions: hours, minutes
Case: white gold, ø 40 mm, height 5.9 mm; sapphire crystal; transparent case back; water-resistant to 3 atm
Band: reptile skin, buckle
Price: $25,100
Variations: pink gold ($23,900); as "Saxonia" ($23,900)

Saxonia (jewelry)

Reference number: 878.029
Movement: manually wound, Lange Caliber L941.2; ø 25.6 mm, height 3.2 mm; 21 jewels; 21,600 vph; 4 screw-mounted gold chatons, hand-engraved balance cock; 45-hour power reserve
Functions: hours, minutes, subsidiary seconds
Case: white gold, ø 35 mm, height 7.9 mm; bezel set with 60 diamonds; sapphire crystal; transparent case back; water-resistant to 3 atm
Band: reptile skin, buckle
Remarks: mother-of-pearl dial
Price: $35,200
Variations: brown mother-of-pearl dial

Caliber L096.1

Manually wound; constant force escapement with intermediate winding spring, stop-seconds; twin spring barrels, 336-hour power reserve

Functions: hours, minutes, subsidiary seconds; power reserve indicator; perpetual calendar with large date, weekday, month, leap year, orbital moon phase with day/night display on case back

Diameter: 37.3 mm; **Height:** 11.1 mm

Jewels: 80; **Balance:** glucydur with weighted screws

Frequency: 21,600 vph

Balance spring: in-house manufacture

Shock protection: Kif

Remarks: three-quarter plate with integrated moon phase display, manufactured according to highest quality criteria and chiefly decorated and assembled by hand, hand-engraved balance bridge

Caliber L072.1

Manually wound; chain and fusée transmission; 1-minute tourbillon with patented second-stop system; single spring barrel, 36-hour power reserve

Functions: hours, minutes, subsidiary seconds; pivoting dial

Diameter: 33.6 mm; **Height:** 7.6 mm

Jewels: 32; **Balance:** glucydur with weighted screws

Frequency: 21,600 vph

Balance spring: in-house manufacture

Shock protection: Kif

Remarks: three-quarter plate of untreated German silver; chiefly decorated and assembled by hand; balance and second bridges engraved by hand; chain made of 636 individual parts, worked by hand

Caliber L951.6

Manually wound; stop-seconds mechanism, jumping minute counter; single spring barrel, 60-hour power reserve

Functions: hours, minutes, subsidiary seconds; power reserve indicator; flyback chronograph; large date

Diameter: 30.6 mm; **Height:** 7.9 mm

Jewels: 46

Balance: glucydur with weighted screws

Frequency: 18,000 vph

Balance spring: in-house manufacture

Shock protection: Kif

Remarks: three-quarter plate of untreated German silver, chiefly decorated and assembled by hand; hand-engraved balance cock

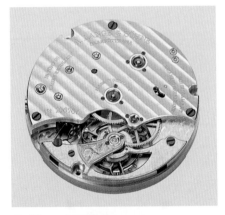

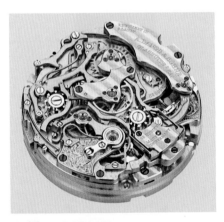

Caliber L102.1

Manually wound; 1-minute tourbillon with balance stop with zero reset hand setting mechanism, single spring barrel; 72-hour power reserve

Functions: hours, minutes, subsidiary seconds

Diameter: 32.6 mm; **Height:** 6.6 mm

Jewels: 20, including 3 screwed-mounted gold chatons

Balance: glucydur with weighted screws

Frequency: 21,600 vph

Balance spring: in-house manufacture

Shock protection: Kif

Remarks: three-quarter plate of untreated German silver, manufactured according to highest quality criteria and chiefly decorated and assembled by hand, hand-engraved balance bridge

Caliber L101.1

Manually wound; swan-neck fine adjustment; single spring barrel; 42-hour power reserve

Functions: hours, minutes, subsidiary seconds; power reserve indicator; rattrapante chronograph; perpetual calendar with date, weekday, month, moon phase, leap year

Diameter: 32.6 mm; **Height:** 9.1 mm

Jewels: 43, including 4 screw-mounted gold chatons

Balance: glucydur with weighted screws

Frequency: 21,600 vph

Shock protection: Kif

Remarks: manufactured according to highest quality criteria and chiefly decorated and assembled by hand

Caliber L034.1

Manually wound, key winding with torque limiter, constant force escapement, stop-seconds mechanism; twin spring barrels, 31-day power reserve with switch-off mechanism

Functions: hours, minutes, subsidiary seconds; power reserve indicator; large date

Diameter: 37.3 mm; **Height:** 9.6 mm

Jewels: 62; **Balance:** glucydur with weighted screws

Frequency: 21,600 vph

Balance spring: Nivarox 1 with special terminal curve and swan-neck fine adjustment

Shock protection: Incabloc

Remarks: three-quarter plate of untreated German silver; chiefly decorated and assembled by hand; hand-engraved balance cock; 2 mainsprings, each 1.85 m long

Caliber L095.3

Manually wound; stop-seconds mechanism; single spring barrel, 72-hour power reserve

Functions: hours, minutes, subsidiary seconds; power reserve display, large date, moon phase

Diameter: 34.1 mm

Height: 4.7 mm

Jewels: 45, including 7 screw-mounted gold chatons

Balance: glucydur with weighted screws

Frequency: 21,600 vph

Shock protection: Kif

Remarks: three-quarter plate of untreated German silver, manufactured according to highest quality criteria and chiefly decorated and assembled by hand, hand-engraved balance cock

Caliber L082.1

Automatic; 1-minute tourbillon with stop-second; 1-way gold rotor with platinum mass; single barrel, 50-hour power reserve

Functions: hours, minutes; subsidiary seconds; day/night; perpetual calendar, large date, weekday, month, moon phase, leap year

Diameter: 34.1 mm; **Height:** 7.8 mm

Jewels: 76, including 6 screwed golden chatons and 1 diamond counter-bearing

Balance: glucydur, eccentric regulating cams;

Frequency: 21,600 vph

Balance spring: in-house manufacture

Shock protection: Incabloc

Remarks: three-quarter plate with untreated German silver mostly hand-assembled, decorated; hand-engraved balance and wheel cock

Caliber L021.1

Manually wound; central rotor with platinum weight and shock-absorbing suspension; single spring barrel, 50-hour power reserve

Functions: hours, minutes, subsidiary seconds; large date, weekday (retrograde)

Diameter: 31.6 mm; **Height:** 6.1 mm

Jewels: 67; **Balance:** glucydur with eccentric regulating cams

Frequency: 21,600 vph

Balance spring: in-house manufacture

Shock protection: Kif

Remarks: plates and bridges of untreated German silver, manufactured according to highest quality criteria and chiefly hand-decorated and assembled, hand-engraved balance cock

Caliber L043.2

Manually wound; jumping minutes; constant force escapement; patent pending on spring barrel mechanism; stop-second system; single spring barrel, 36-hour power reserve

Functions: hours and minutes (digital, jumping), subsidiary seconds; power reserve indicator

Diameter: 36 mm; **Height:** 10 mm

Jewels: 78; **Balance:** glucydur

Frequency: 18,000 vph

Balance spring: in-house manufacture

Shock protection: Incabloc

Remarks: three-quarter plate with untreated German silver; Glashütte ribbing; mostly assembled and decorated by hand; hand-engraved balance cock

Caliber L922.1 SAX-O-MAT

Manually wound; bidirectional winding, finely embossed three-quarter rotor in 21 kt gold and platinum; zero reset hand adjustment; stop-second system; single spring barrel, 46-hour power reserve

Functions: hours, minutes, sweep seconds; additional 24-hour display; perpetual calendar with date, weekday, month, moon phase, leap year day/night indicator

Diameter: 30 mm; **Height:** 5.7 m

Jewels: 43

Balance: glucydur with weighted screws

Frequency: 21,600 vph

Remarks: calendar mechanism with 48-step program disc and precision moon phase system

Caliber L085.1 SAX-O-MAT

Automatic; bidirectional, finely embossed three-quarter rotor of 21 kt gold and platinum, zero reset hand adjustment, stop-seconds mechanism; complete or individual calendar correction; single spring barrel, 46-hour power reserve

Functions: hours, minutes, subsidiary seconds; full calendar with large date, weekday, month, moon phase

Diameter: 30.4 mm; **Height:** 5.4 mm

Jewels: 43; **Balance:** glucydur with weighted screws

Frequency: 21,600 vph

Balance spring: Nivarox 1 with special terminal curve and swan-neck fine adjustment

Shock protection: Kif

Remarks: three-quarter plate of untreated German silver; chiefly decorated and assembled by hand; hand-engraved balance cock

Alpina Watch International
Chemin de la Galaise, 8
CH-1228 Plan-les-Ouates (Geneva)
Switzerland

Tel.:
01141-22-860-87-40

Fax:
01141-22-860-04-64

E-Mail:
info@alpina-watches.com

Website:
www.alpina-watches.com

Founded:
1883

Number of employees:
100

Annual production:
10,000 watches

U.S. distributor:
Alpina Watches USA
877-61-WATCH
info@usa.alpina-watches.com

Most important collections/price range:
Extreme / from approx. $1,200; Startimer
Pilot / from approx. $2,300; Sailing / from
approx. $1,500; Tourbillon / from approx.
$50,000

Alpina

The brand Alpina essentially grew out of a confederation of watchmakers known as the Alpina Union Horlogère, founded by Gottlieb Hauser. The group expanded quickly to reach beyond Swiss borders into Germany, where it opened a factory in Glashütte. For a while in the 1930s, it even merged with Gruen, one of the most important watch companies in the United States. The collaboration fell apart in 1937.

After World War II, the Allied Forces decreed that the name Alpina could no longer be used in Germany, and so that branch was renamed "Dugena" for Deutsche Uhrmacher-Genossenschaft Alpina, or the German Watchmaker Cooperative Alpina.

Today, Geneva-based Alpina is no longer associated with that watchmaker cooperative of yore. Now a sister brand of Frédérique Constant, it has a decidedly modern collection enhanced with its own automatic movement—based, of course, on the caliber of its co-headquartered manufacturer. Owners Peter and Aletta Stas have built an impressive watch *manufacture* in Geneva's industrial district, Plan-les-Ouates. There, they produce about 8,000 of their own watches each year as well as reassembling other timepieces with externally manufactured movements.

Alpina, which celebrated its 130th anniversary during 2013, likes to call itself the inventor of the modern sports watch. Its iconic Block-Uhr of 1933 and the Alpina 4 of 1938, with an in-house automatic movement, set the pace of all sports watches, with a waterproof stainless steel case, an antimagnetic system, and shock absorbers. The timepieces found favor in various branches of the military, notably aviation. This past is now the future as well, as the reconstituted Alpina brand sets its sights on a modern look and seeking out customers who engage in water and aeronautic sports but would also like an outstanding price-performance ratio.

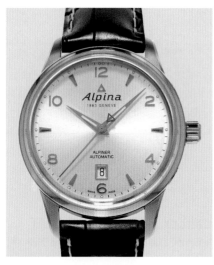

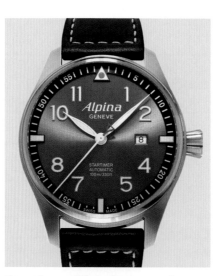

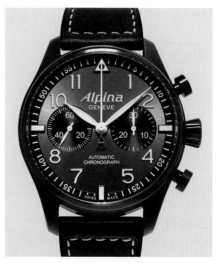

Alpiner Automatic

Reference number: AL-525S4E6
Movement: automatic, Sellita Caliber SW 200-1; ø 25.6 mm, height 4.6 mm; 26 jewels; 28,800 vph; 38-hour power reserve
Functions: hours, minutes, sweep seconds; date
Case: stainless steel, ø 41.5 mm, height 10.8 mm; sapphire crystal, water-resistant to 5 atm
Band: calf leather, buckle
Price: $1,395

Startimer Pilot Automatic

Reference number: AL-525GB4S6
Movement: automatic, Sellita Caliber SW 200-1; ø 25.6 mm, height 4.6 mm; 26 jewels; 28,800 vph; 38-hour power reserve
Functions: hours, minutes, sweep seconds; date
Case: stainless steel, ø 40 mm, height 10.2 mm; sapphire crystal; screw-in crown; water-resistant to 10 atm
Band: calf leather, buckle
Price: $1,495

Startimer Pilot Automatic Chronograph

Reference number: AL-860GB4FBS6
Movement: automatic, Sellita Caliber SW 500; 30 jewels; 28,800 vph; 46-hour power reserve
Functions: hours, minutes, subsidiary seconds
Case: stainless steel with black PVD coating, ø 44 mm, height 14.6 mm; sapphire crystal; screw-in crown, water-resistant to 10 atm
Band: calf leather, buckle
Price: $3,395

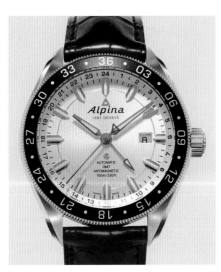

Alpiner 4 GMT

Reference number: AL-550S5AQ6
Movement: automatic, Sellita Caliber; ø 25.6 mm; 26 jewels; 28,800 vph; 38-hour power reserve
Functions: hours, minutes, sweep seconds; additional 24-hour display (2nd time zone); date
Case: stainless steel, ø 44 mm, height 14.2 mm; bidirectional bezel with 360 divisions (compass function), sapphire crystal; water-resistant to 10 atm
Band: calf leather, buckle
Price: $2,495
Variations: stainless steel band ($2,695); black dial

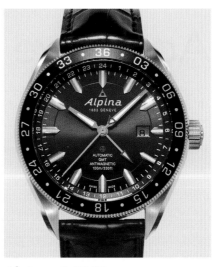

Alpiner 4 GMT

Reference number: AL-550G5AQ6
Movement: automatic, Sellita Caliber; ø 25.6 mm; 26 jewels; 28,800 vph; 38-hour power reserve
Functions: hours, minutes, sweep seconds; additional 24-hour display (2nd time zone); date
Case: stainless steel, ø 44 mm, height 14.2 mm; bidirectional bezel with 360 divisions (compass function), sapphire crystal; water-resistant to 10 atm
Band: reptile skin, buckle
Price: $2,495

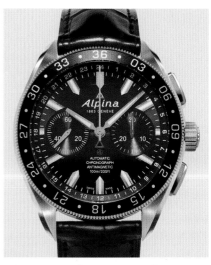

Alpiner 4 Chronograph

Reference number: AL-860S5AQ6
Movement: automatic, Sellita Caliber SW 500; ø 30 mm, height 7.9 mm; 26 jewels; 28,800 vph; 38-hour power reserve
Functions: hours, minutes, subsidiary seconds; chronograph
Case: stainless steel, ø 44 mm, height 15.7 mm; bidirectional bezel with 360 divisions (compass function), sapphire crystal; water-resistant to 10 atm
Band: reptile skin, buckle
Price: $3,495
Variations: white dial; stainless steel bracelet ($3,695)

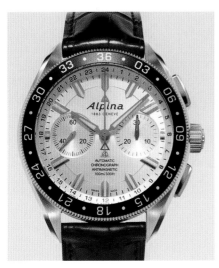

Alpiner 4 Chronograph

Reference number: AL-860B5AQ6
Movement: automatic, Sellita Caliber SW 500; ø 30 mm, height 7.9 mm; 26 jewels; 28,800 vph; 38-hour power reserve
Functions: hours, minutes, subsidiary seconds; chronograph
Case: stainless steel, ø 44 mm, height 15.7 mm; bidirectional bezel with 360 divisions (compass function), sapphire crystal; water-resistant to 10 atm
Band: reptile skin, buckle
Price: $3,495
Variations: black dial

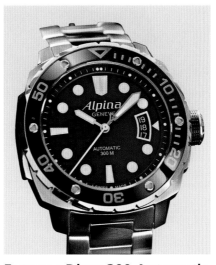

Extreme Diver 300 Automatic Orange

Reference number: AL-525LBO4V26
Movement: automatic, AL Caliber 525 (base Sellita SW 200-1); ø 25.6 mm, height 4.6 mm; 26 jewels; 28,800 vph; 38-hour power reserve
Functions: hours, minutes, sweep seconds; date
Case: stainless steel, ø 44 mm, unidirectional bezel with 60-minute division, sapphire crystal; screw-in crown; water-resistant to 30 atm
Band: stainless steel, safety folding clasp
Price: $1,795
Variations: rubber strap ($1,595)

Extreme Diver 300 Chronograph Automatic

Reference number: AL-725LB4V26
Movement: automatic, AL Caliber 725 (base ETA 7750); ø 30 mm, height 7.9 mm; 25 jewels; 28,800 vph; 46-hour power reserve
Functions: hours, minutes; chronograph; date
Case: stainless steel, ø 44 mm, height 17.2 mm; unidirectional bezel with 60-minute division, sapphire crystal, transparent case back; screw-in crown; water-resistant to 30 atm
Band: rubber, buckle
Price: $3,095
Variations: stainless steel bracelet ($3,295)

Aquadive

AQUADIVE USA

1950 Oleander Street
Baton Rouge, LA 70806

Tel.:
888-397-9363

E-Mail:
info@aquadive.com

Website:
www.aquadive.com

Founded:
1962

Number of employees:
18

Distribution:
direct online sales

Most important collections/price range:
NOS Diver, Bathyscaphe / $1,290 to $2,990
(prices plus shipping)

According to Laver's Law, a style that shows up again at the fifty-year mark is "quaint." So much for the outward impact, maybe. But what about the intrinsic long-term personal and ephemeral value, the sometimes collective memories associated with a particular moment in our lives? Today, the very sight of a watch from times past might bring forth images of a different era, much like hearing the songs of Procol Harum or touching Naugahyde in an old Dodge Dart. Nostalgia is a powerful impulse, especially in an era like ours, which appears enamored by its own frenetic pace and refuses categorically to stop and reflect.

So when a group of watch experts decided to revive an iconic watch of the sixties and seventies, they were bound to strike a positive note. In its day, the Aquadive was considered a solidly built and reliable piece of equipment seriously coveted by professional divers. It might still be around had it not been put out to pasture during the quartz revolution.

In its twenty-first century incarnation, the Aquadive bears many hallmarks of the original. The look is unmistakable: the charmingly awkward hands, the puffy cushion case, the sheer stability it exudes. In fact, some of the components, like the 200 NOS case and sapphire crystal, are leftovers from the old stock. The Swiss-made automatic movements and the gaskets, of course, are new.

Modern technologies, like DLC, and advances in CNC machining have transformed the older concepts. And to ensure reliability, the watches are assembled in Switzerland. The top of the current line is the Bathyscaphe series, machined from a block of stainless steel, and featuring new shock absorbers and an automatic helium release valve.

Bathyscaphe 100

Reference number: 1002.11.36211
Movement: automatic, ETA Caliber 2836-2; ø 25.6 mm, height 4.6 mm; 25 jewels; 28,800 vph; 42-hour power reserve; regulated in 5 positions
Functions: hours, minutes, sweep seconds; date
Case: stainless steel, ø 43 mm, height 14 mm; unidirectional bezel with 60-minute divisions; antimagnetic soft iron inner case; sapphire crystal; screw-in crown; automatic helium release valve; water-resistant to 100 atm
Band: Isofrane, buckle
Price: $1,690, limited to 500 pieces
Variations: mesh bracelet ($1,890); gun metal DLC-coated version ($1,890)

Bathyscaphe 300

Reference number: 3002.11.36211
Movement: automatic, ETA Caliber 2824-2; ø 25.6 mm, height 4.6 mm; 25 jewels; 28,800 vph; 42-hour power reserve; regulated in 5 positions
Functions: hours, minutes, sweep seconds; date
Case: stainless steel, ø 47 mm, height 14 mm; unidirectional bezel with 60-minute divisions; sapphire crystal; screw-in crown; automatic helium release valve; water-resistant to 300 atm
Band: Isofrane rubber, buckle
Price: $2,490

Aquadive 200 (New Old Stock)

Reference number: 200NOS.11.36211
Movement: automatic, ETA Caliber 2824-2; ø 25.6 mm, height 4.6 mm; 25 jewels; 28,800 vph; 42-hour power reserve; regulated in 5 positions
Functions: hours, minutes, sweep seconds; date
Case: stainless steel, ø 37 mm, height 11 mm; bidirectional bezel; NOS fiberglass crystal; screw-in crown; water-resistant to 20 atm
Band: Isofrane, buckle
Remarks: case made from original 1962 stock
Price: $1,290
Variations: NATO strap

Aquadive 77 (New Old Stock)

Reference number: 771.12.365112
Movement: automatic, ETA Caliber 2836-2;
ø 25.6 mm, height 4.6 mm; 25 jewels; 28,800 vph;
42-hour power reserve; regulated in 5 positions
Functions: hours, minutes, sweep seconds; date
Case: stainless steel, 41 x 51 mm, height 16 mm;
unidirectional bezel with 60-minute divisions;
sapphire crystal; screw-in crown; automatic helium
release valve; water-resistant to 100 atm
Band: rubber, buckle
Price: $1,290, limited to supply of old stock parts
Variations: with mesh bracelet ($1,390);
overhauled NOS Anton Schild movement ($1,390)

Bathyscaphe 100 Bronze

Reference number: 1006.13.365311
Movement: automatic, ETA Caliber 2836-2;
ø 25.6 mm, height 4.6 mm; 25 jewels; 28,800 vph;
42-hour power reserve; regulated in 5 positions
Functions: hours, minutes, sweep seconds; date
Case: German bronze alloy, ø 43 mm, height
15 mm; unidirectional bezel with 60-minute
divisions; sapphire crystal; screw-in crown;
automatic helium release valve; water-resistant to
100 atm
Band: Isofrane, buckle
Price: $1,690, limited to 100 pieces

Bathysphere 100 GMT

Reference number: 1001.13.935113
Movement: automatic, ETA Caliber 2893-2;
ø 25.6 mm, height 4.2 mm; 21 jewels; 28,800 vph;
42-hour power reserve; regulated in 5 positions
Functions: hours, minutes, sweep seconds; date,
GMT hand for 24-hour indication
Case: stainless steel case, ø 43 mm, height 15 mm;
unidirectional bezel with 60-minute divisions;
sapphire crystal; screw-in crown; automatic helium
release valve; water-resistant to 100 atm
Band: Isofrane, buckle
Price: $1,990, limited to 300 pieces
Variations: with mesh bracelet ($2,150); DLC-
coated gun metal ($2,090); 2 additional dial colors

Bathysphere 300

Reference number: 2001.13.TB5D5111
Movement: automatic, custom-made Caliber TB5D;
ø 30.1 mm, height 5.9 mm; 45 jewels; 28,800 vph;
120-hour power reserve; regulated in 5 positions
Functions: hours, minutes, sweep seconds; date
Case: stainless steel, ø 42 mm, height 13 mm;
unidirectional bezel with 60-minute divisions;
sapphire crystal; screwed-in crown; automatic
helium release valve; water-resistant to 100 atm
Band: Isofrane, buckle
Price: $3,990
Variations: stainless steel link bracelet or mesh
bracelet

Bathyscaphe 300 DLC

Reference number: 3002.11.36211
Movement: automatic, ETA Caliber 2824-2;
ø 25.6 mm, height 4.6 mm; 25 jewels; 28,800 vph;
42-hour power reserve; regulated in 5 positions
Functions: hours, minutes, sweep seconds; date
Case: Diamond Like Carbon steel, ø 47 mm,
height 14 mm; unidirectional bezel with 60-minute
divisions; sapphire crystal; screw-in crown;
automatic helium release valve; water-resistant to
300 atm
Band: Isofrane rubber, buckle
Price: $2,490

Aquadive 50 Depth Gauge (New Old Stock)

Reference number: 1976.50
Movement: quartz, depth gauge
Functions: hours, minutes, seconds, depth gauge
Case: stainless steel, ø 47 mm, height 17 mm;
unidirectional bezel with 60-minute divisions;
mineral crystal; screw-in crown; water-resistant to
20 atm
Band: Isofrane rubber, buckle
Price: $4,490

Anonimo

Anonimo SA
Chemin des Chalets 9
CH-1279 Chavannes-de-Bogis
Switzerland

Tel.:
01141-22-566-06-06

E-Mail:
info@anonimo.com

Website:
www.anonimo.com

Founded:
1997; relaunched 2013

Distributor:
Network in construction; for inquiries contact
the brand directly.

Most important collections/price range:
Militari Militare / $7,000 to $8,500

The brand Anonimo was launched on the banks of the Arno, in Florence. Watchmaking has a long history in the capital of Tuscany, going back to one Giovanni de Dondi (1318–1389) who built his first planetarium around 1368. Then came the Renaissance man Lorenzo della Volpaia (1446–1512), an architect and goldsmith, who also worked with calendars and astronomical instruments. And finally, there were the likes of the mathematician Galileo and the incomparable Leonardo da Vinci.

In more recent times, the Italian watchmaking industry was busy equipping submarine crews and frogmen with timepieces. The key technology came from Switzerland, but the specialized know-how for making robust, water-resistant watches sprang from small enterprises with competencies in building cases. The founders of Anonimo understood this strength and decided to put it in the service of their "anonymous" brand—a name chosen to "hide" the fact that many small, discreet companies are involved in their superbly finished watches.

In 2013, armed with some fresh capital and a new management team, Anonimo came out with three watch families running on Swiss technology: The mechanical movements are partially complemented with Dubois Dépraz modules or ETA and Sellita calibers. On the whole, though, the collections reflect exquisite conception and manufacturing, and the quality of the materials is unimpeachable: corrosion-resistant stainless steel, fine bronze, and titanium, appreciated for its durability and hypoallergenic properties. As for design, the cases come with some special features. On the military models, the crown has been placed in a protected area between the two upper lugs. Thanks to a clever hinge system, that crown can be pressed onto the case for an impermeable fit or released for time-setting.

Militare Alpini Chrono

Reference number: AM.1110.04.003.A01
Movement: automatic, Sellita Caliber SW300 with Dubois Dépraz module 2035T; ø 26.2 mm, 26 jewels, 28,800 vph; 42 hours power reserve
Functions: hours, minutes, subsidiary seconds; chronograph
Case: bronze; ø 43 mm, height 14.5 mm; stainless steel case back; sapphire crystal; water-resistant to 12 atm
Band: calf leather, buckle
Remarks: crown pressed onto case by upper lug for impermeable seal
Price: $8,500

Militare Chrono

Reference number: AM.1100.05.005A01
Movement: automatic, Sellita Caliber SW300 with Dubois Dépraz module 2035T; ø 26.2 mm, 26 jewels, 28,800 vph; 42 hours power reserve
Functions: hours, minutes, subsidiary seconds; chronograph
Case: bronze; ø 43 mm, height 15.3 mm; sapphire crystal; water-resistant to 12 atm
Band: calf leather, folding clasp
Remarks: crown pressed onto case by upper lug for impermeable seal
Price: $8,500
Variations: stainless steel; stainless steel with black DLC-coating

Militare Alpini Power Reserve

Reference number: AM.1010.04.002.A01
Movement: manually wound, ETA Caliber 7001 with power reserve module; ø 23.3 mm, 17 jewels, 21,600 vph; 42 hours power reserve
Functions: hours, minutes, subsidiary seconds; power reserve indicator
Case: bronze; ø 43 mm, height 14.5 mm; stainless steel case back; sapphire crystal; water-resistant to 12 atm
Band: calf leather, buckle
Remarks: crown pressed onto case by upper lug for impermeable seal
Price: $7,200

Aristo

"If you lie down with dogs, . . ." goes the old saying. And if you work closely with watchmakers . . . you may catch their more beneficial bug and become one yourself. That at any rate is what happened to the watch case and metal bracelet manufacturer Vollmer, Ltd, established in Pforzheim, Germany, by Ernst Vollmer in 1922. Third-generation president Hansjörg Vollmer decided he was interested in producing watches as well.

Vollmer, who studied business in Stuttgart, had the experience, but also the connections with manufacturers in Switzerland. He speaks French fluently, another asset. He acquired Aristo and launched a series of pilot watches in 1998 housed in sturdy titanium cases with bold onion crowns and secured with Vollmer's own light and comfortable titanium bracelets. Bit by bit, thanks to affordable prices and no-nonsense design—reviving some classic dials from World War II—Vollmer's watches caught hold. The collection grew with limited editions and a few chronometers.

In October 2005, Vollmer GmbH and Aristo Watches finally consolidated for a bigger impact. Besides their own lines, they produce quartz watches, automatics, and chronographs under the names Messerschmitt and Aristella. The Aristo brand has been trademarked worldwide and is sold mainly in Europe, North America, and Asia. The collection is divided up into Classic, Design, and Sports with the mechanical segment further split based on elements Land, Water, and Air. The timepieces range from quality wristwatches with historical movements from older Swiss production to attractive ladies watches or replicas of classic military watches, all assembled in Pforzheim. The company also has an established name as a manufacturer of classic pilot watches.

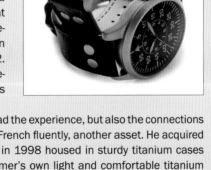

Aristo Vollmer GmbH
Erbprinzenstr. 36
D-75175 Pforzheim
Germany

Tel.:
01149-7231-17031

Fax:
01149-7231-17033

E-Mail:
info@aristo-vollmer.de

Website:
www.aristo-vollmer.de

Founded:
1907 / 1998

Number of employees:
16

Annual production:
6,600 watches and 10,000 bracelets

Distribution:
retail

U.S. distributor:
Marc Time Imports
P.O. Box 10057
Melville, NY 11747
631-213-9112

Most important collections/price range:
Aristo watches starting at $400 up to Vollmer watches at $1,839

XL-Pilot's Chronograph

Reference number: 3H123
Movement: automatic, ETA Caliber 7750; ø 30 mm, height 7.9 mm; 25 jewels, 28,800 vph; 42-hour power reserve
Functions: hours, minutes, subsidiary seconds; chronograph; weekday and date
Case: stainless steel, ø 44 mm, height 14.5 mm; sapphire crystal; transparent case back; water-resistant to 5 atm
Band: calf leather, buckle
Price: $1,495

Chronograph "Tachymeter" Flyer

Reference number: 3H129
Movement: automatic, ETA Caliber 7750; ø 30 mm, height 7.9 mm; 25 jewels; 28,800 vph; 42-hour power reserve
Functions: hours, minutes, subsidiary seconds; chronograph; weekday, date
Case: stainless steel, ø 40.5 mm, height 14.5 mm; mineral glass; transparent case back; water-resistant to 5 atm
Band: stainless steel mesh, folding clasp
Price: $1,490
Variations: calf leather band ($1,390)

Carbon-Watch

Reference number: 7H82
Movement: automatic, Caliber Aristomatic (base Sellita SW200); ø 25.6 mm, height 4.6 mm; 26 jewels; 28,800 vph; 38-hour power reserve
Functions: hours, minutes, sweep seconds
Case: stainless steel, ø 40 mm, height 10.6 mm; bezel with carbon insert, sapphire crystal; water-resistant to 5 atm
Band: carbon fiber, folding clasp
Price: $798
Variations: carbon fiber link bracelet ($675); leather strap ($875)

Armin Strom AG
Bözingenstrasse 46
CH-2502 Biel/Bienne
Switzerland

Tel.:
01141-32-343-3344

Fax:
01141-32-343-3340

E-Mail:
info@arminstrom.com

Website:
www.arminstrom.com

Founded:
1967

Number of employees:
20

Annual production:
approx. 1,000 watches

U.S. distributor:
Contact Armin Strom headquarters.

Most important collections/price range:
Gravity, One Week, Tourbillon, Racing,
Regulator, Skeleton / $10,100 to $131,600

Armin Strom

For more than thirty years, Armin Strom's name was associated mainly with the art of skeletonizing. But this "grandmaster of skeletonizers" then decided to entrust his life's work to the next generation, which turned out to be the Swiss industrialist and art patron Willy Michel.

Michel had the wherewithal to expand the one-man show into a full-blown *manufacture* able to conceive, design, and produce its own mechanical movements. The endeavor attracted Claude Geisler, a very skilled designer, and Michel's own son, Serge, who became business manager. When this triumvirate joined forces, it was able to come up with a technically fascinating movement at the quaint little *manufacture* in the Biel suburb of Bözingen within a brief period of time.

The new movement went on to grow with several variants and derivatives and forms the backbone of a new collection. The acronym ARM stands for "Armin reserve de marche" (a seven-day power reserve), and AMW means "Armin manual winding" (a trimmed down manually wound movement with a single spring barrel). In sum, over the past few years, the brand has managed to gradually modernize its range of models and give itself a more contemporary profile without losing touch with its origins. The in-house movements are showing off their abilities on new, at times daring, dials. As for Strom, he has taken a very well-earned retirement, though he does come into the workshop every now and then to look over shoulders and offer valuable insights from a life of watchmaking.

Gravity Date Air

Reference number: TI14-DA.50
Movement: automatic, Caliber ADD14; ø 36.6 mm, height 6 mm; 30 jewels; 18,000 vph; screw balance with 18 gold weight screws; Breguet spring; microrotor; 120-hour power reserve
Functions: hours, minutes, subsidiary seconds; additional 24-hour display with day/night indicator; date
Case: titanium, ø 43.4 mm, height 13 mm; sapphire crystal; transparent case back; water-resistant to 5 atm
Band: reptile skin, buckle
Remarks: additional leather or rubber bracelet
Price: $21,300; limited to 100 pieces
Variations: Earth, Water, and Fire

Tourbillon Gravity Water

Reference number: ST14-TW.M.50
Movement: automatic, Caliber ATM13; ø 36.6 mm, height 6.2 mm; 26 jewels; 18,000 vph; 1-minute tourbillon; Breguet spring; screw balance with 18 gold weight screws; microrotor; 110-hour power reserve
Functions: hours, minutes, subsidiary seconds
Case: stainless steel, ø 43.4 mm, height 13 mm; sapphire crystal, transparent case back; water-resistant to 5 atm
Band: reptile skin, double folding clasp
Remarks: additional rubber bracelet
Price: $89,900; limited to 50 pieces
Variations: Air, Earth, and Fire

One Week Skeleton

Reference number: RG14-W5.5N
Movement: manually wound, Caliber ARM09-S; ø 36.6 mm, height 6.2 mm; 34 jewels; 18,000 vph; 2 spring barrels; screw balance with 18 gold weight screws; Breguet spring; crown wheels visible on dial side; base plate, hand skeletonized and engraved wheels and spring barrel bridges; 168-hour power reserve
Functions: hours, minutes, subsidiary seconds; power reserve indicator
Case: rose gold, ø 43.4 mm, height 13 mm; sapphire crystal; transparent case back; water-resistant to 5 atm
Band: reptile skin, buckle
Remarks: additional rubber bracelet
Price: $49,900; limited to 50 pieces

Racing Manual

Reference number: ST14-MR.90
Movement: manually wound, Caliber AMW11-MR;
ø 36.6 mm, height 6 mm; 20 jewels; 18,000 vph;
screw balance with gold weight screws; Breguet
spring, bridges of melted Formula 1 engine parts;
120-hour power reserve
Functions: hours, minutes, subsidiary seconds
Case: stainless steel with black PVD coating and
titanium; ø 43.4 mm, height 13 mm; sapphire
crystal; transparent case back; water-resistant to
5 atm
Band: reptile skin with carbon fiber inlay, buckle
Remarks: additional rubber bracelet
Price: $13,800; limited to 50 pieces

Racing Gravity

Reference number: ST14-GR.90
Movement: automatic, Caliber AMR13-MR; ø 36.6
mm, height 6 mm; 32 jewels; 18,000 vph; screw
balance with gold weight screws; Breguet spring;
microrotor visible on dial side; bridges of melted
Formula 1 engine parts; 120-hour power reserve
Functions: hours, minutes, subsidiary seconds
Case: stainless steel with black PVD coating and
titanium; ø 43.4 mm, height 13 mm; titanium bezel,
sapphire crystal; transparent case back; water-
resistant to 5 atm
Band: reptile skin with carbon fiber inlay, buckle
Remarks: additional rubber bracelet
Price: $16,800; limited to 50 pieces

Tourbillon Fire

Reference number: RG13-TF.90
Movement: manually wound, Caliber ATC11; ø
36.6 mm, height 6.2 mm; 24 jewels; 18,000 vph;
1-minute tourbillon; screw balance with gold weight
screws; Breguet spring; 2 spring barrels; crown
wheels visible on dial side; 240-hour power reserve
Functions: hours, minutes, subsidiary seconds
Case: rose gold, ø 43.4 mm, height 13 mm;
sapphire crystal; transparent case back; water-
resistant to 5 atm
Band: reptile skin, double folding clasp
Remarks: with extra rubber bracelet
Price: $121,500; limited to 50 pieces
Variations: Air, Earth, and Water

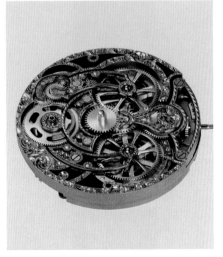

Caliber ATM13

Automatic, 1-minute tourbillon, microrotor visible on
dial; single spring barrel; 110-hour power reserve
Functions: hours, minutes, subsidiary seconds
Diameter: 36.6 mm
Height: 6.2 mm
Jewels: 26
Balance: screw balance with gold weight screws
Frequency: 18,000 vph
Balance spring: Breguet spring
Shock protection: Incabloc
Remarks: fine finishing on movement

Caliber ARM09-S

Manually wound; crown wheels visible on dial side;
platinum, gearwheels and spring barrel bridges
hand-skeletonized and engraved; double spring
barrel; 168-hour power reserve
Functions: hours, minutes, subsidiary seconds
Diameter: 36.6 mm
Height: 6.2 mm
Jewels: 34
Balance: screw balance with gold weight screws
Frequency: 18,000 vph
Balance spring: Breguet spring
Shock protection: Incabloc

Caliber ADD14

Automatic, microrotor; single spring barrel; 120-
hour power reserve
Functions: hours, minutes, subsidiary seconds;
additional 24-hour display with day/night indicator
Diameter: 36.6 mm
Height: 6 mm
Jewels: 30
Balance: screw balance with gold weight screws
Frequency: 18,000 vph
Balance spring: Breguet spring
Shock protection: Incabloc
Remarks: fine finishing on movement

Arnold & Son

38, boulevard des Eplatures
CH-2300 La Chaux-de-Fonds
Switzerland

Tel.:
01141-32-967-9797

Fax:
01141-32-968-0755

E-Mail:
info@arnoldandson.com

Website:
www.arnoldandson.com

Founded:
1995

Number of employees:
approx. 30

U.S. distributor:
Arnold & Son USA
Time Art Distribution
550 Fifth Avenue, Suite 501
New York, NY 10036
212-221-8041

Most important collections/price range:
UTTE, Time Pyramid, DBG, DBS, HMS, TB88,
TE8 (Tourbillon), TBR / from approx. $10,000
to $325,000

Arnold & Son

John Arnold holds a special place among the British watchmakers of the eighteenth and nineteenth centuries because he was the first to literally organize the production of his chronometers along industrial lines. He developed his own standards and employed numerous watchmakers. During his lifetime, he is said to have manufactured around 5,000 marine chronometers which he sold at reasonable prices to the Royal Navy and the West Indies merchant fleet. Arnold chronometers were packed in the trunks of some of the greatest explorers, from John Franklin and Ernest Shackleton to Captain Cook and Dr. Livingstone.

As Arnold & Son was once synonymous with precision timekeeping on the high seas, it stands to reason, then, that the modern brand should also focus its design policies on the interplay of time and geography as well as the basic functions of navigation. Independence from The British Masters Group has meant that the venerable English chronometer brand has been reorienting itself, setting its sights on classic, elegant watchmaking. With the expertise of watch manufacturer La Joux-Perret behind it (and the expertise housed in the building behind the complex on the main road between La Chaux-de-Fonds and Le Locle), it has been able to implement a number of new ideas.

There are two main lines: The Royal Collection celebrates John Arnold's art, with luxuriously designed models that look back in time with delicate complications, tourbillons or world-time displays, or unadorned manual windings featuring the new Caliber A&S 1001 by La Joux-Perret. The Instrument Collection is dedicated to exploring the seven seas and offers a sober look reflecting old-fashioned meters. Typically, these timepieces combine two displays on a single dial: a chronograph with jumping seconds, for example, between the off-center displays of time and the date hand or separate escapements driving a dual time display—left the sidereal time, right the solar time, and between the two, the difference. Perhaps the most remarkable timepiece in the collection is the skeletonized Time Pyramid with a dual power reserve, a crown between the lugs, and an overall modern look.

TEC1

Reference number: 1CTAR.G01A.C112R
Movement: automatic, Arnold & Son Caliber 8305; ø 35 mm, height 8.15 mm; 30 jewels; 28,800 vph; 1-minute tourbillon; pink gold rotor; finely finished; 55-hour power reserve
Functions: hours, minutes; chronograph
Case: pink gold, ø 45 mm, height 16.5 mm; sapphire crystal; transparent case back; water-resistant to 3 atm
Band: reptile skin, buckle
Price: $99,900
Variations: pink gold with blue dial ($106,400; limited to 28 pieces); palladium ($87,850)

HM Perpetual Moon

Reference number: 1GLAR.I01A.C122A
Movement: manually wound, Arnold & Son Caliber 1512; ø 34 mm, height 5.35 mm; 27 jewels; 21,600 vph; astronomically accurate moon phase display over 122 years; 90-hour power reserve
Functions: hours, minutes; moon phase
Case: pink gold, ø 42 mm, height 11.43 mm; sapphire crystal; transparent case back; water-resistant to 3 atm
Band: reptile skin, buckle
Remarks: hand-engraved golden moon disc
Price: $29,950
Variations: pink gold with guillochéed blue dial ($29,950); stainless steel with black dial/silver moon disc ($16,300)

TB88

Reference number: 1TBAS.S01A.C113S
Movement: manually wound, Arnold & Son Caliber 5003; ø 37.8 mm, height 5.9 mm; 32 jewels; 18,000 vph; inverted construction, escapement with dead beat seconds; double spring barrel; 100-hour power reserve
Functions: hours, minutes, subsidiary seconds (jumping)
Case: stainless steel, ø 46 mm, height 12.85 mm; sapphire crystal; transparent case back; water-resistant to 3 atm
Band: reptile skin, buckle
Price: $39,100
Variations: rose gold ($56,550)

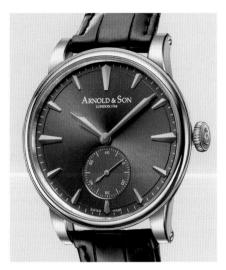

HMS1

Reference number: 1LCAP.S04A.C110A
Movement: manual winding, Arnold & Son Caliber 1101; ø 30 mm, height 2.7 mm; 21 jewels; 21,600 vph; double spring barrel; 80-hour power reserve
Functions: hours, minutes, subsidiary seconds
Case: rose gold, ø 40 mm, height 8 mm; sapphire crystal; transparent case back; water-resistant to 3 atm
Band: reptile skin, buckle
Price: $16,200
Variations: white dial ($16,200); stainless steel with white dial ($9,900) or anthracite dial ($9,900)

DTE

Reference number: 1DTAR.L01A.C120A
Movement: manually wound, Arnold & Son Caliber 8513; ø 37.3 mm, height 8.35 mm; 42 jewels; 21,600 vph; 2 1-minute tourbillons; double spring barrel; finely finished; 90-hour power reserve
Functions: hours, minutes (2 time zones)
Case: pink gold, ø 43.5 mm, height 11.77 mm; sapphire crystal; transparent case back; water-resistant to 3 atm
Band: reptile skin, buckle
Remarks: limited to 28 pieces
Price: $215,850

DSTB

Reference number: 1ATAR.L01A.C120A
Movement: automatic, Arnold & Son Caliber 6003; ø 38 mm, height 7.39 mm; 32 jewels; 28,800 vph; dead beat seconds; escapement visible on dial side; finely finished; 50-hour power reserve
Functions: hours and minutes (off-center), subsidiary seconds (retrograde)
Case: pink gold, ø 43.5 mm, height 13 mm; sapphire crystal; transparent case back; water-resistant to 3 atm
Band: reptile skin, buckle
Remarks: limited to 50 pieces
Price: $48,550

CTB

Reference number: 1CHAS.S02A.C121S
Movement: automatic, Arnold & Son Caliber 7103; ø 30.4 mm, height 8.5 mm; 31 jewels; 28,800 vph; finely finished; 50-hour power reserve
Functions: hours and minutes (off-center), sweep seconds (jumping); chronograph
Case: stainless steel, ø 44 mm, height 14 mm; sapphire crystal; transparent case back; water-resistant to 3 atm
Band: reptile skin, buckle
Price: $27,750
Variations: pink gold ($44,350)

UTTE

Reference number: 1UTAR.S01A.C120A
Movement: manually wound, Arnold & Son Caliber 8200; ø 32 mm; height 2.97 mm; 29 jewels; 21,600 vph; 1-minute tourbillon; finely finished; 90-hour power reserve
Functions: hours and minutes (off-center), subsidiary seconds (on tourbillon cage)
Case: pink gold, ø 42 mm, height 8.34 mm; sapphire crystal; transparent case back; water-resistant to 3 atm
Band: reptile skin, buckle
Price: $73,900
Variations: palladium ($64,200)

Time Pyramid

Reference number: 1TPAR.S01A.C124A
Movement: manual winding, Arnold & Son Caliber 1615; ø 37 mm, height 4.4 mm; 27 jewels; 21,600 vph; skeletonized; pyramidal architecture; 2 spring barrels; 80-hour power reserve
Functions: hours, minutes, subsidiary seconds; double power reserve display
Case: pink gold, ø 44.6 mm, height 10.09 mm; sapphire crystal; transparent case back; water-resistant to 3 atm
Band: reptile skin, buckle
Remarks: inspired by clocks of John and Roger Arnold
Price: $43,200
Variations: stainless steel ($31,900)

ArtyA

Luxury Artpieces SA
Route de Thonon 146
CH-1222 Vésenaz
Switzerland

Tel.:
01141-22-752-4940

Website:
www.artya.com

Founded:
2010

Number of employees:
12

Annual production:
at least 365 (one a day)

U.S. distributor:
Contact headquarters for all enquiries.

Most important collections/price range:
Son of a Gun / $8,800 to $167,000;
Son of Art / $3,800 to $21,000;
Son of Earth / $4,300 to $183,000;
Son of Love / $4,300 to $54,500;
Son of Sound / $4,300 to $22,110;
Son of Gears / $6,550 to $16,550

Shaking up the staid atmosphere of watchmaking can be achieved many ways. The conservative approach is to make some small engineering advance and then talk loudly of tradition and innovation. Yvan Arpa, founder of ArtyA watches, takes another route and enjoys "putting his boot in the anthill," in his own words.

This refreshingly candid personality arrived at watchmaking because, after spending his *Wanderjahre* crossing Papua New Guinea on foot and practicing Thai boxing in its native land, any corporate mugginess back home did not quite cut it for him. Instead he turned the obscure brand Romain Jerome into the talk of the industry with novel material choices: "I looked for antimatter to gentrify common matter," he reflects, "like the rust: proof of the passage of time and the sworn enemy of watchmaking."

After leaving Romain Jerome, he founded his own company, ArtyA, where he could get his "monster" off the slab as it were, with a divine spark. "I had worked with water, rust, dust, and other elements, so then I took fire," says Arpa. Each new ArtyA case was hit with an electrical arc, resulting in something different each time. Inside the cases, besides a solid Swiss-made mechanism, are interesting bits and pieces—from butterfly wings and cut up euros (Bye Bye Euro) to bullets (Son of a Gun). As the brand progresses, the zapped cases are giving way to new and bold shapes in more traditional materials, as in the Son of Sound series with a guitar-shaped case and chrono pushers designed like guitar pegs—Alice Cooper owns one, obviously. He has also launched a second brand, Spero Lucem (I hope for light), a little taunt at Geneva's Calvinistic motto *Post tenebras lux* (after the dark comes light). Arpa often uses the warty skin of toads, a pest in Australia, as straps. Killing rare animals is, he feels, "a little borderline." Arpa wants us not only to wear a watch, but to reflect on aspects of our world and society, the meaning of money, our love-hate relationship with electronics, the passage of time, love and violence, and the significance of music.

ArtyA Son of Sound Broken Glass

Reference number: SoS G BG
Movement: automatic, Artya-Woodstock by Concepto; 27 jewels; 28,800 vph; 48-hour power reserve
Functions: hours, minutes, subsidiary seconds; date; patented active "tuning pegs" system for chronograph functions and date setting; 30-minute counter
Case: stainless steel, 36.62 x 52.3 mm, height 15 mm; water-resistant to 50 atm
Band: reptile skin, buckle
Price: $21,000; limited to 99 pieces

Son of a Gun Russian Roulette

Movement: manually wound, ArtyA patent; ø 32.6 mm, height 5.7 mm; 19 jewels
Functions: hours, minutes
Case: stainless steel, ø 44 mm; Artyor inserts on case; sapphire crystal; transparent case back; water-resistant to 5 atm
Band: reptile skin, buckle
Remarks: single lucky bullet spins rapidly around dial with every move
Price: $8,500; limited to 99 pieces

Son of Earth Classic Butterfly

Movement: automatic COSC movement (Swiss-made); 25 jewels; 42-hour power reserve
Functions: hours, minutes
Case: pink gold; ø 40 mm, height 12 mm; sapphire crystal; transparent case back; water-resistant to 5 atm
Band: reptile skin, buckle
Remarks: dial decorated with genuine iridescent butterfly wings and gold leaf
Price: $16,500; unique piece

A JOURNEY THROUGH TIME.

1960

2014

TRIBUTE TO CONTOGRAF · 1960s ·

Manufacture d'Horlogerie Audemars Piguet
Route de France 16
CH-1348 Le Brassus
Switzerland

Tel.:
01141-21-845-1400

Fax:
01141-21-845-1400

E-Mail:
info@audemarspiguet.com

Website:
www.audemarspiguet.com

Founded:
1875

Number of employees:
approx. 1,100

Annual production:
26,000 watches

U.S. distributor:
Audemars Piguet (North America) Inc.
65 East 57th Street
New York, NY 10022
212-758-8400

Most important collections/price range:
Royal Oak / from approx. $15,400

Audemars Piguet

The history of Audemars Piguet may well be one of the most engaging stories of Swiss watchmaking folklore: Ever since their school days together in the Vallée de Joux, Jules-Louis Audemars (born in 1851) and Edward-Auguste Piguet (born 1853) knew that they would follow in the footsteps of their fathers and grandfathers and become watchmakers. They were members of the same sports association, sang in the same church choir, attended the same vocational school—and both became outstandingly talented watchmakers.

The *manufacture* that was founded 140 years ago by these two is still in family hands. The company was able to make extensive investments in production facilities and new movements thanks to the ongoing success of the sporty Royal Oak collection (launched in 1972) and the profits made from selling off shares in Jaeger-LeCoultre fifteen years ago. The Manufacture des Forges, designed according to the latest ecological and economical standards, opened in August 2009 in Le Brassus and is a key to the future of the traditional brand. The second key is no doubt the atelier Renaud et Papi, which has belonged to AP since 1992 and specializes in the most complex complications.

Something must have clicked, because general manager Philippe C. Merk steered the brand through the recession well, even crossing the CHF 550 million mark. Merk and AP parted ways in May 2012, and the company is currently operating under manager François-Henry Bennahmias, who previously handled the key Asian market.

Royal Oak Tourbillon Concept GMT

Reference number: 26580IO.00.D010CA.01
Movement: manually wound, AP Caliber 2930; ø 35.6 mm, height 9.9 mm; 29 jewels; 21,600 vph; 1-minute tourbillon; fine hand-finishing; 237-hour power reserve
Functions: hours, minutes; additional 24-hour display (2nd time zone) with day/night indicator, crown positions shown for changing functions
Case: titanium, ø 44 mm; ceramic bezel; sapphire crystal; ceramic crown and pushers; water-resistant to 2 atm
Band: rubber, folding clasp
Price: $214,200

Royal Oak Offshore Diver

Reference number: 15707CB.00.A010CA.01
Movement: automatic, AP Caliber 3120; ø 26.6 mm, height 4.26 mm; 40 jewels; 21,600 vph; entirely hand-decorated; 60-hour power reserve
Functions: hours, minutes, sweep seconds; date
Case: ceramic, ø 42 mm, bezel attached with 8 titanium screws; crown adjustable scale ring with 60-minute divisions; sapphire crystal; screw-in crown; water-resistant to 30 atm
Band: rubber, buckle
Price: $23,900

Royal Oak Offshore Chronograph

Reference number: 26470ST.00.A027CA.01
Movement: automatic, AP Caliber 3126/3840 (base AP 3120); ø 29.9 mm, height 7.16 mm; 59 jewels; 21,600 vph; 55-hour power reserve
Functions: hours, minutes, subsidiary seconds; chronograph; date
Case: stainless steel, ø 42 mm, bezel attached with 8 screws; sapphire crystal; transparent case back; ceramic screw-in crown and pusher; water-resistant to 10 atm
Band: rubber, buckle
Price: $25,600

Royal Oak Offshore Chronograph

Reference number: 26470ST.OO.A101CR.01
Movement: automatic, AP Caliber 3126/3840 (base AP 3120); ø 29.92 mm, height 7.16 mm; 59 jewels; 21,600 vph; 55-hour power reserve
Functions: hours, minutes, subsidiary seconds; chronograph; date
Case: stainless steel, ø 42 mm; bezel attached with 8 screws; sapphire crystal; transparent case back; ceramic crown and pushers; water-resistant to 10 atm
Band: reptile skin, buckle
Price: $26,000
Variations: blue dial/rubber strap ($25,700)

Royal Oak Offshore Chronograph

Reference number:
Movement: automatic, AP Caliber 3126/3840 (base AP 3120); ø 29.92 mm, height 7.16 mm; 59 jewels; 21,600 vph; 55-hour power reserve
Functions: hours, minutes, subsidiary seconds; chronograph; date
Case: stainless steel, ø 42 mm; bezel attached with 8 screws; sapphire crystal; transparent case back; ceramic crown and pushers; water-resistant to 10 atm
Band: reptile skin, buckle
Price: $26,000
Variations: black dial

Royal Oak Offshore Chronograph

Reference number: 26402CB.OOA010CA.01
Movement: automatic, AP Caliber 3126/3840 (base AP 3120); ø 29.92 mm, height 7.16 mm; 59 jewels; 21,600 vph; 55-hour power reserve
Functions: hours, minutes, subsidiary seconds; chronograph; date
Case: ceramic, ø 44 mm, height 14.45 mm; bezel attached with 8 white-gold screws; sapphire crystal; screw-in crown and pushers; water-resistant to 10 atm
Band: rubber, buckle
Price: $41,700

Royal Oak Offshore Chronograph

Reference number: 26400RO.OO.A002CA.01
Movement: automatic, AP Caliber 3126/3841 (base AP 3120); ø 29.9 mm, height 7.16 mm; 59 jewels; 21,600 vph; 55-hour power reserve
Functions: hours, minutes, subsidiary seconds; chronograph; date
Case: pink gold, ø 39 mm, height 15 mm; screwed-down bezel; sapphire crystal; transparent case back; screw-in crown; water-resistant to 10 atm
Band: rubber, buckle
Price: $47,100

Royal Oak Offshore Chronograph

Reference number: 26400SO.OO.A002CA.01
Movement: automatic, AP Caliber 3126/3841 (base AP 3120); ø 29.92 mm, height 7.16 mm; 59 jewels; 21,600 vph; 55-hour power reserve
Functions: hours, minutes, subsidiary seconds; chronograph; date
Case: stainless steel, ø 44 mm, height 15 mm; ceramic bezel attached with 8 screws; sapphire crystal; transparent case back; screw-in crown; water-resistant to 10 atm
Band: rubber, buckle
Price: $33,400

Royal Oak Chronograph

Reference number: 26320ST.OO.1220ST.03
Movement: automatic, AP Caliber 2385; ø 26.2 mm, height 5.5 mm; 37 jewels; 21,600 vph; entirely hand-decorated; 40-hour power reserve
Functions: hours, minutes, subsidiary seconds; chronograph; date
Case: stainless steel, ø 41 mm, height 10.8 mm; bezel attached with 8 white-gold screws; screw-in crown; sapphire crystal; screw-in crown and pushers; water-resistant to 5 atm
Band: stainless steel, folding clasp
Price: $24,300

Royal Oak Chronograph

Reference number: 26320OR.OO.D002CR.01
Movement: automatic, AP Caliber 2385;
ø 26.2 mm, height 5.5 mm; 37 jewels; 21,600 vph;
entirely hand-decorated; 42-hour power reserve
Functions: hours, minutes, subsidiary seconds;
chronograph; date
Case: pink gold, ø 39 mm, height 5.25 mm; bezel
attached with 8 white-gold screws; sapphire crystal;
screw-in crown and pushers; water-resistant to
30 atm
Band: reptile skin, folding clasp
Price: $37,900

Royal Oak

Reference number: 15400ST.OO.1220ST.01
Movement: automatic, AP Caliber 3120;
ø 26.6 mm, height 4.25 mm; 40 jewels; 21,600
vph; entirely hand-decorated
Functions: hours, minutes, sweep seconds; date
Case: stainless steel, ø 41 mm, height 9.8 mm;
bezel attached with 8 white-gold screws; sapphire
crystal; transparent case back; screw-in crown;
water-resistant to 30 atm
Band: stainless steel, folding clasp
Price: $17,100
Variations: various dial colors

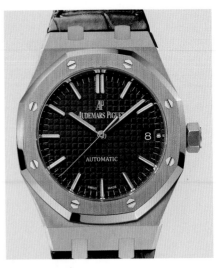

Royal Oak

Reference number: 15450OR.OO.D002CR.01
Movement: automatic, AP Caliber 3120;
ø 26.6 mm, height 4.25 mm; 40 jewels;
21,600 vph; entirely hand-decorated
Functions: hours, minutes, sweep seconds; date
Case: pink gold, ø 37 mm, height 9.8 mm; bezel
attached with 8 white-gold screws; sapphire crystal;
transparent case back; screw-in crown; water-
resistant to 5 atm
Band: reptile skin, folding clasp
Price: $28,600
Variations: various dial colors; stainless steel/
stainless steel bracelet ($16,500)

Royal Oak Jumbo

Reference number: 15202ST.OO.1240ST.01
Movement: automatic, AP Caliber 2121; ø 28 mm,
height 3.05 mm; 36 jewels; 19,800 vph
Functions: hours, minutes; date
Case: stainless steel, ø 39 mm, height 8.1 mm;
bezel attached with 8 white-gold screws; sapphire
crystal; transparent case back; water-resistant to
5 atm
Band: stainless steel, folding clasp
Price: $22,700
Variations: pink gold/pink gold bracelet ($50,800)

Lady Royal Oak

Reference number: 15451ST.ZZ.1256ST.01
Movement: automatic, AP Caliber 3120;
ø 26.6 mm, height 4.26 mm; 40 jewels; 21,600
vph; entirely hand-decorated; 60-hour power
reserve
Functions: hours, minutes, sweep seconds; date
Case: stainless steel, ø 37 mm, height 9.8 mm;
bezel attached with 8 white-gold screws and set
with 40 brilliant-cut diamonds; sapphire crystal;
transparent case back; water-resistant to 5 atm
Band: stainless steel, folding clasp
Price: $25,100

Lady Royal Oak

Reference number: 15402OR.ZZ.D003CR.01
Movement: automatic, AP Caliber 3120;
ø 26.6 mm, height 4.25 mm; 40 jewels; 21,600
vph; entirely hand-decorated; 60-hour power
reserve
Functions: hours, minutes, sweep seconds; date
Case: pink gold, ø 39 mm, height 9.8 mm; bezel
attached with 8 white-gold screws and set with 40
brilliant-cut diamonds; sapphire crystal; transparent
case back; screw-in crown; water-resistant to 5 atm
Band: reptile skin, folding clasp
Remarks: lugs and dial set with diamonds
Price: $82,300

Jules Audemars Chronograph

Reference number: 261530R.OO.D088CR.01
Movement: manually wound, AP Caliber 2908; ø 37.2 mm; 33 jewels; 43,200 vph; 2 spring barrels; balance with variable inertia; inverted design with balance and escapement on dial side; fine hand-finishing; 90-hour power reserve; COSC-tested chronometer
Functions: hours, minutes, subsidiary seconds; power reserve indicator
Case: pink gold, ø 46 mm, height 12.7 mm; sapphire crystal; transparent case back
Band: reptile skin, folding clasp
Price: $212,500

Jules Audemars Extra-Thin

Reference number: 151800R.OO.A002CR.01
Movement: automatic, AP Caliber 2120; ø 28.4 mm, height 2.45 mm; 36 jewels; 19,800 vph; 40-hour power reserve
Functions: hours, minutes
Case: pink gold, ø 41 mm, height 6.7 mm; sapphire crystal; transparent case back
Band: reptile skin, folding clasp
Price: $26,000
Variations: white gold ($28,200)

Jules Audemars Extra-Thin

Reference number: 15180BC.OO.A002CR.01
Movement: automatic, AP Caliber 2120; ø 28.4 mm, height 2.45 mm; 36 jewels; 19,800 vph; 40-hour power reserve
Functions: hours, minutes
Case: white gold, ø 41 mm, height 6.7 mm; sapphire crystal; transparent case back
Band: reptile skin, buckle
Price: $28,200
Variations: pink gold ($26,000)

Millenary Minute Repeater

Reference number: 263710R.OO.D803CR.01
Movement: manually wound, 37.9 x 32.9 mm, height 10.05 mm; 40 jewels; 21,600 vph; 165-hour power reserve
Functions: hours, minutes, subsidiary seconds; minute repeater
Case: rose gold, 47 x 42 mm, height 15.79 mm; sapphire crystal; transparent case back
Band: reptile skin, folding clasp
Remarks: enamel dial
Price: $495,800

Millenary 4101

Reference number: 15350ST.OO.D002CR.01
Movement: automatic, AP Caliber 4101; ø 37.25 mm, height 7.46 mm; 34 jewels; 28,800 vph; inverted design with balance and escapement on dial side
Functions: hours, minutes, subsidiary seconds
Case: stainless steel, ø 47 mm, height 13 mm; sapphire crystal; transparent case back
Band: reptile skin, folding clasp
Price: $24,500
Variations: pink gold ($40,300)

Millenary 4101

Reference number: 153500R.OO.D093CR.01
Movement: automatic, AP Caliber 4101; ø 37.25 mm, height 7.46 mm; 34 jewels; inverted design with balance and escapement on dial side
Functions: hours, minutes, subsidiary seconds
Case: pink gold, ø 47 mm, height 13 mm; sapphire crystal; transparent case back
Band: reptile skin, folding clasp
Price: $40,300
Variations: stainless steel ($24,500)

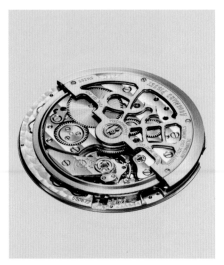

Caliber 2120

Automatic; bidirectional winding rotor; extra-flat design, lateral studs and running ring on movement for stability; single spring barrel, 40-hour power reserve

Functions: hours, minutes
Diameter: 28 mm
Height: 2.45 mm
Jewels: 36
Balance: with variable inertia
Frequency: 19,800 vph
Shock protection: Kif Elastor
Remarks: beveled and polished steel parts, perlage on plate, bridges with côtes de Genève

Caliber 2928

Manually wound, inverted design with AP direct impulse balance; single spring barrel; 165-hour power reserve

Functions: hours, minutes, subsidiary seconds; minute repeater
Measurements: 37.9 x 32.9 mm
Height: 10.05 mm
Jewels: 40
Balance: with variable inertia
Frequency: 21,600 vph
Balance spring: double spring (counterwound)
Remarks: all components decorated by hand, 443 components

Caliber 2121

Automatic; bidirectional winding rotor; extra-flat design, lateral studs and running ring on movement for stability; single spring barrel, 40-hour power reserve

Functions: hours, minutes; date
Diameter: 28 mm
Height: 3.05 mm
Jewels: 36
Balance: with variable inertia
Frequency: 19,800 vph
Shock protection: Kif Elastor
Remarks: beveled and polished steel parts, perlage on plate, bridges with côtes de Genève

Caliber 2324-2825

Automatic; rotor with gold weight segment; single spring barrel, 40-hour power reserve

Functions: hours, minutes; date, weekday, moon phase
Diameter: 26.6 mm
Height: 4.6 mm
Jewels: 45
Balance: with variable inertia
Frequency: 28,800 vph
Shock protection: Kif Elastor
Remarks: beveled and polished steel parts, perlage on plate, bridges with côtes de Genève

Caliber 2329-2846

Automatic; rotor with gold weight segment; single spring barrel, 40-hour power reserve

Functions: hours, minutes; 24-hour display; date; power reserve indicator; day/night indicator
Diameter: 26.6 mm
Height: 4.9 mm
Jewels: 33
Balance: with variable inertia
Frequency: 28,800 vph
Shock protection: Kif Elastor
Remarks: beveled and polished steel parts, perlage on plate, bridges with côtes de Genève

Caliber 2930

Manually wound, 1-minute tourbillon; central front movement bridge of white ceramic; switch for hand setting and winding; single spring barrel, 237-hour power reserve

Functions: hours, minutes; additional 12-hour indicator (2nd time zone)
Diameter: 35.6 mm
Height: 9.9 mm
Jewels: 29
Balance: screw balance
Frequency: 21,600 vph
Remarks: movement of the Royal Oak concept watch of 2014; beveled and polished steel parts, matte mainplate, straight-grain polished bridges

Caliber 2897

Mechanical with automatic winding; hubless peripheral rotor with platinum weight turning on movement edge; column wheel control of chronograph functions; 1-minute tourbillon; simple spring barrel, 65-hour power reserve
Functions: hours, minutes, subsidiary seconds; chronograph
Diameter: 35 mm
Height: 7.75 mm
Jewels: 34
Balance: with variable inertia
Frequency: 21,600 vph
Shock protection: Kif Elastor
Remarks: beveled and guilloché steel parts, perlage on plate

Caliber 2924

Manually wound, 1-minute tourbillon; single spring barrel, 70-hour power reserve
Functions: hours, minutes; power reserve indicator (on movement side)
Diameter: 31.5 mm
Height: 4.46 mm
Jewels: 25
Balance: screw balance
Frequency: 21,600 vph
Shock protection: Kif Elastor
Remarks: beveled and polished steel parts, perlage on plate, bridges with côtes de Genève

Caliber 3120

Mechanical with automatic winding; bidirectional winding gold rotor; single spring barrel, 60-hour power reserve
Functions: hours, minutes, sweep seconds; date
Diameter: 26.6 mm
Height: 4.25 mm
Jewels: 40
Balance: with variable inertia
Frequency: 21,600 vph
Shock protection: Kif Elastor
Remarks: beveled and polished steel parts, perlage on plate, bridges with côtes de Genève

Caliber 3124-3841

Mechanical with automatic winding; bidirectional winding gold rotor; single spring barrel, 60-hour power reserve
Functions: hours, minutes, subsidiary seconds; chronograph
Diameter: 29.94 mm
Height: 7.16 mm
Jewels: 59
Balance: with variable inertia
Frequency: 21,600 vph
Shock protection: Kif Elastor
Remarks: beveled and polished steel parts, perlage on plate, bridges with côtes de Genève

Caliber 3126-3840

Base caliber: 3120
Automatic; bidirectional winding gold rotor; single spring barrel, 60-hour power reserve
Functions: hours, minutes, subsidiary seconds; date
Diameter: 29.94 mm
Height: 7.15 mm
Jewels: 59
Balance: with variable inertia
Frequency: 21,600 vph
Shock protection: Kif Elastor
Remarks: beveled and polished steel parts, perlage on plate, bridges with côtes de Genève

Caliber 4101

Automatic, inverted construction (escapement on dial side); bidirectional winding gold rotor with ceramic ball bearings; single spring barrel, 60-hour power reserve
Functions: hours, minutes, subsidiary seconds
Measurements: 37.25 x 32.9 mm
Height: 7.46 mm
Jewels: 34
Balance: with variable inertia
Frequency: 28,800 vph
Shock protection: Kif Elastor
Remarks: all components decorated by hand; dial side of plate with horizontal côtes de Genève, perlage on back; rhodium-plated bridges, beveled and with decorative graining

Azimuth

Azimuth Watch Co. Sàrl
CH-2503 Bienne/Biel
Switzerland

Tel.:
01141-32-322-2481

Fax:
01141-32-322-2481

E-Mail:
sales@azimuthwatch.com

Website:
www.azimuthwatch.com

Founded:
2004

Number of employees:
10

U.S. distributor:
Coast Time
800 S. Pacific Coast Highway, Suite 8446
Redondo Beach, CA 90277
888-609-1010

Most important collections/price range:
SP-1 / $5,450 to $109,000;
Round-1 / $2,150 to $7,450

Creativity can take on all forms and accept all forms as well. That appears to be the philosophy behind Azimuth, a brand that has sprouted an eclectic and surprising bouquet of watch designs. The company is named for the mathematical term defining the arc of a horizon from a reference point. *Azimuth* is a word of Arabic origin meaning "the route taken by a traveler" or even "the way." It is a term, and indeed a concept, used mainly by astrologers, navigators, and the military—precisely the same sort of people who have placed great stock in accurate timekeeping. But for the company, the path is by no means well-beaten: Azimuth always guarantees a raised eyebrow with avant-garde designs for luxury timepieces. But to hook into tradition, the brand researches, models, and assembles its watches in Switzerland.

Azimuth fans are creative thinkers themselves who appreciate the company's unusual, genuinely innovative timepieces—some known internally as "concept watches." The Mr. Roboto and the Chrono Gauge Mecha-1 are tongue-in-cheek hyperbolic statements about the meaning of a mechanical watch. The SP-1 Mecanique Spaceship and its adventurous mix of displays, powered by a highly modified ETA Unitas 6497, feature a variety of imaginative dials. The single three-dimensional titanium hand vaguely recalls a spaceship. The secret gambler can depress the die-shaped crown of the SP-1 Roulette to send a ball zooming around the dial. The SP-1 Landship has made it over the top (yes, it refers to a World War I tank) after years of tinkering in time for the commemorations of 1914. Given all these complicated devices, the single-hand Back In Time pieces appear as mysterious as a koan.

Retrograde Minutes MOP Fire Dragon

Reference number: RN.RM.SS.L001
Movement: automatic, in-house modified (base ETA); ø 33.1 mm, height 6.4 mm; 21,600/28,800 vph
Functions: retrograde minutes, hours, seconds
Case: stainless steel, ø 42 mm, height 14.8 mm; domed sapphire crystal; water-resistant to 3 atm
Band: calf leather, folding clasp
Remarks: dragon motif engraved on single piece of MOP
Price: $7,450; limited to 25 pieces
Variations: with yellow dragon MOP dial; limited to 25 pieces

Back In Time Beige

Reference number: RN.BT.SS.D007
Movement: automatic, in-house modified (base ETA/Sellita); ø 34.4 mm; height 4.5 mm; 21,600/28,800 vph
Functions: single hand in counterclockwise motion; date
Case: stainless steel, ø 42 mm, height 14.4 mm; domed sapphire crystal; water-resistant to 3 atm
Band: calf leather, buckle
Price: $2,150
Variations: with silver, black, blue, anthracite, etc., dial colors

Frost Gold Retrograde Minutes

Reference number: RN.RM.SS.N003
Movement: automatic, in-house modified (base ETA); ø 33.1 mm; height 6.4 mm; 21,600/28,800 vph
Functions: retrograde minutes, hours, seconds
Case: stainless steel, ø 42 mm, height 14.8 mm; domed sapphire crystal; water-resistant to 3 atm
Band: calf leather, folding clasp
Price: $4,200
Variations: with frost gray dial

SP-1 Spaceship Tiger Eye Stone

Reference number: SP.SS.SS.N003
Movement: manual winding, UNITAS 6497-1 Côtes de Genève modified; ø 36.6 mm; height 4.5 mm; 18,000 vph
Functions: jumping hours, minutes, seconds
Case: stainless steel, ø 47.8 mm; domed sapphire crystal; water-resistant to 3 atm
Band: reptile skin, folding clasp
Remarks: 3D titanium minute hand
Price: $6,650
Variations: PVD case; with calf leather band

SP-1 Spaceship Predator

Reference number: SP.SS.SS.N004
Movement: manual winding, AZM 768 modified and skeletonized; ø 36.6 mm; height 4.5 mm; 18,000 vph
Functions: jumping hours, minutes, seconds
Case: stainless steel, ø 47.8 mm; domed sapphire crystal; water-resistant to 3 atm
Band: calf leather, folding clasp
Remarks: 3D titanium minute hand
Price: $7,100
Variations: PVD case; with reptile skin band

SP-1 Spaceship Blue Aventurine

Reference number: SP.SS.SS.N002
Movement: manual winding, UNITAS 6497-1 Côtes de Genève modified; ø 36.6 mm; height 4.5 mm; 18,000 vph
Functions: jumping hours, minutes, seconds
Case: stainless steel, ø 47.8 mm; domed sapphire crystal; water-resistant to 3 atm
Band: rubber, folding clasp
Remarks: 3D titanium minute hand
Price: $6,650
Variations: PVD case; with calf leather band

SP-1 Twin Barrel Tourbillon

Reference number: SP.TB.TI.L001
Movement: manual winding tourbillon; in-house modified; 36.3 x 32.0 mm, height 6.4 mm; 28,800 vph; twin barrels; 5-day power reserve
Functions: jumping hours, minutes; specially modified twin-disc jumping hour system on 3-dimensional minute hand
Case: titanium with carbon fiber side inserts, 45 x 50 mm, height 18.3 mm; domed sapphire crystal; water-resistant to 5 atm
Band: woven black fiber, folding clasp
Price: $109,000; limited to 25 pieces

SP-1 Mr. Roboto

Reference number: ME.RB.SS.N001
Movement: automatic, in-house modified (base ETA); ø 32.5 mm, height 6.7 mm; 21,600/28,800 vph
Functions: regulator hours, retrograde minutes, seconds; GMT
Case: stainless steel, 43 x 50 mm; sapphire crystal; water-resistant to 5 atm
Band: calf leather, buckle
Price: $5,450
Variations: stainless steel bracelet

SP-1 Landship

Reference number: SP.LS.TI.L001
Movement: automatic, in-house modified (base ETA); ø 32.5 mm, height 6.4 mm; 21,600/28,800 vph
Functions: wandering hour, retrograde minutes
Case: titanium, 55 x 40 mm; water-resistant to 3 atm
Band: rubber, folding clasp
Price: $7,800
Variations: case in handpainted military camouflage

Ball Watch Co.

BALL Watch Company SA
Rue du Châtelot 21
CH-2300 La Chaux-de-Fonds
Switzerland

Tel.:
01141-32-724-53-00

Fax:
01141-32-724-53-01

E-Mail:
info@ballwatch.ch

Website:
www.ballwatch.com

Founded:
1891

U.S. distributor:
BALL Watch USA
1920 Dr. Martin Luther King Jr. St N
Suite D
St. Petersburg, FL 33704
727-896-4278

Most important collections/price range:
Engineer, Fireman, Trainmaster, Conductor /
$1,300 to $6,500

Engineer, Fireman, Trainmaster, Conductor . . . these names for the Ball Watch Co. collections trace back to the company's origins and evoke the glorious age when trains puffing smoke and steam crisscrossed America. Back then, the pocket watch was a necessity to maintain precise rail schedules. By 1893, many companies had adopted the

General Railroads Timepiece Standards, which included such norms as regulation in at least five positions, precision to within thirty seconds per week, Breguet balance springs, and so on. One of the chief players in developing the standards was Webster Clay Ball. This farmboy-turned-watchmaker from Fredericktown, Ohio, decided to leave the homestead for a more lucrative occupation. He apprenticed as a watchmaker, became a salesperson for Dueber watch cases, and finally opened the Webb C. Ball Company in Cleveland. In 1891, he added the position of chief inspector of the Lake Shore Lines to his CV. When a hogshead's watch stopped resulting in an accident, Ball decided to establish quality benchmarks for watches that included antimagnetic technology, and he set up an inspection system for the timepieces.

Today, Ball Watch Co. has maintained its lineage, although now producing in Switzerland. These rugged, durable watches aim to be "accurate in adverse conditions," so the company tagline says—and at a very good price. Functionality remains a top priority, so Ball will go to special lengths to work special technologies into its timepieces. Ball has also developed special oils for cold temperatures, for instance. And it is one of few brands to use tritium gas tubes to light up dials, hands, and markers. For those who need to read the time accurately in dark places—divers, pilots, commandos, hunters, etc.—this is essential.

Engineer Hydrocarbon Airborne S

Reference number: DM2076C-S1CAJ-BK
Movement: automatic, BALL Caliber RR1102-CSL; ø 25.6 mm, height 5.05 mm; 25 or 26 jewels; 28,800 vph; 38-hour power reserve; COSC-certified chronometer
Functions: hours, minutes, sweep seconds; day, date
Case: stainless steel, ø 42 mm, height 13.85 mm; SpringLOCK® antishock system; ceramic unidirectional bezel; sapphire crystal; crown protection system; water-resistant to 12 atm
Band: stainless steel, folding clasp and extension
Remarks: micro gas tube illumination; shock-resistant; antimagnetic
Price: $4,399

Engineer Hydrocarbon Black S

Reference number: DM2176A-P1CAJ-BK
Movement: automatic, BALL Caliber RR1101-CSL; ø 25.6 mm, height 3.6 mm; 21 or 25 jewels; 28,800 vph; 42-hour power reserve; COSC-certified chronometer
Functions: hours, minutes, sweep seconds; magnified date
Case: black DLC & titanium, ø 42 mm, height 13.25 mm; SpringLOCK® antishock system; ceramic unidirectional bezel; 5.3 mm sapphire crystal; patented crown protection system; water-resistant to 30 atm
Band: rubber strap, buckle
Remarks: micro gas tube illumination; shock-resistant; antimagnetic
Price: $4,699

Engineer Hydrocarbon NEDU

Reference number: DC3026A-SC-BK
Movement: automatic, BALL Caliber RR1402-C; ø 30 mm, height 7.9 mm; 25 jewels; 28,800 vph; 48-hour power reserve; COSC-certified chronometer
Functions: hours, minutes, subsidiary seconds; day, date; 12-hour chronograph operable underwater
Case: stainless steel, ø 42 mm, height 17.30 mm; patented helium system; ceramic unidirectional bezel; sapphire crystal; crown protection system; water-resistant to 60 atm
Band: titanium/stainless steel, folding clasp, extension
Remarks: micro gas tube illumination; shock-resistant; antimagnetic
Price: $4,799

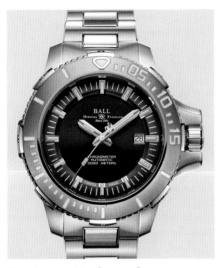

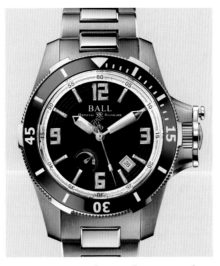

Engineer Hydrocarbon DeepQUEST

Reference number: DM3000A-SCJ-BK
Movement: automatic, BALL Caliber RR1101-C;
ø 25.6 mm, height 3.6 mm; 21 or 25 jewels; 28,800
vph; 42-hour power reserve; COSC-certified chronometer
Functions: hours, minutes, sweep seconds; date
Case: titanium single-block case, ø 43 mm, height 16
mm; unidirectional bezel with patented setting system,
5.3 mm sapphire crystal; crown protection system;
water-resistant to 300 atm
Band: titanium/stainless steel, folding clasp, extension
Remarks: micro gas tube illumination; shock-resistant;
antimagnetic
Price: $4,299

Engineer Hydrocarbon Hunley

Reference number: PM2096B-S1J-BK
Movement: automatic, BALL Caliber RR1702;
ø 25.6 mm, height 4.85 mm; 21 jewels; 28,800
vph; 42-hour power reserve
Functions: hours, minutes, sweep seconds; date;
power reserve indication
Case: stainless steel, ø 42 mm, height 17.3
mm; Amortiser® antishock system, ceramic
unidirectional bezel; sapphire crystal; patented
crown protection; water-resistant to 20 atm
Band: stainless steel, folding clasp and extension
Remarks: micro gas tube illumination; antimagnetic
Price: $3,899; limited to 1,864 pieces

Engineer Master II Diver

Reference number: DM2020A-SA-BKGR
Movement: automatic, BALL Caliber RR1102;
ø 25.6 mm, height 5.05 mm; 25 or 26 jewels;
28,800 vph; 38-hour power reserve
Functions: hours, minutes, sweep seconds; day,
date
Case: stainless steel, ø 42 mm, height 13.3 mm;
inner bezel; sapphire crystal; screw-in crown; water-resistant to 30 atm
Band: stainless steel, folding clasp
Remarks: micro gas tube illumination; shock-resistant; antimagnetic
Price: $2,399
Variations: white inner bezel

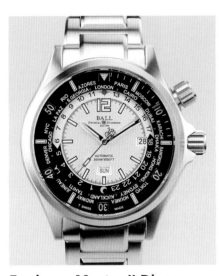

Engineer Master II Diver Worldtime

Reference number: DG2022A-SA-WH
Movement: automatic, BALL Caliber RR1501;
ø 25.6 mm, height 5.05 mm; 25 jewels;
28,800 vph; 38-hour power reserve
Functions: hours, minutes, sweep seconds; day,
date; world-time display
Case: stainless steel, ø 45 mm, height 15.4 mm;
inner bezel, sapphire crystal; screw-in crown; water-resistant to 30 atm
Band: stainless steel, folding clasp
Remarks: micro gas tube illumination; shock-resistant; antimagnetic
Price: $2,999

Engineer Master II Slide Chronograph

Reference number: CM3888C-S1J-BK
Movement: automatic, BALL Caliber RR1402;
ø 30 mm, height 7.9 mm; 25 jewels; 28,800 vph;
48-hour power reserve
Functions: hours, minutes, subsidiary seconds; day,
date; 12-hour patented slide chronograph
Case: stainless steel, ø 47.6 mm, height 15.5 mm;
sapphire crystal; screw-in crown; water-resistant to
10 atm
Band: stainless steel, folding clasp
Remarks: micro gas tube illumination; shock-resistant
Price: $3,399

Engineer Master II Pilot GMT

Reference number: GM3090C-LLAJ-BK
Movement: automatic, BALL Caliber RR1201;
ø 25.6 mm, height 4.1 mm; 21 jewels; 28,800 vph;
42-hour power reserve
Functions: hours, minutes, sweep seconds;
magnified date; 2nd time zone indication
Case: stainless steel, ø 43.5 mm, height 11.9 mm;
aluminum unidirectional bezel; sapphire crystal;
screw-in crown; water-resistant to 10 atm
Band: reptile skin, buckle
Remarks: micro gas tube illumination; shock-resistant; antimagnetic
Price: $2,499

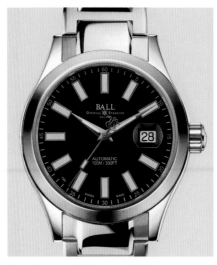

Engineer II Magneto S

Reference number: NM3022C-NCJ-BK
Movement: automatic, BALL Caliber RR1103-CSL; ø 25.6 mm, height 4.6 mm; 25 or 26 jewels; 28,800 vph; 38-hour power reserve; COSC-certified chronometer
Functions: hours, minutes, sweep seconds; date
Case: stainless steel, ø 42 mm, height 12.9 mm; A-PROOF® antimagnetic system; SpringLOCK® antishock system; sapphire crystal; screw-in crown; transparent case back; water-resistant to 10 atm
Band: fabric, buckle
Remarks: micro gas tube illumination; shock-resistant
Price: $3,399

Engineer II Marvelight

Reference number: NM2026C-S6J-BK
Movement: automatic, BALL Caliber RR1103; ø 25.6 mm, height 4.6 mm; 25 or 26 jewels; 28,800 vph; 38-hour power reserve
Functions: hours, minutes, sweep seconds; magnified date
Case: stainless steel, ø 40 mm, height 13.15 mm; sapphire crystal; screw-in crown; water-resistant to 10 atm
Band: stainless steel, folding clasp
Remarks: micro gas tube illumination; shock-resistant; antimagnetic
Price: $1,799
Variations: blue, gray, or silver dial

Trainmaster Cannonball S

Reference number: CM1052D-S2J-GY
Movement: automatic, BALL Caliber RR1401-SL; ø 30 mm, height 7.5 mm; 49 jewels; 28,800 vph; 38-hour power reserve
Functions: hours, minutes, subsidiary seconds; date; 45-minute chronograph
Case: stainless steel, ø 43 mm, height 14.8 mm; SpringLOCK® antishock system; sapphire crystal; transparent case back; screw-in crown; water-resistant to 5 atm
Band: stainless steel, folding clasp
Remarks: micro gas tube illumination; shock-resistant
Price: $3,899

Trainmaster Cleveland Express

Reference number: NM1058D-LCJ-SL
Movement: automatic, BALL Caliber RR1102-C; ø 25.6 mm, height 5.05 mm; 25 or 26 jewels; 28,800 vph; 38-hour power reserve; COSC-certified chronometer
Functions: hours, minutes, sweep seconds; day, date
Case: stainless steel, ø 41 mm, height 12.5 mm; antireflective convex sapphire crystal; sapphire crystal case back; screw-in crown; water-resistant to 5 atm
Band: reptile skin, buckle or clasp
Remarks: satin dial; micro gas tube illumination; shock-resistant
Price: $2,799

Trainmaster One Hundred Twenty

Reference number: NM2888D-PG-LJ-GYGO
Movement: automatic, BALL Caliber RR1101; ø 25.6 mm, height 3.6 mm; 21 or 25 jewels; 28,800 vph; 42-hour power reserve
Functions: hours, minutes, sweep seconds; date
Case: rose gold, ø 39.5 mm, height 10.5 mm; antireflective convex sapphire crystal; screw-in crown; sapphire crystal case back; water-resistant to 5 atm
Band: reptile skin, buckle
Remarks: micro gas tube illumination; shock-resistant
Price: $6,999
Variations: silver dial

Trainmaster Roman

Reference number: NM1058D-L4J-WH
Movement: automatic, BALL Caliber RR1102; ø 25.6 mm, height 5.05 mm; 25 or 26 jewels; 28,800 vph; 38-hour power reserve
Functions: hours, minutes, sweep seconds; day, date
Case: stainless steel, ø 41 mm, height 12.55 mm; antireflective sapphire crystal; screw-in crown; sapphire crystal case back; water-resistant to 5 atm
Band: reptile skin, buckle or clasp
Remarks: micro gas tube illumination; shock-resistant
Price: $1,899
Variations: gray dial

Fireman Storm Chaser Pro

Reference number: CM3090C-L1J-BK
Movement: automatic, BALL Caliber RR1402;
ø 30 mm, height 7.9 mm; 25 jewels; 28,800 vph;
48-hour power reserve
Functions: hours, minutes, subsidiary seconds; day,
date; 12-hour chronograph; telemeter
Case: stainless steel, ø 42 mm, height 15.65 mm;
aluminum bezel, sapphire crystal; screw-in crown;
transparent case back; water-resistant to 10 atm
Band: calf leather, buckle
Remarks: micro gas tube illumination; shock-
resistant
Price: $3,199
Variations: gray or white dial

Ball for BMW Classic

Reference number: NM3010D-LCFJ-BK
Movement: automatic, BALL Caliber RR1101-C;
ø 25.6 mm, height 3.6 mm; 21 or 25 jewels;
28,800 vph; 42-hour power reserve; COSC-certified
chronometer
Functions: hours, minutes, sweep seconds; date
Case: stainless steel, ø 40 mm, height 10.87
mm; Amortiser® antishock system; antireflective
sapphire crystal; screw-in crown; transparent case
back; water-resistant to 50 m
Band: reptile skin, folding clasp
Remarks: micro gas tube illumination; antimagnetic
Price: $3,699

Ball for BMW GMT

Reference number: GM3010C-SCJ-SL
Movement: automatic, BALL Caliber RR1201-C;
ø 25.6 mm, height 4.1 mm; 21 jewels; 28,800 vph;
42-hour power reserve; COSC-certified chronometer
Functions: hours, minutes, sweep seconds; date;
2nd time zone indication
Case: stainless steel, ø 42 mm, height 12.64
mm; Amortiser® antishock system; antireflective
sapphire crystal; screw-in crown; sapphire crystal
case back; water-resistant to 10 atm
Band: stainless steel, folding clasp
Remarks: micro gas tube illumination; antimagnetic
Price: $4,399
Variations: black DLC case; black dial

Ball for BMW Power Reserve

Reference number: PM3010C-P1CFJ-BK
Movement: automatic, BALL Caliber RR1702-C;
ø 25.6 mm, height 4.85 mm; 21 jewels; 28,800
vph; 42-hour power reserve; COSC-certified
chronometer
Functions: hours, minutes, sweep seconds; date;
power reserve indication
Case: stainless steel with black DLC, ø 42 mm,
height 12.64 mm; Amortiser® antishock system;
sapphire crystal; screw-in crown; transparent case
back; water-resistant to 10 atm
Band: rubberized leather, folding clasp
Remarks: micro gas tube illumination; antimagnetic
Price: $4,599
Variations: stainless steel case; silver dial

Ball for BMW Chronograph

Reference number: CM3010C-P1CJ-BK
Movement: automatic, BALL Caliber RR1402-C;
ø 30 mm, height 7.9 mm; 25 jewels; 28,800 vph;
48-hour power reserve; COSC-certified chronometer
Functions: hours, minutes, subsidiary seconds; day,
date; 12-hour chronograph
Case: stainless steel with black DLC, ø 44 mm,
height 16 mm; Amortiser® antishock system;
sapphire crystal; screw-in crown; transparent case
back; water-resistant to 10 atm
Band: rubberized leather, folding clasp
Remarks: micro gas tube illumination; antimagnetic
Price: $4,999
Variations: stainless steel case

Ball for BMW TMT

Reference number: NT3010C-P1CJ-BKF
Movement: automatic, BALL Caliber RR1601-C;
ø 25.6 mm, height 5.1 mm; 21 jewels; 28,800 vph;
42-hour power reserve; COSC-certified chronometer
Functions: hours, minutes, sweep seconds;
mechanical thermometric indication
Case: stainless steel with black DLC, ø 44 mm,
height 13.25 mm; Amortiser® antishock system;
sapphire crystal; screw-in crown; transparent case
back; water-resistant to 10 atm
Band: rubberized leather, folding clasp
Remarks: micro gas tube illumination; antimagnetic
Price: $5,299; limited to 1,000 pieces
Variations: TMT Celsius scale

Baume & Mercier

Baume & Mercier
chemin de la Chênaie 50
CH-1293 Bellevue
Switzerland

Tel.:
01141-022-999-5151

Fax:
01141-44-972-2086

Website:
www.baume-et-mercier.com
register on the website to contact via e-mail

Founded:
1830

U.S. distributor:
Baume & Mercier
Richemont North America
New York, NY 10022
800-MERCIER

Most important collections/price range:
Clifton (men) / $2,700 to $13,950;
Capeland (men) / $4,350 to $19,990;
Hampton (men and women) / $3,450
to $15,000; Linea (women) / $1,950 to
$15,750; Classima / $1,750 to $5,950

Baume & Mercier and its elite watchmaking peers Cartier and Piaget make up the quality nucleus in the Richemont Group's impressive portfolio. The tradition-rich brand counts among the most accessible and affordable watches of the Genevan luxury brands. Recently, it has created a number of remarkable—and often copied—classics. The twelve-sided Riviera and the Catwalk have had to step off the stage, but the classic rectangular Hampton continues to evolve. The company has also worked hard to make gains in the men's market for its Classima Executives line and to build on watchmaking glory of days gone by, when Baume & Mercier was celebrated as a chronograph specialist.

Though the brand has taken up residence in Geneva, most of the watches are produced in a reassembly center built a few years ago in Les Brenets near Le Locle. Individual parts are made by specialized suppliers according to the strictest of quality guidelines. Some of these manufacturers are sister companies within the Richemont Group.

Former Cartier and IWC marketing manager Alain Zimmermann took over as CEO of Baume & Mercier in 2009. The successful luxury salesman's first task was to use the opportunity of the great recession to drastically streamline the retail structure, closing many less-profitable doors. He also introduced the venerable Genevan brand to modern media through Facebook and Twitter. With those tasks under control, the brand has started working on its look and mechanical prowess. The Capeland line has been retuned to late forties, with a masculine dial that is busy but not crowded. The somewhat more restrained fifties are celebrated in the new Clifton line, now boasting a flying tourbillon inspired by an 1892 B&M pocket watch that won a Kew Observatory prize. This model is equipped with a highly precise détente escapement. For women, there is the Linea with pastel-colored straps to suit every mood.

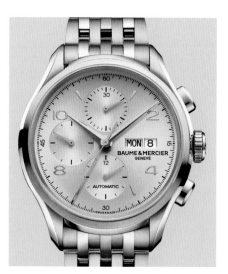

Clifton 1892 with Flying Tourbillon

Reference number: 10143
Movement: manually wound, Fleurier Caliber P591; ø 38.2 mm, height 4.66 mm; 21 jewels; 28,800 vph; flying 1-minute tourbillon; fine finishing; 50-hour power reserve
Functions: hours, minutes, subsidiary seconds
Case: pink gold, ø 45.5 mm; sapphire crystal; transparent case back; water-resistant to 5 atm
Band: reptile skin, buckle
Remarks: limited to 30 pieces
Price: $57,500

Clifton Chronograph

Reference number: 10123
Movement: automatic, ETA Caliber 7750; ø 30 mm, height 7.9 mm; 25 jewels; 28,800 vph; rhodium-plated, perlage and côtes de Genève; 48-hour power reserve
Functions: hours, minutes, subsidiary seconds; chronograph; weekday, date
Case: stainless steel, ø 43 mm, height 14.95 mm; sapphire crystal; transparent case back; water-resistant to 5 atm
Band: reptile skin, double folding clasp
Price: $3,800
Variations: brown leather strap; stainless steel band

Clifton Chronograph

Reference number: 10130
Movement: automatic, ETA Caliber 7750; ø 30 mm, height 7.9 mm; 25 jewels; 28,800 vph; rhodium-plated, perlage and côtes de Genève; 48-hour power reserve
Functions: hours, minutes, subsidiary seconds; chronograph; weekday, date
Case: stainless steel, ø 43 mm, height 14.95 mm; sapphire crystal; transparent case back; water-resistant to 5 atm
Band: stainless steel, double folding clasp
Price: $3,900
Variations: brown or black leather strap

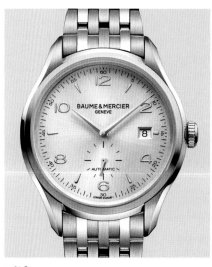

Clifton Retrograde

Reference number: 10149
Movement: automatic, Soprod Caliber 9094; 30 jewels; 28,800 vph; finely finished, côtes de Genève on rotor; 42-hour power reserve
Functions: hours, minutes, sweep seconds; power reserve indicator (retrograde); date and weekday (retrograde)
Case: stainless steel, ø 43 mm, height 12.05 mm; sapphire crystal; transparent case back; water-resistant to 5 atm
Band: reptile skin, double folding clasp
Price: $5,700

Clifton Two-Tone

Reference number: 10139
Movement: automatic, Sellita Caliber SW260-1; ø 25.6 mm, height 5.6 mm; 31 jewels; 28,800 vph; côtes de Genève on rotor; 38-hour power reserve
Functions: hours, minutes, subsidiary seconds; date
Case: stainless steel, ø 41 mm, height 11.54 mm; pink gold-plated bezel; sapphire crystal; transparent case back; water-resistant to 5 atm
Band: reptile skin, double folding clasp
Price: $3,850
Variations: stainless steel/stainless steel band ($4,750)

Clifton

Reference number: 10141
Movement: automatic, Sellita Caliber SW260-1; ø 25.6 mm, height 5.6 mm; 31 jewels; 28,800 vph; côtes de Genève on rotor; 38-hour power reserve
Functions: hours, minutes, subsidiary seconds; date
Case: stainless steel, ø 41 mm, height 11.54 mm; sapphire crystal; transparent case back; water-resistant to 5 atm
Band: stainless steel, double folding clasp
Price: $2,900
Variations: pink gold-plated bezel; stainless steel bracelet; 30 mm case

Clifton 30mm

Reference number: 10152
Movement: automatic, ETA Caliber 2671; ø 17.2 mm, height 4.8 mm; 25 jewels; 28,800 vph; côtes de Genève on rotor; 38-hour power reserve
Functions: hours, minutes, sweep seconds; date
Case: stainless steel, ø 30 mm, height 9.94 mm; pink gold-plated bezel; sapphire crystal; transparent case back; water-resistant to 5 atm
Band: stainless steel with rose gold elements, double folding clasp
Price: $4,450
Variations: stainless steel; dial set with diamonds

Classima

Reference number: 10144
Movement: quartz
Functions: hours, minutes; date
Case: stainless steel, ø 42 mm, height 6 mm; sapphire crystal, water-resistant to 3 atm
Band: reptile skin, buckle
Price: $1,750
Variations: with 33 mm case; dial set with diamonds

Classic Automatic

Reference number: 08688
Movement: automatic, ETA Caliber 2824-2; ø 25.6 mm, height 4.6 mm; 25 jewels; 28,800 vph; 38-hour power reserve
Functions: hours, minutes, sweep seconds
Case: stainless steel, ø 42 mm, height 9.5 mm; sapphire crystal; transparent case back; water-resistant to 3 atm
Band: reptile skin, buckle
Price: $3,250

Bell & Ross Ltd.
8 rue Copernic
F-75116 Paris
France

Tel.:
01133-1-73-73-93-00

Fax:
01133-1-73-73-93-01

E-Mail:
sav@bellross.com

Website:
www.bellross.com

Founded:
1992

U.S. distributor:
Bell & Ross, Inc.
605 Lincoln Road, Suite 300
Miami Beach, FL 33139
888-307-7887; 305-672-3840 (fax)
www.bellross.com

Most important collections/price range:
Instrument BR 01 and BR 03 / approx.
$3,100 to $200,000

Bell & Ross

Known for robust, "large-print" watches with a military look, Paris-headquartered Bell & Ross develops, manufactures, assembles, and regulates its famed timepieces in a modern factory in La Chaux-de-Fonds in the Jura mountains of Switzerland. In recent years, working with outside specialists, the company has dared to design even more complicated watches such as tourbillons and wristwatches with uncommon shapes. This kind of ambitious innovation has only been possible since perfume and fashion specialist Chanel—which also maintains a successful watch line in its own right—became a significant Bell & Ross shareholder and brought the watchmaker access to the production facilities where designers Bruno Belamich and team can to create more complicated, more interesting designs for their aesthetically unusual "instrument" watches.

Belamich continues to prove his skills where technical features and artful proportions are concerned, and what sets Bell & Ross timepieces apart from those of other, more traditional professional luxury makers is their special, roguish look—a delicate balance between striking, martial, and poetic. And it is this beauty for the eye to behold that makes the company's wares popular with style-conscious "civilians" as well as with the pilots, divers, astronauts, sappers, and other hard-riding professionals drawn to Bell & Ross timepieces for their superior functionality.

BR 03-90 B-Rocket

Movement: automatic, Soprod Caliber 9090; 28,800 vph; 40 hours power reserve
Functions: hours, minutes, sweep seconds; power reserve indicator; large date
Case: stainless steel, 42 x 42 mm; crown-adjustable inner bezel with 60-minute divisions, sapphire crystal; water-resistant to 10 atm
Band: calf leather, folding clasp
Price: $5,800

BR 03-92 Black Matte Ceramic

Movement: automatic, ETA Caliber 2824-2; ø 25.6 mm, height 4.6 mm; 25 jewels; 28,800 vph; 38 hours power reserve
Functions: hours, minutes, sweep seconds; date
Case: ceramic, 42 x 42 mm; sapphire crystal; water-resistant to 10 atm
Band: rubber, buckle
Price: $4,000

BR 03-92 Commando Ceramic

Reference number: BR0392-COMMANDO
Movement: automatic, ETA Caliber 2824-2; ø 25.6 mm, height 4.6 mm; 25 jewels; 28,800 vph; 38 hours power reserve
Functions: hours, minutes, sweep seconds; date
Case: ceramic, 42 x 42 mm, height 12.3 mm; bezel screwed to monocoque case with 4 screws, sapphire crystal; water-resistant to 10 atm
Band: rubber, buckle
Price: $4,300

BR 03-90 Steel & Rose Gold

Reference number: BR0390-STEELROSEGOLD
Movement: automatic, Soprod Caliber 9090;
28,800 vph; 40 hours power reserve
Functions: hours, minutes, sweep seconds; power
reserve indicator; large date
Case: stainless steel, 42 x 42 mm; rose gold bezel
screwed to monocoque case with 4 screws, sapphire
crystal; water-resistant to 5 atm
Band: calf leather, buckle
Price: $6,500

BR 03-94 Golden Heritage

Reference number: BR0394-ST-G-HE/SCA
Movement: automatic, ETA Caliber 2836-2;
ø 28.6 mm, height 6.1 mm; 37 jewels; 28,800 vph;
42 hours power reserve
Functions: hours, minutes, subsidiary seconds;
chronograph; date
Case: stainless steel, 42 x 42 mm, height 12.3 mm;
bezel screwed to monocoque case with 4 screws,
sapphire crystal; water-resistant to 10 atm
Band: calf leather, folding clasp
Price: $5,800

Vintage BR 123 GMT Officer

Movement: automatic, ETA Caliber 2893-2;
ø 25.6 mm, height 4.1 mm; 21 jewels; 28,800 vph;
42 hours power reserve
Functions: hours, minutes, sweep seconds;
additional 24-hour display (2nd time zone); date
Case: stainless steel, ø 42 mm; sapphire crystal;
water-resistant to 10 atm
Band: rubber, with textile insert, buckle
Price: $3,600

Vintage BR 126 Sport Heritage GMT & Flyback

Movement: automatic, modified ETA Caliber 2894;
ø 28.6 mm, height 6.1 mm; 37 jewels; 28,800 vph;
40 hours power reserve
Functions: hours, minutes, subsidiary seconds;
additional 24-hour display (2nd time zone); flyback
chronograph; date
Case: stainless steel, ø 43 mm; bezel with
aluminum inlay, sapphire crystal; transparent case
back; water-resistant to 10 atm
Band: calf leather, folding clasp
Remarks: limited to 500 pieces
Price: $7,900

Vintage BR126 Sport Heritage

Reference number: BRV126-ST-HER/SRB
Movement: automatic, ETA Caliber 2894-2;
ø 28.6 mm, height 6.1 mm; 37 jewels, 28,800 vph;
42 hours power reserve
Functions: hours, minutes, subsidiary seconds;
chronograph; date
Case: stainless steel, ø 41 mm, height 13.3 mm;
sapphire crystal; water-resistant to 10 atm
Band: rubber, folding clasp
Price: $4,500
Variations: stainless steel bracelet ($4,800)

Vintage WW2 Military Tourbillon Rose Gold

Movement: manually wound, 1-minute tourbillon,
rose gold tourbillon cage; 120 hours power reserve
Functions: hours (off-center), minutes; power
reserve display; trust index
Case: titanium, ø 45 mm; bezel with protective lid,
sapphire crystal; transparent case back; water-
resistant to 5 atm
Band: calf leather, buckle
Remarks: limited to 20 pieces
Price: $147,000

Benzinger "unique timepieces"
Dietlinger Strasse 17
D-75179 Pforzheim
Germany

Tel.:
01149-7231-464-233

Fax:
01149-7231-467-362

E-Mail:
info@jochenbenzinger.de

Website:
www.jochenbenzinger.de

Founded:
1985

Number of employees:
6

Annual production:
approx. 50 of his own watches and 100
movements for third parties

U.S. distributor:
WatchBuys
888-333-4895
www.watchbuys.com

Price range:
from approx. $9,850 (in stainless steel)

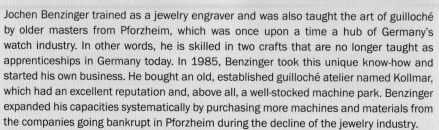

Benzinger

Jochen Benzinger trained as a jewelry engraver and was also taught the art of guilloché by older masters from Pforzheim, which was once upon a time a hub of Germany's watch industry. In other words, he is skilled in two crafts that are no longer taught as apprenticeships in Germany today. In 1985, Benzinger took this unique know-how and started his own business. He bought an old, established guilloché atelier named Kollmar, which had an excellent reputation and, above all, a well-stocked machine park. Benzinger expanded his capacities systematically by purchasing more machines and materials from the companies going bankrupt in Pforzheim during the decline of the jewelry industry.

It has been a while since Benzinger has burnished a precious stone; at some point he found delight in decorating watches. In the 1990s, his first customers included Jörg Schauer and Martin Braun, who came to Pforzheim to have their movements decorated. Chronoswiss went so far as to release a complete edition with phenomenal guilloché and engraved works from the Benzinger atelier (the Zeitzeichen collection). In the meantime, the high quality of his work has made the rounds. Even high-end Swiss watchmakers commission him to improve their movements and components. Indeed, Benzinger's name is not always found on Benzinger's art. But it is fully present in masterpieces like the Zeitmaschine II or the Regulateur, which turn the three basic units of time into individual ballet dancers performing their pirouettes on the dial at different speeds.

Open Subscription IV
Movement: manually wound, modified ETA Caliber 6498; ø 36.6 mm, height 4.5 mm; 17 jewels, 18,000 vph; entirely skeletonized, guillochéed, and engraved by hand; blued screws, blue platinum-coated mainplate, white screw balance; skeletonized ratchet wheel and crown wheel
Functions: hours and minutes (off-center), subsidiary seconds
Case: stainless steel, ø 42 mm, height 10.5 mm; sapphire crystal; transparent case back
Band: reptile skin, double folding clasp
Remarks: hand-guilloché sterling silver dial
Price: $11,200
Variations: rose and white gold (on request)

Black T - 24h
Movement: manually wound, modified ETA Caliber 6498; ø 36.6 mm, height 4.5 mm; 17 jewels; 18,000 vph; completely hand-engraved and guillochéed, hand-guillochéed mainplate, blued screws; 38-hour power reserve
Functions: hours (24-hour scale), minutes, subsidiary seconds
Case: stainless steel, ø 42 mm; sapphire crystal; transparent case back
Band: reptile skin, double folding clasp
Remarks: hand-guillochéed sterling silver dial
Price: $13,400
Variations: white or rose gold (on request)

Régulateur White
Movement: manually wound, modified ETA Caliber 6498; ø 36.6 mm, height 4.5 mm; 17 jewels; 18,000 vph; entirely skeletonized, guillochéed, and engraved by hand; blued screws, rhodium-plated screw balance; 38-hour power reserve
Functions: hours and minutes (off-center), subsidiary seconds
Case: rose gold, ø 42 mm, height 10.5 mm; sapphire crystal; transparent case back
Band: reptile skin, double folding clasp
Remarks: 2-part hand-guillochéed sterling silver dial
Price: on request
Variations: stainless steel ($12,500)

Blancpain

Blancpain SA
Le Rocher 12
CH-1348 Le Brassus
Switzerland

Tel.:
01141-21-796-3636

Website:
www.blancpain.com

Founded:
1735

U.S. distributor:
Blancpain
The Swatch Group (U.S.), Inc.
1200 Harbor Boulevard
Weehawken, NJ 07087
201-271-1400

Most important collections/price range:
L'Evolution, Villeret, Fifty Fathoms
Bathyscaphe, Le Brassus / $6,800 to
$450,000

In its advertising, the Blancpain watch brand has always proudly declared that, since 1735, the company has never made quartz watches and never will. Indeed, Blancpain is Switzerland's oldest watchmaker, and by sticking to its ideals, the company was put out of business by the "quartz boom" of the 1970s.

The Blancpain brand we know today came into being in the mid-eighties, when Jean-Claude Biver and Jacques Piguet purchased the venerable name. The company was subsequently moved to the Frédéric Piguet watch factory in Le Brassus, where it quickly became largely responsible for the renaissance of the mechanical wristwatch. This success caught the attention of the Swatch Group—known at that time as SMH. In 1992, it swooped in and purchased both companies to add to its portfolio. Movement fabrication and watch production were melded to form the Blancpain Manufacture in mid-2010.

Over the past several years, Blancpain president Marc A. Hayek has put a great deal of energy into the company's technical originality. He is frank about the fact that the development of the new *manufacture* caliber harnessed most of Blancpain's creative potential, leaving little to apply to its existing collection of watches. Still, in terms of complications, Blancpain watches have always been in a class of their own. And now even more models are being introduced, watches that feature the company's own basic movement and a choice of manual or automatic winding, like the new collection, the Fifty Fathoms Bathyscaphe, a modern interpretation of the classic diver's watch of 1953. As part of the planned consolidation of the entire collection, the other major families—the Villeret, Le Brassus, L'Evolution, and Sport—will be reworked over time.

Le Brassus Carrousel Répétition Minutes Chronograph Flyback

Reference number: 2358-3631-55B
Movement: automatic, Blancpain Caliber 2358; ø 32.8 mm, height 11.7 mm; 59 jewels; 21,600 vph; escapement system with 1-minute flying tourbillon, 1-minute carrousel
Functions: hours, minutes; minute repeater; flyback chronograph with 30-minute sweep counter
Case: pink gold, ø 45 mm, height 17.8 mm; sapphire crystal; transparent case back; water-resistant to 3 atm
Band: reptile skin, folding clasp
Remarks: enamel dial
Price: $449,600

Le Brassus Tourbillon Carrousel

Reference number: 2322-3631-55B
Movement: manually wound, Blancpain Caliber 2322; ø 35.3 mm, height 5.85 mm; 70 jewels; escapement system with 1-minute flying tourbillon, 1-minute carrousel, and differential compensation; 3 spring barrels; 168-hour power reserve
Functions: hours, minutes; power reserve indicator (on case back); date
Case: pink gold, ø 44.6 mm, height 11.94 mm; sapphire crystal; transparent case back; water-resistant to 3 atm
Band: reptile skin, folding clasp
Remarks: enamel dial
Price: $319,000

Villeret Tourbillon Volant Une Minute 12 Jours

Reference number: 66240-3431-55B
Movement: automatic, Blancpain Caliber 242; ø 30.6 mm; height 6.1 mm; 43 jewels; 28,800 vph; flying 1-minute tourbillon; 288-hour power reserve
Functions: hours, minutes; power reserve display (on case back)
Case: platinum, ø 42 mm, height 11.65 mm; sapphire crystal; transparent case back; water-resistant to 3 atm
Band: reptile skin, folding clasp
Remarks: mother-of-pearl dial
Price: $148,800; limited to 188 pieces
Variations: pink gold ($127,400)

Villeret Carrousel Phases de Lune

Reference number: 6622L-3631-55B
Movement: automatic, Blancpain Caliber 225L; ø 31.9 mm, height 6.86 mm; 40 jewels; 28,800 vph; flying 1-minute carrousel; 120-hour power reserve
Functions: hours, minutes; date; moon phase
Case: pink gold, ø 42 mm, height 12.74 mm; sapphire crystal; transparent case back; water-resistant to 3 atm
Band: reptile skin, folding clasp
Remarks: enamel dial
Price: $129,600
Variations: platinum ($151,000; limited to 88 pieces)

Villeret Traditional Chinese Calendar

Reference number: 0888-3631-55B
Movement: automatic, Blancpain Caliber 3638; ø 32 mm, height 8.3 mm; 39 jewels; 28,800 vph; 3 spring barrels; 168-hour power reserve
Functions: hours, minutes; annual calendar with double hours, date, month, moon phase, zodiac, elements, celestial stems
Case: rose gold, ø 45 mm, height 15 mm; sapphire crystal, transparent case back; water-resistant to 3 atm
Band: reptile skin, folding clasp
Price: $66,400
Variations: platinum ($87,800; limited to 20 pieces per zodiac)

Villeret Perpetual Calendar 8 Days Power Reserve

Reference number: 6659-3631-55B
Movement: automatic, Blancpain Caliber 5939A; ø 32 mm, height 7.25 mm; 42 jewels; 28,800 vph; 192-hour power reserve
Functions: hours, minutes, subsidiary seconds; perpetual calendar with date, weekday, month, moon phase, leap year
Case: pink gold, ø 42 mm, height 13.5 mm; sapphire crystal; transparent case back; water-resistant to 3 atm
Band: reptile skin, folding clasp
Price: $58,900
Variations: pink gold Milanese mesh bracelet ($78,200); platinum ($80,300; limited edition)

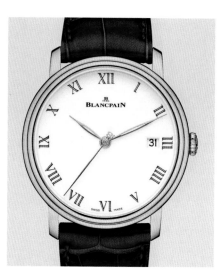

Villeret 8 Days

Reference number: 6630-3631-55B
Movement: automatic, Blancpain Caliber 1335; ø 30.6 mm, height 5.65 mm; 35 jewels; 28,800 vph; 192-hour power reserve
Functions: hours, minutes, sweep seconds; date
Case: pink gold, ø 42 mm, height 11.25 mm; sapphire crystal; transparent case back
Band: reptile skin, double folding clasp
Remarks: enamel dial
Price: $28,900
Variations: white gold ($48,200)

Villeret Ultra-Slim

Reference number: 6223C-1529-55A
Movement: automatic, Blancpain Caliber 1150; ø 26.2 mm, height 3.25 mm; 28 jewels; 21,600 vph; 2 spring barrels; 100-hour power reserve
Functions: hours, minutes, sweep seconds; date
Case: white gold, ø 38 mm, height 9.15 mm; sapphire crystal
Band: reptile skin, buckle
Price: $17,300
Variations: pink gold ($15,500); with opaline dial or stainless steel ($8,400), with white dial

Villeret Retrograde Small Seconds

Reference number: 6653Q-1529-55B
Movement: automatic, Blancpain Caliber 7663Q; ø 27 mm, height 4.57 mm; 34 jewels; 28,800 vph; 72-hour power reserve
Functions: hours, minutes, subsidiary seconds (retrograde); date
Case: white gold, ø 40 mm, height 10.83 mm; sapphire crystal; transparent case back; water-resistant to 3 atm
Band: reptile skin, folding clasp
Price: $22,500
Variations: pink gold ($22,500)

Villeret Complete Calendar

Reference number: 6654-1529-55B
Movement: automatic, Blancpain Caliber 6654;
ø 32 mm, height 5.32 mm; 28 jewels; 28,800 vph;
72-hour power reserve
Functions: hours, minutes, sweep seconds; full
calendar with date, weekday, month, moon phase
Case: white gold, ø 40 mm, height 10.74 mm;
sapphire crystal; transparent case back; water-
resistant to 3 atm
Band: reptile skin, folding clasp
Price: $25,700
Variations: red gold ($24,100); red gold on bracelet
($45,000); stainless steel ($14,900)

Villeret Ultra-Slim

Reference number: 6102C-1929-55A
Movement: automatic, Blancpain Caliber 951; ø 21
mm, height 3.25 mm; 21 jewels; 21,600 vph; 2
spring barrels; 40-hour power reserve
Functions: hours, minutes, sweep seconds; date
Case: white gold, ø 29.2 mm, height 8.7 mm;
sapphire crystal
Band: reptile skin, buckle
Remarks: dial set with 8 diamonds
Price: $18,800

X Fathoms

Reference number: 5018-1230-64A
Movement: automatic, Blancpain Caliber 9918B
(base Blancpain 1315); ø 36 mm, height 13 mm;
48 jewels; 28,800 vph; 3 spring barrels; 120-hour
power reserve
Functions: hours, minutes, sweep seconds;
mechanical depth gauge (split scale) with display of
maximum diving depth; 5-minute countdown
Case: titanium, ø 55.65 mm, height 24 mm,
unidirectional bezel with 60-minute divisions;
sapphire crystal; helium valve; water-resistant to
30 atm
Band: rubber, buckle
Price: $40,700

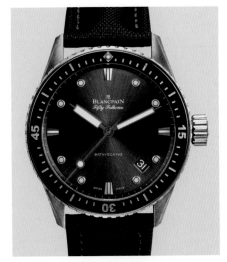

Fifty Fathoms Flyback Chronograph

Reference number: 5085F.A-3630-52B
Movement: automatic, Blancpain Caliber F185;
ø 26.2 mm, height 5.5 mm; 37 jewels; 21,600 vph
Functions: hours, minutes, subsidiary seconds;
flyback chronograph; date
Case: pink gold, ø 45 mm, height 15.5 mm;
unidirectional bezel with 60-minute divisions;
sapphire crystal; screw-in crown and pushers; water-
resistant to 30 atm
Band: textile, folding clasp
Price: $33,700

Fifty Fathoms Bathyscaphe Flyback Chronograph

Reference number: 5200-0130-NAB A
Movement: automatic, Blancpain Caliber F385;
ø 31.8 mm, height 6.65 mm; 37 jewels; 36,000 vph;
silicon spring; 50-hour power reserve
Functions: hours, minutes, subsidiary seconds;
flyback chronograph; date
Case: ceramic, ø 43.6 mm, height 15.25 mm;
unidirectional bezel with 60-minute divisions;
sapphire crystal; water-resistant to 30 atm
Band: textile, buckle
Price: $17,200

Fifty Fathoms Bathyscaphe

Reference number: 5000-1110-B52A
Movement: automatic, Blancpain Caliber 1315; ø
30.6 mm, height 5.65 mm; 35 jewels; 28,800 vph
Functions: hours, minutes, sweep seconds; date
Case: stainless steel, ø 43 mm, height 13.4
mm; unidirectional bezel with ceramic insert with
60-minute divisions; sapphire crystal; screw-in
crown; water-resistant to 30 atm
Band: textile, buckle
Price: $10,500
Variations: various textile bands; titanium
($11,600)

Fifty Fathoms Bathyscaphe

Reference number: 5100-1127-W52 A
Movement: automatic, Blancpain Caliber 1150;
ø 26.2 mm, height 3.37 mm; 28 jewels; 28,800
vph; silicon spring; 100-hour power reserve
Functions: hours, minutes, sweep seconds; date
Case: stainless steel, ø 38 mm, height 10.77 mm;
unidirectional ceramic bezel, 60-minute divisions;
sapphire crystal; transparent case back; screw-in
crown; water-resistant to 30 atm
Band: textile, buckle
Price: $9,500

L'Evolution Tourbillon

Reference number: 8822-15B30-53B
Movement: automatic, Blancpain Caliber 4225G;
ø 27.6 mm, height 8.68 mm; 46 jewels; 21,600 vph;
1-minute tourbillon; 168-hour power reserve
Functions: hours, minutes; power reserve indicator
on case back; large date
Case: white gold, ø 43.5 mm, height 14.9 mm;
sapphire crystal, transparent case back; water-
resistant to 3 atm
Band: reptile skin, folding clasp
Price: $158,400
Variations: pink gold ($158,400)

L'Evolution Rattrapante Chronograph

Reference number: 8886F-1503-52B
Movement: automatic, Blancpain Caliber 69F9;
ø 32 mm, height 8.4 mm; 44 jewels; 21,600 vph;
40-hour power reserve
Functions: hours, minutes, subsidiary seconds;
rattrapante chronograph; large date
Case: white gold, ø 43 mm, height 16.04 mm;
carbon-fiber bezel; sapphire crystal, transparent
case back; water-resistant to 30 atm
Band: textile, folding clasp
Remarks: carbon-fiber dial
Price: $55,700
Variations: pink gold ($55,700)

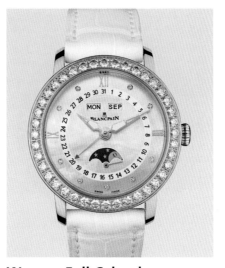

Women Chronograph Large Date

Reference number: 3626-2954-58A
Movement: automatic, Blancpain Caliber 26F8G;
ø 25.6 mm, height 7 mm; 44 jewels; 28,800 vph
Functions: hours and minutes (off-center);
chronograph; large date
Case: pink gold, ø 38.6 mm, height 13.1 mm; bezel
set with diamonds; sapphire crystal; diamond on
crown; water-resistant to 3 atm
Band: ostrich leather, buckle
Remarks: mother-of-pearl dial set with diamonds
Price: $43,900

Women Full Calendar

Reference number: 3663-2954-55B
Movement: automatic, Blancpain Caliber 6763;
ø 27 mm, height 4.9 mm; 30 jewels; 21,600 vph
Functions: hours, minutes, subsidiary seconds; full
calendar with date, weekday, month, moon phase
Case: pink gold, ø 35 mm, height 10.57 mm; bezel
set with diamonds; sapphire crystal, transparent
case back; water-resistant to 3 atm
Band: reptile skin, folding clasp
Remarks: mother-of-pearl dial set with 9 diamonds
Price: $28,900
Variations: stainless steel ($18,700)

Women

Reference number: 3650-1944L-58B
Movement: automatic, Blancpain Caliber 2653;
ø 26 mm, height 4.47 mm; 28 jewels; 28,800 vph;
72-hour power reserve
Functions: hours and minutes (off-center)
Case: white gold, ø 36.8 mm, height 10.3 mm;
bezel set with diamonds; sapphire crystal; diamond
cabochon on crown; water-resistant to 3 atm
Band: ostrich leather, folding clasp
Remarks: mother-of-pearl dial
Price: $35,300

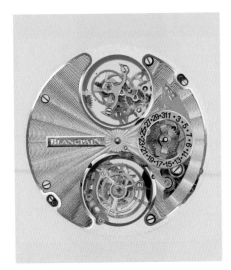

Caliber 2322

Manually wound; 2 independent escapement systems (1-minute carrousel and 1-minute tourbillon) with differential gearbox between the 2; 3 spring barrels; 168-hour power reserve

Functions: hours, minutes, date
Diameter: 35.3 mm
Height: 5.85 mm
Jewels: 70
Balance: glucydur with regulating screws (2x)
Frequency: 21,600 vph
Remarks: hand-guillochéed bridges, fine finishing on movement; 379 components

Caliber 2358

Automatic, escapement with 1-minute carrousel; single spring barrel; 65-hour power reserve

Functions: hours, minutes, minute repeater with cathedral gong; flyback chronograph 30-minute sweep counter
Diameter: 32.8 mm
Height: 11.7 mm
Jewels: 59
Balance: glucydur with gold regulating screws
Frequency: 28,800 vph
Balance spring: flat hairspring
Shock protection: Kif
Remarks: hand-engraved bridges and rotor; 546 components

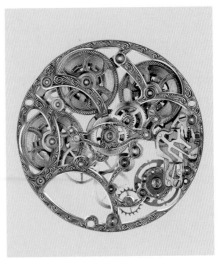

Caliber 1333SQ

Manually wound; entirely skeletonized and engraved by hand; 3 spring barrels; 192-hour power reserve

Functions: hours, minutes, sweep seconds
Diameter: 30.6 mm
Height: 4.2 mm
Jewels: 30
Balance: titanium with adjustable inertia
Frequency: 21,600 vph
Balance spring: Breguet
Shock protection: Kif

Caliber 152B

Manually wound; inverted movement structure with time display on case back, bridges with black ceramic inserts; single spring barrel; 40-hour power reserve

Functions: hours, minutes
Diameter: 35.64 mm
Height: 2.95 mm
Jewels: 21
Balance: screw balance
Frequency: 21,600 vph
Balance spring: flat hairspring
Shock protection: Kif

Caliber F385

Automatic; column wheel control of chronograph functions; single spring barrel; 50-hour power reserve

Functions: hours, minutes, subsidiary seconds; flyback chronograph; date
Diameter: 31.8 mm
Height: 6.65 mm
Jewels: 37
Balance: silicon
Frequency: 36,000 vph
Balance spring: flat hairspring
Shock protection: Kif
Remarks: fine finishing on movement, bridges with côtes de Genève

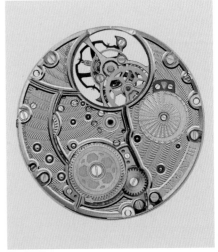

Caliber 242

Automatic, flying 1-minute tourbillon with silicon balance and anchor horns; hubless peripheral rotor at edge of movement; 4 spring barrels; 288-hour power reserve

Functions: hours, minutes; power reserve indicator (on case back)
Diameter: 30.6 mm
Height: 6.1 mm
Jewels: 43
Balance: silicon
Frequency: 21,600 vph
Remarks: very fine finishing of movement, hand-guillochéed bridges; 243 components

Borgward

It is not unusual for prospective watch brand founders to search for the name of a dormant or even defunct horological company to connect their business with a glorious past. Watchmaker Jürgen Betz looked elsewhere when he launched a series of watches under the name Borgward. This former automobile concern had a reputation for outstanding quality, reliability, and durability. For connoisseurs and fans, Borgward meant technical prowess, perfect styling, and precision engineering.

Carl F. Borgward began his career as an automobile designer in 1924 when he built a small three-wheeled van. In the early 1930s, his budding company took over the Hansa-Lloyd automobile factory and went on to conquer a global market with the Lloyd, Goliath, and Borgward brands. The real Borgward legend, however, began in the 1950s with the "Goddess," the famed Isabella Coupé, whose elegant lines and state-of-the-art technology literally heralded a new era in automotive design in Germany. In 1961, the company went bankrupt due to poor management. But the legend lives on and became the inspiration for Betz when building his Borgward watch B511. Support came from his friend Eric Borgward, grandson of Carl, who confirmed: "My grandfather would have liked it." Since the Borgward Zeitmanufaktur was founded in July 2010, it has produced three collections: the B511 limited to 511 pieces, the P100 limited to 1,890 pieces, and the B2300 limited to 1,942 pieces. They are all "made in Germany" but based on Swiss technology. At the heart of each watch is either an ETA 2824 with three hands and calendar or the famous ETA 7750 Valjoux chronograph automatic.

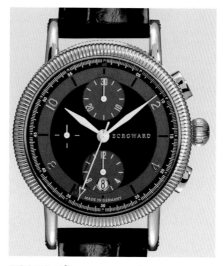

**Borgward
Zeitmanufaktur GmbH & Co. KG**
Markgrafenstrasse 16
D-79588 Efringen-Kirchen
Germany

Tel.:
01149-7628-805-7840

Fax:
01149-7628-805-7841

E-Mail:
manufaktur@borgward.ag

Website:
www.borgward.ag

Founded:
2010

Number of employees:
3

Annual production:
approx. 350

Distribution:
Please contact Borgward directly for enquiries.

Most important collections:
P100, B2300, and B511

P100 Chronograph

Reference number: P100.CL.01
Movement: automatic, ETA Caliber 7750; ø 30 mm, height 7.9 mm; 25 jewels, 28,800 vph; with perlage, blackened rotor; 38-hour power reserve
Functions: hours, minutes, subsidiary seconds; chronograph; date
Case: stainless steel, ø 40 mm, height 16 mm; sapphire crystal, transparent case back; water-resistant to 5 atm
Band: calf leather, buckle
Price: $3,050
Variations: black or silver-plated dial

B2300 Chronograph

Reference number: B2300.CL.02
Movement: automatic, ETA Caliber 7750; ø 30 mm, height 7.9 mm; 25 jewels, 28,800 vph; with perlage, blackened rotor; 38-hour power reserve
Functions: hours, minutes, subsidiary seconds; chronograph; date
Case: stainless steel, ø 44 mm, height 15 mm; sapphire crystal, transparent case back; water resistant to 5 atm
Band: calf leather, buckle
Price: $3,180

B511 Automatic

Reference number: B511.AL.04
Movement: automatic, ETA Caliber 2824-2; ø 25.6 mm, height 4.6 mm; 25 jewels, 28,800 vph; with perlage, blackened rotor; 38-hour power reserve
Functions: hours, minutes, sweep seconds; date
Case: stainless steel, ø 40.5 mm, height 12 mm; sapphire crystal, transparent case back; water-resistant to 5 atm
Band: calf leather, buckle
Remarks: limited to 511 pieces
Price: $2,460
Variations: black or white dial

Bovet Fleurier S.A.
109 Pont-du-Centenaire
CP183 CH-1228 Plan-les-Ouates
Switzerland

Tel.:
01141-22-731-4638

Fax:
01141-22-884-1450

E-Mail:
info@bovet.com

Website:
www.bovet.com

Founded:
1822

Annual production:
2,000 watches

U.S. distributor:
Bovet LLC USA
3363 NE 163rd Street, Suite 703
North Miami Beach, FL 33160
888-909-1822

Most important collections/price range:
Pininfarina, Amadeo Fleurier,
Sportster / $18,500 to $725,250

Bovet

If any brand can claim real connections to China, it is Bovet, founded by Swiss businessman Edouard Bovet. Bovet emigrated to Canton, China in 1818 and sold four watches of his own design there. On his return to Switzerland in 1822, he set up a company for shipping his Fleurier-made watches to China. The company name, pronounced "Bo Wei" in Mandarin, became a synonym for "watch" in Asia and at one point had offices in Canton. For more than eighty years, Bovet and his successors supplied the Chinese ruling class with valuable timepieces.

In 2001, the brand was bought by entrepreneur Pascal Raffy. He ensured the company's industrial independence by acquiring several other companies as well, notably the high-end watchmaker Swiss Time Technology (STT) in Tramelan, which he renamed Dimier 1738. In addition to creating its own line of watches, this *manufacture* produces complex technical components such as tourbillons for Bovet watches. Assembly of Bovet creations takes place at the headquarters in the thirteenth-century Castle of Môtiers in Val-de-Travers not far from Fleurier.

Bovet watches have several distinctive features—undoubtedly a reason for their growing fame. The first is intricate dial work, featuring not only complex architecture, but also very fine enameling. The second is the lugs and crown at 12 o'clock, recalling Bovet's tasteful pocket watches of the nineteenth century. On some models, the wristbands are made to be easily removed so the watch can be worn on a chain or cord. Other watches convert to table clocks.

Amadeo Fleurier Tourbillon Virtuoso III

Reference number: AIQPR003
Movement: manually wound, Bovet Caliber Virtuoso III; ø 38 mm; 59 jewels; 21,600 vph; 1-minute tourbillon; 120-hour power reserve
Functions: hours, minutes, subsidiary seconds; perpetual calendar with date (retrograde), weekday, month, leap year, power reserve indicator (dial); hours and minutes (off-center; on back)
Case: red gold, ø 46 mm, height 18.3 mm; sapphire crystal; transparent back; water-resistant to 3 atm
Band: reptile skin, buckle
Price: $350,000; limited to 39 pieces
Variations: white gold (limited to 39 pieces)

Amadeo Fleurier 43

Reference number: AF43039
Movement: automatic, Bovet Caliber 11BA12; ø 25.87 mm, height 10.72 mm; 28,800 vph; red gold rotor, 72-hour power reserve
Functions: hours, minutes, subsidiary seconds; power reserve display
Case: rose gold, ø 43 mm, height 12.33 mm; sapphire crystal; water-resistant to 3 atm
Band: reptile skin, buckle
Remarks: flexible lugs for converting to pocket watch or table clock
Price: $46,000
Variations: white gold, various dials

Récital 11 "Miss Alexandra"

Reference number: DTR11-RG-0B0-C1-01
Movement: automatic, Bovet Caliber 11DA16-MP; ø 25.6 mm; 28,800 vph; 72-hour power reserve
Functions: hours, minutes (off-center); moon phase
Case: red gold, 37 x 41 mm, height 11.35 mm; sapphire crystal; transparent case back; water-resistant to 3 atm
Band: reptile skin, buckle
Remarks: mother-of-pearl dial set with 10 diamonds
Price: $89,700
Variations: white gold

Récital 15

Reference number: DTR15-42RG-0B0-W1-01
Movement: manually wound, Bovet Caliber Virtuoso II Spécialité 13.75-70-001-HSMR; ø 30 mm; 21,600 vph; 120-hour power reserve
Functions: hours (digital), minutes (retrograde), subsidiary seconds on front and back (coaxial, with corrected inverted rotational direction); power reserve indicator on back
Case: pink gold, ø 42 mm, height 12.8 mm; bezel set with 64 diamonds, sapphire crystal; transparent case back; water-resistant to 3 atm
Band: reptile skin, buckle
Price: $126,600; limited to 60 pieces
Variations: white gold w/o diamonds (limited to 60 pieces)

Récital 16

Reference number: DTR16-46RG-000-B1-01
Movement: manually wound, Bovet Caliber Rising Star II Spécialité OM3-70-DIM; ø 36 mm; 21,600 vph; 1-minute tourbillon; 168-hour power reserve
Functions: hours, minutes, subsidiary seconds (on tourbillon cage); 2nd and 3rd time zone with additional reference city division and day/night indicator; power reserve display
Case: pink gold, ø 46 mm, height 15.3 mm; sapphire crystal; transparent back; water-resistant to 3 atm
Band: reptile skin, buckle
Price: $299,000; limited to 20 pieces
Variations: white gold with diamonds (limited to 20 pieces)

Récital 12 "Monsieur Dimier"

Reference number: DTR12-42RG-000-B1-01
Movement: manual winding, Bovet Caliber Virtuoso II Spécialité 13.75-70-AI; ø 30 mm, height 3.9 mm; 21,600 vph; 168-hour power reserve; inverted design with balance and escapement on dial side
Functions: hours and minutes (off-center), subsidiary seconds; power reserve display
Case: pink gold, ø 42 mm, height 9.1 mm; sapphire crystal; transparent back; water-resistant to 3 atm
Band: reptile skin, buckle
Price: $43,700; limited to 100 pieces
Variations: white gold with diamonds (limited to 100 pieces)

Saguaro 46 Chronograph

Reference number: SP0452-MA
Movement: automatic, Bovet Caliber 13BA01; ø 29.81 mm, height 14.93 mm; 28 jewels; 28,800 vph; blued stainless steel rotor, blued screws, côtes de Genève; 42-hour power reserve
Functions: hours, minutes, subsidiary seconds; chronograph; large date
Case: stainless steel with black DLC coating, ø 46 mm; sapphire crystal; rose gold crown and pusher; water-resistant to 30 atm
Band: rubber, buckle
Remarks: converts to pocket watch or table clock
Price: $27,600
Variations: stainless steel; rose gold, meteorite dial

Pininfarina "Sergio" Split Second Chronograph

Reference number: SEPIN001
Movement: automatic, Bovet Caliber 13BA09-R; ø 29.81 mm; 28,800 vph; 50-hour power reserve
Functions: hours, minutes, subsidiary seconds; power reserve indicator; split-second chronograph
Case: stainless steel, ø 45 mm; sapphire crystal; transparent case back; black DLC coating on crown and pusher; water-resistant to 3 atm
Band: rubber, buckle
Remarks: converts to pocket watch or table clock
Price: $34,500; limited to 250 pieces
Variations: blue, black, or silver-plated dial

Pininfarina Chronograph Cambiano Cambiano

Reference number: CHPIN010
Movement: automatic, Bovet Caliber 13BA08; ø 29.81 mm, height 14.25 mm; 28,800 vph; 48-hour power reserve
Functions: hours, minutes, subsidiary seconds; chronograph; large date
Case: stainless steel, ø 45 mm, height 15.6 mm; sapphire crystal, water-resistant to 10 atm
Band: rubber, buckle
Remarks: totalizer scale of Venetian wood; converts to pocket watch or table clock
Price: $32,200; limited to 80 pieces

Breguet

Montres Breguet SA

CH-1344 L'Abbaye
Switzerland

Tel.:
01141-21-841-9090

Fax:
01141-21-841-9084

Website:
www.breguet.com

Founded:
1775 (Swatch Group since 1999)

U.S. distributor:
Breguet
The Swatch Group (U.S.), Inc.
1200 Harbor Boulevard
Weehawken, NJ 07087
201-271-1400

Most important collections:
Classique, Héritage, Marine, Reine de Naples,
Type XX

We never quite lose that attachment to the era in which we were born and grew up, nor do some brands. Abraham-Louis Breguet (1747–1823), who hailed from Switzerland, brought his craft to Paris in the *Sturm und Drang* atmosphere of the late eighteenth century. It was fertile ground for one of the most inventive watchmakers in the history of horology, and his products soon found favor with the highest levels of society.

Little has changed two centuries later. After a few years of drifting, in 1999 the brand carrying this illustrious name became the prize possession of the Swatch Group and came under the personal management of Nicolas G. Hayek, CEO. Hayek worked assiduously to restore the brand's roots, going as far as rebuilding the legendary Marie Antoinette pocket watch and contributing to the restoration of the Petit Trianon at Versailles.

Breguet is a full-fledged *manufacture,* and this has allowed it to forge ahead uncompromisingly with upscale watches and even jewelry. In modern facilities on the shores of Lake Joux, traditional craftsmanship still plays a significant role in the production of its fine watches, but at the same time, Breguet is one of the few brands to work with modern materials for its movements. This is not just a PR trick, but rather a sincere attempt to improve quality and rate precision. Many innovations have debuted at Breguet, for instance pallet levers and balance wheels made of silicon, the first Breguet hairspring with the arched terminal curve made of this glassy material, or even a mechanical high-frequency balance beating at 72,000 vph. Other innovations include the electromagnetic regulation of a minute repeater or the use of two micro-magnets to achieve contactless anchoring of a balance wheel staff.

Breguet, now under the auspices of Nicolas G. Hayek's grandson, Marc A. Hayek, continues to explore the edges of the technologically possible in watchmaking.

Classique "Chronométrie"

Reference number: 7727BR 12 9WU
Movement: manually wound, Breguet Caliber 574 DR; ø 31.6 mm, height 3.5 mm; 45 jewels, 72,000 vph; double balance spring, silicon pallet lever and escape wheel; magnetic bearing of balance pivot; 2 spring barrels; 60-hour power reserve
Functions: hours, minutes, subsidiary seconds (1/10 second display); power reserve display
Case: rose gold, ø 41 mm, height 9.65 mm; sapphire crystal; transparent case back; water-resistant to 3 atm
Band: reptile skin, folding clasp
Price: $40,000
Variations: white gold ($40,500)

Classique Tourbillon Ultra-Thin

Reference number: 5377BR 12 9WU
Movement: automatic, Breguet Caliber 581 DR; ø 36 mm, height 3 mm; 42 jewels; 28,800 vph; 1-minute tourbillon in titanium cage, silicon hairspring; hubless peripheral rotor; 90-hour power reserve
Functions: hours, minutes, subsidiary seconds (on tourbillon cage); power reserve display
Case: platinum, ø 42 mm, height 7 mm; sapphire crystal; transparent case back; water-resistant to 3 atm
Band: reptile skin, double folding clasp
Remarks: currently thinnest automatic tourbillon movement
Price: $149,500
Variations: rose gold ($163,800)

Classique

Reference number: 5277BR 12 9V6
Movement: manually wound, Breguet Caliber 515 DR; ø 34.4 mm, height 3.6 mm; 23 jewels; 28,800 vph; silicon hairspring; 96-hour power reserve
Functions: hours, minutes, subsidiary seconds; power reserve indicator
Case: rose gold, ø 38 mm, height 8 mm; sapphire crystal; transparent case back; water-resistant to 3 atm
Band: reptile skin, buckle
Price: $19,000
Variations: white gold ($19,500)

Classique Chronograph

Reference number: 5287BB 92 9ZV
Movement: manually wound, Breguet Caliber 533.3; ø 27 mm, height 5.57 mm; 24 jewels; 21,600 vph; Breguet spring; 48-hour power reserve
Functions: hours, minutes, subsidiary seconds; chronograph
Case: white gold, ø 42.5 mm, height 12.1 mm; sapphire crystal; transparent case back; water-resistant to 3 atm
Band: reptile skin, double folding clasp
Price: $50,200
Variations: light dial; rose gold ($49,700)

Classique "La Musicale"

Reference number: 7800BR AA 9Y V02
Movement: automatic, Breguet Caliber 901; ø 38.9 mm, height 8.7 mm; 59 jewels; 28,800 vph; silicon anchor/anchor escape wheel, Breguet balance with regulating screws; music box with peg disc/gong strips playing Bach's "Badinerie," hand-guillochéed sonorous liquid metal membrane, magnetic striking regulator; 45-hour power reserve
Functions: hours, minutes, sweep seconds; power reserve display; alarm clock with music mechanism and function display
Case: yellow gold, ø 48 mm, height 16.6 mm; sapphire crystal, water-resistant to 3 atm
Band: reptile skin, folding clasp
Price: $89,600

Classique Hora Mundi

Reference number: 5717PT EU 9ZU
Movement: automatic, Breguet Caliber 77F0; ø 36 mm, height 6.15 mm; 39 jewels; 28,800 vph; silicon pallet lever, escape wheel, and hairspring
Functions: hours, minutes, sweep seconds; world-time display (2nd time zone); day/night indicator; date
Case: platinum, ø 44 mm, height 13.55 mm; sapphire crystal; transparent case back; water-resistant to 3 atm
Band: reptile skin, folding clasp
Price: $94,200
Variations: rose gold ($78,900); 3 different dials (Asia, America, Europe/Africa)

Classique Grande Complication Tourbillon Perpetual Calendar

Reference number: 3797BR 1E 9WU
Movement: manually wound, Breguet Caliber 558QP2; 37.09 mm; 21 jewels; 18,000 vph; 1-minute tourbillon, Breguet spring, balance with gold weight screws; 50-hour power reserve
Functions: hours/minutes (off-center), subsidiary seconds (on tourbillon cage); perpetual calendar with date (retrograde), weekday, month, leap year
Case: rose gold, ø 41 mm, height 11.6 mm; sapphire crystal; transparent case back; water-resistant to 3 atm
Band: reptile skin, double folding clasp
Price: $164,900; limited to 300 pieces

Classique Grande Complication

Reference number: 7637BB 12 9ZU
Movement: manually wound, Breguet Caliber 567/2; ø 28 mm, height 5.8 mm; 31 jewels; 18,000 vph; hand-decorated
Functions: hours, minutes, subsidiary seconds; additional 24-hour display (2nd time zone); hour, quarter-hour, and minute repeater
Case: white gold, ø 42 mm, height 12.35 mm; sapphire crystal, transparent case back; water-resistant to 3 atm
Band: reptile skin, folding clasp
Price: $237,000
Variations: pink gold ($236,400)

Classique Moon Phase

Reference number: 7337BR 1E 9V6
Movement: automatic, Breguet Caliber 502.3 QSE1; ø 31 mm, height 3.8 mm; 35 jewels; 21,600 vph; numbered and signed
Functions: hours and minutes (off-center), subsidiary seconds; full calendar with date, weekday, moon phase and age
Case: rose gold, ø 39 mm, height 9.9 mm; sapphire crystal; transparent case back; water-resistant to 3 atm
Band: reptile skin, folding clasp
Remarks: silvered, hand-guillochéed gold dial
Price: $39,400
Variations: white gold ($39,900); yellow gold ($38,800)

Tradition GMT

Reference number: 7067BR G1 9W6
Movement: manually wound, Breguet Caliber 507 DRF; ø 32.8 mm, height 6.92 mm; 40 jewels; 21,600 vph; Breguet spring, silicon pallet lever and escape wheel, central barrel spring; 50-hour power reserve
Functions: hours, minutes; 2nd time zone (additional 12-hour indicator); power reserve display
Case: rose gold, ø 40 mm, height 12.65 mm; sapphire crystal, transparent case back; water-resistant to 3 atm
Band: reptile skin, folding clasp
Price: $39,200
Variations: white gold ($40,000)

Tradition Grande Complication

Reference number: 7047BR G9 9ZU
Movement: manually wound, Breguet Caliber 569; ø 36 mm, height 10.82 mm; 43 jewels; 18,000 vph; Breguet silicon spring; torque regulator with chain and worm screw; 1-minute tourbillon, 50-hour power reserve
Functions: hours, minutes; power reserve display on case back
Case: pink gold, ø 41 mm, height 15.95 mm; sapphire crystal; transparent case back; water-resistant to 3 atm
Band: reptile skin, folding clasp
Price: $175,600
Variations: yellow gold ($174,800); platinum ($189,700)

Type XXII

Reference number: 3880BR Z2 9XV
Movement: automatic, Breguet Caliber 589F; ø 30 mm, height 8.3 mm; 27 jewels; 72,000 vph; high-frequency silicon escapement, sweep minute counter; 40-hour power reserve
Functions: hours, minutes, subsidiary seconds; additional 12-hour display (2nd time zone); flyback chronograph; date
Case: rose gold, ø 44 mm, height 18.05 mm; bidirectional bezel with 60-minute divisions; sapphire crystal; transparent case back; screw-in crown; water-resistant to 10 atm
Band: reptile skin, folding clasp
Price: $35,500
Variations: stainless steel ($21,600)

Marine GMT

Reference number: 5857BR Z2 5ZU
Movement: automatic, Breguet Caliber 517F; ø 26.2 mm; 28 jewels; 28,800 vph; Breguet silicon lever escapement and hairspring; 65-hour power reserve
Functions: hours, minutes, sweep seconds; additional 12-hour display (2nd time zone); date
Case: pink gold, ø 42 mm, height 12.25 mm; sapphire crystal, transparent case back; water-resistant to 10 atm
Band: rubber, folding clasp
Price: $35,900
Variations: stainless steel ($26,200)

Marine Royale

Reference number: 5847BR Z2 5ZV
Movement: automatic, Breguet Caliber 519 R; ø 27.6 mm, height 6.2 mm; 36 jewels; 28,800 vph
Functions: hours, minutes, sweep seconds; power reserve display; alarm clock with function indicator; date
Case: rose gold, ø 45 mm, height 17.45 mm; unidirectional bezel with 60-minute divisions, sapphire crystal; transparent case back; screw-in crown; water-resistant to 30 atm
Band: rubber, folding clasp
Price: $46,300
Variations: rose gold dial ($46,300); rose gold bracelet ($61,800); white gold ($42,900)

Marine Ladies Chronograph

Reference number: 8827ST 5W 986
Movement: automatic, Breguet Caliber 550; ø 23.9 mm, height 6 mm; 47 jewels; 28,800 vph; silicon anchor and lever escapement; 45-hour power reserve
Functions: hours, minutes, subsidiary seconds; chronograph; date
Case: stainless steel, ø 34.6 mm, height 12.3 mm; sapphire crystal; water-resistant to 5 atm
Band: reptile skin, folding clasp
Remarks: mother-of-pearl dial
Price: $19,500
Variations: blue dial; rose gold ($60,800)

Héritage Chronograph

Reference number: 5400BB 12 9V6
Movement: automatic, Breguet Caliber 550/1;
ø 23.9 mm, height 6 mm; 47 jewels; 21,600 vph;
Breguet spring, silicon pallet lever and escape
wheel; 52-hour power reserve
Functions: hours, minutes, subsidiary seconds;
chronograph; date
Case: white gold, 35 x 42 mm, height 14.45 mm;
sapphire crystal
Band: reptile skin, folding clasp
Price: $44,100
Variations: pink gold ($43,000)

Héritage

Reference number: 8860BR 11 386
Movement: manually wound, Breguet Caliber 586L;
ø 20 mm; 38 jewels; 21,600 vph; Breguet spring,
silicon pallet lever and escape wheel; 36-hour power
reserve
Functions: hours, minutes; moon phase
Case: rose gold, 25 x 35 mm, height 9.75 mm;
sapphire crystal, water-resistant to 3 atm
Band: leather, folding clasp
Price: $28,700
Variations: with diamonds ($33,300); white gold
($29,700); white gold set with diamonds ($54,800)

Classique Dame

Reference number: 9068BB 12 976 DD00
Movement: automatic, Breguet Caliber 591A; ø
26 mm, height 3.15 mm; 25 jewels; 28,800 vph;
silicon lever escapement and hairspring; 38-hour
power reserve
Functions: hours, minutes, sweep seconds; date
Case: white gold, ø 33.5 mm
Band: reptile skin, buckle
Price: $26,600
Variations: rose gold ($26,100)

Reine de Naples

Reference number: 8967ST 51 J50
Movement: automatic, Breguet Caliber 591C;
ø 25.6 mm, height 2.95 mm; 25 jewels; 28,800
vph; silicon anchor and lever escapement; 38-hour
power reserve
Functions: hours, minutes
Case: stainless steel, 34.95 x 43 mm, height 9.58
mm; sapphire crystal; transparent case back;
sapphire cabochon on crown
Band: stainless steel, double folding clasp
Remarks: mother-of-pearl dial
Price: $18,500
Variations: various dials

Reine de Naples
Complications Day/Night

Reference number: 8999BB 8D 874 DD0D
Movement: automatic, Breguet Caliber 78CS;
45 jewels; 25,200 vph; silicon hairspring; 57-hour
power reserve
Functions: hours, minutes; day/night indication via
rotating titanium disk
Case: white gold, 34 x 42.05 mm, height 10.8
mm; bezel and dial set with 73 diamonds; sapphire
crystal; transparent case back; diamond cabochon
on crown, lugs set with 35 diamonds
Band: satin, double folding clasp set with 26
diamonds
Price: $225,200

Reine de Naples Princess

Reference number: 8968BRX1 986 0D0D
Movement: automatic, Breguet Caliber 591C;
ø 26 mm, height 2.95 mm; 25 jewels; 28,800
vph; silicon anchor and lever escapement; 38-hour
power reserve
Functions: hours, minutes
Case: rose gold, 34.95 x 43 mm, height 9.58 mm;
sapphire crystal; transparent case back; diamond
cabochon on crown, bezel set with 16 diamonds;
water-resistant to 3 atm
Band: reptile skin, buckle set with 29 diamonds
Price: $28,200
Variations: silver-plated dial

Breitling
Schlachthausstrasse 2
CH-2540 Grenchen
Switzerland

Tel.:
01141-32-654-5454

Fax:
01141-32-654-5400

E-Mail:
info@breitling.com

Website:
www.breitling.com

Founded:
1884

Annual production:
700,000 (estimated)

U.S. distributor:
Breitling U.S.A. Inc.
206 Danbury Road
Stamford, CT 06897
800-641-7343
www.breitling.com

Most important collections:
Navitimer Avenger, Trancsocean, Superocean, Cockpit, Breitling for Bentley

Breitling

In 1884, Léon Breitling opened his workshop in St. Imier in the Jura mountains and immediately began specializing in integrated chronographs. His business strategy was to focus consistently on instrument watches with a distinctive design. High quality standards and the rise of aviation completed the picture.

Today, Breitling's relationship with air sports and commercial and military aviation is clear from its brand identity. The watch company hosts a series of aviation days, owns an aerobatics team, and sponsors several aviation associations.

The unveiling of its own, modern chronograph movement at the 2009 Basel Watch Fair was a major milestone in the company's history and also a return to its roots. The new design was to be "100 percent Breitling" and industrially produced in large numbers at a reasonable cost. Breitling's headquarters in Grenchen and its subsidiary Breitling Chronométrie in La Chaux-de-Fonds both boast state-of-the-art equipment. Nevertheless, the contract for the new chronograph was awarded to a small team in Geneva. By the spring of 2005, the initial design plans were on the table. By the end of that year, the first parts of the watch were ready, and just a few months later, prototypes were available for testing. In 2006, the brand-new Caliber B01 made the COSC grade with flying colors and has enjoyed great popularity ever since. For the team of designers, the innovative centering system on the reset mechanism that requires no manual adjustment was one of the great achievements.

The in-house caliber has evolved. It now comes as the B04 with a second time zone, the B05 with world time, and the B06 with a 30-second chrono display for the Breitling for Bentley series. And in 2014, the calibers were used in the Navitimers as well as the Chronomats, which celebrated their thirtieth anniversary.

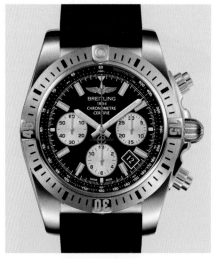

Chronomat GMT

Reference number: AB041012/BA69
Movement: automatic, Breitling Caliber 04 (base Breitling 01); ø 30 mm, height 7.4 mm; 47 jewels; 28,800 vph; column wheel control of chronograph functions; 70-hour power reserve; COSC-certified
Functions: hours, minutes, subsidiary seconds; additional 24-hour display (2nd time zone); chronograph; date
Case: stainless steel, ø 47 mm, height 18.35 mm; unidirectional bezel with 60-minute divisions; sapphire crystal; screw-in crown and pushers; water-resistant to 50 atm
Band: stainless steel, folding clasp
Price: $10,020
Variations: calf-leather band/buckle ($9,360)

Chronomat 44 Airborne

Reference number: AB01154G/BD13
Movement: automatic, Breitling Caliber 01; ø 30 mm, height 7.2 mm; 47 jewels; 28,800 vph; column wheel control of chronograph functions; 70-hour power reserve; COSC-certified chronometer
Functions: hours, minutes, subsidiary seconds; chronograph; date
Case: stainless steel, ø 44 mm, height 16.95 mm; unidirectional bezel with 60-minute divisions; sapphire crystal; screw-in crown and pushers; water-resistant to 50 atm
Band: textile, folding clasp
Price: $8,030
Variations: stainless steel bracelet ($9,060)

Chronomat 41 Airborne

Reference number: AB01442J/G787
Movement: automatic, Breitling Caliber 01; ø 30 mm, height 7.2 mm; 47 jewels; 28,800 vph; column wheel control of chronograph functions; 70-hour power reserve; COSC-certified chronometer
Functions: hours, minutes, subsidiary seconds; chronograph; date
Case: stainless steel, ø 41 mm, height 16.95 mm; unidirectional bezel with 60-minute divisions; sapphire crystal; screw-in crown and pushers; water-resistant to 30 atm
Band: textile, folding clasp
Price: $8,030
Variations: stainless steel bracelet ($9,060)

Navitimer 01 (46 mm)

Reference number: AB012721/BD09
Movement: automatic, Breitling Caliber 01;
ø 30 mm, height 7.2 mm; 47 jewels; 28,800 vph;
column wheel control of chronograph functions;
70-hour power reserve; COSC-certified chronometer
Functions: hours, minutes, subsidiary seconds;
chronograph; date
Case: stainless steel, ø 46 mm, height 15.5 mm;
bidirectional bezel with integrated slide rule and
tachymeter scale; sapphire crystal, water-resistant
to 3 atm
Band: calf leather, buckle
Price: $8,840
Variations: stainless steel band ($9,620)

Navitimer GMT

Reference number: AB044121/BD24
Movement: automatic, Breitling Caliber 04 (base
Breitling 01); ø 30 mm, height 7.4 mm; 47 jewels;
28,800 vph; column wheel control of chronograph
functions; 70-hour power reserve; COSC-certified
Functions: hours, minutes, subsidiary seconds;
additional 24-hour display; chronograph; date
Case: stainless steel, ø 48 mm, height 18.35 mm;
bidirectional bezel with integrated slide rule and
tachymeter scale; sapphire crystal; transparent case
back; screw-in crown and pushers; water-resistant
to 3 atm
Band: calf leather, buckle
Price: $9,680
Variations: stainless steel bracelet ($10,460)

Navitimer 1461 Blacksteel

Reference number: M1938022/BD20
Movement: automatic, Breitling Caliber 19
(base ETA 2892-A2); ø 25.6 mm; 28,800 vph;
COSC-certified chronometer
Functions: hours, minutes, subsidiary seconds;
chronograph; full calendar with week, month, moon
phase, weekday, date, leap year
Case: stainless steel, with black DLC coating; ø
48 mm, height 15.5 mm; bidirectional bezel with
integrated slide rule and tachymeter, sapphire
crystal; water-resistant to 3 atm
Band: textile, buckle
Price: $11,165
Variations: rubber band and folding clasp
($11,845)

Montbrillant 01

Reference number: AB013012/G709
Movement: automatic, Breitling Caliber 01;
ø 30 mm, height 7.2 mm; 47 jewels; 28,800 vph;
column wheel control of chronograph functions;
70-hour power reserve; COSC-certified chronometer
Functions: hours, minutes, subsidiary seconds;
chronograph; date
Case: stainless steel, ø 40 mm, height 13.5 mm;
bidirectional bezel with integrated slide rule,
sapphire crystal; water-resistant to 5 atm
Band: stainless steel, folding clasp
Price: $8,895; limited to 2,000 pieces
Variations: reptile skin, tang buckle ($8,115)

Transocean Chronograph Unitime

Reference number: AB0510U4/BB62
Movement: automatic, Breitling Caliber 05 (base
Breitling 01); ø 30 mm, height 8.1 mm; 56 jewels;
28,800 vph; 70-hour power reserve; COSC-certified
chronometer
Functions: hours, minutes, subsidiary seconds; 24
time zones shown simultaneously on dial (world-
time display); chronograph; date
Case: stainless steel, ø 46 mm, height 14.8 mm;
crown rotates inner ring with reference city names;
sapphire crystal; water-resistant to 10 atm
Band: calf leather, folding clasp
Price: $11,640
Variations: Milanese mesh bracelet ($11,575)

Transocean Chronograph 1461

Reference number: A1931012/G750
Movement: automatic, Breitling Caliber 19 (base
ETA 2892-A2); ø 25.6 mm; 38 jewels; 28,800 vph;
COSC-certified chronometer
Functions: hours, minutes, subsidiary seconds;
chronograph; perpetual calendar with date,
weekday, week, month, moon phase, leap year
Case: stainless steel, ø 43 mm, height 15.25 mm;
sapphire crystal; water-resistant to 5 atm
Band: reptile skin, buckle
Price: $10,220
Variations: stainless steel Milanese mesh bracelet
($10,155)

Transocean Chronograph 38

Reference number: U4131012/Q600
Movement: automatic, Breitling Caliber 41 (base ETA 2892-A2); ø 30 mm, height 7.6 mm; 38 jewels, 28,800 vph; 42-hour power reserve
Functions: hours, minutes, subsidiary seconds; chronograph; date
Case: stainless steel, ø 38 mm, height 14.25 mm; pink gold bezel; sapphire crystal; water-resistant to 10 atm
Band: reptile skin, buckle
Price: $7,700
Variations: stainless steel Milanese mesh bracelet ($7,635)

Transocean Chronograph

Reference number: AB015212/BA99
Movement: automatic, Breitling Caliber 01; ø 30 mm, height 7.2 mm; 47 jewels; 28,800 vph; column wheel control of chronograph functions; 70-hour power reserve; COSC-certified
Functions: hours, minutes, subsidiary seconds; chronograph; date
Case: stainless steel, ø 43 mm, height 14.35 mm; sapphire crystal; transparent case back; water-resistant to 10 atm
Band: stainless steel Navitimer bracelet, folding clasp
Price: $8,395
Variations: calf leather band, tang buckle ($7,565)

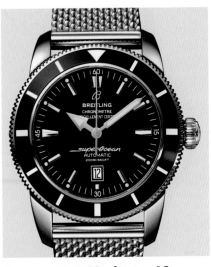

Superocean Heritage 46

Reference number: A1732024/B868
Movement: automatic, Breitling Caliber 17 (base ETA 2824-2); ø 25.6 mm, height 4.6 mm; 25 jewels; 28,800 vph; COSC-certified chronometer
Functions: hours, minutes, sweep seconds; date
Case: stainless steel, ø 46 mm, height 16.4 mm; unidirectional bezel with reference markers; sapphire crystal; screw-in crown; water-resistant to 20 atm
Band: stainless steel Milanese mesh, folding clasp
Price: $4,405
Variations: rubber band, folding clasp ($4,090)

Superocean Heritage 42

Reference number: U1732112/BA61
Movement: automatic, Breitling Caliber 17 (base ETA 2824-2); ø 25.6 mm, height 4.6 mm; 25 jewels, 28,800 vph; COSC-certified chronometer
Functions: hours, minutes, sweep seconds; date
Case: stainless steel, ø 42 mm, height 12.95 mm; unidirectional bezel with pink gold insert and reference markers, sapphire crystal; screw-in crown; water-resistant to 20 atm
Band: stainless steel Milanese mesh, folding clasp
Price: $5,670
Variations: rubber band, folding clasp ($5,200)

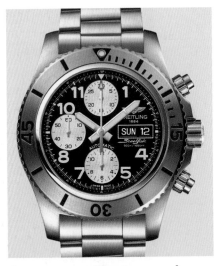

Superocean Chronograph Steelfish

Reference number: A13341C3/BD19
Movement: automatic, Breitling Caliber 13 (base ETA 7750); ø 30 mm, height 7.9 mm; 25 jewels; 28,800 vph; COSC-certified chronometer
Functions: hours, minutes, subsidiary seconds; chronograph; date
Case: stainless steel, ø 44 mm, height 17.2 mm; unidirectional bezel with rubber inlay, with 60-second divisions, sapphire crystal; screw-in crown and pushers; water-resistant to 50 atm
Band: stainless steel, folding clasp
Price: $6,250
Variations: rubber band, folding clasp

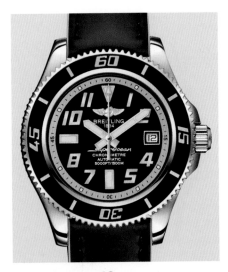

Superocean 42

Reference number: A1736402/BA32
Movement: automatic, Breitling Caliber 17 (base ETA 2824-2); ø 25.6 mm, height 3.6 mm; 21 jewels; 28,800 vph; COSC-certified chronometer
Functions: hours, minutes, sweep seconds; date
Case: stainless steel, ø 42 mm, height 15 mm; unidirectional bezel with rubber inlay and 60-minute divisions, sapphire crystal; screw-in crown; helium valve; water-resistant to 150 atm
Band: calf leather, tang buckle
Price: $3,295
Variations: stainless steel bracelet ($3,520)

Superocean 44

Reference number: A1739102/BA78
Movement: automatic, Breitling Caliber 17 (base ETA 2824-2); ø 25.6 mm, height 4.6 mm; 25 jewels; 28,800 vph; COSC-certified chronometer
Functions: hours, minutes, sweep seconds; date
Case: stainless steel, ø 44 mm, height 16.7 mm; unidirectional bezel with rubber inlay and 60-minute divisions, sapphire crystal, screw-in crown; helium valve; water-resistant to 200 atm
Band: stainless steel, folding clasp
Price: $4,130
Variations: rubber band, buckle ($3,930)

Galactic 36

Reference number: A3733053/A717
Movement: automatic, Breitling Caliber 37 (base ETA 2892-A2); ø 25.6 mm, height 3.6 mm; 27 jewels; 28,800 vph; 42-hour power reserve
Functions: hours, minutes, subsidiary seconds; date
Case: stainless steel, ø 36 mm, height 12.3 mm; unidirectional bezel set with diamonds; sapphire crystal
Band: calf leather, buckle
Price: $9,235
Variations: stainless steel bracelet ($10,735)

Super Avenger II

Reference number: A1337111/BC29
Movement: automatic, Breitling Caliber 13 (base ETA 7750); ø 30 mm, height 7.9 mm; 25 jewels; 28,800 vph; 42-hour power reserve; COSC-certified chronometer
Functions: hours, minutes, subsidiary seconds; chronograph; date
Case: stainless steel, ø 48 mm, height 17.75 mm; unidirectional bezel with 60-minute divisions, sapphire crystal; screw-in crown; water-resistant to 30 atm
Band: stainless steel, folding clasp
Price: $5,835
Variations: rubber band, folding clasp ($6,025)

Bentley 6.75 Midnight Carbon

Reference number: M4436413/BD27
Movement: automatic, Breitling Caliber 44B (base Sellita 2892-A2 with Dubois Dépraz module); ø 30 mm, height 7.6 mm; 38 jewels; 28,800 vph; 42-hour power reserve; COSC-certified chronometer
Functions: hours, minutes, subsidiary seconds; chronograph; large date
Case: stainless steel, with black DLC coating, ø 49 mm, height 15.5 mm; bidirectional bezel with integrated slide rule, sapphire crystal; screw-in crown; water-resistant to 10 atm
Band: rubber, folding clasp
Price: $10,990

Bentley B06

Reference number: AB061112/BC42
Movement: automatic, Breitling Caliber 06 (base Breitling 01); ø 30 mm; 47 jewels; 28,800 vph; 70-hour power reserve; chronograph with 30-second sweep minute totalizer; COSC-certified
Functions: hours, minutes, subsidiary seconds; chronograph; date
Case: stainless steel, ø 49 mm; bidirectional bezel with tachymeter scale; sapphire crystal, transparent case back; screw-in crown; water-resistant to 10 atm
Band: stainless steel, folding clasp
Price: $12,370
Variations: calf leather band, tang buckle ($11,015)

Bentley GMT Light Body B04

Reference number: EB043210/BD23
Movement: automatic, Breitling Caliber 04 (base Breitling 01); ø 30 mm, height 7.4 mm; 47 jewels; 28,800 vph; column wheel control of chronograph functions; 70-hour power reserve; COSC-certified chronometer
Functions: hours, minutes, subsidiary seconds; additional 24-hour display (2nd time zone); chronograph; date
Case: titanium, ø 49 mm, height 17.35 mm; crown rotates inner ring with reference city names; sapphire crystal; transparent case back; screw-in crown; water-resistant to 10 atm
Band: rubber, folding clasp
Price: $13,665

Bremont Watch Company

PO Box 4741
Henley-on-Thames
RG9 9BZ
Great Britain

Tel.:
01144-845-094-0690

Fax:
01144-870-762-0475

E-Mail:
info@bremont.com

Website:
www.bremont.com

Founded:
2002

Number of employees:
60+

Annual production:
several thousand watches

U.S. distributor:
Mike Pearson
1-855-BREMONT
michael@bremont.com

Most important collections/price range:
ALT1, MB, SOLO, U-2, and limited editions /
$3,900 to $30,000

Bremont

At the 2012 Olympic Games in London, stuntman Gary Connery parachuted into the stadium wearing a silvery wig and a frumpy dress that made him look suspiciously like the queen. He was also the first to jet suit out of a helicopter. On both occasions he was wearing a Bremont watch. And so do many other adventurous types, like polar explorer Ben Saunders or free diver Sara Campbell.

Bremonts are tough stuff, created by brothers Nick and Giles English, themselves dyed-in-the-wool pilots and restorers of vintage airplanes. They understand that flying safety relies on outstanding mechanics, so they took their time engineering their watches. Naming their brand required some thought, however. The solution came when they remembered an adventure they had had in southern France when they were forced to land their vintage biplane in a field to avoid a storm. The farmer, himself an enthusiastic restorer of vintage engines, was more than happy to put them up. His name: Antoine Bremont.

Ever since the watches hit the market in 2007, the brand has grown by leaps and bounds. These Swiss-made timepieces reflect sobriety, functionality, history, and ruggedness. They would fit as well in an old Spitfire as on a vintage yacht. They use a sturdy in-house automatic movement, especially hardened steel, a patented shock-absorbing system, and a rotor whose cutout design recalls a flight of planes. All chronographs are COSC certified. The brand continues to explore various cultural icons in British history, including the Spitfire, Bletchley Park (where the German codes were broken during World War II), or Jaguar sports cars. Recently, though, it tied the knot, so to speak, with Boeing and produced an elegant watch with a leather-polymer composite strap and a seconds hand with a Boeing-blue tip shaped like part of the Seattle firm's famous logo.

ALTI-C/CR

Movement: automatic, Caliber BE-50AE; ø 28.04 mm, height 10.5 mm; 28 jewels; 28,800 vph; 42-hour power reserve; Bremont decorated rotor; COSC-certified chronometer
Functions: hours, minutes, subsidiary seconds; chronograph; date
Case: stainless steel; ø 43 mm, height 16 mm; transparent case back; sapphire crystal; water-resistant to 10 atm
Band: leather, stainless steel deployment clasp
Price: $5,900
Variations: cream, anthracite, black, green, or silver dial

ALT1-WT/BL

Movement: automatic, modified Caliber BE-54AE; ø 28.04 mm, height 10.5 mm; 25 jewels; 28,800 vph; Bremont molded and decorated rotor; COSC-certified chronometer; 42-hour power reserve
Functions: hours, minutes, subsidiary seconds; 2nd time zone; world-time display; chronograph; date
Case: stainless steel; ø 43 mm, height 16 mm; transparent case back; sapphire crystal; water-resistant to 10 atm
Band: leather, stainless steel deployment clasp
Price: $6,250
Variations: black or white dial

Boeing Model 1

Movement: automatic, modified Caliber BE-36AE; ø 28 mm, height 7.5 mm; 25 jewels; 28,800 vph; 38-hour power reserve; Bremont molded and decorated rotor; COSC-certified chronometer
Functions: hours, minutes, subsidiary seconds; date
Case: custom stainless steel; ø 43 mm, height 16 mm; crown-adjustable bezel; transparent case back; sapphire crystal; water-resistant to 10 atm
Band: leather-polymer composite (Seattle Hybrid), buckle
Remarks: comes with NATO strap
Price: $5,450
Variations: in Boeing aviation-grade titanium (price on request)

U-2/BL

Movement: automatic, modified Caliber BE-36AE; ø 28 mm, height 7.5 mm; 25 jewels; 28,800 vph; 38 hours power reserve; Bremont molded and decorated rotor; COSC-certified chronometer
Functions: hours, minutes, seconds; weekday, date
Case: stainless steel; ø 43 mm, height 16 mm; antimagnetic soft iron core; crown-adjustable bidirectional inner bezel; sapphire crystal; transparent case back; water-resistant to 10 atm
Band: leather strap, buckle
Remarks: optional NATO military strap
Price: $5,450
Variations: U-2/SS, U-2/DLC both with closed case back and faraday cage

MBIII

Movement: automatic, modified Caliber BE-93-2AE; ø 29.89 mm; 21 jewels; 28,800 vph; Bremont skeletonized rotor; COSC-certified; 42 hours power reserve
Functions: hours, minutes, sweep seconds; sweep 24-hour hand (2nd time zone); date
Case: hardened stainless steel; ø 43 mm, height 14.35 mm; crown-operated bidirectional inner bezel; antimagnetic cage; screwed-down case back; sapphire crystal; water-resistant to 10 atm
Band: leather, buckle
Remarks: comes with NATO military strap
Price: $5,995
Variations: bronze, orange, or anthracite barrel

SOLO/WH-SI

Movement: automatic, modified Caliber BE-36AE; ø 28 mm, height 7.5 mm; 25 jewels; 28,800 vph; 38 hours power reserve; Bremont decorated rotor; COSC-certified chronometer
Functions: hours, minutes, seconds; date
Case: stainless steel; ø 43 mm, height 16 mm; transparent case back; sapphire crystal, water-resistant to 10 atm
Band: leather with stainless steel pin buckle
Price: $4,250
Variations: white dial with silver markers, black dial with white or cream hands and markers

Terra Nova

Movement: automatic, modified Caliber BE-93-2AE; ø 29.89 mm; 21 jewels; 28,800 vph; Bremont skeletonized rotor; COSC-certified; 42 hours power reserve
Functions: hours, minutes, sweep seconds; sweep 24-hour hand (2nd time zone); date
Case: titanium satin and polished; ø 43 mm, height 16.47 mm; bidirectional bezel; protected crown; antimagnetic cage; automatic helium valve; sapphire crystal; water-resistant to 50 atm
Band: rubber, buckle
Price: $5,995; limited to 300 pieces
Variations: titanium bracelet

S2000

Movement: automatic, modified Caliber BE-36AE; ø 28 mm, height 7.5 mm; 25 jewels; 28,800 vph; 38 hours power reserve; Bremont molded and decorated rotor; shock absorbers; COSC-certified chronometer
Functions: hours, minutes, seconds; weekday, date
Case: stainless steel; ø 45 mm, height 16 mm; antimagnetic soft iron cage; unidirectional bezel; screw-down case back; sapphire crystal; water-resistant to 200 atm
Band: rubber, buckle
Price: $5,900

ALT1-C/RG

Movement: automatic, Caliber BE-50AE; ø 28 mm, height 10.5 mm; 28 jewels; 28,800 vph; 42 hours power reserve; Bremont decorated rotor; COSC-certified chronometer
Functions: hours, minutes, subsidiary seconds; chronograph; date
Case: rose gold; ø 43 mm, height 16 mm; transparent case back; sapphire crystal; water-resistant to 10 atm
Band: reptile skin, buckle
Price: $18,250

BRM
(Bernard Richards Manufacture)
2 Impasse de L'Aubette
ZA des Aulnaies
F-95420 Magny en Vexin
France

Tel.:
01133-1-61-02-00-25

Fax:
01133-1-61-02-00-14

Website:
www.brm-manufacture.com

Founded:
2003

Number of employees:
20

Annual production:
approx. 2,000 pieces

U.S. distributor:
BRM Manufacture North America
25 Highland Park Village, Suite 100-777
Dallas, TX 75205
214-231-0144
usa@brm-manufacture.com

Most important collections/price range:
$3,000 to $150,000

BRM

Is luxury on the outside or the inside? The answer to this question can tear the veil from the hype and reveal the true craftsman. For Bernard Richards, the true sign of luxury lies in "technical skills and perfection in all stages of manufacture." The exterior of the product is of course crucial, but all of BRM's major operations for making a wristwatch—such as encasing, assembling, setting, and polishing—are performed by hand in his little garage-like factory located outside Paris in Magny-sur-Vexin.

The look: 1940s, internal combustion, axle grease, pinups, real pilots, and a can-do attitude. The inside: custom-designed components, fitting perfectly into Richards's automotive ideal. And since the beginning of 2009, BRM aficionados have been able to engage in this process to an even greater degree: When visiting the BRM website, the client can now construct his or her own V12-44-BRM model. A luxury watch that is a collaboration between the client and Richards is simply a click away.

BRM's unusual timepieces have mainly been based on the tried and trusted Valjoux 7750. But Richards has lofty goals for himself and his young venture, for he intends to set up a true *manufacture* in his French factory. His Birotor model is thus outfitted with the Precitime, an autonomous caliber conceived and manufactured on French soil. The movement features BRM shock absorbers mounted on the conical springs of its so-called Isolastic system. Plates and bridges are crafted in Arcap, while the rotors are made of Fortale and tantalum. The twin rotors, found at 12 and 6 o'clock, are mounted on double rows of ceramic bearings that require no lubrication. And for the real deal in car feel, Richards uses seat belt material for some models.

RG 46

Reference number: RG46 MK AR
Movement: automatic, modified ETA Caliber 2824; ø 25.6 mm, height 4.6 mm; 25 jewels; 28,800 vph; 6 shock absorbers connected to movement; BRM designed and manufactured rotor; 38-hour power reserve
Functions: hours, minutes, sweep seconds; stop mechanism function
Case: makrolon, ø 46 mm, height 14 mm; Fortale HR lugs and crown with black PVD; sapphire crystal; transparent case back; water-resistant to 10 atm
Band: seat belt material, buckle
Price: $13,550
Variations: rose gold

BiRotor

Reference number: BRT-01
Movement: automatic, Precitime Caliber Birotor; 24 x 32 mm; 35 jewels; 28,800 vph; 45-hour power reserve; Fortale HR and tantalum double rotors on ceramic ball bearings; patented Isolastic system with 4 shock absorbers, arcap plates, bridges
Functions: hours, minutes, subsidiary seconds
Case: titanium with rose gold crown and strap lugs, 40 x 48 mm, height 9.9 mm; domed sapphire crystal; antireflective on both sides; domed sapphire crystal transparent case back; water-resistant to 30 m
Band: nomex, buckle
Price: $68,500

TriRotor

Movement: automatic, Precitime Caliber TriRotor; ø 48 mm; 29 jewels; 28,800 vph; 45-hour power reserve; Fortale HR main rotors with 3 macro rotors in Fortale HR with tantalum on ceramic ball bearings; patented Isolastic system with 3 shock absorbers, arcap plates, bridges
Functions: hours, minutes, subsidiary seconds
Case: titanium with rose gold crown and strap lugs, ø 48 mm, height 9.9 mm; domed sapphire crystal; antireflective on both sides; domed sapphire crystal transparent case back; water-resistant to 10 atm
Band: nomex, buckle
Price: $47,950
Variations: rose gold; yellow, red, or orange hands

R50 MK

Movement: automatic, heavily modified ETA Caliber 2161; ø 38 mm; 35 jewels; 28,800 vph; 48-hour power reserve; patented Isolastic system with 3 shock absorbers; Fortale HR, tantalum, and aluminum rotor; handpainted Gulf colors
Functions: hours, minutes, sweep seconds; power reserve indication
Case: makrolon with rose gold crown and strap lugs, ø 50 mm, height 13.2 mm; sapphire crystal; antireflective on both sides; exhibition case back; water-resistant to 3 atm
Band: leather, buckle
Price: $28,550; limited to 30 pieces
Variations: rose gold ($65,000)

TR1 Tourbillon

Movement: automatic, Precitime Caliber; ø 30 mm, height 7.9 mm; 26 jewels; 28,800 vph; 46-hour power reserve; 105-second tourbillon in arcap with reversed cage for visible escapement and suspended by 2 micro springs; patented Isolastic system with 4 shock absorbers; automatic assembly with ceramic ball bearings
Functions: hours, minutes, sweep seconds
Case: titanium, ø 52 mm; sapphire crystal; antireflective on both sides; transparent case back; water-resistant to 10 atm
Band: leather, buckle
Price: $145,350
Variations: 48 mm ($136,150)

RG 46AB

Movement: automatic, Precitime Caliber; ø 30 mm, height 7.9 mm; 27 jewels; 28,800 vph; self-locking rotor mounted on 2 rows of ceramic ball bearings, 6 shock absorbers; suspended between 3 angled shock absorbers and vertical hydraulic cylinders; 42-hour power reserve
Functions: hours, minutes, subsidiary seconds
Case: polymer, ø 46 mm; sapphire crystal; exhibition case back; water-resistant to 10 atm
Band: technical fabric, buckle
Price: $12,950
Variations: hands and markers in yellow, orange, red, or lime green

V6-44 SA

Movement: automatic, ETA Valjoux Caliber 2824 modified; ø 30 mm, height 7.90 mm; 27 jewels; 28,800 vph; shock absorbers connected to block; 42-hour power reserve
Functions: hours, minutes, sweep seconds
Case: polished stainless steel case with black PVD; lugs, crown from single titanium block; sapphire crystal; transparent case back; water-resistant to 10 atm
Band: leather, buckle
Remarks: skeletonized dial with red hands
Price: $5,600

BT12 Gulf

Movement: automatic, ETA Valjoux Caliber 7753; ø 30 mm, height 7.90 mm; 27 jewels; 28,800 vph; 42-hour power reserve, Gulf logo and color strip
Functions: hours, minutes, subsidiary seconds; date; chronograph
Case: grade 5 titanium, black PVD, 41 x 42 mm; sapphire crystal; transparent case back; water-resistant to 10 atm
Band: seat belt material, buckle
Price: $9,550; limited to 100 pieces

V12-44-MK ABL

Movement: automatic, ETA Valjoux Caliber 7753; ø 30 mm, height 7.90 mm; 27 jewels; 28,800 vph; 42-hour power reserve
Functions: hours, minutes, subsidiary seconds; date; chronograph
Case: makrolon (polycarbonate), ø 45 mm; pushers, lugs, crown from single titanium block; sapphire crystal; exhibition case back; water-resistant to 10 atm
Band: technical fabrics for extra lightness
Remarks: lightest automatic chronograph ever made; skeleton dial with blue hands
Price: $13,450
Variations: many options with configurator

Bulgari Horlogerie SA

rue de Monruz 34
CH-2000 Neuchâtel
Switzerland

Tel.:
01141-32-722-7878

Fax:
01141-32-722-7933

E-Mail:
info@bulgari.com

Website:
www.bulgari.com

Founded:
1884 (Bulgari Horlogerie was founded in the early 1980s as Bulgari Time.)

U.S. distributor:
Bulgari Corporation of America
625 Madison Avenue
New York, NY 10022
212-315-9700

Most important collections/price range:
Bulgari-Bulgari / from approx. $4,700 to $30,300; Diagono / from approx. $3,200; Octo / from approx. $9,500 to $690,000 and above; Daniel Roth and Gérald Genta collections

Bulgari

Although Bulgari is one of the largest jewelry manufacturers in the world, watches have always played an important role for the brand. The purchase of Daniel Roth and Gérald Genta opened new perspectives for its timepieces, thanks to specialized production facilities and the watchmaking talent in the Vallée de Joux—especially where complicated timepieces are concerned.

The Bulgari family is originally from Greece, and the watches, though designed in Rome, echo classic Hellenistic architecture in many ways. They are timeless and elegant, with style elements that border on the abstract. Manufacturing is done in Switzerland. Following a move from its old location in Neuchâtel to a modern building in the industrial zone of La Chaux-de-Fonds, the company threw its energies behind its movements. It has produced, among others, the Caliber 168 automatic based on a Leschot design that managing director Guido Terrini calls "the tractor," because it provided the "pull" to guarantee the company's independence. The year 2014 saw the simple Octo built on the double-barreled Caliber 193.

In March 2011, luxury goods giant Louis Vuitton Moët Hennessy (LVMH) secured all the Bulgari family shares in exchange for 16.5 million LVMH shares and a say in the group's future. The financial backing of the mega-group boosted the company's strategy to become fully independent. In mid-2013, Jean-Christophe Babin, the man who turned TAG Heuer into a leading player in sports watches, was chosen to head the venerable brand. He also managed to build up a manufacturing structure from scratch at TAG Heuer, which is exactly the direction Bulgari's watch division is headed in.

Bulgari Bulgari

Reference number: BBP39WGLD
Movement: automatic, Bulgari Caliber BVL 191; ø 26.2 mm, height 3.8 mm; 26 jewels; 28,800 vph; finely finished with côtes de Genève; 42-hour power reserve
Functions: hours, minutes, sweep seconds; date
Case: rose gold, ø 39 mm; sapphire crystal; water-resistant to 3 atm
Band: reptile skin, folding clasp
Price: $19,900
Variations: stainless steel ($6,600)

Bulgari Bulgari

Reference number: BB41WSLD
Movement: automatic, Bulgari Caliber BVL 191; ø 26.2 mm, height 3.8 mm; 26 jewels; 28,800 vph; finely finished with côtes de Genève; 42-hour power reserve
Functions: hours, minutes, sweep seconds; date
Case: stainless steel, ø 41 mm; sapphire crystal; water-resistant to 5 atm
Band: reptile skin, folding clasp
Price: $6,600
Variations: rose gold ($19,900)

Bulgari Bulgari Chronograph

Reference number: BB41BSSDCH
Movement: automatic, Bulgari Caliber BVL 328 (base Zenith "El Primero"); ø 30.5 mm, height 6.62 mm; 31 jewels; 36,000 vph; côtes de Genève; 50-hour power reserve
Functions: hours, minutes, subsidiary seconds; chronograph; date
Case: stainless steel, ø 41 mm; sapphire crystal: screw-in crown; water-resistant to 10 atm
Band: stainless steel, folding clasp
Price: $10,200

Octo

Reference number: BGO41BSSD
Movement: automatic, Bulgari Caliber BVL 193; ø 25.6 mm, height 3.7 mm; 28 jewels; 28,800 vph; double spring barrel; 50-hour power reserve
Functions: hours, minutes, sweep seconds; date
Case: stainless steel, ø 41.5 mm, height 10.55 mm; sapphire crystal, transparent case back
Band: stainless steel, folding clasp
Price: $9,550

Octo

Reference number: BGOP41BGLD
Movement: automatic, Bulgari Caliber BVL 193; ø 25.6 mm, height 3.7 mm; 28 jewels; 28,800 vph; double spring barrel; 50-hour power reserve
Functions: hours, minutes, sweep seconds; date
Case: rose gold, ø 41.5 mm, height 10.55 mm; sapphire crystal, transparent case back
Band: reptile skin, double folding clasp
Price: $23,900

Octo Velocissimo

Reference number: BGO41BSLDCH
Movement: automatic, Bulgari Caliber Velocissimo (base Zenith "El Primero"); ø 30 mm, height 6.62 mm; 31 jewels, 36,000 vph; column wheel control of chronograph functions, silicon escapement; 50-hour power reserve
Functions: hours, minutes, subsidiary seconds; chronograph; date
Case: stainless steel, ø 41.5 mm; screw-in crown
Band: reptile skin, buckle
Price: $9,900
Variations: stainless steel bracelet ($11,000); rose gold ($29,000)

Octo Finissimo

Reference number: BGO40BPLXT
Movement: manually wound, Bulgari Caliber Finissimo; ø 36.6 mm, height 2.23 mm; 26 jewels; 28,800 vph; fine finishing; 70-hour power reserve
Functions: hours, minutes, subsidiary seconds
Case: platinum, ø 40 mm, height 5 mm; sapphire crystal; transparent case back; water-resistant to 3 atm
Band: reptile skin, buckle
Price: $26,200

Octo Finissimo Tourbillon

Reference number: BGO40BPLTBXT
Movement: manually wound, Bulgari Caliber Finissimo Tourbillon; ø 32 mm, height 1.95 mm; 26 jewels; 21,600 vph; flying 1-minute tourbillon; fine finishing; 55-hour power reserve
Functions: hours, minutes
Case: platinum, ø 40 mm, height 5 mm; sapphire crystal; transparent case back; water-resistant to 3 atm
Band: reptile skin, buckle
Price: $138,000

Octo Grande Sonnerie Tourbillon

Reference number: BGOW44BGLTBGS
Movement: automatic, Gérald Genta GG31002; ø 31.5 mm, height 10.65 mm; 95 jewels; 21,600 vph; 1-minute tourbillon
Functions: hours (retrograde), hours/minutes (digital, jumping); 2 power reserve indicators; large repeater with Westminster chimes on 3 gongs
Case: white gold, ø 44 mm, height 15.76 mm; sapphire crystal; transparent case back; falcon-eye cabochon on crown; water-resistant to 3 atm
Band: reptile skin, double folding clasp
Price: on request

Magsonic Grande Sonnerie

Reference number: BGGP51GLTBGS
Movement: manually wound, Gérald Genta Caliber GG 31001; ø 31.5 mm, height 7.31 mm; 55 jewels; 21,600 vph; 1-minute tourbillon; 48-hour power reserve
Functions: hours, minutes (off-center); grande sonnerie minute repeater with Westminster chimes (4 hammers) gong; power reserve indicators
Case: rose gold, ø 51 mm, height 16.27 mm; sapphire crystal; pushers for large/small striking mechanisms and muting; water-resistant to 3 atm
Band: reptile skin, double folding clasp
Price: on request

Bulgari-Bulgari Tourbillon

Reference number: BBW41BGLTB
Movement: automatic, Bulgari Caliber BVL 263; ø 28.6 mm, height 5.95 mm; 40 jewels; 21,600 vph; 1-minute tourbillon; rose gold oscillating mass, fine finishing; 64-hour power reserve
Functions: hours, minutes
Case: rose gold, ø 41.5 mm; sapphire crystal; transparent case back; water-resistant to 5 atm
Band: reptile skin, buckle
Price: $86,000
Variations: white gold ($86,000)

Commedia dell'Arte

Reference number: BGGW54GLCA/PU
Movement: manually wound, Bulgari Caliber BVL 618; ø 36 mm, height 11 mm; 91 jewels; 18,000 vph; 48-hour power reserve
Functions: hours (jumping), minutes (retrograde); automaton with 5 figures
Case: white gold, ø 54 mm, height 16.36 mm; sapphire crystal, transparent case back; water-resistant to 3 atm
Band: reptile skin, buckle
Price: price upon request; limited to 8 pieces

Papillon Voyageur

Reference number: BRRP46C14GLGMTP
Movement: automatic, Daniel Roth Caliber DR 1307; ø 25.6 mm, height 6.78 mm; 26 jewels; 28,800 vph; 45-hour power reserve
Functions: hours (digital, jumping), minutes (retrograde), subsidiary seconds (segment display with double hand); additional 24-hour indicator (2nd time zone)
Case: rose gold, 43 x 46 mm, height 15.2 mm; sapphire crystal; transparent case back; pusher to advance 24-hour display; water-resistant to 3 atm
Band: reptile skin, double folding clasp
Price: $51,000

Carillon Tourbillon

Reference number: BRRP48GLTBMR
Movement: manually wound, Daniel Roth Caliber DR 3300; ø 34.6 mm, height 8.35 mm; 35 jewels; 21,600 vph; 1-minute tourbillon; double spring barrel; partially skeletonized, black finishing; 75-hour power reserve
Functions: hours, minutes; 3-hammer minute repeater
Case: rose gold, 45 x 48 mm, height 14.9 mm; sapphire crystal, transparent case back; water-resistant to 3 atm
Band: reptile skin, double folding clasp
Remarks: skeletonized dial; limited edition
Price: $257,000

Diagono Calibro 303

Reference number: DG42C6SPGLDCH
Movement: automatic, Bulgari Caliber BVL 303 (base Frédéric Piguet 1185); ø 25.6 mm, height 5.5 mm; 37 jewels; 21,600 vph; column wheel control of chronograph functions, 40-hour power reserve
Functions: hours, minutes, subsidiary seconds; chronograph; date
Case: stainless steel, ø 42 mm, height 11.7 mm; rose gold bezel, sapphire crystal; transparent case back; screw-in crown; water-resistant to 10 atm
Band: reptile skin, double folding clasp
Price: $13,900
Variations: white gold bezel

Diagono Ceramic

Reference number: DGP42BGCVDCH
Movement: automatic, Bulgari Caliber BVL 130; ø 25.6 mm; 37 jewels; 28,800 vph; 42-hour power reserve
Functions: hours, minutes, subsidiary seconds; chronograph; date
Case: rose gold, ø 42 mm, height 12.68 mm; ceramic bezel; sapphire crystal, transparent case back; ceramic pushers and crown
Band: rubber, buckle
Price: $25,600
Variations: white ceramic bezel

Endurer Chronosprint

Reference number: BRE56BSVDCHS
Movement: automatic, Daniel Roth Caliber DR1306; ø 25.6 mm, height 6.1 mm; 34 jewels; 28,800 vph; single pusher for chronograph functions
Functions: hours, minutes; chronograph; large date
Case: stainless steel, 51 x 56 mm, height 14.55 mm; sapphire crystal; transparent case back; water-resistant to 10 atm
Band: rubber, buckle
Price: $16,000

Sotirio Bulgari Tourbillon Perpetual Calendar

Reference number: SB43BPLTBPC
Movement: automatic, Bulgari Caliber BVL 465; ø 28.6 mm, height 8.3 mm; 46 jewels; 21,600 vph; 1-minute tourbillon; 2 spring barrels; fine finishing; 64-hour power reserve
Functions: hours, minutes, subsidiary seconds; perpetual calendar with date, weekday, month, day (on 4 retrograde counters)
Case: platinum, ø 43 mm, height 14.26 mm; sapphire crystal, transparent case back
Band: reptile skin, buckle
Price: $257,000; limited to 30 pieces

Ammiraglio del Tempo

Reference number: BRRP50BGLDEMR
Movement: manually wound, Bulgari Caliber; ø 38 mm, height 9.38 mm; 56 jewels; 14,400 vph; minute repeater, Westminster chimes and chronometer escapement, 4 hammers and gongs; constant force mechanism; cylindrical balance spring; triple shock absorbing system; fine finishing; 48-hour power reserve
Functions: hours, minutes; minute repeater
Case: rose gold, 45.75 x 50 mm, height 14.9 mm; sapphire crystal; transparent case back
Remarks: mobile lug at 7 to activate chimes
Price: $359,000
Variations: white gold ($359,000)

Tourbillon Lumière

Reference number: BRR44PLTBSK
Movement: manually wound, Gérald Genta Caliber GG 8000; ø 32.6 mm, height 7.85 mm; 19 jewels; 21,600 vph; 1-minute tourbillon; skeletonized plate and bridges of gold; 70-hour power reserve
Functions: hours, minutes; power reserve indicator on case back
Case: platinum, ø 53 mm, height 14.89 mm; sapphire crystal; transparent case back; water-resistant to 3 atm
Band: reptile skin, buckle
Price: on request
Variations: rose gold

Tourbillon Sapphire

Reference number: BGGW53GLTBSK
Movement: manually wound, Gérald Genta Caliber GG 8000; ø 32.6 mm, height 7.85 mm; 19 jewels; 21,600 vph; 1-minute tourbillon, skeletonized; 70-hour power reserve
Functions: hours, minutes
Case: white gold, ø 53 mm, height 14.89 mm; bezel set with diamonds, sapphire crystal; transparent case back; water-resistant to 3 atm
Band: reptile skin, double folding clasp
Price: $240,000; limited to 25 pieces

Bucherer Montres SA
Langensandstrasse 27
CH-6002 Lucerne
Switzerland

Tel.:
01141-41-369-7070

Fax:
01141-41-369-7072

E-Mail:
info@carl-f-bucherer.com

Website:
www.carl-f-bucherer.com

Founded:
1919, repositioned under the name Carl F.
Bucherer in 2001

Number of employees:
approx. 100

Annual production:
approx. 20,000 watches

U.S. distributor:
Carl F. Bucherer North America
1805 South Metro Parkway
Dayton, OH 45459
937-291-4366
info@cfbna.com; www.carl-f-bucherer.com

Most important collections/price range:
Patravi, Manero, and Alacria / core price
segment $5,000 to $30,000

Carl F. Bucherer

While luxury watch brand Carl F. Bucherer is still rather young, the Lucerne-based Bucherer jewelry dynasty behind it draws its vast know-how from more than ninety years of experience in the conception and design of fine wristwatches.

The summer of 2005 ushered in a new age for the watch brand: company decision makers decided to develop and manufacture an in-house mechanical movement. Together with Bucherer's longtime, Sainte-Croix-headquartered cooperative partner, Techniques Horlogères Appliquées SA (THA), an ambitious plan was hatched. When it became clear that such sophisticated construction could not be realized using outside suppliers, the next logical step was to purchase its partner's renowned atelier in the Jura mountains.

THA was integrated into the Bucherer Group, and the watch company was renamed Carl F. Bucherer Technologies SA (CFBT). At present, the Sainte-Croix operation is led by technical director Dr. Albrecht Haake, who oversees a staff of about twenty. Dr. Haake is currently focusing much of his energy on putting into place industrial structures that will allow for the further development of capacities at the workshop. "Industrialization is not a question of cost, but rather a question of quality," says Haake.

This very successful family-run business celebrated its 125th anniversary in 2013. Its birthday present to itself included a classic tourbillon and a two-tone Alacria with an in-house quartz engine. Carl F. Bucherer has also been quietly pursuing a strategy of boutique openings as a way to give its customers the right surroundings. A new store launched in Macau in March 2013, while the group opened the world's largest watch store in Paris, a favorite shopping city for travelers from Asia.

Pathos Queen

Reference number: 00.10550.07.25.21
Movement: automatic, Caliber CFB 1969;
ø 17.5 mm, height 4.8 mm; 25 jewels; 28,800 vph;
38-hour power reserve
Functions: hours, minutes, sweep seconds; date
Case: stainless steel and rose gold, ø 26.5 mm,
height 9.08 mm; rose gold bezel; sapphire crystal;
water-resistant to 3 atm
Band: stainless steel with rose gold elements,
folding clasp
Price: $8,400
Variations: stainless steel ($4,400); set with 38
diamonds ($13,100); stainless steel/set with 38
diamonds ($9,400)

Manero Tourbillon
Limited Edition

Reference number: 00.10918.03.33.01
Movement: manually wound, Caliber CFB T1001;
ø 33 mm, height 6.2 mm; 35 jewels; 28,800 vph;
1-minute tourbillon, exclusively developed by APRP;
70-hour power reserve
Functions: hours, minutes, subsidiary seconds (on
tourbillon cage); additional 24-hour display (2nd
time zone); power reserve indicator; date
Case: rose gold, ø 41.8 mm, height 12.58 mm;
sapphire crystal; transparent case back; water-
resistant to 3 atm
Band: reptile skin, folding clasp
Price: $98,800
Variations: white dial

Patravi ScubaTec

Reference number: 00.10632.24.53.21
Movement: automatic, Caliber CFB 1950.1;
ø 26.2 mm, height 4.8 mm; 26 jewels; 28,800 vph;
38-hour power reserve; COSC-certified chronometer
Functions: hours, minutes, sweep seconds; date
Case: stainless steel, ø 44.6 mm, height 13.45 mm;
rose gold unidirectional bezel with ceramic inserts,
with 60-minute divisions, sapphire crystal; screw-in
crown, helium valve; water-resistant to 50 atm
Band: stainless steel with rose gold elements,
folding clasp with extension link
Price: $14,700
Variations: black or white dial; rubber strap
($11,700); stainless steel/stainless steel band
($6,800); stainless steel/rubber band ($6,400)

Patravi ChronoGrade

Reference number: 00.10623.08.63.01
Movement: automatic, Caliber CFB 1902; ø 30 mm, height 7.3 mm; 51 jewels; 28,800 vph; 42-hour power reserve
Functions: hours, minutes, subsidiary seconds; power reserve indicator; flyback chronograph with retrograde hour totalizer; full calendar with large date, month
Case: stainless steel, ø 44.6 mm, height 14.1 mm; sapphire crystal, transparent case back; screw-in crown; water-resistant to 5 atm
Band: leather, folding clasp
Price: $10,900
Variations: rose gold ($33,900)

Patravi TravelTec Four-X

Reference number: 00.10620.22.93.01
Movement: automatic, Caliber CFB 1901; ø 28.6 mm, height 7.3 mm; 39 jewels; 28,800 vph; 42-hour power reserve
Functions: hours, minutes, subsidiary seconds; second 24-hour display (2nd time zone); chronograph; date
Case: pink gold, ø 46.6 mm, height 15.5 mm; ceramic bezel, pusher-activated inner bezel with 24-hour division (3rd time zone); sapphire crystal; screw-in crown; water-resistant to 5 atm
Band: rubber, buckle
Price: $52,900
Variations: palladium ($52,900)

Patravi T-Graph

Reference number: 00.10615.08.33.01
Movement: automatic, Caliber CFB 1960; ø 30 mm, height 7.3 mm; 47 jewels; 28,800 vph; 42-hour power reserve
Functions: hours, minutes, subsidiary seconds; power reserve indicator; chronograph; large date
Case: stainless steel, 39 x 42 mm; sapphire crystal; screw-in crown; water-resistant to 5 atm
Band: leather, folding clasp
Price: $7,500

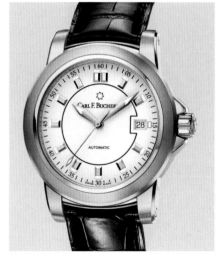

Patravi EvoTec DayDate

Reference number: 00.10625.08.33.01
Movement: automatic, Caliber CFB A1001; ø 32 mm, height 6.3 mm; 33 jewels; 28,800 vph; 55-hour power reserve
Functions: hours, minutes, subsidiary seconds; large date, weekday
Case: stainless steel, 43.75 x 44.5 mm, height 13.95 mm; sapphire crystal; transparent case back; screw-in crown; water-resistant to 5 atm
Band: calf leather, folding clasp
Price: $9,900

Patravi ChronoDate

Reference number: 00.10624.08.33.01
Movement: automatic, Caliber CFB 1956; ø 30 mm, height 7.3 mm; 49 jewels; 28,800 vph; 42-hour power reserve
Functions: hours, minutes, subsidiary seconds; chronograph; large date
Case: stainless steel, ø 44.6 mm; sapphire crystal, screw-in crown; water-resistant to 5 atm
Band: leather, folding clasp
Price: $6,300

Patravi AutoDate

Reference number: 00.10617.08.23.01
Movement: automatic, Caliber CFB 1950; ø 26.2 mm, height 4.8 mm; 26 jewels; 28,800 vph; 38-hour power reserve
Functions: hours, minutes, sweep seconds; date
Case: stainless steel, ø 38 mm, height 10.85 mm; sapphire crystal, transparent case back; screw-in crown; water-resistant to 5 atm
Band: reptile skin, folding clasp
Price: $3,000

Manero ChronoPerpetual Limited Edition

Reference number: 00.10907.03.13.01
Movement: automatic, Caliber CFB 1904; ø 30 mm, height 7.6 mm; 49 jewels; 28,800 vph; 50-hour power reserve
Functions: hours, minutes, sweep seconds; flyback chronograph; perpetual calendar with date, weekday, month, moon phase, leap year
Case: rose gold, ø 42.5 mm, height 14.3 mm; sapphire crystal; transparent case back; water-resistant to 3 atm
Band: reptile skin, folding clasp
Price: $52,600

Manero PowerReserve

Reference number: 00.10912.08.13.01
Movement: automatic, Caliber CFB A1011; ø 32 mm, height 6.3 mm; 33 jewels; 28,800 vph; 55-hour power reserve
Functions: hours, minutes, subsidiary seconds; power reserve indicator; large date, weekday
Case: stainless steel, ø 42.5 mm, height 12.54 mm; sapphire crystal; transparent case back; screw-in crown; water-resistant to 5 atm
Band: leather, folding clasp
Price: $11,000

Manero AutoDate

Reference number: 00.10908.08.13.01
Movement: automatic, Caliber CFB 1965; ø 26.2 mm, height 4.8 mm; 26 jewels; 28,800 vph; 42-hour power reserve
Functions: hours, minutes, sweep seconds; date
Case: rose gold, ø 42 mm, height 11.98 mm; sapphire crystal; transparent case back; screw-in crown, water-resistant to 3 atm
Band: reptile skin, buckle
Price: $2,800

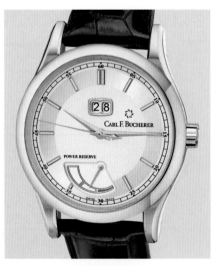

Manero BigDate Power

Reference number: 00.10905.08.13.01
Movement: automatic, Caliber CFB 1964; ø 26.2 mm, height 5.1 mm; 28 jewels; 28,800 vph; 42-hour power reserve
Functions: hours, minutes, sweep seconds; power reserve indicator; large date
Case: stainless steel, ø 40 mm, height 11.5 mm; sapphire crystal; transparent case back, water-resistant to 3 atm
Band: reptile skin, buckle
Price: $5,800
Variations: pink gold ($16,600)

Manero CentralChrono

Reference number: 00.10910.08.13.01
Movement: automatic, Caliber CFB 1967; ø 30 mm, height 7.4 mm; 47 jewels; 28,800 vph; chronograph with sweep minute totalizer; 40-hour power reserve
Functions: hours, minutes, subsidiary seconds; additional 24-hour display; chronograph; date
Case: stainless steel, ø 42.5 mm, height 14.24 mm; sapphire crystal; transparent case back; water-resistant to 3 atm
Band: reptile skin, buckle
Price: $7,100
Variations: stainless steel bracelet ($7,700)

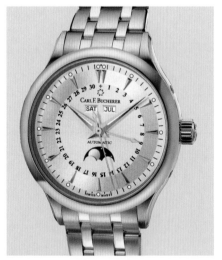

Manero MoonPhase

Reference number: 00.10909.03.13.21
Movement: automatic, Caliber CFB 1966; ø 26.2 mm, height 5.2 mm; 21 jewels; 28,800 vph; 42-hour power reserve
Functions: hours, minutes, sweep seconds; full calendar with date, weekday, month, moon phase
Case: pink gold, ø 38 mm, height 10.85 mm; sapphire crystal; transparent case back; water-resistant to 3 atm
Band: pink gold, folding clasp
Price: $27,200
Variations: reptile skin band ($12,900)

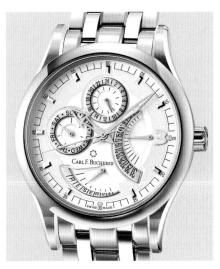

Manero AutoDate

Reference number: 00.10908.08.13.01
Movement: automatic, Caliber CFB 1965; ø 26.2 mm, height 3.6 mm; 25 jewels; 28,800 vph; 42-hour power reserve
Functions: hours, minutes, sweep seconds; date
Case: stainless steel, ø 38 mm, height 8.75 mm; sapphire crystal; water-resistant to 3 atm
Band: reptile skin, buckle
Price: $2,800
Variations: pink gold ($9,000)

Manero RetroGrade

Reference number: 00.10901.08.26.21
Movement: automatic, Caliber CFB 1903; ø 26.2 mm, height 5.1 mm; 34 jewels; 42-hour power reserve
Functions: hours, minutes, sweep seconds; additional 24-hour display (2nd time zone); power reserve indicator; full calendar with date (retrograde), weekday
Case: stainless steel, ø 40 mm, height 11.5 mm; sapphire crystal; transparent case back; water-resistant to 3 atm
Band: stainless steel, folding clasp
Price: $7,900
Variations: pink gold ($36,900)

Alacria RoyalRose

Reference number: 00.10702.02.90.18
Movement: quartz
Functions: hours, minutes
Case: white gold, 26.5 x 38 mm, height 7.4 mm; sapphire crystal
Band: calf leather, buckle
Remarks: limited to 125 pieces
Price: $69,000

Alacria Mini TwoTone

Reference number: 00.10701.07.15.21
Movement: quartz
Functions: hours, minutes
Case: stainless steel with pink gold sides; 21 x 30 mm, height 6.2 mm; sapphire crystal, water-resistant to 3 atm
Band: stainless steel with pink gold links, folding clasp
Price: $8,500
Variations: bezel set with 40 brilliant-cut diamonds ($13,200)

Adamavi

Reference number: 00.10308.03.16.01
Movement: quartz
Functions: hours, minutes
Case: pink gold, ø 26 mm, height 4.75 mm; sapphire crystal; water-resistant to 3 atm
Band: leather, buckle
Price: $4,800

Caliber CFB A1000

Automatic, bidirectional rotor, peripheral rotor on edge of movement with spring-held support bearings; precision fine adjustment; single spring barrel, 55-hour power reserve
Functions: hours, minutes, subsidiary seconds
Diameter: 30 mm; **Height:** 4.3 mm
Jewels: 33
Balance: glucydur
Balance spring: flat hairspring
Shock protection: Incabloc
Related calibers: CFB A1002 (with large date, weekday, and power reserve indicator); CFB A1003 (with large date and weekday)

Cartier SA
boulevard James-Fazy 8
CH-1201 Geneva
Switzerland

Tel.:
01141-022-818-4321

Fax:
01141-022-310-5461

E-Mail:
info@cartier.ch

Website:
www.cartier.de

Founded:
1847

Number of employees:
approx. 1,300 (watch manufacturing)

U.S. distributor:
Cartier North America
767 Fifth Avenue
New York, NY 10153
800-223-4000

Most important collections:
Calibre, Santos, Rotonde de Cartier, Ballon
Bleu, Tank, Pasha

Cartier

Since the Richemont Group's founding, Cartier has played an important role in the luxury concern as its premier brand and instigator of turnover. Although it took a while for Cartier to find its footing and convince the male market of its masculinity, any concerns about Cartier's seriousness and potential are being dispelled by facts. "We aimed to become a key player in *haute horlogerie*, and we succeeded," said CEO Bernard Fornas at a July 2012 press conference at the company's main manufacturing site in La Chaux-de-Fonds. His optimism is well founded. The company is growing by leaps and bounds—a components manufacturing site that will employ 400 people is in the works.

It was Richemont Group's purchase of the Roger Dubuis *manufacture* in Geneva a few years ago that paved the way to the brand's independence and vertical integration. Cartier currently produces nineteen movements, among them the 1904, which made its debut in the Calibre model. With a diameter of 42 mm, this strikingly designed men's watch is also well positioned in the segment. The designation 1904 MC is a reference to the year in which Louis Cartier developed the first wristwatch made for men—a pilot's watch custom designed for his friend and early pioneer of aviation, Alberto Santos-Dumont.

The automatic movement is a largely unadorned, yet efficient machine, powered by twin barrels. The central rotor sits on ceramic ball bearings, and the adjustment of the conventional escapement is by excenter screw. The Cartier developers have also forged ahead with two concept watches each featuring a unique barrel spring made of microfiber able to store more energy. All this research and development has produced a number of outstanding models like the Astrocalendaire, with a fully visible calendar and a tourbillon to boot, or the new diver in the Calibre collection.

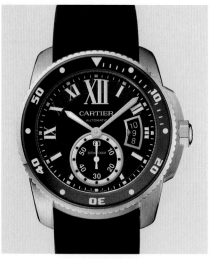

Calibre de Cartier Diver

Reference number: W7100056
Movement: automatic, Cartier Caliber 1904 MC; ø 25.6 mm, height 4 mm; 27 jewels; 28,800 vph; 2 spring barrels; 48 hours power reserve
Functions: hours, minutes, sweep seconds; date
Case: stainless steel, ø 42 mm, height 11 mm; black DLC-coated unidirectional bezel with 60-minute division; sapphire crystal; screw-in crown; water-resistant to 30 atm
Band: rubber, buckle
Price: $8,200
Variations: pink gold ($28,100)

Calibre de Cartier

Reference number: W7100016
Movement: automatic, Cartier Caliber 1904-PS; ø 25.6 mm, height 4 mm; 27 jewels; 28,800 vph; 2 spring barrels; 48 hours power reserve
Functions: hours, minutes, subsidiary seconds; date
Case: stainless steel, ø 42 mm, height 9.64 mm; sapphire crystal; transparent case back; water-resistant to 3 atm
Band: stainless steel, folding clasp
Price: $8,050
Variations: white dial

Calibre de Cartier Chronograph

Reference number: W7100045
Movement: automatic, Cartier Caliber 1904-CH MC; ø 25.6 mm, height 5.71 mm; 35 jewels; 28,800 vph; côtes de Genève; 48 hours power reserve
Functions: hours, minutes; chronograph; date
Case: stainless steel, ø 42 mm, height 12.66 mm; sapphire crystal; transparent case back; water-resistant to 10 atm
Band: stainless steel, double folding clasp
Price: $11,200
Variations: pink gold/reptile skin band ($11,200)

Rotonde de Cartier Astrocalendaire

Reference number: W1556242
Movement: automatic, Cartier Caliber 9459 MC; ø 31.38 mm, height 8.1 mm; 51 jewels; 21,600 vph; 1-minute tourbillon; 50 hours power reserve; Geneva Seal
Functions: hours, minutes; perpetual calendar with date, weekday
Case: platinum, ø 45 mm, height 15.1 mm; sapphire crystal; transparent case back; sapphire cabochon on crown; water-resistant to 3 atm
Band: reptile skin, folding clasp
Price: $204,000; limited to 100 pieces

Rotonde de Cartier Tourbillon Chronograph

Reference number: W1556245
Movement: manually wound, Cartier Caliber 9438 MC; ø 33.8 mm, height 8.15 mm; 31 jewels; 21,600 vph; 1-minute tourbillon; 192 hours power reserve
Functions: hours, minutes, subsidiary seconds; chronograph; power reserve indicator
Case: pink gold, ø 45 mm, height 16.4 mm; transparent case back; sapphire cabochon on crown; water-resistant to 3 atm
Band: reptile skin, folding clasp
Price: $183,000; limited to 50 pieces

Rotonde de Cartier Earth & Moon

Reference number: W1556222
Movement: manually wound, Cartier Caliber 9440 MC; ø 38.8 mm, height 5.65 mm; 40 jewels; 21,600 vph; 1-minute tourbillon; partially skeletonized; 72 hours power reserve
Functions: hours, minutes; additional 24 hours indicator (2nd time zone); moon phase with "moon shadow" that swivels via a pusher
Case: platinum, ø 47 mm, height 16.65 mm; sapphire crystal; transparent case back; sapphire cabochon crown; water-resistant to 3 atm
Band: reptile skin, double folding clasp
Price: $271,000; limited to 50 pieces

Rotonde de Cartier Day & Night

Reference number: W1556243
Movement: automatic, Cartier Caliber 9912 MC; ø 25.6 mm, height 6.44 mm; 44 jewels; 28,800 vph; 48 hours power reserve
Functions: hours, minutes; day/night indicator; moon phase (retrograde)
Case: pink gold, ø 43.5 mm, height 12.77 mm; sapphire crystal; transparent case back; sapphire cabochon on crown; water-resistant to 3 atm
Band: reptile skin, double folding clasp
Price: $42,500
Variations: palladium ($45,500)

Rotonde de Cartier 40 mm

Reference number: W1556252
Movement: manually wound, Cartier Caliber 9753 MC; ø 20.5 mm; 20 jewels; 21,600 vph; 40 hours power reserve
Functions: hours, minutes; power reserve indicator; date
Case: rose gold, ø 40 mm, height 8.94 mm; sapphire crystal; transparent case back; sapphire cabochon on crown
Band: reptile skin, folding clasp
Price: $22,300

Rotonde de Cartier Mystérieuse

Movement: manually wound, Cartier Caliber 9981 MC; ø 31.9 mm, height 4.61 mm; 27 jewels; 28,800 vph; 48 hours power reserve
Functions: hours, minutes (off-center); floating hands
Case: pink gold, ø 42 mm, height 11.6 mm; sapphire crystal; transparent case back; sapphire cabochon on crown; water-resistant to 3 atm
Band: reptile skin, double folding clasp
Price: $59,000
Variations: white gold; white or pink gold set with diamonds ($63,000)

Rotonde de Cartier Double Tourbillon Mystérieux

Reference number: W1556210
Movement: manually wound, Cartier Caliber 9454 MC; ø 35 mm, height 5 mm; 25 jewels; 21,600 vph; double flying tourbillon between 2 sapphire discs; 52 hours power reserve; Geneva Seal
Functions: hours, minutes (off-center)
Case: platinum, ø 45 mm, height 12.45 mm; sapphire crystal, transparent case back; sapphire cabochon on crown
Band: reptile skin, double folding clasp
Price: $177,000

Ballon Bleu Flying Tourbillon

Reference number: W6920105
Movement: automatic, Cartier Caliber 9452 MC; ø 24.5 mm, height 4.5 mm; 19 jewels; 21,600 vph; flying 1-minute tourbillon; Geneva Seal
Functions: hours, minutes, subsidiary seconds (on tourbillon cage)
Case: white gold, ø 39 mm, height 11.4 mm; sapphire crystal; sapphire cabochon on crown; water-resistant to 3 atm
Band: reptile skin, folding clasp
Remarks: guilloché dial with enamel layer
Price: $119,000; limited to 100 pieces

Ballon Bleu Flying Tourbillon

Reference number: W6920104
Movement: automatic, Cartier Caliber 9452 MC; ø 24.5 mm, height 4.5 mm; 19 jewels; 21,600 vph; flying 1-minute tourbillon; Geneva Seal
Functions: hours, minutes, subsidiary seconds (on tourbillon cage)
Case: pink gold, ø 39 mm, height 11.4 mm; sapphire crystal, sapphire cabochon on crown; water-resistant to 3 atm
Band: reptile skin, folding clasp
Price: $99,500

Tank Louis Cartier Skeleton

Reference number: W5310012
Movement: manually wound, Cartier Caliber 9616 MC; 26 x 26.3 mm, height 3.6 mm; 21 jewels; 28,800 vph; skeletonized; 72 hours power reserve
Functions: hours, minutes
Case: white gold, 30 x 39.2 mm, height 7.45 mm; sapphire crystal; transparent case back; sapphire cabochon on crown; water-resistant to 3 atm
Band: reptile skin, double folding clasp
Price: $53,500

Tank MC Skeleton

Reference number: W5310040
Movement: manually wound, Cartier Caliber 9619 MC; 28.6 x 28.6 mm, height 3.97 mm; 20 jewels; 28,800 vph; skeleton design with integrated roman numerals; 2 spring barrels; 72 hours power reserve
Functions: hours, minutes
Case: pink gold, 34.5 x 43.8 mm, height 9.3 mm; sapphire crystal; transparent case back; sapphire cabochon on crown; water-resistant to 3 atm
Band: reptile skin, buckle
Price: $56,000

Tank MC Chronograph

Reference number: W5330008
Movement: automatic, Cartier Caliber 1904-CH MC; ø 25.6 mm, height 5.71 mm; 35 jewels; 28,800 vph; 2 spring barrels; 48 hours power reserve
Functions: hours, minutes; chronograph; date
Case: stainless steel, 34.3 x 43.9 mm, height 11.7 mm; sapphire crystal; transparent case back; sapphire cabochon on crown
Band: reptile skin, folding clasp
Price: $10,300

Tank MC

Reference number: W5330003
Movement: automatic, Cartier Caliber 1904-PS MC;
ø 25.6 mm, height 4 mm; 27 jewels; 28,800 vph; 2
spring barrels; 48 hours power reserve
Functions: hours, minutes, subsidiary seconds;
date
Case: stainless steel, 34.3 x 44 mm, height 9.5
mm; sapphire crystal; transparent case back;
sapphire cabochon on crown; water-resistant to 3
atm
Band: reptile skin, folding clasp
Price: $6,600

Tortue Multiple Time Zone

Movement: manually wound, Cartier Caliber
9914 MC; ø 35.1 mm, height 7.18 mm; 27 jewels;
28,800 vph; 48 hours power reserve
Functions: hours, minutes; world-time display
(pusher-activated reference cities in lateral case
window)
Case: pink gold, 45.6 x 51 mm, height 17.2 mm;
mineral glass; transparent case back; sapphire
cabochon on crown; water-resistant to 3 atm
Band: reptile skin, double folding clasp
Price: $43,600
Variations: white gold ($46,700); white gold set
with diamonds ($46,700)

Tortue Perpetual Calendar

Reference number: W1580045
Movement: automatic, Cartier Caliber 9422 MC;
ø 32 mm, height 5.88 mm; 33 jewels; 28,800 vph;
52 hours power reserve
Functions: hours, minutes; perpetual calendar with
date, weekday, month, leap year
Case: pink gold, 45.6 x 51 mm, height 16.8 mm;
sapphire crystal, transparent case back; sapphire
cabochon on crown; water-resistant to 3 atm
Band: reptile skin, double folding clasp
Price: $63,000
Variations: white gold ($67,500)

Ronde Louis Cartier

Reference number: W6801005
Movement: automatic, Cartier Caliber 1904 MC;
ø 25.6 mm, height 4 mm; 27 jewels; 28,800 vph; 2
spring barrels; 48 hours power reserve
Functions: hours, minutes, subsidiary seconds;
date
Case: rose gold, ø 40 mm, height 9.19 mm;
sapphire crystal; sapphire cabochon on crown
Band: reptile skin, folding clasp
Price: $17,000

Santos Dumont Carbon Skeleton

Reference number: W2020052
Movement: manually wound, Cartier Caliber 9431
MC; 28.6 x 28.6 mm, height 3.97 mm; 20 jewels;
21,600 vph; skeletonized with integrated roman
numerals; 2 spring barrels; 72 hours power reserve
Functions: hours, minutes
Case: titanium with black ADLC coating, 38.7 x 47.4
mm, height 9.4 mm; sapphire crystal; transparent
case back; water-resistant to 3 atm
Band: reptile skin, double folding clasp
Price: $48,000

Santos Dumont Skeleton

Reference number: W2020033
Movement: manually wound, Cartier Caliber 9431
MC; 28.6 x 28.6 mm, height 3.97 mm; 20 jewels;
21,600 vph; skeletonized with integrated roman
numerals; 2 spring barrels; 72 hours power reserve
Functions: hours, minutes
Case: white gold, 38.7 x 47.4 mm, height 9.4 mm;
sapphire crystal; transparent case back; water-
resistant to 3 atm
Band: reptile skin, double folding clasp
Price: $53,500

Caliber 1904-PS MC

Automatic; 2 spring barrels; 48-hour power reserve
Functions: hours, minutes, subsidiary seconds; date
Diameter: 25.6 mm
Height: 4 mm
Jewels: 27
Balance: glucydur
Frequency: 28,800 vph
Balance spring: flat hairspring
Remarks: finely finished with côtes de Genève

Caliber 1904-CH MC

Automatic; column wheel control of chronograph functions; 2 spring barrels; 48-hour power reserve
Functions: hours, minutes; chronograph; date
Diameter: 25.6 mm
Height: 5.71 mm
Jewels: 35
Balance: glucydur
Frequency: 28,800 vph
Balance spring: flat hairspring
Remarks: finely finished with côtes de Genève

Caliber 9459 MC

Automatic; flying 1-minute tourbillon; forward and backward calendar adjusting on demand; patented central control unit; 2 spring barrels; 50-hour power reserve; Geneva Seal
Functions: hours, minutes; perpetual calendar with date, weekday, month, and leap year (on back); forward and backward setting
Diameter: 31.38 mm
Height: 8.1 mm
Jewels: 51
Balance: glucydur
Frequency: 21,600 vph
Balance spring: flat hairspring

Caliber 9440 MC

Manually wound; 1-minute tourbillon; skeletonized movement; 2 spring barrels; 72-hour power reserve
Functions: hours, minutes; additional 24-hour display (2nd time zone); moon phase display with pusher-activated moon shadow
Diameter: 38.8 mm
Height: 5.65 mm
Jewels: 40
Balance: glucydur
Frequency: 21,600 vph
Balance spring: flat hairspring

Caliber 9616 MC

Manually wound; skeletonized movement, 2 spring barrels; 72-hour power reserve
Functions: hours, minutes
Measurements: 26 x 26.3 mm
Height: 3.6 mm
Jewels: 21
Balance: glucydur
Frequency: 28,800 vph
Balance spring: flat hairspring
Remarks: fine finishing with beveled edges

Caliber 9619 MC

Manually wound; skeletonized movement with integrated Roman numerals; 2 spring barrels; 72-hour power reserve
Functions: hours, minutes
Measurements: 28.6 x 28.6 mm
Height: 3.97 mm
Jewels: 20
Balance: glucydur
Frequency: 28,800 vph
Balance spring: flat hairspring
Remarks: finely finished, gold-plated mainplate with beveled edges

Villeret Collection

Chanel

Chanel

135, avenue Charles de Gaulle
F-92521 Neuilly-sur-Seine Cedex
France

Tel.:
01133-1-41-92-08-33

Website:
www.chanel.com

Founded:
1914

Distribution:
retail and 200 Chanel boutiques worldwide

U.S. distributor:
Chanel Fine Jewelry and Watches
733 Madison Avenue
New York, NY 10021
800-550-0005
www.chanel.com

Most important collections:
J12, Première

After having put the occasional jewelry watch onto the market earlier in its history, Chanel, a family-owned business headquartered in Paris, opened its own horology division in 1987, a move that gave the brand instant access to the world of watchmaking art. Chanel boasts its own studio and logistics center, both in La Chaux-de-Fonds. While the brand's first collections were still directed exclusively at its female clientele, it was actually with the rather simple and masculine J12 that Chanel finally achieved a breakthrough. Designer Jacques Helleu says he mainly designed the unpretentious ceramic watch for himself. "I wanted a timeless watch in glossy black," shares the likable eccentric. Indeed, it's not hard to imagine that the J12 will still look modern a number of years down the road—especially given the fact that the watch now comes in white and shiny, polished titanium/ceramic as well.

The J12 collection showpiece, the Rétrograde Mystérieuse, was a stroke of genius—courtesy of the innovative think tank Renaud et Papi. It propelled Chanel into the world of *haute horlogerie* in one fell swoop. And the brand has not been resting on any laurels. It has continued developing the J12, keeping the octagonal shape of Place Vendôme in Paris (home of the brand) and the famous Chanel No. 5 bottle stopper, but narrowing the bezel somewhat for a finer look.

J12 Chromatic Beige Gold

Reference number: H4185
Movement: automatic, ETA Caliber 2824-2; ø 25.6 mm, height 4.6 mm; 25 jewels; 28,800 vph; 42-hour power reserve
Functions: hours, minutes, sweep seconds; date
Case: titanium, ø 38 mm, height 13 mm; bidirectional bezel with beige gold inlay, with 60-minute division, sapphire crystal; screw-in crown; water-resistant to 20 atm
Band: titanium, double folding clasp
Price: $10,000
Variations: 33 mm case ($9,200)

J12 Intense Black

Reference number: H 3829
Movement: automatic, ETA Caliber 2824-2; ø 25.6 mm, height 4.6 mm; 25 jewels; 28,800 vph; 42-hour power reserve
Functions: hours, minutes, sweep seconds
Case: ceramic, ø 38 mm, height 13 mm; bezel in white gold with ceramic inlays, sapphire crystal; screw-in crown; water-resistant to 20 atm
Band: ceramic, double folding clasp
Price: $6,100
Variations: 33 mm ($5,600) or 29 mm case ($5,200)

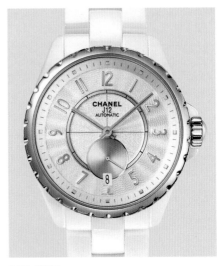

J12-365

Reference number: H 3836
Movement: automatic, ETA Caliber 2895-1; ø 25.6 mm, height 4.35 mm; 30 jewels; 28,800 vph; 42-hour power reserve
Functions: hours, minutes, subsidiary seconds; date
Case: ceramic, ø 36.5 mm; bezel in stainless steel, sapphire crystal; screw-in crown; water-resistant to 10 atm
Band: ceramic, double folding clasp
Price: $6,200
Variations: beige gold bezel ($11,000) set with diamonds; black ceramic ($20,500)

Chopard

The Chopard *manufacture* was founded by Louis-Ulysse Chopard in 1860 in the tiny village of Sonvillier in the Jura mountains of Switzerland. In 1963, it was purchased by Karl Scheufele, a goldsmith from Pforzheim, Germany, and revived as a producer of fine watches and jewelry.

The past seventeen years have seen a breathtaking development, when Karl Scheufele's son, Karl-Friedrich, and his sister, Caroline, decided to create watches with in-house movements, thus restoring the old business launched by Louis-Ulysse back in the nineteenth century.

In the 1990s, literally out of nowhere, Chopard opened up its watchmaking *manufacture* in the sleepy town of Fleurier. Since 1996, the company has created no fewer than nine *manufacture* calibers, reassembled to create more than fifty watch variations ranging from the three-hand automatic to the tourbillon. The aim of Chopard's Fleurier Ebauches SA is to revive the long-standing tradition of *ébauche* production in that town.

The factory's debut caliber, the 01.03-C, is featured in its Impériale ladies watch. In 2011, Chopard produced more than 3,000 "Fleurier" watches. In 2012 came the men's version, the 01.04-C. The number of movements is scheduled to reach 15,000 by the year 2015. And the engineers are not resting on their laurels: A chronograph caliber is already in the making. The company also continues to support the Geneva Watchmaking School with special *ébauches* for the students, a demonstration of its commitment to the industry. So, with its wide range of *manufacture* watch models and over 130 boutiques worldwide, the brand enjoys firm footing in the rarified air of *haute horlogerie*. Mission accomplished.

Chopard & Cie. SA
8, rue de Veyrot
CH-1217 Meyrin (Geneva)
Switzerland

Tel.:
01141-22-719-3131

E-Mail:
info@chopard.ch

Website:
www.chopard.ch

Founded:
1860

Distribution:
145 boutiques

U.S. distributor:
CHOPARD USA
21 East 63rd Street
New York, NY 10065
1-800-CHOPARD
www.us.chopard.com

Most important collections/price range:
Superfast / $9,320 to $33,190; L.U.C / $8,670 to $434,540; Imperiale / $4,390 to $617,010; Classic Racing / $4,170 to $57,130; Happy Sport / $5,120 to $287,330

Grand Prix de Monaco Historique Automatic

Reference number: 168568-3001
Movement: automatic, ETA Caliber A07.111; ø 37.2 mm, height 7.9 mm; 24 jewels; 28,800 vph; 46-hour power reserve; COSC-certified
Functions: hours, minutes, sweep seconds; date
Case: titanium, ø 44.5 mm, height 13.9 mm; stainless steel bezel with aluminum inlay, sapphire crystal; water-resistant to 10 atm
Band: calf leather, folding clasp
Price: $5,570
Variations: stainless steel/titanium bracelet ($7,260); stainless steel with titanium/rose gold parts ($8,950)

Grand Prix de Monaco Historique Power Control

Reference number: 168569-3001
Movement: automatic, ETA Caliber A07.161; ø 37.2 mm, height 7.9 mm; 24 jewels; 28,800 vph; 46-hour power reserve; COSC-certified
Functions: hours, minutes, sweep seconds; power reserve indicator; date
Case: titanium, ø 44.5 mm, height 13.9 mm; stainless steel bezel with aluminum inlay, sapphire crystal; water-resistant to 10 atm
Band: calf leather, folding clasp
Price: $6,990
Variations: stainless steel with titanium/rose gold parts ($10,250.)

Grand Prix de Monaco Historique Chrono

Reference number: 168570-3001
Movement: automatic, ETA Caliber A07.211; ø 37.2 mm, height 7.9 mm; 24 jewels; 28,800 vph; 46-hour power reserve; COSC-certified
Functions: hours, minutes, sweep seconds; chronograph; date
Case: titanium, ø 44.5 mm, height 13.9 mm; stainless steel bezel with aluminum inlay, sapphire crystal; water-resistant to 10 atm
Band: calf leather, folding clasp
Price: $7,640
Variations: stainless steel/titanium bracelet ($8,680); stainless steel with titanium/rose gold parts ($11,590)

Classic Racing Superfast Chrono

Reference number: 168535-3001
Movement: automatic, Chopard Manufacture Caliber 03.05-M; ø 28.8 mm, height 7.6 mm; 45 jewels; 28,800 vph; 60-hour power reserve; COSC-certified chronometer
Functions: hours, minutes, subsidiary seconds; flyback chronograph; date
Case: stainless steel, ø 45 mm, height 15.2 mm; sapphire crystal; transparent back; screw-in crown with rubber coating; water-resistant to 10 atm
Band: rubber, folding clasp
Price: $12,740
Variations: rose gold ($33,190)

Classic Racing Superfast Power Control

Reference number: 168537-3001
Movement: automatic, Chopard Manufacture Caliber 01.02-M; ø 28.8 mm, height 4.95 mm; 37 jewels; 28,800 vph; 60-hour power reserve; COSC-certified chronometer
Functions: hours, minutes, subsidiary seconds; power reserve indicator; date
Case: stainless steel, ø 45 mm, height 12.4 mm; sapphire crystal; transparent back; screw-in crown with rubber coating; water-resistant to 10 atm
Band: rubber, folding clasp
Price: $10,350
Variations: rose gold ($28,690)

Classic Racing Superfast Power Control

Reference number: 161291-5001
Movement: automatic, Chopard Manufacture Caliber 01.02-M; ø 28.8 mm, height 4,95 mm; 37 jewels; 28,800 vph; 60-hour power reserve; COSC-certified chronometer
Functions: hours, minutes, subsidiary seconds; power reserve indicator; date
Case: rose gold, ø 45 mm, height 12.4 mm; sapphire crystal; transparent case back; screw-in crown with rubber coating; water-resistant to 10 atm
Band: rubber, folding clasp
Price: $28,690
Variations: stainless steel ($10,350)

Classic Racing Mille Miglia 2014

Reference number: 168511-3036
Movement: automatic, ETA Caliber 2894-2; ø 28.6 mm, height 6.1 mm; 37 jewels; 28,800 vph; 42-hour power reserve; COSC-certified chronometer
Functions: hours, minutes, subsidiary seconds; chronograph; date
Case: stainless steel, ø 42 mm, height 12.31 mm; sapphire crystal; transparent case back; water-resistant to 5 atm
Band: calf leather, buckle
Price: $5,520; limited to 2,014 pieces
Variations: rose gold ($19,110; limited to 250 pieces)

Classic Racing Mille Miglia 2014

Reference number: 161274-5006
Movement: automatic, ETA Caliber 2894-2; ø 28.6 mm, height 6.1 mm; 37 jewels; 28,800 vph; 42-hour power reserve; COSC-certified chronometer
Functions: hours, minutes, subsidiary seconds; chronograph; date
Case: rose gold, ø 42 mm, height 12.31 mm; sapphire crystal; transparent case back; water-resistant to 5 atm
Band: calf leather, buckle
Price: $19,110; limited to 250 pieces
Variations: stainless steel ($5,520; limited to 2,014 pieces)

L.U.C 8 HF Power Control

Reference number: 168575-9001
Movement: automatic, L.U.C Caliber 01.09-L; ø 28.8 mm, height 4.95 mm; 24 jewels, 57,600 vph; high-frequency escapement with silicone lever and escape wheel; 60-hour power reserve; COSC-certified chronometer
Functions: hours, minutes, subsidiary seconds; power reserve indicator; date
Case: ceramic, ø 42 mm, height 11.2 mm; sapphire crystal, transparent case back; water-resistant to 10 atm
Band: textile, buckle
Price: $20,820; limited to 250 pieces

L.U.C Lunar One

Reference number: 161927-5001
Movement: automatic, L.U.C Caliber 96.13-L;
ø 33 mm, height 6 mm; 32 jewels; 28,800 vph;
65-hour power reserve; Geneva Seal, COSC-certified
Functions: hours, minutes, subsidiary seconds;
perpetual calendar with large date, weekday, month,
orbital moon phase display, leap year
Case: rose gold, ø 43 mm, height 11.47 mm;
sapphire crystal; transparent case back; water-
resistant to 5 atm
Band: reptile skin, folding clasp
Price: $63,600
Variations: bezel set with diamonds ($98,550);
white gold ($63,600)

L.U.C Lunar Big Date

Reference number: 161969-1001
Movement: automatic, L.U.C Caliber 96.20-L;
ø 33 mm, height 5.25 mm; 33 jewels; 28,800 vph;
65-hour power reserve; COSC-certified chronometer
Functions: hours, minutes, subsidiary seconds;
large date; moon phase
Case: white gold, ø 42 mm, height 11.04 mm;
sapphire crystal; transparent case back; water-
resistant to 5 atm
Band: reptile skin, buckle
Price: $31,730
Variations: rose gold ($31,730)

L.U.C Lunar Twin

Reference number: 161934-1001
Movement: automatic, L.U.C Caliber 96.21-L;
ø 33 mm, height 5.1 mm; 33 jewels; 28,800 vph;
bridges with côtes de Genève; 65-hour power
reserve; COSC-certified chronometer
Functions: hours, minutes, subsidiary seconds;
date; moon phase
Case: white gold, ø 40 mm, height 9.97 mm;
sapphire crystal; transparent case back; water-
resistant to 3 atm
Band: reptile skin, buckle
Price: $26,550
Variations: rose gold ($26,550)

L.U.C Tourbillon Qualité Fleurier Fairmined Gold

Reference number: 161929-5006
Movement: manually wound, L.U.C Caliber 02.13-L;
ø 29.7 mm, height 6.1 mm; 33 jewels; 28,800 vph;
1-minute tourbillon, bridges with côtes de Genève;
216-hour power reserve; COSC-certified chronometer,
Qualité Fleurier
Functions: hours, minutes, subsidiary seconds; power
reserve indicator
Case: rose gold, ø 43 mm, height 11.15 mm; sapphire
crystal; transparent case back; water-resistant to 5 atm
Band: reptile skin, buckle
Remarks: case of Fairmined-certified gold
Price: $144,570; limited to 25 pieces

L.U.C Triple Certification Tourbillon

Reference number: 161929-5001
Movement: manually wound, L.U.C Caliber 02.01-L;
ø 29.7 mm, height 6.1 mm; 33 jewels; 28,800
vph; 1-minute tourbillon; 216-hour power reserve;
Geneva Seal, COSC-certified, Qualité Fleurier
Functions: hours, minutes, subsidiary seconds;
power reserve indicator
Case: rose gold, ø 43 mm, height 11.15 mm;
sapphire crystal; transparent case back; water-
resistant to 5 atm
Band: reptile skin, buckle
Price: $146,270; limited to 100 pieces

L.U.C Qualité Fleurier

Reference number: 161896-5003
Movement: automatic, L.U.C Caliber 96.09-L;
ø 27.4 mm, height 3.3 mm; 29 jewels; 28,800
vph; 65-hour power reserve; COSC-certified
chronometer, Qualité Fleurier
Functions: hours, minutes, subsidiary seconds
Case: rose gold, ø 39 mm, height 8.92 mm;
sapphire crystal, transparent case back; water-
resistant to 3 atm
Band: reptile skin, buckle
Price: $19,280

L.U.C 1963 Hand-wound

Reference number: 161963-5001
Movement: manually wound, L.U.C Caliber 63.01-L; ø 38 mm, height 5.5 mm; 20 jewels; 28,800 vph; 60-hour power reserve; Geneva Seal, COSC-certified chronometer
Functions: hours, minutes, subsidiary seconds
Case: rose gold, ø 44 mm, height 11.5 mm; sapphire crystal; transparent case back; water-resistant to 5 atm
Band: reptile skin, buckle
Price: $37,580; limited to 50 pieces
Variations: platinum ($43,650; limited to 50 pieces)

L.U.C 1963 Chronograph

Reference number: 161964-5001
Movement: manually wound, L.U.C Caliber 03.07-L; ø 28.8 mm, height 5.62 mm; 38 jewels; 28,800 vph; 60-hour power reserve; Geneva Seal, COSC-certified chronometer
Functions: hours, minutes, subsidiary seconds; flyback chronograph; date
Case: rose gold, ø 42 mm, height 11.5 mm; sapphire crystal; transparent case back; water-resistant to 5 atm
Band: reptile skin, buckle
Price: $44,440; limited to 50 pieces

L.U.C XPS

Reference number: 161920-5002
Movement: automatic, L.U.C Caliber 96.12-L; ø 27.4 mm; height 3.3 mm; 29 jewels; 28,800 vph; bridges with côtes de Genève; 65-hour power reserve; COSC-certified chronometer
Functions: hours, minutes, subsidiary seconds
Case: rose gold, ø 39.5 mm, height 7.13 mm; sapphire crystal; transparent case back; water-resistant to 3 atm
Band: reptile skin, buckle
Price: $16,780
Variations: white gold ($16,780)

L.U.C XPS Poinçon de Genève 125th Anniversary Edition

Reference number: 161932-5001
Movement: automatic, L.U.C Caliber 96-01-L; ø 27.4 mm, height 3.3 mm; 29 jewels; 28,800 vph; 2 double spring barrel; 65-hour power reserve; Geneva Seal, COSC-certified chronometer
Functions: hours, minutes, subsidiary seconds; date
Case: rose gold, ø 39.5 mm, height 7.13 mm; sapphire crystal; transparent case back; water-resistant to 3 atm
Band: reptile skin, buckle
Price: $19,320; limited to 125 pieces

L.U.C XPS 35 mm

Reference number: 131968-5001
Movement: automatic, L.U.C 96.12-L; ø 27.4 mm, height 3.3 mm; 29 jewels; 28,800 vph; bridges with côtes de Genève; 65-hour power reserve; COSC-certified chronometer
Functions: hours, minutes, subsidiary seconds
Case: rose gold, ø 35 mm, height 7.1 mm; bezel set with diamonds; sapphire crystal; transparent case back; water-resistant to 5 atm
Band: reptile skin, buckle
Remarks: dial set with diamonds
Price: $27,080
Variations: white gold ($27,080); w/o diamonds ($16,710)

Imperiale

Reference number: 384241-5005
Movement: automatic, Chopard Caliber 01.01-C; ø 28.8 mm, height 4.95 mm; 31 jewels; 28,800 vph; 60-hour power reserve
Functions: hours, minutes, sweep seconds; date
Case: rose gold, ø 40 mm, height 10.28 mm; sapphire crystal; transparent case back; amethyst cabochons on crown and lugs; water-resistant to 5 atm
Band: reptile skin, buckle
Price: $20,640

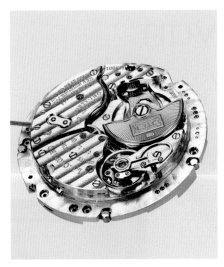

Caliber L.U.C 96.13-L

Automatic, microrotor; 2 double spring barrels; 65-hour power reserve; Geneva Seal, COSC-certified chronometer
Functions: hours, minutes, subsidiary seconds, perpetual calendar with large date, weekday, month, moon phase, leap year
Diameter: 33 mm
Height: 6 mm
Jewels: 32
Balance: glucydur
Frequency: 28,800 vph
Balance spring: flat hairspring, Nivarox 1

Caliber L.U.C 96.12-L

Automatic, microrotor; 2 double spring barrels; 65-hour power reserve; COSC-certified chronometer
Functions: hours, minutes, subsidiary seconds
Diameter: 27.4 mm
Height: 3.3 mm
Jewels: 29
Balance: glucydur
Frequency: 28,800 vph
Balance spring: flat hairspring, Nivarox 1

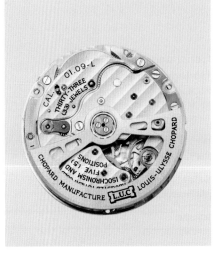

Caliber L.U.C 01.09-L

Automatic, high-frequency escapement with silicon pallet lever and balance wheel; single spring barrel; 60-hour power reserve; COSC-certified chronometer
Functions: hours, minutes, subsidiary seconds; power reserve indicator; date
Diameter: 28.8 mm
Height: 4.95 mm
Jewels: 33
Balance: glucydur
Frequency: 57,600 vph
Balance spring: flat hairspring, Nivarox 1

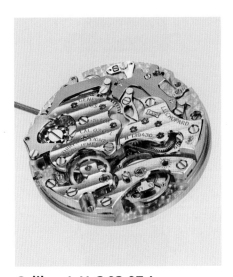

Caliber L.U.C 03.07-L

Manually wound; column wheel control of chronograph functions, vertical chronograph clutch; single spring barrel; 60-hour power reserve; Geneva Seal, COSC-certified chronometer
Functions: hours, minutes, subsidiary seconds; date
Diameter: 28.8 mm; **Height:** 5.62 mm
Jewels: 38
Balance: Variner with 4 weighted screws
Frequency: 28,800 vph
Balance spring: flat hairspring
Remarks: perlage on plate, beveled bridges with côtes de Genève, polished steel parts and screw heads

Caliber 03.05-M

Automatic, column wheel control of chronograph functions, vertical chronograph clutch; single spring barrel; 65-hour power reserve; COSC-tested chronometer
Functions: hours, minutes, subsidiary seconds; flyback chronograph; date
Diameter: 28.8 mm
Height: 7.6 mm
Jewels: 45
Balance: glucydur
Frequency: 28,800 vph
Balance spring: flat hairspring
Remarks: slitted movement bridges; gray finishing; skeletonized winding rotor

Caliber L.U.C 02.13-L (1.02 QF)

Manually wound; 1-minute tourbillon; 2 double spring barrels; 216-hour power reserve; Geneva Seal, COSC-certified chronometer, Qualité Fleurier
Functions: hours, minutes, subsidiary seconds (on tourbillon cage); power reserve indicator
Diameter: 29.7 mm
Height: 6.1 mm
Jewels: 33
Frequency: 28,800 vph
Balance spring: flat hairspring
Remarks: triply certified movement (COSC, QF, and Geneva Seal), very fine finishing

**Christiaan van der Klaauw
Horloge Atelier b.v.**

P.O. Box 87
NL-8440 AB Heerenveen
The Netherlands

Tel.:
01131-513-624-906

E-Mail:
info@klaauw.com

Website:
www.klaauw.com

Founded:
1974

Annual production:
500–1,000 watches

U.S. distributor:
Kaufmann de Suisse
210 Worth Avenue
Palm Beach, FL 33480
561-832-4918

Most important collections:
astronomical watches

Christiaan van der Klaauw

Christiaan van der Klaauw was one of the earliest members of the famous AHCI, the Académie Horlogère des Créateurs Indépendents (Horological Academy of Independent Creators), in Switzerland. His main focus since 1976 has been on astronomical watches. He did not have to search long for a role model: The most obvious choice was Christiaan Huygens. The famous physicist and mathematician built the first pendulum clock. Like van der Klaauw, he too came from the Netherlands. And so did the astronomer Eise Eisinga, who set up a model of the solar system in his living room in 1774 to prove to people that the moon, Mars, Jupiter, Mercury, and Venus would not collide with our own planet.

During his studies of microengineering, van der Klaauw worked in the world's oldest observatory (founded by J. H. Oort in 1633) and had already begun building astrolabes, planetaria, and complicated calendar watches.

The astronomical watch he completed in 1990 turned out to be his passport to the AHCI. From then on, van der Klaauw drove the watch world forward with his many elaborate creations. He also won numerous awards, most notably the Baselworld Gold Medal in 1992. In 2012, he accepted the financial and administrative assistance of a small group of Dutch watch collectors. The move was strategic, allowing him to put more time and talent into developing modern interpretations of astronomical displays and making his watches available to a greater public.

Real Moon Joure 40Y

Reference number: CKRJ3384
Movement: automatic, Caliber CK7382 (base TT 738); ø 30 mm, height 4.35 mm; 35 jewels; 28,800 vph; twin spring barrels, hand-engraved gold rotor; 96-hour power reserve
Functions: hours, minutes; moon phase (3D moon)
Case: stainless steel, ø 40 mm, height 14.8 mm; sapphire crystal; transparent case back
Band: reptile skin, buckle
Remarks: limited to 40 pieces commemorating 40th anniversary
Price: $25,840
Variations: various colors; rose gold ($42,900); white gold ($50,500)

Planetarium

Reference number: CKPT3304
Movement: automatic, Caliber CK7386 (base TT 738); ø 30 mm, height 4.35 mm; 35 jewels; 28,800 vph; twin spring barrels, hand-engraved gold rotor; 96-hour power reserve
Functions: hours, minutes; orbits of main planets; calendar with date, month
Case: stainless steel, ø 40 mm, height 14.8 mm; sapphire crystal; transparent case back; water-resistant to 5 atm
Band: reptile skin, folding clasp
Remarks: world's smallest heliocentric planetarium
Price: $46,500
Variations: rose gold ($56,500); white gold (69,500); platinum ($76,500)

Real Moon 1980

Reference number: CKRL1124
Movement: automatic, Caliber CK7384 (base TT 738); ø 30 mm, height 4.35 mm; 35 jewels; 28,800 vph; twin spring barrels, hand-engraved gold rotor; 96-hour power reserve
Functions: hours, minutes; calendar with date, month, moon phase (sculptural moon), sun's zenith (with sun declination); sun and moon eclipse displays
Case: rose gold, ø 40 mm, height 13 mm; sapphire crystal; transparent case back
Band: reptile skin, buckle
Price: $55,950
Variations: white gold ($61,950); stainless steel ($38,900)

Christophe Claret

Individuals like Christophe Claret are authentic horological engineers who eat, drink, and breathe watchmaking and have developed careers based on pushing the envelope to the very edge of what's possible.

By the age of twenty-three, the Lyon-born Claret was in Basel alongside Journe, Calabrese, and other independents, where he was spotted by the late Rolf Schnyder of Ulysse Nardin and commissioned to make a minute repeater with jacquemarts. In 1989, he opened his *manufacture* in a nineteenth-century mansion tastefully extended with a state-of-the-art machining area. Claret embraces the potential in modern tools to create the precise pieces needed to give physical expression to exceedingly complex ideas.

Over the years, Claret created complications and movements for many companies. In 2004, he came out with the Harry Winston Opus IV, a reversible moon phase with tourbillon and a minute repeater. And twenty years after establishing his business, Claret finally launched his own complex watches: models like the DualTow, with its hours and minutes on two tracks, minute repeater, and complete view of the great ballet of arms and levers inside. Then came the Adagio, also a minute repeater, with a clear dial that manages a second time zone and large date. In 2011, Claret wowed the watch world with a humorous, on-the-wrist gambling machine telling time and playing blackjack, craps, or roulette. It was followed by the stunning X-TREM-1, a turbocharged DualTow with two spheres controlled by magnets hovering along the numeral tracks to tell the time plus a tourbillon, and the Kantharos, named after a top-notch thoroughbred. One of his latest productions is the Margot, a play on the gambling theme, but for women—or men, in fact—who want to hazard determining the feelings of a partner or prospect via "He loves me, he loves me not."

Christophe Claret SA

Route du Soleil d'Or 2
CH-2400 Le Locle
Switzerland

Tel.:
01141-32-933-0000

Fax:
01141-32-933-8081

E-Mail:
info@christopheclaret.com

Website:
www.christopheclaret.com

Founded:
manufacture 1989, brand 2010

Number of employees:
100

Distribution:
For sales information, contact the *manufacture* directly.

Most important collections:
DualTow, Adagio, Blackjack, Maestoso, X-TREM-1, Soprano, Kantharos, Baccara, Poker, Margot

Maestoso

Movement: manually wound, Caliber DTC 07; ø 31 mm, height 8.6 mm; 44 jewels; 14,400 vph; constant force escapement, sprung suspension; anti-over-banking system; screw balance with cylindrical spring and hacking second on pulling crown; 2 spring barrels; 80-hour power reserve
Functions: hours, minutes
Case: rose gold, ø 44 mm, height 13.6 mm; sapphire crystal; transparent case back
Band: reptile skin, double folding clasp
Price: CHF 186,000
Variations: white gold/titanium (CHF 182,000); rose gold/titanium (CHF 178,000)

Margot

Movement: automatic, Caliber EMT 17; ø 38.4 mm, height 9.76 mm; 95 jewels; 28,800 vph; 2 spring barrels; 72-hour power reserve
Functions: hours, minutes; mechanical randomness generator via case pusher with sound signal
Case: white gold, ø 42.5 mm, height 14.5 mm; baguette diamonds on bezel and lugs; sapphire crystal; transparent case back
Band: double folding clasp
Remarks: "He loves me, he loves me not..." game, answer at 4 o'clock, with delicate sound (hammer visible at mother-of-pearl dial near 8)
Price: CHF 278,000
Variations: with "snowflake" diamonds on bezel (CHF 198,000)

Poker

Movement: automatic, Caliber PCK 05; ø 38.6 mm, height 9.92 mm; 72 jewels; 28,800 vph; 72-hour power reserve
Functions: hours, minutes; mechanical randomness generator via case pusher with sound signal
Case: titanium, white gold, ø 45 mm, height 15.95 mm; sapphire crystal; transparent case back
Band: reptile skin, double folding clasp
Remarks: randomness generator starts Texas hold'em for 3 people with flops and rivers on dial side or roulette on movement side
Price: CHF 172,000
Variations: rose gold (CHF 168,000); titanium with black PVD coating (CHF 160,000)

Chronoswiss AG
Löwenstrasse 16a
CH-6004 Lucerne
Switzerland

Tel.:
01141-41-552-2100

Fax:
01141-41-552-2109

E-Mail:
mail@chronoswiss.com

Website:
www.chronoswiss.com

Founded:
1983

Number of employees:
approx. 40

Annual production:
4,000–6,000 wristwatches

U.S. distributor:
Please contact brand headquarters in
Switzerland.

Most important collections/price range:
approx. 30 models including Sirius
Régulateur, Sirius Triple Date, Sirius
Artist, Timemaster Big Date, Timemaster
Chronograph GMT / approx. $3,900 to
$60,000

Chronoswiss

Chronoswiss has been assembling its signature watches—which boast such features as coin edge bezels and onion crowns—since 1983. Chronoswiss founder Gerd-Rüdiger Lang loved to joke about having "the only Swiss watch factory in Germany" as the brand has always adhered closely to the qualities of the Swiss watch industry while still contributing a great deal to reviving mechanical watches from its facilities in Karlsfeld near Munich, with concepts and designs "made in Germany." The fact is, however, that the watches are equipped with Swiss movements and cases, as well as many other important parts. The company's financial brawn is also Swiss, ever since Eva and Oliver Ebstein bought up all Chronoswiss shares in order to ensure the brand's survival. Oliver, as a passionate watch man, is continuing the brand tradition and producing top-drawer mechanical timepieces. The spacious sun-drenched facilities in Karlsfeld are now focused on distribution and servicing.

With such developments as the *manufacture* caliber C.122—based on an old Enicar automatic movement with a patented rattrapante mechanism—and its Chronoscope chronograph, Chronoswiss has earned a solid reputation for technical prowess. The Pacific and Sirius models, additions to the classic collection, point the company in a new stylistic direction designed to help win new buyers and the attention of the international market. As for the successful Timemaster chrono, it has appeared in a new skeletonized version, giving a deep insight into the brand's own modification of an ETA Valjoux.

Sirius Régulateur

Reference number: CH 1241.1 R
Movement: automatic, Chronoswiss Caliber C.122 (base Enicar 165); ø 30 mm, height 5.2 mm; 30 jewels; 21,600 vph; skeletonized rotor; finely finished with côtes de Genève; 40-hour power reserve
Functions: hours (off-center), minutes, subsidiary seconds
Case: pink gold, ø 40 mm, height 11 mm; sapphire crystal; transparent back; water-resistant to 3 atm
Band: reptile skin, buckle
Remarks: sterling silver dial
Price: $18,400
Variations: stainless steel ($7,400)

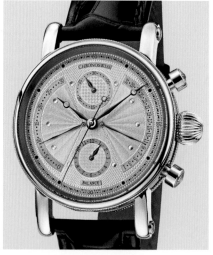

Sirius Chronograph Retrograde

Reference number: CH 7543 B R
Movement: automatic, Chronoswiss Caliber C.831 (base LJP 8310); ø 30 mm, height 7.9 mm; 39 jewels; 28,800 vph; skeletonized rotor; finely finished with côtes de Genève
Functions: hours, minutes, subsidiary seconds (retrograde); chronograph; date (retrograde)
Case: stainless steel, ø 42 mm, height 14.75 mm; sapphire crystal; transparent case back; water-resistant to 3 atm
Band: reptile skin, buckle
Price: $11,875
Variations: pink gold ($26,625)

Sirius Chronograph Moon Phase

Reference number: CH 7541 L R
Movement: automatic, Chronoswiss Caliber C.755 (base ETA 7750); ø 30 mm, height 7.9 mm; 25 jewels; 28,800 vph; côtes de Genève, perlage on plate, skeletonized rotor
Functions: hours, minutes, subsidiary seconds; chronograph; date, moon phase
Case: pink gold, ø 42 mm, height 14.75 mm; sapphire crystal; transparent case back; water-resistant to 3 atm
Band: reptile skin, buckle
Price: $23,775
Variations: stainless steel ($8,700)

Sirius Small Seconds

Reference number: CH 8021 R
Movement: automatic, Chronoswiss Caliber C.285; ø 30 mm, height 5.2 mm; 25 jewels; 28,800 vph; perlage on bridges and plates, skeletonized rotor with côtes de Genève; 42-hour power reserve
Functions: hours, minutes, subsidiary seconds
Case: pink gold, ø 40 mm, height 10.12 mm; sapphire crystal, transparent case back; water-resistant to 3 atm
Band: reptile skin, buckle
Price: $14,900
Variations: stainless steel ($5,400)

Sirius Medium

Reference number: CH 8923 D
Movement: automatic, Chronoswiss Caliber C.281 (base ETA 2892-A2); ø 25.6 mm, height 3.6 mm; 21 jewels; 28,800 vph; perlage on plate and bridges, skeletonized rotor with côtes de Genève; 42-hour power reserve
Functions: hours, minutes, sweep seconds; date
Case: stainless steel, ø 34 mm, height 9.4 mm; sapphire crystal; transparent case back; water-resistant to 3 atm
Band: reptile skin, buckle
Remarks: dial set with diamonds
Price: $11,400
Variations: w/o diamonds ($6,400); rose gold ($20,300 with diamond bezel); diamonds on dial, w/o diamond bezel ($15,200)

Sirius Retrograde Day

Reference number: CH 8121 R cp
Movement: automatic, Chronoswiss Caliber C.286; ø 30 mm, height 5.2 mm; 22 jewels; 28,800 vph; perlage on plate and bridges, skeletonized rotor with côtes de Genève; 42-hour power reserve
Functions: hours, minutes, sweep seconds; large date and weekday (retrograde)
Case: pink gold, ø 40 mm, sapphire crystal, transparent case back
Band: reptile skin, buckle
Price: $17,800
Variations: stainless steel ($7,100)

Sirius Triple Date

Reference number: CH 9343
Movement: automatic, Chronoswiss Caliber C.931 (base ETA 2892-A2); ø 25.6 mm, height 5.75 mm; 21 jewels; 28,800 vph; skeletonized rotor, côtes de Genève; 42-hour power reserve
Functions: hours, minutes, sweep seconds; full calendar with date, weekday, month, moon phase
Case: stainless steel, ø 40 mm, height 9.9 mm; sapphire crystal; transparent case back; water-resistant to 3 atm
Band: reptile skin, buckle
Price: $9,025
Variations: pink gold ($18,675)

Sirius Artist

Reference number: CH 6421 RE4 wh
Movement: manually wound, Chronoswiss Caliber C.642 (base Unitas 6425); ø 29.4 mm, height 4.6 mm; 17 jewels; 21,600 vph; hand-skeletonized, finely decorated; 47-hour power reserve
Functions: hours, minutes, subsidiary seconds
Case: pink gold, ø 40 mm, height 11 mm; sapphire crystal, transparent case back; water-resistant to 3 atm
Band: reptile skin, buckle
Remarks: fired enamel sterling silver dial
Price: $37,200

Sirius Artist

Reference number: CH 6421 RE3
Movement: manually wound, Chronoswiss Caliber C.642 (base Unitas 6425); ø 29.4 mm, height 4.6 mm; 17 jewels; 21,600 vph; hand-skeletonized, finely decorated; 47-hour power reserve
Functions: hours, minutes, subsidiary seconds
Case: pink gold, ø 40 mm, height 11 mm; sapphire crystal; transparent case back; water-resistant to 3 atm
Band: reptile skin, buckle
Remarks: hand-guilloché and fired enamel sterling silver dial
Price: $37,200

Sirius Artist

Reference number: CH 2893.1 E bl
Movement: automatic, Chronoswiss Caliber C.281;
ø 25.6 mm, height 3.6 mm; 21 jewels; 28,800 vph;
skeletonized rotor, perlage on plates, bridges with
côtes de Genève; 42-hour power reserve
Functions: hours, minutes, seconds, date window
(at 6)
Case: stainless steel, ø 40 mm, height 11 mm;
sapphire crystal, transparent case back; water-
resistant to 3 atm
Band: reptile skin, buckle
Remarks: hand-guilloché and fired enamel sterling
silver dial
Price: $8,900

Timemaster Chronograph Skeleton

Reference number: CH 9043 SB bk
Movement: automatic, Chronoswiss Caliber C.741 S
(base ETA 7750); ø 30 mm, height 7.9 mm; 25 jewels;
28,800 vph; perlage on bridges and plates, skeletonized
rotor with côtes de Genève; 46-hour power reserve
Functions: hours, minutes, subsidiary seconds;
chronograph; date
Case: stainless steel, ø 44 mm, height 15.3 mm; bezel
with black DLC coating, sapphire crystal; water-resistant
to 10 atm
Band: rubber, folding clasp
Remarks: skeletonized dial
Price: $13,900
Variations: skeletonized silver-plated dial

Timemaster Chronograph Day Date

Reference number: CH 9043 B db
Movement: automatic, Chronoswiss Caliber C.771
(base ETA 7750); ø 30 mm, height 7.9 mm; 25 jewels;
28,800 vph; perlage on bridges and plates, skeletonized
rotor with côtes de Genève; 46-hour power reserve
Functions: hours, minutes, subsidiary seconds; date,
weekday
Case: stainless steel, ø 44 mm, height 15.3 mm; bezel
with black DLC coating, sapphire crystal; water-resistant
to 10 atm
Band: rubber, folding clasp
Price: $7,700
Variations: bezel w/o DLC ($7,300)

Timemaster Chronograph GMT

Reference number: CHD 7555.1
Movement: automatic, Chronoswiss Caliber C.754
(base La-Joux-Perret); ø 30.4 mm, height 7.9 mm;
25 jewels; 28,800 vph; skeletonized and gold-
plated rotor, finely finished with côtes de Genève;
46-hour power reserve
Functions: hours, minutes; additional 24-hour
display (2nd time zone); chronograph; date
Case: stainless steel with black DLC coating; ø
44 mm, height 16.25 mm; bezel with 24-hour
division, sapphire crystal; water-resistant to 10 atm
Band: rubber, folding clasp
Price: $8,700
Variations: w/o DLC ($7,850)

Timemaster Retrograde Day

Reference number: CH 8145 wh
Movement: automatic, Chronoswiss Caliber C.286;
ø 30 mm, height 5.2 mm; 22 jewels; 28,800 vph;
perlage on bridges and plates, skeletonized rotor
with côtes de Genève; 42-hour power reserve
Functions: hours, minutes, sweep seconds; large
date and weekday (retrograde)
Case: stainless steel with black DLC coating; ø
44 mm, height 15.1 mm; sapphire crystal; water-
resistant to 10 atm
Band: rubber, folding clasp
Price: $6,900
Variations: w/o DLC ($6,300)

Timemaster Big Date

Reference number: CH 3563.1
Movement: automatic, Chronoswiss Caliber C.351
(base LJP 3513); ø 25.6 mm, height 4.95 mm;
21 jewels; 28,800 vph; rotor rhodium-plated and
skeletonized with black DLC coating; finely finished
with côtes de Genève
Functions: hours, minutes, sweep seconds; power
reserve indicator; large date
Case: stainless steel, ø 44 mm, height 13.8 mm;
bezel with 60-minute division, sapphire crystal;
water-resistant to 10 atm
Band: rubber, folding clasp
Price: $5,950
Variations: black dial and stainless steel case
($5,750); black dial and DLC ($6,475)

Caliber C.111

Base caliber: Marvin 700
Manually wound; power reserve 46 hours
Functions: hours, minutes, subsidiary seconds
Diameter: 29.4 mm
Height: 3.3 mm
Jewels: 17
Balance: glucydur, 3-legged
Frequency: 21,600 vph
Balance spring: Nivarox 1
Shock protection: Incabloc
Remarks: polished pallet lever, escapement wheel and screws, bridges with côtes de Genève

Caliber C.122

Automatic; skeletonized and gold-plated rotor on ball bearings, with côtes de Genève; power reserve approx. 40 hours
Functions: hours, minutes, subsidiary seconds
Diameter: 26.8 mm
Height: 5.3 mm
Jewels: 30
Balance: glucydur, 3-legged
Frequency: 21,600 vph
Balance spring: Nivarox 1
Shock protection: Incabloc
Remarks: pallet lever, escape wheel and screws, perlage on plate, bridges with côtes de Genève; individually numbered

Caliber C.126

Automatic; E94 striking module (Dubois Dépraz), all-or-nothing strike train and 2 gongs; power reserve 35 hours
Functions: hours, minutes, subsidiary seconds; quarter hour repeater
Diameter: 28 mm
Height: 8.35 mm
Jewels: 38
Balance: glucydur, 3-legged
Frequency: 21,600 vph
Balance spring: Nivarox 1
Shock protection: Incabloc
Remarks: base plate with perlage; beveled bridges with perlage; côtes de Genève decoration; individually numbered

Caliber C.127

Automatic; calendar module with a left-side moon phase; skeletonized and gold-plated rotor on ball bearings, with côtes de Genève; power reserve 40 hours
Functions: hours, minutes, sweep seconds; perpetual calendar with months, moon phase, leap year, weekday, date
Diameter: 26.8 mm; **Height:** 8.79 mm
Jewels: 30; **Balance:** glucydur, 3-legged
Frequency: 21,600 vph
Balance spring: Nivarox 1
Shock protection: Incabloc
Remarks: polished pallet lever, escapement wheel and screws, perlage on plate, bridges with côtes de Genève; individually numbered

Caliber C.673

Base caliber: ETA 6498
Manually wound; power reserve 46 hours
Functions: hours (off-center), minutes, subsidiary seconds
Diameter: 37.2 mm
Height: 4.5 mm
Jewels: 17
Balance: glucydur screw balance with stop second
Frequency: 18,000 vph
Balance spring: Nivarox 1
Shock protection: Incabloc
Remarks: polished pallet lever, escape wheel and screws; côtes de Genève and hand perlage on bridges, balance cocks, sunburst pattern on crown and ratchet wheel; individually numbered

Caliber C.741 S

Base caliber: ETA 7750
Automatic; completely skeletonized; skeletonized and gold-plated rotor on ball bearings, with côtes de Genève; power reserve approx. 46 hours
Functions: hours, minutes, subsidiary seconds; chronograph; date
Diameter: 30 mm; **Height:** 7.9 mm; **Jewels:** 25
Balance: glucydur, 3-legged
Frequency: 28,800 vph
Balance spring: Nivarox 1
Shock protection: Incabloc
Remarks: polished pallet lever, escape wheel and screws; perlage on plate, skeletonized and beveled levers and wheels

Montres Corum Sàrl
Rue du Petit-Château 1
Case postale 374
CH-2301 La Chaux-de-Fonds
Switzerland

Tel.:
01141-32-967-0670

Fax:
01141-32-967-0800

E-Mail:
info@corum.ch

Website:
www.corum.ch

Founded:
1955

Number of employees:
160 worldwide

Annual production:
16,000 watches

U.S. distributor:
Montres Corum USA
14050 NW 14th Street, Suite 110
Sunrise, Florida 33323
954-279-1220; 954-279-1780 (fax)
www.corum.ch

Most important collections/price range:
Admiral's Cup, Corum Bridges and Heritage,
Romvlvs and Artisan, 150 models in total /
approx. $4,100 to over $1,000,000

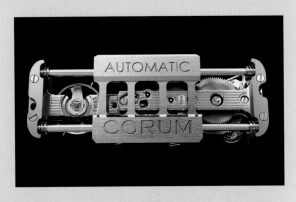

Corum

Making a name for itself since 1955, Switzerland's youngest luxury watch brand, Corum, is known for unusual—and sometimes outlandish—case and dial designs. In 1999, the company was purchased by Severin Wunderman, who had enjoyed twenty-three years of creating highly successful wristwatches for fashion giant Gucci. After a number of overly daring forays into the shimmering world of fashion watches, he led Corum back to the straight and narrow before dying of a stroke, on June 25, 2008, at the age of 69.

Together with Wunderman's son, Michael, CEO Antonio Calce turned the focus of the collection toward the brand's two "draft horses." The legendary Golden Bridge baguette movement received a complete makeover, featuring a totally new technical interpretation in modern materials and such complicated mechanisms as a flying tourbillon. The development of these extraordinary movements requires great watchmaking craftsmanship. In fact, the company has added a number of professional watchmakers to its workforce, who make good use of the new technical equipment in Corum's workshops. The product development department also underwent expansion and modernization in preparation for the development of even more innovations.

The brand's expansive policies cost money, so to secure its future, Corum was sold to China Haidian Group for over $90 million in April 2013. Calce welcomed the move not only for the financial independence it is bringing, but also for the access it allows to the crucial Chinese market.

Golden Bridge Automatic

Reference number: 313.165.95 0001 GL10R
Movement: automatic, Caliber CO 313; 11.25 x 33.18 mm; 26 jewels; 28,800 vph; variable inertia balance; baguette with gold bridges and main plate; linear winding with sliding platinum weight
Functions: hours, minutes
Case: titanium with black PVD, 51.8 x 37.2 mm, height 13.7 mm; sapphire crystal, transparent case back; water-resistant to 3 atm
Band: reptile skin, buckle
Remarks: lateral window on case
Price: $40,000
Variations: white gold ($54,800); pink gold ($52,700)

Golden Bridge Automatic

Reference number: 313.165.55 0002 GL10R
Movement: manually wound, Caliber CO113; 4.9 x 34 mm, height 3 mm; 26 jewels; 28,800 vph; baguette, gold bridges and plate, hand-engraved
Functions: hours, minutes
Case: pink gold, 37.2 x 51.8 mm, height 13.7 mm; sapphire crystal; transparent back; water-resistant to 3 atm
Band: reptile skin, buckle
Remarks: lateral window for full view of caliber
Price: $52,700
Variations: white gold/white gold band ($54,800)

Golden Bridge

Reference number: 313.165.59 0001 GLI0G
Movement: manually wound, Caliber CO113; 4.9 x 34 mm, height 3 mm; 26 jewels; 28,800 vph; baguette, gold bridges and plate, hand-engraved
Functions: hours, minutes
Case: white gold, 51 x 34 mm, height 10.9 mm; sapphire crystal, transparent case back; water-resistant to 3 atm
Band: reptile skin, buckle
Remarks: lateral window on case for full view of movement but not wrist
Price: $54,800
Variations: pink gold/pink gold bracelet ($76,500)

Golden Bridge Tourbillon Panoramique

Reference number: 100.160.55 OF01 0000
Movement: manually wound, Caliber CO 100;
ø 29 mm; 22 jewels; 21,600 vph; flying 1-minute
tourbillon; baguette; sapphire crystal bridges and
plate; 90-hour power reserve
Functions: hours, minutes
Case: pink gold, 37.6 x 56 mm, height 12.35 mm;
sapphire crystal, transparent case back; water-
resistant to 3 atm
Band: reptile skin, folding clasp
Remarks: lateral window on case
Price: $185,300
Variations: white gold ($193,700)

Ti-Bridge Automatic Dual Winder

Reference number: 207.201.04 OF61 0000
Movement: automatic, Caliber CO 207;
37.9 x 12.27 mm; 30 jewels, 28,800 vph; baguette;
bridges and plate of titanium; 2 winding rotors with
tungsten oscillating weights coupled by pushrod;
72-hour power reserve
Functions: hours, minutes
Case: titanium, 52 x 42 mm, height 15 mm;
sapphire crystal; transparent case back; water-
resistant to 3 atm
Band: leather/rubber, folding clasp
Price: $22,300
Variations: pink gold/leather strap ($51,000)

Ti-Bridge Power Reserve

Reference number: 107.201.05 OF81 0000
Movement: manually wound, Caliber CO113;
12.37 x 38.25 mm, height 4.4 mm; 25 jewels;
28,800 vph; baguette; PVD-coated titanium
chassis; 72-hour power reserve
Functions: hours, minutes; power reserve indicator
Case: pink gold, 52 x 42 mm, height 13.23 mm;
sapphire crystal; water-resistant to 5 atm
Band: reptile skin, double folding clasp
Price: $47,800
Variations: titanium ($19,200)

Admiral's Cup AC-One 45 Double Tourbillon

Reference number: 108.101.04/OF01 AN01
Movement: manually wound, CO Caliber 1008;
ø 31.7 mm; 21,600 vph; 2 1-minute tourbillons,
connected via differential; full hour corrector for
precision setting of time near top of hour
Functions: hours, minutes; date (retrograde)
Case: titanium, ø 45 mm, height 14.4 mm; sapphire
crystal; transparent case back; water-resistant to
3 atm
Band: reptile skin, double folding clasp
Price: $76,000
Variations: pink gold ($96,500)

Admiral's Cup Seafender 47 Tourbillon Chronograph

Reference number: 398.550.55 0001 AN10
Movement: automatic, Caliber CO 398; ø 36.25
mm; 28 jewels; 28,800 vph; 1-minute tourbillon;
winding rotor coated in black ruthenium; 45-hour
power reserve
Functions: hours, minutes, subsidiary seconds;
chronograph; date
Case: pink gold, ø 47 mm, height 15.72 mm;
sapphire crystal; transparent case back; water-
resistant to 5 atm
Band: reptile skin, buckle
Price: $88,800
Variations: aluminum ($57,600)

Admiral's Cup AC-One 45 Regatta

Reference number: 040.101.04 OF61 AN10
Movement: automatic, Caliber CO 040 (base ETA
7750 with Corum module); ø 30 mm; 25 jewels;
28,800 vph; 48-hour power reserve
Functions: hours, minutes; chronograph with
adjustable regatta countdown
Case: titanium, ø 45 mm, height 15.2 mm;
bezel with black PVD coating; sapphire crystal;
transparent case back; water-resistant to 30 atm
Band: stainless steel, folding clasp
Price: $11,525
Variations: titanium band ($12,100)

Admiral's Cup AC-One 45 Skeleton

Reference number: 082.401.04/0F01 FH10
Movement: automatic, Caliber CO 082; ø 25.6 mm; 27 jewels, 28,800 vph; platinum, skeletonized bridges and rotors; 42-hour power reserve
Functions: hours, minutes, sweep seconds; date
Case: titanium, ø 45 mm, height 13.3 mm; sapphire crystal; transparent back; water-resistant to 30 atm
Band: reptile skin, double folding clasp
Remarks: skeletonized dial
Price: $11,500

Admiral's Cup AC-One 45 Tides

Reference number: 277.101.04/F373 AB12
Movement: automatic, Caliber CO 277 (base ETA 2892-A2 with Dubois Dépraz tides module); ø 25.9 mm, height 5.2 mm; 21 jewels; 28,800 vph; COSC chronometer
Functions: hours, minutes, sweep seconds; tides display with current strength; date; moon phase
Case: titanium, ø 45 mm, height 14.3 mm; sapphire crystal, screw-in crown; water-resistant to 30 atm
Band: rubber, buckle
Price: $9,350
Variations: pink gold/leather strap ($32,700); titanium and rubber bracelet ($11,300)

Admiral's Cup AC-One 45 Chronograph

Reference number: 132.201.05 OF01 AN11
Movement: automatic, Caliber CO 132 (base Sellita 2892-A2, Dubois Dépraz module); ø 28.6 mm, height 6.1 mm; 39 jewels; 28,800 vph; black PVD coating on rotor; 42-hour power reserve
Functions: hours, minutes, subsidiary seconds; chronograph; date
Case: titanium, ø 45 mm, height 14.3 mm; pink gold bezel, sapphire crystal; transparent case back; water-resistant to 30 atm
Band: reptile skin, folding clasp
Price: $18,450
Variations: titanium bezel and bracelet ($10,150)

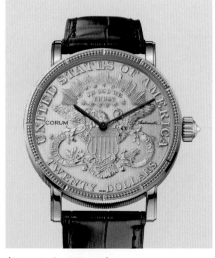

Admiral's Cup Legend 42 Chronograph

Reference number: 984.101.20 V705 AB10
Movement: automatic, Caliber CO 984 (base ETA 2892-2); ø 28.6 mm, height 6.1 mm; 37 jewels; 28,800 vph; 42-hour power reserve; COSC chronometer
Functions: hours, minutes, subsidiary seconds; chronograph; date
Case: stainless steel, ø 42 mm, height 11.6 mm; sapphire crystal; transparent case back; water-resistant to 3 atm
Band: stainless steel, double folding clasp
Price: $6,550
Variations: pink gold/leather strap ($10,000)

Admiral's Cup Legend 42 Chronograph

Reference number: 984.101.98 F502 AN46
Movement: automatic, Caliber CO 984 (base ETA 2892-2); ø 28.6 mm, height 6.1 mm; 37 jewels, 28,800 vph; 42-hour power reserve; COSC chronometer
Functions: hours, minutes, subsidiary seconds; chronograph; date
Case: stainless steel, with gray PVD coating, ø 42 mm, height 11.6 mm; sapphire crystal; transparent case back; water-resistant to 3 atm
Band: calf leather, double folding clasp
Price: $7,350

$20 Coin Watch

Reference number: 293.645.56/0001 MU51
Movement: automatic, Caliber CO 293 (base Frédéric Piguet 1150); ø 25.6 mm, height 3.25 mm mm; 30 jewels; 28,800 vph; 70-hour power reserve
Functions: hours, minutes
Case: yellow gold, ø 36 mm, height 6.4 mm; sapphire crystal; water-resistant to 3 atm
Band: reptile skin, buckle
Remarks: dial and case back made of original Double Eagle dollar coin
Price: $20,800

Cuervo y Sobrinos

Cuba means a lot of things to different people. Today it seems to be the last bastion of genuine retro in an age of frenzied technology. However, turn the clock back to the early twentieth century and you find that Ramón Rio y Cuervo and his sister's sons kept a watchmaking workshop and an elegant store on Quinto Avenida where they sold fine Swiss pocket watches—and more modest American models as well. With the advent of tourism from the coast of Florida, their business developed with wristwatches, whose dials Don Ramón soon had printed with Cuervo y Sobrinos— Cuervo and Nephews.

An Italian watch enthusiast and a Spanish businessman got together to resuscitate Cuervo y Sobrinos in 2002 and started manufacturing in the Italian-speaking region of Switzerland and in cooperation with various Swiss workshops. The tagline, "Latin soul, Swiss brand," says it all. These timepieces epitomize—or even romanticize—the island's heyday. The colors hint at cigar leaves and sepia photos in frames of old gold. The lines are at times elegant and sober, like the Esplendido, or radiate the ease of those who still have time on their hands, like the Prominente. Playfulness is also a Cuervo y Sobrinos quality: The Piratas have buttons shaped like the muzzle of a blunderbuss, a cannonball crown, and a porthole flange. Lately, CyS has been modernizing (the Manjuari dive watch or the Robusto Day-Date have a younger feel), and they have introduced a line of writing implements as accessories for the genuine lover of fine things and the mechanical world.

Cuervo y Sobrinos Habana SA
Via Carlo Maderno 54
CH-6825 Capolago
Switzerland

Tel.:
01141-91-921-2773

Fax:
01141-91-921-2775

E-Mail:
info@cuervoysobrinos.com

Website:
www.cuervoysobrinos.com

Founded:
1882

Annual production:
3,500 watches

U.S. distributor:
Cuervo y Sobrinos Swiss Watches
P.O. Box 347890
Coral Gables, FL 33234
214-704-3000

Most important collections/price range:
Esplendido, Historiador, Prominente, Torpedo, Robusto / $3,200 to $16,000; higher for perpetual calendars and tourbillon models

Historiador Flameante Blue Edition

Reference number: 3130.1FB-US
Movement: manually wound, ETA Caliber 7001; ø 23.3 mm, height 2.5 mm; 17 jewels; 28,800 vph; 42-hour power reserve
Functions: hours, minutes, subsidiary seconds; date
Case: stainless steel, ø 40 mm, height 6.2 mm; sapphire crystal; transparent case back; water-resistant to 3 atm
Band: reptile skin, folding clasp
Remarks: 10th Anniversary USA Commemorative
Price: $3,300

Robusto Manjuari

Reference number: 2808.1NR3
Movement: automatic, Sellita Caliber SW 200-1; ø 25.6 mm, height 4.6 mm; 26 jewels; 28,800 vph; 38-hour power reserve
Functions: hours, minutes, sweep seconds; date
Case: stainless steel and titanium, ø 43 mm, height 14.95 mm; titanium and sapphire bezel, black ring rubber with Cuervo y Sobrinos in relief; sapphire crystal; screwed-down case back with Manjuari fish engraving; water-resistant to 60 atm
Band: rubber, folding clasp
Price: $5,100

Historiador Retrogrado

Reference number: 3194.1A
Movement: automatic, 9094/2892-A2 ETA; ø 25.6 mm, height 5.1 mm; 30 jewels; 28,800 vph; 42-hour power reserve
Functions: hours, minutes, sweep seconds; retrograde date; day of the week; power reserve
Case: stainless steel, ø 40 mm, height 11.25 mm; double curved sapphire crystal; transparent case back; water-resistant to 3 atm
Band: reptile skin, folding buckle
Price: $5,500

Cvstos
2, rue Albert Richard
CH-1201 Geneva
Switzerland

Tel.:
01141-22-989-1010

Fax:
01141-22-989-1019

E-Mail:
info@cvstos.com

Website:
www.cvstos.com

Founded:
2005

U.S. distributor:
Cvstos USA, Inc.
207 W. 25th Street, 8th Floor
New York, NY 10001
212-463-8898

Most important collections/price range:
Challenge, Challenge-R, Concept-S,
Evosquare, High Fidelity / $10,000 to
$315,000

Cvstos

Dials in a conventional sense are something that one can search for in vain at Cvstos (Latin for guardian); technology rules the roost at the brand, and thus these extroverted, stately timepieces show what they're made of, quite literally. The look is cultivated throughout the collection, which veers sharply from the appearance of traditional *haute horlogerie*, targeting a clientele that doesn't necessarily include elements such as *côtes de Genève*, gold, and guilloché in their watchmaking ideal.

Although it may not seem so at first sight, a great deal of watchmaking know-how goes into the making of a Cvstos, and that is no surprise for a brand that is the spiritual child of Sassoun Sirmakes, son of Vartan Sirmakes, the man who led Genevan watchmaker Franck Muller to world fame. Under the tutelage of his father, the cofounder of the Watchland *manufacture* in Genthod, young Sassoun was introduced to the hands-on side of watchmaking. In 2005, fate brought him together with designer and watchmaker Antonio Terranova, who had made a name for himself in the Swiss watch industry with the timepieces he designed and produced for leading brands. Even though he had freelanced for some of the more staid brands, Terranova had the heart of an avant-gardist willing to break free of the constraints of traditional forms—he collaborated on some of the early Richard Mille pieces, for example. So a Cvstos has all the thrilling complications, but expect some technoid materials and high engineering art.

Challenge Jetliner SL

Reference number: CHJETLINERSLSTB
Movement: automatic, Cvstos Caliber 350; 21 jewels; 28,800 vph; special plasma finish, skeletonized disc; 42-hour power reserve
Functions: hours, minutes, sweep seconds; date
Case: stainless steel, 41 x 53.7 mm, height 13.35 mm; sapphire crystal; screw-in crown; transparent case back; water-resistant to 10 atm
Band: rubber, folding clasp
Price: $9,200
Variations: rose gold ($22,000)

Challenge Pilot RC Yellow

Reference number: CHPILOTNRTTBY
Movement: automatic, Cvstos Caliber 357; 25 jewels; 28,800 vph; special plasma finish; 48-hour power reserve
Functions: hours, minutes, subsidiary seconds; chronograph; date
Case: titanium with black and yellow plasma coating, 41 x 53.7 mm, height 16 mm; sapphire crystal; screw-in crown; transparent case back; water-resistant to 10 atm
Band: rubber, folding clasp
Price: $20,000
Variations: blue or red alloy with titanium ($20,000); rose gold ($31,000)

Challenge Jet Liner GT Daedalus Edition

Reference number: CHGTJETSLSTDAEDALUS
Movement: automatic, Cvstos Caliber CVS350; 25 jewels; 28,800 vph; skeletonized; black plasma and rhodium treatment; 42-hour power reserve
Functions: hours, minutes, subsidiary seconds; chronograph; date; power reserve indicator
Case: polished titanium, ø 59 x 45 mm, height 15.45 mm; titanium bezel; screw-in crown with Nitril insert; sapphire crystal; transparent case back; water-resistant to 10 atm
Remarks: titanium honeycomb dial, pierced hands
Band: rubber, folding clasp
Price: $10,500

Challenge Jet Liner Carbon

Reference number: CHJETSLCARB5NB
Movement: automatic, Cvstos Caliber CVS350; 25
jewels; 28,800 vph; skeletonized; black plasma and
rhodium treatment; 42-hour power reserve
Functions: hours, minutes, sweep seconds;
chronograph; date
Case: rose gold and lacquered carbon, 53.7 x
41 mm, height 13.45 mm; sapphire crystal;
transparent case back; water-resistant to 10 atm
Band: carbon, carbon folding clasp
Price: $25,000

Chrono II Power Reserve

Reference number: C-R50CHF
CHR50CCNRHFBC3STB-A
Movement: automatic, Cvstos Caliber 577; 25
jewels; 28,800 vph; 42-hour power reserve
Functions: hours, minutes, subsidiary seconds;
chronograph; date; power reserve indicator
Case: titanium with pink gold lateral elements,
53.70 x 41 mm; height 16 mm; sapphire crystal;
transparent case back; water-resistant to 10 atm
Band: rubber, folding clasp
Price: $31,000; limited to 100 pieces
Variations: black steel ($31,200)

Challenge Minute Repeater Tourbillon

Reference number: CHRMTSNRTT
Movement: manually wound, Cvstos Caliber 76510;
32 jewels; 18,000 vph; flying 1-minute tourbillon;
partially skeletonized; 60-hour power reserve
Functions: hours, minutes, subsidiary seconds (on
tourbillon cage); hour, quarter-hour, minute repeater
Case: titanium with black plasma coating,
45 x 53.7 mm, height 16 mm; sapphire crystal;
transparent back; screw-in crown; water-resistant
to 10 atm
Band: rubber, folding clasp
Price: $333,400

Challenge GP Black Steel

Reference number: CHCCGPNRSTBR
Movement: automatic, Cvstos Caliber 577; 25
jewels; 28,800 vph; special finish, plasma-coated,
satinized, and polished; 60-hour power reserve
Functions: hours, minutes, subsidiary seconds;
chronograph; date; power reserve indicator
Case: aluminum with black plasma coating,
41 x 53.7 mm, height 16 mm; sapphire crystal;
transparent case back; water-resistant to 10 atm
Band: reptile skin, folding clasp
Price: $17,000; limited to 100 pieces
Variations: with large case and red, blue, and yellow
colors ($20,000)

CTR-S Tourbillon Chronograph

Reference number: CTR-S GT
Movement: manually wound, Cvstos Caliber 555;
48 jewels; 18,000 vph; flying 1-minute tourbillon;
satinized and polished finish; partially skeletonized;
192-hour power reserve
Functions: hours and minutes (off-center),
subsidiary seconds; split-seconds chronograph
Case: titanium with black plasma coating, 45 x 53.7
mm, height 16 mm; sapphire crystal; transparent
case back; screw-in crown; water-resistant to 10 atm
Band: rubber, folding clasp
Price: $277,800; limited to 5 pieces

Sea Liner

Reference number: CHSEALINERSTBL5NW
Movement: automatic, Cvstos Caliber CV350; 21
jewels; 28,800 vph; skeletonized; côtes de Genève;
42-hour power reserve
Functions: hours, minutes, sweep seconds; date
(on skeletonized disc); power reserve indicator
Case: blue steel and pink gold, 53.7 x 41 mm,
height 13.35 mm; sapphire crystal; transparent
case back; screw-in crown with Nitril insert; water-
resistant to 10 atm
Band: reptile skin, folding clasp
Remarks: teak base dial with gold/rhodium
Price: $18,000

D. Dornblüth & Sohn
Westpromenade 7
D-39624 Kalbe/Milde
Germany

Tel.:
01149-39080-3206

Fax:
01149-39080-72796

E-Mail:
info@dornblueth.com

Website:
www.dornblueth.com

Founded:
1962

Number of employees:
5

Annual production:
approx. 120 watches

U.S. distributor:
Dornblüth & Sohn
WatchBuys
888-333-4895
www.watchbuys.com

Most important collections/price range:
men's wristwatches / between $3,000 and
$24,000

D. Dornblüth & Sohn

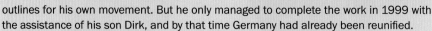

D. Dornblüth & Sohn is a two-generation team of master watchmakers. Their workshop in Kalbe, near Magdeburg in eastern Germany, turns out remarkable wristwatches with large manual winding mechanisms, three-quarter plates, screw balances, swan-neck fine adjustments, and a clever power reserve indicator.

The history of the "Dornblüth Caliber" goes back to the 1960s in the Erz mountains in East Germany. Dieter Dornblüth, the father in this father-and-son team, had sketched the first outlines for his own movement. But he only managed to complete the work in 1999 with the assistance of his son Dirk, and by that time Germany had already been reunified.

The strength of the tiny *manufacture* lies in the high level of skill that goes into producing these classical, manually wound watches in the old-fashioned way, i.e., without any CNC machines.

The 99 series is based on the reliable ETA Unitas 6497 pocket watch movement. Dirk redesigns about one-half of it by putting in a three-quarter plate and other elements. The dials are created in-house, using the 250-year-old "filled engraving" technique. They are then given a lustrous frosted layer of matte silver plating to complement the traditional *grainage* look.

The brand's fiftieth anniversary in 2012 saw the birth of the Q-2010, which features a special Maltese cross drive that reduces linear torque between two serially positioned barrel springs. The movement drives the latest models, like the Auf & Ab and Klassik. A specially designed lowered escape wheel minimizes position errors caused by the anchor escapement. The 99.0 collection has a new model, too: the 99.5, with a hand date and power reserve indicator on the traditionally classical Dornblüth dial.

Caliber 99.5

Reference number: 99.5 (1) ST
Movement: manually wound, Dornblüth Caliber 99.5 (base ETA 6497); ø 37 mm, height 5.4 mm; 20 jewels; 18,000 vph; indirect sweep seconds driven by seconds wheel, screw balance, swan-neck fine adjustment, finely finished with côtes de Genève
Functions: hours, minutes, sweep seconds; power reserve indicator; date
Case: stainless steel, ø 42 mm, height 12.5 mm; sapphire crystal; transparent case back
Band: reptile skin, buckle
Price: $11,950
Variations: various dials; rose gold (on request)

Klassik

Reference number: Q-2010.1(GR)ST
Movement: manually wound, Dornblüth Caliber Q-2010 Classic; ø 34.3 mm, height 4.7 mm; 29 jewels; 18,000 vph; double spring barrel; driven by indirectly controlled Maltese cross spring producing almost linear torque; short anchor escapement with lower escape wheel; Breguet spring
Functions: hours, minutes, subsidiary seconds
Case: stainless steel, ø 38.5 mm, height 10 mm; sapphire crystal; transparent case back
Band: reptile skin, buckle
Price: $12,350
Variations: various dials; rose gold (on request)

Auf & Ab

Reference number: Q-2010.2(GR)ST
Movement: manually wound, Dornblüth Caliber Q-2010 Auf-Ab; ø 34.3 mm, height 4.7 mm; 29 jewels; 18,000 vph; double spring barrel; driven by indirectly controlled Maltese cross spring producing almost linear torque; short anchor escapement with lower escape wheel; Breguet spring
Functions: hours, minutes, subsidiary seconds; power reserve indicator
Case: stainless steel, ø 38.5 mm, height 10 mm; sapphire crystal; transparent case back
Band: reptile skin, buckle
Price: $14,975
Variations: various dials; rose gold (on request)

Davosa

Davosa has come a long way from its beginnings in 1861. Back then, farmer Abel Frédéric Hasler spent the long winter months in Tramelan, in Switzerland's Jura mountains, making silver pocket watch cases. Later, two of his brothers ventured out to the city of Geneva and opened a watch factory. The third brother also opted to engage with the watch industry and moved to Biel. The entire next generation of Haslers went into watchmaking as well.

The name Hasler & Co. appeared on the occasional package mailed in Switzerland or overseas. Playing the role of unassuming private-label watchmakers, the Haslers remained in the background and let their customers in Europe and the United States run away with the show. It wasn't until after World War II that brothers Paul and David Hasler dared produce their own timepieces.

In 1987, the brothers developed their own line of watches under the brand name Davosa and took on the sales and marketing roles. The sustained development of the brand began in 1993, when the Haslers signed a partnership with the German distributor Bohle. In Germany, mechanical watches were experiencing a boom, so the brand was able to evolve quickly. In 2000, Corinna Bohle took over as manager of strategic development. Meanwhile, Davosa has reached well beyond Switzerland's borders and is now an integral part of the world of mechanical watches.

Hasler & Co. SA
CH-2720 Tramelan
Switzerland

E-Mail:
info@davosa.com

Website:
www.davosa.com

Founded:
1861

U.S. distributor:
D. Freemont Inc.
P.O. Box 417
232 Karda Drive
Hollidaysburg, PA 16648
877-236-9248
david@freemontwatches.com
www.davosawatches.com

Most important collections/price range:
Argonautic, Classic, Gentleman, Pilot, Simplex, Ternos, Titanium, Vanguard, X-Agon / $650 to $2,600

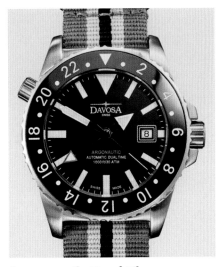

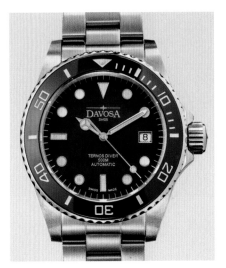

Argonautic Lumis Chronograph

Reference number: 161.508.80
Movement: automatic, ETA Caliber 7750; ø 30 mm, height 7.9 mm; 25 jewels; 28,800 vph; 42-hour power reserve
Functions: hours, minutes, subsidiary seconds; chronograph; date
Case: stainless steel with gray PVD coating; ø 42.5 mm, height 17.5 mm; unidirectional bezel with 60-minute division, sapphire crystal; screw-in crown, helium valve; water-resistant to 30 atm
Band: stainless steel, safety folding clasp
Price: $2,200
Variations: 3-hand automatic ($910)

Argonautic Dual Time Automatic

Reference number: 161.512.20
Movement: automatic, ETA Caliber 2893-2; ø 25.6 mm, height 4.3 mm; 21 jewels; 28,800 vph; 38-hour power reserve
Functions: hours, minutes, sweep seconds; additional 24-hour display (2nd time zone); date
Case: stainless steel, ø 42 mm, height 14 mm; unidirectional bezel with 24-hour divisions, sapphire crystal; helium valve; water-resistant to 30 atm
Band: textile, buckle
Price: $1,300
Variations: gray PVD coating ($1,400)

Ternos Professional Automatic

Reference number: 161.556.40
Movement: automatic, ETA Caliber 2824-2; ø 25.6 mm, height 4.6 mm; 25 jewels; 28,800 vph; 38-hour power reserve
Functions: hours, minutes, sweep seconds; date
Case: stainless steel, ø 42 mm, height 15.5 mm; unidirectional bezel with 60-minute divisions, sapphire crystal; screw-in crown
Band: stainless steel, folding clasp, with safety clasp, with extension link
Price: $900
Variations: black dial/bezel ($900)

World Traveller Chronograph

Reference number: 161.502.45
Movement: automatic, ETA Caliber 7754; ø 30 mm, height 7.9 mm; 25 jewels; 28,800 vph; finely finished with Geneva stripes, blued screws, perlage on bridges; 42-hour power reserve
Functions: hours, minutes, subsidiary seconds; additional 24-hour display; chronograph; date
Case: stainless steel, ø 44 mm, height 15.7 mm; unidirectional bezel with 24-hour time zone, sapphire crystal; transparent back; water-resistant to 5 atm
Band: calf leather, buckle
Price: $2,450
Variations: silver or black dial; 3-hand ($1,300)

Vintage Rallye Pilot Chronograph

Reference number: 161.008.46
Movement: automatic, ETA Caliber 7750; ø 30 mm, height 7.9 mm; 25 jewels; 28,800 vph; finely finished with Geneva stripes, blued screws, perlage on bridges; 42-hour power reserve
Functions: hours, minutes, subsidiary seconds; chronograph; date
Case: stainless steel, ø 42 mm, height 15.6 mm; sapphire crystal, transparent case back; water-resistant to 10 atm
Band: calf leather, buckle
Price: $2,100
Variations: black dial

Pilot Chronograph

Reference number: 161.004.56
Movement: automatic, ETA Caliber 7750; ø 30 mm, height 7.9 mm; 25 jewels; 28,800 vph; finely finished with Geneva stripes, blued screws, and perlage on bridges; 42-hour power reserve
Functions: hours, minutes, subsidiary seconds; chronograph; date and weekday
Case: stainless steel, ø 42 mm, height 15.6 mm; sapphire crystal; transparent case back
Band: calf leather, buckle
Price: $2,100
Variations: stainless steel bracelet; vintage model with tachymeter/telemeter display ($2,100)

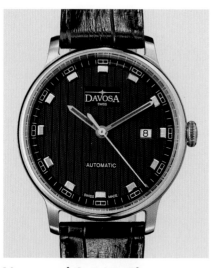

Vanguard Automatic

Reference number: 161.513.55
Movement: automatic, ETA Caliber 28 92-2; ø 26.2 mm, height 4.85 mm; 21 jewels; 28,800 vph; 38-hour power reserve
Functions: hours, minutes, sweep seconds; date
Case: stainless steel, ø 40 mm, height 9 mm; sapphire crystal; transparent case back; water-resistant to 5 atm
Band: calf leather, buckle
Remarks: comes with 2 additional leather bands
Price: $900
Variations: silver dial

Classic Skeleton Automatic

Reference number: 161.010.15
Movement: automatic, Sellita Caliber SW 200-1; ø 25.6 mm, height 4.6 mm; 26 jewels; 28,800 vph; 38-hour power reserve; fully skeletonized and engraved
Functions: hours, minutes, sweep seconds
Case: stainless steel, ø 40 mm, height 9.8 mm; sapphire crystal; transparent case back; water-resistant to 5 atm
Band: calf leather, buckle
Price: $1,950
Variations: stainless steel bracelet ($2,050)

Military Automatic

Reference number: 161.511.94
Movement: automatic, ETA Caliber 2824-2; ø 25.6 mm, height 4.6 mm; 25 jewels; 28,800 vph; 38-hour power reserve
Functions: hours, minutes, sweep seconds; date
Case: stainless steel with black PVD coating, ø 42 mm, height 12.5 mm; sapphire crystal; screw-in crown; water-resistant to 20 atm
Band: calf leather, buckle
Price: $780
Variations: without PVD coating with green dial ($830)

De Bethune

De Bethune's technical director, Denis Flageollet, has more than twenty years of experience under his belt with regard to the research, conception, and successful implementation of more than 120 different, extremely prestigious timepieces—all for other firms. He and David Zanetta, a well-known consultant for a number of high-end watch brands, founded their own company in 2002, and De Bethune was born. Together, they bought what used to be the village pub and turned it into a stunning factory. The modern CNC machinery, combined with the expertise of an experienced watchmaking team, allows Flageollet to produce prototypes in the blink of an eye and make small movement series with great dispatch. In order to become even more independent of suppliers, the little factory now also produces its own cases, dials, and hands, which guarantees a high level of excellence with regard to quality control.

Since its founding, De Bethune has developed a manually wound caliber with a power reserve of up to eight days, a self-regulating double barrel, a balance wheel in titanium and platinum that allows for an ideal inertia/mass ratio, a balance spring with a patented De Bethune end curve, a triple "parachute" shock-absorbing system, and the lightest and one of the fastest silicon/titanium tourbillons on the market. Another project was research into acoustic vibrations as a power regulator. The control of the "Resonique" escapement utilizes a flying magnet that regulates the escape wheel without touching it. The logical extension of the titanium-platinum balance wheel is the eighteen-month development of an in-house silicon hairspring.

As for the recent Dreamwatch No. 5, it is a genuine sculpture for the wrist by Zanetta and Flageollet. Some elements from its predecessors were retained to form a harmonious ensemble in the new model. The dial is nothing but a cutout revealing jumping hours and minutes and a three-dimensional moon. Keeping things simple is a design guideline.

De Bethune SA

Granges Jaccard 6
CH-1454 La Chaux L'Auberson
Switzerland

Tel.:
01141-24-454-2281

Fax:
01141-24-454-2317

E-Mail:
info@debethune.ch

Website:
www.debethune.ch

Founded:
2002

Number of employees:
60

Annual production:
400

Distribution:
For all inquiries from the U.S., contact the *manufacture* directly.

DB28 Skybridge

Reference number: DB28CE
Movement: manually wound, De Bethune Caliber DB 2105; ø 30 mm; 27 jewels; 28,800 vph; double spring barrel, silicon balance; 144-hour power reserve
Functions: hours, minutes; spherical moon phase
Case: titanium, ø 42.6 mm, height 11.4 mm; sapphire crystal; transparent case back
Band: reptile skin, buckle
Remarks: concave dial with golden spheres as heavenly bodies; completely sculptural moon
Price: $106,000

DB 28 T

Reference number: DB28TTIS8
Movement: manually wound, Caliber DB 2019; ø 30 mm, height 6.95 mm; 31 jewels; 36,000 vph; 30-second tourbillon with silicon balance and platinum frame; double spring barrel; 120-hour power reserve
Functions: hours, minutes, subsidiary seconds (on tourbillon cage); power reserve display (on case back)
Case: titanium, ø 42.60 mm, height 11.3 mm; sapphire crystal
Band: reptile skin, buckle
Price: $199,000

DB 27 Titan Hawk Silver

Reference number: DB27S1
Movement: automatic, De Bethune Caliber S233; ø 32.95 mm, height 3.55 mm; 31 jewels; 144-hour power reserve
Functions: hours, minutes; date
Case: titanium, ø 43 mm, height 11 mm; sapphire crystal; window at 6 o'clock opens on balance wheel.
Band: reptile skin, buckle
Price: $39,900

de Grisogono

de Grisogono SA
Route de St-Julien 176 bis
CH-1228 Plan-les-Ouates (Geneva)
Switzerland

Tel.:
01141-22-817-8100

Fax:
01141-22-817-8188

E-Mail:
marco@degrisogono.com

Website:
www.degrisogono.com

Founded:
1993

Number of employees:
approx. 150

U.S. distributor:
De Grisogono, Inc.
824 Madison Avenue, 3rd Floor
New York, NY 10021
866-DEGRISO

Most important collections/price range:
Instrumento N°Uno / starting at $39,900;
Tondo / starting at $36,200

Watch connoisseurs frequently look down on jewelers who suddenly develop an interest for their trade. The brand de Grisogono had to deal with this somewhat odd prejudice when it made its debut in horology, but the critics quickly fell silent once it became obvious that brand head Fawaz Gruosi was not just producing quartz watches with lots of glitz, but was intending to grow his portfolio with a line of very high-end mechanical watches.

His jewelry pieces are renowned for showcasing precious stones of the highest quality. Gruosi applied the same standard to the manufacturing of his watches. Not only are they unusually sophisticated technically, but the actual manufacturing quality has stood the test of even the toughest experts.

Right from the start, Gruosi opted for unusual case shapes and novel ways of displaying time. He took the high road, as it were, producing, for instance, the Instrumento Doppio Tre, with a single spring barrel that drives three separate sets of hands to display three time zones, or watches with dials that open and close like camera shutters or can be turned to change the display.

For the most part, de Grisogono watches have no historical models—which is quite rare nowadays. The Meccanico dG, a large rectangular watch with a hint of 1970s chic, has an imitation digital display produced mechanically with engineering that literally reaches absurd boundaries: Twenty-three tiny multi-surface tube-like segments turn on their longitudinal axis to shape squarish numbers.

All this innovation came at a cost—exacerbated by huge setbacks from the 2009 recession. In March 2012, de Grisogono announced it had brought a number of investors on board. Ever since, it has been consolidating its existing portfolio, developing the Tondos in sharp, trendy colors, and focusing on jewelry.

Instumento N° UNO

Reference number: UNO BIG DATE N01
Movement: automatic, ETA Caliber with large date module; ø 31.6 mm, height 5.6 mm; 22 jewels; 28,800 vph; 42-hour power reserve
Functions: hours, minutes; large date
Case: rose gold, 44.15 x 57.51 mm, height 18.13 mm; sapphire crystal; transparent case back; water-resistant to 5 atm
Band: reptile skin, rose gold/steel folding clasp with brown PVD coating
Price: $31,200
Variations: white gold ($31,200)

Instrumentino

Reference number: Tino S36 AT
Movement: automatic, ETA Caliber 2004 with 2nd time zone module; ø 23.9 mm; 20 jewels; 28,800 vph
Functions: hours, minutes; additional 12-hour indicator (2nd time zone)
Case: rose gold, 33.95 x 42.2 mm, height 14.8 mm; bezel set with 124 diamonds; dial set with 82 diamonds; sapphire crystal; transparent case back; black diamond cabochon on crown; water-resistant to 3 atm
Band: ray skin, folding clasp (set with 112 diamonds)
Price: $63,600

Allegra Watch

Reference number: Allegra Acier S12
Movement: quartz
Functions: hours, minutes
Case: stainless steel with black PVD coating; 35 x 35 mm; bezel set with 44 precious stones, sapphire crystal; black diamond cabochon on crown; water-resistant to 3 atm
Band: leather cords, magnetic clasp with safety clicks
Price: $13,000
Variations: various colors

DeWitt

It has become clear over the last few years just how fruitful and enriching it can be for the watchmaking industry when outsiders without any technical knowledge approach its challenges simply because they are curious and interested. A good example of this is DeWitt, a brand that has been highly successful with a strategy of blending traditional horology with truly unconventional ideas.

Jérôme de Witt comes from a long line of illustrious personalities reaching back on one side to the Dutch lawyer and politician Johan de Witt, who was murdered in 1672 by supporters of the royal house of Orange-Nassau. The other side boasts Jérôme Bonaparte and German royal lines Sachsen-Coburg, Württemberg, and Hohenzollern.

De Witt spent a significant number of years in the construction industry, building houses and bridges all over the world. A general interest in technology and a passion for restoring vintage cars were the springboard for his ideas for original mechanical solutions for these watches. "I see myself more as a sort of conductor," says De Witt.

The team at DeWitt tirelessly experiments with new materials and has now become famous for characteristic "toothed" bezels (derived from the cam shaft of a 2CV Citroën) and special in-house dials. DeWitt's demanding founder is a man of exacting standards. He believes that this is the only way to realize his visions, such as a silicon dial made of forty-seven individual parts. In the past years, however, DeWitt has tamed the brand's technophile tendencies, and some of the more recent models, notably in the Classic line, are showing signs of rococo and classicistic elegance, even delicacy.

Montres DeWitt SA
Rue du Pré-de-la-Fontaine
CH-1217 Meyrin 2
Switzerland

Tel.:
01141-22-750-9797

Fax:
01141-22-750-9799

E-Mail:
info@dewitt.ch

Website:
www.dewitt.ch

Founded:
2003

Number of employees:
70

Annual production:
over 1,500 watches (estimated)

U.S. distributor:
Montres DeWitt America
4330 NE 2nd Avenue
Miami, FL 33137
305-572-9812

Most important collections/price range:
Academia / from approx. $30,000
Furtive / from approx. $12,000
Classic / from approx. $23,000
Twenty-8-Eight / from approx. $28,000

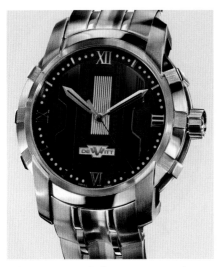

Glorious Knight Automatic

Reference number: FTV.HMS.001
Movement: automatic, DeWitt Caliber DWHMS; ø 25.60 mm; 21 jewels; 28,800 vph; DeWitt rotor with côtes de Genève; 42-hour power reserve
Functions: hours, minutes, sweep seconds
Case: steel with black PVD coating on case band; ø 42 mm, height 11.40 mm; sapphire crystal; clous de Paris on case back; water-resistant to 3 atm
Remarks: open-worked white gold hands
Band: stainless steel, folding clasp
Price: $12,300
Variations: black or white dial

Twenty-8-Eight Full Moon

Reference number: T8.FM.001
Movement: automatic, DeWitt Caliber DW.0160; ø 33 mm; 21 jewels; 28,800 vph; DeWitt rotor with côtes de Genève; 42-hour power reserve
Functions: hours, minutes; moon phase
Case: polished titanium; ø 43 mm, height 12.25 mm; sapphire crystal; clous de Paris on case back; water-resistant to 3 atm
Band: reptile skin, folding clasp
Remarks: mother-of-pearl moon passes through applique aperture
Price: $30,600

Twenty-8-Eight Tourbillon Prestige

Reference number: T8.TP.001
Movement: automatic, DeWitt Caliber 8015; ø 37 mm; 36 jewels; 18,000 vph; DeWitt Automatic Sequential Winding (A.S.W.) device; variable inertia balance; 72-hour power reserve
Functions: hours, minutes; dead beat seconds connected to tourbillon carriage; tourbillon; power reserve indicator
Case: rose gold, ø 46 mm, height 12.10 mm; sapphire crystal; clous de Paris on back; water-resistant to 3 atm
Band: reptile skin, triple folding clasp
Remarks: open-worked tourbillon cage
Price: $269,200; limited to 99 pieces

Alma

Reference number: AL.001
Movement: automatic, DeWitt Caliber 0162; ø 25.6 mm; 25 jewels; 28,800 vph; 42-hour power reserve
Functions: hours, minutes, sweep seconds; additional 24-hour display (2nd time zone) with reference cities; date
Case: rose gold oval case, 38.38 x 32.50 mm, height 11.09 mm; cambered sapphire crystal, transparent case back; water-resistant to 3 atm
Band: reptile skin, buckle
Remarks: open-worked pink gold hands; clous de Paris on dial center
Price: $31,900

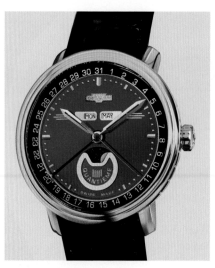

Classic Quantième

Reference number: CLA.QUA.003
Movement: automatic, DeWitt Caliber DW.9000; ø 26.20 mm; 21 jewels; 28,800 vph; 42-hour power reserve
Functions: hours, minutes, sweep seconds; annual calendar, day (sweep hand), weekday, month; moon phase
Case: rose gold, 40 mm, height 10.60 mm; sapphire crystal; transparent case back; water-resistant to 3 atm
Band: reptile skin, buckle
Remarks: blue dial with rose gold indices
Price: $36,100
Variations: white or black dial

Academia Mirabilis

Reference number: AC.MI.004
Movement: automatic, Caliber DW0090 (base Concepto C-2220); ø 30.4 mm, height 4.3 mm; 23 jewels; 28,800 vph; 48-hour power reserve
Functions: hours, minutes, sweep seconds
Case: white gold and titanium with blue PVD, ø 44 mm, height 13.25 mm; white gold and blue PVD-coated bezel; sapphire crystal; transparent case back; water-resistant to 3 atm
Band: rubber, buckle
Price: $36,000
Variations: titanium/pink gold with bronze-colored PVD coating (price on request)

Classic Jumping Hour

Reference number: CLA.HSA.002
Movement: automatic, DeWitt Caliber DWHSA; ø 26.20 mm; 21 jewels; 28,800 vph; De Witt rotor with côtes de Genève; 42-hour power reserve
Functions: hours (jumping), minutes (sweep)
Case: rose gold, 40 mm, height 10.60 mm; sapphire crystal; transparent case back; water-resistant to 3 atm
Band: reptile skin, buckle
Remarks: sunburst pattern on dial
Price: $31,900
Variations: blue or black dial

Tourbillon Imperial

Reference number: AC.TI.002
Movement: manually wound, DeWitt Caliber DW0082; ø 31.3 mm, height 9.55 mm; 29 jewels; 21,600 vph; 1-minute tourbillon; black-gold finish, pink gold wheels, balance; 84 diamonds on lower tourbillon bridge; split-second chronograph with 2 control wheels; 50-hour power reserve
Functions: hours, minutes, subsidiary seconds; split-second chronograph; date, moon phase
Case: titanium, ø 46 mm, height 15.15 mm; sapphire crystal, transparent case back; water-resistant to 3 atm
Band: reptile skin, folding clasp
Price: $361,000; limited to 10 pieces

Hora Mundi

Reference number: NAC.HMI.001
Movement: automatic, DeWitt Caliber 2021; ø 26.2 mm; 46 jewels; 28,800 vph; 42-hour power reserve
Functions: hours, minutes, sweep seconds; additional 24-hour display (2nd time zone) with reference cities; date
Case: steel, ø 43 mm, height 10.2 mm; sapphire crystal, transparent case back; water-resistant to 3 atm
Band: stainless steel, folding clasp
Remarks: 10th anniversary edition
Price: $12,200; limited to 200 pieces
Variations: rubber strap ($12,200)

Dodane 1857

For pilots of all aircraft, time is not money; it is life and death. So not surprisingly, the specifications for on-board instruments put out by the world's air forces are particularly stringent. In the 1950s, the French Air Force approached several companies to produce watches that could withstand the extreme accelerations and pressure changes imposed by the new generation of jet-propelled aircraft. Pilots also needed a flyback chronograph to measure speed and distances in case of instrument failure.

One of those companies was Dodane, a small family enterprise situated in Besançon just a few miles from the Swiss border and the horologically prolific "Jurassic Arc." The company had been founded in 1857 by Alphonse Dodane on the banks of the Doubs River and produced watch components and watches. It was Alphonse's son, Alphonse Gabriel, who set the course on aviation, though. During World War I, he developed a chronograph that allowed flyers to target their payload more accurately. From then on, inventing instruments for airplanes became the main business. Among the later Dodane developments was an altimetric chronograph used by night parachutists to tell them when to pull the cord.

The Dodane range of watches is limited to the Type 21 and the Type 23, also available in quartz with many functions for sporty types. These products are authentic military—rugged, resistant, and perhaps a touch rabble-rousing. After all, they have to appeal to pilots as well as meeting the high standards of the French defense ministry.

Dodane 1857
2, Chemin des Barbizets
F-25870 Châtillon le Duc
France

Tel.:
01133-3-81-58-88-02

Fax:
01133-3-81-58-92-27

E-Mail:
info@dodane1857.com

Website:
www.Dodane1857.com

Founded:
1857

U.S. distributor:
Totally Worth It, LLC
76 Division Avenue
Summit, NJ 07901-2309
201-894-4710
info@totallyworthit.com
www.TotallyWorthIt.com

Most important collections:
Type 21 and Type 23 chronographs used by the French military

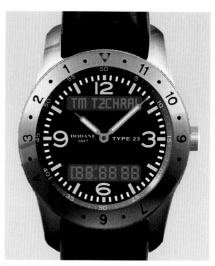

TYPE 21

Reference number: 21NLN
Movement: automatic, Caliber Dubois Dépraz 42022; ø 30 mm, height 6.8 mm; 57 jewels; 28,800 vph; 42-hour power reserve; chronometer; côtes de Genève, blued screws, cocks with perlage
Functions: hours, minutes, subsidiary seconds; date; 1/5th-second 3-hand flyback chronograph with 30-minute counter
Case: stainless steel, ø 41.5 mm, height 13.7 mm; unidirectional black anodized bezel with ratchet wheel; sapphire crystal; transparent case back; water-resistant to 10 atm
Band: reptile skin, with double folding buckle
Price: $5,750; limited to 400

TYPE 23

Reference number: 23-CF10R
Movement: automatic, Caliber Dubois Dépraz 42030; ø 30 mm, height 6.5 mm; 45 jewels; 28,800 vph
Functions: hours, minutes, sweep seconds; chronograph
Case: stainless steel, ø 42.5 mm, height 12.3 mm; sapphire crystal; transparent case back; bidirectional brushed steel bezel with ratchet wheel; sapphire crystal; transparent case back; hinged back cover for pilot ID tag; water-resistant to 10 atm
Band: reptile skin, double folding clasp
Price: $4,750
Variations: black anodized and polished steel bezel; various straps, NATO clasp

Dodane Type 23 Quartz

Reference number: 23-C7N
Movement: quartz, ETA 988.333; digital and analog display
Functions: hours, minutes, seconds; day, date, perpetual calendar; various chronograph functions (1/100th seconds); alarm; second time zone
Case: stainless steel, ø 42.5 mm, height 12.3 mm; sapphire crystal; transparent case back; bidirectional brushed steel bezel with ratchet wheel; sapphire crystal; transparent case back; water-resistant to 10 atm
Band: calf, rubber, double folding clasp
Price: $2,250

Doxa

Doxa Watches USA

5847 San Felipe, 17th Floor
Houston, TX 77057

Tel.:
877-255-5017

Fax:
866-230-2922

E-Mail:
customersupport@doxawatches.com

Website:
www.doxawatches.com

Founded:
1889

Number of employees:
48

Distribution:
direct sales only

Most important collections/price range:
Doxa SUB dive watch collection / $1,500 to
$3,500

Watch aficionados who have visited the world-famous museum in Le Locle will know that the little castle in which it is housed once belonged to Georges Ducommun, the founder of Doxa. The *manufacture* was launched as a backyard operation in 1889 and originally produced pocket watches. Quality products and good salesmanship quickly put Doxa on the map, but the company's real game-changer came in 1967 with the uncompromising SUB 300, a heavy, bold diver's watch. It featured a unidirectionally rotating bezel with the official U.S. dive table engraved on it. The bright orange dial was notable for offering the best legibility under water. It also marked the beginning of a trend for colorful dials.

Doxa continued to develop successful diver's watches in the 1970s in collaboration with U.S. Divers, Spirotechnique, and Aqualung. Their popularity increased with the commercialization of diving. Thriller writer Clive Cussler, chairman and founder of the National Underwater and Marine Agency, NUMA, even chose a Doxa as gear for his action hero Dirk Pitt.

Doxa makes watches for other occasions as well. The Ultraspeed and Régulateur are just two examples combining a classic look, fine workmanship, and an affordable price. Today, the brand has also resurrected some of the older designs from the late sixties, but with improved technology, enabling divers to go down to 1,500 meters and still read the time.

SUB 300T-Graph "Sharkhunter"

Reference number: 877.10.101.10
Movement: automatic, ETA Caliber 2894-2; ø 28.6 mm, height 6.1 mm; 37 jewels; 28,800 vph; 42-hour power reserve
Functions: hours, minutes, subsidiary seconds; chronograph; date
Case: stainless steel, ø 47 mm, height 19 mm; unidirectional bezel with 60-minute divisions, sapphire crystal; screw-in crown; water-resistant to 30 atm
Band: stainless steel, folding clasp with safety lock and extension link
Price: $2,990; limited to 250 pieces
Variations: orange dial ($2,990); rubber strap ($2,790)

SUB 1200T "Searambler"

Reference number: 872.10.021.10
Movement: automatic, Soprod Caliber A10; ø 25.6 mm, height 4.6 mm; 25 jewels; 28,800 vph; 42-hour power reserve
Functions: hours, minutes, sweep seconds; date
Case: stainless steel, ø 42 mm, height 14 mm; unidirectional bezel with engraved decompression scale, sapphire crystal; screw-in crown; helium valve; water-resistant to 120 atm
Band: stainless steel, folding clasp with extension link
Remarks: new of 1969 original; with rubber strap
Price: $1,990
Variations: Sharkhunter/black dial ($1,990); Professional/orange dial ($1,990)

SUB 4000T "Professional"

Reference number: 875.10.351.10
Movement: automatic, ETA Caliber 2897-2; ø 25.6 mm, height 4.85 mm; 21 jewels; 28,800 vph; 42-hour power reserve
Functions: hours, minutes, sweep seconds; date; power reserve indicator
Case: stainless steel, ø 47 mm, height 16 mm; unidirectional bezel with 60-minute divisions, sapphire crystal; screw-in crown; helium valve; water-resistant to 120 atm
Band: stainless steel, folding clasp with extension link
Price: $2,590
Variations: Sharkhunter/black dial ($2,590)

SUB 800Ti

Reference number: 880.10.101N-WH
Movement: automatic, ETA Caliber 2824-2;
ø 25.6 mm, height 4.6 mm; 25 jewels; 28,800 vph
Functions: hours, minutes, sweep seconds; date
Case: titanium, ø 44.7 mm, height 15 mm;
unidirectional bezel with engraved decompression
table, sapphire crystal; screw-in crown; water-
resistant to 80 atm
Band: fabric, buckle
Remarks: reissue of 1969 original; with orange
NATO fabric strap
Price: $2,790; limited to 1,000 pieces
Variations: Sharkhunter/black dial ($2,790);
Professional/orange hands ($2,790)

SUB MISSION 31

Reference number: 801.50.351-WH
Movement: automatic, ETA Caliber 2824-2;
ø 25.6 mm, height 4.6 mm; 25 jewels; 28,800 vph
Functions: hours, minutes, sweep seconds; date
Case: titanium, ø 44 mm, height 15 mm;
unidirectional bezel with engraved decompression
table, sapphire crystal; screw-in crown; water-
resistant to 100 atm
Band: BOR titanium, folding clasp with extension
link
Remarks: reissue of 1969 original; comes with
orange NATO fabric strap
Price: $2,890; limited to 331 pieces

SUB 5000T Military Sharkhunter Black Ed.

Reference number: 880.30.101N.11
Movement: automatic, ETA Caliber 2892-2;
ø 25.6 mm, height 4.85 mm; 21 jewels; 28,800 vph
Functions: hours, minutes, sweep seconds; date
Case: stainless steel, ø 45 mm; helium valve;
unidirectional bezel with engraved decompression
table, sapphire crystal; screw-in crown; water-
resistant to 150 atm
Band: stainless steel, folding clasp with extension
link
Price: $2,490
Variations: Sharkhunter/orange dial ($2,490);
Caribbean/blue dial ($2,490)

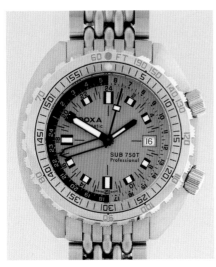

SUB 750T GMT

Reference number: 850.10.351N.10
Movement: automatic, ETA Caliber 2893-2;
ø 25.6 mm, height 4.1 mm; 21 jewels; 28,800 vph
Functions: hours, minutes, sweep seconds; 24-hour
display (3 time zones); date
Case: stainless steel, ø 45 mm, height 16 mm;
unidirectional rotating bezel with engraved
decompression table (patented), sapphire crystal;
screw-in crown; water-resistant to 750 m
Band: stainless steel, folding clasp
Price: $2,790
Variations: Professional/orange dial ($2,790);
Sharkhunter/black dial ($2,790); Divingstar/yellow
dial ($2,790); Caribbean/blue dial ($2,790)

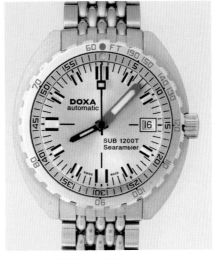

DOXA SUB 200T

Reference number: 802.10.021.10
Movement: automatic, ETA Caliber 2671;
ø 17.2 mm, height 4.8 mm; 25 jewels; 28,800 vph
Functions: hours, minutes, sweep seconds
Case: stainless steel, ø 35 mm, height 9 mm;
unidirectional rotating bezel with engraved
decompression table (patented), sapphire crystal;
screw-in crown; water-resistant to 20 atm
Band: stainless steel, folding clasp
Price: $1,649
Variations: Seamaid/black dial ($1,649)

SUB 1500T "Professional"

Reference number: 1500.10.P.03
Movement: automatic, ETA Caliber 2894-2;
ø 26.2 mm, height 3.6 mm; 21 jewels, 28,800 vph;
42-hour power reserve
Functions: hours, minutes, sweep seconds; date
Case: stainless steel, ø 45 mm, height 13 mm;
unidirectional bezel with engraved decompression
table, sapphire crystal; screw-in crown; water-
resistant to 150 atm
Band: stainless steel, folding clasp with extension
link
Remarks: new edition of the 1969 original; comes
with rubber strap
Price: $2,490

Eberhard & Co.

Eberhard & Co.
5, rue du Manège
CH-2502 Biel/Bienne
Switzerland

Tel.:
01141-32-342-5141

Fax:
01141-32-341-0294

E-Mail:
info@eberhard-co-watches.ch

Website:
www.eberhard-co-watches.ch

Founded:
1887

U.S. distributor:
ABS Distributors
22600 Savi Ranch Parkway
Suite 274
Yorba Linda, CA 92887
www.absdist.com
714-453-1622
714-998-0181 (fax)

Most important collections/price range:
Chrono 4, Champion V, Tazio Nuvolari, 8 Jours, Extra Forte, Gilda, Contograph / $3,000 to $25,000

Chronographs weren't always the main focus of the Eberhard & Co. brand. In 1887, Georges-Emile Eberhard rented a workshop in La Chaux-de-Fonds to produce a small series of pocket watches, but it was the unstoppable advancement of the automotive industry that gave the young company its inevitable direction. By the 1920s, Eberhard was producing timekeepers for the first auto races. In Italy, Eberhard & Co. functioned well into the 1930s as the official timekeeper for all important events relating to motor sports. And the Italian air force later commissioned some split-second chronographs from the company, one of which went for 56,000 euros at auction.

Eberhard & Co. is still doing well, thanks to the late Massimo Monti. In the 1990s, he associated the brand with legendary racer Tazio Nuvolari. The company dedicated a chronograph collection to Nuvolari and sponsored the annual Gran Premio Nuvolari oldtimer rally in his hometown of Mantua.

With the launch of its four-counter chronograph, this most Italian of Swiss watchmakers underscored its expertise and ambitions where short time/sports time measurement is concerned. Indeed, Eberhard & Co.'s Chrono 4 chronograph, featuring four little counters all in a row, has brought new life to the chronograph in general. CEO Mario Peserico has continued to develop it, putting out versions with new colors and slightly altered looks.

The brand is pure vintage, so it was no surprise when, in 2014, it reissued the two-totalizer Contograph chrono from the 1960s, which originally allowed the user to calculate phone units exactly (*conto* = bill).

Chrono 4 Géant Full Injection

Reference number: 31062 CU
Movement: automatic, Eberhard Caliber EB 251-12 1/2 (base ETA 2894-2); ø 33 mm, height 7.5 mm; 53 jewels; 28,800 vph; 4 totalizers in a row
Functions: hours, minutes, subsidiary seconds; additional 24-hour display; chronograph; date
Case: stainless steel with carbon diffusion and DLC coating; ø 46 mm, height 14.1 mm; unidirectional bezel with 60-minute divisions, sapphire crystal; screw-in crown/pushers; water-resistant to 200 m
Band: rubber, buckle
Price: $10,200; limited to 500 pieces

Chrono 4 Grande Taille Colors

Reference number: 31067 CU
Movement: automatic, Eberhard Caliber EB 251-12 1/2 (base ETA 2894-2); ø 33 mm, height 7.5 mm; 53 jewels; 28,800 vph; 4 totalizers in a row
Functions: hours, minutes, subsidiary seconds; additional 24-hour display; chronograph; date
Case: stainless steel, ø 43 mm, height 13.32 mm; sapphire crystal; screw-in crown; water-resistant to 50 m
Band: rubber, buckle
Price: $7,600; limited to 600 pieces
Variations: various dial designs

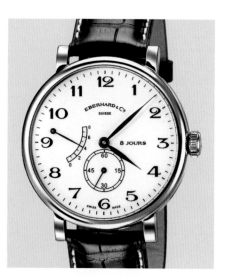

8 Jours Grande Taille

Reference number: 21027 CP
Movement: manually wound, Eberhard Caliber EB 896 10½ (base ETA 7001); ø 34 mm, height 5 mm; 25 jewels; 21,600 vph; 2 winding springs; 8 days power reserve
Functions: hours, minutes, subsidiary seconds; power reserve indicator
Case: stainless steel, ø 41 mm, height 10.85 mm; sapphire crystal, transparent case back; water-resistant to 3 atm
Band: reptile skin, buckle
Price: $4,950

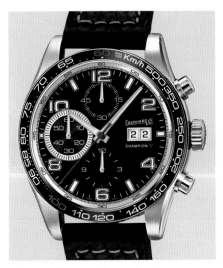

Champion V Grande Date

Reference number: 31064 CP
Movement: automatic, LJP Caliber 8210; ø 30 mm, height 8 mm; 25 jewels; 28,800 vph
Functions: hours, minutes, subsidiary seconds; chronograph; large date
Case: stainless steel, ø 42.8 mm, height 14.45 mm; sapphire crystal; screw-in crown; water-resistant to 50 m
Band: calf leather, buckle
Price: $4,300

Contograf

Reference number: 31069 CP
Movement: automatic, LJP Caliber 8147 (base ETA 7750 13 1/4); ø 30 mm, height 8.40 mm; 25 jewels; 28,800 vph; 42-hour power reserve
Functions: hours, minutes, subsidiary seconds; chronograph; date
Case: stainless steel, ø 42 mm, height 14.7 mm; unidirectional bezel with 60-minute divisions, sapphire crystal; screw-in crown; water-resistant to 50 m
Band: calf leather, buckle
Price: $5,750
Variations: stainless steel bracelet ($6,350); black dial

Extra-fort RAC 125ème Anniversaire

Reference number: 31125 CPD
Movement: automatic, LJP Caliber 8150 (base ETA Caliber 7750); ø 30 mm, height 8.85 mm; 28 jewels; 28,800 vph; column wheel control of chronograph functions
Functions: hours, minutes, subsidiary seconds; chronograph; large date
Case: stainless steel, ø 41 mm, height 15 mm; sapphire crystal; transparent case back; water-resistant to 50 m
Band: reptile skin, folding clasp
Price: $8,300; limited to 500 pieces

Tazio Nuvolari Vanderbilt Cup "Naked"

Reference number: 31068 CP
Movement: automatic, LJP Caliber (base ETA 7750); ø 30 mm, height 8.4 mm; 30 jewels; 28,800 vph; crown pusher for zero reset; bridges with perlage, rotor with côtes de Genève; 42-hour power reserve
Functions: hours, minutes, subsidiary seconds; chronograph
Case: stainless steel, ø 42 mm, height 13.45 mm; sapphire crystal; water-resistant to 3 atm
Band: calf leather, buckle
Price: $7,900

Tazio Nuvolari Data

Reference number: 31066 CP
Movement: automatic, ETA Caliber 7750; ø 30 mm, height 7.9 mm; 25 jewels; 28,800 vph; 42-hour power reserve
Functions: hours, minutes, chronograph; date
Case: stainless steel, ø 43 mm, height 13 mm; sapphire crystal; screw-in crown; water-resistant to 3 atm
Band: reptile skin, buckle
Price: $5,500

Tazio Nuvolari Gold Car

Reference number: 31038 CP
Movement: automatic, ETA Caliber 7750; ø 30 mm, height 7.9 mm; 25 jewels; 28,800 vph; 42-hour power reserve
Functions: hours, minutes; chronograph; date
Case: stainless steel, ø 43 mm, height 13 mm; sapphire crystal; transparent case back; screw-in crown; water-resistant to 3 atm
Band: reptile skin, buckle
Remarks: gold, stylized Alfa Romeo on rotor
Price: $5,800

Edox & Vista SA
CH-2714 Les Genevez
Switzerland

Tel.:
01141-32-484-7010

Fax:
01141-32-484-7019

E-Mail:
info@edox.ch

Website:
www.edox.ch

Founded:
1884

Number of employees:
100

Annual production:
approx. 50,000 watches

U.S. distributor:
Edox
Gevril Group
9 Pinecrest Road
Valley Cottage, NY 10989
845-425-9882; lea@gevril.net
www.edox.ch

Most important collections/price range:
Classe Royale, Royal Lady, Les Bémonts,
Les Vauberts, Grand Ocean, Class-1, WRC /
approx. $750 to $4,700

Edox

Edox is interested in motion and extreme feats, and that has given its timepieces a consistently sporty look. Since the company took its place as official timekeeper of the FIA World Rally Championship, it has come out with a striking collection of timer watches with "race car" character, most recently the X-treme Pilot III. And already in the sixties, Edox had gotten more than just its feet wet in the special domain of water-resistant watches, producing the legendary Delfin and Hydrosub, which could submerge up to 500 meters. This was long before the brand became the official timekeeper of offshore yacht racing several years ago. That, too, inspired a stunning sports line. And so have car racing, bicycle racing, flying . . . and climbing up walls, since the company has associated itself with the Spider-Man film franchise.

Edox is more than 125 years old: The company started out in a tiny atelier in Biel in 1884 where owner Christian Rüefli-Flury refined *ébauches*. Edox was one of the first watchmakers to concentrate solely on wristwatches, a move it made in the 1920s. In 1973, Edox shares were sold to the ASUAG, a predecessor of today's Swatch Group. However, the success this partnership hoped to achieve never panned out, and in 1983, Victor Strambini, still president of the company today, bought back the shares and with them Edox's independence. Strambini subsequently relocated Edox to Les Genevez, a village in the heart of the Swiss Jura and one of the cradles of the country's watch industry. Today, the state-of-the-art factory houses 100 employees.

Grand Ocean Day Date Automatic

Reference number: 83006 357 B BUIN
Movement: automatic, Edox Caliber 83 (base ETA 2834-2); ø 29 mm, height 5.05 mm; 25 jewels; 28,800 vph; 42-hour power reserve
Functions: hours, minutes, sweep seconds; date and weekday
Case: stainless steel, ø 45 mm, height 12.7 mm; sapphire crystal; transparent case back; screwed-down crown; water-resistant to 10 atm
Band: reptile skin, folding clasp
Price: $3,950
Variations: with brown dial ($3,300), black dial ($3,650), or silver dial ($3,025)

Class-1 Chronoffshore Automatic

Reference number: 01115 3 NIN
Movement: automatic, Edox Caliber 011 (base ETA Valjoux 7750); ø 30 mm, height 7.9 mm; 25 jewels; 28,800 vph; 46-hour power reserve
Functions: hours, minutes, subsidiary seconds; chronograph; date and weekday
Case: stainless steel, ø 45 mm, height 17 mm; unidirectional ceramic bezel, 60-minute division, sapphire crystal; screwed-down crown; water-resistant to 50 atm
Band: rubber, folding clasp
Price: $5,300
Variations: blue dial ($5,300); black PVD ($5,775); PVD stainless steel case/bracelet ($5,775)

Chronorally Automatic

Reference number: 01110 37N PN GIN
Movement: automatic, Edox Caliber 011 (base ETA Valjoux 7750); ø 30 mm, height 7.9 mm; 25 jewels; 28,800 vph; 46-hour power reserve
Functions: hours, minutes, subsidiary seconds; chronograph; date and weekday
Case: stainless steel, ø 45 mm, height 17.5 mm; sapphire crystal; case back with rubber inlay; screwed-down crown; color anodized start-stop pusher; water-resistant to 10 atm
Band: rubber, buckle
Price: $4,225
Variations: black dial ($4,225)

Epos

This brand's roots trace back to 1925, the Vallée de Joux, and founder James Aubert. Today, its fate is in the hands of Ursula Forster, who comes from a family of watchmakers,

and her husband, Tamdi Chonge, who hails from Tibet and spent many years working in the industry in Switzerland. Together with movement designer Jean Fillon—the son-in-law of the founder's nephew, Jean Aubert—they make sure that the calibers are given an exclusive touch by adding in-house complications as well as skillful decoration. And the Epos collection is impressive in its breadth, covering practically the whole spectrum of complications from simple three-hand watches, chronographs with and without flyback function, and horizontal and vertical large date displays to regulators, moon phase indicators, jumping hours, repeaters, and even tourbillons. Regardless of the complication, the look is always serene; there always seems to be space on the dial. Epos has even ventured into complicated mechanical women's watches, and its portfolio includes a number of very exciting pocket watches.

According to *Merriam-Webster's Collegiate Dictionary*, an epos is an "epic poem or a number of poems that treat an epic theme but are not formally united." That seems to describe rather well the strategy of this Swiss specialist in mechanical watches—if you add the word "successful." Its chances are quite good: Epos has an epic portfolio of top-notch, affordable timepieces for every taste. The brand has earned a good reputation abroad; now all it needs to do is convince the home market.

Montres EPOS SA
Solothurnstrasse 44
CH-2543 Lengnau
Switzerland

Tel.:
01141-32-323-8182

Fax:
01141-32-323-6494

E-Mail:
info@epos.ch

Website:
www.epos.ch

Founded:
1925

U.S. distributor:
Please consult Epos directly.

Price range:
$700 to $4,000 (higher prices for special timepieces)

Collection Originale

Reference number: 3420
Movement: automatic, ETA Caliber 2892-A2; ø 25.6 mm, height 3.6 mm; 21 jewels; 28,800 vph; finely decorated; 42-hour power reserve
Functions: hours, minutes, sweep seconds; date
Case: stainless steel with rose gold-colored PVD coating, ø 40 mm, height 7.7 mm; sapphire crystal; transparent case back; water-resistant to 3 atm
Band: calf leather, buckle
Price: $1,300
Variations: with stainless steel bracelet ($1,450); without PVD coating ($1,200)

Collection Emotion

Reference number: 3390SK
Movement: automatic, ETA Caliber 2824-A2; ø 25.6 mm, height 4.6 mm; 25 jewels; 28,800 vph; skeletonized and hand-decorated; 38-hour power reserve
Functions: hours, minutes, sweep seconds
Case: stainless steel, ø 41 mm, height 8 mm; sapphire crystal; transparent case back; water-resistant to 5 atm
Band: stainless steel, buckle
Price: $1,990

Collection Sophistiquée

Reference number: 3424SK
Movement: manually wound, ETA Caliber 6497-1; ø 36.6 mm, height 4.5 mm; 17 jewels; 21,600 vph; skeletonized, finely decorated, and black-coated; 38-hour power reserve
Functions: hours, minutes, subsidiary seconds
Case: stainless steel, ø 42 mm, height 10.4 mm; sapphire crystal; transparent case back; water-resistant to 5 atm
Band: calf leather, buckle
Remarks: skeletonized dial
Price: $2,025
Variations: case with black or rose gold-colored PVD coating ($2,085); stainless steel with uncoated movement ($1,735)

Ernst Benz

Ernst Benz
7 Route de Crassier
CH-1262 Eysins
Switzerland

E-Mail:
info@ernstbenz.com

Website:
www.ernstbenz.com

Founded:
early 1960s

U.S. distributor:
Ernst Benz North America
177 S. Old Woodward
Birmingham, MI 48009
248-203-2323; 248-203-6633 (fax)

Most important collections:
Great Circle, ChronoScope, ChronoLunar,
ChronoRacer

Necessity is really the mother of creativity and then invention. Ernst Benz was an engineer by trade, an inventor by design, and a multitalented person who dabbled in many technologies including record player styluses. And as a passionate flier, he needed solid, reliable, and readable watches that could be used in the cockpits of small aircraft and gliders, so he gradually slipped into making timepieces. Size and clarity were determining factors, hence his clean dials and 47 mm diameters. Reliability is guaranteed by a no-nonsense Valjoux 7750. These elements save pilots' lives. At first, Benz made what he called the Great Circle Chronograph and later the ChronoScope just for fellow aviators. He also engineered other aviation instruments now standard in many small aircraft.

In 2005, the brand was bought by the Khankins, a watchmaking family with generations of experience in complicated horology. Leonid Khankin, who has spent a lifetime in the hands-on side of the business, expanded the brand both geographically and by creating exciting new models. The ChronoScope received black PVC coating and was retooled as the ChronoDiver for those attracted to water rather than air. He was also quick to adopt ultra-hard DLC coating.

Khankin, who knows every nook and cranny of the horological world, is taking the brand places. He uses the broad dial of these distinct timepieces as a platform for adding thrilling design elements. On the style side, Ernst Benz has collaborated with fashion designer John Varvatos and Food Network chef Mario Batali on a series with distinct hands and color schemes. As for Ernst Benz, he has retired, but passion is a flame that always burns bright.

ChronoScope ChronoRacer CR1

Reference number: GC10100/CR1-DLC
Movement: automatic, Valjoux Caliber 7750; ø 30 mm, height 7.9 mm; 25 jewels; 28,800 vph
Functions: hours, minutes, subsidiary seconds; day, date; chronograph with hours, minutes, sweep seconds
Case: black DLC brushed stainless steel, ø 47 mm, height 16 mm; sapphire crystal; screwed-down transparent case back; double O-ring sealed crown; water-resistant to 5 atm
Band: double-stitch handmade alligator strap
Price: $6,500; limited edition of 50 pieces, individually numbered dials

ChronoScope ChronoRacer CR2

Reference number: GC10100/CR2
Movement: automatic, Valjoux Caliber 7750; ø 30 mm, height 7.9 mm; 25 jewels; 28,800 vph
Functions: hours, minutes, subsidiary seconds; date, day; chronograph with hours, minutes, sweep seconds
Case: brushed stainless steel, ø 47 mm, height 16 mm; sapphire crystal; screwed-down transparent case back; double O-ring sealed crown; water-resistant to 5 atm
Band: reptile skin, buckle
Price: $5,700; limited edition of 50 pieces, individually numbered dials

ChronoScope ChronoCombat CC2

Reference number: GC10100/CC2 DLC
Movement: automatic, Valjoux Caliber 7750; ø 30 mm, height 7.9 mm; 25 jewels; 28,800 vph
Functions: hours, minutes, subsidiary seconds; date, day; chronograph with hours, minutes, sweep seconds
Case: black DLC brushed stainless steel, ø 47 mm, height 16 mm; sapphire crystal; screwed-down transparent case back; double O-ring sealed crown; water-resistant to 5 atm
Band: reptile skin, buckle
Price: $6,500; limited edition of 50 pieces, individually numbered dials

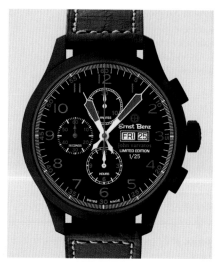

ChronoLunar Officer

Reference number: GC10381
Movement: automatic, Valjoux 7751; ø 30 mm, height 7.9 mm; 25 jewels; 28,800 vph
Functions: hours, minutes, subsidiary seconds; day, date, month, moon phase; 24-hour display; chronograph with hours, minutes, sweep seconds
Case: polished stainless steel, ø 47 mm, height 16 mm; sapphire crystal; screwed-down transparent case back; double O-ring sealed crown; water-resistant to 5 atm
Band: reptile skin, buckle
Price: $7,625

ChronoLunar Traditional DLC

Reference number: GC10311-DLC
Movement: automatic, Valjoux 7751; ø 30 mm, height 7.9 mm; 25 jewels; 28,800 vph
Functions: hours, minutes, subsidiary seconds; day, date, month, moon phase; 24-hour display; chronograph with hours, minutes, sweep seconds
Case: black DLC polished stainless steel; ø 47 mm, height 16 mm; water-resistant to 5 atm
Band: reptile skin, buckle
Price: $8,175
Variations: 44 mm case ($7,575)

Ernst Benz by John Varvatos ChronoScope DLC

Reference number: GC10410/JV6-DLC
Movement: automatic, Valjoux Caliber 7750; ø 30 mm, height 7.9 mm; 25 jewels; 28,800 vph
Functions: hours, minutes, subsidiary seconds; day, date; chronograph with hours, minutes, sweep seconds
Case: black DLC-coated brushed stainless steel, ø 47 mm, height 16 mm; angled and polished bezel, sapphire crystal; screwed-down transparent case back; double O-ring sealed crown; water-resistant to 5 atm
Band: reptile skin, buckle
Price: $7,800; limited edition of 25 pieces, individually numbered dials

ChronoSport ChronoCombat

Reference number: GC10200/CC1-DLC
Movement: automatic, ETA Caliber 2836-2; ø 30 mm, height 5.05 mm; 25 jewels; 28,800 vph; 38-hour power reserve
Functions: hours, minutes, sweep seconds; weekday, date
Case: black DLC brushed stainless steel, ø 47 mm, height 16 mm; sapphire crystal; screwed-down transparent case back; double O-ring sealed crown; water-resistant to 5 atm
Band: reptile skin, buckle
Price: $4,525; limited numbered edition of 50 pieces
Variation: 44 mm black brushed DLC case ($3,925)

ChronoSport Nautical Star

Reference number: GC10200/NS2
Movement: automatic, ETA Caliber 2836-2; ø 30 mm, height 5.05 mm; 25 jewels; 28,800 vph; 38-hour power reserve
Functions: hours, minutes, sweep seconds; weekday, date
Case: brushed stainless steel, ø 47 mm, height 16 mm; sapphire crystal; screwed-down transparent case back; double O-ring sealed crown; water-resistant to 5 atm
Band: reptile skin, buckle
Price: $3,925; limited edition of 25 pieces, individually numbered dials
Variations: black DLC brushed stainless steel case ($4,725)

ChronoScope Traditional DLC

Reference number: GC10118-DLC
Movement: automatic, Valjoux Caliber 7750; ø 30 mm, height 7.9 mm; 25 jewels; 28,800 vph
Functions: hours, minutes, subsidiary seconds; day, date; chronograph with hours, minutes, sweep seconds
Case: black DLC-coated brushed stainless steel, ø 47 mm, height 16 mm; sapphire crystal; screwed-down transparent case back; double O-ring sealed crown; water-resistant to 5 atm
Band: reptile skin, buckle
Price: $6,225

Erwin Sattler OHG

Grossuhrenmanufaktur
Lohenstr. 6
D-82166 Gräfelfing
Germany

Tel.:
01149-89-895-5806-0

Fax:
01149-89-895-5806-28

E-Mail:
info@erwinsattler.de

Website:
www.erwinsattler.de

Founded:
1958

Number of employees:
31

Annual production:
approx. 1,200 clocks and watches

Distribution:
direct through company in Germany

Most important collections/price range:
wristwatches, precision clocks, winders,
table clocks, marine chronometers / approx.
$1,000 to $200,000

Erwin Sattler

In 2008, for the fiftieth anniversary of their clock *manufacture*, managing directors Stephanie Sattler-Rick and Richard Müller presented something unexpected: In addition to a large pendulum clock outfitted with a perpetual calendar and an elegant table clock, the company released an impressive, limited edition of fifty of the "Trilogy" set, comprising a table clock, watch winder, and wristwatch. The wristwatch, offered only in precious metal as part of the Trilogy, was in high demand—leading Sattler to add an unlimited stainless steel version of the wristwatch regulator to its line in 2009.

The Sattler wristwatches are actually the result of a collaboration with the Austrian watchmaking couple Maria and Richard Habring. They turned to the tried-and-true ETA Valjoux Caliber 7750—a chronograph movement, actually—as their base, modifying it to accommodate the regulator display and adding a special technical detail: The second hand jumps in one-second increments just like its role model, one of Sattler's full-size pendulum clocks.

The dial, a miniature version of the popular Sattler wall clock regulator, features four screws and is made of solid sterling silver. The clock specialist paid a great deal of attention to the steel hands of the wristwatches. They are vaulted, hardened, and polished. Like those of their large clock cousins, the watches' hour and minute hands have steel sockets with polished grooves.

This small collection was extended in 2013 by a very interesting automatic chronograph featuring a regulator dial and a classic crown control system between the two lower lugs.

Régulateur "Classica Secunda"

Movement: automatic, Sattler Caliber ES 01 (base ETA 7750); ø 30 mm, height 7.9 mm; 28 jewels; 28,800 vph; modified to include regulator display with jumping seconds; rotor skeletonized, engraved, and guillochéed by hand; 42-hour power reserve
Functions: hours (off-center), minutes, subsidiary seconds (retrograde)
Case: stainless steel, ø 44 mm, height 15 mm; sapphire crystal; water-resistant to 5 atm
Band: reptile skin, double folding clasp
Price: $12,100

Régulateur "Classica Secunda" Medium

Movement: manually wound, Sattler Caliber ES 02 (base Habring A09MS); ø 30 mm, height 6.25 mm; 28 jewels; 28,800 vph; modified for regulator display with jumping seconds; rotor skeletonized, engraved, and guillochéed by hand
Functions: hours (off-center), minutes, subsidiary seconds (retrograde)
Case: stainless steel, ø 38 mm, height 12 mm; sapphire crystal; water-resistant to 5 atm
Band: reptile skin, double folding clasp
Price: $11,200

Chronograph Classica Secunda

Movement: automatic, Sattler Caliber ES 03 (base ETA 7750); ø 30 mm, height 7.9 mm; 25 jewels; 28,800 vph; modified for central time display and crown-activated chronograph control; hand-engraved and guillochéed rotor; 42-hour power reserve
Functions: hours, minutes (off-center), subsidiary seconds; chronograph
Case: stainless steel, ø 44 mm, height 15.5 mm; rose gold bezel; sapphire crystal; transparent back
Band: reptile skin, folding clasp
Price: $26,000; limited to 28 pieces
Variations: stainless steel ($16,200)

Eterna

The brand Eterna has truly left its mark on the watchmaking industry. Founded in 1856 as Dr. Girard & Schild, the company became a *manufacture,* producing pocket watches under Urs Schild in 1870. Among its earliest claims to fame was the first wristwatch with an alarm, released in 1908, by which time the company had taken on the name Eterna. Forty years later, came the legendary Eterna-matic, featuring micro ball bearings for an automatic winding rotor. At the slightest movement of the watch, the rotor began to turn and set in motion what was another newly developed system of two ratchet wheels, which, independent of the rotational direction, lifted the mainspring over the automatic gears. Today, the five micro ball bearings used to cushion that rotor are the inspiration for Eterna's stylized pentagon-shaped logo. The invention itself is now standard in millions of watch movements.

In 2007, the company launched its Caliber 39 project with two distinct goals: the first, to develop an automatic chronograph with three totalizers, and the second, to optimize manufacturing costs. Gradually, this led to the establishment of an entire family of movements whose particular design allowed them to be flexibly built up on a single base movement, the 88. Modules for additional indicators or functions could be affixed with just a few screws or connected by way of a bridge. The Royal KonTiki Two Time Zones is the first model making use of this base caliber. Thanks to the famous ball bearing-mounted Spherodrive winding mechanism, the movement has a power reserve of sixty-eight hours.

So ironically perhaps, Eterna, whose original movement division became a separate company called ETA (now with the Swatch Group), has returned to building its own movements. In 1995, Eterna was acquired by F.A. Porsche Beteiligungen GmbH and started manufacturing for Porsche Design. But in 2011, International Volant Ltd., a wholly owned subsidiary of China Haidian, bought up the Porsche-owned shares in Eterna, opening many opportunities in Asia through Haidian's chain of retailers. In March 2014, Eterna and Porsche finally separated, freeing up Eterna's technical and financial resources to focus on its own growth.

Eterna SA
Schützenstrasse 40
CH-2540 Grenchen
Switzerland

Tel.:
01141-32-654-7211

Website:
www.eterna.com

Founded:
1856

Number of employees:
approx. 50

Distribution:
Contact headquarters for all enquiries.

Most important collections:
1948, Vaughan; Madison; KonTiki; Contessa

1948 Legacy Small Second

Reference number: 7682.47.11.1320
Movement: automatic, Eterna Caliber 3903A;
ø 30 mm, height 5.6 mm; 27 jewels; 28,800 vph;
ball-bearing mounted spring barrel (Spherodrive);
68-hour power reserve
Functions: hours, minutes, subsidiary seconds;
date
Case: stainless steel, ø 41.5 mm, height 11.45
mm; rose gold bezel and crown; sapphire crystal;
transparent case back; water-resistant to 5 atm
Band: reptile skin, folding clasp
Price: $6,900
Variations: stainless steel bezel; black or silver-
plated dial

Royal KonTiki Two TimeZones

Reference number: 7740.40.41.1289
Movement: automatic, Eterna Caliber 3945A;
ø 30 mm, height 5.9 mm; 28 jewels; 28,800 vph; 2
ball-bearing mounted spring barrels (Spherodrive);
68-hour power reserve
Functions: hours, minutes, sweep seconds;
additional 24-hour display (2nd time zone); date
Case: stainless steel, ø 42 mm, height 12.3 mm;
sapphire crystal, transparent case back; water-
resistant to 10 atm
Band: rubber, buckle
Price: $5,600

Heritage Military

Reference number: 1939.43.46.1299
Movement: automatic, ETA Caliber 2824-2;
ø 25.6 mm, height 4.6 mm; 25 jewels; 28,800 vph;
38-hour power reserve
Functions: hours, minutes, sweep seconds; date
Case: stainless steel with black PVD coating, ø
40 mm, height 11.7 mm; sapphire crystal; water-
resistant to 5 atm
Band: calf leather, buckle
Price: $2,390
Variations: stainless steel without PVD coating

Adventic GMT

Reference number: 7661.41.46.1702
Movement: automatic, Eterna Caliber 3914A;
ø 30 mm, height 5.9 mm; 27 jewels; 28,800 vph;
ball-bearing mounted spring barrel (Spherodrive);
68-hour power reserve
Functions: hours, minutes, subsidiary seconds;
additional 24-hour display (2nd time zone); date
Case: stainless steel, ø 42 mm, height 12.6 mm;
sapphire crystal; transparent case back; water-
resistant to 5 atm
Band: stainless steel, folding clasp
Price: $4,790
Variations: white dial

Madison Eight-Days Spherodrive

Reference number: 7720.41.53.1231
Movement: manually wound, Eterna Caliber
3510; 27.2 x 33.2 mm, height 6.6 mm; 22 jewels;
28,800 vph; 2 ball-bearing mounted spring barrels
(Spherodrive); 192-hour power reserve
Functions: hours, minutes, sweep seconds; power
reserve indicator; large date
Case: stainless steel, 38.5 x 53.3 mm, height
13.25 mm; sapphire crystal; transparent case back;
water-resistant to 3 atm
Band: reptile skin, folding clasp
Price: $9,500
Variations: black or white dial and leather band

Grace Three-Hands

Reference number: 2944.54.76.1334
Movement: manual winding, Sellita SW 300-1;
28,800 vph; 42-hour power reserve
Functions: hours, minutes, seconds; date
Case: stainless steel, 34 mm, height 8.85 mm;
case band with 6 diamonds; sapphire crystal; water-
resistant to 5 atm
Remarks: 3 diamond indices
Band: satin, pin buckle
Price: $2,450
Variations: rose gold plated case set with 60
diamonds, white dial, steel/PVD bracelet (price on
request)

KonTiki Chronograph

Reference number: 1241.43.41.1306
Movement: automatic, ETA Caliber 7750; ø 30 mm,
height 7.9 mm; 25 jewels; 28,800 vph; 48-hour
power reserve
Functions: hours, minutes, subsidiary seconds;
chronograph; date
Case: stainless steel with black PVD coating; ø
42 mm, height 16 mm; sapphire crystal, water-
resistant to 20 atm
Band: calf leather, buckle
Price: $4,150
Variations: various dials; rubber band

Super KonTiki Limited Edition 1973

Reference number: 1973.41.41.1230
Movement: automatic, ETA Caliber 2824-2;
ø 25.6 mm, height 4.6 mm; 25 jewels; 28,800 vph;
38-hour power reserve
Functions: hours, minutes, sweep seconds; date
Case: stainless steel, ø 44 mm, height 13.7 mm;
unidirectional bezel with 60-minute divisions,
sapphire crystal; screw-in crown; water-resistant to
20 atm
Band: stainless steel Milanese bracelet, folding
clasp with extension link
Price: $2,460

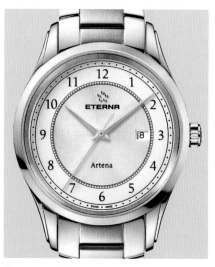

Artena Gent

Reference number: 2520.41.64.0274
Movement: quartz, ETA Caliber 955.412
Functions: hours, minutes, sweep seconds; date
Case: stainless steel, ø 40 mm, height 8.37 mm;
sapphire crystal
Band: stainless steel, folding clasp
Price: $1,120
Variations: various bands and dials

Tangaroa Three-Hands

Reference number: 2948.41.51.1261
Movement: automatic, Sellita Caliber SW200-1;
ø 25.6 mm, height 4.6 mm; 26 jewels; 28,800 vph;
38-hour power reserve
Functions: hours, minutes, sweep seconds; date
Case: stainless steel, ø 42 mm, height 10.8 mm;
sapphire crystal; transparent case back; water-
resistant to 5 atm
Band: calf leather, buckle
Price: $1,640
Variations: various bands and dials

Vaughan Big Date

Reference number: 7630.41.61.1185
Movement: automatic, Eterna Caliber 3030; ø
30 mm, height 4.6 mm; 27 jewels; 28,800 vph
Functions: hours, minutes, sweep seconds; large
date
Case: stainless steel, ø 42 mm, height 9.8 mm;
sapphire crystal; transparent case back; water-
resistant to 5 atm
Band: reptile skin, folding clasp
Price: $6,180
Variations: various bands and dials

Contessa Two-Hands

Reference number: 2410.48.67.1247
Movement: quartz, ETA Caliber 901.001
Functions: hours, minutes
Case: stainless steel, 25.75 x 40 mm, height
6.5 mm; bezel set with 46 diamonds; sapphire
crystal; water-resistant to 5 atm
Band: reptile skin, folding clasp
Remarks: dial set with 12 diamonds
Price: $5,550
Variations: various bands and dials

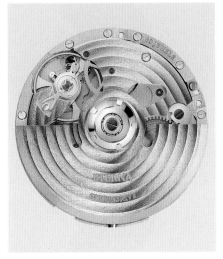

Caliber 3945A

Automatic, ball bearing-mounted spring barrel and
rotor; single spring barrel, 68-hour power reserve
Functions: hours, minutes, sweep seconds;
additional 24-hour indicator (2nd time zone); date
Diameter: 30 mm
Height: 5.9 mm
Jewels: 28
Balance: glucydur
Frequency: 28,800 vph
Balance spring: flat hairspring
Shock protection: Incabloc

Caliber 3843

Automatic; ball bearing-mounted spring barrel and
rotor; single spring barrel; 72-hour power reserve
Functions: hours, minutes, subsidiary seconds; 2nd
time zone (additional 24-hour display); date
Diameter: 30.4 mm
Height: 6.1 mm
Jewels: 26
Balance: glucydur
Frequency: 28,800 vph

Caliber 3510

Mechanical with manual winding; 2 ball bearing-
mounted spring barrels; 192-hour power reserve
Functions: hours, minutes, sweep seconds; power
reserve display
Dimensions: 27.2 x 33.2 mm
Height: 6.6 mm
Jewels: 22
Balance: glucydur
Frequency: 28,800 vph
Shock protection: Incabloc

Fortis Uhren AG

Lindenstrasse 45
CH-2540 Grenchen
Switzerland

Tel.:
01141-32-653-3361

Fax:
01141-32-652-5942

E-Mail:
info@fortis-watches.com

Website:
www.fortis-watches.com

Founded:
1912

U.S. distributor:
Gevril Group
9 Pinecrest Road
Valley Cottage, NY 10989
845-425-9882; 845-425-9897 (fax)
www.gevrilgroup.com

Most important collections/price range:
Flieger, Official Cosmonauts, Marinemaster,
Stratoliner, Art Edition / $1,400 to $9,500

Fortis

From March to September 2012, anyone visiting the Museum of Cultural History in Grenchen, Switzerland, could have enjoyed an in-depth look at one century's worth of Fortis. The exhibition was appropriately called "From Grenchen into Space." And knowing Grenchen, that is quite a step.

The 102-year history of the Fortis brand has been marked by many memorable events. The biggest milestone dates to the 1920s, when the company began the first serial production of wristwatches with automatic winding.

The word *Fortis* comes from the Latin term for "strong." With its striking and sturdy watches, the brand itself has always enjoyed a reputation for reliability and consistency. But perhaps its greatest claim to fame comes from the clients it serves: These days, if you say "Fortis," the first thing that springs to mind is aeronautics and space travel. For the past seventeen years, Fortis has been collaborating with specialists from the European space agency to test how the company's first generation of space chronographs would hold up in truly extreme conditions. This resulted in approval for use aboard the Russian space station *Mir*. Since then, Fortis chronographs have become part of the official equipment of the Russian space program and, from there, on the *International Space Station*.

The competencies acquired from work in space continue to flow back into the company's traditional pilot's watches, which have long served as the role models for modern cockpit wristwatches. It's hardly astonishing that many international squadrons wear Fortis watches. Aside from such high-performance, space-traveling timepieces, Fortis also regularly enjoys creating limited edition art and design timepieces in collaboration with artists.

B-42 Black Mars 500 Day/Date

Reference number: 647.28.13.L13
Movement: automatic, ETA Caliber 2836-2; ø 30 mm, height 5.05 mm; 25 jewels; 28,800 vph; 38-hour power reserve
Functions: hours, minutes, sweep seconds; weekday, date
Case: titanium with black PVD coating, ø 42 mm, height 13 mm; unidirectional bezel with 60-minute divisions, sapphire crystal; water-resistant to 20 atm
Band: calf leather, buckle
Price: $3,025; limited to 2,012 pieces
Variations: silicon band ($3,325)

B-47 Big Steel

Reference number: 675.10.81 L
Movement: automatic, Fortis Caliber F-2016 (base ETA 2836-2); ø 25.6 mm, height 5.05 mm; 26 jewels; 28,800 vph; 42-hour power reserve
Functions: hours, minutes, sweep seconds; weekday, date
Case: stainless steel, ø 47 mm, height 13.3 mm; unidirectional bezel with 60-minute divisions, sapphire crystal, water-resistant to 20 atm
Band: calf leather, buckle
Remarks: sapphire crystal dial
Price: $3,450; limited to 2,012 pieces
Variations: steel/PVD black ($4,000)

B-42 Marinemaster Chronograph Yellow

Reference number: 671.24.14 K
Movement: automatic, ETA Caliber 7750; ø 30 mm, height 7.9 mm; 25 jewels; 28,800 vph; 42-hour power reserve
Functions: hours, minutes, subsidiary seconds; chronograph; weekday, date
Case: stainless steel, ø 42 mm, height 16 mm; unidirectional bezel with 60-minute divisions, sapphire crystal; water-resistant to 20 atm
Band: rubber, folding clasp
Price: $4,025
Variations: various bands; Day/Date version ($2,050)

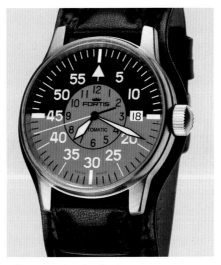

F-43 Flieger Chronograph Alarm GMT Certified Chronometer

Reference number: 703.10.81 LC01
Movement: automatic, Fortis Caliber F-2012 (base ETA 7750); ø 30 mm, height 7.9 mm; 39 jewels; 28,800 vph; 36-hour power reserve; COSC-certified
Functions: hours, minutes, subsidiary seconds; additional 24-hour display; double power reserve display; alarm clock; chronograph; day/night indicator; date
Case: stainless steel, ø 43 mm, height 16.3 mm; sapphire crystal; water-resistant to 5 atm
Band: reptile skin, folding clasp
Price: $20,750; limited to 100 pieces

Flieger Cockpit Date

Reference number: 595.11.13 L01
Movement: automatic, ETA Caliber 2824-2; ø 25.6 mm, height 4.6 mm; 25 jewels; 28,800 vph; 38-hour power reserve
Functions: hours, minutes, sweep seconds; date
Case: stainless steel, ø 40 mm, height 14.6 mm; sapphire crystal; water-resistant to 20 atm
Band: calf leather, buckle
Price: $1,300
Variations: various bands; yellow/black and olive/black dial

Flieger Chronograph

Reference number: 597.11.11 L01
Movement: automatic, ETA Caliber 7750; ø 30 mm, height 7.9 mm; 25 jewels, 28,800 vph; 42-hour power reserve
Functions: hours, minutes, subsidiary seconds; chronograph; weekday and date
Case: stainless steel, ø 40 mm, height 14.6 mm; sapphire crystal; water-resistant to 10 atm
Band: calf leather, buckle
Price: $2,825
Variations: various bands; 3-hand automatic ($3,825)

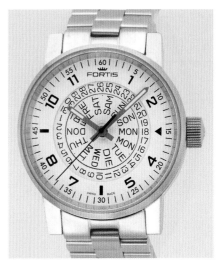

B-42 Official Cosmonauts Chronograph

Reference number: 638.10.11 M
Movement: automatic, ETA Caliber 7750; ø 30 mm, height 7.9 mm; 25 jewels; 28,800 vph; 42-hour power reserve
Functions: hours, minutes, subsidiary seconds; chronograph; weekday and date
Case: stainless steel, ø 42 mm, height 16 mm; unidirectional bezel with 60-minute divisions, sapphire crystal, water-resistant to 20 atm
Band: stainless steel, folding clasp
Price: $4,100
Variations: various bands; Day/Date ($2,250); alarm chronograph ($11,675)

B-47 Calculator GMT 3 Time Zones

Reference number: 669.10.31 L16
Movement: automatic, ETA Caliber 2893-2; ø 25.6 mm, height 4.1 mm; 21 jewels; 28,800 vph; 42-hour power reserve
Functions: hours, minutes, sweep seconds; additional 24-hour display (2nd time zone); date
Case: stainless steel, ø 47 mm, height 13.5 mm; bidirectional bezel with 24-hour division; crown-activated scale ring inner with 24-hour division and slide rule; sapphire crystal; water-resistant to 20 atm
Band: calf leather, buckle
Price: $3,500; limited to 2,012 pieces
Variations: stainless steel bracelet ($3,975); rubber strap ($3,675)

Spacematic Classic White-Red

Reference number: 623.10.52 M
Movement: automatic, ETA Caliber 2836-2; ø 25.6 mm, height 5.05 mm; 25 jewels; 28,800 vph; 38-hour power reserve
Functions: hours, minutes, sweep seconds; weekday, date
Case: stainless steel, ø 40 mm, height 10.4 mm; sapphire crystal; water-resistant to 10 atm
Band: stainless steel, double folding clasp
Price: $1,975
Variations: calf leather band ($1,575); silicone band ($1,875)

**Groupe Franck Muller
Watchland SA**
22, route de Malagny
CH-1294 Genthod
Switzerland

Tel.:
01141-22-959-8888

Fax:
01141-22-959-8882

E-Mail:
info@franckmuller.ch

Website:
www.franckmuller.com

Founded:
1997

Number of employees:
approx. 500 (estimated)

U.S. distributor:
Franck Muller USA, Inc.
207 W. 25th Street, 8th Floor
New York, NY 10001
212-463-8898
www.franckmuller.com

Most important collections:
Giga, Aeternitas, Revolution, Evolution 3-1

Franck Muller

Francesco "Franck" Muller has been considered one of the great creative minds in the industry ever since he designed and built his first tourbillon watch back in 1986. In fact, he never ceased amazing his colleagues and competition ever since, with his astounding timepieces combining complications in a new and fascinating manner.

Recently, the "master of complications" has been stepping away from the daily business of the brand, leaving space for the person who had paved young Muller's way to fame, Vartan Sirmakes. It was Sirmakes, previously a specialist in watch cases, who had contributed to the development of the double-domed, tonneau-shaped Cintrée Curvex case, with its elegant, 1920s retro look. The complications never stop either. The latest Gigatourbillons are 20 millimeters across; the Revolution series has a tourbillon that rises toward the crystal.

It was in 1997 that Muller and Sirmakes founded the Franck Muller Group Watchland, which now holds the majority interest in thirteen other companies, eight of which are watch brands. During the 2009 economic crisis, the company downsized somewhat and put all its ambitious plans for expansion on hold. Franck Muller remains the leading brand in the Watchland portfolio, but via far-reaching synergies within the group, two brands specializing in complicated movements, Pierre Kunz and Pierre-Michel Golay, play a part in the founding brand's success.

Giga Tourbillon

Reference number: 8889 T G SQT BR NR
Movement: manually wound, FM Caliber 2100 TS; 34.4 x 41.4 mm, height 8.5 mm; 29 jewels; 18,000 vph; flying 1-minute, 20 mm tourbillon; 4 spring barrels; fully skeletonized; 216-hour power reserve
Functions: hours, minutes; power reserve indicator
Case: rose gold, 43.7 x 59.2 mm, height 14 mm; sapphire crystal; transparent case back; water-resistant to 3 atm
Band: reptile skin, buckle
Price: $242,200
Variations: white gold ($264,400); black PVD steel ($242,200)

Aeternitas 2

Reference number: 8888 Aeternitas 2 (8888TPRACE)
Movement: automatic, FM Caliber 3405 T PR; 34.4 x 41.4 mm, height 7.55 mm; 45 jewels; 18,000 vph; 1-minute tourbillon, Breguet spring, platinum rotor with côtes de Genève; 192-hour power reserve
Functions: hours, minutes; power reserve indicator
Case: stainless steel, 38.2 x 57.6 mm, height 13.49 mm; sapphire crystal
Band: reptile skin, buckle
Price: $166,700

Aeternitas Mega 4

Reference number: 8888 Aternitas Mega 4 (8888 GSW T CC R QPS)
Movement: automatic, FM Caliber 3420; 33.8 x 40.8 mm, height 13 mm; 21,600 vph; flying 1-minute tourbillon, microrotor; 96-hour power reserve
Functions: hours, minutes; 2 24-hour displays; equation of time indicator; minute repeater; grande and petite sonnerie; split-second chronograph; perpetual secular calendar with date (retrograde), weekday, month, moon phase, year, leap year
Case: platinum, 42 x 61 mm, height 23.05 mm; sapphire crystal; transparent case back
Band: reptile skin, buckle
Price: $2,600,000

7 Days Power Reserve Skeleton

Reference number: 7045 S6 SQT
Movement: manually wound, FM Caliber 1740 RS; ø 33.4 mm, height 5.3 mm; 21 jewels; 18,000 vph; Breguet spring, double spring barrel, skeletonized plate and bridges, finely finished with côtes de Genève and perlage; 168-hour power reserve
Functions: hours, minutes, subsidiary seconds
Case: rose gold, ø 45 mm, height 11.2 mm; sapphire crystal; transparent case back
Band: reptile skin, buckle
Price: $9,800
Variations: stainless steel ($40,800)

Cintrée Curvex 7 Days Power Reserve

Reference number: 7885BS6PRVIN5NW
Movement: manually wound, FM Caliber 1700; ø 31 mm, height 5 mm; 27 jewels; 18,000 vph; double spring barrel, Breguet spring, finely finished with côtes de Genève and perlage; 168-hour power reserve
Functions: hours, minutes, subsidiary seconds; power reserve indicator
Case: rose gold, 36 x 50.4 mm, height 10.3 mm; sapphire crystal; transparent case back; water-resistant to 3 atm
Band: reptile skin, buckle
Price: $22,000

Vanguard

Reference number: V45SCDTTT5NGR-WG
Movement: automatic, FM Caliber 800; ø 25.6 mm, height 3.6 mm; 21 jewels; 28,800 vph; finely finished with perlage and côtes de Genève; 42-hour power reserve
Functions: hours, minutes, sweep seconds; date
Case: titanium, black PVD-coated; 44 x 53.7 mm, height 12.8 mm; sapphire crystal; transparent case back
Band: rubber, with reptile skin inserts, folding clasp
Price: $8,800

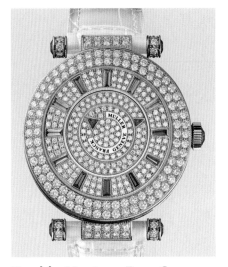

Tourbillon Revolution 3

Reference number: 9800 T REV 3
Movement: manually wound, FM Caliber 2004; 32.46 x 39.48 mm, height 9.5 mm; 23 jewels; 18,000 vph; spherically suspended triple-axis tourbillon (rotation duration of 1-8-60 minutes); 2 spring barrels; 240-hour power reserve
Functions: hours, minutes; 2 retrograde revolution displays for inner tourbillon cage
Case: platinum, 35.3 x 48.7 mm, height 18 mm; sapphire crystal
Band: reptile skin, buckle
Price: $1,355,600

Sunrise

Reference number: 8035 QZ SNR D CD.OG
Movement: quartz
Functions: hours, minutes
Case: white gold, ø 35 mm, height 7.9 mm; bezel set with 136 diamonds; sapphire crystal
Band: reptile skin, buckle
Remarks: mother-of-pearl dial set with 128 diamonds
Price: $26,800

Double Mystery Four Seasons

Reference number: 42 DCD2 COL.OG
Movement: automatic, FM Caliber 2800; ø 25.6 mm, height 3.6 mm; 21 jewels; 28,800 vph; disc displays; finely finished; 42-hour power reserve
Functions: mysterious hour and minute display (without visible hand arbor)
Case: white gold, ø 42 mm, height 10 mm; bezel set with 240 diamonds, sapphire crystal; transparent case back; water-resistant to 3 atm
Band: reptile skin, buckle (set with 8 diamonds)
Remarks: dial set with 218 diamonds
Price: $94,200

Montres Journe SA
17 rue de l'Arquebuse
CH-1204 Geneva
Switzerland

Tel.:
01141-22322-09-09

Fax:
01141-22-322-09-19

E-Mail:
info@fpjourne.com

Website:
www.fpjourne.com

Founded:
1999

Number of employees:
120

Annual production:
850–900 watches

U.S. distributor:
Montres Journe America
4330 NE 2nd Avenue
Miami, FL 33137
305-572-9802
phalimi@fpjourne.com

Most important collections/price range:
Souveraine, Octa, Vagabondage, Elegante
(Prices are in Swiss francs. Use daily exchange
rate for calculations.)

François-Paul Journe

Born in Marseilles in 1957, François-Paul Journe might have become something else had he concentrated better in school. He was kicked out and apprenticed with a watchmaking uncle in Paris instead. And he has never looked back. By the age of twenty he had made his first tourbillon and soon was producing watches for connoisseurs.

He then moved to Switzerland, where he started out with handmade creations for a limited circle of clients and developing the most creative and complicated timekeepers for other brands before taking the plunge and founding his own in the heart of Geneva.

The timepieces he basically single-handedly and certainly single-mindedly—hence his tagline *invenit et fecit*—conceives and produces are of such extreme complexity that it is no wonder that they leave his workshop in relatively small quantities. Journe has won numerous top awards, some several times over. He particularly values the Prix de la Fondation de la Vocation Bleustein-Blanchet since it came from his peers.

His collection is divided into two pillars: the automatic Octa line with its somewhat more readily understandable complications and the manually wound Souveraine line, which contains horological treasures that can't be found anywhere else. The latter includes a *grande sonnerie*, a minute repeater, a constant force tourbillon with deadbeat seconds, and even a timepiece containing two escapements beating in resonance—and providing chronometer-precise timekeeping.

Journe never stops surprising the watch world. His most recent creation is a woman's timepiece, the Elégante. Incredibly, it features a microprocessor that electronically notes when the watch is immobile, stops the mechanical movement to preserve energy, and starts it up again when the watch is once again in motion.

Chronomètre à Résonance

Movement: manually wound, F.P.Journe Caliber 1499.3; ø 32.6 mm, height 4.2 mm; 36 jewels; 21,600 vph; unique concept of 2 escapements mutually influencing and thus stabilizing each other utilizing resonance; pink gold plate and bridges
Functions: hours, minutes, subsidiary seconds; 2nd time zone; power reserve indicator
Case: platinum, ø 40 mm, height 9 mm; sapphire crystal; transparent case back
Band: reptile skin, platinum buckle
Price: CHF 84,100
Variations: pink gold (CHF 75,600)

Sonnerie Souveraine

Movement: manually wound, F.P.Journe Caliber 1505; ø 35.8 mm, height 7.8 mm; 42 jewels; 21,600 vph; 18 kt rose gold plate and bridges; repeater chimes hours/quarter hours, automatically or on demand; on/off function; 422 components; 10 patents
Functions: hours, minutes (off-center), subsidiary seconds; grande sonnerie; power reserve indicator; chime indicator
Case: stainless steel, ø 42 mm; height 12.25 mm; sapphire crystal; screw-in crown and pusher; transparent case back
Band: reptile skin with double folding clasp or stainless steel bracelet
Price: CHF 702,000

Répétition Souveraine

Movement: manually wound, F.P.Journe Caliber 1408; ø 32.2 mm, height 4 mm; 33 jewels; 21,600 vph; pink gold plate and bridges
Functions: hours, minutes, subsidiary seconds; hour, quarter-hour, and minute repeater; power reserve indicator
Case: stainless steel, ø 40 mm, height 8.8 mm; sapphire crystal; transparent case back
Band: reptile skin, double folding clasp
Price: CHF 185,700

Centigraphe Souverain

Movement: manually wound, F.P.Journe Caliber 1506; ø 34.4 mm, height 5.6 mm; 50 jewels; 21,600 vph; pink gold plate and bridges; simultaneous drive from spring barrel (movement) and barrel arbor (chronograph)
Functions: hours, minutes, subsidiary seconds; chronograph 10-minute, 20-second, and 1/100th second counters
Case: platinum, ø 40 mm, height 10.7 mm; sapphire crystal; transparent case back; slide pusher for chronograph functions
Band: reptile skin, buckle
Price: CHF 64,500
Variations: pink gold (CHF 55,600)

Chronomètre Optimum

Movement: manually wound, F.P.Journe Caliber 1510; ø 34.4 mm, height 3.75 mm; 44 jewels; 21,600 vph; pink gold plate and bridges; with double barrel, constant force remontoire, EPHB high-performance biaxial escapement, balance spiral with Phillips curve, deadbeat seconds on back
Functions: hours, minutes, subsidiary seconds; power reserve indicator
Case: platinum, ø 40 mm, height 10.1 mm; sapphire crystal; transparent case back
Band: reptile skin, buckle
Price: CHF 90,200
Variations: pink gold (CHF 85,800)

Chronomètre Bleu

Movement: manually wound, F.P.Journe Caliber 1304; ø 30.4 mm, height 3.75 mm; 22 jewels; 21,600 vph; pink gold plate and bridges; chronometer balance with "invisible" connection to gear train; 2 spring barrels
Functions: hours, minutes, subsidiary seconds
Case: tantalum, ø 39 mm, height 8.6 mm; sapphire crystal; transparent case back
Band: reptile skin, tantalum buckle
Price: CHF 19,800

Octa Automatique Lune

Movement: automatic, F.P.Journe Caliber 1300.3; ø 30.8 mm, height 5.7 mm; 39 jewels; 21,600 vph; 120-hour power reserve; pink gold plate and bridge; silver guilloché dial with clous de Paris
Functions: central hours, minutes, subsidiary seconds; large date; moon phase; power reserve indicator
Case: platinum, ø 40 mm, height 10.6 mm; sapphire crystal; transparent case back
Band: reptile skin, platinum buckle
Price: CHF 49,000
Variations: pink gold (CHF 41,900)

Octa Sport

Movement: automatic, F.P.Journe Caliber 1303.3; ø 30.8 mm, height 5.70 mm; 40 jewels; 21,600 vph; plate and movement entirely aluminum alloy; 120-hour power reserve
Functions: central hours, minutes, subsidiary seconds; large date; power reserve; day/night indicator
Case: titanium, ø 42 mm, height 11.6 mm; sapphire crystal; transparent case back
Band: rubber, titanium clasp
Price: CHF 26,460
Variations: titanium bracelet (CHF 31,860)

Elégante

Movement: electromechanical, F.P.Journe Caliber 1210; 28.5 x 28.3 mm, height 3.13 mm; 18 jewels; quartz frequency 32,000 Hz; autonomy 10 years/18 years stand-by mode; 120-hour power reserve; pink gold plate and bridge
Functions: hours, minutes, subsidiary seconds; large date; power reserve indicator
Case: pink gold, 34 x 35 mm, height 7.35 mm; sapphire crystal; transparent case back
Band: reptile skin, platinum buckle
Remarks: stand-by mode after 30 minutes motionless
Price: CHF 29,160
Variations: titanium set (CHF 15,120); platinum set (CHF 33,260)

Frédérique Constant SA
Chemin du Champ des Filles 32
CH-1228 Plan-les-Ouates (Geneva)
Switzerland

Tel.:
01141-22-860-0440

Fax:
01141-22-860-0464

E-Mail:
info@frederique-constant.com

Website:
www.frederique-constant.com

Founded:
1988

Number of employees:
100

Annual production:
110,000 watches

U.S. distributor:
Frederic Constant USA
877-61-WATCH
info@usa.frederique-constant.com

Most important collections/price range:
Slimline Manufacture Automatic / from approx.
$2,800; Heart Beat Manufacture / from
approx. $6,000; Lady Automatic / from approx.
$2,800; Runabout / from approx. $2,500;
Vintage Rally / from approx. $1,700; Art Deco /
approx. $1,100; Classics / from approx. $800

Frédérique Constant

Time flies when you're having fun, even in the watch business. It's been ten years since the brand Frédérique Constant went public with its first movement entirely produced in-house and equipped with innovative silicon components. And the idea of being a full-fledged *manufacture* has supported the speed and rhythm of the brand's evolution. In 2013, Frédérique Constant sold about 130,000 timepieces at 2,800 doors in roughly 100 countries. This represents an 8 percent increase over the previous year. The production of Heart Beat calibers has more than doubled, allowing the brand to get a lot closer to achieving its goal of offering affordable luxury to everyone.

Since 1991, the Dutch couple Peter und Aletta Stas have genuinely lived up to the tagline they use for their Swiss brand: "live your passion." The watch brand, named for Aletta's great-grandmother, Frédérique Schreiner, and Peter's great-grandfather, Constant Stas, was conceived in the late 1980s. The new company had its work cut out for it: Frédérique Constant had to compete in a watch market truly saturated with brands.

After their Heart Beat *manufacture* model met with award-winning enthusiasm in 2003, the Stases decided to invest in their own watch factory, an impressive, four-floor facility with ample room for a spacious atelier, administrative offices, conference rooms, fitness area, and cafeteria, in Geneva's industrial section, Plan-les-Ouates. Frédérique Constant moved into its new home in 2006, joined shortly after by its sister brand Alpina. The Heart Beat collection continues to make waves; the Double Heart Beat is even being used to fund charities ($50 per watch sold). But the brand is growing in other directions as well. In 2009, Frédérique Constant backed the founding of the exclusive Ateliers de Monaco. And as evidence that the Stases are genuinely interested in spreading their passion about watches, they have created a kind of sub-brand, Frédérique Constant Junior, aimed at teenagers.

Classics Manufacture Worldtimer

Reference number: FC-718MC4H6B
Movement: automatic, Caliber FC-718 (base ETA 2893-1); ø 25.6 mm, height 4.1 mm; 26 jewels; 28,800 vph; 42-hour power reserve
Functions: hours, minutes, sweep seconds; world-time display (2nd time zone); date
Case: stainless steel, ø 42 mm, crown-adjustable inner bezel with 24-hour divisions, reference cities, sapphire crystal; transparent case back; water-resistant to 5 atm
Band: stainless steel, folding clasp
Price: $4,095

Classics Manufacture Worldtimer

Reference number: FC-718WM4H6B
Movement: automatic, Caliber FC-718 (base ETA 2893-1); ø 25.6 mm, height 4.1 mm; 26 jewels; 28,800 vph; 42-hour power reserve
Functions: hours, minutes, sweep seconds; world-time display (2nd time zone); date
Case: stainless steel, ø 42 mm, crown-adjustable inner bezel with 24-hour divisions, reference cities, sapphire crystal; transparent case back; water-resistant to 5 atm
Band: stainless steel, folding clasp
Price: $4,095

Slimline Moonphase Manufacture

Reference number: FC-705S4S6B
Movement: automatic, Caliber FC-705; ø 30 mm, height 6.3 mm; 26 jewels; 28,800 vph; côtes de Genève; 42-hour power reserve
Functions: hours, minutes; date, moon phase
Case: stainless steel, ø 42 mm; sapphire crystal; transparent case back; water-resistant to 3 atm
Band: stainless steel, folding clasp
Price: $3,795

Slimline Moonphase Manufacture

Reference number: FC-705N4S6B
Movement: automatic, Caliber FC-705; ø 30 mm, height 6.3 mm; 26 jewels; 28,800 vph; côtes de Genève; 42-hour power reserve
Functions: hours, minutes; date, moon phase
Case: stainless steel, ø 42 mm; sapphire crystal; transparent case back; water-resistant to 3 atm
Band: stainless steel, folding clasp
Price: $3,795

Healey GMT

Reference number: FC-350CH5B4
Movement: automatic, Sellita Caliber SW 200; ø 25.6 mm, height 6.1 mm; 26 jewels; 28,800 vph; 38-hour power reserve
Functions: hours, minutes, sweep seconds; additional 24-hour display (2nd time zone); date
Case: stainless steel with rose gold-colored PVD coating, ø 40 mm, height 12.5 mm; sapphire crystal; water-resistant to 5 atm
Band: calf leather, buckle
Remarks: limited to 2,888 pieces
Price: $2,795

Healey GMT

Reference number: FC-350HS5B6
Movement: automatic, Sellita Caliber SW 200; ø 25.6 mm, height 6.1 mm; 26 jewels; 28,800 vph; 38-hour power reserve
Functions: hours, minutes, sweep seconds; additional 24-hour display (2nd time zone); date
Case: stainless steel, ø 40 mm, height 12.5 mm; sapphire crystal; water-resistant to 5 atm
Band: calf leather, buckle
Remarks: limited to 2,888 pieces
Price: $2,295

Heart Beat Manufacture

Reference number: FC-945MC4H9
Movement: automatic, Caliber FC-945; ø 30.5 mm, height 6.38 mm; 26 jewels; 28,800 vph; silicon escapement; finely finished with côtes de Genève; 42-hour power reserve
Functions: hours, minutes; additional 24-hour display (2nd time zone); date, moon phase
Case: rose gold, ø 42 mm, height 11.6 mm; sapphire crystal; transparent back; water-resistant to 5 atm
Band: reptile skin, buckle
Remarks: dial with opening
Price: $15,500; limited to 1,888 pieces

Runabout Moonphase

Reference number: FC-330RM6B6
Movement: automatic, Caliber FC-330 (base Sellita SW 200); ø 25.6 mm, height 6.1 mm; 26 jewels, 28,800 vph; 38-hour power reserve
Functions: hours, minutes, sweep seconds; date; moon phase
Case: stainless steel, ø 43 mm, height 10.9 mm; sapphire crystal; transparent case back; water-resistant to 10 atm
Band: calf leather, folding clasp
Remarks: limited to 1,888 pieces
Price: $2,795

Art Déco Oval

Reference number: FC-200MPW2VD6B
Movement: quartz
Functions: hours, minutes
Case: stainless steel, 25 x 30 mm; bezel and lugs set with 78 diamonds; sapphire crystal; water-resistant to 3 atm
Band: stainless steel, folding clasp
Price: $2,995

Genesis

Genesis
Jaffestr. 6
D-21109 Hamburg
Germany

Tel.:
01149-40-414-9880-0

E-Mail:
info@genesis-uhren.de

Website:
www.genesis-uhren.de

Founded:
2005

Number of employees:
2

U.S. distributor:
direct sales only

Most important collections/price range:
$2,500 to $3,800
Prices may vary due to exchange
rate fluctuations.

These days, the graduating classes of watchmaking schools comprise more and more women who are passionate about precision handcrafting. Many of them have already become masters of their trade. Hamburg-based watchmaker Christine Genesis is one of these women—and her last name, the biblical term for the story of creation, can be seen as the theme of her horological activities. In addition to teaming up with designer Jorn Lund to create her own series of timelessly elegant, reliable, and affordable wristwatches in an old factory building in Hamburg's south end, Genesis, who studied at the watchmaking school of Pforzheim, also makes use of her longtime experience repairing clocks, maintaining mechanical wristwatches, and working on such larger complications as perpetual calendars. Her timepieces, however, are never overbearing. Genesis has bucked the trend toward ever larger watches and complicated dials, opting instead for uncluttered elegance, with complications subtly integrated in timepieces that are hardly ostentatious.

Genesis Carpe Diem

Reference number: 39.14.2
Movement: automatic, ETA Caliber 7750; ø 30 mm, height 7.9 mm; 25 jewels; 28,800 vph; finely finished with perlage and côtes de Genève; 42-hour power reserve
Functions: hours, minutes, subsidiary seconds; weekday, date
Case: stainless steel, ø 39.6 mm, height 14 mm; sapphire crystal; transparent case back
Band: various leathers, buckle
Price: $3,850; limited to 50 pieces
Variations: hands in various colors; light-colored dial

Genesis 1

Reference number: 38.01.1
Movement: automatic, Soprod Caliber 9060 (base ETA 2892-A2); ø 25.6 mm, height 5.1 mm; 26 jewels; 28,800 vph; finely finished with perlage and côtes de Genève, engraved rotor
Functions: hours, minutes, sweep seconds; power reserve indicator; weekday, date
Case: stainless steel, ø 38.5 mm, height 10.5 mm; sapphire crystal; transparent case back
Band: various leathers, buckle
Price: $3,100; limited to 44 pieces
Variations: black dial; black DLC-coating ($3,500)

Genesis Classic

Reference number: 38.11.1
Movement: automatic, Soprod Caliber A10; ø 25.6 mm, height 3.6 mm; 25 jewels; 28,800 vph; finely finished with perlage and côtes de Genève
Functions: hours, minutes, sweep seconds; date
Case: stainless steel, ø 38.5 mm, height 9.5 mm; sapphire crystal; transparent case back
Band: various leathers, buckle
Price: $2,600; limited to 50 pieces
Variations: various dial colors

Girard-Perregaux
1, Place Girardet
CH-2300 La Chaux-de-Fonds
Switzerland

Tel.:
01141-32-911-3333

Fax:
01141-32-913-0480

Website:
www.girard-perregaux.com

Founded:
1791

Number of employees:
280

Annual production:
approx. 12,000 watches

U.S. distributor:
Girard-Perregaux
Tradema of America, Inc.
201 Route 17 North
Rutherford, NJ 07070
877-846-3447
www.girard-perregaux.com

Most important collections/price range:
Vintage 1945 / approx. $7,010 to $650,000;
ww.tc / $12,400 to $210,000; GP 1966 /
$13,600 to $290,850

Girard-Perregaux

When Girard-Perregaux CEO Luigi ("Gino") Macaluso died in 2010, the former minority partner of Sowind Group, PPR (Pinault, Printemps, Redoute) increased its equity stake to 51 percent. Under the leadership of Michele Sofisti since 2011, the brand has been charting a rather bold course that includes some technically sharp developments with the support

of a strong development team and an excellently equipped production department. Under his guidance, the company has reduced its multitude of references but continues treading the fine line between fashionable watches and technical miracles. In January 2012, the manufacturing team was reinforced with one of the most scintillating figures in horology, master watchmaker Dominique Loiseau, who is working on a new, modular movement for the brand.

The various combinations of tourbillons and the gold bridges remain the company specialty. The elegant GP 1966 line and the very feminine Cat's Eye are still available, of course. The Vintage 45 is another standout, featuring striking rectangular and arched cases. But the most dazzling talking piece lately has undoubtedly been the Constant Escapement, a new concept that stores energy by buckling an ultra-thin silicium blade and then releasing it to the balance wheel. Like many sophisticated systems, it was born of the banal: Inventor Nicolas Déhon was absentmindedly bending a train ticket one day when he was suddenly struck by the simple thought. As the ticket bent, it collected energy that was released in even bursts when it straightened up.

Another technical development is the triple-axis tourbillon. On the other side of the scale, one finds the manually wound chronograph caliber 03800, with column wheel and jumping minute counter, which maintains the brand's line of classic virtues.

Constant Escapement L.M.

Reference number: 93500-52-731-BA6D
Movement: manually wound, GP Caliber 09100-0002; ø 39.2 mm, height 7.9 mm; 28 jewels; 21,600 vph; escapement with constant force, 2 escape wheels and flat silicon blade spring to provide impulses; 2 spring barrels; 168-hour power reserve
Functions: hours and minutes (off-center), sweep seconds; linear power reserve indicator
Case: rose gold, ø 48 mm, height 14.63 mm; sapphire crystal; transparent case back; water-resistant to 3 atm
Band: reptile skin, folding clasp
Remarks: dedicated to Luigi ("Gino") Macaluso
Price: $123,500

Tourbillon with Three Bridges

Reference number: 99270-52-000-BA6A
Movement: automatic, GP Caliber 9400-0001; ø 36.6 mm, height 8.21 mm; 27 jewels; 21,600 vph; 1-minute tourbillon under 3 PVD-coated titanium bridges, white gold microrotor; 70-hour power reserve
Functions: hours, minutes, subsidiary seconds (on tourbillon cage)
Case: rose gold, ø 45 mm, height 14.45 mm; sapphire crystal; transparent case back; water-resistant to 3 atm
Band: reptile skin, folding clasp
Price: $153,150

Tri-Axial Tourbillon

Reference number: 99815-52-251-BA6A
Movement: manually wound, GP Caliber 09300-0001; ø 36.1 mm, height 16.83 mm; 34 jewels; 21,600 vph; 1-minute tourbillon held in 2 cages positioned at 90° with 30-second and 2-minute rotation speed; balance with gold weight screws, fine finishing; 52-hour power reserve
Functions: hours, minutes; power reserve indicator
Case: rose gold, ø 48 mm, height 17.51 mm (with 20.27 mm tourbillon dome); sapphire crystal; transparent case back; water-resistant to 3 atm
Band: reptile skin, folding clasp
Remarks: lateral sapphire crystal
Price: $484,750; limited to 10 pieces

GP 1966 Column Wheel Chronograph

Reference number: 49529-52-231-BA6A
Movement: automatic, GP Caliber 03800-0001;
ø 25.6 mm; 31 jewels; 28,800 vph; balance
with gold weight screws, column wheel control of
chronograph functions; 58-hour power reserve
Functions: hours, minutes, subsidiary seconds;
chronograph; date
Case: rose gold, ø 40 mm, height 11.25 mm;
sapphire crystal; transparent case back; water-
resistant to 3 atm
Band: reptile skin, buckle
Price: $37,700
Variations: silver-plated dial

GP 1966

Reference number: 49525-52-432-BB4A
Movement: automatic, GP Caliber 03300-0030;
ø 25.6 mm; 27 jewels; 28,800 vph; 46-hour power
reserve
Functions: hours, minutes, sweep seconds; date
Case: rose gold, ø 38 mm, height 8.62 mm;
sapphire crystal; transparent case back; water-
resistant to 3 atm
Band: reptile skin, buckle
Price: $16,300
Variations: silver-plated or black dial

GP 1966 Annual Calendar and Equation of Time

Reference number: 49538-52-231-BK6A
Movement: automatic, GP Caliber 033M0;
ø 25.6 mm, height 4.85 mm; 44 jewels; 28,800
vph; 46-hour power reserve
Functions: hours, minutes, subsidiary seconds;
annual calendar with date, month, equation of time
indicator
Case: rose gold, ø 40 mm, height 10.72 mm;
sapphire crystal; transparent case back; water-
resistant to 3 atm
Band: reptile skin, buckle
Price: $33,400
Variations: white gold ($37,300)

Vintage 1945 XXL Large Date

Reference number: 25882-11-121-BB6B
Movement: automatic, GP Caliber 03300-00062;
ø 25.6 mm, height 4.9 mm; 32 jewels; 28,800 vph;
46-hour power reserve
Functions: hours, minutes, subsidiary seconds;
large date; moon phase
Case: stainless steel, 35.25 x 36.1 mm, height
11.74 mm; sapphire crystal; transparent case back;
water-resistant to 3 atm
Band: reptile skin, folding clasp
Price: $12,200

Vintage 1945 XXL Chronograph

Reference number: 25883-52-121-BB6C
Movement: automatic, GP Caliber 03300-0058;
ø 25.6 mm, height 5.5 mm; 32 jewels; 28,800 vph;
46-hour power reserve
Functions: hours, minutes, subsidiary seconds;
chronograph
Case: rose gold, 36 x 36.96 mm, height 13.09 mm;
sapphire crystal; transparent case back; water-
resistant to 3 atm
Band: reptile skin, folding clasp
Price: $32,500

Vintage 1945 XXL Small Seconds

Reference number: 25880-11-221-BB6A
Movement: automatic, GP Caliber 3300-0051;
ø 26.2 mm, height 4.2 mm; 32 jewels; 28,800 vph;
48-hour power reserve
Functions: hours, minutes, subsidiary seconds
Case: stainless steel, 35.25 x 36.2 mm, height
10.83 mm; sapphire crystal; transparent case back;
water-resistant to 3 atm
Band: reptile skin, folding clasp
Price: $10,450
Variations: silver or anthracite dial; rose gold
($27,600)

Traveller Large Date

Reference number: 49650-11-131-BB6A
Movement: automatic, GP Caliber 03300-0080; ø 31 mm; 35 jewels; 28,800 vph; 46-hour power reserve
Functions: hours, minutes, subsidiary seconds; power reserve indicator; large date; moon phase
Case: stainless steel, ø 44 mm, height 12.1 mm; sapphire crystal; transparent case back; water-resistant to 10 atm
Band: reptile skin, folding clasp
Price: $12,950
Variations: black dial

Traveller ww.tc

Reference number: 49700-52-134-BB6B
Movement: automatic, GP Caliber 03300-0084; ø 30 mm, height 6.2 mm; 63 jewels; 28,800 vph; 46-hour power reserve
Functions: hours, minutes, subsidiary seconds; world-time display; day/night indicator; chronograph; date
Case: rose gold, ø 44 mm, height 13.65 mm; crown-adjustable inner bezel with reference cities; sapphire crystal; transparent case back; water-resistant to 10 atm
Band: reptile skin, folding clasp
Price: $34,750
Variations: black dial; stainless steel

Traveller ww.tc

Reference number: 49700-21-132-HBBB
Movement: automatic, GP Caliber 03300-0084; ø 30 mm, height 6.2 mm; 63 jewels; 28,800 vph; 46-hour power reserve
Functions: hours, minutes, subsidiary seconds; world-time display; day/night indicator; chronograph; date
Case: stainless steel, ø 44 mm, height 13.65 mm; crown-adjustable inner bezel with reference cities, sapphire crystal; transparent case back; water-resistant to 10 atm
Band: calf leather, folding clasp
Price: $18,300

 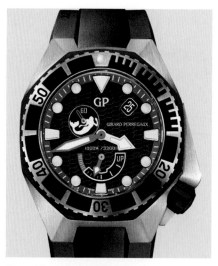 

Hawk Chronograph

Reference number: 49970-11-431-11A
Movement: automatic, GP Caliber 03300-0073; ø 29 mm; 61 jewels; 28,800 vph; 46-hour power reserve
Functions: hours, minutes, subsidiary seconds; chronograph; date
Case: stainless steel, ø 44 mm, height 15.45 mm; sapphire crystal; screw-in crown; water-resistant to 10 atm
Band: stainless steel, folding clasp
Price: $15,100
Variations: calf leather band ($13,900)

Sea Hawk Edition "Mission of Mermaid"

Reference number: 49960-19-1305SFK6A
Movement: automatic, GP Caliber 03300-0074; ø 25.6 mm; 27 jewels; 28,800 vph; 46-hour power reserve
Functions: hours, minutes, subsidiary seconds; power reserve indicator; date
Case: stainless steel, ø 46.2 mm, height 17.1 mm; unidirectional bezel with 60-minute divisions, sapphire crystal; screw-in crown; water-resistant to 100 atm
Band: rubber, folding clasp
Price: $11,750

Hawk Ceramic Chronograph

Reference number: 49970-32-631-FK6A
Movement: automatic, GP Caliber 03300-0076; ø 25.6 mm; 61 jewels; 28,800 vph; 46-hour power reserve
Functions: hours, minutes, subsidiary seconds; chronograph; date
Case: ceramic, ø 44 mm, height 15.45 mm; sapphire crystal; transparent case back; screw-in crown; water-resistant to 10 atm
Band: rubber, folding clasp
Price: $17,000

Caliber GP 3200

Automatic, rotor with ceramic ball bearing, stop-second system; single spring barrel, 42-hour power reserve
Functions: hours, minutes, sweep seconds or subsidiary seconds at 9 o'clock; date
Diameter: 23.3 mm
Height: 3.2 mm
Jewels: 27
Balance: glucydur
Frequency: 28,800 vph
Balance spring: flat hairspring, fine adjustment
Shock protection: Kif
Remarks: 185 components

Caliber GP 3300

Automatic, rotor with ceramic ball bearing, stop-second system; single spring barrel, 46-hour power reserve
Functions: hours, minutes, sweep seconds or subsidiary seconds at 9 o'clock; date
Diameter: 25.6 mm
Height: 3.2 mm
Jewels: 27
Balance: glucydur
Frequency: 28,800 vph
Balance spring: flat hairspring, fine adjustment
Shock protection: Kif
Remarks: 191 components

Caliber GP 3800

Manually wound; column wheel control of chronograph functions; single spring barrel, 58-hour power reserve
Functions: hours, minutes, subsidiary seconds; chronograph
Diameter: 25.6 mm
Height: 5.4 mm
Jewels: 31
Balance: Microvar with adjustable inertia
Frequency: 28,800 vph
Balance spring: flat hairspring
Shock protection: Kif
Remarks: 312 components

Caliber GP 09400

Automatic, 1-minute tourbillon, bidirectional winding rotor; tourbillon bridges in PVD-coated titanium; single spring barrel; 70-hour power reserve
Functions: hours, minutes, subsidiary seconds (on tourbillon cage)
Diameter: 36.6 mm
Height: 8.21 mm
Jewels: 27
Balance: screw balance
Frequency: 21,600 vph
Remarks: modern version of the classic Tourbillon under 3 Gold Bridges

Caliber GP 09300

Manually wound; 1-minute tourbillon held in 2 cages positioned at 90° with 30-second and 2-minute rotation speed; single spring barrel; 52-hour power reserve
Functions: hours, minutes; power reserve indicator
Diameter: 36.1 mm
Height: 16.83 mm
Jewels: 34
Balance: screw balance
Frequency: 21,600 vph

Caliber GP 3330-6LM00

Automatic; unidirectional rotor, stop-second system; single spring barrel, 46-hour power reserve
Functions: hours, minutes, subsidiary seconds; large date; moon phase
Measurements: 25.6 x 28.8 mm
Height: 4.9 mm
Jewels: 32
Balance: glucydur
Frequency: 28,800 vph
Balance spring: flat hairspring, fine adjustment
Shock protection: Kif

Glashütter Uhrenbetrieb GmbH
Altenberger Strasse 1
D-01768 Glashütte
Germany

Tel.:
01149-350-53-460

Fax:
01149-350-53-46-205

E-Mail:
info@glashuette-original.com

Website:
www.glashuette-original.com

Founded:
1994

Annual production:
approx. 5,000 watches (estimated)

U.S. distributor:
Glashütte Original
The Swatch Group (U.S.), Inc.
1200 Harbor Boulevard
Weehawken, NJ 07087
201-271-1400

Most important collections/price range:
Senator, PanoMatic, Ladies / approx. $5,000
to $170,000

Glashütte Original

Is there a little nostalgia creeping into the designers at Glashütte Original? Or is it just understated ecstasy for older looks? The retro touches that started appearing again a few years ago with the Sixties Square Tourbillon are still in vogue as the company delves into its own past for inspiration, such as the use of a special silver treatment on dials.

The Glashütte Original *manufacture* was once subsumed in the VEB Glashütter Uhrenbetriebe, a group of Glashütte watchmakers and suppliers who were collectivized as part of the former East German system. After reunification, the company took up its old moniker of Glashütte Original, and in 1995, the *manufacture* released an entirely new collection. Later, it purchased Union Glashütte. In 2000, the *manufacture* was sold to the Swiss Swatch Group, which invested a sizable amount in production space expansion at Glashütte Original headquarters.

All movements are designed by a team of experienced in-house engineers, while the components comprising them such as plates, screws, pinions, wheels, levers, spring barrels, balance wheels, and tourbillon cages are manufactured in the upgraded production areas. These parts are lavishly finished by hand before assembly by a group of talented watchmakers. The large and elegant Senator Chronometer is a highlight of recent years with its classic design. It also boasts second and minute hands that automatically jump to zero when the crown is pulled, allowing for extremely accurate time setting. And to prove that the company is not just about tradition, it has even created a Senator-based smartphone app.

Grande Cosmopolite Tourbillon

Reference number: 1-89-01-03-03-04
Movement: manually wound, GO Caliber 89-01; ø 39.2 mm, height 7.5 mm; 70 jewels, 2 diamond endstones; 21,600 vph; flying 1-minute tourbillon; Breguet spring, 18 weighted screws on screw balance, gold chatons; 72-hour power reserve
Functions: hours, minutes, subsidiary seconds (on tourbillon cage); 37-zone world-time display, day/night indicator, power reserve on back; perpetual calendar
Case: platinum, ø 48 mm, height 16 mm; sapphire crystal; transparent case back; water-resistant to 5 atm
Band: reptile skin, folding clasp
Price: on request; limited to 25 pieces

Senator Tourbillon

Reference number: 1-94-03-04-04-04
Movement: automatic, GO Caliber 94-03; ø 32.2 mm, height 7.65 mm; 50 jewels, 2 diamond endstones; 21,600 vph; flying 1-minute tourbillon; screw balance with 18 weighted screws, skeletonized rotor with gold oscillating weight; 48-hour power reserve
Functions: hours, minutes, subsidiary seconds (on tourbillon cage); date
Case: white gold, ø 42 mm, height 13.7 mm; sapphire crystal; transparent case back; water-resistant to 5 atm
Band: reptile skin, folding clasp
Price: $118,600

PanoLunarTourbillon

Reference number: 1-93-02-05-05-05
Movement: automatic, GO Caliber 93-02; ø 32.2 mm, height 7.65 mm; 48 jewels, 2 diamond endstones; 21,600 vph; flying 1-minute tourbillon; screw balance with 18 weighted screws
Functions: hours and minutes (off-center), subsidiary seconds (on tourbillon cage); panorama date; moon phase
Case: pink gold, ø 40 mm, height 13.1 mm; sapphire crystal, transparent case back; water-resistant to 5 atm
Band: reptile skin, folding clasp
Price: $117,400
Variations: with black leather strap

PanoGraph

Reference number: 1-61-03-25-15-04
Movement: manually wound, GO Caliber 61-03; ø 32.2 mm, height 7.2 mm; 41 jewels; 28,800 vph; screw balance with 18 weighted screws; swan-neck fine adjustment; hand-engraved balance bridge; 42-hour power reserve
Functions: hours, minutes, subsidiary seconds (all off-center); flyback chronograph; 30-minute counter; stop seconds; panorama date
Case: red gold, ø 40 mm, height 13.7 mm; sapphire crystal; transparent case back; water-resistant to 5 atm
Band: reptile skin, folding clasp
Price: $34,500

PanoReserve

Reference number: 1-65-01-22-12-04
Movement: manually wound, GO Caliber 65-01; ø 32.2 mm, height 6.1 mm; 48 jewels; 28,800 vph; three-quarter plate, 18 weighted screws on screw balance, duplex swan-neck fine adjustment, hand-engraved balance bridge and second cock; 42-hour power reserve
Functions: hours and minutes (off-center), subsidiary seconds; power reserve indicator; panorama date
Case: stainless steel, ø 40 mm, height 11.7 mm; sapphire crystal; transparent case back; water-resistant to 5 atm
Band: reptile skin, folding clasp
Price: $11,300
Variations: pink gold ($23,000)

PanoMaticInverse

Reference number: 1-91-02-01-05-30
Movement: automatic, GO Caliber 91-02; ø 38.2 mm, height 7.1 mm; 49 jewels; 28,800 vph; 18 weighted screws on screw balance; duplex swan-neck fine adjustment; inverted structure; three-quarter plate with Glashütte ribbing, hand-engraved balance bridge, skeletonized rotor with gold oscillating weight; 42-hour power reserve
Functions: hours and minutes (off-center), subsidiary seconds; panorama date
Case: pink gold, ø 42 mm, height 12.3 mm; sapphire crystal; transparent back; water-resistant to 5 atm
Band: reptile skin, folding clasp
Price: $29,700
Variations: stainless steel

Senator Chronograph Panorama Date

Reference number: 1-37-01-02-03-30
Movement: automatic, GO Caliber 37-01; ø 31.6 mm, height 8 mm; 65 jewels; 28,800 vph; screw balance with 4 gold regulating screws, swan-neck fine adjustment; mainplate with Glashütte stripe finishing; blued screws, skeletonized rotor with gold oscillating weight; 70-hour power reserve
Functions: hours, minutes, subsidiary seconds; power reserve indicator; flyback chronograph; panorama date
Case: platinum, ø 42 mm, height 14 mm; sapphire crystal; transparent case back; blue sapphire on crown; water-resistant to 5 atm
Band: reptile skin, folding clasp
Price: $55,600

Senator Chronometer

Reference number: 1-58-01-01-01-04
Movement: manually wound, GO Caliber 58-01; ø 35 mm, height 6.5 mm; 58 jewels; 28,800 vph; Glashütte three-quarter plate, second reset via crown for precise minute setting; screw balance with 18 weighted screws, swan-neck fine adjustment; 45-hour power reserve; DIN-tested chronometer
Functions: hours, minutes, subsidiary seconds; second stop and reset function, day/night and power reserve indicator; panorama date
Case: rose gold, ø 42 mm, height 12.3 mm; sapphire crystal; transparent back; water-resistant to 5 atm
Band: reptile skin, folding clasp
Price: $30,300
Variations: white gold ($32,000)

Senator Chronometer Regulator

Reference number: 1-58-04-04-04-04
Movement: manually wound, GO Caliber 58-04; ø 35 mm, height 6.5 mm; 58 jewels; 28,800 vph; Glashütte three-quarter plate, swan-neck fine adjustment, hand-engraved balance bridge, 18 weighted screws on screw balance; 45-hour power reserve; DIN-tested chronometer
Functions: hours (off-center), minutes, subsidiary seconds; day/night and power reserve indicators; panorama date
Case: white gold, ø 42 mm, height 12.47 mm; sapphire crystal; transparent case back; water-resistant to 5 atm
Band: reptile skin, folding clasp
Price: $33,300

Senator Observer

Reference number: 100-14-05-02-05
Movement: automatic, GO Caliber 100-14;
ø 31.15 mm, height 6.5 mm; 60 jewels; 28,800 vph;
screw balance, swan-neck fine adjustment; three-
quarter plate with Glashütte ribbing, skeletonized rotor
with gold oscillating weight; 55-hour power reserve
Functions: hours, minutes, subsidiary seconds; power
reserve indicator; hacking seconds; panorama date
Case: stainless steel, ø 44 mm, height 12 mm;
sapphire crystal; transparent case back; water-
resistant to 5 atm
Band: calf leather, folding clasp
Price: $11,800

Senator Panorama Date

Reference number: 100-03-32-42-04
Movement: automatic, GO Caliber 100-03; ø 31.15 mm,
height 5.8 mm; 51 jewels; 28,800 vph; screw balance
with 18 weighted screws, swan-neck fine adjustment;
three-quarter plate with Glashütte stripe, skeletonized
rotor with gold oscillating weight; 55-hour power reserve
Functions: hours, minutes, sweep seconds; panorama
date
Case: stainless steel, ø 40 mm, height 11.52 mm;
sapphire crystal; transparent case back; water-resistant
to 5 atm
Band: reptile skin, folding clasp
Price: $9,800
Variations: pink gold ($21,500)

Senator Panorama Date Moon Phase

Reference number: 100-04-32-15-04
Movement: automatic, GO Caliber 100-04; ø 31.15 mm,
height 5.8 mm; 55 jewels; 28,800 vph; screw balance
with 18 weighted screws, swan-neck fine adjustment;
three-quarter plate with Glashütte stripe, skeletonized
rotor with gold oscillating weight; 55-hour power reserve
Functions: hours, minutes, sweep seconds; panorama
date; moon phase
Case: pink gold, ø 40 mm, height 11.52 mm;
transparent back; water-resistant to 5 atm
Band: reptile skin, folding clasp
Price: $22,800
Variations: stainless steel case/bracelet ($12,000)

Senator Perpetual Calendar

Reference number: 100-02-25-05-04
Movement: automatic, GO Caliber 100-02;
ø 31.15 mm, height 7.1 mm; 59 jewels; 28,800 vph;
screw balance with 18 weighted screws, swan-neck fine
adjustment; zero reset mechanism; skeletonized rotor
with gold oscillating weight; 55-hour power reserve
Functions: hours, minutes, sweep seconds; perpetual
calendar with panorama date, weekday, month, moon
phase, leap year
Case: pink gold, ø 42 mm, height 13.6 mm; sapphire
crystal; transparent back; water-resistant to 5 atm
Band: rubber, folding clasp
Price: $36,500
Variations: stainless steel ($22,000); silver dial

Senator Diary

Reference number: 100-13-01-01-04
Movement: automatic, GO Caliber 100-13;
ø 34 mm, height 8.4 mm; 86 jewels; 28,800 vph;
screw balance, swan-neck fine adjustment, zero
reset mechanism; three-quarter plate with Glashütte
stripe, skeletonized rotor with gold oscillating weight;
55-hour power reserve
Functions: hours, minutes, sweep seconds;
panorama date; memory function (appointment day/
hour) with 80 second sonorous signal; on/off switch
Case: rose gold, ø 42 mm, height 14.4 mm; sapphire
crystal, transparent case back; water-resistant to
5 atm
Band: reptile skin, folding clasp
Price: $38,000

PanoMaticCounter XL

Reference number: 1-96-01-02-02-04
Movement: automatic, GO Caliber 96-01;
ø 32.2 mm, height 8.9 mm; 72 jewels; 28,800 vph;
screw balance with 18 weighted screws, swan-
neck fine adjustment, skeletonized rotor with gold
oscillating weight; 42-hour power reserve
Functions: hours and minutes (off-center),
subsidiary seconds; 2-digit counter (pusher-
controlled, forward/backward); flyback chronograph;
hacking seconds on 2nd dial level; panorama date
Case: stainless steel, ø 44 mm, height 16 mm;
sapphire crystal, transparent case back; water-
resistant to 5 atm
Band: reptile skin, folding clasp
Price: $25,100

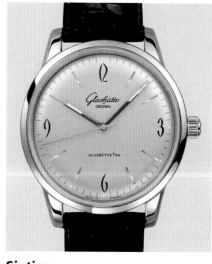

Seventies Chronograph Panorama Date

Reference number: 1-37-02-03-02-30
Movement: automatic, GO Caliber 37-02; ø 31.6 mm, height 8 mm; 65 jewels, 28,800 vph; screw balance with 4 gold regulating screws, swan-neck fine adjustment; mainplate with Glashütte stripes finish, blued screws, skeletonized rotor with gold oscillating weight; 70-hour power reserve
Functions: hours, minutes, subsidiary seconds; power reserve indicator; flyback chronograph; panorama date
Case: stainless steel, 40 x 40 mm, height 13.5 mm; transparent case back; water-resistant to 10 atm
Band: reptile skin, folding clasp
Price: $14,900

Seventies Panorama Date

Reference number: 2-39-47-12-12-14
Movement: automatic, GO Caliber 39-47; ø 30.95 mm, height 5.9 mm; 39 jewels; 28,800 vph; swan-neck fine adjustment, three-quarter plate with Glashütte stripe, skeletonized rotor with gold oscillating weight; 40-hour power reserve
Functions: hours, minutes, sweep seconds; panorama date
Case: stainless steel, 40 x 40 mm, height 11.5 mm; sapphire crystal; transparent case back; screw-in crown; water-resistant to 10 atm
Band: stainless steel, folding clasp
Price: $11,100
Variations: blue or silver dial; reptile skin or rubber strap ($10,100)

Sixties

Reference number: 1-39-52-01-02-04
Movement: automatic, GO Caliber 39-52; ø 26 mm, height 4.3 mm; 25 jewels; 28,800 vph; 40-hour power reserve
Functions: hours, minutes, sweep seconds
Case: stainless steel, ø 39 mm, height 9.4 mm; sapphire crystal; transparent case back
Band: reptile skin, buckle
Price: $7,100
Variations: black or blue dial ($7,100); rose gold ($14,300)

Lady Serenade

Reference number: 1-39-22-14-11-44
Movement: automatic, GO Caliber 39-22; ø 26 mm, height 4.3 mm; 25 jewels; 28,800 vph; three-quarter plate, swan-neck fine adjustment, skeletonized rotor; 40-hour power reserve
Functions: hours, minutes, sweep seconds; date
Case: rose gold, ø 36 mm, height 10.2 mm; bezel set with 52 brilliant-cut diamonds, sapphire crystal; transparent case back; water-resistant to 5 atm
Band: reptile skin, buckle
Remarks: mother-of-pearl dial set with brilliant-cut diamonds
Price: $26,300
Variations: without diamond bezel ($20,000); various bands and dials with stainless steel case ($7,100)

PanoMatic Luna

Reference number: 1-90-12-01-12-04
Movement: automatic, GO Caliber 90-12; ø 32.6 mm, height 7 mm; 47 jewels; 28,800 vph; 42-hour power reserve
Functions: hours, minutes, subsidiary seconds; panorama date; moon phase
Case: stainless steel, ø 39.4 mm, height 12 mm; bezel set with 64 brilliant-cut diamonds, sapphire crystal, transparent case back; water-resistant to 3 atm
Band: rubber, buckle
Price: $19,800
Variations: reptile skin band ($19,800); dark mother-of-pearl dial ($19,800)

Pavonina

Reference number: 1-03-01-05-34-30
Movement: quartz
Functions: hours, minutes; date
Case: white gold, 31 x 31 mm, height 7.5 mm; sapphire crystal; water-resistant to 5 atm
Band: satin, buckle
Remarks: set with 513 brilliant-cut diamonds, only available in Glashütte Original boutiques
Price: $41,400
Variations: various bands, dials and cases (from $4,900)

Caliber 37

Automatic; single barrel spring, 70-hour power reserve

Functions: hours, minutes, subsidiary seconds; power reserve indicator; flyback chronograph; panorama date

Diameter: 31.6 mm; **Height:** 8 mm; **Jewels:** 65

Balance: screw balance with 4 gold regulating screws

Frequency: 28,800 vph

Balance spring: flat hairspring, swan-neck fine adjustment

Remarks: finely finished movement, beveled edges, polished steel parts, blued screws, mainplate with Glashütte ribbing, skeletonized rotor with 21 kt gold oscillating mass

Caliber 39

Automatic; 40-hour power reserve

Functions: hours, minutes, sweep seconds (base caliber)

Diameter: 26.2 mm; **Height:** 4.3 mm

Jewels: 25

Frequency: 28,800 vph

Balance spring: flat hairspring, swan-neck fine adjustment

Shock protection: Incabloc

Related calibers: 39-55 (GMT, 40 jewels); 39-52 (automatic, 25 jewels); 39-50 (perpetual calendar, 48 jewels); 39-41/39-42 (panorama date, 44 jewels); 39-31 (chronograph, 51 jewels); 39-21/39-22 (date, 25 jewels)

Caliber 58-01

Manually wound; approx. 44-hour power reserve, second reset when crown is pulled allows precise setting of minutes and seconds

Functions: hours (off-center), minutes (off-center), subsidiary seconds; date (retrograde); power reserve indication with planetary gear; large date

Diameter: 35 mm; **Height:** 6.5 mm; **Jewels:** 58

Balance: screw balance with 18 weighted screws

Frequency: 28,800 vph

Remarks: components finely finished, beveled edges, polished steel parts, screw-mounted gold chatons, blued screws, swan-neck fine adjustment, three-quarter plate with Glashütte ribbing, hand-engraved balance cock

Caliber 60

Manually wound; single spring barrel, 42-hour power reserve

Functions: hours, minutes, subsidiary seconds; chronograph with flyback and countdown function; acoustic signal via gong; large date

Diameter: 32.2 mm; **Height:** 7.2 mm; **Jewels:** 54

Balance: screw balance with 18 gold screws

Frequency: 28,800 vph; **Balance spring:** flat hairspring, swan-neck fine adjustment

Remarks: components finely finished; beveled edges, polished steel parts, screw-mounted gold chatons, blued screws, winding wheels with double sunburst decoration, bridges and cocks with Glashütte ribbing, hand-engraved balance cock

Caliber 61

Manually wound; 42-hour power reserve

Functions: hours, minutes, subsidiary seconds; chronograph with flyback function; panorama date

Diameter: 32.2 mm; **Height:** 7.2 mm

Jewels: 41

Balance: screw balance with 18 gold screws

Frequency: 28,800 vph

Balance spring: flat hairspring, swan-neck fine adjustment

Remarks: components finely finished, beveled edges, polished steel parts, screw-mounted gold chatons, blued screws, winding wheels with double sunburst pattern, bridges and cocks decorated with Glashütte ribbing, hand-engraved balance cock

Caliber 65

Manually wound; single spring barrel, 42-hour power reserve

Functions: hours (off-center), minutes (off-center), subsidiary seconds; power reserve indication

Diameter: 32.2 mm

Height: 6.1 mm

Jewels: 48

Balance: screw balance with 18 weighted screws

Frequency: 28,800 vph

Balance spring: flat hairspring, duplex swan-neck fine adjustment (for rate and beat)

Remarks: components finely finished, beveled edges, polished steel parts, screw-mounted gold chatons, blued screws

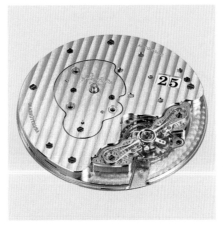

Caliber 90

Automatic; single spring barrel, 42-hour power reserve

Functions: hours, minutes (off-center), sweep seconds; panorama date; moon phase
Diameter: 32.6 mm; **Height:** 7 mm
Jewels: 41, 47, or 61; **Frequency:** 28,800 vph
Balance: screw balance with 18 gold screws
Balance spring: flat hairspring, duplex swan-neck fine adjustment (for rate and beat)
Shock protection: Incabloc
Remarks: components finely finished; hand-engraved balance cock; beveled edges, polished steel parts; three-quarter plate with Glashütte ribbing; off-center skeletonized rotor with 21 kt gold oscillating weight

Caliber 91-02

Automatic; inverted movement with rate regulator on dial side; single spring barrel; 42-hour power reserve
Functions: hours and minutes (off-center), subsidiary seconds; panorama date
Diameter: 38.2 mm; **Height:** 7.1 mm
Jewels: 49
Balance: screw balance with 18 weighted screws
Frequency: 28,800 vph
Balance spring: flat hairspring, duplex swan-neck fine adjustment (for rate and beat)
Shock protection: Incabloc
Remarks: finely finished movement, beveled edges, polished steel parts, three-quarter plate with blued screws, with côtes de Genève, skeletonized rotor with 21 kt gold oscillating mass, hand-engraved balance bridge

Caliber 93-02

Automatic; flying tourbillon, single spring barrel, 48-hour power reserve
Functions: hours, minutes (off-center), subsidiary seconds (on tourbillon cage); panorama date; moon phase
Diameter: 32.2 mm; **Height:** 7.65 mm
Jewels: 48
Balance: screw balance with 18 weighted screws in rotating frame
Frequency: 21,600 vph
Balance spring: flat hairspring
Remarks: finely finished movement, hand-engraved balance cock, beveled edges, polished steel parts, mainplate with Glashütte ribbing; oscillating, eccentric, skeletonized, 21 kt gold weight

Caliber 94-03

Automatic; flying tourbillon; single spring barrel, 48-hour power reserve
Functions: hours, minutes, subsidiary seconds (on tourbillon cage); panorama date
Diameter: 32.2 mm
Height: 7.65 mm
Jewels: 50
Balance: screw balance with 18 weighted screws in rotating frame
Frequency: 21,600 vph
Balance spring: flat hairspring
Remarks: finely finished movement, beveled edges, polished steel parts, mainplate with Glashütte ribbing; oscillating, eccentric, skeletonized, 21 kt gold weight

Caliber 96-01

Automatic; twin spring barrel, 2-speed bidirectional winding via stepped reduction gear, 42-hour power reserve
Functions: hours and minutes (off-center), subsidiary seconds; 2-digit counter (pusher-controlled, forward and backward); split-seconds chronograph with flyback function; large date
Diameter: 32.2 mm; **Height:** 8.9 mm; **Jewels:** 72
Balance: screw balance with 18 gold weight screws
Frequency: 28,800 vph
Balance spring: flat hairspring, swan-neck fine adjustment; **Shock protection:** Incabloc
Remarks: separate wheel bridges for winding and chronograph, finely finished, beveled edges, polished steel parts, screwed-in gold chatons, blued screws, hand-engraved balance cock

Caliber 100

Automatic; skeletonized rotor; reset mechanism for second hand via button on case; 55-hour power reserve
Functions: hours, minutes, sweep seconds; panorama date
Diameter: 31.15 mm
Height: 7.1 mm
Jewels: 59
Balance: screw balance with 18 gold screws
Frequency: 28,800 vph
Balance spring: flat hairspring
Related calibers: 100-01 (power reserve display); 100-02 (perpetual calendar); 100-03 (large date); 100-04 (moon phase); 100-05 (53 weeks); 100-06 (full calendar, moon phase)

Graham

Boulevard des Eplatures 38
CH-2300 La Chaux-de-Fonds
Switzerland

Tel.:
01141-32-910-9888

Fax:
01141-32-910-9889

E-Mail:
info@graham1695.com

Website:
www.graham1695.com

Founded:
1995

Number of employees:
approx. 30

Annual production:
5,000–7,000 watches

U.S. distributor:
Graham USA
510 W. 6th Street, Suite 309
Los Angeles, CA 90014
213-622-1716

Most important collections:
Tourbillograph, Chronofighter, Silverstone,
Swordfish

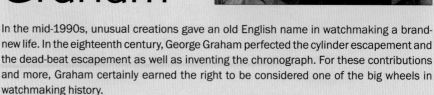

Graham

In the mid-1990s, unusual creations gave an old English name in watchmaking a brand-new life. In the eighteenth century, George Graham perfected the cylinder escapement and the dead-beat escapement as well as inventing the chronograph. For these contributions and more, Graham certainly earned the right to be considered one of the big wheels in watchmaking history.

Despite his merits in the development of precision timekeeping, it was the mechanism he invented to measure short times—the chronograph—that became the trademark of his wristwatch company. To this day, the fundamental principle of the chronograph hasn't changed at all: A second set of hands can be engaged to or disengaged from the constant flow of energy of the movement. Given The British Masters' aim to honor this English inventor, it is certainly no surprise that the Graham collection includes quite a number of fascinating chronograph variations.

In 2000, the company released its Chronofighter, whose striking thumb-controlled lever mechanism—a modern twist on a function designed for WW II British fighter pilots, who couldn't activate the crown button of their flight chronographs with their thick gloves on—is a perfect example of why luxury watches are one of the male world's most beloved toys. Recently, Graham has also added comparatively conventionally designed watches to its collection. For lovers of special pieces, there are the models of the Geo.Graham series. It was the name used by the brilliant watchmaker-inventor, and The Moon, developed in collaboration with Christophe Claret, is a perfect exemplar of the line featuring a beautifully finished flying tourbillon with a stunning retrograde moon phase.

Geo.Graham Tourbillon Orrery

Reference number: 2GGBP.B01A
Movement: manually wound, Graham Caliber G1800 (Christophe Claret base); ø 39 mm, height 10.5 mm; 35 jewels; 21,600 vph; 1-minute tourbillon, mechanical model of solar system with sculptural planets, 2 spring barrels; côtes de Genève; 72-hour power reserve
Functions: hours, minutes, (off-center); 100-year calendar with date and month indicator, zodiac and year display (case back); sculptural planets
Case: red gold, ø 48 mm, height 17.6 mm; sapphire crystal; transparent case back; water-resistant to 5 atm
Band: reptile skin, buckle
Price: on request; limited to 20 pieces

Geo.Graham "The Moon"

Reference number: 2GGAW.B01A.C154Y
Movement: manually wound, Graham Caliber G1769; ø 31.2 mm, height 8 mm; 29 jewels; 21,600 vph; flying 1-minute tourbillon; 96-hour power reserve
Functions: hours, minutes, subsidiary seconds (on tourbillon cage); moon phase
Case: white gold, ø 46 mm, height 17 mm; sapphire crystal; transparent case back; cabochon on crown; water-resistant to 3 atm
Band: reptile skin, folding clasp
Remarks: dial set with 68 diamonds
Price: on request; limited to 8 pieces

Chronofighter Oversize Black Sahara

Reference number: 2CCAU.B02A.T13N
Movement: automatic, Graham Caliber G 1747; ø 30 mm, height 8 mm; 25 jewels; 28,800 vph; 48-hour power reserve
Functions: hours, minutes, subsidiary seconds; chronograph; date
Case: stainless steel with black PVD coating, ø 47 mm, height 15 mm; ceramic bezel, sapphire crystal; transparent case back; crown, pusher, and carbon finger lever on left; water-resistant to 10 atm
Band: textile, ceramic buckle
Price: $6,900

Silverstone RS Endurance 12H

Reference number: 2STCB.B04A.K98H
Movement: automatic, Graham Caliber G1735; ø 30 mm, height 7.9 mm; 25 jewels; 28,800 vph; 46-hour power reserve
Functions: hours, minutes, subsidiary seconds; chronograph; date
Case: stainless steel with black PVD coating, ø 46 mm, height 15 mm; ceramic bezel with aluminum ring, sapphire crystal; transparent case back; crown secured with bayonet fixing; water-resistant to 10 atm
Band: rubber, folding clasp
Price: $10,430

Chronofighter Oversize Black Arrow

Reference number: 2CCAU.G02A.K94N
Movement: automatic, Graham Caliber G 1747; ø 30 mm, height 8 mm; 25 jewels; 28,800 vph; 48-hour power reserve
Functions: hours, minutes, subsidiary seconds; chronograph; date
Case: stainless steel with black PVD coating; ø 47 mm, height 15 mm; ceramic bezel, sapphire crystal; transparent case back; crown, pusher, and carbon finger lever on left; water-resistant to 10 atm
Band: rubber, ceramic buckle
Price: $8,050

Chronofighter Oversize Superlight Carbon

Reference number: 2CCBK.B11A.K95K
Movement: automatic, Graham Caliber G 1747; ø 30 mm, height 8 mm; 25 jewels; 28,800 vph; 48-hour power reserve
Functions: hours, minutes, subsidiary seconds; chronograph; date
Case: carbon nanofiber composite; ø 47 mm, height 15 mm; sapphire crystal; transparent case back; crown, pusher, and carbon finger lever on left; water-resistant to 10 atm
Band: rubber, buckle
Price: $11,550

Silverstone RS Endurance 24H

Reference number: 2STCB.B03A.K89H
Movement: automatic, Graham Caliber G1751; ø 30 mm; 25 jewels; 28,800 vph; single pusher for chronograph functions; chrono function control, separate, controllable 24-hour counter with flyback function; 48-hour power reserve
Functions: hours, minutes, subsidiary seconds; chronograph; date
Case: stainless steel with black DLC coating, ø 46 mm, height 15 mm; ceramic bezel with aluminum ring, sapphire crystal; transparent case back; crown with bayonet locking; water-resistant to 10 atm
Band: rubber, folding clasp
Price: $14,580

Chronofighter Oversize Prodive Professional

Reference number: 2CDAV.B01A.K81F
Movement: automatic, Graham Caliber G 1750; ø 37 mm, height 8.75 mm; 25 jewels; 28,800 vph; 48-hour power reserve
Functions: hours, minutes, subsidiary seconds; chronograph; date
Case: stainless steel, ø 45 mm, height 19 mm; unidirectional bezel with PVD coating, with 60-minute division, sapphire crystal; screw-in crown (with bayonet fixing), pusher, and finger lever on left; helium valve; water-resistant to 60 atm
Band: rubber, folding clasp
Remarks: Laboratoire Dubois SA diving certification
Price: $15,750; limited to 200 pieces

Swordfish Booster Iris

Reference number: 2SWBB.B39L.C125N
Movement: automatic, Graham Caliber G1710; ø 30 mm; 34 jewels; 28,800 vph; 48-hour power reserve
Functions: hours, minutes; chronograph
Case: stainless steel with iridescent PVD coating; ø 48 mm, height 15 mm; sapphire crystal; transparent case back; screw-in crown and pusher; water-resistant to 10 atm
Band: reptile skin, buckle
Remarks: black mother-of-pearl dial
Price: $17,500

Greubel Forsey SA
Eplatures-Grise 16
CH-2301 La Chaux-de-Fonds
Switzerland

Tel.:
01141-32-925-4545

Fax:
01141-32-925-4500

E-Mail:
info@greubelforsey.com

Website:
www.greubelforsey.com

Founded:
2004

Number of employees:
approx. 75

Annual production:
approx. 100 watches

U.S. distributor:
Time Art Distribution
550 Fifth Avenue
New York, NY 10036
212-221-5842
info@timeartdistribution.com

Greubel Forsey

Each year, at the SIHH, the journalists visit brands. But they congregate at the Greubel Forsey booth to take part in something close to a religious experience, an initiation into the esoteric art of *ultra-haute horlogerie*.

In 2004, when Alsatian Robert Greubel and Englishman Stephen Forsey presented a new movement at Baselworld, eyes snapped open: Their watch featured not one, but *two* tourbillon carriages working at a 30° incline. In their design, Forsey and Greubel not only took up the basic Abraham-Louis Breguet idea of cancelling out the deviations of the balance by the continuous rotation of the tourbillon cage, but they went further, creating a quadruple tourbillon.

Greubel Forsey's success as an independent brand has been remarkable. In 2010, they moved into new facilities at a renovated farmhouse between Le Locle and La Chaux-de-Fonds and a brand-new modern building. After capturing an Aiguille D'Or for the magical Double Tourbillon 30° and the Grand Prix d'Horlogerie in Geneva, these two specialists snatched up the top prize at the International Chronometry Competition in Le Locle for the Double Tourbillon 30°.

Greubel and Forsey continue to stun the highest-end fans with some spectacular pieces, like the Quadruple Tourbillon Secret, which shows the complex play of the tourbillons through the case back, and the Greubel Forsey GMT with the names of world cities and a huge floating globe. Nothing seems impossible to these two tourbillonists. Their first Art Piece came out in 2013, a most natural collaboration with British miniaturist Willard Wigan, who can sculpt the head of a pin. The special technical challenge for Greubel and Forsey: integrating a 20x magnifier into the watch. And they have promised more of the same.

GMT

Reference number: 9100 1776
Movement: manually wound, Caliber GF 05; ø 36.4 mm, height 9.8 mm; 50 jewels; 21,600 vph; 24-second tourbillon cage with variable inertia balance at 25°; 2 coaxial series-coupled barrels; 72-hour power reserve
Functions: hours, minutes, subsidiary seconds; 12-hour/24-hour world-time display; day/night indicator; summer/winter DST; power reserve
Case: pink gold, ø 43.5 mm, height 16.14 mm; transparent back; water-resistant to 3 atm
Band: reptile skin, folding clasp
Price: $605,000
Variations: white gold or platinum (on request)

Double Tourbillon Asymétrique

Reference number: 9100 1775
Movement: manually wound, Caliber GF 02A2; ø 36.4 mm, height 9.48 mm; 39 jewels, 21,600 vph; escapement with variable inertia; 4-minute tourbillon with inner 1-minute tourbillon inclined at 30°; 72-hour power reserve
Functions: hours, minutes, subsidiary seconds; 4-minute indication on large tourbillon; power reserve indicator
Case: white gold, ø 43.5 mm, height 16.13 mm; sapphire crystal; transparent case back; water-resistant to 3 atm
Band: reptile skin, folding clasp
Price: $560,000; limited to 11 pieces

Tourbillon 24 Secondes Contemporain

Reference number: 9100 1781
Movement: manually wound, Caliber GF 01s; ø 36.4 mm, height 10.9 mm; 40 jewels; 21,600 vph; 24-second tourbillon cage with variable inertia balance inclined at 25°, 72-hour power reserve
Functions: hours, minutes, subsidiary seconds; 24-second display on tourbillon cage; power reserve
Case: pink gold, ø 43.5 mm, height 15.2 mm; transparent back; water-resistant to 3 atm
Band: reptile skin, folding clasp
Price: on request; limited to 33 pieces
Variations: titanium movement; white gold with titanium movement

H. Moser & Cie.

Rundbuckstrasse 10
CH-8212 Neuhausen am Rheinfall
Switzerland

Tel.:
01141-52-674-0050

Fax:
01141-52-674-0055

E-Mail:
info@h-moser.com

Website:
www.h-moser.com

Founded:
1828

Number of employees:
50

Annual production:
approx. 1,000 watches

Distribution:
Please contact headquarters directly.

Most important collections/price range:
Endeavour Small Seconds / approx. $18,300;
Endeavour Centre Seconds / approx. $24,400
to $31,000; Endeavour Dual Time / approx.
$36,500 to $47,500; Endeavour Perpetual
Calendar / approx. $52,000 to $78,000;
Perpetual Moon / approx. $41,500 to $56,700;
Venturer Small Seconds / $19,500

H. Moser & Cie.

H. Moser & Cie. is not a new name in the watch industry: In Schaffhausen between 1820 and 1824 Heinrich Moser had learned watchmaking from his father, who, like his grandfather, fulfilled the role of "city watchmaker." Afterward, Moser went to Le Locle and, in 1825, founded his own company at twenty-one. Soon after, he moved to Saint Petersburg, where ambitious watchmakers were enjoying a good market. In 1828, H. Moser & Cie. was brought to life—a brand resuscitated in modern times by a group of investors and watch experts together with Moser's great-grandson, Roger Nicholas Balsiger.

Under the technical leadership of Dr. Jürgen Lange, H. Moser & Cie. has focused on the fundamentals. The company has made movements that contain a separate, interchangeable escapement module supporting the pallet lever, escape wheel, and balance. The latter is fitted with the Straumann spring, made by Precision Engineering, another one of the Moser Group companies—in the case of the Henry Double Hairspring watch, of course, the balance has two Straumann springs.

This small company has considerable technical know-how, which is probably what attracted MELB Holding, owners of Hautlence. Edouard Meylan became CEO of the brand in May 2013 and set out to streamline and refocus its energy on the core look and feel: understatement, soft tones, and subtle technicity. It's all in the name of the latest collection, the Venturer.

Venturer Small Seconds

Reference number: 2327-0402
Movement: manually wound, Moser Caliber HMC 327; ø 32 mm, height 4.4 mm; 28 jewels; 18,000 vph; 72-hour power reserve
Functions: hours, minutes, subsidiary seconds; power reserve indicator on case back
Case: pink gold, ø 39 mm, height 12.5 mm; sapphire crystal; transparent case back
Band: reptile skin, pink gold buckle
Price: $19,500
Variations: argenté or red gold fumé dial

Endeavour Dual Time

Reference number: 346.133-005
Movement: automatic, Moser Caliber HMC 346; ø 34 mm, height 6.5 mm; 29 jewels; 18,000 vph; interchangeable Moser escapement with Straumann hairspring; gold oscillating mass; 72-hour power reserve
Functions: hours, minutes, subsidiary seconds; additional 12-hour display (2nd time zone), day/night indicator
Case: rose gold, ø 40.8 mm, height 10.97 mm; sapphire crystal; transparent case back
Band: reptile skin, rose gold buckle
Price: $36,500
Variations: platinum ($56,700)

Endeavour Perpetual Calendar

Reference number: 341.501-022
Movement: manually wound, Moser Caliber HMC 341; ø 34 mm, height 5.8 mm; 28 jewels; 18,000 vph; interchangeable Moser escapement with Straumann hairspring; "flash calendar" functions correctable forward and backward; 168-hour power reserve
Functions: hours, minutes, subsidiary seconds; power reserve; perpetual calendar with large date, small month display in middle; leap year display (back)
Case: rose gold, ø 40.8 mm, height 11.05 mm; sapphire crystal; transparent case back
Price: $60,000
Variations: white gold ($60,000); platinum ($78,000); Golden Edition ($123,000)

Endeavour Moon

Reference number: 348.901-015
Movement: manually wound, Moser Caliber
HMC 348; ø 34 mm, height 5.8 mm; 26 jewels;
18,000 vph; interchangeable Moser escapement
with Straumann hairspring; 168-hour power reserve
Functions: hours, minutes, sweep seconds; power
reserve indicator on case back; "eternal" moon
phase
Case: platinum, ø 40.8 mm, height 11.05 mm;
sapphire crystal; transparent case back
Band: reptile skin, platinum folding clasp
Price: $56,700
Variations: rose gold ($41,500)

Endeavour Centre Seconds

Reference number: 343.505-010
Movement: manually wound, Moser Caliber
HMC 343; ø 34 mm, height 5.8 mm; 28 jewels;
18,000 vph; interchangeable Moser escapement
with Straumann hairspring; 168-hour power reserve
Functions: hours, minutes, sweep seconds; power
reserve indicator on case back
Case: white gold, ø 40.8 mm, height 10.85 mm;
sapphire crystal; transparent case back
Band: alligator strap, white gold buckle
Price: $24,400
Variations: rose gold ($24,400)

Endeavour Small Seconds

Reference number: 321.131-021
Movement: manually wound, Moser Caliber
HMC 321; ø 32 mm, height 4.8 mm; 27 jewels;
18,000 vph; interchangeable Moser escapement
with Straumann hairspring; 72-hour power reserve
Functions: hours, minutes, subsidiary seconds;
power reserve indicator on case back
Case: pink gold, ø 38.8 mm, height 9.3 mm;
sapphire crystal; transparent case back
Band: reptile skin, pink gold buckle
Price: $18,300
Variations: white gold ($18,300)

Caliber HMC 341

Manually wound; interchangeable Moser escapement,
hardened gold pallet fork and escapement wheel; twin
spring barrels, "flash calendar"; 168-hour power reserve
Functions: hours, minutes, subsidiary seconds; power
reserve indicator; perpetual calendar with large date
and small month display in middle; leap year display
(back)
Diameter: 34 mm; **Height:** 5.8 mm
Jewels: 28
Balance: Moser balance wheel with gold screws
Frequency: 18,000 vph
Balance spring: Straumann with Breguet overcoil
Shock protection: Incabloc
Remarks: date adjustable forward and backward;
double-pull crown switch between crown rest positions

Caliber HMC 346

Automatic, interchangeable Moser escapement,
pallet fork and escapement wheel of hardened gold;
pure gold rotor; 72-hour power reserve
Functions: hours, minutes, subsidiary seconds;
additional 12-hour display (2nd time zone), day/
night indicator
Diameter: 34 mm
Height: 6.51 mm
Jewels: 29
Balance: Moser balance wheel with gold screws
Frequency: 18,000 vph
Balance spring: Straumann with Breguet overcoil
Shock protection: Incabloc
Remarks: double-pull crown mechanism for easy
switching of crown position

Caliber HMC 327

Manually wound, silicon anchor with ruby pallets
and silicon escapement hours power reserve
Functions: hours, minutes, subsidiary seconds;
power reserve indicator on case back
Diameter: 32 mm
Height: 4.4 mm
Jewels: 28
Balance: Moser balance wheel with gold screws
Frequency: 18,000 vph
Balance spring: Straumann with Breguet overcoil
Shock protection: Incabloc

Habring Uhrentechnik OG

Hauptplatz 16
A-9100 Völkermarkt
Austria

Tel.:
01143-4232-51-300

Fax:
01143-4232-51-300-4

E-Mail:
habring@aon.at

Website:
www.habring2.com; www.habring.com

Founded:
1997

Number of employees:
4

Annual production:
100 watches

U.S. distributors:
Martin Pulli (USA-East)
215-508-4610
www.martinpulli.com
Passion Fine Jewelry (USA-West)
858-794-8000
www.passionfinejewelry.com

Most important collections/price range:
Time Only / from $3,850; Jumping Second /
from $5,250; Doppel 3 / from $9,150;
Chrono COS / from $7,850

Habring²

Fine mechanical works of art are created containing smaller and larger complications in a small workshop in Austria's Völkermarkt, where the name Habring² stands for an unusual joint project. "We only come in a set," Maria Kristina Habring jokes. Her husband, Richard, adds with a grin, "You get double for your money here." The couple's first watch labeled with their own name came out in 2004: a simple, congenial three-handed watch based on a refined and unostentatiously decorated ETA pocket watch movement, the Unitas 6498-1. In connoisseur circles the news spread like wildfire that exceptional quality down to the smallest detail was hidden behind its inconspicuous specifications.

Since then, they have put their efforts into such projects as completely revamping the Time Only, which is powered by brand-new base movement Caliber A09. All the little details that differentiate this caliber are either especially commissioned or are made in-house. Caliber A09, jokingly referred to as "the tractor" by the Habrings, is available both as a manually wound movement (A09M) and a bidirectionally wound automatic with an exclusive gear system. Its sporty incarnation drives a pilot's watch. Also more or less in-house are the components of the Seconde Foudroyante. Because the drive needs a lot of energy, the foudroyante mechanism has been given its own spring barrel. In the Caliber A07F, the eighth of a second is driven by a gear train that is directly coupled with the movement without surrendering any reliability, power reserve, or amplitude.

For the twentieth anniversary of the IWC double chronograph, Habring² has built a limited, improved edition. The movement, based on the ETA 7750 "Valjoux," was conceived in 1991/1992 with an additional module between the chronograph and automatic winder. Richard was working as a designer at IWC back then. For 2013, the horological couple followed up the prizewinning Doppel 2 chronograph with the Doppel 3, whose pushers are arranged in traditional style at 10 and 2.

Doppel 3

Reference number: Doppel 3
Movement: manually wound, Caliber A08MR-MONO; ø 30 mm, height 8.4 mm; 23 jewels; 28,800 vph; Triovis fine adjustment; 48-hour power reserve
Functions: hours, minutes, subsidiary seconds; split-seconds chronograph
Case: titanium, ø 42 mm, height 13 mm; sapphire crystal; transparent case back; water-resistant to 5 atm
Band: leather, buckle
Remarks: limited to 20 pieces
Price: $11,250
Variations: stainless steel ($9,550)

Doppel 3

Reference number: Doppel 3
Movement: manually wound, Caliber A08MR-MONO; ø 30 mm, height 8.4 mm; 23 jewels; 28,800 vph; Triovis fine adjustment; 48-hour power reserve
Functions: hours, minutes, subsidiary seconds; split-seconds chronograph
Case: stainless steel, ø 42 mm, height 13 mm; sapphire crystal; transparent case back; water-resistant to 5 atm
Band: leather, buckle
Remarks: limited to 20 pieces
Price: $9,550
Variations: various dial designs

Chrono COS

Reference number: Chrono COS
Movement: automatic, Caliber A08COS; ø 30 mm, height 7.9 mm; 25 jewels; 28,800 vph; Triovis fine adjustment; crown control of chronograph functions ("Crown Operation System")
Functions: hours, minutes, subsidiary seconds; chronograph
Case: stainless steel, ø 42 mm, height 13 mm; sapphire crystal; transparent case back; water-resistant to 5 atm
Band: calf leather, buckle
Price: $8,250
Variations: titanium ($9,700); manual winding ($8,250); various dials

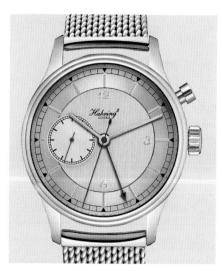

Chrono ZM

Reference number: Chrono ZM
Movement: manually wound, Caliber A08MZM-MONO; ø 30 mm, height 7.9 mm; 17 jewels; 28,800 vph; Triovis fine adjustment; central minute totalizer
Functions: hours, minutes, subsidiary seconds; chronograph
Case: stainless steel, ø 42 mm, height 13 mm; sapphire crystal; transparent case back; water-resistant to 5 atm
Band: stainless steel Milanese mesh, folding clasp
Price: $6,550

Time Only Pilot

Reference number: Time Only Pilot
Movement: manually wound, Caliber A09M; ø 30 mm, height 6.25 mm; 17 jewels; 48-hour power reserve
Functions: hours, minutes, subsidiary seconds
Case: stainless steel, ø 42 mm, height 13 mm; sapphire crystal; transparent case back; water-resistant to 5 atm
Band: calf leather, buckle
Price: $4,150
Variations: automatic ($4,550)

Time Date Pilot

Reference number: Time Date Pilot
Movement: automatic, Caliber A09D; ø 30 mm, height 7.25 mm; 24 jewels; 28,800 vph; 48-hour power reserve
Functions: hours, minutes, subsidiary seconds; date
Case: stainless steel, ø 42 mm, height 13 mm; sapphire crystal; transparent case back; water-resistant to 5 atm
Band: calf leather, buckle
Price: $5,150
Variations: date display ($4,550); manual winding ($4,150)

Jumping Second Pilot

Reference number: Jumping Second Pilot
Movement: manually wound, Caliber A09MS; ø 36.6 mm, height 7 mm; 20 jewels; 28,800 vph; Triovis fine adjustment
Functions: hours, minutes, sweep dead beat seconds
Case: stainless steel, ø 42 mm, height 13 mm; sapphire crystal; transparent case back; water-resistant to 5 atm
Band: calf leather, buckle
Price: $5,550
Variations: automatic ($5,550); various dials

Jumping Second Date

Reference number: Jumping Second Date
Movement: automatic, Caliber A09MSD; ø 30 mm, height 7.9 mm; 24 jewels; 28,800 vph
Functions: hours, minutes, sweep seconds (jumping); date
Case: stainless steel, ø 42 mm, sapphire crystal; transparent case back
Band: calf leather, buckle
Price: $6,150
Variations: date display ($5,550); various dials

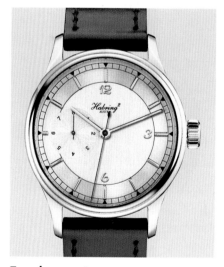

Foudroyante

Reference number: Foudroyante
Movement: manually wound, Caliber A09MF; ø 30 mm, height 7 mm; 24 jewels; 28,800 vph; Triovis fine adjustment
Functions: hours, minutes, dead beat seconds, eighth of a second display (flashing second or "foudroyante")
Case: stainless steel, ø 42 mm, height 13 mm; sapphire crystal; transparent case back; water-resistant to 5 atm
Band: leather, buckle
Price: $6,950
Variations: automatic ($7,500); power reserve display ($8,350); various dials

Hamilton International Ltd.

Mattenstrasse 149
CH-2503 Biel/Bienne
Switzerland

Tel.:
01141-32-343-4004

Fax:
01141-32-343-4006

Email:
info@hamiltonwatch.com

Website:
www.hamiltonwatch.com

Founded:
1892

U.S. distributor:
Hamilton
The Swatch Group, Inc.
1200 Harbor Boulevard
Weehawken, NJ 07087
201-271-1400
www.hamilton-watch.com

Price range:
between approx. $500 and $2,200

Hamilton

The Hamilton Watch Co. was founded in 1892 in Lancaster, Pennsylvania, and, within a very brief period, grew into one of the world's largest *manufactures*. Around the turn of the twentieth century, every second railway employee in the United States was carrying a Hamilton watch in his pocket, not only to make sure the trains were running punctually, but also to assist in coordinating them and organizing schedules. And during World War II, the American army officers' kits included a service Hamilton.

Hamilton is the sole survivor of the large U.S. watchmakers—if only as a brand within the Swiss Swatch Group. At one time, Hamilton had itself owned a piece of the Swiss watchmaking industry in the form of the Büren brand in the 1960s and 1970s. As part of a joint venture with Heuer-Leonidas, Breitling, and Dubois Dépraz, Hamilton-Büren also made a significant contribution to the development of the automatic chronograph. Just prior in its history, the tuning fork watch pioneer was all the rage when it took the new movement technology and housed it in a modern case created by renowned industrial designer Richard Arbib. The triangular Ventura hit the watch-world ground running in 1957, in what was truly a frenzy of innovation. The American spirit of freedom and belief in progress this model embodies, something evoked in Hamilton's current marketing, are taken quite seriously by its designers—even those working in Biel, Switzerland. The collection today is dominated by models that recall the glory days of the 1950s and 1960s. As such, they are absolutely trendy.

Railroad Auto Chrono

Reference number: H40656731
Movement: automatic, Hamilton Caliber H-21 (base ETA 7750); ø 30 mm, height 7.9 mm; 25 jewels; 28,800 vph; 60-hour power reserve
Functions: hours, minutes, subsidiary seconds; chronograph; date
Case: stainless steel, ø 44 mm; sapphire crystal; transparent case back; water-resistant to 5 atm
Band: calf leather, folding clasp
Price: $1,995

Pan Europ Day-Date

Reference number: H35405741
Movement: automatic, Hamilton Caliber H30 (base ETA 2834-2); ø 25.6 mm, height 5.05 mm; 29 jewels; 28,800 vph; 80-hour power reserve
Functions: hours, minutes, sweep seconds; date, weekday
Case: stainless steel, ø 42 mm; unidirectional bezel with 60-minute divisions, sapphire crystal; transparent case back; water-resistant to 5 atm
Band: calf leather, folding clasp
Remarks: leather band comes with NATO strap and changing tool
Price: $1,195

Khaki Takeoff Limited Edition

Reference number: H76786735
Movement: automatic, Hamilton Caliber H-31 (base ETA 7753); ø 30 mm, height 7.9 mm; 27 jewels; 28,800 vph; 60-hour power reserve
Functions: hours, minutes, subsidiary seconds; chronograph; date
Case: stainless steel with black PVD coating, ø 46.3 mm; bidirectional bezel with 60-minute division, sapphire crystal; transparent case back; water-resistant to 5 atm
Band: calf leather, buckle
Price: $3,295

Khaki X-Wind Limited Edition

Reference number: H77766131
Movement: automatic, Hamilton Caliber H-21;
ø 30 mm, height 7.9 mm; 25 jewels; 28,800 vph;
60-hour power reserve
Functions: hours, minutes, subsidiary seconds;
chronograph; date, weekday
Case: stainless steel, ø 45 mm; inner ring rotated
with crown, with integrated slide rule to measure
flight altitude; sapphire crystal; transparent case
back; water-resistant to 10 atm
Band: stainless steel, folding clasp
Price: $2,395

Khaki Pilot Pioneer Auto Aluminum

Reference number: H80405865
Movement: automatic, Hamilton Caliber H-10 (base
ETA 2824-2); ø 25.6 mm, height 4.6 mm; 25 jewels;
28,800 vph; 80-hour power reserve
Functions: hours, minutes, sweep seconds; date
Case: aluminum, ø 41 mm; crown-adjustable inner
bezel with 60-minute divisions, sapphire crystal;
water-resistant to 10 atm
Band: textile, buckle
Price: $1,145

Khaki Field Day-Date

Reference number: H70505833
Movement: automatic, Hamilton Caliber H-30 (base
ETA 2834-2); ø 25.6 mm, height 5.05 mm; 29
jewels; 28,800 vph; 80-hour power reserve
Functions: hours, minutes, sweep seconds; date,
weekday
Case: stainless steel, ø 42 mm; sapphire crystal;
transparent case back; water-resistant to 5 atm
Band: suede, buckle
Price: $895

Spirit of Liberty

Reference number: H42445551
Movement: automatic, Hamilton Caliber H-10 (base
ETA 2824-2); ø 25.6 mm, height 4.6 mm; 25 jewels;
28,800 vph; 80-hour power reserve
Functions: hours, minutes, sweep seconds; date
Case: stainless steel with rose gold-colored PVD
coating, ø 42 mm, height 14.75 mm; sapphire
crystal; water-resistant to 5 atm
Band: calf leather, folding clasp
Price: $1,145

Jazzmaster Auto Chrono

Reference number: H32546781
Movement: automatic, Hamilton Caliber H-21 (base
ETA 7750); ø 30 mm, height 7.9 mm; 25 jewels;
28,800 vph; 60-hour power reserve
Functions: hours, minutes, subsidiary seconds;
chronograph; date
Case: stainless steel with rose gold-colored PVD
coating, ø 42 mm, height 15.23 mm; sapphire
crystal; transparent case back; water-resistant to
10 atm
Band: calf leather, buckle
Price: $1,195

Bagley

Reference number: H12451855
Movement: quartz
Functions: hours, minutes, subsidiary seconds
Case: stainless steel, 30 x 36 mm; sapphire crystal;
water-resistant to 5 atm
Band: ostrich leather, buckle
Price: $695

Hanhart AG
Hauptstrasse 33
D-78148 Gütenbach
Germany

Tel.:
01149-7723-93-44-0

Fax:
01149-7723-93-44-0

E-Mail:
info@hanhart.de

Website:
www.hanhart.com

Founded:
1882 in Diessenhofen, Switzerland; operating
in Germany since 1902

Number of employees:
31

Annual production:
approx. 1,000 chronographs and 150,000
stopwatches

Distribution:
Please contact the main office in Germany for
information

Most important collections/price range:
Mechanical stopwatches / from approx.
$660; Pioneer / from approx. $2,550;
Primus / from approx. $6,600

Hanhart

In 2012, Hanhart celebrated its 130th anniversary. But its reputation really goes back to the twenties and thirties. At the time, the brand manufactured affordable and robust stopwatches, pocket watches, and chronograph wristwatches. These core timepieces were what the fans of instrument watches wanted, and so they were thrilled as the company slowly abandoned its quartz dabbling of the eighties and reset its sights on the brand's rich and honorable tradition. A new collection was in the wings, raising expectations of great things to come. Support by the shareholding Gaydoul Group provided the financial backbone to get things moving.

The first step was to move company headquarters to the Swiss town of Diessenhofen, leaving the factory and technical offices in the Black Forest town of Gütenbach, Germany. The company's motto has thus become "German engineering, Swiss made," and its goal is expanding exports into new key markets using three solid collections: two chronographs, the Pioneer and Primus, and the ClassicTimer stopwatches.

In spite of effort and money, however, Hanhart ran into some difficulties carving out a path for itself. After some fits and starts, the brand, now in the hands of Jan Endöcs, has moved back to the Black Forest. The characteristic red start/stop pusher continues to grace the new collections, even on the bi-compax chronos of the Racemasters, which come with a smooth bezel.

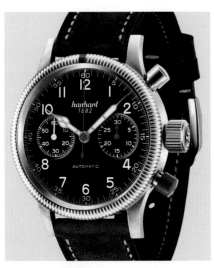

Pioneer Mk II

Reference number: 716.210-0110
Movement: automatic, Caliber HAN3703 (base ETA Caliber 7753); ø 30 mm, height 7.9 mm; 27 jewels; 28,800 vph; 42-hour power reserve
Functions: hours, minutes, subsidiary seconds; chronograph
Case: stainless steel, ø 40 mm, height 15 mm; bidirectional bezel with reference marker, sapphire crystal; water-resistant to 10 atm
Band: calf leather, buckle
Price: $3,850
Variations: bright dial; stainless steel bracelet ($4,650)

Pioneer Racemaster GTM

Reference number: 737.670-0010
Movement: automatic, Caliber HAN4212 (base Sellita SW500); ø 30 mm, height 7.9 mm; 31 jewels; 28,800 vph; single pusher for chronograph functions; 42-hour power reserve
Functions: hours, minutes, subsidiary seconds; chronograph
Case: stainless steel, ø 45 mm, height 16 mm; sapphire crystal, water-resistant to 10 atm
Band: calf leather, buckle
Price: $8,800

Primus Desert Pilot

Reference number: 740.250-3720
Movement: automatic, Caliber HAN3809 (base Sellita SW500); ø 30 mm, height 7.9 mm; 28 jewels; 28,800 vph
Functions: hours, minutes, subsidiary seconds; chronograph; date
Case: stainless steel, ø 44 mm, height 15 mm; sapphire crystal; transparent case back; screw-in crown; water-resistant to 10 atm
Band: textile, folding clasp
Remarks: mobile lugs
Price: $7,950
Variations: various bands and dials

Harry Winston

Swatch Group's purchase of the luxury brand Harry Winston in early 2013 for $1 billion came as something of a surprise. But then, banking on a proven high-end luxury brand would seem obvious. Founder Harry Winston (1896–1978) bought, recut, and set some of the twentieth century's greatest precious gems. He was succeeded by his son Ronald, also a gifted craftsman with several patents in precious metals processing.

It was Ronald who added watches to the company's portfolio, inaugurating two lines: one showcasing the finest precious gems to dovetail with the company's overall focus and one containing clever, complicated timepieces resulting in the stunning Opus line launched by Harry Winston Rare Timepieces. Each of the thirteen models has been developed in conjunction with one exceptional independent watchmaker per year in very small series. The roster of artist-engineers who have participated reads like a *Who's Who* of independent watchmaking, including François-Paul Journe, Vianney Halter, Felix Baumgartner, and Greubel Forsey all the way to Denis Giguet and Emmanuel Bouchet. For the Opus XIII, the brand tapped Ludovic Ballouard. An extremely complex movement flicks fifty-nine metal pins to show the minutes and eleven triangles to show the hours. At twelve and noon, the dial cover opens to reveal the Harry Winston logo.

In May 2013, Nayla Hayek, daughter of Swatch founder Nicolas Hayek, became brand CEO, suggesting that Harry Winston will be staying the course in ultra-high-end watches. A year later, the brand was already releasing its first new models, a feat it owes to the synergies within the group, notably the expertise of new sister brand Blancpain. But Harry Winston hasn't lost track of its stony past. In May 2014, it picked up a blue, pear-shaped diamond at an auction in Geneva: The "Winston Vivid Blue" cost over $23 million.

Harry Winston, Inc.
718 Fifth Avenue
New York, NY 10019
800-848-3948

Website:
www.harrywinston.com

Founded:
1989

Most important collections:
Avenue, Midnight, Premier, Ocean, Opus

Histoire de Tourbillon 5

Reference number: HCOMTT47RR001
Movement: manually wound, Harry Winston Caliber HW4303; ø 40.4 mm, height 17.3 mm; 57 jewels; 21,600 vph; triaxial tourbillon (45, 75, and 300 seconds rotation), variable inertia balance with gold adjustment screws; Philips end curve, 2 spring barrels, 50-hour power reserve
Functions: hours and minutes (off-center disc display), subsidiary seconds (on tourbillon cage); power reserve indicator
Case: rose gold, ø 47 mm, height 21.7 mm; sapphire crystal; transparent case back; water-resistant to 3 atm
Band: reptile skin, buckle
Price: $655,200; limited to 20 pieces

Project Z8

Reference number: OCEATZ44ZZ009
Movement: automatic, Harry Winston Caliber HW3502; ø 32 mm, height 5.2 mm; 32 jewels; 28,800 vph; balance-spring, skeletonized rotor in white gold, fine finishing with circular côtes de Genève
Functions: hours, minutes (off-center); additional 12-hour indicator (2nd time zone, retrograde); day/night indicator; date, shuriken-shaped power reserve indicator
Case: Zalium, ø 44.2 mm, height 21.7 mm; sapphire crystal; transparent case back; water-resistant to 10 atm
Band: rubber, buckle
Price: $20,300; limited to 300 pieces

Harry Winston Midnight Moon Phase Automatic 42mm

Reference number: MIDAMP42RR002
Movement: automatic, Harry Winston Caliber HW3202; ø 26.2 mm, height 5.37 mm; 28 jewels; 28,800 vph; balance-spring, skeletonized rotor in white gold, fine finishing with circular côtes de Genève
Functions: hours, minutes (off-center); date (retrograde); moon phase
Case: rose gold, ø 42.5 mm, height 10.6 mm; sapphire crystal; transparent case back; water-resistant to 3 atm
Band: reptile skin, buckle
Price: $28,400
Variations: white gold; various bands and dials

Premier Chronograph 40 mm

Reference number: PRNQCH40RR002
Movement: quartz
Functions: hours, minutes, subsidiary seconds; chronograph; date
Case: rose gold, ø 40 mm, height 9.5 mm; bezel set with 57 brilliant-cut diamonds, sapphire crystal; diamond on crown; water-resistant to 3 atm
Band: reptile skin, buckle, set with 42 brilliant-cut diamonds
Remarks: mother-of-pearl dial set with 135 brilliant-cut diamonds
Price: $48,100
Variations: various bands and dials

Premier Precious Marquetry 36 mm

Reference number: PRNQHM36WW015
Movement: quartz
Functions: hours, minutes
Case: white gold, ø 36 mm, height 9.5 mm; bezel set with 63 brilliant-cut diamonds, sapphire crystal; diamond on crown; water-resistant to 3 atm
Band: reptile skin, buckle
Remarks: dial with enamel pailloné and mother-of-pearl inlays and set with 11 pear-shape cabochon sapphires and 54 brilliant-cut diamonds
Price: $92,900

Harry Winston Avenue C Precious Marquetry

Reference number: AVCQHM19WW139
Movement: quartz
Functions: hours, minutes
Case: white gold, 19 x 39.5 mm, height 6.7 mm; bezel set with 43 brilliant-cut diamonds, sapphire crystal; water-resistant to 3 atm
Band: reptile skin, buckle
Remarks: dial with marquetry of various mother-of-pearl colors inlays and set with 44 brilliant-cut diamonds
Price: $41,500

Harry Winston Avenue Classic

Reference number: AVEQHM21WW283
Movement: quartz
Functions: hours, minutes, subsidiary seconds
Case: white gold, 21 x 36.1 mm, height 6.7 mm; bezel set with 29 brilliant-cut diamonds, sapphire crystal; diamond on crown; water-resistant to 3 atm
Band: reptile skin, folding clasp
Price: $37,600
Variations: various bands; rose gold

Harry Winston Avenue C Art Deco

Reference number: AVCQHM19WW130
Movement: quartz
Functions: hours, minutes
Case: white gold, 19 x 39.5 mm, height 7.8 mm; bezel set with 43 brilliant-cut diamonds, sapphire crystal; diamond on crown; water-resistant to 3 atm
Band: reptile skin, folding clasp
Price: $34,800
Variations: rose gold; various bands and dials

Harry Winston Avenue C Mini Lily Cluster

Reference number: AVCQHM16RR042
Movement: quartz
Functions: hours, minutes
Case: rose gold, 15.6 x 32.3 mm, height 9.5 mm; bezel set with 47 brilliant-cut diamonds, sapphire crystal; diamond on crown; water-resistant to 3 atm
Band: rose gold, folding clasp
Remarks: mother-of-pearl dial set with 34 brilliant-cut diamonds
Price: $31,100
Variations: white gold; various bands

HAUTLENCE
Rue Numa-Droz 150
2300 La Chaux-de-Fonds
Switzerland

Tel.:
01141-32-924-00-62

Fax:
01141-32-924-00-64

E-Mail:
info@hautlence.com

Website:
www.hautlence.com

Founded:
2004

Number of employees:
10

Annual production:
130 watches

U.S. distributor:
Westime
132 South Rodeo Drive, Fourth Floor
Beverly Hills, CA 90212
310-205-5555
info@westime.com
www.westime.com

Most important collections:
Origine, Avant-Garde, Concepts d'Exception

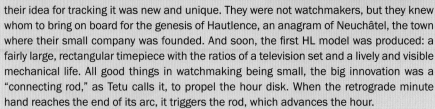

Hautlence

Time can be read in so many ways. Back in 2004, after spending years in the Swiss watch industry, Guillaume Tetu and Renaud de Retz decided that their idea for tracking it was new and unique. They were not watchmakers, but they knew whom to bring on board for the genesis of Hautlence, an anagram of Neuchâtel, the town where their small company was founded. And soon, the first HL model was produced: a fairly large, rectangular timepiece with the ratios of a television set and a lively and visible mechanical life. All good things in watchmaking being small, the big innovation was a "connecting rod," as Tetu calls it, to propel the hour disk. When the retrograde minute hand reaches the end of its arc, it triggers the rod, which advances the hour.

Having survived the Great Recession, Hautlence persists with fewer staff and without de Retz. The watches have evolved, developing shape and character. Design and mechanics are increasingly integrated, as inspiration from other industrial segments bears fruit. For the HLq, the movement has been reengineered for a round case. Instead of a tourbillon, Hautlence has found a way to have the whole escapement rotate four times a day.

In 2012, Hautlence became the first member of the brand-new MELB Holding, headed by Georges-Henri Meylan (formerly of Audemars Piguet) and former Breguet CFO Bill Muirhead. The experience and contacts of these two horological powerhouses have energized the brand. Besides opening outlets in Dubai and Los Angeles, Hautlence has refreshed its collection with the Avant-Garde series. The stark industrial look is now tempered with daubs of color, but the price is far more attractive to less-well-heeled collectors. Affordability was also one of the ideas behind the new Destination models, which offer the brand's typical steampunkish look but driven by a trusty Soprod engine, an excellent way of lowering costs while maintaining quality.

Destination 02

Movement: automatic, Soprod Caliber 9351/A10-2; ø 25.6 mm, height 5.1 mm; 25 jewels; 28,800 vph; côtes de Genève finishing; 42-hour power reserve
Functions: hours, minutes; large date; 2nd time zone on sapphire disk; day/night indicator
Case: titanium, 37 x 43.5 mm, height 13 mm; silvered opaline base dial; extra-hardened antireflective sapphire crystal; titanium case back with time zones; water-resistant to 3 atm
Band: reptile skin, folding buckle
Remarks: rhodium hour markers and blue Superluminova; honeycomb open-worked dial
Price: $21,400

Avant-Garde HL RQ 03

Movement: manually wound, in-house caliber; 32 jewels; 21,600 vph; hand-beveled bridges and connecting rods; côtes de Genève; 40-hour power reserve
Functions: jumping hour, retrograde minutes; jumping date with quick corrector
Case: DLC steel, black titanium, ø 44 mm, height 12.5 mm; polished DLC steel bezel, crown, and lugs; antireflective, beveled sapphire crystal; screwed-down sapphire case back; water-resistant to 3 atm
Band: black rubber, folding buckle
Remarks: mineral glass hour disc with rhodium-treated hour markers and orange Superluminova
Price: $35,800; limited to 88 pieces

HL2.4

Movement: automatic, in-house caliber with gear train and automatic winding system; ID HL2.3 on No. plate; 37.8 x 33.2 mm, height 12.35 mm; 18,000 vph; 92 jewels; rotating mobile bridge with oscillator; 2 spring barrels; 45-hour power reserve
Functions: half-trailing hours on chain, 3-4 seconds for change, retrograde minutes; power reserve indication
Case: titanium in satin, polished and microbille finishing; 50 x 42 mm, height 17.8 mm; 3D sapphire crystal; rose gold horns and case back screws; water-resistant to 3 atm
Band: reptile skin, folding buckle
Remarks: sapphire dial
Price: $192,500; limited to 28 pieces

M 29 Classic Kleine Sekunde

Since 1869, Mühle-Glashütte is all about precise measurement. Already at the end of the 19th century, Robert Mühle created measuring devices capable of measurement accuracy to within hundredths or even thousandths of millimetres. In order to read these values precisely, the millimetres were displayed by a small macro dial gauge, and the large micro dial gauge made the fractions of the measuring unit visible. The new M 29 Classic Kleine Sekunde invokes this design and reinvents it in the language of timepieces by Nautische Instrumente Mühle-Glashütte.

――――――――――――――――― For more information please contact: ―――――――――――――――――

Mühle-Glashütte USA • 727-896-8453 • www.muehle-glashuette.de

E.D. Marshall Jewelers Scottsdale, AZ | Topper Jewelers Burlingame, CA | Feldmar Watch Co. Los Angeles, CA | Leo Hamel Fine Jewelers San Diego, CA
Partita Custom Design San Francisco, CA | Ravits Watches & Jewelry San Francisco, CA | Right Time Denver & Highlands Ranch, CO | Exquisite Timepieces Naples, FL
Old Northeast Jewelers St. Petersburg & Tampa, FL | Little Treasury Jewelers Gambrills, MD | Continental Diamond Minneapolis, MN
Joseph Edwards New York, NY | Martin Pulli Phliadelphia, PA | Marvin Scott & Co. Yardley, PA | Jack Ryan Fine Jewelry Austin, TX
Timeless Luxury Watches Frisco, TX | Fox's Gem Shop Seattle, WA | Trident Jewels and Time St. Thomas, USVI

La Montre Hermès

Erlenstrasse 31A
CH-2555 Brügg
Switzerland

Tel.:
01141-32-366-7100

Fax:
01141-32-366-7101

E-Mail:
info@montre-hermes.ch

Website:
www.hermes.ch

Founded:
1978

Number of employees:
150

U.S. distributor:
Hermès of Paris, Inc.
55 East 59th Street
New York, NY 10022
800-441-4488
www.hermes.com

Most important collections/price range:
Arceau, Cape Cod, Clipper, Dressage, H-Our,
Kelly, Kelly 2, Medor / $2,150 to $34,000

Hermès

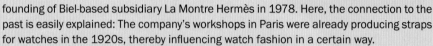

This company founded in Paris in 1837 by Thierry Hermès originally specialized in the robust leather accessories that gentlemen needed for travel: chiefly headgear for horses as well as bags and suitcases. Although, over time, Hermès has largely diversified its range of products—handbags, foulards, fashion, porcelain, glass, and gold jewelry are found in its portfolio—a link has always remained to its roots. The production of watches began with the founding of Biel-based subsidiary La Montre Hermès in 1978. Here, the connection to the past is easily explained: The company's workshops in Paris were already producing straps for watches in the 1920s, thereby influencing watch fashion in a certain way.

Unlike so many other manufacturers of lifestyle products, Hermès does not have its watches simply assembled by so-called private labelers, but instead has maintained its own little watch factory in Biel since the beginning. Some interesting little complications have been produced in collaboration with external designers, such as the unusual hand movements with varying speeds or "parking options."

In 2006, Hermès invested close to 25 million Swiss francs in its movement production, securing 25 percent of the Vaucher Manufacture's stock. This didn't particularly surprise insiders, especially since Hermès has been continuously investing in and intensifying the relationship since it began working with this arm of the Sandoz empire four years ago. La Montre Hermès is directly positioned at the mouth of a grand source of first-class movements—something that is reflected in the complicated watch collection the company is now offering. By the same token, as a brand it keeps to its roots, as shown by the new Arceau Bridon series with a bridoon at 12 o'clock serving as a strap holder.

Dressage "L'Heure Masquée"

Reference number: DR5.870.221/MHA
Movement: automatic, Hermès Caliber H1925; ø 32 mm, height 6.5 mm; 35 jewels; 28,800 vph; pressing crown makes hour hand appear from hiding place behind minute hand; 45-hour power reserve
Functions: hours (on demand), minutes; additional 24-hour display (2nd time zone; only on pressing crown)
Case: rose gold, ø 40.5 mm; sapphire crystal; water-resistant to 5 atm
Band: reptile skin, buckle
Price: $43,750
Variations: stainless steel ($20,750)

Dressage "L'Heure Masquée"

Reference number: DR5.810.220/MHA
Movement: automatic, Hermès Caliber H1925; ø 32 mm, height 6.5 mm; 35 jewels; 28,800 vph; pressing crown makes hour hand appear from hiding place behind minute hand; 45-hour power reserve
Functions: hours (on demand), minutes; additional 24-hour display (2nd time zone; only on pressing crown)
Case: stainless steel, ø 40.5 mm; sapphire crystal; water-resistant to 5 atm
Band: reptile skin, buckle
Price: $20,750
Variations: rose gold ($43,750)

Dressage Chronograph Black

Reference number: DR5.910.330/MNO
Movement: automatic, Hermès Caliber H1925 with Vaucher module; ø 30 mm, height 6.8 mm; 68 jewels; 28,800 vph; 45-hour power reserve
Functions: hours, minutes, subsidiary seconds; chronograph; date
Case: stainless steel, ø 40.5 mm; sapphire crystal; water-resistant to 5 atm
Band: reptile skin, folding clasp
Price: $11,200

Arceau Chrono Classique Bridon

Reference number: AR4.910.220/VBA2
Movement: automatic, ETA Caliber 2894;
ø 28.2 mm, height 6.1 mm; 37 jewels; 28,800 vph;
42-hour power reserve
Functions: hours, minutes, subsidiary seconds;
chronograph; date
Case: stainless steel, ø 43 mm, height 12.48 mm;
sapphire crystal; transparent case back; water-resistant to 5 atm
Band: calf leather, folding clasp
Price: $6,950

Arceau Lift

Reference number: AR5.970.220/MHA
Movement: manually wound, Hermès Caliber
H1923; ø 32.6 mm, height 5.75 mm; 21,600 vph;
flying 1-minute tourbillon (La Joux-Perret); 90-hour
power reserve
Functions: hours, minutes
Case: rose gold, ø 43 mm; sapphire crystal;
transparent case back; water-resistant to 3 atm
Band: reptile skin, buckle
Remarks: tourbillon cage spring barrel decorated
with double H as in Paris headquarters
Price: price on request; limited to 176 pieces

Cape Cod GMT

Reference number: CD6.910.220/MHA
Movement: automatic, ETA Caliber 2892 with
Soprod module 9351; ø 26 mm, height 3.6 mm; 25
jewels; 28,800 vph; plate and bridges with perlage,
rotor with côtes de Genève; 42-hour power reserve
Functions: hours, minutes, sweep seconds;
additional 12-hour display (2nd time zone); day/
night indicator; large date
Case: stainless steel, 35.4 x 36.5 mm; sapphire
crystal; transparent case back; water-resistant to
5 atm
Band: reptile skin, folding clasp with safety lock
Price: $7,550
Variations: blue dial ($7,550)

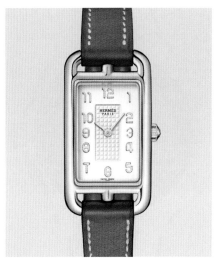

Cape Cod Nantucket Silver

Reference number: NA2.250.220/WW18
Movement: quartz
Functions: hours, minutes
Case: silver, 20 x 27 mm; sapphire crystal; water-resistant to 3 atm
Band: calf leather, buckle
Price: $3,600
Variations: set with diamonds ($12,850)

Cape Cod Tonneau GM Silver

Reference number: CT1.750.220/WW9T
Movement: quartz
Functions: hours, minutes, sweep seconds; date
Case: silver, 30 x 33.6 mm; sapphire crystal; water-resistant to 3 atm
Band: calf leather, buckle
Price: $4,050
Variations: set with diamonds ($16,500)

Faubourg

Reference number: FG1.170.111/VRH
Movement: quartz
Functions: hours, minutes
Case: rose gold, ø 15.5 mm; sapphire crystal; water-resistant to 3 atm
Band: calf leather, buckle
Price: $6,500
Variations: rose gold band ($13,000); with
diamonds ($8,700); set with diamonds and rose
gold band ($15,200)

Hublot SA
Chemin de la Vuarpillière 33
CH-1260 Nyon
Switzerland

Tel.:
01141-22-990-9900

E-Mail:
info@hublot.ch

Website:
www.hublot.com

Founded:
1980

Number of employees:
approx. 450

Annual production:
approx. 40,000 watches

U.S. distributor:
Hublot of America, Inc.
The International Building, ST-402
2455 East Sunrise Blvd.
Fort Lauderdale, FL 33304
800-536-0636

Most important collections/price range:
Big Bang / $15,000 to $1,000,000;
King Power / $20,000 to $200,000;
Classic Fusion / $7,000 to $130,000,
MasterPieces / $100,000 to $450,000

Hublot

Ever since Hublot moved into a new, modern, spacious factory building in Nyon, near Geneva—in the midst of a recession, no less—the brand has evolved with stunning speed. The growth has been such that Hublot has even built a second factory, which is even bigger than the first. The ground-breaking ceremony took place on March 3, 2014, and the man holding the spade was Hublot chairman Jean-Claude Biver, who is also head of LVMH's Watch Division.

Hublot grew and continues to grow thanks to its innovative approach to watchmaking in which scientific research is leveraged to discover new high-tech materials, for example. In 2011, the brand introduced the first scratchproof precious metal, an alloy of gold and ceramic named "Magic Gold," which is produced in a dedicated facility in Nyon. And the experimentation continues. At Baselworld 2014, Hublot came out with a watch whose dial is made of osmium, one of the world's rarest metals. Using a new patented process, Hublot has also implemented a unique concept of cutting wafer-thin bits of glass that are set in the open spaces of a skeletonized movement plate.

In 2014, Hublot connected with the FIFA Soccer World Cup as an official timekeeper. It was the impetus for the Big Bang Unico Chrono Bi-Retrograde. The in-house caliber running the piece, the HUB 1260, cost the company 18 months' hard work. A patent was filed for the movement, which drives a double retrograde chronograph from the center. Biver was in fact the first in the industry to introduce a luxury brand to soccer. Among the Hublot ambassadors are such legends as Pelé, Falcao, and Luiz Felipe Scolari, plus the famous trainer José Mourinho. Hublot also has partnerships with several clubs, notably FC Bayern München, Paris Saint-Germain, and Juventus Turin.

Big Bang Ferrari King Gold

Reference number: 401.OX.0123.VR
Movement: automatic, Caliber HUB 1241 "Unico"; ø 30 mm, height 8.05 mm; 38 jewels; 28,800 vph; black-coated plate and bridges; 72-hour power reserve
Functions: hours, minutes, subsidiary seconds; flyback chronograph; date
Case: pink gold, ø 45.5 mm, height 2.57 mm; bezel screwed through to case back with 6 screws, sapphire crystal; transparent case back; water-resistant to 10 atm
Band: calf leather, folding clasp
Price: $45,900; limited to 500 pieces

Big Bang Ferrari Ceramic Carbon

Reference number: 401.CQ.0129.VR
Movement: automatic, Caliber HUB 1241 "Unico"; ø 30 mm, height 8.05 mm; 38 jewels; 28,800 vph; black-coated plate and bridges; 72-hour power reserve
Functions: hours, minutes, subsidiary seconds; flyback chronograph; date
Case: ceramic, ø 45.5 mm, height 16.7 mm; carbon fiber bezel screwed to case back with 6 titanium screws, sapphire crystal; transparent case back; water-resistant to 10 atm
Band: calf leather, folding clasp
Price: $29,800; limited to 1,000 pieces

Big Bang Ferrari White Ceramic Carbon

Reference number: 401.HQ.0121.VR
Movement: automatic, Caliber HUB 1241 "Unico"; ø 30 mm, height 8.05 mm; 38 jewels; 28,800 vph; black-coated plate and bridges; 72-hour power reserve
Functions: hours, minutes, subsidiary seconds; flyback chronograph; date
Case: ceramic, ø 45.5 mm, height 16.7 mm; carbon fiber bezel screwed to case back with 6 titanium screws, sapphire crystal; transparent case back; water-resistant to 10 atm
Band: calf leather, folding clasp
Price: Price: $29,800; limited to 500 pieces

Big Bang Unico Carbon

Reference number: 411.QX.1170.RX
Movement: automatic, Caliber HUB 1242 "Unico"; ø 30 mm, height 9.8 mm; 38 jewels; 28,800 vph; black-coated plate and bridges; 72-hour power reserve
Functions: hours, minutes, subsidiary seconds; flyback chronograph; date
Case: carbon fiber, ø 45.5 mm, height 15.55 mm; bezel screwed to case back with 6 titanium screws, sapphire crystal; transparent case back; water-resistant to 10 atm
Band: rubber, folding clasp
Price: $24,000

Big Bang Unico Chrono Bi-Retrograde Ceramic Carbon FIFA World Cup Official Watch

Reference number: 412.CQ1127.RX
Movement: automatic, Caliber HUB 1260 "Unico"; ø 30 mm, height 11.85 mm; 44 jewels; 28,800 vph; 72-hour power reserve
Functions: hours, minutes, (off-center); twin retrograde chrono to measure soccer halftime and extra time; date
Case: ceramic, ø 45.5 mm, height 16.25 mm; carbon fiber bezel screwed to case back with 6 titanium screws, sapphire crystal; transparent case back; water-resistant to 10 atm
Band: rubber, folding clasp
Price: $26,300; limited to 200 pieces
Variations: pink gold ($42,400; limited to 100 pieces)

Big Bang Unico Chrono Bi-Retrograde King Gold Carbon FIFA World Cup Official Watch

Reference number: 412.OQ1128.RX
Movement: automatic, Caliber HUB 1260 "Unico"; ø 30 mm, height 11.85 mm; 44 jewels, 28,800 vph; 72-hour power reserve
Functions: hours, minutes, (off-center); twin retrograde chrono to measure soccer halftime and extra time; date
Case: rose gold, ø 45.5 mm, height 16.25 mm; carbon fiber bezel screwed to case back with 6 titanium screws, sapphire crystal; transparent case back; water-resistant to 10 atm
Band: rubber, folding clasp
Price: $42,400; limited to 100 pieces
Variations: ceramic ($26,300; limited to 200)

Big Bang Unico King Gold Ceramic

Reference number: 411.QM.1180.RX
Movement: automatic, Caliber HUB 1242 "Unico"; ø 30 mm, height 9.8 mm; 38 jewels; 28,800 vph; black-coated plate and bridges; 72-hour power reserve
Functions: hours, minutes, subsidiary seconds; flyback chronograph; date
Case: rose gold, ø 45.5 mm, height 15.45 mm; ceramic bezel screwed to case back with 6 titanium screws, sapphire crystal; transparent case back; water-resistant to 10 atm
Band: rubber, folding clasp
Price: $40,100

Big Bang All Black Shiny

Reference number: 341.CX.1210.VR.1100
Movement: automatic, Caliber HUB 4300 (base ETA 2894-2); ø 28.6 mm, height 6.9 mm; 37 jewels; 28,800 vph; 42-hour power reserve
Functions: hours, minutes, subsidiary seconds; chronograph; date
Case: ceramic, ø 41 mm, height 12.75 mm; PVD-coated stainless steel bezel screwed to case back with 6 titanium screws, sapphire crystal; transparent case back; water-resistant to 10 atm
Band: calf leather, folding clasp
Price: $21,700

King Power King Gold Blue Carbon

Reference number: 701.OQ.0138.GR.SP014
Movement: automatic, Caliber HUB 1240 "Unico"; ø 30 mm, height 8.05 mm; 38 jewels; 28,800 vph; black-coated plate/bridges; 72-hour power reserve
Functions: hours, minutes, subsidiary seconds; flyback chronograph; date
Case: rose gold, ø 48 mm, height 17.4 mm; carbon fiber bezel screwed to case back with 6 titanium screws, sapphire crystal; transparent case back; water-resistant to 10 atm
Band: reptile skin, folding clasp
Price: $44,700; limited to 100 pieces
Variations: titanium ($24,500; limited to 250)

Classic Fusion Tourbillon Firmament

Reference number: 502.CX.0002.LR
Movement: manual winding, Caliber HUB 6017; ø 34.4 mm, height 5.3 mm; 19 jewels; 21,600 vph; 1-minute tourbillon; base plate skeletonized, openings filled with osmium crystals; 120-hour power reserve
Functions: hours, minutes
Case: ceramic, ø 45 mm, height 11.15 mm; bezel screwed to case back with 6 titanium screws, sapphire crystal; transparent case back; water-resistant to 3 atm
Band: reptile skin, folding clasp
Price: $172,000

Classic Fusion Tourbillon Ceramic Blue Vitrail

Reference number: 502.CX.0003.LR
Movement: manual winding, Caliber HUB 6017; ø 34.4 mm, height 5.3 mm; 19 jewels; 21,600 vph; 1-minute tourbillon; base plate skeletonized, openings filled with leaded glass; 120-hour power reserve
Functions: hours, minutes
Case: ceramic, ø 45 mm, height 11.15 mm; bezel screwed to case back with 6 titanium screws, sapphire crystal; transparent case back; water-resistant to 3 atm
Band: reptile skin, folding clasp
Price: $109,000; limited to 20 pieces
Variations: titanium ($103,000; limited to 20 pieces)

Classic Fusion Power Reserve 8 Days King Gold

Reference number: 516.OX.1480.LR
Movement: automatic, Caliber HUB 1601; ø 34.4 mm, height 4 mm; 33 jewels; 21,600 vph; 192-hour power reserve
Functions: hours, minutes, subsidiary seconds; power reserve indicator; date
Case: rose gold, ø 45 mm, height 11.15 mm; bezel screwed to case back with 6 titanium screws, sapphire crystal; transparent case back
Band: reptile skin, folding clasp
Price: $32,500
Variations: titanium ($16,400)

Classic Fusion Chronograph Forbidden X

Reference number: 521.OC.0589.VR.OPX14
Movement: automatic, Caliber HUB 1143; height 6.9 mm; 59 jewels; 28,800 vph; 42-hour power reserve
Functions: hours, minutes, subsidiary seconds; chronograph; date
Case: rose gold, ø 45 mm, ceramic bezel screwed to case back with 6 titanium screws, sapphire crystal; transparent case back; water-resistant to 5 atm
Band: calf leather, folding clasp
Price: $36,700; limited to 150 pieces
Variations: titanium ($14,800; limited to 250)

Classic Fusion Pelé Aerofusion Chronograph

Reference number: 525.CM.0179.VR.PEL14
Movement: automatic, Hublot Caliber 1155 "Aero"; ø 30 mm, height 7.1 mm; 60 jewels; 28,800 vph; skeletonized and rhodium-plated, tungsten carbide oscillating mass; 42-hour power reserve
Functions: hours, minutes, subsidiary seconds; chronograph; date
Case: ceramic, ø 45 mm, height 13.4 mm; bezel screwed to case back with 6 titanium screws, sapphire crystal; transparent case back; water-resistant to 5 atm
Band: calf leather, folding clasp
Price: $18,700; limited to 500 pieces
Variations: gold ($39,400; limited to 200)

Classic Fusion Cathedral Tourbillon Minute Repeater

Reference number: 504.NX.0170.LR
Movement: manual winding, Caliber HUB 8001; height 6.35 mm; 30 jewels; 21,600 vph; flying 1-minute tourbillon; 120-hour power reserve
Functions: hours, minutes; minute repeater
Case: titanium, ø 45 mm, height 14.3 mm; bezel screwed to case back with 6 titanium screws, sapphire crystal; transparent case back; water-resistant to 3 atm
Band: reptile skin, folding clasp
Price: $264,000; limited to 99 pieces
Variations: red gold ($299,000; limited to 50)

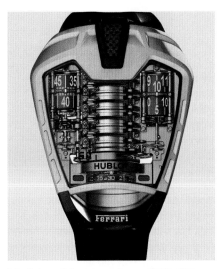

Hublot Masterpiece MP-05 "LaFerrari" Titanium

Reference number: 905.NX.0001.RX
Movement: automatic, Caliber HUB 9005.H1.6;
39.5 x 45.8 mm, height 17.6 mm; 108 jewels;
21,600 vph; vertically suspended flying tourbillon;
indication of hours, minutes, seconds, power
reserve on black anodized aluminum cylinders; 11
spring barrels; 50-day power reserve
Functions: hours, minutes, seconds (on cylinders);
power reserve display
Case: titanium; sapphire crystal; transparent case
back; water-resistant to 3 atm
Band: rubber, folding clasp
Price: $345,000; limited to 50 pieces

Classic Fusion Black Skull Full Pavé

Reference number: 511.ND.9100.LR.1700.SKULL
Movement: automatic, Caliber HUB 1110;
ø 34.7 mm, height 4.25 mm; 21 jewels; 28,800 vph;
42-hour power reserve
Functions: hours, minutes, sweep seconds
Case: titanium with black PVD coating, 218 black
diamonds; ø 45 mm, height 10 mm; bezel screwed
to case back with 6 titanium screws with 126 black
diamonds, sapphire crystal; transparent case back;
water-resistant to 5 atm
Band: reptile skin, folding clasp
Price: $47,000; limited to 50 pieces
Variations: titanium with white diamonds ($45,900)

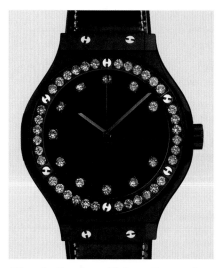

Classic Fusion Shiny Ceramic Green

Reference number: 565.CX.1210.VR.1222
Movement: automatic, Caliber HUB 1110; ø
34.7 mm, height 4.25 mm; 21 jewels; 28,800 vph;
42-hour power reserve
Functions: hours, minutes, sweep seconds
Case: ceramic, ø 38 mm, height 9.6 mm; bezel
screwed to case back with 6 titanium screws with
126 black diamonds, sapphire crystal; transparent
case back
Band: calf leather, folding clasp
Remarks: dial set with 11 diamonds
Price: $12,500

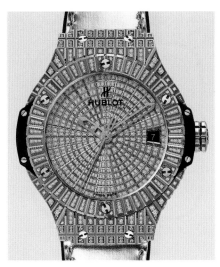

Big Bang Steel Caviar Full Pavé

Reference number: 346.SX.9000.VR.1704
Movement: automatic, Caliber HUB 1143; height
8.9 mm; 21 jewels; 28,800 vph; 42-hour power
reserve
Functions: hours, minutes, subsidiary seconds;
date
Case: stainless steel, set with 430 diamonds,
ø 41 mm; bezel set with 168 diamonds, sapphire
crystal; transparent case back
Band: calf leather, folding clasp
Price: $49,300

Caliber HUB1240

Automatic; column wheel control of chronograph
functions; silicon anchor and anchor escape wheel;
removable escapement; double-pawl automatic
winding (Pellaton system), winding rotor with
ceramic ball bearing, simple barrel spring, 70-hour
power reserve
Functions: hours, minutes, subsidiary seconds;
flyback chronograph; date
Diameter: 30.4 mm; **Height:** 8.05 mm
Jewels: 38
Balance: glucydur
Frequency: 28,800 vph
Balance spring: flat hairspring with fine regulation
Shock protection: Incabloc
Remarks: 330 individual components

Caliber HUB1300

Manually wound; skeletonized movement; structural
sections with black PVD coating; double spring
barrel; 90 hours power reserve
Functions: hours, minutes, subsidiary seconds
Diameter: 28 mm
Height: 2.9 mm
Jewels: 23
Balance: glucydur
Frequency: 21,600 vph
Balance spring: flat hairspring with fine regulation
Shock protection: Incabloc
Remarks: 123 individual components

Itay Noy
P.O. Box 16661
Tel Aviv 61166
Israel

Tel.:
011-972-352-47-380

Fax:
011-972-352-47-381

E-Mail:
studio@itay-noy.com

Website:
www.itay-noy.com

Founded:
2000

Number of employees:
4

Annual production:
200–300 pieces

U.S. distributor:
Bareti, California
949-715-7084
info@bareti.com
www.bareti.com

Most important collections/price range:
Hyper Scape, X-ray, Identity, Point of View /
$2,500 to $7,500

Itay Noy

Israeli watchmaker Itay Noy started his career as a jeweler, so it comes as no surprise that his watches weigh in heavily on the form side, while the functional aspects are left to the solid technology generated by the Swiss. Noy focuses on his own cases and dials and makes his own straps, which give his timepieces such a distinct look. He reveals himself to be a pensive, philosophical storyteller who makes each timepiece a unique, encapsulated tale of sorts. The City Squares model, for example, gives the time on the backdrop of a map of the owner's favorite or native city, thus creating an intimate connection with, perhaps, a past moment. At Baselworld 2013, Noy showcased a square watch run on a Technotime automatic movement with a face-like dial that changes with the movement of the hands, a reminder of how our life has become dominated by the rectangular frame of mobile gadgets. The Cityscape, square as well, represents a modern urban landscape. The skeletonization of the Point of View dial, his 2014 model, creates a harmonious collage of the world's religious symbols superimposed on the inexorable passage of time. Its numerals are remarkable: sculpted and raised to form a crown-like structure.

Noy is generous with his talent: Once a year he teaches a course in timepiece design for the Department of Jewelry and Fashion at Bezalel Academy of Art and Design Jerusalem. A glance at the imaginative works his students turn out suggests the beginning of a new strain of DNA.

His timepieces are quite affordable, especially considering they are made in limited and numbered editions. They are often found in museums and special exhibitions, notably the C. Bronfman Collection in New York, the Droog Design Collection in Amsterdam, and the collection of the Israel Museum in Jerusalem.

Point Of View

Reference number: POV-R.G
Movement: automatic, Caliber 90S5; ø 25.6 mm, height 3.9 mm; 24 jewels; 28,800 vph; 42-hour power reserve
Functions: hours, minutes, sweep seconds
Case: stainless steel, ø 42.4 mm, height 10 mm; sapphire crystal; screw-down case back; water-resistant to 5 atm
Band: handmade leather band
Remarks: numbered limited edition of 99 pieces
Price: $2,000
Variations: black or brown leather band

Hyper Scape

Reference number: LANDSCAPE.B
Movement: automatic, Caliber TT651-24H; ø 26.2 mm, height 5.25 mm; 21 jewels; 28,800 vph; 42-hour power reserve
Functions: hours, minutes, sweep seconds; quick-set big date window; 2nd time zone, 24-hour disc and day/night
Case: stainless steel, 42.4 x 42.4 mm, height 11.6 mm; sapphire crystal; transparent case back; water-resistant to 5 atm
Band: rubber, double folding clasp
Remarks: numbered limited edition of 24 pieces
Price: $5,800
Variations: black or cream dial; handmade leather band

Mask

Reference number: MASK02.W
Movement: automatic, Caliber TT651-24H; ø 26.2 mm, height 5.25 mm; 21 jewels; 28,800 vph; 42-hour power reserve
Functions: hours, minutes, sweep seconds; quick-set big date window; 2nd time zone, 24-hour disc and day/night
Case: stainless steel, 42.4 x 42.4 mm, height 11.6 mm; sapphire crystal; transparent case back; water-resistant to 5 atm
Band: rubber band or handmade leather band, double folding clasp
Remarks: numbered limited edition of 24 pieces
Price: $5,800
Variations: black or cream dial

Skeleton

Reference number: SKEL6498G
Movement: manually wound, ETA Caliber 6498-1;
ø 36.6 mm, height 4.5 mm; 17 jewels; 21,600 vph;
38-hour power reserve
Functions: hours, minutes, subsidiary seconds
Case: stainless steel, 41.6 x 44.6 mm, height
10 mm; sapphire crystal; screw-down case back;
water-resistant to 5 atm
Band: handmade leather band, double folding clasp
Remarks: numbered limited edition of 99 pieces
Price: $3,900
Variations: black or brown leather band

X-ray

Reference number: XRAY6498
Movement: manually wound, ETA Caliber 6498-1;
ø 36.6 mm, height 4.5 mm; 17 jewels; 21,600 vph;
38-hour power reserve
Functions: hours, minutes, subsidiary seconds
Case: stainless steel, 41.6 x 44.6 mm, height 10
mm; sapphire crystal; screw-down case back; water-
resistant to 5 atm
Band: handmade leather band, double folding clasp
Remarks: numbered limited edition of 99 pieces
Price: $3,640
Variations: gold plated dial ($3,900); black or
brown leather band

DiaLOG

Reference number: DiaLOG.Num
Movement: manually wound, ETA Caliber 6498-1;
ø 36.6 mm, height 4.5 mm; 17 jewels; 21,600 vph;
38-hour power reserve
Functions: hours, minutes, subsidiary seconds
Case: stainless steel, 41.6 x 44.6 mm, height
10 mm; sapphire crystal; screw-down case back;
water-resistant to 5 atm
Band: dark blue handmade leather band, double
folding clasp
Remarks: numbered limited edition of 99 pieces
Price: $3,900

Maximalism

Reference number: MAX-DECO
Movement: automatic, ETA Caliber 2824-2;
ø 25.6 mm, height 4.6 mm, 25 jewels; 28,800 vph;
38-hour power reserve
Functions: hours, minutes, sweep seconds; quick-
set date window
Case: stainless steel, ø 42.4 mm, height 10 mm;
sapphire crystal; screw-down case back; water-
resistant to 5 atm
Band: handmade leather band
Remarks: numbered limited edition
Price: $2,400
Variations: black or brown leather band

Identity-Hebrew

Reference number: ID-HEB
Movement: automatic, ETA Caliber 2824-2;
ø 25.6 mm, height 4.6 mm; 25 jewels; 28,800 vph;
38-hour power reserve
Functions: hours, minutes, sweep seconds; quick-
set date window
Case: stainless steel, ø 42.4 mm, height 10 mm;
sapphire crystal; screw-down case back; water-
resistant to 5 atm
Band: handmade leather band
Remarks: numbered limited edition of 99 pieces
Price: $2,550
Variations: black or brown leather band

City Squares - San-Pietro, Rome

Reference number: CS-Rome
Movement: automatic, ETA Caliber 2824-2;
ø 25.6 mm, height 4.6 mm; 25 jewels; 28,800 vph;
38-hour power reserve
Functions: hours, minutes, sweep seconds; quick-
set date window
Case: stainless steel, ø 42.4 mm, height 10 mm;
sapphire crystal; screw-down case back; water-
resistant to 5 atm
Band: hand-stitched leather
Remarks: numbered limited edition of 99 pieces
Price: $3,640
Variations: London, Paris, Rome, Tel Aviv,
Copenhagen

IWC

International Watch Co.

Baumgartenstrasse 15
CH-8201 Schaffhausen
Switzerland

Tel.:
01141-52-635-6565

Fax:
01141-52-635-6501

E-Mail:
info@iwc.com

Website:
www.iwc.com

Founded:
1868

Number of employees:
approx. 750

U.S. distributor:
IWC North America
645 Fifth Avenue, 5th Floor
New York, NY 10022
800-432-9330

Most important collections/price range:
Da Vinci, Pilot's, Portuguese, Ingenieur,
Aquatimer / approx. $4,000 to $260,000

It was an American who laid the cornerstone for an industrial watch factory in Schaffhausen—now modern and environmentally state-of-the-art facilities. In 1868, Florentine Ariosto Jones, watchmaker and engineer from Boston, crossed the Atlantic and came to the then low-wage country of Switzerland to open the International Watch Company Schaffhausen.

Jones was not only a savvy businessperson, but also a talented designer, who had a significant influence on the development of watch movements. Soon, he gave the IWC its own seal of approval, the *Ingenieursmarke* (Engineer's Brand), a standard it still maintains today. As it always has, IWC is synonymous with excellently crafted watches that meet high technical benchmarks. Not even a large variety of owners over the past 100 years has been able to change the company's course, though it did ultimately end up in the hands of the Richemont Group in 2000.

Technical milestones from Schaffhausen include the Jones caliber, named for the IWC founder, and the pocket watch caliber 89, introduced in 1946 as the creation of then technical director Albert Pellaton. Four years later, Pellaton created the first IWC automatic movement and, with it, a company monument. Over the years, IWC has made a name for itself with its pilot's watches. The technical highlight of the present day is no doubt the Perpetual Calendar, which is programmed to run until the year 2499.

Georges Kern, the current CEO at IWC, has pursued the development of in-house movements, such as those found in the company's Da Vinci, Portuguese, and Ingenieur models. The watches are retro-styled, and the branding is always connected to some sort of active pursuit, like car racing or flying. Lately, IWC has revisited its Aquatimer and brought out the Deep Three, with, among other things, two depth gauges, one of which records how deep the diver has gone.

Aquatimer Perpetual Calendar Digital Date-Month

Reference number: IW379401
Movement: automatic, IWC Caliber 89801; ø 37 mm, height 9.86 mm; 51 jewels; 28,800 vph; 68 hours power reserve
Functions: hours, minutes, subsidiary seconds; flyback chronograph; perpetual calendar with large date, month (digital), leap year
Case: titanium with black rubber coating, ø 49 mm, height 19 mm; rose gold bezel and case back; bidirectional bezel activates inside timing bezel; sapphire crystal; transparent case back; screw-in crown; water-resistant to 10 atm
Price: $56,300; limited to 50 pieces

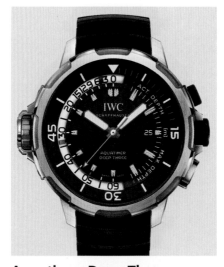

Aquatimer Deep Three

Reference number: IW355701
Movement: automatic, IWC Caliber 30120 (base ETA 2892-A2); ø 25.6 mm, height 3.6 mm; 21 jewels; 28,800 vph; 42 hours power reserve
Functions: hours, minutes, sweep seconds, depth gauges with split seconds function; date
Case: titanium, ø 46 mm, height 16.5 mm; bidirectional bezel activates inside timing bezel; sapphire crystal; screw-in crown; water-resistant to 10 atm
Band: rubber, buckle
Price: $19,100

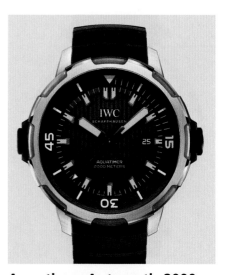

Aquatimer Automatic 2000

Reference number: IW358002
Movement: automatic, IWC Caliber 80110; ø 30 mm, height 7.23 mm; 28 jewels; 28,800 vph; 44 hours power reserve
Functions: hours, minutes, sweep seconds; date
Case: titanium, ø 46 mm, height 20.5 mm; bidirectional bezel activates inside timing bezel; sapphire crystal; screw-in crown; water-resistant to 200 atm
Band: rubber, buckle
Price: $10,100

Aquatimer Chronograph Edition "Galapagos Islands"

Reference number: IW379502
Movement: automatic, IWC Caliber 89365; ø 30 mm, height 7.46 mm; 35 jewels; 28,800 vph; 68 hours power reserve
Functions: hours, minutes, subsidiary seconds; chronograph; date
Case: stainless steel with black rubber coating, ø 44 mm, height 17 mm; bidirectional bezel activates inside timing bezel; sapphire crystal; screw-in crown; water-resistant to 30 atm
Band: rubber, buckle
Price: $11,100

Aquatimer Chronograph Edition "50 Years Science for Galapagos"

Reference number: IW379504
Movement: automatic, IWC Caliber 89365; ø 30 mm, height 7.46 mm; 35 jewels; 28,800 vph; 68 hours power reserve
Functions: hours, minutes, subsidiary seconds; chronograph; date
Case: stainless steel with black rubber coating, ø 44 mm, height 17 mm; bidirectional bezel activates inside timing bezel; sapphire crystal; screw-in crown; water-resistant to 30 atm
Band: rubber, buckle
Price: $11,200; limited to 500 pieces

Aquatimer Chronograph Edition "Expedition Charles Darwin"

Reference number: IW379503
Movement: automatic, IWC Caliber 89365; ø 30 mm, height 7.46 mm; 35 jewels; 28,800 vph; 68 hours power reserve
Functions: hours, minutes, subsidiary seconds; chronograph; date
Case: bronze; ø 44 mm, height 17 mm; bidirectional bezel activates inside timing bezel; sapphire crystal; screw-in crown; water-resistant to 30 atm
Band: rubber, buckle
Price: $11,100

Aquatimer Chronograph Edition "Expedition Jacques-Yves Cousteau"

Reference number: IW376805
Movement: automatic, IWC Caliber 79320 (base ETA 7750); ø 30 mm, height 7.9 mm; 25 jewels; 28,800 vph; 44 hours power reserve
Functions: hours, minutes, subsidiary seconds; chronograph; weekday, date
Case: stainless steel, ø 44 mm, height 17 mm; bidirectional bezel activates inside timing bezel; sapphire crystal; screw-in crown; water-resistant to 30 atm
Band: rubber, buckle
Price: $7,200

Aquatimer Chronograph

Reference number: IW376804
Movement: automatic, IWC Caliber 79320 (base ETA 7750); ø 30 mm, height 7.9 mm; 25 jewels; 28,800 vph; 44 hours power reserve
Functions: hours, minutes, subsidiary seconds; chronograph; weekday, date
Case: stainless steel, ø 44 mm, height 17 mm; bidirectional bezel activates inside timing bezel; sapphire crystal; screw-in crown; water-resistant to 30 atm
Band: stainless steel, folding clasp
Price: $8,000
Variations: silver-plated dial/rubber strap ($7,000)

Aquatimer Automatic

Reference number: IW329001
Movement: automatic, IWC Caliber 30120 (base ETA 2892-A2); ø 25.6 mm, height 3,6 mm; 21 jewels; 28,800 vph; 42 hours power reserve
Functions: hours, minutes, sweep seconds; date
Case: stainless steel, ø 42 mm, height 14 mm; bidirectional bezel activates inside timing bezel; sapphire crystal; screw-in crown; water-resistant to 30 atm
Band: rubber, buckle
Price: $5,750
Variations: silver-plated dial; stainless steel bracelet ($6,750)

Portuguese Tourbillon Mystère Rétrograde

Reference number: IW504401
Movement: automatic, IWC Caliber 51900; ø 37.8 mm, height 8.9 mm; 44 jewels; 19,800 vph; flying 1-minute tourbillon; Pellaton winding; yellow gold oscillating mass; 168 hours power reserve
Functions: hours, minutes; power reserve indicator; date (retrograde)
Case: platinum, ø 44.2 mm, height 15.5 mm; sapphire crystal; transparent case back; water-resistant to 3 atm
Band: reptile skin, folding clasp
Price: $136,000; limited to 250 pieces
Variations: pink gold ($114,000; limited to 500 pieces)

Portugieser Chronograph Classic

Reference number: IW390405
Movement: automatic, IWC Caliber 89361; ø 30 mm, height 7.46 mm; 38 jewels; 28,800 vph; double-pawl automatic winding system; 68 hours power reserve
Functions: hours, minutes, subsidiary seconds; flyback chronograph; date
Case: pink gold, ø 42 mm, height 14.5 mm; sapphire crystal; transparent case back; water-resistant to 3 atm
Band: reptile skin, buckle
Price: $24,200
Variations: stainless steel ($13,000)

Portuguese Yacht Club Chronograph

Reference number: IW390211
Movement: automatic, IWC Caliber 89361; ø 30 mm, height 7.46 mm; 38 jewels; 28,800 vph; double-pawl automatic winding system; 68 hours power reserve
Functions: hours, minutes, subsidiary seconds; flyback chronograph; date
Case: stainless steel, ø 45.4 mm, height 14.5 mm; sapphire crystal; transparent case back; screw-in crown, water-resistant to 6 atm
Band: rubber, folding clasp
Price: $14,000
Variations: pink gold ($26,400); special stainless steel edition "Laureus Sport for Good Foundation" ($10,800)

Portuguese Perpetual Calendar

Reference number: IW503202
Movement: automatic, IWC Caliber 51614; ø 37.8 mm; 62 jewels; 21,600 vph; Pellaton winding; power reserve mechanically limited to 7 days, 168 hours power reserve
Functions: hours, minutes, subsidiary seconds; power reserve indicator; perpetual calendar with month, weekday, double moon phase (for southern and northern hemispheres), 4-digit year display
Case: pink gold, ø 44.2 mm, height 15.5 mm; sapphire crystal; water-resistant to 3 atm
Band: reptile skin, folding clasp
Price: $37,900
Variations: white gold ($41,900)

Portofino Hand-Wound Eight Days

Reference number: IW510104
Movement: manually wound, IWC Caliber 59210; ø 37.8 mm, height 5.8 mm; 30 jewels; 28,800 vph; 192 hours power reserve
Functions: hours, minutes, subsidiary seconds; power reserve indicator; date
Case: pink gold, ø 45 mm, height 12 mm; sapphire crystal; transparent case back; water-resistant to 3 atm
Band: reptile skin, buckle
Price: $20,200
Variations: stainless steel ($10,800)

Ingenieur Constant-Force Tourbillon

Reference number: IW590001
Movement: manually wound, IWC Caliber 94800; ø 37.8 mm, height 7.7 mm; 43 jewels; 18,000 vph; 1-minute tourbillon; constant force escapement; 96 hours power reserve
Functions: hours, minutes, subsidiary seconds; power reserve indicator; double moon phase
Case: platinum, ø 46 mm, height 14 mm; sapphire crystal; transparent case back; water-resistant to 12 atm
Band: rubber with reptile skin inserts, buckle
Price: $290,000

Ingenieur Automatic AMG Black Series Ceramic

Reference number: IW322503
Movement: automatic, IWC Caliber 80110;
ø 30 mm, height 7.23 mm; 28 jewels; 28,800 vph;
Pellaton winding; 44 hours power reserve
Functions: hours, minutes, sweep seconds; date
Case: ceramic, ø 46 mm, height 14.5 mm; sapphire
crystal; transparent case back; screw-in crown;
water-resistant to 12 atm
Band: rubber with calf leather insert, buckle
Price: $12,300
Variations: brown dial and strap

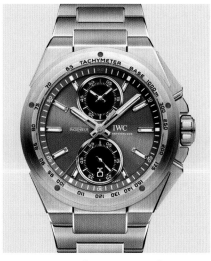

Ingenieur Chronograph Racer

Reference number: IW378508
Movement: automatic, IWC Caliber 89361;
ø 30 mm, height 7.46 mm; 38 jewels; 28,800 vph;
double-pawl automatic winding system; 68 hours
power reserve
Functions: hours, minutes, subsidiary seconds;
flyback chronograph; date
Case: stainless steel, ø 45 mm, height 14.5 mm;
sapphire crystal, screw-in crown; water-resistant to
12 atm
Band: stainless steel, folding clasp
Price: $14,300
Variations: black dial; rubber strap ($13,100)

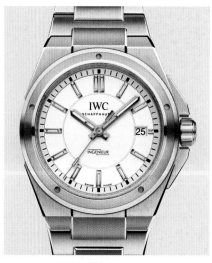

Ingenieur Automatic

Reference number: IW323906
Movement: automatic, IWC Caliber 30110 (base
ETA 2892-A2); ø 25.6 mm, height 3.6 mm; 21
jewels; 28,800 vph; soft iron cap for antimagnetic
protection; 42 hours power reserve
Functions: hours, minutes, sweep seconds; date
Case: stainless steel, ø 40 mm, height 10 mm;
sapphire crystal; screw-in crown; water-resistant to
12 atm
Band: stainless steel, folding clasp
Price: $6,600
Variations: black or silver dial

Big Pilot's Watch "Top Gun" Miramar

Reference number: IW388002
Movement: automatic, IWC Caliber 51111;
ø 37.8 mm, height 7.53 mm; 42 jewels; 21,600
vph; Pellaton automatic winding system; 168 hours
power reserve
Functions: hours, minutes, sweep seconds; power
reserve indicator; date
Case: ceramic and titanium, ø 48 mm, height
15 mm; sapphire crystal; screw-in crown; water-
resistant to 6 atm
Band: textile, buckle
Price: $12,700
Variations: "Top Gun" version with black dial/band
($18,200)

Big Pilot's Watch "Top Gun"

Reference number: IW388001
Movement: automatic, IWC Caliber 51111;
ø 37.8 mm, height 7.53 mm; 42 jewels; 21,600
vph; Pellaton automatic winding system; 168 hours
power reserve
Functions: hours, minutes, sweep seconds; power
reserve indicator; date
Case: ceramic and titanium, ø 48 mm, height
16 mm; sapphire crystal; screw-in crown; water-
resistant to 6 atm
Band: textile, buckle
Price: $12,700

Big Pilot's Watch

Reference number: IW500901
Movement: automatic, IWC Caliber 51111;
ø 37.8 mm, height 7.53 mm; 42 jewels; 21,600 vph;
Pellaton automatic winding system; soft iron cap for
antimagnetic protection; 168 hours power reserve
Functions: hours, minutes, sweep seconds; power
reserve indicator; date
Case: stainless steel, ø 46 mm, height 16 mm;
sapphire crystal, screw-in crown; water-resistant to
6 atm
Band: reptile skin, folding clasp
Price: $15,400

Caliber 51111

Base caliber: 5000
Automatic; double-pawl automatic winding
(Pellaton system); single spring barrel, 7-day power
reserve
Functions: hours, minutes, sweep seconds; date;
power reserve indicator
Diameter: 37.8 mm
Height: 7.53 mm
Jewels: 44
Balance: balance with variable inertia
Frequency: 21,600 vph
Balance spring: Breguet
Shock protection: Incabloc

Caliber 51900

Base caliber: 5000
Automatic; double-pawl automatic winding
(Pellaton system); flying 1-minute tourbillon; single
spring barrel, 7-day power reserve
Functions: hours, minutes; date (retrograde); power
reserve indicator
Diameter: 37.8 mm
Height: 8.9 mm
Jewels: 44
Balance: glucydur
Frequency: 19,800 vph
Balance spring: Breguet
Shock protection: Incabloc

Caliber 51011

Base caliber: 5000
Automatic; double-pawl automatic winding
(Pellaton system); single spring barrel, 7-day power
reserve
Functions: hours, minutes, subsidiary seconds;
power reserve indicator
Diameter: 37.8 mm
Height: 7.6 mm
Jewels: 42
Balance: balance with variable inertia
Frequency: 21,600 vph
Balance spring: Breguet
Shock protection: Incabloc

Caliber 59210

Manual winding; single spring barrel, 8-day power
reserve
Functions: hours, minutes, subsidiary seconds;
date; power reserve indicator
Diameter: 37.8 mm
Height: 5.8 mm
Jewels: 30
Balance: balance with variable inertia
Frequency: 28,800 vph
Balance spring: Breguet
Shock protection: Incabloc

Caliber 89361

Base caliber: 89360
Automatic; double-pawl automatic winding
(Pellaton system); column wheel control of
chronograph functions; single spring barrel, 68-hour
power reserve
Functions: hours, minutes, subsidiary seconds;
flyback chronograph; date
Diameter: 30 mm; **Height:** 7.46 mm
Jewels: 38
Balance: balance with variable inertia
Frequency: 28,800 vph
Balance spring: flat hairspring
Shock protection: Incabloc
Remarks: concentric chronograph counter for
minutes and hours

Caliber 98295 "Jones"

Manual winding; characteristic long regulator index;
single spring barrel, 46-hour power reserve
Functions: hours, minutes, subsidiary seconds
Diameter: 38.2 mm
Height: 5.3 mm
Jewels: 18
Balance: screw balance with precision adjustment
cams on balance arms
Frequency: 18,000 vph
Balance spring: Breguet
Shock protection: Incabloc
Remarks: three-quarter plate of German silver,
hand-engraved balance cocks

Manufacture Jaeger-LeCoultre
Rue de la Golisse, 8
CH-1347 Le Sentier
Switzerland

Tel.:
01141-21-852-0202

Fax:
01141-21-852-0505

E-Mail:
info@jaeger-lecoultre.com

Website:
www.jaeger-lecoultre.com

Founded:
1833

Number of employees:
over 1,000

Annual production:
approx. 50,000 watches

U.S. distributor:
Jaeger-LeCoultre
645 Fifth Avenue
New York, NY 10022
800-JLC-TIME
www.jaeger-lecoultre.com

Most important collections/price range:
Reverso, Rendez-Vous, Duomètre, Master,
AMVOX / approx. $6,000 to $130,000 and higher for
limited editions and Grandes Complications models

Jaeger-LeCoultre

The Jaeger-LeCoultre *manufacture* has a long and tumultuous history. In 1833, Antoine LeCoultre opened his own workshop for the production of gear wheels. Having made his fortune, he then did what many other artisans did: In 1866, he had a large house built and brought together all the craftspeople needed to produce timepieces, from the watchmakers to the turners and polishers. He outfitted the workshop with the most modern machinery of the day, all powered by a steam engine. "La Grande Maison" was the first watch *manufacture* in the Vallée de Joux.

At the start of the twentieth century, the grandson of the company founder, Jacques-David LeCoultre, built slender, complicated watches for the Paris manufacturer Edmond Jaeger. The Frenchman was so impressed with these that, after a few years of fruitful cooperation, he engineered a merger of the two companies.

In the 1970s, the *manufacture* hit hard times and was taken over by the German VDO Group (later Mannesmann). Under the leadership of Günter Blümlein, Jaeger-LeCoultre weathered the quartz crisis, and during the mechanical watch renaissance in the 1980s, the company finally recouped its status as an innovative, high-performance *manufacture*.

When Mannesmann's watch division (JLC, IWC, A. Lange & Söhne) sold Jaeger-LeCoultre to the Richemont Group in 2000, words like "competence" and "capacities" were used in the sales pitch. Those qualities, plus a decade of continual expansion and growth made it a great buy. Today, Jaeger-LeCoultre boasts more than 1,000 employees, making it the largest employer in the Vallée de Joux—just as it was back in the 1860s.

Duomètre à Quantième Lunaire

Reference number: 604 35 E1
Movement: manual winding, JLC Caliber 381; ø 33.7 mm, height 7.25 mm; 40 jewels; 21,600 vph; 2 spring barrels and 2 separate gear trains for watch and foudroyante mechanism; 50-hour power reserve
Functions: hours and minutes (off-center); foudroyante sixth-second counter (2nd foudroyante); date; moon phase and age; double power reserve display
Case: white gold, ø 40.5 mm, height 13.4 mm; sapphire crystal; transparent case back; water-resistant to 5 atm
Band: reptile skin, buckle
Price: $62,500
Variations: rose gold ($38,600)

Duomètre Unique Travel Time

Reference number: 606 25 20
Movement: manually wound, JLC Caliber 383; ø 33.7 mm, height 7.25 mm; 54 jewels; 28,800 vph; 2 separate spring barrels and 2 separate gear works for 2 time displays, 50-hour power reserve
Functions: hours and minutes (off-center), sweep seconds; 2nd time zone (digital, jumping hours, minutes), world-time display; separate power reserve indicator for each spring barrel
Case: pink gold, ø 42 mm, height 13.65 mm; sapphire crystal
Band: reptile skin, buckle
Price: $46,300

Duomètre à Chronographe

Reference number: 601 25 21
Movement: manually wound, JLC Caliber 380A; ø 33.7 mm, height 6.95 mm; 47 jewels; 21,600 vph; 2 separate spring barrels, separate mechanisms for time and chronograph; chronograph functions controlled by switch on foudroyante mechanism; 50-hour power reserve
Functions: hours and minutes (off-center), sweep seconds; power reserve display; chronograph
Case: rose gold, ø 39.5 mm, height 13.6 mm; sapphire crystal; transparent case back; water-resistant to 5 atm
Band: reptile skin, buckle
Price: $49,800

Master Grande Tradition Tourbillon Cylindrique à Quantième Perpétuel

Reference number: 504 25 20
Movement: automatic, JLC Caliber 985; ø 30 mm, height 8.15 mm; 49 jewels; 28,800 vph; flying 1-minute tourbillon with cylindrical balance-spring; 48-hour power reserve
Functions: hours, minutes, subsidiary seconds; perpetual calendar with date, weekday, month, moon phase, year display (digital, 4 digits)
Case: pink gold, ø 42 mm, height 13.1 mm; sapphire crystal; transparent back; water-resistant to 5 atm
Band: reptile skin, platinum buckle
Price: $143,000

Master Grande Tradition à Quantième Perpétuel 8 Jours Squelette

Reference number: 506 35 SQ
Movement: manually wound, JLC Caliber 876SQ; ø 30 mm height 6.6 mm; 37 jewels; 28,800 vph; skeletonized; 2 spring barrels; 192-hour power reserve
Functions: hours, minutes, day/night indicator, power reserve indicator; perpetual calendar with date, weekday, month, moon phase, 2-digit year until 2100
Case: white gold, ø 42 mm, height 11.6 mm; sapphire crystal; transparent case back; water-resistant to 5 atm
Band: reptile skin, buckle
Remarks: skeletonized enamel dial
Price: $121,000

Master Compressor Chronograph Ceramic

Reference number: 205 C5 70
Movement: automatic, JLC Caliber 757; ø 25.6 mm, height 6.27 mm; 45 jewels; 28,800 vph; fine hand-finishing; 65-hour power reserve
Functions: hours, minutes, subsidiary seconds; additional 12-hour display (2nd time zone); day/night indicator; chronograph; date
Case: ceramic, ø 46 mm; sapphire crystal; water-resistant to 10 atm
Band: calf leather, buckle
Remarks: limited to 500 pieces
Price: $15,600

Hybris Mechanica 11

Reference number: 131 35 20
Movement: automatic, JLC Caliber 362; ø 33.3 mm, height 4.8 mm; 21,600 vph; flying tourbillon with flying balance; hubless peripheral rotor; 45-hour power reserve
Functions: hours, minutes; minute repeater
Case: white gold, ø 41 mm, height 7.9 mm; sapphire crystal; transparent back; pusher for minute repeater sunken into case; water-resistant to 3 atm
Band: reptile skin, buckle
Price: $143,472; limited to 75 pieces

Master Ultra Thin

Reference number: 127 25 10
Movement: automatic, JLC Caliber 896; ø 26 mm, height 3.98 mm; 32 jewels; 28,800 vph; 43-hour power reserve
Functions: hours, minutes, subsidiary seconds
Case: pink gold, ø 38.5 mm, height 7.58 mm; sapphire crystal; transparent case back; water-resistant to 5 atm
Band: reptile skin, buckle
Price: $15,200
Variations: stainless steel ($8,500)

Master Ultra Thin

Reference number: 127 84 20
Movement: automatic, JLC Caliber 896; ø 26 mm, height 3.98 mm; 32 jewels; 28,800 vph; 43-hour power reserve
Functions: hours, minutes, subsidiary seconds
Case: stainless steel, ø 38.5 mm, height 7.58 mm; sapphire crystal; transparent case back; water-resistant to 5 atm
Band: reptile skin, buckle
Price: $8,500
Variations: pink gold ($15,200)

Master Ultra Thin Date

Reference number: 128 25 10
Movement: automatic, JLC Caliber 899; ø 26 mm, height 3.3 mm; 32 jewels; 28,800 vph; 43-day power reserve
Functions: hours, minutes, sweep seconds; date
Case: pink gold, ø 40 mm, height 7.4 mm; sapphire crystal; transparent case back; water-resistant to 5 atm
Band: reptile skin, buckle
Price: $16,700

Master Ultra Thin Perpetual

Reference number: 130 35 20
Movement: automatic, JLC Caliber 868; height 4.72 mm; 46 jewels; 28,800 vph; 38-hour power reserve
Functions: hours, minutes, sweep seconds; perpetual calendar with date, weekday, month, moon phase, year display (4 digits)
Case: white gold, ø 39 mm, height 9.2 mm; sapphire crystal; transparent case back; water-resistant to 5 atm
Band: reptile skin, buckle
Price: $35,900
Variations: rose gold ($32,800), stainless steel ($20,800)

Master Ultra Thin Perpetual

Reference number: 130 25 20
Movement: automatic, JLC Caliber 868; height 4.72 mm; 46 jewels; 28,800 vph; 38-hour power reserve
Functions: hours, minutes, sweep seconds; perpetual calendar with date, weekday, month, moon phase, year display (4 digits)
Case: pink gold, ø 39 mm, height 9.2 mm; sapphire crystal; transparent case back; water-resistant to 5 atm
Band: reptile skin, buckle
Price: $32,800
Variations: white gold ($35,900), stainless steel ($20,800)

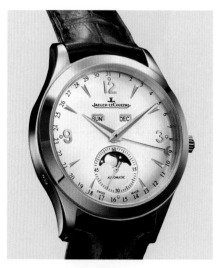

Master Ultra Thin Grand Feu

Reference number: Q129 35 E1
Movement: manually wound, JLC Caliber 849; ø 20.8 mm, height 1.85 mm; 19 jewels; 21,600 vph; 35-hour power reserve
Functions: hours, minutes
Case: white gold, ø 39 mm, height 5.04 mm; sapphire crystal; transparent case back; water-resistant to 3 atm
Band: reptile skin, buckle
Remarks: enamel dial
Price: $32,200

Master Calendar

Reference number: 155 25 20
Movement: automatic, JLC Caliber 866; height 5.65 mm; 32 jewels; 28,800 vph; fine hand-finishing; 43-hour power reserve
Functions: hours, minutes, subsidiary seconds; full calendar with date, weekday, month, moon phase
Case: pink gold, ø 39 mm, height 10.6 mm; sapphire crystal; transparent case back; water-resistant to 5 atm
Band: reptile skin, buckle
Price: $24,300
Variations: stainless steel with folding clasp ($11,300)

Master Ultra Thin 1907

Reference number: 129 25 20
Movement: manually wound, JLC Caliber 849; ø 20.8 mm, height 1.85 mm; 19 jewels; 21,600 vph; 35-hour power reserve
Functions: hours, minutes
Case: pink gold, ø 39 mm, height 4.1 mm; sapphire crystal; water-resistant to 3 atm
Band: reptile skin, buckle
Price: $18,600

Geophysic 1958

Reference number: 800 85 20
Movement: automatic, JLC Caliber 898/1; ø 26 mm height 3.30 mm; 30 jewels, 28,800 vph; 43-hour power reserve
Functions: hours, minutes, seconds
Case: pink gold, ø 38.5 mm, height 11.32 mm; water-resistant to 10 atm
Band: reptile skin, buckle
Price: $20,800; limited to 800 pieces
Variations: stainless steal ($9,800; limited to 300 pieces); platinum ($32,000; limited to 58 pieces)

Grande Reverso Ultra Thin 1931

Reference number: 278 25 60
Movement: manually wound, JLC Caliber 822-2; 17.20 x 22 mm, height 2.94 mm; 19 jewels; 21,600 vph; fine finishing; 45-hour power reserve
Functions: hours, minutes, subsidiary seconds
Case: pink gold, 27.4 x 46.8 mm, height 7.3 mm; sapphire crystal; water-resistant to 3 atm
Band: reptile skin, buckle
Remarks: case pivots 180°; with 2nd strap
Price: $18,800

Grande Reverso Night & Day

Reference number: 380 25 20
Movement: automatic, JLC Caliber 967B; height 4.05 mm; 28 jewels; 28,800 vph; fine finishing by hand; 42-hour power reserve
Functions: hours, minutes; 24-hour display
Case: pink gold, 27.4 x 46.8 mm, height 9.14 mm; sapphire crystal; water-resistant to 3 atm
Band: reptile skin, buckle
Remarks: case pivots 180°
Price: $19,200
Variations: stainless steel ($9,750)

Grande Reverso Calendar

Reference number: 375 25 20
Movement: manually wound, JLC Caliber 843; height 4.29 mm; 21 jewels; 21,600 vph; 45-hour power reserve
Functions: hours, minutes; full calendar with date, weekday, month, moon phase
Case: rose gold, 29.5 x 48.5 mm, height 10.24 mm; sapphire crystal; water-resistant to 3 atm
Band: reptile skin, buckle
Remarks: case pivots 180°
Price: $23,200
Variations: stainless steel ($13,100)

Rendez-Vous Date

Reference number: 351 25 20
Movement: automatic, JLC Caliber 966; ø 20 mm, height 4.2 mm; 28 jewels; 28,800 vph; 42-hour power reserve
Functions: hours, minutes, sweep seconds; date
Case: pink gold, ø 27.5 mm, height 8.24 mm; bezel set with 60 diamonds; sapphire crystal; transparent case back; water-resistant to 3 atm
Band: reptile skin, buckle
Price: $20,400

Rendez-Vous Night & Day

Reference number: 346 25 90
Movement: automatic, JLC Caliber 967A; ø 20 mm, height 4.05 mm; 28 jewels; 28,800 vph
Functions: hours, minutes, seconds; day/night indicator
Case: stainless steel, ø 29 mm, height 8.7 mm; sapphire crystal; transparent case back; water-resistant to 3 atm
Band: reptile skin, buckle
Remarks: dial set with 11 diamonds
Price: $10,300
Variations: pink gold ($18,100)

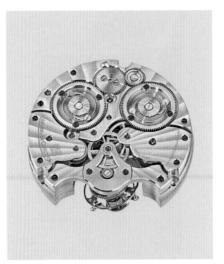

Caliber 381

Manually wound; 2 spring barrels and 2 separate gear trains for watch and foudroyante mechanism; 50-hour power reserve
Functions: hours, minutes, foudroyante sixth-second counter (2nd foudroyante); date; moon phase and age; double power reserve indicator
Diameter: 33.7 mm
Height: 7.25 mm
Jewels: 40
Balance: screw balance with weights
Frequency: 21,600 vph
Remarks: 369 components

Caliber 382

Manually wound; 2 barrel springs and 2 separate mechanisms for watch and double-axis tourbillon, double-axis tourbillon with -20° tilt, 15- or 30-second revolution, pull crown to reset second hand; twin spring barrels, 50-hour power reserve
Functions: hours, minutes, subsidiary seconds; 2nd time zone (additional 24-hour display); annual calendar with date; double power reserve display
Diameter: 33.7 mm; **Height:** 10.45 mm
Jewels: 33
Balance: glucydur
Frequency: 21,600 vph
Balance spring: cylindrical

Caliber 383

Manually wound; 2 separate spring barrels and 2 separate gear works for 2 time displays, pull crown to reset second hand; 50-hour power reserve
Functions: hours and minutes (off-center), sweep seconds; 2nd time zone (digital, jumping hours, minutes), world-time display, separate power reserve indicator for each spring barrel
Diameter: 34.3 mm
Height: 7.25 mm
Jewels: 54
Balance: glucydur
Frequency: 28,800 vph

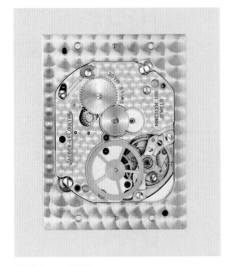

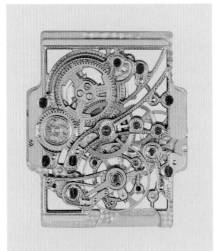

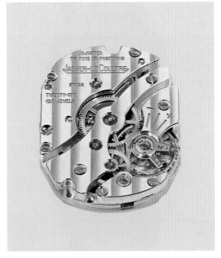

Caliber 986

Manually wound; 48-hour power reserve
Functions: hours, minutes, subsidiary seconds; 24-hour display (2nd time zone); date
Measurements: 22.6 x 25.6 mm
Height: 4.15 mm
Jewels: 19
Frequency: 28,800 vph
Balance spring: flat hairspring
Shock protection: Kif
Remarks: perlage on plate

Caliber 849 RSQ

Manually wound; fully skeletonized and engraved by hand; simple barrel spring, 35-hour power reserve
Functions: hours, minutes
Measurements: 20 x 23.5 mm
Height: 2.09 mm
Jewels: 19
Balance: glucydur
Frequency: 21,600 vph
Balance spring: flat spring with swan-neck fine adjustment
Shock protection: Kif
Remarks: 128 components

Caliber 843

Manually wound; single spring barrel, 45-hour power reserve
Functions: hours, minutes; full calendar with date, weekday, month, moon phase
Measurements: 22.6 x 25.6 mm
Height: 4.29 mm
Jewels: 21
Balance: glucydur with weighted screws
Frequency: 21,600 vph
Balance spring: flat hairspring
Shock protection: Kif

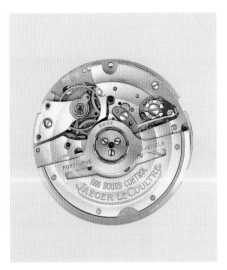

Caliber 757

Automatic; column wheel control of the chronograph functions; 2 spring barrels, 65-hour power reserve
Functions: hours, minutes, subsidiary seconds; additional 12-hour display (2nd time zone), day/night indicator; chronograph; date
Diameter: 28 mm
Height: 6.26 mm
Jewels: 45
Balance: glucydur with 4 weighted screws
Frequency: 28,800 vph
Balance spring: flat hairspring
Shock protection: Kif

Caliber 849

Manually wound; single spring barrel, 35-hour power reserve
Functions: hours, minutes
Diameter: 26 mm
Height: 1.85 mm
Jewels: 19
Balance: glucydur
Frequency: 21,600 vph
Balance spring: flat hairspring
Shock protection: Kif
Remarks: finely finished movement, bridges with côtes de Genève; 123 components

Caliber 898A

Automatic; single spring barrel, 43-hour power reserve
Functions: hours, minutes, sweep seconds; day/night indicator
Diameter: 26 mm
Height: 3.3 mm
Jewels: 30
Balance: glucydur with 4 weighted screws
Frequency: 28,800 vph
Balance spring: flat hairspring
Shock protection: Kif

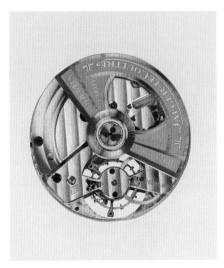

Caliber 978

Automatic; 1-minute tourbillon; full gold rotor; single spring barrel, 48-hour power reserve
Functions: hours, minutes, small seconds (on tourbillon cage); additional 24-hour display; hand date (jumps from 15th to 16th of month)
Diameter: 31 mm
Height: 7.05 mm
Jewels: 33
Balance: glucydur with weighted screws
Frequency: 28,800 vph
Balance spring: Breguet spring
Shock protection: Kif
Remarks: perlage on plate, bridges with côtes de Genève

Caliber 982

Automatic; 1-minute tourbillon; full gold rotor; single spring barrel, 48-hour power reserve
Functions: hours, minutes, subsidiary seconds (on tourbillon cage)
Diameter: 30 mm
Height: 6.4 mm
Jewels: 33
Balance: glucydur with weighted screws
Frequency: 28,800 vph
Balance spring: Breguet spring
Shock protection: Kif
Remarks: perlage on plate, bridges with côtes de Genève

Caliber 985

Automatic, flying 1-minute tourbillon; full gold rotor; single spring barrel, 48-hour power reserve
Functions: hours, minutes, subsidiary seconds (on tourbillon cage); perpetual calendar with date, weekday, month, moon phase, year display (digital, 4 digits)
Diameter: 30.7 mm
Height: 8.25 mm
Jewels: 49
Balance: glucydur with 4 weighted screws
Frequency: 28,800 vph
Balance spring: cylindrical

Jaquet Droz

Montres Jaquet Droz SA
CH-2300 La Chaux-de-Fonds
Switzerland

Tel.:
01141-32-924-2888

Fax:
01141-32-924-2882

E-Mail:
info@jaquet-droz.com

Website:
www.jaquet-droz.com

Founded:
1738

U.S. distributor:
The Swatch Group (U.S.), Inc.
1200 Harbor Boulevard
Weehawken, NJ 07086
201-271-1400
www.swatchgroup.com

Most important collections/price range:
Urban: London; Legend: Geneva;
Complication: La Chaux-de-Fonds; Majestic:
Beijing; Elegance: Paris; Les Ateliers D'Art /
starting at $8,400

Though this watch brand first gained real notice when it was bought by the Swatch Group in 2001, Jaquet Droz looks back on a long tradition. Pierre Jaquet-Droz (1721–1790) was actually supposed to be a pastor, but instead followed the call to become a mechanic and a watchmaker. In the mid-eighteenth century, he began to push the limits of micromechanics, and his enthusiasm for it quickly led him to work on watch mechanisms and more complicated movements, which he attempted to operate through purely mechanical means.

Jaquet-Droz became famous in Europe for his automatons. More than once, he had to answer to religious institutions, whose guardians of public morals suspected there might be some devil's work and witchcraft behind his mechanical children, scribes, and organists. He even designed prostheses. A small enterprise in La Chaux-de-Fonds still produces items of this applied art, proof that the name Jaquet-Droz is still alive and well in the Jura mountains. The true wealth of the Jaquet-Droz family's output, however, was shown in the stunning exhibition "Automats and Marvels" organized in Neuchâtel, La Chaux-de-Fonds, and Le Locle in 2012.

The Swatch Group has developed an aesthetically and technically sophisticated collection based on an outstanding Frédéric Piguet movement. In recent years, the classically beautiful watch dials have taken on a slightly modern look without losing any of their identity. The spirit of the maverick founder of the brand still hovers about. In fact, Jaquet Droz is a top representative in the Swatch Group's portfolio. Its CEO is Marc A. Hayek, who is also CEO of Breguet and Blancpain.

The Bird Repeater

Reference number: J031033200
Movement: manual winding, Jaquet Droz Caliber RMA88; ø 35 mm, height 8.8 mm; 69 jewels; 18,000 vph; 48-hour power reserve
Functions: hours and minutes (off-center); minute repeater
Case: pink gold, ø 47 mm, height 18.7 mm; sapphire crystal
Band: reptile skin, folding clasp
Remarks: hand-painted mother-of-pearl dial
Price: $472,500; limited to 8 pieces
Variations: white gold ($493,500; limited to 8 pieces)

Petite Heure Minute Relief Horse

Reference number: J005023275
Movement: automatic, Jaquet Droz Caliber 2653; ø 26.2 mm, height 4.47 mm; 28 jewels; 28,800 vph; double spring barrel, oscillating mass of pink gold and white mother-of-pearl with hand-engraved cobra; 68-hour power reserve
Functions: hours and minutes (off-center)
Case: pink gold set with 309 diamonds; ø 41 mm, height 13.77 mm; sapphire crystal, water-resistant to 3 atm
Band: reptile skin, buckle
Remarks: mother-of-pearl dial, hand-engraved horse
Price: $62,000; limited to 88 pieces
Variations: black enamel dial and low relief ($57,800)

The Eclipse Mother of Pearl

Reference number: J012614570
Movement: automatic, Jaquet Droz Caliber 6553L2; ø 27 mm, height 5.02 mm, 28 jewels; 28,800 vph; double spring barrel, white gold oscillating weight, 68-hour power reserve
Functions: hours, minutes; full calendar with date, weekday, month, moon phase (retrograde)
Case: white gold, ø 39 mm, height 12.7 mm; bezel and lugs set with 248 diamonds; sapphire crystal; transparent case back; water-resistant to 3 atm
Band: satin, buckle set with 24 diamonds
Remarks: mother-of-pearl dial
Price: $36,500
Variations: pink gold w/o diamonds ($29,300)

Perpetual Calendar Eclipse Ivory Enamel

Reference number: J030533201
Movement: automatic, Jaquet Droz Caliber 5853LR; ø 32 mm, height 6.22 mm; 34 jewels; 28,800 vph; double spring barrel, white gold oscillating mass; 68-hour power reserve
Functions: hours, minutes; perpetual calendar with retrograde date, weekday, month, moon phase, leap year
Case: pink gold, ø 43 mm, height 13.2 mm; sapphire crystal; water-resistant to 3 atm
Band: reptile skin, folding clasp
Price: $54,600
Variations: black dial ($54,600)

Petite Heure Minute Paillonnée

Reference number: J005013240
Movement: automatic, Jaquet Droz Caliber 2653; ø 26.2 mm, height 4.47 mm; 30 jewels; 28,800 vph; double spring barrel, white gold and white mother-of-pearl oscillating mass, hand-engraved; 68-hour power reserve
Functions: hours and minutes (off-center)
Case: pink gold, ø 39 mm, height 11.52 mm; sapphire crystal; water-resistant to 3 atm
Band: reptile skin, buckle
Remarks: enamel dial with paillette decoration
Price: $39,900; limited to 8 pieces
Variations: as Grande Seconde Paillonnée ($42,000); pocket watch ($47,300)

Grande Seconde Quantieme Ivory Enamel

Reference number: J007033200
Movement: automatic, Jaquet Droz Caliber 2660Q2; ø 26.2 mm, height 4.52 mm; 30 jewels; 28,800 vph; double spring barrel, silicon, pink gold oscillating mass; 68-hour power reserve
Functions: hours and minutes (off-center), subsidiary seconds; date
Case: pink gold, ø 43 mm, height 12.21 mm; sapphire crystal; water-resistant to 3 atm
Band: reptile skin, buckle
Remarks: enamel dial
Price: $20,000
Variations: 39 mm case ($19,400)

Grande Seconde SW Steel

Reference number: J029020241
Movement: automatic, Jaquet Droz Caliber 2663A-S; ø 26.2 mm, height 4.52 mm; 30 jewels; 28,800 vph; double spring barrel, white gold oscillating mass with black PVD finish; 68-hour power reserve
Functions: hours and minutes (off-center), subsidiary seconds
Case: stainless steel, ø 41 mm, height 10.89 mm; sapphire crystal; transparent case back; crown with rubber sheathing; water-resistant to 5 atm
Band: reptile skin, folding clasp
Price: $17,700
Variations: anthracite or light gray dial and 45 mm case

Lady 8 Mother-of-Pearl

Reference number: J014503270
Movement: automatic, Jaquet Droz Caliber 1153; ø 26.2 mm, height 3.37 mm; 28 jewels; 28,800 vph; double spring barrel, white gold oscillating mass; 68-hour power reserve
Functions: hours and minutes (off-center)
Case: pink gold, ø 35 mm, height 12.7 mm; bezel set with 128 diamonds; pearl at 12; sapphire crystal; cabochon on crown; water-resistant to 3 atm
Band: reptile skin, folding clasp (set with 47 diamonds)
Remarks: mother-of-pearl dial
Price: $35,600
Variations: black or white ceramic ($14,600)

Petite Heure Minute 35 mm Aventurine

Reference number: J005000271
Movement: automatic, Jaquet Droz Caliber 2653; ø 26.2 mm, height 4.52 mm; 28 jewels; 28,800 vph; double spring barrel, oscillating mass of heavy metal; 68-hour power reserve
Functions: hours and minutes (off-center)
Case: stainless steel, ø 35 mm, height 10.4 mm; bezel set with 160 diamonds, sapphire crystal; water-resistant to 3 atm
Band: folding clasp
Remarks: aventurine dial
Price: $15,200
Variations: w/o diamonds ($8,400)

Jeanrichard SA

129, rue du Progrès
CH-2300 La Chaux-de-Fonds
Switzerland

Tel.:
01141-32-911-3636

Fax:
01141-32-911-3637

Website:
www.jeanrichard.com

Founded:
1988

Number of employees:
100

Annual production:
4,000 watches

U.S. distributor:
Tradema of America, Inc.
201 Route 17 North, 8th Floor
Rutherford, NJ 07070
201-804-1904

Most important collections/price range:
1681 / approx. $4,900 to $21,400;
Terrascope, Aeroscope, Aquascope / approx.
$2,900 to $8,500

Jeanrichard

Daniel Jeanrichard (1665–1741) is one of the seminal figures in the art of watchmaking in the Jura region above Neuchâtel, though myth and reality may well have become a little mixed up. When he was fourteen, allegedly, a passing horse dealer noticed the filigree silver jewelry the boy had made and gave him a timepiece to repair. When he returned a few weeks later, the watch was fixed, and Daniel had caught the watchmaking bug. He ultimately moved to Le Locle, opened a small *manufacture,* taught his five sons watchmaking, and rebuilt a gear-cutting machine that had been an industrial secret in Geneva.

Jeanrichard, today, is a part of the Sowind Group, with access to all the technology needed for serious timepieces. For a while, that meant playing little sister to the more dashing Girard-Perregaux, but between the Group CEO Michele Sofisti and COO Bruno Grande, a formula was devised simplifying the message through the product. The flagship 1681 series survived, and earth, air, and water are now celebrated by the Terrascope, Aeroscope, and Aquascope collections. The retro (as in sixties) cushion-shaped cases house a robust in-house automatic movement, and the price ceiling is around $6,000. The designers have a free hand in multiplying these models with colored dials, suggesting that the brand is on its way to serving a larger market. A sign of this is the bold collaboration with the London Arsenal Football Club, which also spawned an Aeroscope Chrono with a black titanium bezel and a brilliant red dial.

Terrascope

Reference number: 60500-11-601-11A
Movement: automatic, JR Caliber JR60 (base Sellita SW 300); ø 25.6 mm, height 4.6 mm; 26 jewels; 28,800 vph; 38-hour power reserve
Functions: hours, minutes, sweep seconds; date
Case: stainless steel; ø 44 mm, height 12.6 mm; sapphire crystal; water-resistant to 10 atm
Band: stainless steel bracelet, folding clasp
Price: $3,500
Variations: rubber strap, folding clasp ($2,900)

Aquascope

Reference number: 60400-11B402-FK4A
Movement: automatic, JR Caliber JR60 (base Sellita SW 300); ø 25.6 mm, height 4.6 mm; 26 jewels; 28,800 vph; 38-hour power reserve
Functions: hours, minutes, sweep seconds; date
Case: stainless steel, ø 44 mm, height 13.05 mm; unidirectional bezel with 60-minute division, sapphire crystal; screw-in crown; water-resistant to 30 atm
Band: stainless steel, folding clasp
Remarks: engraved dial with floating indexes
Price: $3,300
Variations: stainless steel bracelet ($3,800)

Aeroscope Arsenal FC Limited Edition

Reference number: 60650-21PH51-FKHB
Movement: automatic, JR Caliber JR66 (base Sellita SW300 with Dubois Dépraz chronograph module); ø 28.6 mm, height 6.1 mm; 43 jewels; 28,800 vph; 42-hour power reserve
Functions: hours, minutes, subsidiary seconds; chronograph; date
Case: titanium with black DLC coating, ø 44 mm, height 12.8 mm; engraved tachymeter-scale bezel, sapphire crystal; water-resistant to 10 atm
Band: rubber, folding clasp
Remarks: Arsenal emblem acts as constant seconds hand
Price: $6,200; limited to 250 pieces

Jörg Schauer

Jörg Schauer's watches are first and foremost cool. The cases have been carefully worked, the look is planned to draw the eye. After all, he is a perfectionist and leaves nothing to chance. He works on every single case himself, polishing and performing his own brand of magic for as long as it takes to display his personal touch. This time-consuming process is one that Schauer believes is absolutely necessary. "I do this because I place a great deal of value on the fact that my cases are absolutely perfect," he explains. "I can do it better than anyone, and I would never let anyone else do it for me."

Schauer, a goldsmith by training, has been making watches since 1990. He began by doing one-off pieces in precious metals for collectors and then opened his business and simultaneously moved to stainless steel. His style is to produce functional, angular cases with visibly screwed-down bezels and straightforward dials in plain black or white. Forget finding any watch close to current trends in his collection; Schauer only builds timepieces that he genuinely likes.

Purchasing a Schauer is not that easy. He has chosen a strategy of genuine quality over quantity and only produces to about 500 annually. This includes special watches like the One-Hand Durowe, with a movement from one of Germany's movement manufacturers, Durowe, which Schauer acquired in 2002. His production structure is a vital part of his success and includes prototyping, movement modification, finishing, case production, dial painting and printing—all done in Schauer's own workshop in Engelsbrand. Any support he needs from the outside he prefers to search out among regional specialists.

Jörg Schauer
c/o Stowa GmbH &CO. KG
Gewerbepark 16
D-75331 Engelsbrand
Germany

Tel.:
01149-7082-9306-0

Fax:
01149-7082-9306-2

E-Mail:
info@schauer-germany.com

Website:
www.schauer-germany.com

Founded:
1990

Number of employees:
20

Annual production:
max. 500 watches and 4,000 watches for Stowa

Distribution:
direct sales; please contact the address in Germany

Edition 9

Reference number: Ed9
Movement: automatic, ETA Caliber 7751; ø 30 mm, height 7.9 mm; 28 jewels; 28,800 vph; decorative ribbing, blued screws, exclusive engraved Schauer rotor; 42-hour power reserve
Functions: hours, minutes, subsidiary seconds; additional 24-hour display; chronograph; full calendar with month, moon phase, weekday, date
Case: stainless steel, ø 42 mm, height 15 mm; bezel secured with 12 screws; antireflective sapphire crystal on front and back; water-resistant to 5 atm
Band: stainless steel Milanese mesh, folding clasp
Price: $5,410
Variations: calf leather band ($4,630); reptile band ($4,710); manually wound ($5,590)

Edition 10

Reference number: Ed10
Movement: automatic, ETA Caliber 7753; ø 30 mm, height 7.9 mm; 27 jewels; 28,800 vph; finished with ornamental stripes and blued screws, exclusive engraved Schauer rotor; 42-hour power reserve
Functions: hours, minutes, subsidiary seconds; chronograph
Case: stainless steel, ø 42 mm, height 15 mm; bezel fixed with 12 screws; sapphire crystal on front and back, antireflective inside; water-resistant to 5 atm
Band: calf leather, double folding clasp
Price: $4,360
Variations: reptile band ($4,450); stainless steel bracelet ($4,780); manually wound ($4,900)

Edition 15

Reference number: Ed15
Movement: automatic, ETA Caliber 7753; ø 30 mm, height 7.9 mm; 27 jewels; 28,800 vph; finished with ornamental stripes and blued screws, exclusive engraved Schauer rotor; 40-hour power reserve
Functions: hours, minutes, subsidiary seconds; chronograph; date
Case: stainless steel, ø 44 mm, height 15 mm; bezel fixed with 12 screws; sapphire crystal on front and back, antireflective inside; water-resistant to 5 atm
Band: rubber, double folding clasp
Price: $4,100
Variations: leather strap ($4,225); stainless steel bracelet ($4,250); manually wound ($4,640)

Juvenia Montres S.A.
Rue du Chatelot 21
CH-2304 La Chaux-de-Fonds
Switzerland

Tel.:
01141-32-925-7000

Fax:
01141-32-925-7008

E-Mail:
info@juvenia.ch

Website:
www.juvenia.ch

Founded:
1860

Number of employees:
30

Annual production:
10,000 watches

U.S. distributor:
Carat n Karat, Flushing Meadows, NY
718-888-3590; www.caratco.com
Westime, Beverly Hills, CA
310-271-0000
Hing Wa Lee, San Gabriel, CA
909-831-8888

Most important collections:
Sextant, Classic, J., Planet, specialties

Juvenia

The benefits of marketing are well illustrated by the Swiss brand Juvenia. In Hong Kong and other points east, its classic looking three-handers and two-handers are well-known. The largest Juvenia case is 41 millimeters in diameter, making these timepieces almost ideal for slimmer Asian wrists. But in the Occident, mentioning Juvenia could crease a few brows, because not many know of or remember it. Yet it is a brand whose history stretches back over 150 uninterrupted years.

It was founded in 1860 by an Alsatian watchmaker named Jacques Didisheim in the Swiss horological hub of La Chaux-de-Fonds. It became quite a powerful operation at one time, a full-fledged *manufacture* with a catalogue that served the Swiss Patent Office as a reference guide to check new filings for originality. Among its claims to fame is the smallest single lever movement ever made, which was unveiled in 1914: 9.5 by 2.5 millimeters.

The quartz crisis left Juvenia on the ropes. It reacted by cultivating the Asian markets, which turned out to be a lucrative strategy. With new stability and investments, Juvenia is now beginning to move back into Europe and the United States with a mostly staid, well-built set of timepieces. There is the Sextant, looking curiously Masonic with its protractor and compass pointer as the hour and second hand respectively. (Johnny Depp was wearing an older version in a shoot for *Esquire*.) The understated Planets fit anywhere, and the tourbillon in the specialty series is for real watch fans. Juvenia has also revived its iconic Attraction, originally released in 1951 and based on a stick movement that powers a small two-hand watch almost buried in diamonds.

Sextant

Reference number: SXA1.6.096.21
Movement: automatic, Juvenia J015; ø 25.6 mm, height 3.6 mm; 25 jewels; 28,800 vph; 42-hour power reserve
Functions: hours, minutes, sweep seconds; date
Case: red gold, ø 40 mm, height 9.35 mm; sapphire crystal; transparent case back; water-resistant to 3 atm
Band: reptile skin, buckle
Remarks: seconds hand acts as compass, minute hands as ruler; hour hand as protractor; BlackOr dial
Price: $11,000

Slimatic

Reference number: SLA1.6.536.21
Movement: automatic, Juvenia J09; ø 32.5 mm, height 4.51 mm; 26 jewels; 21,600 vph; 38-hour power reserve
Functions: hours, minutes, date
Case: pink gold, 40 mm, height 10.05 mm; sapphire crystal; screw-in crown; transparent case back; water-resistant to 3 atm
Band: reptile skin, buckle
Price: $14,200

Power Reserve

Reference number: PRA2.4.514.20
Movement: automatic, Juvenia J017; ø 25.6 mm, height 5.1 mm; 26 jewels; 28,800 vph; 42-hour power reserve
Functions: hours, minutes, sweep seconds; weekday, date; power reserve indicator
Case: stainless steel, ø 40 mm, height 10 mm; sapphire crystal; transparent case back; water-resistant to 3 atm
Band: reptile skin, folding clasp
Price: $5,100

Moon Phase

Reference number: MPA2.4.514.20
Movement: automatic, Juvenia J019; ø 25.6 mm, height 5.2 mm; 25 jewels; 28,800 vph; 42-hour power reserve
Functions: hours, minutes, sweep seconds; weekday, month, date; moon phase
Case: stainless steel, ø 40 mm, height 10 mm; sapphire crystal; transparent case back; water-resistant to 3 atm
Band: reptile skin, buckle
Price: $6,000

World Time

Reference number: WTA1.6.056.21
Movement: automatic, Juvenia J07-A; ø 34 mm, height 4.3 mm; 23 jewels; 28,800 vph; 40-hour power reserve
Functions: hours, minutes, sweep seconds; date; second time zone, day/night display; 24-hour display with reference cities and places
Case: pink gold, ø 40 mm, height 10 mm; sapphire crystal; transparent case back; water-resistant to 3 atm
Band: reptile skin, buckle
Remarks: BlackOr dial
Price: $19,100

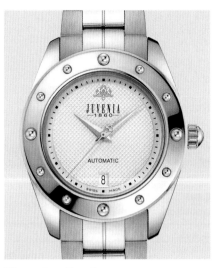

Planet – Gents

Reference number: PLA1.4.594.04
Movement: automatic, Juvenia J026-G; ø 25.6 mm, height 3.6 mm; 25 jewels; 28,800 vph; 42-hour power reserve
Functions: hours, minutes, sweep seconds; date
Case: stainless steel, ø 40 mm, height 12.45 mm; screw-in crown; sapphire crystal; water-resistant to 10 atm
Band: stainless steel, folding clasp
Price: $3,600

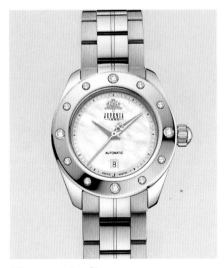

Planet – Ladies

Reference number: PLB1.5.994.04
Movement: automatic, Juvenia J026-L; ø 17.2 mm, height 4.8 mm; 25 jewels; 28,800 vph; 38-hour power reserve
Functions: hours, minutes, sweep seconds; date
Case: stainless steel, ø 29 mm, height 10.35 mm; screw-in crown; sapphire crystal; bezel set with 12 diamonds; water-resistant to 10 atm
Band: stainless steel, folding clasp
Price: $4,600

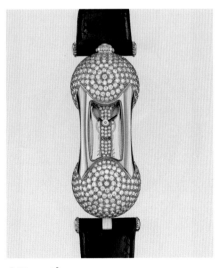

Attraction

Reference number: ATT1.7.700.71
Movement: manually wound, straight Juvenia J02; height 4.17 mm; 17 jewels; 21,600 vph; 35-hour power reserve
Functions: hours, minutes
Case: pink gold, set with 426 diamonds, height 9.15 mm; transparent case back; sapphire crystal; water-resistant to 3 atm
Band: reptile skin, buckle
Price: $78,700

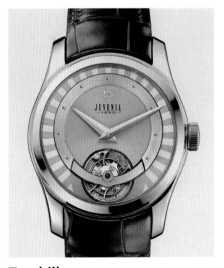

Tourbillon

Reference number: TBC1.6.646.21
Movement: manually wound, Juvenia J020; ø 32.8 mm, height 5.76 mm; 29 jewels; 21,600 vph; tourbillon; 56-hour power reserve
Functions: hours, minutes
Case: pink gold, ø 38 mm, height 10.85 mm; sapphire crystal; transparent case back; water-resistant to 3 atm
Band: reptile skin, buckle
Price: $77,100

Kobold Watch Company, LLC
1801 Parkway View Drive
Pittsburgh, PA 15205

Tel.:
724-533-3000

E-Mail:
info@koboldwatch.com

Website:
www.koboldwatch.com

Founded:
1998

Number of employees:
12

Annual production:
maximum 2,500 watches

Distribution:
factory-direct, select retailers

Most important collections/price range:
Soarway / $1,950 to $35,000

Kobold

Like many others in the field, Michael Kobold had already developed an interest in the watch industry in childhood. As a young man, he found a mentor in Chronoswiss founder Gerd-Rüdiger Lang, who encouraged him to start his own brand. This he did in 1998—at the age of nineteen while he was still a student at Carnegie Mellon University. Today, Kobold Watch Company has twelve employees split between Amish Country in Pennsylvania and a subsidiary in Kathmandu, Nepal. The latter operation is run by two former sherpas, Namgel and Thundu, who trained under Kobold watchmakers in Pittsburgh in 2011 and now oversee the first mechanical watch company in the Himalayas. The company's motto—Embrace Adventure—is reflected in the adventure-themed watches it turns out worn by explorers such as Sir Ranulph Fiennes, whom the *Guinness Book of Records* describes as "the world's greatest living explorer."

In 2014, Kobold inaugurated new headquarters on a 170-year-old farm. There, the company manufactures cases, movement components, dials, hands, and even straps. Kobold has contributed to the renaissance of American watchmaking and has set his sights even higher, namely, on an in-house U.S.-made movement.

The brand's centerpiece is the Soarway collection and the fabled Soarway case, which was originally created in 1999 by Sir Ranulph, master watchmaker and Chronoswiss founder Lang, as well as company founder Kobold. The Soarway collection includes several novelties this year, including the Soarway Transglobe, a watch with a second time zone that displays minutes as well as hours.

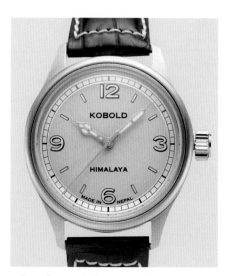

Soarway Transglobe

Reference number: KN 266853
Movement: automatic, Caliber K.793 (base ETA 2892-A2); ø 36 mm, height 4.95 mm; 26 jewels; 28,800 vph; 46-hour power reserve
Functions: hours, minutes, sweep seconds; date; second time zone with hours and minutes
Case: stainless steel, ø 44 mm, height 14.3 mm; sapphire crystal; screwed-down case back; water-resistant to 30 atm
Band: canvas, signed buckle
Price: $3,600

Himalaya

Reference number: KN 880121
Movement: automatic, ETA Caliber 2824-A2; ø 30.4 mm, height 10.35 mm; 25 jewels; 28,800 vph; 42-hour power reserve
Functions: hours, minutes, sweep seconds
Case: stainless steel, ø 44 mm, height 11.3 mm; antireflective sapphire crystal; screwed-down case back; water-resistant to 10 atm
Band: calf leather, buckle
Price: $2,950
Variations: black or white dial

Himalaya 41

Reference number: KN 830854
Movement: automatic, ETA Caliber 2824-A2; ø 30.4 mm, height 10.35 mm; 25 jewels; 28,800 vph; 42-hour power reserve
Functions: hours, minutes, sweep seconds
Case: stainless steel, ø 41 mm, height 12.6 mm; antireflective sapphire crystal; screwed-down case back; water-resistant to 10 atm
Band: reptile, buckle
Price: $2,450

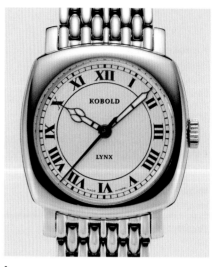

Phantom Tactical Chronograph

Reference number: KD 924451
Movement: automatic, ETA Valjoux Caliber 7750;
ø 30 mm, height 8.1 mm; 25 jewels; 28,800 vph;
46-hour power reserve; côtes de Genève, perlage,
engraved and skeletonized gold-plated rotor
Functions: hours, minutes, subsidiary seconds;
date, day; chronograph
Case: PVD-coated stainless steel, made in USA, ø
41 mm, height 15.3 mm; unidirectional bezel with
60-minute divisions; screwed-in crown and buttons;
sapphire crystal; screwed-down case back; water-
resistant to 300 m
Band: PVD-coated stainless steel, folding clasp
Price: $4,150

Phantom Chronograph

Reference number: KD 924453
Movement: automatic, ETA Valjoux Caliber 7750;
ø 30 mm, height 8.1 mm; 25 jewels; 28,800 vph;
46-hour power reserve
Functions: hours, minutes, subsidiary seconds;
perpetual calendar, date, weekday; chronograph
Case: stainless steel, made in USA, ø 41 mm, height
15.3 mm; unidirectional bezel with 60-minute
divisions; screwed-in crown and buttons; sapphire
crystal; screwed-down case back; water-resistant
to 30 atm
Band: canvas, folding clasp
Price: $3,250

Lynx

Reference number: KD 415752
Movement: automatic, ETA Caliber 2892-A2;
ø 28 mm, height 3.6 mm; 25 jewels; 28,800 vph;
46-hour power reserve
Functions: hours, minutes, sweep seconds
Case: stainless steel, made in USA, ø 36 mm,
height 10.2 mm; antireflective sapphire crystal;
screwed-down case back; water-resistant to 10 atm
Band: stainless steel bracelet, folding clasp
Price: $2,450
Variations: dial made from Mt. Everest summit rock,
mother-of-pearl, diamond bezel

Polar Surveyor

Reference number: KD 915151
Movement: automatic, Caliber K.751 (base ETA
7750); ø 26.2 mm, height 5.3 mm; 28 jewels;
28,800 vph; 42-hour power reserve
Functions: hours, minutes, sweep seconds;
perpetual calendar, date; chronograph; day/night
indicator
Case: stainless steel, made in USA, ø 41 mm, height
15.3 mm; antireflective sapphire crystal; screwed-
down case back; screwed-in crown; water-resistant
to 30 atm
Band: canvas, signed buckle
Price: $4,050

Soarway Diver

Reference number: KD 212441
Movement: automatic, ETA Caliber 2892-A2;
ø 28 mm, height 3.6 mm; 25 jewels; 28,800 vph;
46-hour power reserve
Functions: hours, minutes, sweep seconds; date
Case: stainless steel, made in USA; ø 43.5 mm,
height 15 mm; unidirectional bezel; soft iron core;
antireflective sapphire crystal; screwed-down case
back; screw-in crown; water-resistant to 50 atm
Band: canvas, buckle
Price: $1,950
Variations: standard, non-California dial, Arctic
Blue dial

SMG-2

Reference number: KD 956853
Movement: automatic, Caliber ETA 2893-A2;
ø 26.2 mm, height 6.1 mm; 21 jewels; 28,800 vph;
40-hour power reserve
Functions: hours, minutes, sweep seconds; second
time zone; date
Case: stainless steel, made in USA; ø 43 mm,
height 12.75 mm; unidirectional bezel; soft iron
core; antireflective sapphire crystal; screwed-down
case back; screwed-in crown; water-resistant to 30
atm
Band: canvas, buckle
Price: $3,450

Kudoke Uhren

Tannenweg 5
D-15236 Frankfurt (Oder)
Germany

Tel.:
01141-335-280-0409

E-Mail:
info@kudoke.eu

Website:
www.kudoke.eu

Founded:
2007

Number of employees:
1

Annual production:
30–50 watches

U.S. distributor:
Kudoke
WatchBuys
888-333-4895
www.watchbuys.com

Most important collections/price range:
between approx. $4,500 and $11,500

Kudoke

Stefan Kudoke, a watchmaker from Frankfurt/Oder, has made a name for himself as an extremely skilled and imaginative creator of timepieces. He apprenticed with two experienced watchmakers and graduated as the number one trainee in the state of Brandenburg. This earned him a stipend from a federal program promoting gifted individuals. He then moved on to one of the large *manufactures* in Glashütte, where he refined his skills in its workshop for complications and prototyping. At the age of twenty-two, with a master's diploma in his pocket, he decided to get an MBA and then devote himself to building his own company.

His guiding principle is individuality, and that is not possible to find in a serial product. So Kudoke began building unique pieces. By realizing the special wishes of customers, he manages to reflect each person's uniqueness in each watch. And he has produced some out-of-the-ordinary pieces, like the ExCentro1 and 2, whose dials are off-center and hint at a feeling for the absurd, à la Dali.

His specialties include engraving and goldsmithing. Within his creations bridges may in fact be graceful bodies, or the fine skeletonizing of a plate fragment, a world of figures and garlands. In 2012, he presented the ladies' White Flower, frankly romantic and surprisingly simple. A close look at the bridges and fragments of the mainplate reveals small works of art—the shape of a grasping octopus, the sensuous body of a woman, or a skull with a bone, giving the term "skeleton watch" a special meaning.

ExCentro II

Movement: automatic, ETA Caliber 2824-2; ø 25.6 mm, height 4.6 mm; 25 jewels; 28,800 vph; partly hand-skeletonized and engraved, gold-plated rotor; 38-hour power reserve
Functions: hours, minutes, sweep seconds; date
Case: stainless steel, ø 42 mm, height 10.5 mm; sapphire crystal; transparent case back; water-resistant to 5 atm
Band: reptile skin, buckle
Remarks: ring to hold movement, customizable
Price: $5,400

HR1-Ring

Movement: manually wound, modified ETA Caliber 6498; ø 36.6 mm, height 4.5 mm; 17 jewels; 18,000 vph; hand-skeletonized and engraved; 38-hour power reserve
Functions: hours, minutes
Case: stainless steel, ø 42 mm, height 10.5 mm; sapphire crystal; transparent case back
Band: reptile skin, buckle
Remarks: hand-guilloché silver dial
Price: $10,600

Real Skeleton

Movement: manually wound, modified ETA Caliber 6498; ø 36.6 mm, height 4.5 mm; 17 jewels; 18,000 vph; screw balance, polished pallet lever and escape wheel, hand-skeletonized and engraved; 38-hour power reserve
Functions: hours, minutes
Case: stainless steel, ø 42 mm, height 10.5 mm; sapphire crystal; transparent case back
Band: reptile skin, buckle
Remarks: real bone hands, hand-made, skull eyes set with diamonds
Price: $13,650

Linde Werdelin

There are sports watches, and then there are watches for sports. Morton Linde and Jorn Werdelin, two Danes, were just teenagers when they started comparing their iconic acquisitions, like their Cartier Santos Octogonal, their Reversos, their Royal Oaks. Werdelin went on to study business; Linde became an industrial designer—the chairs in Copenhagen's park are from his drawing board.

The two men also shared a love of sports, particularly skiing. One day, when Werdelin was recovering from a severe skiing accident, the two friends dreamed up the idea of launching a sports watch. Thus Linde Werdelin was founded in 2002, and their idea gradually grew into a full-fledged concept, bold and quite literally out-of-the-box. Why confine oneself to mechanics, when electronics do some things better? A separate clip-on instrument box with a sophisticated mini-computer could be affixed to the base watch to display and log all the parameters of the activity being performed: The Reef, for divers, displays dive time, ascent rate, temperature, decompression stops, and more. For climbers, the Rock features a chronometer, altimeter, thermometer, three-point compass, incline indicator, and much more. As for the watch itself, without its IT unit, it spices up refinement with a dose of industrial ruggedness and hell-raiser edginess. So the collections were born: the Founders—the Elemental and 2-Timer—the Oktopus, and the SpidoSpeed, a three-way summit between tradition, high-tech, and style for the active and athletic with clip-ons for diving and skiing.

Divers looking for the thrill and romance of a moonlit plunge now have the Oktopus MoonLite, launched at Baselworld 2014 alongside the new-generation SpidoSpeed RoseGold Black and Green. These three new models push the young brand's venture into building in-house movements and experimenting with unusual materials like Alloy Linde Werdelin (ALW), an ultralight aerospace zirconium, aluminum, and magnesium-based alloy. All timepieces are manufactured in Geneva and Zurich.

Linde Werdelin
Studio 7, 27a Pembridge Villas
London W11 3EP
United Kingdom

Tel.:
01144-207-727-6577

Fax:
01144-207-900-1722

E-Mail:
info@lindewerdelin.com

Website:
www.lindewerdelin.com

Founded:
2002

Number of employees:
20+

Annual production:
between 600–1,000

U.S. distributor:
Totally Worth It, LLC
76 Division Avenue
Summit, NJ 07901-2309
201-894-4710
info@totallyworthit.com

Most important collections/price range:
SpidoSpeed, SpidoLite, Oktopus / $11,000 to $44,200

Linde WerdelinOktopus MoonLite

Movement: automatic, modified ETA 2892; ø 25.6 mm, height 3.6 mm; 23 jewels; 28,800 vph; in-house moon phase; 5-layer skeletonized dial; 42-hour power reserve
Functions: hours, minutes, sweep seconds; moon phase
Case: colorless ALW alloy, 44 x 46 mm, height 15.25 mm; 2.5 mm antireflective sapphire crystal; screwed-in titanium crown with microbille/satin finishing; screwed-down case back with octopus engraving; water-resistant to 30 atm
Band: rubber, ardillon buckle
Remarks: luminous moon disk
Price: $21,600; limited to 59 numbered pieces

SpidoSpeed Green

Movement: automatic, LW06 Caliber (custom-made by Concepto); ø 30 mm, height 8.4 mm; 27 jewels; 28,800 vph; LW customized rotor bridge; 48-hour power reserve
Functions: hours, minutes, sweep seconds; chronograph
Case: outer case carbon, inner case DLC-coated titanium; 44 x 46 mm, height 15 mm; black ceramic bezel; Start/Stop and Reset engraved at pushers; antireflective sapphire crystal; transparent case back; water-resistant to 10 atm
Band: calfskin, DLC-coated titanium buckle
Remarks: flange and dial with circular satin finishing.
Price: $25,200; limited to 99 numbered pieces

SpidoSpeed Rosegold Black

Movement: automatic, LW06 Caliber (custom-made by Concepto); ø 30 mm, height 8.4 mm; 27 jewels; 28,800 vph; LW customized rotor; 48-hour power reserve
Functions: hours, minutes, sweep seconds; chronograph
Case: outer case rose gold, inner case DLC-coated titanium; 44 x 46 mm, height 15 mm; black ceramic bezel; Start/Stop and Reset engraved at pushers; antireflective sapphire crystal; transparent case back; water-resistant to 10 atm
Band: calfskin, DLC-coated titanium buckle
Remarks: flange and dial with rose gold treatment and circular satin finishing.
Price: $38,400; limited to 99 numbered pieces

Longines Watch Co.
CH-2610 St.-Imier
Switzerland

Tel.:
01141-32-942-5425

Fax:
01141-32-942-5429

E-Mail:
info@longines.com

Website:
www.longines.com

Founded:
1832

Number of employees:
worldwide approx. 560

U.S. distributor:
Longines
The Swatch Group (U.S.), Inc.
1200 Harbor Boulevard
Weehawken, NJ 07087
201-271-1400
www.longines.com

Most important collections/price range:
Saint-Imier, Master Collection, PrimaLuna,
Sport Collection, Heritage Collection / from
approx. $1,350 to $6,500

Longines

The Longines winged hourglass logo is the world's oldest trademark, according to the World Intellectual Property Organization (WIPO). Since its founding in 1832, the brand has manufactured somewhere in the region of 35 million watches, making it one of the genuine heavyweights of the Swiss watch world. In 1983, Nicolas G. Hayek merged the two major Swiss watch manufacturing groups ASUAG and SIHH into what would later become the Swatch Group. Longines, the leading ASUAG brand, barely missed capturing the same position in the new concern; that honor went to Omega, the SIHH frontrunner. However, from a historical and technical point of view, this brand has what it takes to be at the helm of any group. Was it not Longines that equipped polar explorer Roald Amundsen and air pioneer Charles Lindbergh with their watches? It has also been the timekeeper at many Olympic Games and, since 2007, the official timekeeper for the French Open at Roland Garros. In fact, this brand is a major sponsor at many sports events, from riding to archery.

It is not surprising then to find that this venerable Jura company also has an impressive portfolio of in-house calibers in stock, from simple manual winders to complicated chronographs. This broad technological base has benefited the company. As a genuine "one-stop shop," the brand can supply the Swatch Group with anything from cheap, thin quartz watches to heavy gold chronographs and calendars with quadruple retrograde displays. Longines does have one particular specialty, besides elegant ladies' watches and modern sports watches, in that it often has the luxury of rebuilding the classics from its own long history.

Elegant Collection

Reference number: L4.309.5.88.7
Movement: automatic, Caliber L595 (base ETA 2000-1); ø 19.4 mm, height 3.6 mm; 20 jewels; 28,800 vph; 40-hour power reserve
Functions: hours, minutes, sweep seconds; date
Case: stainless steel, ø 25.5 mm, height 8.3 mm; rose gold bezel set with 52 diamonds, sapphire crystal; transparent case back; water-resistant to 3 atm
Band: stainless steel with rose gold elements, double folding clasp
Remarks: mother-of-pearl dial set with 12 diamonds
Price: $4,600

Elegant Collection

Reference number: L4.809.5.72.7
Movement: automatic, Caliber L619 (base ETA 2892-A2); ø 25.6 mm, height 3.6 mm; 21 jewels; 28,800 vph; 42-hour power reserve
Functions: hours, minutes, sweep seconds; date
Case: stainless steel, ø 34.5 mm, height 8.4 mm; rose gold bezel, sapphire crystal; transparent case back; water-resistant to 3 atm
Band: stainless steel with rose gold elements, double folding clasp
Price: $2,700

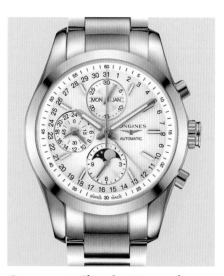

Conquest Classic Moonphase

Reference number: L2.798.4.72.6
Movement: automatic, Caliber L678 (base ETA 7751); ø 30 mm, height 7.9 mm; 25 jewels; 28,800 vph; 48-hour power reserve
Functions: hours, minutes, subsidiary seconds; chronograph; full calendar with date, weekday, month, moon phase
Case: stainless steel, ø 42 mm, height 14.4 mm; sapphire crystal; transparent case back; water-resistant to 5 atm
Band: stainless steel, double folding clasp
Price: $3,900

Conquest Classic Chronograph

Reference number: L2.786.4.56.6
Movement: automatic, Caliber L688 (base ETA A08.L01); ø 30 mm, height 7.9 mm; 27 jewels; 28,800 vph; 54-hour power reserve
Functions: hours, minutes, subsidiary seconds; chronograph; date
Case: stainless steel, ø 41 mm, height 14.2 mm; sapphire crystal; transparent case back; water-resistant to 5 atm
Band: stainless steel, folding clasp
Price: $3,175

Conquest Classic

Reference number: L2.285.5.88.7
Movement: automatic, Caliber L595 (base ETA 2000-1); ø 19.4 mm, height 3.6 mm; 20 jewels; 28,800 vph; 40-hour power reserve
Functions: hours, minutes, sweep seconds; date
Case: stainless steel, ø 29.5 mm, height 9.1 mm; rose gold bezel set with 30 diamonds, sapphire crystal; transparent case back; rose gold crown; water-resistant to 5 atm
Band: stainless steel with rose gold elements, folding clasp
Remarks: mother-of-pearl dial
Price: $3,900

St. Imier Collection Chronograph

Reference number: L2.784.4.53.6
Movement: automatic, Caliber L688 (base ETA A08.L01); ø 30 mm, height 7.9 mm; 27 jewels; 28,800 vph; column wheel control of chronograph functions; 54-hour power reserve
Functions: hours, minutes, subsidiary seconds; chronograph; date
Case: stainless steel, ø 43 mm, height 14.33 mm; sapphire crystal, transparent case back; water-resistant to 3 atm
Band: stainless steel, double folding clasp
Price: $3,275

Master Collection

Reference number: L2.893.4.78.3
Movement: automatic, Caliber L888 (base ETA A31.L01); ø 25.6 mm, height 3.85 mm; 21 jewels; 25,200 vph; 64-hour power reserve
Functions: hours, minutes, sweep seconds; date
Case: stainless steel, ø 42 mm; sapphire crystal; transparent case back; water-resistant to 3 atm
Band: reptile skin, folding clasp
Price: $2,350
Variations: stainless steel bracelet ($2,450)

Master Collection

Reference number: L2.793.4.78.6
Movement: automatic, Caliber L888 (base ETA A31.L01); ø 25.6 mm, height 3.85 mm; 21 jewels; 25,200 vph; 64-hour power reserve
Functions: hours, minutes, sweep seconds; date
Case: stainless steel, ø 40 mm, height 9.8 mm; sapphire crystal; transparent case back; water-resistant to 3 atm
Band: stainless steel, double folding clasp
Price: $2,250
Variations: reptile skin band ($2,150)

Master Collection Moon Phase

Reference number: L2.673.4.78.3
Movement: automatic, Caliber L678 (base ETA 7751); ø 30 mm, height 7.9 mm; 25 jewels; 28,800 vph; 48-hour power reserve
Functions: hours, minutes, subsidiary seconds; additional 24-hour display; chronograph; full calendar with date, weekday, month, moon phase
Case: stainless steel, ø 40 mm, height 14.24 mm; sapphire crystal; transparent case back; water-resistant to 3 atm
Band: reptile skin, folding clasp
Price: $2,250
Variations: stainless steel bracelet ($2,150)

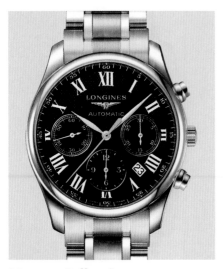

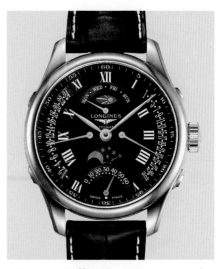

Master Collection Chronograph

Reference number: L2.759.4.51.6
Movement: automatic, Caliber L688 (base ETA A08.L01); ø 30 mm, height 7.9 mm; 27 jewels; 28,800 vph; 54-hour power reserve
Functions: hours, minutes, subsidiary seconds; chronograph; date
Case: stainless steel, ø 42 mm, height 14.2 mm; sapphire crystal; transparent case back; water-resistant to 5 atm
Band: stainless steel, folding clasp
Price: $2,825
Variations: leather band ($2,725)

Master Collection Retrograde Moonphase

Reference number: L2.739.4.71.3
Movement: automatic, Caliber L707.2 (base ETA A07.L31); ø 36.6 mm, height 10 mm; 25 jewels; 28,800 vph; 46-hour power reserve
Functions: hours, minutes, subsidiary seconds (retrograde); additional 24-hour display (2nd time zone); day/night indicator (retrograde); full calendar with date, weekday, moon phase
Case: stainless steel, ø 44 mm, height 16.48 mm; sapphire crystal; transparent case back; water-resistant to 3 atm
Band: reptile skin, double folding clasp
Price: $3,600

Master Collection Retrograde Moonphase

Reference number: L2.738.4.51.7
Movement: automatic, Caliber L707.2 (base ETA A07.L31); ø 36.6 mm, height 10 mm; 25 jewels; 28,800 vph; 46-hour power reserve
Functions: hours, minutes, subsidiary seconds, (retrograde), additional 24-hour display, day/night indicator (2nd time zone), retrograde; full calendar with date, weekday, moon phase
Case: stainless steel, ø 41 mm, height 16.4 mm; sapphire crystal; transparent case back; water-resistant to 3 atm
Band: reptile skin, double folding clasp
Price: $3,700
Variations: 44 mm case ($3,600)

Legend Diver Watch

Reference number: L3.674.4.50.9
Movement: automatic, Caliber L633 (base ETA 2824-2); ø 25.6 mm, height 4.6 mm; 25 jewels; 28,800 vph; 38-hour power reserve
Functions: hours, minutes, sweep seconds; date
Case: stainless steel, ø 42 mm, height 13.6 mm; crown-adjustable inner bezel with 60-minute divisions, sapphire crystal; screw-in crown; water-resistant to 30 atm
Band: rubber, folding clasp
Price: $2,650

Hydro Conquest

Reference number: L3.695.4.53.6
Movement: automatic, Caliber L633 (base ETA 2824-2); ø 25.6 mm, height 4.6 mm; 25 jewels; 28,800 vph; 38-hour power reserve
Functions: hours, minutes, sweep seconds; date
Case: stainless steel, ø 41 mm, height 11.65 mm; unidirectional bezel with aluminum inlay and 60-minute divisions, sapphire crystal; screw-in crown; water-resistant to 30 atm
Band: stainless steel, folding clasp
Price: $1,275

Hydro Conquest Chronograph

Reference number: L3.696.4.53.6
Movement: automatic, Caliber L688 (base ETA A08.L01); ø 30 mm, height 7.9 mm; 27 jewels; 28,800 vph; 54-hour power reserve
Functions: hours, minutes, subsidiary seconds; chronograph; date
Case: stainless steel, ø 41 mm, height 15.55 mm; unidirectional bezel with aluminum inlay and 60-minute divisions, sapphire crystal; screw-in crown; water-resistant to 30 atm
Band: stainless steel, folding clasp
Price: $3,325
Variations: rubber strap ($1,275)

Louis Moinet

In the race to be the first to invent something new, Louis Moinet (1768–1853) emerged as a notable winner: In 2013, a *Compteur de tierces* from 1816 was shown to the public, a chronograph that counts one-sixtieth of a second with a frequency of 216,000 vph. It was proudly signed by Moinet. This professor at the Academy of Fine Arts in Paris and president of the Société Chronométrique was in fact one of the most inventive, multitalented men of his time. He worked with such eminent watchmakers as Breguet, Berthoud, Winnerl, Janvier, and Perrelet. Among his accomplishments is an extensive two-volume treatise on horology. Moinet's timepieces were considered extremely complex, but they did find customers among the aristocracy.

Following in such footsteps is hardly an easy task, but Jean-Marie Schaller and Micaela Bertolucci decided that their idiosyncratic creations were indeed imbued with the spirit of the great Frenchman. They work with a team of independent designers, watchmakers, movement specialists, and suppliers to produce the most unusual wristwatches filled with clever functions and surprising details. The Jules Verne chronographs have hinged levers, for example, and the second hand on the Tempograph changes direction every ten seconds. The new Mecanograph is a complex watch, with transparent subsidiary seconds on a split dial that boldly exhibits "rolling" *côtes du Jura* decoration under classic dewdrop hands.

And every limited edition has a little secret of sorts: A piece of rock that was chipped off the moon roughly 2,000 years ago by an asteroid is secured behind a discreet porthole located at 9 o'clock on the case—visible only to those who are looking for it.

Les Ateliers Louis Moinet SA
Rue du Temple 1
CH-2072 Saint-Blaise
Switzerland

Tel.:
01141-32-753-6814

E-Mail:
info@louismoinet.com

Website:
www.louismoinet.com

Founded:
1806 (refounded in 2005)

U.S. distributor:
Louis Moinet
Milestone Distribution
297 Dividend Drive, Suite B
Peachtree City, GA 30269
678-827-7900; 678-827-7903 (fax)
info@cysusa.com

Most important collections:
Jules Verne, Tempograph, Vertalis, Geograph, Astralis

Mecanograph New York

Reference number: LM-31.50.NY
Movement: automatic, Caliber LM31, developed with Concepto; ø 30 mm, height 7.24 mm; 26 jewels; 28,800 vph; winding rotor with ceramic ball bearing; 48-hour power reserve
Functions: hours, minutes, subsidiary seconds
Case: rose gold, ø 43.5 mm, height 15.6 mm; sapphire crystal; transparent case back; water-resistant to 5 atm
Band: reptile skin, double folding clasp
Remarks: New York skyline set with meteorite on dial
Price: $55,000; limited to 60 pieces
Variations: titanium ($29,900; limited to 60 pieces)

Tempograph 20 Seconds

Reference number: LM-39.20.80
Movement: automatic, Caliber LM39, developed with Concepto; ø 30.4 mm, height 8.29 mm; 36 jewels; 28,800 vph; winding rotor with ceramic ball bearing; 48-hour power reserve
Functions: hours and minutes (off-center), 20 sweep second display (retrograde)
Case: titanium, ø 43.5 mm, height 15.6 mm; sapphire crystal; transparent back; water-resistant to 5 atm
Band: reptile skin, double folding clasp
Remarks: skeletonized dial
Price: $25,000; limited to 365 pieces
Variations: rose gold ($49,500; limited to 60 pieces)

Vertalor

Reference number: LM-35.50.55
Movement: manually wound, ø 34 mm, height 5.7 mm; 19 jewels; 21,600 vph; 1-minute tourbillon; 72-hour power reserve
Functions: hours, minutes
Case: rose gold, ø 47 mm, height 14.1 mm; sapphire crystal; transparent case back; water-resistant to 3 atm
Band: reptile skin, double folding clasp
Price: $199,500; limited to 28 pieces
Variations: white gold ($199,500; limited to 28 pieces)

Louis Vuitton Malletier

2, rue du Pont Neuf
F-75034 Paris, Cedex 01
France

Tel.:
01133-1-55-80-41-40

Fax:
01133-1-55-80-41-40

Website:
www.vuitton.com

Founded:
1854

U.S. distributor:
Louis Vuitton
1-866-VUITTON
www.louisvuitton.com

Most important collection/price range:
Tambour / starting at $3,250

Louis Vuitton

The philosophy of this over 150-year-old brand states that any product bearing the name Louis Vuitton must be manufactured in the company's own facilities. That is why Louis Vuitton has allowed itself the luxury of building its own workshop in Switzerland, specifically in La Chaux-de-Fonds, at the technology center of LVMH (Louis Vuitton, Moët & Hennessy).

Designing is carried out in Paris at the company headquarters, and it is obvious that it would not suit an upscale watch to simply cobble together various parts supplied by outside workshops. The cases and dials with all the details and the hands are all exclusive Louis Vuitton designs, as are other components, such as the pushers and the band clasps, in other words, all that is needed to ensure a unique look. In 2011, Louis Vuitton purchased the dial maker Léman Cadran and the movement specialist Fabrique du Temps (both in Geneva), giving the company a great deal of independence vis-à-vis other brands in the group.

You cannot buy a Louis Vuitton watch at your corner jewelry store, but solely through one of the 450 Louis Vuitton boutiques worldwide. What you will find there, for instance, is the 2014 novelty, the unconventional Escale world-time watch with handpainted scale fields in the style of the monograms that Louis Vuitton uses to mark its bags to avoid loss or confusion when loading the bags for an overseas voyage. Those little labels were also always painted by hand.

Escale Worldtime

Reference number: Q5EK00
Movement: automatic, LV Caliber 106; ø 37 mm, height 6.65 mm; 26 jewels; 28,800 vph; 38-hour power reserve
Functions: hours, minutes, world-time display (2nd time zone) for 24 time zones on handpainted rotating discs
Case: white gold, ø 41 mm, height 9.75 mm; sapphire crystal; transparent case back; water-resistant to 3 atm
Band: reptile skin, buckle
Price: $67,500

Tambour Twin Chronograph Grand Sport

Reference number: Q1B700
Movement: automatic, LV Caliber 175; ø 37 mm, height 6.53 mm; 80 jewels; 28,800 vph; 4 barrel springs, 4 balance systems, 3 for chrono display, single pusher for 2 control wheels/4 functions; 35-hour power reserve
Functions: hours, minutes, subsidiary seconds; chronograph with 2 50-minute counters and difference indicator
Case: white gold, ø 45.5 mm, height 14.35 mm; sapphire crystal; transparent back; water-resistant to 10 atm
Band: reptile skin, folding clasp
Price: $81,000

Tambour eVolution Flying Tourbillon

Reference number: Q1EB11
Movement: automatic, LV Caliber 81; ø 37.4 mm, height 4.6 mm; 28 jewels; 28,800 vph; flying 1-minute tourbillon, microrotor; 40-hour power reserve
Functions: hours, minutes, subsidiary seconds (on tourbillon cage)
Case: aluminum oxide (MMC), ø 43 mm, height 12.66 mm; rose gold bezel, sapphire crystal; transparent case back; water-resistant to 10 atm
Band: rose gold, folding clasp
Price: $103,500

Tambour Bleu GMT

Reference number: Q11570
Movement: automatic, ETA Caliber 2893-2; ø 26.2 mm, height 4.25 mm; 21 jewels; 28,800 vph; 42-hour power reserve
Functions: hours, minutes, sweep seconds; additional 24-hour display (2nd time zone); date
Case: stainless steel, ø 39.5 mm, height 10.5 mm; sapphire crystal; water-resistant to 10 atm
Band: reptile skin, buckle
Price: $4,650
Variations: chronograph ($7,100)

Tambour Heures du Monde

Reference number: Q10550
Movement: automatic, LV Caliber, 28,800 vph
Functions: hours, minutes, sweep seconds; additional 24-hour display (2nd time zone); date
Case: stainless steel, ø 44 mm; sapphire crystal; transparent case back
Band: reptile skin, buckle
Price: $9,450

Tambour LV 277 Chronograph

Reference number: Q114A0
Movement: automatic, LV Caliber 277 (base Zenith El Primero); ø 30 mm, height 6.6 mm; 31 jewels; 36,000 vph; 50-hour power reserve; COSC-tested chronometer
Functions: hours, minutes, subsidiary seconds; chronograph; date
Case: stainless steel, ø 44 mm, height 13.25 mm; sapphire crystal; water-resistant to 10 atm
Band: reptile skin, folding clasp
Price: $13,800

Tambour eVolution Chronograph GMT

Reference number: Q10520
Movement: automatic, LV Caliber 92; ø 30 mm, height 8.4 mm; 26 jewels; 28,800 vph; 42-hour power reserve
Functions: hours, minutes, subsidiary seconds; additional 12-hour display (2nd time zone), day/night indicator; chronograph; date
Case: stainless steel, ø 45 mm, height 15.84 mm; sapphire crystal; transparent case back; water-resistant to 10 atm
Band: stainless steel, folding clasp
Price: $10,200

Tambour in Black GMT

Reference number: Q113I0
Movement: automatic, ETA Caliber 2893-2; ø 26.2 mm, height 4.25 mm; 21 jewels; 28,800 vph; 42-hour power reserve
Functions: hours, minutes, sweep seconds; additional 24-hour display (2nd time zone); date
Case: stainless steel with black DLC coating; ø 41.5 mm, height 12.65 mm; sapphire crystal; water-resistant to 10 atm
Band: rubber, buckle
Price: $5,750

Tambour Diving II Automatic Chronograph

Reference number: Q102F0
Movement: automatic, LV Caliber 105 (base ETA 7750); ø 30 mm, height 7.9 mm; 31 jewels; 28,800 vph; 42-hour power reserve
Functions: hours, minutes, subsidiary seconds; chronograph; date
Case: stainless steel with black rubber coating; ø 45.5 mm, height 14.5 mm; unidirectional bezel with 60-minute divisions, sapphire crystal; water-resistant to 30 atm
Band: rubber, folding clasp
Price: $10,100

Maîtres du Temps

Maîtres du Temps
Rue Daniel Jeanrichard 18
CP 926 CH-2301 La Chaux-de-Fonds
Switzerland

Tel.:
01141-32-911-1717

Fax:
01141-32-911-1718

E-Mail:
info@maitresdutemps.com

Website:
www.maitresdutemps.com

Founded:
2005

U.S. distributor:
Helvetia Time Inc.
100 N. Wilkes-Barre Blvd., Suite 303
Wilkes-Barre, PA 18702
570-970-8888; 570-822-4699 (fax)

Most important collections/price range:
Chapter One / from approx. CHF 474,000;
Chapter Two TCR / from approx. CHF 69,000;
Chapter Three Reveal / from approx. CHF 94,500
Prices in Swiss francs only, calculated according to daily exchange rate.

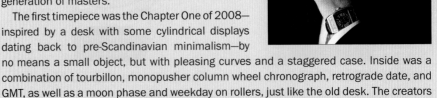

Too many cooks can spoil the soup, but what about too many watchmakers spoiling a watch? After more than twenty-five years in the industry, Steven Holtzman decided to strike out on his own with a special concept: seeing what happens when the top people in the industry work on a piece together. The idea is not only to cross-pollinate, but also, perhaps, to compel each watchmaker to leave some room for a good colleague. Holtzman's plan, he says, "is to be actively involved in passing the craft and skills of more experienced master watchmakers to the next generation of masters."

The first timepiece was the Chapter One of 2008—inspired by a desk with some cylindrical displays dating back to pre-Scandinavian minimalism—by no means a small object, but with pleasing curves and a staggered case. Inside was a combination of tourbillon, monopusher column wheel chronograph, retrograde date, and GMT, as well as a moon phase and weekday on rollers, just like the old desk. The creators of this tour de force: Peter Speake-Marin and Christophe Claret.

In 2009, Speake-Marin and Daniel Roth came up with a triple-calendar watch. The tonneau shape was back, so were the rollers, which could instantaneously switch dates. The dial: less busy, a little more staid, with large numerals. Early 2012 unveiled the Chapter Three Reveal by Kari Voutilainen and Andreas Strehler. At first glance the blue guilloché dial in a round case seems to be a radical departure from the previous two. Where are the rollers? A pusher in the crown opens up a panel in the dial to reveal them displaying a second time zone and day/night indicator. And for 2013, Chapter One has returned with a paper-thin sapphire dial that is lighter than the first edition and lets one look deep into the heart of this mechanical labyrinth.

Chapter One Tonneau Transparence Titanium

Reference number: C1T.TO.2E.60-0
Movement: Caliber SHC02.1; 52 x 32 mm; 58 jewels; 1-minute tourbillon; crown-pusher activation of chronograph functions; correctors with integrated locking system; black finish on chrono bridge; 21,600 vph; 1-minute tourbillon; 60-hour power reserve
Functions: hours, minutes, subsidiary seconds; chronograph; retrograde world time and date, day, moon phase on barrels
Case: titanium, 62.6 x 45.9 mm, height 18 mm; sapphire crystal; transparent case back
Band: reptile skin, white gold buckle
Price: CHF 509,000; limited edition of 11 pieces

Chapter Two TCR

Reference number: C2R.TT0.21.110
Movement: automatic, Caliber SHC01; 45 x 32 mm, height 9 mm; 32 jewels; finished with sunburst côtes de Genève, panier guilloché, perlage and beveling; 28,800 vph; 50-hour power reserve
Functions: hours, minutes, seconds; instant triple calendar with large date, weekday, month
Case: titanium; 56 x 44 mm; height 15 mm; transparent case back with ceramic bezel; white gold crown, screws, pushers; sapphire crystal; transparent case back
Band: rubber, folding clasp
Price: CHF 70,900
Variations: titanium, black PVD with gold elements

Chapter Three Reveal

Reference number: C3R.00.00.185
Movement: manually wound, Caliber SHC03; ø a35.6 mm, height 8.2 mm; 39 jewels; twin spring barrels; Straumann balance spring with Breguet overcoil; côtes de Genève and perlage, polished screw heads; 21,600 vph; 36-hour power reserve
Functions: hours, minutes, seconds; date; moon phase; 2nd time zone; day/night indication
Case: white gold, ø 42 mm; sapphire crystal; transparent case back; water-resistant to 3 atm
Band: reptile skin, tang buckle
Price: CHF 94,500

WE SOW A LOVE OF DETAILS, DEVOTION AND RESPONSIBILITY, FERTILIZE WITH PERSONALITY AND HARVEST HONEST PRODUCTS OF THE UTMOST QUALITY, MADE FOR GENERATIONS TO COME.

Maria Kristina & Richard Habring

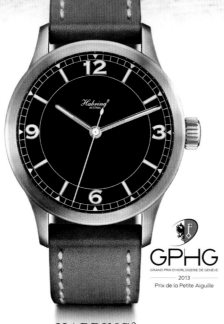

GPHG
GRAND PRIX D'HORLOGERIE DE GENÈVE
2013
Prix de la Petite Aiguille

HABRING²
CHRONO COS

HABRING²
JUMPING SECOND
„PILOT"

HABRING²
DOPPEL 3

HABRING Uhrentechnik OG • Hauptplatz 16, 9100 Völkermarkt, AUSTRIA
Fon +43-4232-51300, info@habring.com   www.habring2.com

Maurice Lacroix SA
Rüschlistrasse 6
CH-2502 Biel/Bienne
Switzerland

Tel.:
01141-44-209-1111

E-Mail:
info@mauricelacroix.com

Website:
www.mauricelacroix.com

Founded:
1975

Number of employees:
about 250 worldwide

Annual production:
approx. 90,000 watches

U.S. distributor:
DKSH Luxury & Lifestyle North America Inc.
103 Carnegie Center, Ste. 300
Princeton, NJ 08540
609-750-8800

Most important collections/price range:
Miros / $1,000 to $2,000; Les Classiques /
$1,500 to $3,500; Fiaba (ladies) / $1,500
to 3,500; Pontos / $2,500 to $5,000;
Masterpiece *manufacture* models / $6,800
to $30,000

Maurice Lacroix

In Maurice Lacroix headquarters in Zürich, administration offices coexist with the worldwide sales and marketing department. After all, Maurice Lacroix watches are found in sixty countries. And the brand has joined in the love for Asia by having singer/actor Dicky Cheung as a brand ambassador in 2011. The heart of the company, however, remains the production facilities in the highlands of the Jura, in Saignelégier and Montfaucon. The company built a workshop there called La Manufacture des Franches-Montagnes SA (MFM) for the production of very specific individual parts and movement components and outfitted with state-of-the-art CNC technology.

The watchmaker can thank the clever interpretations of "classic" pocket watch characteristics for its steep ascent in the 1990s. Since then, the *manufacture* has redesigned the complete collection, banning every lick of Breguet-like bliss from its watch designs. In the upper segment, *manufacture* models such as the chronograph and the retrograde variations on Unitas calibers set the tone. In the lower segment, modern "little" complications outfitted with module movements based on ETA and Sellita are the kings. The brand is mainly associated with the hypnotically turning square wheel, the "roue carrée." It picked up a red dot award in 2012 for design, as did its Masterpiece Double Rétrograde.

All this has ensured Maurice Lacroix a strong position on all major markets, with flagship stores and its own boutiques. Furthermore, the brand was taken over in 2011 by DKSH (Diethelm Keller & SiberHegner), a Swiss holding company specializing in international market expansions with 600 establishments throughout the world.

Masterpiece Gravity

Reference number: MP6118-SS001-110
Movement: automatic, Caliber ML 230; ø 37.2 mm, height 9.05 mm; 35 jewels; 18,000 vph; inverted design with dial-side escapement, silicon pallet lever and escape wheel; 50-hour power reserve
Functions: hours and minutes (off-center), subsidiary seconds
Case: stainless steel, ø 43 mm, height 16.2 mm; sapphire crystal; transparent case back; water-resistant to 5 atm
Band: reptile skin, folding clasp
Price: $13,900

Masterpiece Mystery

Reference number: MP6558-SS001-095
Movement: automatic, Caliber ML 215; ø 38.2 mm, height 9.33 mm; 48 jewels; 18,000 vph; rhodium-plated, with côtes de Genève; 50-hour power reserve
Functions: hours and minutes (off-center), subsidiary seconds ("mysterious" time display with "floating" seconds hand)
Case: stainless steel, ø 43 mm, height 13.86 mm; sapphire crystal, transparent case back; water-resistant to 5 atm
Band: reptile skin, folding clasp
Price: $13,900

Masterpiece Square Wheel

Reference number: MP7158-SS001-301
Movement: manually wound, Caliber ML 156; ø 36.6 mm, height 6.15 mm; 34 jewels; 18,000 vph; 45-hour power reserve
Functions: hours, minutes, subsidiary seconds (with square wheel display); power reserve display
Case: stainless steel, ø 43 mm, height 14.1 mm; sapphire crystal; transparent case back; water-resistant to 5 atm
Band: reptile skin, folding clasp
Remarks: dial directly engraved on main plate, with "grand colimaçon" decoration
Price: $9,900

Masterpiece Le Chronographe Squelette

Reference number: MP7128-SS001-400
Movement: manually wound, Caliber ML 106;
ø 36.6 mm, height 6.9 mm; 22 jewels; 18,000 vph;
skeletonized with black coating; 42-hour power
reserve
Functions: hours, minutes, subsidiary seconds;
chronograph
Case: stainless steel with black PVD coating; ø
45 mm, height 16 mm; sapphire crystal; screw-in
crown; water-resistant to 10 atm
Band: reptile skin, folding clasp
Remarks: skeletonized dial
Price: $17,800

Masterpiece Squelette

Reference number: MP7228-SS001-000
Movement: manually wound, Caliber ML 134;
ø 37.2 mm, height 4.5 mm; 17 jewels; 18,000 vph;
PVD-coated parts, skeletonized and finely finished
by hand
Functions: hours, minutes, subsidiary seconds
Case: stainless steel, ø 43 mm, height 13 mm;
sapphire crystal; transparent case back; water-
resistant to 5 atm
Band: reptile skin, folding clasp
Price: $6,800

Masterpiece Double Retrograde

Reference number: MP6518-SS001-130
Movement: automatic, Caliber ML 191; ø 36.6 mm,
height 8.2 mm; 74 jewels; 18,000 vph; COSC-
certified chronometer
Functions: hours, minutes, subsidiary seconds;
additional 24-hour display (2nd time zone); power
reserve indicator; date (retrograde)
Case: stainless steel, ø 43 mm, height 16 mm;
sapphire crystal; transparent case back; water-
resistant to 5 atm
Band: reptile skin, folding clasp
Price: $7,900

Les Classiques Chronographe Phases de Lune

Reference number: LC6078-SS001-131
Movement: automatic, Caliber ML 154 (base
ETA 7751); ø 30 mm, height 7.9 mm; 25 jewels;
28,800 vph
Functions: hours, minutes; additional 24-hour
indicator (2nd time zone); chronograph; full
calendar with date, weekday, month, moon phase
Case: stainless steel, ø 41 mm, height 14.8 mm;
sapphire crystal; transparent case back; water-
resistant to 3 atm
Band: calf leather, folding clasp
Price: $3,880
Variations: various bands and dials

Les Classiques Date

Reference number: LC6027-SS002-133
Movement: automatic, Caliber ML 115 (base Sellita
SW200); ø 25.6 mm, height 4.6 mm; 25 jewels;
28,800 vph; 38-hour power reserve
Functions: hours, minutes, sweep seconds; date
Case: stainless steel, ø 38 mm, height 10.6 mm;
sapphire crystal; transparent case back; water-
resistant to 3 atm
Band: stainless steel, folding clasp
Price: $1,680
Variations: leather strap ($1,480)

Les Classiques Date

Reference number: LC6027-SS001-311
Movement: automatic, Caliber ML 115 (base Sellita
SW200); ø 25.6 mm, height 4.6 mm; 25 jewels;
28,800 vph; 38-hour power reserve
Functions: hours, minutes, sweep seconds; date
Case: stainless steel, ø 38 mm; sapphire crystal;
transparent case back; water-resistant to 3 atm
Band: calf leather, buckle
Price: $1,480
Variations: stainless steel bracelet ($1,680)

Pontos S Supercharged

Reference number: PT6009-PVB01-330
Movement: automatic, Caliber ML 140 (based on ETA Valgranges); ø 37.32 mm, height 7.9 mm; 25 jewels; 28,800 vph; 46-hour power reserve
Functions: hours, minutes, subsidiary seconds; chronograph; date
Case: stainless steel with black DLC-coating; ø 48 mm, height 16.2 mm; crown-adjustable inner bezel with 60-minute divisions, sapphire crystal; screw-in crown; water-resistant to 20 atm
Band: calf leather with laser decoration and rubberized sections, buckle
Price: $4,950

Pontos S Extreme

Reference number: PT6028-ALB11-331
Movement: automatic, Caliber ML 112 (base ETA 7750); ø 30 mm, height 7.9 mm; 25 jewels; 28,800 vph; 46-hour power reserve
Functions: hours, minutes, subsidiary seconds; chronograph; date
Case: composite material ("Powerlite"); ø 43 mm, height 15.7 mm; crown-controlled inner bezel with 60-minute divisions, sapphire crystal; screw-in crown; water-resistant to 20 atm
Band: calf leather, buckle
Price: $5,900
Variations: green or blue anodized case ($6,900)

Pontos S

Reference number: PT6018-SS001-330
Movement: automatic, Caliber ML157 (based on ETA 7753); ø 30 mm, height 7.9 mm; 25 jewels; 28,800 vph; 46-hour power reserve
Functions: hours, minutes, subsidiary seconds; chronograph; date
Case: stainless steel, ø 43 mm, height 15.5 mm; sapphire crystal; water-resistant to 20 atm
Band: textile, buckle
Price: $4,900
Variations: various bands and dials

Pontos S

Reference number: PT6008-SS002-331
Movement: automatic, Caliber ML157 (based on ETA 7750); ø 30 mm, height 7.9 mm; 25 jewels; 28,800 vph; 46-hour power reserve
Functions: hours, minutes, subsidiary seconds; chronograph; date
Case: stainless steel, ø 43 mm, height 15.5 mm; sapphire crystal; water-resistant to 20 atm
Band: stainless steel, folding clasp
Price: $4,500
Variations: various bands and dials

Pontos S Diver

Reference number: PT6248-SS001-330
Movement: automatic, Caliber ML 115 (base Sellita SW200); ø 25.6 mm, height 4.6 mm; 26 jewels; 28,800 vph; 38-hour power reserve
Functions: hours, minutes, sweep seconds; date
Case: stainless steel, ø 43 mm; crown-controlled inner bezel with 60-minute divisions, sapphire crystal; screw-in crown; automatic helium valve; water-resistant to 60 atm
Band: calf leather, buckle
Price: $3,400
Variations: stainless steel bracelet ($3,400)

Pontos Chronographe

Reference number: PT6288-SS001-330
Movement: automatic, Caliber ML 112 (base Sellita SW500); ø 30 mm, height 7.9 mm; 25 jewels; 28,800 vph; 42-hour power reserve
Functions: hours, minutes, subsidiary seconds; chronograph; date
Case: stainless steel, ø 43 mm, height 14.9 mm; sapphire crystal; transparent case back; water-resistant to 5 atm
Band: reptile skin, folding clasp
Price: $3,900
Variations: white dial

Pontos Day Date

Reference number: PT6158-SS001-231
Movement: automatic, Caliber ML 143-2 (base Sellita SW220); ø 25.6 mm, height 5.05 mm; 25 jewels; 28,800 vph; 42-hour power reserve
Functions: hours, minutes, sweep seconds; weekday, date
Case: stainless steel, ø 40 mm, height 12 mm; sapphire crystal; transparent case back; water-resistant to 5 atm
Band: reptile skin, folding clasp
Price: $2,900
Variations: black dial

Pontos Date Full Black

Reference number: PT6148-PVB01-330
Movement: automatic, Caliber ML 115 (base Sellita SW300); ø 25.6 mm, height 3.6 mm; 25 jewels; 28,800 vph; 38-hour power reserve
Functions: hours, minutes, sweep seconds; date
Case: stainless steel with black PVD coating, ø 40 mm, height 11.8 mm; sapphire crystal; transparent case back; water-resistant to 5 atm
Band: calf leather, buckle
Remarks: hands and indices coated with black luminescent mass
Price: $2,900

Pontos Date

Reference number: PT6148-SS001-230
Movement: automatic, Caliber ML 115 (base Sellita SW300); ø 25.6 mm, height 3.6 mm; 25 jewels; 28,800 vph; 38-hour power reserve
Functions: hours, minutes, sweep seconds; date
Case: stainless steel, ø 40 mm; sapphire crystal; transparent case back; water-resistant to 5 atm
Band: calf leather, buckle
Price: $2,700
Variations: black PVD coating ($2,900)

Caliber ML 230

Manually wound; inverted movement design with dial-side escapement, silicon pallet lever and escape wheel, single spring barrel; 50-hour power reserve
Functions: hours and minutes (off-center); subsidiary seconds
Jewels: 35
Balance: glucydur
Frequency: 18,000 vph
Remarks: rhodium finish, three-quarter plate (movement side) with côtes de Genève; dial assembled directly onto mainplate

Caliber ML 106-2

Manually wound; column wheel control of chronograph functions; single spring barrel; 42-hour power reserve
Functions: hours, minutes, subsidiary seconds; chronograph
Diameter: 36.6 mm
Height: 6.9 mm
Jewels: 22
Balance: screw balance with weights
Frequency: 18,000 vph
Balance spring: swan-neck fine adjustment
Shock protection: Kif Elastor
Remarks: anodized movement finishing, bridges with "grand colimaçon" decoration, 2 gold chatons

Caliber ML 156

Manually wound; single spring barrel; 45-hour power reserve
Functions: hours, minutes, subsidiary seconds; power reserve indicator
Diameter: 36.6 mm
Height: 6.3 mm
Jewels: 34
Balance: screw balance
Frequency: 18,000 vph
Remarks: rhodium finish, three-quarter plate with "grand colimaçon" decoration, dial engraved directly on mainplate

MB&F

Terrasse Agrippa d'Aubigné 6
Case postale 3466
CH-1211 Geneva 3
Switzerland

Tel.:
01141-22-786-3618

Fax:
01141-22-786-3624

E-Mail:
info@mbandf.com

Website:
www.mbandf.com

Founded:
2005

Number of employees:
14

Annual production:
approx. 170 watches

U.S. distributor:
Westime Los Angeles
310-470-1388; 310-475-0628 (fax)
info@westime.com
Provident Jewelry, Florida
561-747-4449; nick@providentjewelry.com

Most important collections/price range:
Horological Machines / from $63,000; Legacy
Machines / from $92,000

MB&F

Maximilian Büsser & Friends (MB&F) goes beyond the standard notion of a brand. Perhaps calling it a tribe would be better: a tribe that aims to create unique works of horological art. At any rate, MB&F is doing something unconventional in an industry that usually takes its innovation in small doses.

After seeing the Opus projects to fruition at Harry Winston Rare Timepieces, Max Büsser decided that it was time to set the creators free. At MB&F he acts as initiator, organizer, and coordinator. His Horological Machines, of which there are now five, are developed and realized in cooperation with highly specialized watchmakers, inventors, and designers in an "idea collective" creating unheard-of mechanical timepieces of great inventiveness, complication, and exclusivity. The composition of this collective varies as much as the shape and function of each machine. When you look at Number 4, the Thunderbolt, you find a miniature jet with two engines. Number 5 ("On the Road Again") is an homage to the 1970s, when the streamlined rather than unsubtle brawn represented true strength. The display in the lateral window is reflected by a prism. The "top" of the watch opens to let in light to charge the Superluminova numerals on the discs. Contrasting sharply with the modern productions is the 2011 Legacy Machine 1, an ultratraditional timepiece with a quirky balance wheel beating away above the dial.

The spirit of Büsser is always present in each new timepiece, but it is now vented freely in the M.A.D. Gallery in Geneva, where the visitor finds "mechanical art objects" that are beautiful, intriguing, technically impeccable, and sometimes perfectly useless except to entertain. They have their own muse, obviously.

Legacy Machine N°2

Reference number: LM2
Movement: manually wound, MB&F Caliber LM2; ø 37.2 mm, height 13 mm; 44 jewels; 18,000 vph; inverted design with 2 balances floating over dial; planetary differential carries average rate of 2 balances to wheelworks; finely finished with côtes de Genève
Functions: hours, minutes
Case: pink and white gold, ø 44 mm, height 20 mm; sapphire crystal; transparent case back
Band: reptile skin, buckle
Price: $138,000
Variations: platinum ($168,000; limited to 18 pieces)

HM3 MegaWind

Reference number: HM3 MegaWind
Movement: automatic, MB&F Caliber HM3 (modified); 39.3 x 42.7 mm, height 11.6 mm; 36 jewels; 28,800 vph; 3-part winding rotor (titanium hub, 2 gold oscillating weights)
Functions: hours (left-hand display dome), minutes (right-hand display dome)
Case: white gold, 47 x 50 mm, height 16 mm; sapphire crystal; transparent case back; screw-in crown; water-resistant to 3 atm
Band: reptile skin, folding clasp
Price: $92,000
Variations: pink gold ($92,000)

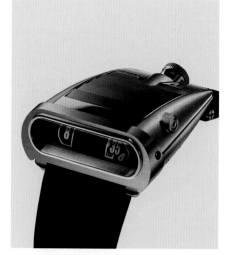

HM5 RT "On the Road Again"

Reference number: HM5 On the Road Again
Movement: automatic, MB&F Caliber HM5; 30.5 x 36.1 mm, height 7.2 mm; 30 jewels; 28,800 vph; gold rotor, disc display reflected through prisms in window; 42-hour power reserve
Functions: hours (digital, jumping) and minutes (digital)
Case: pink gold, titanium case back; 51.5 x 49 mm, height 22.5 mm; sapphire crystal; transparent case back; water-resistant to 3 atm
Band: rubber, buckle
Price: $82,000

Meccaniche Veloci

The recipe almost seems too simplistic: watches and cars. With speed and exhaust fumes, the race clock ticking away . . . suddenly men become boys again. For a watch brand, choosing this aesthetic strategy is a risky game. Perhaps the trick is to be really frank about it, possibly even "in your face." Meccaniche Veloci, a young brand that was founded in 2006, has even made its name a sort of tagline: fast engineering. Its timepieces are all saturated with the techno look—inside are Swiss movements; outside, Italian design.

The company made its automotive theme clear from the outset: Its first watch, the Quattro Valvole, featuring such auto construction elements as piston ring grooves and four embedded valve seat pockets, pushed all the right buttons with its target audience. Each year, the collection grows by a number of models building upon the original, car-inspired idea. Later designs include a watch with two valve seat pockets as the dials; clean-lined, three-hand watches; and timepieces that feature cases set with gemstones or made of special materials, such as sintered carbon ceramic, the stuff used in brake discs for high-performance sports cars courtesy of Italian brake manufacturer Brembo. Meccaniche Veloci now has chronographs and the Only One collection, which contains bits of a Formula-1 racer.

Meccaniche Veloci Srl.
Via Piazzon, 82
I-36051 Olmo di Creazzo (Vi)
Italy

Tel.:
01139-444-99-0100

Fax:
01139-444-34-9488

E-Mail:
info@meccanicheveloci.com

Website:
www.meccanicheveloci.com

Founded:
2006

Most important collections/price range:
Quattro Valvole / from $2,300; Due Valvole / from $1,900; Only One / from $3,100

Quattro Valvole 48 Strokes Tyre – Limited Edition

Reference number: W 124K409
Movement: automatic, 4 separate ETA Caliber 2671; ø 17.2 mm, height 4.8 mm; 25 jewels; 28,800 vph; 38-hour power reserve
Functions: hours and minutes (4 time zones), sweep seconds; date
Case: titanium, ø 48 mm, height 16 mm; sapphire crystal; 4 screw-in crowns; water-resistant to 10 atm
Band: rubber, buckle
Price: $5,200
Variations: dial with red or green parts

Quattro Valvole 44 Chronograph Limited Edition

Reference number: W 123K140
Movement: automatic, ETA Caliber 7750; ø 30 mm, height 7.9 mm; 25 jewels; 28,800 vph; 42-hour power reserve
Functions: hours, minutes, subsidiary seconds; chronograph
Case: titanium with black PVD coating, ø 44 mm, height 15.1 mm; sapphire crystal; screw-in crown; water-resistant to 10 atm
Band: rubber, buckle
Price: $4,200

Due Valvole "Only One"

Reference number: W 125K019
Movement: automatic, 2 x ETA Caliber 2671; ø 17.2 mm, height 4.8 mm; 25 jewels; 28,800 vph; 38-hour power reserve
Functions: hours and minutes (2 time zones), sweep seconds; date
Case: titanium with black PVD coating; ø 44 mm, height 16 mm; sapphire crystal; screw-in crowns; water-resistant to 10 atm
Band: rubber, buckle
Remarks: dial made of body of genuine Formula 1 car
Price: $3,400

MeisterSinger GmbH & Co. KG
Hafenweg 46
D-48155 Münster
Germany

Tel.:
01149-251-133-4860

E-Mail:
info@meistersinger.de

Website:
www.meistersinger.de

Founded:
2001

Number of employees:
9

Annual production:
approx. 8,000 watches

U.S. distributor:
Duber Time
1920 Dr. MLK Jr. Street North
St. Petersburg, FL 33704
727-202-3262
damir@meistersingertime.com

Most important collections/price range:
from approx. $1,200 to $7,000

MeisterSinger

In 2014, MeisterSinger completed a long process of re-orientation, setting the German brand in redux mode. At Baselworld 2014, it presented a portfolio of exclusively one-hand watches, the actual core of the brand. These watches express a relaxed and self-determined approach to the perception of time apparent in the special diurnal rituals that everyone knows, young, old, in private or at work. These rituals actually divide up and define certain moments. And it is the reiteration of these moments which leads to order, or at least avoiding chaos.

Founder Martin Brassler launched his little collection of stylistically neat one-hand dials at the beginning of the new millennium. Looking at these ultimately simplified dials does tempt one to classify the one-hand watch as an archetype. The single hand simply cannot be reduced any further, and the 144 minutes for 12 hours around the dial do have a normative function of sorts. In a frenetic era when free time has become so rare, these watches slow things down a little.

"A customer once wrote me that his MeisterSinger was a symbol of leisure time for him," Brassler grins. "It measures the time in intervals of five minutes; you don't need to know what time it is any more precisely than that." The most recent one-hander does provide the hour, jumping very precisely in a window under 12 o'clock—hence its Italian name "Salthora," or jumping hour.

Nevertheless, Brassler has put a few three-hand watches on the market, like the Paleograph, but the hour hand remains the dominant feature on the dials. A new series geared toward women exudes its own simplicity, with just a slight breeze of color. Design, product planning, service, and management are all done in Münster, Germany. The watches, however, are Swiss made, with ETA and Sellita movements.

N° 01

Reference number: AM 3301
Movement: manually wound, ETA Caliber 2801-2; ø 35.6 mm, height 3.35 mm; 17 jewels; 28,800 vph; 42-hour power reserve
Functions: hours (each line stands for 5 minutes)
Case: stainless steel, ø 43 mm, height 11.5 mm; sapphire crystal, transparent case back; water-resistant to 5 atm
Band: calf leather, buckle
Price: $1,595
Variations: ivory-colored or anthracite dial; reptile skin or stainless steel Milanese mesh band

Salthora

Reference number: SH 908
Movement: automatic, ETA Caliber 2824-2 or Sellita SW200-1 with module for jumping hour; ø 25.6 mm, height 6.9 mm; 26 jewels; 28,800 vph; 38-hour power reserve; côtes de Genève
Functions: hours (digital, jumping), minutes
Case: stainless steel, ø 40 mm, height 13.3 mm; sapphire crystal; transparent case back; water-resistant to 5 atm
Band: calf leather, double folding clasp
Price: $3,425
Variations: white, ivory-colored, or anthracite dial; reptile skin or stainless steel Milanese mesh band

Paleograph

Reference number: SC 103
Movement: manually wound, Meistersinger Caliber MSYN13 (base ETA 6497); ø 36.6 mm, height 7.6 mm; 20 jewels; 18,000 vph; column wheel control of chronograph functions; 46-hour power reserve
Functions: hours (each line stands for 5 minutes), subsidiary seconds; chronograph
Case: stainless steel, ø 43 mm, height 15.8 mm; sapphire crystal; transparent case back; water-resistant to 5 atm
Band: reptile skin, double folding clasp
Price: $8,175
Variations: blue dial; stainless steel Milanese mesh band

Perigraph

Reference number: AM1007
Movement: automatic, ETA 2824-2 or Sellita SW200-1; ø 25.6 mm, height 4.6 mm; 25 or 26 jewels; 28,800 vph; with côtes de Genève; 38-hour power reserve
Functions: hours (each line stands for 5 minutes); date (disc display)
Case: stainless steel, ø 43 mm, height 11.5 mm; sapphire crystal; transparent case back; water-resistant to 5 atm
Band: calf leather, buckle
Price: $2,375
Variations: silver-white or ivory-colored dial; reptile skin or stainless steel Milanese mesh band

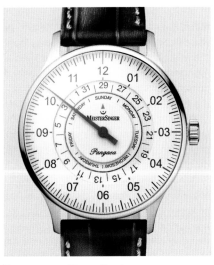

Pangaea Day Date

Reference number: PDD903
Movement: automatic, ETA Caliber 2836-2 or Sellita Caliber SW220-1; ø 25.6 mm, height 5.05 mm; 26 jewels; 28,800 vph; with côtes de Genève; 38-hour power reserve
Functions: hours (each line stands for 5 minutes); date and weekday (disc display)
Case: stainless steel, ø 40 mm, height 10.5 mm; sapphire crystal; transparent case back; water-resistant to 5 atm
Band: calf leather, buckle
Price: $2,825
Variations: white or anthracite dial; reptile skin or stainless steel Milanese mesh band

Neo

Reference number: NE 901
Movement: automatic, ETA 2824-2 or Sellita SW200-1; ø 25.6 mm, height 4.6 mm; 25 or 26 jewels; 28,800 vph; 38-hour power reserve
Functions: hours (each line stands for 5 minutes); date
Case: stainless steel, ø 36 mm, height 9.7 mm; plexiglass, water-resistant to 3 atm
Band: calf leather, buckle
Price: $1,350
Variations: ivory-colored, anthracite, or blue dial; with reptile skin or stainless steel Milanese mesh band

Singulator

Reference number: SIM 101
Movement: manually wound, Caliber MS.0109 (base ETA 6498); ø 36.6 mm, height 5.1 mm; 17 jewels; 18,000 vph; swan-neck fine adjustment, glucydur screw balance, blued screws, skeletonized bridges, finely finished with côtes de Genève; 46-hour power reserve
Functions: hours, minutes (off-center), subsidiary seconds
Case: stainless steel, ø 43 mm, height 13.3 mm; transparent case back; water-resistant to 5 atm
Band: reptile skin, double folding clasp
Price: $7,450
Variations: black or ivory-colored dial; stainless steel Milanese mesh band

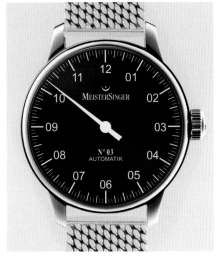

N° 03

Reference number: AM 908MIL
Movement: automatic, ETA Caliber 2824-2 or Sellita SW220-1; ø 25.6 mm, height 4.6 mm; 25 or 26 jewels; 28,800 vph; with côtes de Genève; 38-hour power reserve
Functions: hours (each line stands for 5 minutes)
Case: stainless steel, ø 43 mm, height 11.5 mm; sapphire crystal; transparent case back; water-resistant to 5 atm
Band: stainless steel Milanese mesh, double folding clasp
Price: $2,150
Variations: silver-white, ivory-colored, or anthracite dial; calf or reptile skin band

Caliber MSYN13

Base caliber: ETA 6497
Manually wound; simple barrel spring; 46-hour power reserve
Functions: hours, subsidiary seconds; chronograph
Diameter: 36.6 mm
Height: 7.6 mm
Jewels: 20
Balance: glucydur
Frequency: 18,000 vph
Shock protection: Incabloc

Milus

Milus International SA

Rue de Reuchenette 19
CH-2502 Biel/Bienne
Switzerland

Tel.:
01141-32-344-3939

Fax:
01141-32-344-3938

E-Mail:
info@milus.com

Website:
www.milus.com

Founded:
1919

U.S. distributor:
Totally Worth It, LLC
76 Division Avenue
Summit, NJ 07901-2309
201-894-4710
info@totallyworthit.com

Most important collections/price range:
Milus Tirion Répétition Minutes TriRetrograde / from approx. $308,000; Tirion TriRetrograde / from approx. $9,300; Merea TriRetrograde / from approx. $7,000; Snow Star Heritage / $3,290

Milus was founded by Paul William Junod in Biel/Bienne and remained in family hands until the year 2002. A new era began then with the founding of Milus International SA under the able guidance of Jan Edöcs and with investments from the giant Peace Mark Group from Hong Kong.

Within a few years, the brand had moved into the edgy segment of the watch industry with a triple retrograde seconds indicator, which was developed together with the specialists at Agenhor in Geneva. And that made all the difference in the Milus image. In the 1970s, the brand had a considerable reputation for jewelry. Now, however, it has become a genuine and respected watchmaker, one producing top-drawer horological complications. The TriRetrograde function is a Milus trademark and can be found in a host of models all named after constellations (Tirion, Merea, Zetios). Fans of retrogrades will have a feast. There are watches with three separate second hands showing twenty seconds each before passing the baton to the next one or the lively "five-hand watch" or even the spectacular Tirion Répétition Minutes TriRetrograde, which also features a delicate minute repeater.

Meanwhile, the Peace Mark Group collapsed in 2008, but Milus quickly found another investor in the Chow Tai Fook Group owned by Dr. Cheng Yu-tung. In 2011, Cyril Dubois took over at the head of the company. Quietly, but surely, the brand has been expanding on several fronts with the triretrogrades in the lead, and the more sporty-elegant Zetios line coming in a close second. Models like the Merea look back to a time when Milus made top-of-the-line jewelry as well. The brand's Snow Star Instant Date from the 1940s was also rebuilt for vintage fans. Finally, Milus has been intensively communicating a collection of eye-catching cuff links it began launching in 2006—before many others—already featuring real rotor systems.

Tirion TriRetrograde

Reference number: TIRI742
Movement: automatic, ETA Caliber 2892-A2 with Milus special module 3838; ø 30 mm; 37 jewels; 28,800 vph; 40-hour power reserve
Functions: hours, minutes, triretrograde seconds
Case: pink gold, ø 45 mm, height 13.91 mm; carbon bezel; DLC-treated crown; sapphire crystal; screwed-down transparent case back; water-resistant to 3 atm
Band: reptile skin, buckle
Remarks: second hands shaped like oscillating rotor
Price: $36,200

Tirion TriRetrograde

Reference number: TIRI022
Movement: automatic, ETA Caliber 2892-A2 with Milus special module 3838; ø 30 mm; 37 jewels; 28,800 vph; 40-hour power reserve
Functions: hours, minutes, triretrograde seconds (on black bridges); date
Case: DLC-treated stainless steel, ø 45 mm, height 13.91 mm; carbon bezel; screwed-in transparent case back; water-resistant to 3 atm
Band: reptile skin, folding clasp
Remarks: skeleton hour, minute, and second hands
Price: $13,500

Tirion Répétition Minutes TriRetrograde

Reference number: TIRM600
Movement: manually wound, Milus Caliber M08-35RM module; ø 26.2 mm, height 5.2 mm; 25 jewels; 28,800 vph; 96-hour power reserve; COSC-certified
Functions: hours, minutes, subsidiary triretrograde seconds; date; minute repeater
Case: pink gold, ø 46 mm, height 13.92 mm; sapphire crystal; screwed-down back; water-resistant to 3 atm
Band: reptile skin, buckle
Remarks: blued hands, retrograde seconds displayed on three 20-second gold arcs
Price: $350,000

Zetios Classic

Reference number: ZETK401
Movement: automatic, ETA Caliber 2892-A2 with Dubois Dépraz 14070 module; ø 26.2 mm, height 5.2 mm; 25 jewels; 28,800 vph; 42-hour power reserve
Functions: hours, minutes, sweep seconds
Case: pink gold, ø 42 mm, 12.4 mm; screwed-down case back; sapphire crystal; water-resistant to 3 atm
Band: reptile skin, folding clasp
Remarks: dial with clous de Paris decoration
Price: $26,500

Zetios Regulator

Reference number: ZETR400
Movement: automatic, ETA Caliber 2892-A2 with Dubois Dépraz 14070 module; ø 26.2 mm, height 5.2 mm; 25 jewels; 28,800 vph; 42-hour power reserve
Functions: hours, minutes, subsidiary seconds; date
Case: pink gold, ø 42 mm; sapphire crystal; screwed-down case back; water-resistant to 3 atm
Band: reptile skin, buckle
Remarks: galvanic dial with *grain de riz* decoration, blued hands
Price: $23,500

Zetios Chronograph

Reference number: ZETC028
Movement: automatic, ETA Caliber 2892 with Dubois Dépraz 4500 module; ø 30 mm, height 7.5 mm; 49 jewels; 28,800 vph; 40-hour power reserve
Functions: hours, minutes, subsidiary seconds; chronograph; 30-minute and 12-hour counter; date
Case: stainless steel with black DLC, ø 45 mm, height 14.5 mm; sapphire crystal; screwed-down case back; water-resistant to 3 atm
Band: calf leather, buckle
Remarks: carbon dial with silver indexes, partly luminescent hands; red counter hands
Price: $7,100
Variations: pink gold (starting at $33,400)

Snow Star Heritage

Reference number: HKIT001
Movement: automatic, Sellita SW200; ø 25.6 mm, height 4.6 mm; 28,800 vph
Functions: hours, minutes, seconds; date
Case: stainless steel, ø 40 mm; sapphire crystal with magnifying glass at 3; water-resistant to 3 atm
Band: calf leather, buckle
Remarks: comes with interchangeable NATO strap, compass and propeller cufflinks, and military ID tag
Price: $3,290; limited to 1,940 pieces
Variations: pink gold ($32,900; limited to 99 pieces)

Merea TriRetrograde

Reference number: MER027
Movement: automatic, ETA Caliber 2892-A2 with Milus special module 3838; ø 30 mm; 37 jewels; 28,800 vph; 40-hour power reserve
Functions: hours, minutes, triple retrograde subsidiary seconds
Case: stainless steel, 35.8 x 36.8 mm, height 12.9 mm; case, crown, and attachments partially set with 115 white diamonds; sapphire crystal; screwed-down case back; water-resistant to 3 atm
Band: reptile skin, buckle
Price: $15,200

Milus Cufflinks

Reference number: CUF011D
Movement: with original Milus rotor rotating 360°, ø 19 mm; set with 104 diamonds
Case: stainless steel, rotor with côtes de Genève decoration
Remarks: Milus started manufacturing cufflinks in 2006 using original movement parts
Price: $1,850
Variations: white gold, pink gold, PVD-coated, rose gold and yellow gold plated (starting at $485)

Mk II

Mk II Corporation
303 W. Lancaster Avenue, #283
Wayne, PA 19087

E-Mail:
info@mkiiwatches.com

Website:
www.mkiiwatches.com

Founded:
2002

Number of employees:
3

Annual production:
800 watches

Distribution:
direct sales

Most important collections/price range:
Professional series / $1,200 to $2,000;
Specialist series / $799 to $1,150

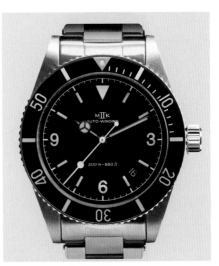

If vintage and unserviceable watches had their say, they would probably be naturally attracted to Mk II for the name alone, which is a military designation for the second generation of equipment. The company, which was founded by watch enthusiast and maker Bill Yao in 2002, not only puts retired designs back into service, but also modernizes and customizes them. Before the screwed-down crown, diving watches were not nearly as reliably sealed, for example. And some beautiful old pieces were made with plated brass cases or featured Bakelite components, which are either easily damaged or have aged poorly. Mk II not only substitutes proven modern materials, but also modern manufacturing methods and techniques to ensure a better outcome.

These are material issues that the team at Mk II handles with great care. They will not, metaphorically speaking, airbrush a Model-T. As genuine watch lovers themselves, they make sure that the final design is in the spirit of the watch itself, which still leaves a great deal of leeway for many iterations given a sufficient number of parts. In the company's output, vintage style and modern functionality are key. The watches are assembled by hand at the Mk II workshop in Pennsylvania—and subjected to a rigorous regime of testing. The components are individually inspected, the cases tested at least three times for water resistance, and at the end the whole watch is regulated in six positions. Looking to the future, Mk II aspires to carry its clean vintage style into the development of what it hopes will be future classics of its own.

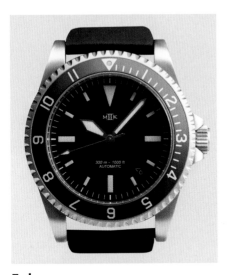

Fulcrum

Reference number: CD06-1003
Movement: automatic, Caliber Soprod A10; ø 26.2 mm, height 3.60 mm; 25 jewels; 28,800 vph; 42-hour power reserve; rhodium-plated; rotor decorated with côtes de Genève
Functions: hours, minutes, sweep seconds; date
Case: stainless steel, ø 42.1 mm, height 15.1 mm; 120-click unidirectional bezel, domed sapphire crystal with antireflective coating; screwed-down case back; screw-in crown; automatic helium release valve; water-resistant to 30 atm
Band: rubber strap, buckle
Price: $1,595
Variations: black 12-hour GMT bezel

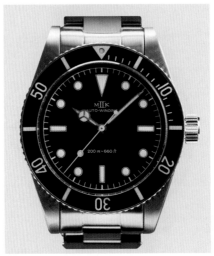

Nassau

Reference number: CD05.1-1002B
Movement: automatic, Caliber ETA 2836-2; ø 26 mm, height 5.05 mm; 25 jewels; 28,800 vph; 38-hour power reserve; rhodium-plated, rotor decorated with côtes de Genève
Functions: hours, minutes, sweep seconds
Case: stainless steel; ø 39.20 mm, height 14.50 mm; unidirectional steel/aluminum bezel, domed sapphire crystal with antireflective coating; screwed-down case back; screw-in crown; water-resistant to 20 atm
Band: steel bracelet
Price: $945
Variations: nylon strap

Nassau 369 Date

Reference number: CD05.1-2002B
Movement: automatic, Caliber ETA 2836-2; ø 26 mm, height 5.05 mm; 25 jewels; 28,800 vph; rhodium-plated rotor decorated with côtes de Genève; 38-hour power reserve
Functions: hours, minutes, sweep seconds; date
Case: stainless steel; ø 39.2 mm, height 14.5 mm; unidirectional bezel; domed sapphire crystal with antireflective coating; screwed-down case back; screw-in crown; water-resistant to 20 atm
Band: stainless steel, folding clasp
Remarks: 2-tone lacquered dial
Price: $1,095
Variations: nylon strap

Montana Watch Company

Back in the nineteenth and early twentieth centuries, the American watch industry was a sizable affair, with manufacturers producing timepieces of superior craftsmanship, reliability, and simplicity, including their own movements in some instances. A century later, the Montana Watch Company in Livingston, Montana, decided to produce wristwatches that hark back to the days of old, boldly retro and therefore distinctive. Just looking at a Montana can make you hear horses galloping and banjos twanging.

The trick is in the design and the choice of materials. Think rich hand-engraved motifs, gems, and custom-designed cases. These often unique pieces are created by designer and horologist Jeffrey Nashan, who works individually with each client from concept to completion to achieve heirloom timepieces.

The traditional exterior, however, belies the state-of-the-art interior. Each case is machined in-house from a single piece of solid stock. Custom design with SolidWorks 3-D modeling CAD software and state-of-the-art CNC machines allows production of small runs in all variety of metals, notably silver.

Nashan has assembled a team of master engravers well versed in every style of metal engraving, inlay, and gem setting, and one of the most highly skilled and innovative leathersmiths in the American West to produce the brand's bespoke straps. The watches featuring vignettes from John Banovich wildlife paintings using a special engraving technique are very popular. And in 2013, for the brand's fifteenth anniversary, Nashan rereleased newer versions of the watch that started the company—the 1915—with some especially florid engraving.

Montana Watch Company
124 N. Main Street
Livingston, Montana 59047

Tel.:
406-222-8899

E-Mail:
info@montanawatch.com

Website:
www.montanawatch.com

Founded:
1998

Number of employees:
6

Annual production:
100 watches

Distribution:
direct distribution

Most important collection/price range:
Model 1915 / starting at $6,500; Bridger Field Watch / starting at $3,200; Model 1925 / starting at $5,150; Officer's Watch / starting at $6,100; Model 1920 / starting at $3,850; Model 1930 / starting at $5,650; Highline Aviator / starting at $3,550; Miles City Pocket Watch / starting at $3,350; Montana Travler / starting at $3,750

Highline Aviator "Spaghetti Western"

Movement: manually wound, ETA Caliber 6498; ø 36.6 mm, height 4.5 mm; 17 jewels; 18,000 vph
Functions: hours, minutes, subsidiary seconds
Case: sterling silver, ø 43 mm, height, 10.5 mm; gold crown; wire lugs; sapphire crystal; transparent case back; water-resistant to 3 atm
Band: saddle leather, silver buckle
Remarks: custom hand-engraved dial with horse motif; engraved case
Price: $24,200
Variations: all custom variations available (from $3,650)

Ladies Bridger Field Watch

Movement: automatic, ETA Caliber 2824-2; ø 25.6 mm, height 4.6 mm; 25 jewels; 28,800 vph
Functions: hours, minutes, sweep seconds
Case: Argentium silver, ø 37 mm, height 9.75 mm; gold crown; sapphire crystal; transparent case back; water-resistant to 3 atm
Band: silver bracelet, buckle
Remarks: case with western bright-cut engraving
Price: $9,900
Variations: custom variations available (from $3,300)

Reissue, Western Design Premium

Movement: automatic, Soprod Caliber A10-2; ø 25.6 mm, height 3.6 mm; 25 jewels; 28,800 vph
Functions: hours, minutes, sweep second
Case: Argentium silver, ø 37 mm, height 9.75 mm; gold crown; sapphire crystal; transparent case back
Band: saddle leather, buckle
Remarks: case with western single-point hand-engraving in deep relief, gold overlays, set with rubies; grand feu enamel dial; sterling silver buckle
Price: $15,000
Variations: unadorned variations (starting at $6,500)

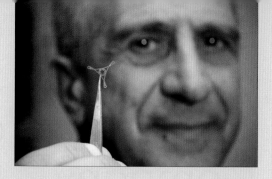

Montblanc Montre SA
10, chemin des Tourelles
CH-2400 Le Locle
Switzerland

Tel.:
01141-32-933-8888

Fax:
01141-32-933-8880

E-Mail:
service@montblanc.com

Website:
www.montblanc.com

Founded:
1997 (1906 in Hamburg)

Number of employees:
worldwide approx. 3,000

U.S. distributor:
Montblanc International
26 Main Street
Chatham, NJ 07928
908-508-2301
www.montblanc.com

Most important collections:
Meisterstück, Star, Star Nicolas Rieussec,
Star 4810, TimeWalker, Collection Villeret

Montblanc

The fact that, in a period of fifteen years, a company once famous only for its exclusive writing implements managed to transform itself into a distinguished watch brand is one of the most impressive stories in the watch industry.

It was with great skill and cleverness that Nicolas Rieussec used the invention of a special chronograph—the "Time Writer," a device that released droplets of ink onto a rotating sheet of paper—to make a name for himself. And nowadays, the range of chronographs driven by in-house calibers is impressive: from simple automatic stopwatches to flagship pieces with two independent spring barrels for time and "time-writing."

The Richemont Group, owner of Montblanc, has placed great trust in its "daughter" company, having put the little *manufacture* Minerva, which it purchased at the beginning of 2007, at the disposal of Montblanc. The Minerva Institute serves as a kind of think tank for the future, a place where young watchmakers can absorb the old traditions and skills, as well as the wealth of experience and mind-set of the masters.

In the summer of 2013, Jerôme Lambert from sister brand Jaeger-LeCoultre took over the presidency and refocused the brand on the almost-luxury price segment and a bit away from the boisterous complicated watches of recent years. The new Meisterstück Heritage collection is a sober reminder of ninety years of Montblanc history. It features entry-level models at around $2,900.

Collection Villeret 1858 ExoTourbillon Rattrapante

Reference number: 111823
Movement: manually wound, Montblanc Caliber MB M16.61; ø 38.4 mm, height 11.9 mm; 18,000 vph; 4-minute tourbillon; column wheel control of chronograph functions by crown pusher; fine finishing; 50-hour power reserve
Functions: hours (off-center), minutes, subsidiary seconds; additional 12-hour display (2nd time zone), day/night indicator; rattrapante chronograph
Case: white gold, ø 47 mm, height 18.2 mm; sapphire crystal; transparent case back; water-resistant to 3 atm
Band: reptile skin, buckle
Price: $322,500; limited to 18 pieces

"Homage to Nicolas Rieussec"

Reference number: 111592
Movement: automatic, Montblanc Caliber MB R200; ø 31 mm, height 8.46 mm; 40 jewels; 28,800 vph; 2 spring barrels; column wheel control of chronograph functions with single pusher; 72-hour power reserve
Functions: hours and minutes (off-center), subsidiary seconds; chronograph; date
Case: pink gold, ø 43 mm, height 14.8 mm; sapphire crystal; transparent case back; water-resistant to 3 atm
Band: reptile skin, buckle
Price: $34,400; limited to 193 pieces
Variations: stainless steel ($11,500; limited to 565 pieces)

Nicolas Rieussec Rising Hours

Reference number: 108789
Movement: automatic, Montblanc Caliber MB R220; 42 jewels; 28,800 vph; flat hairspring; column wheel control of chronograph functions with single pusher; 72-hour power reserve
Functions: hours (disc, day/night color change), minutes; chronograph; date, weekday; power reserve indicator (on back)
Case: pink gold, ø 43 mm, height 15.3 mm; sapphire crystal; water-resistant to 3 atm
Band: reptile skin, triple folding clasp
Price: $35,100
Variations: stainless steel ($12,800); platinum ($62,600; limited to 28 pieces)

Meisterstück Heritage Perpetual Calendar

Reference number: 110714
Movement: automatic, Montblanc Caliber MB 29.15 (base ETA 2892 with Dubois Dépraz module); 25 jewels; 28,800 vph; 42-hour power reserve
Functions: hours, minutes; perpetual calendar with date, weekday, month, moon phase, leap year
Case: pink gold, ø 39 mm, height 10.27 mm; sapphire crystal; transparent case back; water-resistant to 3 atm
Band: reptile skin, buckle
Price: $21,600
Variations: stainless steel ($12,800)

Meisterstück Heritage Pulsograph

Reference number: 111626
Movement: manually wound, Montblanc Caliber MB M13.21; 22 jewels; 18,000 vph; column wheel control of chronograph functions; 55-hour power reserve
Functions: hours, minutes, subsidiary seconds; chronograph
Case: pink gold, ø 41 mm, height 11.8 mm; sapphire crystal; transparent case back; water-resistant to 3 atm
Band: reptile skin, buckle
Price: $34,500

Meisterstück Heritage Date Automatic

Reference number: 111580
Movement: automatic, Montblanc Caliber MB 24.17 (base ETA 2824-2); ø 25.6 mm, height 4.6 mm; 26 jewels; 28,800 vph; 38-hour power reserve
Functions: hours, minutes, sweep seconds; date
Case: stainless steel, ø 41 mm, height 9.7 mm; sapphire crystal; transparent case back; water-resistant to 3 atm
Band: reptile skin, buckle
Price: $2,670

Meisterstück Heritage Moonphase

Reference number: 110699
Movement: automatic, Montblanc Caliber MB 29.14; 25 jewels; 28,800 vph; 42-hour power reserve
Functions: hours, minutes; date; moon phase
Case: stainless steel, ø 39 mm, height 10.24 mm; sapphire crystal; transparent case back; water-resistant to 3 atm
Band: reptile skin, buckle
Price: $4,500

TimeWalker Chronograph 100

Reference number: 111285
Movement: manually wound, Montblanc Caliber MB M66-25; ø 38,4 mm, height 7.63 mm; 37 jewels; 18,000 and 360,000 vph (chronograph); separate mechanisms and escapements for movement and chronograph; 1/100th of second display; 100-hour power reserve, 45-minute (chronograph)
Functions: hours, minutes, subsidiary seconds; chronograph
Case: titanium with carbon fiber layer, ø 45.6 mm, height 15.48 mm; black DLC coating on bezel, sapphire crystal; transparent back; water-resistant to 3 atm
Band: reptile skin, buckle
Price: $63,900; limited to 100 pieces

TimeWalker TwinFly Chronograph

Reference number: 109134
Movement: automatic, Caliber MB LL100; ø 31 mm, height 7.9 mm; 36 jewels; 28,800 vph; 72-hour power reserve; sweep minute counter
Functions: hours, minutes, subsidiary seconds; 2nd time zone (additional 24-hour display); flyback chronograph; date
Case: stainless steel, ø 43 mm, height 15.3 mm; sapphire crystal; transparent case back; water-resistant to 3 atm
Band: reptile skin, double folding clasp
Price: $8,400
Variations: stainless steel bracelet ($8,500)

TimeWalker Extreme Chronograph DLC

Reference number: 111197
Movement: automatic, Montblanc Caliber 4810/507 (base ETA 7750); ø 30 mm, height 7.9 mm; 25 jewels; 28,800 vph; 46-hour power reserve
Functions: hours, minutes, subsidiary seconds; chronograph; date
Case: stainless steel with black DLC coating; ø 43 mm, height 14.4 mm; sapphire crystal; transparent case back; water-resistant to 3 atm
Band: calf-leather on rubber base, buckle
Price: $6,400

TimeWalker Date Automatic

Reference number: 110338
Movement: automatic, Montblanc Caliber MB 4810/409 (base ETA 2824-2); ø 25.6 mm, height 4.6 mm; 25 jewels; 28,800 vph; 42-hour power reserve
Functions: hours, minutes, sweep seconds; date
Case: stainless steel, ø 42 mm, height 11.2 mm; sapphire crystal; transparent case back; water-resistant to 3 atm
Band: reptile skin, buckle
Price: $3,435

TimeWalker World-Time Hemispheres

Reference number: 108956
Movement: automatic, Montblanc Caliber MB 4810/410 (base ETA 2893-1); ø 25.6 mm, height 4.1 mm; 21 jewels; 28,800 vph; 42-hour power reserve
Functions: hours, minutes, sweep seconds; world-time display (2nd time zone); date
Case: stainless steel, ø 42 mm, height 12.05 mm; titanium bezel, sapphire crystal; transparent case back; water-resistant to 3 atm
Remarks: crown-activated disc with 24 northern hemisphere reference cities on peripheral ring
Band: calf leather, pin buckle
Price: $5,700
Variations: southern hemisphere reference cities

Star Twin Moonphase

Reference number: 110642
Movement: automatic, Montblanc Caliber MB 29.13; 25 jewels; 28,800 vph; 42-hour power reserve
Functions: hours, minutes, sweep seconds; date, moon phase representing northern and southern hemispheres
Case: stainless steel, ø 42 mm, height 12.17 mm; sapphire crystal; transparent case back; water-resistant to 3 atm
Band: reptile skin, double folding clasp
Price: $5,300

Star Chronograph GMT Automatic

Reference number: 36967
Movement: automatic, Montblanc Caliber MB 4810/503 (base ETA 7753); ø 30 mm, height 7.9 mm; 25 jewels; 28,800 vph; 46-hour power reserve
Functions: hours, minutes, subsidiary seconds; 2nd time zone (additional 24-hour display); chronograph
Case: stainless steel, ø 42 mm, height 14.5 mm; sapphire crystal; transparent case back; water-resistant to 3 atm
Band: reptile skin, double folding clasp
Price: $5,000

Star Classique Lady Small Second

Reference number: 110643
Movement: Montblanc Caliber MB 4810/160 quartz
Functions: hours, minutes, subsidiary seconds
Case: pink gold, ø 30 mm, height 7.36 mm; pink gold bezel set with 62 diamonds, sapphire crystal; water-resistant to 3 atm
Band: stainless steel with pink gold elements, double folding clasp
Remarks: mother-of-pearl dial set with 11 diamonds
Price: $8,300

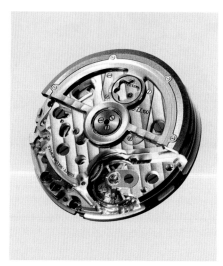

Caliber MB LL100

Automatic; column wheel control of chronograph functions; vertical disc clutch; central minute and second counter with double flyback function; double spring barrel, 72-hour power reserve
Functions: hours, minutes, sweep seconds; additional 24-hour display; flyback chronograph; date
Diameter: 31 mm; **Height:** 7.9 mm
Jewels: 36
Balance: glucydur with variable inertia
Frequency: 28,800 vph
Balance spring: flat hairspring
Shock protection: Incabloc
Remarks: perlage on plate, bridges with côtes de Genève

Caliber MB R200

Automatic; column wheel control using separate chronograph pushers; vertical chronograph clutch; stop-seconds; double spring barrel, 72-hour power reserve
Functions: hours, minutes, sweep seconds; additional 12-hour display; chronograph; date; power reserve indicator
Diameter: 31 mm
Height: 8.46 mm
Jewels: 40
Balance: screw balance
Frequency: 28,800 vph
Balance spring: flat hairspring
Remarks: rhodium-plated plate with perlage, bridges with côtes de Genève

Caliber MB R110

Manually wound; column wheel control using separate chronograph pushers; vertical disc clutch; double spring barrel, 72-hour power reserve
Functions: hours, minutes, subsidiary seconds; chronograph; date; power reserve indicator on case back
Diameter: 31 mm
Height: 7.6 mm
Jewels: 33
Balance: balance with variable inertia
Frequency: 28,800 vph
Balance spring: flat hairspring
Shock protection: Incabloc
Remarks: rhodium-plated plate with perlage, bridges with côtes de Genève

Caliber MB M13.21

Manually wound; column wheel control of chronograph functions; single spring barrel, 60-hour power reserve
Functions: hours, minutes, subsidiary seconds; chronograph
Diameter: 29.5 mm
Height: 6.4 mm
Jewels: 22
Balance: screw balance with weights
Frequency: 18,000 vph
Balance spring: with Phillips end curve
Shock protection: Incabloc
Remarks: plates and bridges of rhodium-plated German silver, partial perlage and beveled by hand

Caliber MB M16.29

Manually wound; column wheel control of chronograph functions with separate pushers; single spring barrel, 55-hour power reserve
Functions: hours, minutes, subsidiary seconds; chronograph
Diameter: 38.4 mm
Height: 6.3 mm
Jewels: 22
Balance: screw balance
Frequency: 18,000 vph
Balance spring: with Phillips end curve
Remarks: rhodium-plated plate with perlage; bridges with côtes de Genève; gold-plated movement

Caliber MB M66.25

Manually wound; two separate gear works and escapements for time and chronograph with 1/100th of a second display; 100-hour power reserve or 45 minutes (chronograph); 2 spring barrels
Functions: hours, minutes, subsidiary seconds; ultra-high frequency chronograph (1/100th)
Diameter: 38.4 mm
Height: 7.63 mm
Jewels: 37
Balance: screw balance with weights and ring balance (chronograph)
Frequency: 18,000 and 360,000 vph (chronograph)

Mühle Glashütte GmbH
Nautische Instrumente und
Feinmechanik

Altenberger Strasse 35
D-01768 Glashütte
Germany

Tel.:
01149-35053-3203-0

Fax:
01149-35053-3203-136

E-Mail:
info@muehle-glashuette.de

Website:
www.muehle-glashutte.de

Founded:
first founding 1869; second founding 1993

Number of employees:
47

U.S. distributor:
Mühle Glashütte
Old Northeast Jewelers
1131 4th Street North
Saint Petersburg, FL 33701
800-922-4377
www.muehle-glashuette.com

Most important collections/price range:
mechanical wristwatches / approx. $1,399
to $5,400

Mühle-Glashütte

Mühle Glashütte has survived all the ups and downs of Germany's history. The firm Rob. Mühle & Sohn was founded by its namesake in 1869. At that time, the company made precision measuring instruments for the local watch industry and the German School of Watchmaking. In the early 1920s, the firm established itself as a supplier for the automobile industry, making speedometers, automobile clocks, tachometers, and other measurement instruments.

Having manufactured instruments for the military during the war, the company was not only bombarded by the Soviet air force, but was also nationalized in 1945, as it was in the eastern part of the country. After the fall of the Iron Curtain, it was reestablished as a limited liability corporation. In 2007, Thilo Mühle took over the helm from his father, Hans-Jürgen Mühle.

The company's wristwatch business was launched in 1996 and now somewhat overshadows the nautical instruments that had made the name Mühle Glashütte famous, especially among owners of luxury yachts and cruise ships. Its collection comprises mechanical wristwatches at entry-level and mid-level prices. For these, the company uses Swiss base movements that are equipped with such in-house developments as a patented woodpecker-neck regulation and the Mühle rotor. Chronographs are additionally fitted with the Glashütte three-quarter plate. All movement surfaces are finished in the typical Mühle style.

S.A.R. Rescue-Timer

Reference number: M1-41-03-MB
Movement: automatic, modified Sellita Caliber SW 200-1; ø 25.6 mm, height 4.6 mm; 26 jewels; 28,800 vph; woodpecker-neck fine adjustment; Mühle rotor; special Mühle finish; 38-hour power reserve
Functions: hours, minutes, sweep seconds; date
Case: stainless steel, ø 42 mm, height 13.5 mm; rubber bezel, sapphire crystal; screw-in crown; water-resistant to 100 atm
Band: stainless steel, folding clasp with extension link
Price: $2,699
Variations: rubber strap ($2,599)

S.A.R. Flieger-Chronograph

Reference number: M1-41-33-KB
Movement: automatic, Caliber MU 9408 (base ETA 7750); ø 30 mm, height 7.9 mm; 25 jewels; 28,800 vph; woodpecker-neck fine adjustment; three-quarter plate, Mühle rotor; special Mühle finish; 48-hour power reserve
Functions: hours, minutes, subsidiary seconds; chronograph; date
Case: stainless steel, ø 44 mm, height 16.2 mm; bidirectional bezel with 60-minute divisions, sapphire crystal; transparent back; screw-in crown; water-resistant to 10 atm
Band: rubber, safety folding clasp with extension
Price: $4,699

Seebataillon GMT

Reference number: M1-28-62-KB
Movement: automatic, ETA Caliber 2893-2; ø 25.6 mm, height 4.1 mm; 21 jewels; 28,800 vph; woodpecker-neck fine adjustment; Mühle rotor; special Mühle finish; 42-hour power reserve
Functions: hours, minutes, sweep seconds; additional 24-hour display (2nd time zone); date
Case: titanium, ø 44 mm, height 12.7 mm; bidirectional bezel with 60-minute divisions, sapphire crystal; screw-in crown; water-resistant to 30 atm
Band: rubber, folding clasp
Price: $3,899

Kampfschwimmer

Reference number: M1-28-92-NB
Movement: automatic, Sellita Caliber SW200-1;
ø 25.6 mm, height 2.6 mm; 26 jewels; 28,800 vph;
woodpecker-neck fine adjustment; special Mühle
finish; 38-hour power reserve
Functions: hours, minutes, sweep seconds; date
Case: stainless steel, ø 44 mm, height 15.1 mm;
unidirectional bezel with 60-minute divisions,
sapphire crystal; screw-in crown; water-resistant to
30 atm
Band: rubber, buckle
Price: $3,899

M 29 Classic Small Seconds

Reference number: M1-25-67-LB
Movement: automatic, Sellita Caliber SW290-1;
ø 25.6 mm; 28,800 vph; woodpecker-neck fine
adjustment; special Mühle finish; 38-hour power
reserve
Functions: hours, minutes, subsidiary seconds;
date
Case: stainless steel, ø 42.4 mm, height 12.2 mm;
sapphire crystal; transparent case back; screw-in
crown; water-resistant to 10 atm
Band: calf leather, buckle
Price: $2,699
Variations: stainless steel bracelet ($2,799)

Antaria Day/Date

Reference number: M1-39-97-LB
Movement: automatic, Sellita Caliber SW220-1;
ø 25.6 mm, height 5.05 mm; 26 jewels; 28,800
vph; woodpecker-neck fine adjustment; special
Mühle finish; 38-hour power reserve
Functions: hours, minutes, sweep seconds;
weekday, date
Case: stainless steel, ø 42 mm, height 11.5 mm;
pink gold-plated bezel, sapphire crystal; transparent
case back; screw-in crown; water-resistant to 5 atm
Band: calf leather, double folding clasp
Price: $3,199

Teutonia II Chronograph

Reference number: M1-30-95-LB
Movement: automatic, Caliber MU 9413 (base
ETA 7750); ø 30 mm, height 7.9 mm; 25 jewels;
28,800 vph; woodpecker-neck fine adjustment;
three-quarter Glashütte plate; special Mühle finish;
48-hour power reserve
Functions: hours, minutes, subsidiary seconds;
chronograph; weekday, date
Case: stainless steel, ø 42 mm, height 15.5 mm;
sapphire crystal; transparent case back; screw-in
crown; water-resistant to 10 atm
Band: reptile skin, double folding clasp
Price: $4,399
Variations: stainless steel bracelet ($4,599)

Teutonia III Hand Wound

Reference number: M1-08-01-LB
Movement: manually wound, Caliber MU 9412; ø
25.6 mm, height 3.4 mm; 18 jewels; 28,800 vph;
woodpecker-neck fine adjustment; three-quarter
Glashütte plate; special Mühle finish; 42-hour power
reserve
Functions: hours, minutes, sweep seconds; date
Case: stainless steel, ø 42 mm, height 11.2 mm;
sapphire crystal; transparent case back; water-
resistant to 10 atm
Band: leather, double folding clasp
Price: $2,999
Variations: stainless steel bracelet ($3,099)

MU 9412.

Manually wound; stop-seconds system;
woodpecker-neck fine adjustment, regulated in
6 positions; single spring barrel, 42-hour power
reserve
Functions: hours, minutes, sweep seconds; date
Diameter: 25.6 mm
Height: 3.4 mm
Jewels: 18
Balance: nickel, gold-plated
Frequency: 28,800 vph
Shock protection: Incabloc
Remarks: Glashütte three-quarter plate and typical
surface finishing

Nienaber Bünde

Bahnhofstrasse 33a
D-32257 Bünde
Germany

Tel.:
01149-5223-12292

E-Mail:
info@nienaber-uhren.de

Website:
www.nienaber-uhren.de

Founded:
1984

Number of employees:
1

Annual production:
approx. 50 watches

Distribution:
Please contact Nienaber Bünde directly.

Most important collections/price range:
watches with retrograde displays / approx.
$4,000 to $27,000
Prices are determined from the daily euro
exchange rate.

Nienaber Bünde

For over a quarter-century, Rainer Nienaber has manufactured, sold, and repaired watches in Bünde, Germany. Although his work has spanned large, small, simple, complicated, expensive, and inexpensive watches, they all share one trait: uniqueness. One of his particular specialties is retrograde displays, which he continually rearranges in various combinations to create new models. Nienaber uses Swiss movements; the rest is, however, "made in Germany" (cases, dials, bands). He doesn't like being called a "*manufacture*," opting instead for the term "atelier."

No one can doubt his inventiveness. He has produced watches with decimal time, a pair of watches called the Day and Night Watch (for more, visit the collections on his website). His Anterograde is designed to look like the tachometer of a classic car. Although this conceit is not that unusual in the watchmaking industry, in this case the result happens to be an unusual one-handed watch. The five-minute divisions along the dial still allow the user to read the time with considerable precision. But Nienaber has added another extraordinary feature: When the hour hand reaches the 12 o'clock mark, which is a little off-center, it jumps ahead to a "0" mark to the right of center, to begin the next 12-hour period of the day. Hence the name "anterograde." This is no mean feat given the unavoidable tooth flank backlash in the display movement.

Decimal Watch

Movement: manually wound, Unitas Caliber 6325; ø 29.6 mm, height 4.2 mm; 17 jewels; 21,600 vph
Functions: hours and minutes (decimal); additional hours and minutes (sexagesimal)
Case: ø 43 mm, height 14 mm; sapphire crystal
Band: calf leather, buckle
Price: $4,375
Variations: various dial colors; with black PVD coating

Antero

Movement: manually wound, base ETA Caliber 6497; ø 36.5 mm, height 4.5 mm; 17 jewels; 18,000 vph; finely finished
Functions: hours (anterograde), subsidiary seconds
Case: stainless steel, ø 44 mm, height 12 mm; sapphire crystal, transparent case back; water-resistant to 3 atm
Band: calf leather, buckle
Remarks: anterograde means jumping forward: the single hour hand jumps over a segment of several degrees past 9 o'clock
Price: $4,600

Regulator Version-1

Movement: manually wound, base ETA 6497; ø 36.6 mm, height 4.5 mm; 17 jewels; 18,000 vph
Functions: hours (off-center), minutes, subsidiary seconds
Case: stainless steel, ø 44 mm, height 12 mm; sapphire crystal; transparent case back
Band: calf leather, buckle
Remarks: gold-plated brass dial
Price: $4,500
Variations: silver dial

Nivrel

In 1891, master goldsmith Friedrich Jacob Kraemer founded a jewelry and watch shop in Saarbrücken that proved to be the place to go for fine craftsmanship. Gerd Hofer joined the family business in 1956, carrying it on into the fourth generation. However, his true passion was for watchmaking. In 1993, he and his wife, Gitta, bought the rights to use the Swiss name Nivrel, a brand that had been established in 1936, and integrated production of these watches into their German-based operations.

Today, Nivrel is led by the Hofers' daughter Anja, who is keeping both lineages alive. Mechanical complications with Swiss movements of the finest technical level and finishing as well as gold watches in the high-end design segment of the industry are manufactured with close attention to detail and an advanced level of craftsmanship. In addition to classic automatic watches, the brand has introduced everything from complicated chronographs and skeletonized watches to perpetual calendars and tourbillons. The movements and all the "habillage" of the watches—case, dial, crystal, crown, etc.—are made in Switzerland. Watch design, assembly, and finishing are done in Saarbrücken.

Nivrel watches are a perfect example of how quickly a watch brand incorporating a characteristic style and immaculate quality can make a respected place for itself in the industry. Affordable prices also play a significant role in this brand's success, but they do not keep the brand from innovating. Nivrel has teamed up with the Department of Metallic Materials of Saarland University to develop a special alloy for repeater springs that is softer and does not need as much energy to press.

Nivrel Uhren

Gerd Hofer GmbH
Kossmannstrasse 3
D-66119 Saarbrücken
Germany

Tel.:
01149-681-584-6576

Fax:
01149-681-584-6584

E-Mail:
info@nivrel.com

Website:
www.nivrel.com

Founded:
1978

Number of employees:
10, plus external staff members

Distribution:
Please contact headquarters for enquiries.

Most important collections/price range:
mechanical watches, most with complications / approx. $600 to $45,000

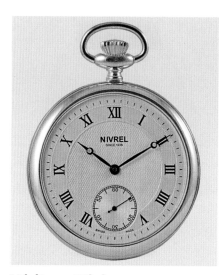

Héritage Minier

Reference number: N 323.001 SAAB
Movement: manually wound, ETA Caliber 6497-1; ø 36.6 mm, height 4.5 mm; 17 jewels; 18,000 vph; 46-hour power reserve
Functions: hours, minutes, subsidiary seconds
Case: sterling silver; ø 45 mm, height 13 mm; mineral crystal
Band: stainless steel chain with 2 snap hooks
Remarks: limited to 200 pieces
Price: $1,380

Réplique Manuelle

Reference number: N 322.001 CASDS
Movement: manually wound, ETA Caliber 6497-1; ø 36.6 mm, height 4.5 mm; 17 jewels; 18,000 vph; blued screws, côtes de Genève; 46-hour power reserve
Functions: hours, minutes, subsidiary seconds
Case: stainless steel, ø 44 mm, height 13 mm; sapphire crystal; transparent case back; water-resistant to 5 atm
Band: calf leather, buckle
Price: $1,100
Variations: white dial

Réplique Lémania Limited

Reference number: N 151.001 CAAHS
Movement: manually wound, Lemania Caliber 8810; ø 25.6 mm, height 2.95 mm; 17 jewels; 28,800 vph; double spring barrel; 40-hour power reserve
Functions: hours, minutes, sweep seconds; date
Case: stainless steel, ø 40 mm, height 7.4 mm; sapphire crystal; transparent case back; water-resistant to 5 atm
Band: calf leather, buckle
Remarks: limited to 30 pieces
Price: $2,750

NOMOS Glashütte
Ferdinand-Adolph-Lange-Platz 2
D-01768 Glashütte
Germany

Tel.:
01149-35053-4040

Fax:
01149-35053-40480

E-Mail:
nomos@glashuette.com

Website:
www.nomos-watches.com

Founded:
1990

Number of employees:
approx. 200

U.S. distributor:
For the U.S. market, please contact Nomos directly.

Most important collections/price range:
Ahoi / $3,940 to $4,500; Tangente / $1,630 to $3,270; Tangomat / $2,700 to $4,570; Orion / $1,780 to $2,850; Ludwig / $1,570 to $3,500; Tetra / $1,840 to $2,730; Club / $1,450 to $3,320; Zürich / $3,800 to $5,760; Sundial / $175

Nomos

Still waters run deep, and discreet business practices at times travel far. Nomos, founded in 1990, has suddenly become a full-fledged *manufacture* with brand-new facilities and a smart policy of only so much growth as the small team gathered around the founder Roland Schwertner and his associate Uwe Ahrendt can easily absorb.

The collection is based on five or six basic models, though the number of calibers available is growing at an impressive rate, including two luxury manually wound movements with fine finishings. The most striking advance, however, has been in Nomos's core business. Over the past years the brand has invested heavily in the design and construction of an in-house escapement with a spring "made in Germany." The escapement made its debut at Baselworld under the name DUW 4401 (Deutsche Uhrenwerke Nomos Glashütte) and will gradually be used in the entire collection.

In 2005, Nomos moved into new space in the former Glashütte train station, but nearly ten years later, the factory is already bursting at the seams. Since 2010, the staff virtually doubled in size to about 200 people, including about 30 in Berlin and Zurich, who are mostly employed in design and communication. The company has also managed to double its revenues during the same period, and it intends to repeat that feat by 2017. Its phenomenal growth could be a lesson to many brands: Use outstanding watches at an affordable price, a simple look full of subtle details, and marketing that is bold and humorous, as for the 2009 Orion models with dials in various shades of gray symbolizing the Berlin Wall, which had fallen twenty years earlier, or the prizewinning Ahoi (as in "ship ahoy!"), a swimmer's watch with an optional synthetic strap like those that carry locker keys at Germany's public swimming pools.

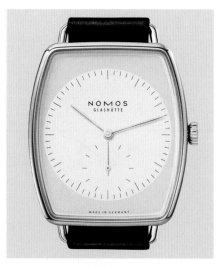

Lambda Rosegold

Reference number: 930
Movement: manually wound, Nomos Caliber DUW 1001; ø 32 mm, height 3.6 mm; 29 jewels; screw balance with swan-neck fine adjustment; screwed gold chatons, hand-engraved balance cock; double spring barrel; 84-hour power reserve
Functions: hours, minutes, subsidiary seconds; power reserve display
Case: rose gold, ø 42 mm, height 8.9 mm; sapphire crystal; transparent case back; water-resistant to 3 atm
Band: horse leather, buckle
Price: $18,500

Lambda Weissgold

Reference number: 931
Movement: manually wound, Nomos Caliber DUW 1001; ø 32 mm, height 3.6 mm; 29 jewels; screw balance with swan-neck fine adjustment; screwed gold chatons, hand-engraved balance cock; double spring barrel; 84-hour power reserve
Functions: hours, minutes, subsidiary seconds; power reserve display
Case: white gold, ø 42 mm, height 8.9 mm; sapphire crystal; transparent case back; water-resistant to 3 atm
Band: horse leather, buckle
Price: $20,000

Lux Weissgold

Reference number: 920
Movement: manually wound, Nomos Caliber DUW 2002; 28.8 x 32.6 mm, height 3.6 mm; 23 jewels; screw balance with swan-neck fine adjustment; screwed gold chatons, hand-engraved balance cock; double spring barrel; 84-hour power reserve
Functions: hours, minutes, subsidiary seconds
Case: white gold, 36 x 40.5 mm, height 8.95 mm; sapphire crystal; transparent case back; water-resistant to 3 atm
Band: horse leather, buckle
Price: $21,500

Metro Datum Gangreserve

Reference number: 1101
Movement: manually wound, Nomos Caliber DUW 4401; ø 32.1 mm, height 2.8 mm; 23 jewels; 21,600 vph; 43-hour power reserve
Functions: hours, minutes, subsidiary seconds; power reserve indicator; date
Case: stainless steel, ø 37 mm, height 7.65 mm; sapphire crystal; transparent case back; water-resistant to 3 atm
Band: horse leather, buckle
Price: $3,780

Tangente 33

Reference number: 122
Movement: manually wound, Nomos Caliber Alpha; ø 23.3 mm, height 2.6 mm; 17 jewels; 21,600 vph
Functions: hours, minutes, subsidiary seconds
Case: stainless steel, ø 32.8 mm, height 6.45 mm; sapphire crystal; water-resistant to 3 atm
Band: suede, buckle
Price: $1,760

Orion 38 grau

Reference number: 383
Movement: manually wound, Nomos Caliber Alpha; ø 23.3 mm, height 2.6 mm; 17 jewels; 21,600 vph
Functions: hours, minutes, subsidiary seconds
Case: stainless steel, ø 38 mm, height 8.86 mm; sapphire crystal; transparent case back; water-resistant to 3 atm
Band: horse leather, buckle
Price: $2,620

Tetra Goldelse

Reference number: 491
Movement: manually wound, Nomos Caliber Alpha; ø 23.3 mm, height 2.6 mm; 17 jewels; 21,600 vph
Functions: hours, minutes, subsidiary seconds
Case: stainless steel, 29.5 x 29.5 mm, height 6.3 mm; sapphire crystal; transparent case back; water-resistant to 3 atm
Band: suede, buckle
Remarks: dial with brushed finish
Price: $2,390

Tetra Kleene

Reference number: 492
Movement: manually wound, Nomos Caliber DUW 4301; ø 23.3 mm, height 2.8 mm; jewels; 21,600 vph; 43-hour power reserve
Functions: hours, minutes, subsidiary seconds; power reserve display
Case: stainless steel, 29.5 x 29.5 mm, height 6.3 mm; sapphire crystal; transparent case back; water-resistant to 3 atm
Band: suede, buckle
Price: $2,920

Tetra Clärchen

Reference number: 489
Movement: manually wound, Nomos Caliber Alpha; ø 23.3 mm, height 2.6 mm; 17 jewels; 21,600 vph
Functions: hours, minutes, subsidiary seconds
Case: stainless steel, 29.5 x 29.5 mm, height 6.3 mm; sapphire crystal; transparent case back; water-resistant to 3 atm
Band: suede, buckle
Price: $2,320

Ahoi Atlantik

Reference number: 552
Movement: automatic, Nomos Caliber Epsilon;
ø 31 mm, height 4.3 mm; 26 jewels; 21,600 vph
Functions: hours, minutes, subsidiary seconds
Case: stainless steel, ø 40 mm, height 10.64 mm;
sapphire crystal; transparent case back; screw-in
crown; water-resistant to 20 atm
Band: textile, buckle
Price: $4,060

Ahoi Datum

Reference number: 551
Movement: automatic, Nomos Caliber Zeta;
ø 31 mm, height 4.3 mm; 26 jewels; 21,600 vph
Functions: hours, minutes, subsidiary seconds;
date
Case: stainless steel, ø 40 mm, height 10.64 mm;
sapphire crystal; transparent case back; screw-in
crown; water-resistant to 20 atm
Band: textile, buckle
Price: $4,660

Tangomat GMT

Reference number: 635
Movement: automatic, Nomos Caliber Xi; ø 31 mm,
height 5.7 mm; 26 jewels; 21,600 vph
Functions: hours, minutes, subsidiary seconds;
world-time display (2nd time zone)
Case: stainless steel, ø 40 mm, height 10.85 mm;
sapphire crystal; transparent case back; water-
resistant to 3 atm
Band: horse leather, buckle
Price: $4,920

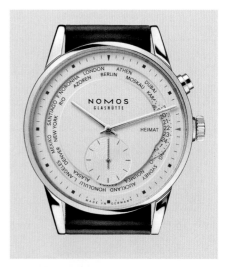

Zürich

Reference number: 801
Movement: automatic, Nomos Caliber Epsilon;
ø 31 mm, height 4.3 mm; 26 jewels; 21,600 vph
Functions: hours, minutes, subsidiary seconds
Case: stainless steel, ø 39.7 mm, height 9.65 mm;
sapphire crystal; transparent case back; water-
resistant to 3 atm
Band: horse leather, buckle
Price: $4,480

Zürich blaugold

Reference number: 822
Movement: automatic, Nomos Caliber Epsilon;
ø 31 mm, height 4.3 mm; 26 jewels; 21,600 vph
Functions: hours, minutes, subsidiary seconds
Case: stainless steel, ø 39.7 mm, height 9.65 mm;
sapphire crystal; transparent case back; water-
resistant to 3 atm
Band: horse leather, buckle
Remarks: dial with Glashütte ribbing
Price: $4,770

Zürich Weltzeit

Reference number: 805
Movement: automatic, Nomos Caliber Xi; ø 31 mm,
height 5.65 mm; 26 jewels; 21,600 vph
Functions: hours, minutes, subsidiary seconds;
world-time display (2nd time zone)
Case: stainless steel, ø 39.9 mm, height 10.85 mm;
sapphire crystal; transparent case back; water-
resistant to 3 atm
Band: horse leather, buckle
Price: $6,100

Omega SA
Jakob-Stämpfli-Strasse 96
CH-2502 Biel/Bienne
Switzerland

Tel.:
01141-32-343-9211

E-Mail:
info@omegawatches.com

Website:
www.omegawatches.com

Founded:
1848

Annual production:
750,000 (estimated)

U.S. distributor:
Omega
The Swatch Group (U.S.), Inc.
1200 Harbor Boulevard
Weehawken, NJ 07087
201-271-1400
www.omegawatches.com

Most important collections/price range:
Seamaster / approx. $3,900 to $138,500;
Constellation / approx. $4,500 to $50,700;
Speedmaster / approx. $4,950 to $11,900

Omega

When it comes to price—and perhaps prestige as well—there are some *manufactures* within the Swatch Group that have overtaken Omega. Nevertheless, the brand with the last letter of the Greek alphabet as its logo still manages to command respect as the flagship of the group and as the timekeeper for the more recent incarnations of James Bond as well as the Vancouver Winter Olympics in 2010.

It has also played a major role in the history of the watch business in Switzerland. The brand was originally founded in 1848. In 1930, it merged with Tissot to form SIHH, which in turn merged with another watch conglomerate, ASUAG, to form the Swatch Group in 1983, of which Omega was the leading brand. In the 1990s, the brand managed to expand incrementally into the Chinese market and thus established a firm foothold in Asia. This also led to a steep growth in production numbers, putting it neck-and-neck with Rolex.

And today, Omega has once again put itself back in the competition with technology as the key. It introduced the innovative coaxial escapement to several collections, which has pushed the brand back into the technological frontrunners in its segment. Swatch Group subsidiary Nivarox-FAR has finally mastered the production of the difficult, oil-free parts of the system designed by the Englishman George Daniels, although the escapement continues to include lubrication as the long-term results of "dry" coaxial movements are less than satisfactory. Thus the most important plus for this escapement design remains high rate stability after careful regulation. Omega has even revived the Ladymatic, adding a silicon spring and the trademark coaxial escapement.

In July 2013, Omega officially unveiled a brand-new 15,000 Gauss antimagnetic movement, which will be spread throughout the brand's models in years to come. The Seamaster Aqua Terra that uses it can go into an MRI machine without stopping. Omega has also been tapping into the broad Swatch Group know-how to explore new materials, such as ceramics in various bright colors, as well as "liquid metal."

Speedmaster Mark II

Reference number: 327.10.43.50.06.001
Movement: automatic, Omega Caliber 3330; ø 30 mm, height 7.9 mm; 31 jewels; 28,800 vph; coaxial escapement, silicon balance and balance spring; 52-hour power reserve; COSC-certified chronometer
Functions: hours, minutes, subsidiary seconds; chronograph; date
Case: stainless steel, 42.4 x 46.2 mm, height 14.85 mm; sapphire crystal
Band: stainless steel, folding clasp
Price: $6,250

Constellation "Pluma"

Reference number: 123.15.27.20.57.001
Movement: automatic, Omega Caliber 8520; ø 20 mm, height 5.3 mm; 28 jewels; 25,200 vph; coaxial escapement, silicon balance and balance spring; antimagnetic to 15,000 Gauss; 50-hour power reserve; COSC-tested chronometer
Functions: hours, minutes, sweep seconds; date
Case: stainless steel with rose gold elements; ø 27 mm, height 12.25 mm; sapphire crystal; water-resistant to 10 atm
Band: stainless steel, folding clasp
Remarks: mother-of-pearl dial with diamonds
Price: $8,000
Variations: w/o diamonds on bezel ($8,000); with diamonds and pink gold ($11,800)

Seamaster 300

Reference number: 233.30.41.21.01.001
Movement: automatic, Omega Caliber 8400; 38 jewels; 25,200 vph; coaxial escapement, silicon balance and balance spring; antimagnetic to 15,000 Gauss; 60-hour power reserve; COSC-certified chronometer
Functions: hours, minutes, sweep seconds
Case: stainless steel, ø 41 mm, height 14.65 mm; unidirectional bezel with 60-minute divisions, sapphire crystal; water-resistant to 30 atm
Band: stainless steel, folding clasp
Price: $6,600
Variations: titanium ($9,000); pink gold ($34,200)

Seamaster Planet Ocean GMT Titanium

Reference number: 232.92.44.22.03.001
Movement: automatic, Omega Caliber 8605;
ø 29 mm, height 6 mm; 38 jewels; 25,200 vph;
coaxial escapement, silicon balance and balance
spring; 60-hour power reserve; COSC-certified
chronometer
Functions: hours, minutes, sweep seconds;
additional 24-hour display (2nd time zone); date
Case: titanium, ø 43.5 mm, height 17.25 mm;
bidirectional ceramic bezel, 24-h divisions, sapphire
crystal; screw-in crown; water-resistant to 60 atm
Band: rubber, folding clasp
Price: $9,500

Seamaster Planet Ocean Good Planet GMT

Reference number: 232.30.44.22.03.001
Movement: automatic, Omega Caliber 8605;
ø 29 mm, height 6 mm; 38 jewels; 25,200 vph; coaxial
escapement, silicon balance and balance spring;
60-hour power reserve; COSC-tested chronometer
Functions: hours, minutes, sweep seconds; additional
24-hour display (2nd time zone); date
Case: stainless steel, ø 43.5 mm, height 17.25 mm;
bidirectional bezel with 24-hour divisions, sapphire
crystal; screw-in crown; water-resistant to 60 atm
Band: stainless steel, folding clasp
Price: $8,100
Variations: rubber strap ($8,000)

Seamaster Aqua Terra

Reference number: 231.10.42.21.03.003
Movement: automatic, Omega Caliber 8500;
ø 29 mm, height 5.5 mm; 39 jewels; 25,200 vph;
coaxial escapement, silicon balance and balance
spring; fully antimagnetic to 15,000 Gauss; 60-hour
power reserve; COSC-tested chronometer
Functions: hours, minutes, sweep seconds; date
Case: stainless steel, ø 41.5 mm, height 12.95 mm;
sapphire crystal; screw-in crown; automatic helium
valve; water-resistant to 15 atm
Band: stainless steel, folding clasp
Price: $6,600
Variations: various dials; leather band ($8,400);
pink gold bezel ($8,400); yellow gold ($33,500)

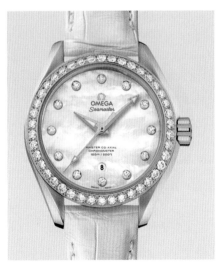

Seamaster Aqua Terra Master Co-Axial

Reference number: 231.28.34.20.55.003
Movement: automatic, Omega Caliber 8520;
ø 20 mm, height 5.3 mm; 28 jewels; 25,200 vph;
coaxial escapement, silicon balance and balance
spring; antimagnetic to 15,000 Gauss; 50-day
power reserve; COSC-certified chronometer
Functions: hours, minutes, sweep seconds; date
Case: stainless steel, ø 34 mm, height 12.5 mm;
pink gold bezel set with diamonds, sapphire crystal
Band: reptile skin, folding clasp
Remarks: mother-of-pearl dial with diamonds
Price: $23,400
Variations: w/o diamonds ($9,250)

Seamaster Aqua Terra Chrono GMT

Reference number: 231.20.43.52.06.001
Movement: automatic, Omega Caliber 9605;
ø 32.5 mm, height 8.35 mm; 54 jewels; 28,800 vph;
coaxial escapement, silicon balance and balance spring;
60-hour power reserve; COSC-certified chronometer
Functions: hours, minutes, subsidiary seconds;
additional 24-hour display; chronograph; date
Case: stainless steel, ø 43 mm, height 16.95 mm; pink
gold bezel, sapphire crystal; transparent case back;
ceramic crown and pushers; water-resistant to 15 atm
Band: stainless steel with rose gold elements, folding
clasp
Price: $13,300

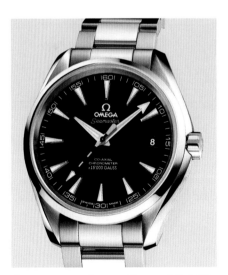

Seamaster Aqua Terra 15,000 Gauss

Reference number: 231.10.42.21.01.002
Movement: automatic, Omega Caliber 8500;
ø 29 mm, height 5.5 mm; 39 jewels; 25,200 vph;
coaxial escapement, silicon balance and balance
spring; fully antimagnetic to 15,000 Gauss; 60-hour
power reserve; COSC-tested chronometer
Functions: hours, minutes, sweep seconds; date
Case: stainless steel, ø 41.5 mm, height 14.3 mm;
sapphire crystal; screw-in crown; automatic helium
valve; water-resistant to 15 atm
Band: stainless steel, folding clasp
Price: $6,600
Variations: leather strap ($6,500)

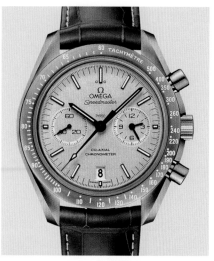

Seamaster Aqua Terra Day-Date

Reference number: 231.10.42.22.03.001
Movement: automatic, Omega Caliber 8602; ø 29 mm, height 6.5 mm; 39 jewels; 25,200 vph; coaxial escapement, silicon balance and balance spring; 55-hour power reserve; COSC-tested chronometer
Functions: hours, minutes, sweep seconds; weekday, date
Case: stainless steel, ø 41.5 mm, height 14.3 mm; sapphire crystal, transparent case back; screw-in crown; water-resistant to 15 atm
Band: stainless steel, folding clasp
Price: $7,800
Variations: pink gold ($35,400)

Seamaster Diver 300M Co-Axial Chronograph

Reference number: 212.30.44.50.03.001
Movement: automatic, Omega Caliber 3330; ø 30 mm, height 7.9 mm; 31 jewels; 28,800 vph; coaxial escapement, silicon balance and balance spring; 60-hour power reserve; COSC-tested chronometer
Functions: hours, minutes, subsidiary seconds; chronograph; date
Case: stainless steel, ø 44 mm, height 17.27 mm; unidirectional bezel with 60-minute divisions, sapphire crystal; screw-in crown; automatic helium valve; water-resistant to 30 atm
Band: stainless steel, folding clasp
Price: $6,000
Variations: black dial ($6,000); 41.5 mm case ($6,000)

Speedmaster Dark Side of the Moon "Lunar Dust"

Reference number: 311.93.44.51.99.001
Movement: automatic, Omega Caliber 9300; ø 32.5 mm, height 7.6 mm; 54 jewels; 28,800 vph; coaxial escapement, silicon balance and balance spring; 60-hour power reserve; COSC-certified chronometer
Functions: hours, minutes, subsidiary seconds; chronograph; date
Case: ceramic, ø 44.25 mm, height 16.14; sapphire crystal; water-resistant to 5 atm
Band: reptile skin, folding clasp
Price: $12,000

Speedmaster Moonwatch "Dark Side of the Moon"

Reference number: 311.92.44.51.01.003
Movement: automatic, Omega Caliber 9300; ø 32.5 mm, height 7.6 mm; 54 jewels; 28,800 vph; coaxial escapement, silicon balance and balance spring; 60-hour power reserve; COSC-tested chronometer
Functions: hours, minutes, subsidiary seconds; chronograph; date
Case: ceramic, ø 44.25 mm, height 15.79 mm; sapphire crystal; transparent case back; water-resistant to 5 atm
Band: nylon, folding clasp
Price: $12,000

Speedmaster "Apollo 11" 45th Anniversary Limited Edition

Reference number: 311.62.42.30.06.001
Movement: manually wound, Omega Caliber 1861 (base Lemania 1873); ø 27 mm, height 6.87 mm; 18 jewels; 21,600 vph; 48-hour power reserve
Functions: hours, minutes, subsidiary seconds; chronograph
Case: titanium, ø 42 mm, height 14.15 mm; pink gold bezel; sapphire crystal
Band: textile, buckle
Remarks: limited to 1,969 pieces
Price: $7,700

Speedmaster Moonwatch

Reference number: 311.90.44.51.03.001
Movement: automatic, Omega Caliber 9300; ø 32.5 mm, height 7.6 mm; 54 jewels; 28,800 vph; coaxial escapement, silicon balance and balance spring; 60-hour power reserve; COSC-tested chronometer
Functions: hours, minutes, subsidiary seconds; chronograph; date
Case: titanium, ø 44.25 mm, height 15.82 mm; sapphire crystal; water-resistant to 10 atm
Band: titanium, folding clasp
Price: $11,400
Variations: blue leather strap ($10,700)

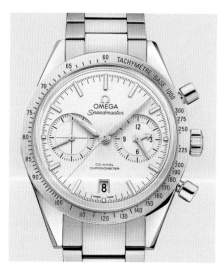

Speedmaster 57

Reference number: 331.10.42.51.02.002
Movement: automatic, Omega Caliber 9300;
ø 32.5 mm, height 7.6 mm; 54 jewels; 28,800 vph;
coaxial escapement, silicon balance and balance
spring; 60-hour power reserve; COSC-tested
chronometer
Functions: hours, minutes, subsidiary seconds;
chronograph; date
Case: stainless steel, ø 41.5 mm, height 16.17 mm;
sapphire crystal; water-resistant to 10 atm
Band: stainless steel, folding clasp
Price: $9,200
Variations: rose gold bezel ($15,000)

Speedmaster 57

Reference number: 331.12.42.51.03.001
Movement: automatic, Omega Caliber 9300;
ø 32.5 mm, height 7.6 mm; 54 jewels; 28,800 vph;
coaxial escapement, silicon balance and balance
spring; 60-hour power reserve; COSC-tested
chronometer
Functions: hours, minutes, subsidiary seconds;
chronograph; date
Case: stainless steel, ø 41.5 mm, height 15.82 mm;
sapphire crystal; water-resistant to 10 atm
Band: leather, folding clasp
Price: $8,900
Variations: various dials; rose gold bezel ($11,000)

De Ville Trésor

Reference number: 432.53.40.21.02.001
Movement: automatic, Omega Caliber 8511;
ø 29 mm; 25,200 vph; coaxial escapement,
silicon balance and balance spring; antimagnetic
to 15,000 Gauss; 60-hour power reserve; COSC-
certified chronometer
Functions: hours, minutes, sweep seconds; date
Case: yellow gold, ø 40 mm, height 10.6 mm;
sapphire crystal
Band: reptile skin, folding clasp
Price: $13,800
Variations: pink gold ($13,800)

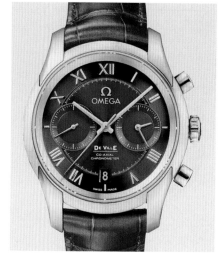

De Ville Ladymatic

Reference number: 425.27.34.20.63.001
Movement: automatic, Omega Caliber 8520;
ø 20 mm, height 5.3 mm; 28 jewels; 25,200 vph;
coaxial escapement, silicon balance and balance
spring; 50-hour power reserve; COSC-tested
chronometer
Functions: hours, minutes, sweep seconds; date
Case: stainless steel with ceramic and rose gold
elements; ø 34 mm, height 11.95 mm; bezel set
with diamonds, sapphire crystal; water-resistant to
10 atm
Band: stainless steel, pink gold elements, folding
clasp
Remarks: dial set with 11 diamonds
Price: $24,600

De Ville Prestige Power Reserve

Reference number: 424.53.40.21.03.002
Movement: automatic, Omega Caliber 2627; 29
jewels; 25,200 vph; coaxial escapement; 48-hour
power reserve; COSC-tested chronometer
Functions: hours, minutes, subsidiary seconds;
power reserve indicator; date
Case: pink gold, ø 39.5 mm, height 10.6 mm;
sapphire crystal; water-resistant to 3 atm
Band: reptile skin, buckle
Price: $11,200
Variations: stainless steel ($4,800)

De Ville Chronograph

Reference number: 431.53.42.51.02.001
Movement: automatic, Omega Caliber 9301;
ø 32.5 mm, height 7.6 mm; 54 jewels; 25,200 vph;
coaxial escapement, silicon balance and balance
spring; 60-hour power reserve; COSC-tested
chronometer
Functions: hours, minutes, subsidiary seconds;
chronograph; date
Case: pink gold, ø 42 mm, height 15.9 mm;
sapphire crystal; transparent case back; water-
resistant to 10 atm
Band: reptile skin, folding clasp
Price: $29,000
Variations: black dial and strap

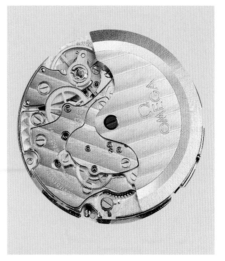

Caliber 9300

Automatic; coaxial escapement; column wheel control of chronograph functions; twin spring barrels, 60-hour power reserve; COSC-certified chronometer
Functions: hours, minutes, subsidiary seconds; chronograph; date
Diameter: 32.5 mm; **Height:** 7.7 mm
Jewels: 54
Balance: silicon, without regulator
Frequency: 28,800 vph
Balance spring: silicon
Shock protection: Nivachoc
Remarks: base plate, bridges, and rotor with "arabesque" côtes de Genève, balance and screws blackened

Caliber 9301

Base caliber: 9300
Automatic; coaxial escapement; column wheel control of chronograph functions; twin spring barrels, 60-hour power reserve; COSC-certified chronometer
Functions: hours, minutes, subsidiary seconds; chronograph; date
Diameter: 32.5 mm; **Height:** 7.7 mm
Jewels: 54; **Balance:** silicon, without regulator
Frequency: 28,800 vph
Balance spring: silicon
Shock protection: Nivachoc
Remarks: base plate, bridges, and rotor with "arabesque" côtes de Genève, rotor and balance bridges in pink gold, balance and screws blackened

Caliber 3313

Automatic; coaxial escapement; column wheel control of chronograph functions; single spring barrel, 52-hour power reserve; COSC-certified chronometer
Functions: hours, minutes, subsidiary seconds; chronograph; date
Diameter: 27 mm
Height: 6.85 mm
Jewels: 37
Balance: without regulator
Frequency: 28,800 vph
Balance spring: freely oscillating
Remarks: perlage on plate, bridges and balance cock with côtes de Genève, gold-plated engravings; rotor hub screw of blued steel

Caliber 8605

Automatic; coaxial escapement; twin spring barrels, 60-hour power reserve; COSC-certified chronometer
Functions: hours, minutes, sweep seconds; second time zone (additional 24-hour indicator); date
Diameter: 29 mm; **Height:** 5.9 mm
Jewels: 38
Balance: silicon, without regulator
Frequency: 25,200 vph
Balance spring: silicon
Shock protection: Nivachoc
Remarks: base plate, bridges, and rotor with "arabesque" côtes de Genève, rhodium-plated, balance and screws blackened (Caliber 8615 with rotor and balance bridge in pink gold)

Caliber 8501

Base caliber: 8500
Automatic; coaxial escapement; twin spring barrels, 60-hour power reserve; COSC-certified chronometer
Functions: hours, minutes, sweep seconds; date
Diameter: 29 mm; **Height:** 5.6 mm
Jewels: 39
Balance: silicon, without regulator
Frequency: 25,200 vph
Balance spring: silicon
Shock protection: Nivachoc
Remarks: platinum, bridges and rotor with "arabesque" côtes de Genève, rotor and balance bridges in pink gold, balance and screws blackened (base Caliber 8500 without gold finishing)

Caliber 8520

Automatic; coaxial escapement; twin spring barrels, 60-hour power reserve; COSC-certified chronometer
Functions: hours, minutes sweep seconds; date
Diameter: 20 mm
Height: 5.3 mm
Jewels: 28
Balance: silicon, without regulator
Frequency: 25,200 vph
Balance spring: silicon
Shock protection: Nivachoc
Remarks: platinum, bridges and rotor with "arabesque" côtes de Genève, rhodium-plated, balance and screws blackened (Caliber 8251 with rotor and balance bridge in pink gold)

[P R I M E D]

Mk II FULCRUM

In our continuing pursuit of perfection we are pleased to offer the Mk II Fulcrum. The successor to the Mk II LRRP, the Fulcrum features a new case with vintage-styled high-domed sapphire crystal and our new Lume-brik dial markers. Each timepiece is driven by a high-grade Swiss Made automatic movement and hand assembled and tested in the USA.

Oris SA

Ribigasse 1
CH-4434 Hölstein
Switzerland

Tel.:
01141-61-956-1111

E-Mail:
info@oris

Website:
www.oris.ch

Founded:
1904

Number of employees:
90

U.S. distributor:
Oris Watches USA
50 Washington Street, Suite 412
Norwalk, CT 06854
203-857-4769; 203-857-4782 (fax)

Most important collections/price range:
Diver, Big Crown, Artelier, BC3, BC4 / approx.
$1,100 to $4,000

Oris

Oris has been producing mechanical watches in the little town of Hölstein in northwestern Switzerland, near Basel, since 1904, so 2014 was a celebratory year. What the brand has always aimed for is quality with an advantageous price-performance ratio. This particular strategy has allowed Oris to expand in a segment being relinquished by other big-name competitors as they sought their fortune in the higher-end markets. The result has been growing international success for Oris, whose portfolio is divided up into four "product worlds," each with its own distinct identity: aviation, motor sports, diving, and culture. In utilizing specific materials and functions based on these types, Oris makes certain that each will fit perfectly into the world for which it was designed. Yet the heart of every watch houses a small, high-quality "high-mech" movement identifiable by the brand's standard red rotor.

The brand surprised everyone for its 110th birthday by signing off on in-house Caliber 110, an unembellished and technically efficient manually wound movement. The designers clearly concentrated on proper energy use, the key to good efficiency. In collaboration with the engineers from the Technical College of Le Locle, Oris developed a massive barrel spring containing a 6-foot (1.8 m) spring. With numerous trials and lots of tweaking, the unwinding of this very long spring was optimized, giving the movement a full ten days of power of even torque. The power reserve indicator on the right of the dial does not move evenly, however, due to the transmission ratio. Toward the end, the markers are somewhat longer to give a more accurate idea of the remaining power in the spring.

110 Years Limited Edition

Reference number: 110 7700 6081
Movement: manually wound, Oris Caliber 110;
ø 34 mm, height 6 mm; 40 jewels; 21,600 vph;
240-hour power reserve
Functions: hours, minutes, subsidiary seconds;
power reserve indicator (progressive display)
Case: rose gold, ø 43 mm, height 12.3 mm;
sapphire crystal; transparent back; water-resistant
to 3 atm
Band: reptile skin, buckle
Remarks: limited to 110 pieces
Price: $17,500
Variations: folding clasp; stainless steel ($6,500;
limited to 110 pieces)

Artelier Jumping Hour

Reference number: 917 7702 4051
Movement: automatic, Oris Caliber 917 (base
Sellita SW300 with Dubois Dépraz module
14400A); ø 25.6 mm, height 5.2 mm; 31 jewels;
28,800 vph; 42-hour power reserve
Functions: hours (digital, jumping), minutes (off-
center), subsidiary seconds
Case: stainless steel, ø 40.5 mm, height 11.1 mm;
sapphire crystal; transparent case back; water-
resistant to 5 atm
Band: calf leather, folding clasp
Price: $4,600
Variations: reptile band ($4,900); stainless steel
bracelet ($4,800)

Big Crown ProPilot Chronograph GMT

Reference number: 677 7699 4164
Movement: automatic, Oris Caliber 677 (base
ETA 7754); ø 30 mm, height 7.9 mm; 25 jewels;
28,800 vph; 48-hour power reserve
Functions: hours, minutes, subsidiary seconds;
additional 24-hour display (2nd time zone);
chronograph; date
Case: stainless steel, ø 44 mm, height 15.5 mm;
sapphire crystal; transparent case back; screw-in
crown; water-resistant to 10 atm
Band: textile, folding clasp
Price: $4,100
Variations: stainless steel bracelet ($4,300)

Big Crown Timer Chronograph

Reference number: 675 7648 4234
Movement: automatic, Oris Caliber 675 (base ETA 7750); ø 30 mm, height 7.9 mm; 25 jewels; 28,800 vph; 48-hour power reserve
Functions: hours, minutes, subsidiary seconds; chronograph; date
Case: stainless steel with gray PVD coating, ø 46 mm, height 15.5 mm; bidirectional bezel, with 60-second divisions, sapphire crystal; transparent case back; screw-in crown; water-resistant to 3 atm
Band: calf leather, buckle
Price: $3,700

Big Crown ProPilot Day Date

Reference number: 752 7698 4164
Movement: automatic, Oris Caliber 752 (base Sellita SW220); ø 32.2 mm, height 5.25 mm; 26 jewels; 28,800 vph; 38-hour power reserve
Functions: hours, minutes, sweep seconds; weekday, date
Case: stainless steel, ø 45 mm, height 12.6 mm; sapphire crystal; transparent case back; screw-in crown; water-resistant to 10 atm
Band: textile, folding clasp
Price: $1,750
Variations: stainless steel bracelet ($1,950)

Greenwich Mean Time Limited Edition

Reference number: 690 7690 4081
Movement: automatic, Oris Caliber 690 (base ETA 2836-2); ø 25.6 mm, height 5.05 mm; 30 jewels; 28,800 vph; 38-hour power reserve
Functions: hours, minutes, subsidiary seconds; additional 12-hour display (2nd time zone), day/night indication; date
Case: stainless steel, ø 42 mm, height 12.4 mm; sapphire crystal, water-resistant to 5 atm
Band: stainless steel, folding clasp
Price: $4,250; limited to 2,000 pieces
Variations: reptile skin ($4,200) or leather band ($3,900)

Artelier Chronograph

Reference number: 774 7686 4051
Movement: automatic, Oris Caliber 774 (base Sellita SW500); ø 30 mm, height 7.9 mm; 25 jewels; 28,800 vph; 48-hour power reserve
Functions: hours, minutes, subsidiary seconds; chronograph; date
Case: stainless steel, ø 44 mm, height 14.7 mm; sapphire crystal; transparent case back; water-resistant to 5 atm
Band: calf leather, folding clasp
Price: $3,700
Variations: reptile band ($4,000); stainless steel bracelet ($3,900)

Artix Pointer Moon Date

Reference number: 761 7691 4054
Movement: automatic, Oris Caliber 761 (base Sellita SW220); ø 25.6 mm, height 5.05 mm; 26 jewels; 28,800 vph; 38-hour power reserve
Functions: hours, minutes, sweep seconds; date; moon phase
Case: stainless steel, ø 42 mm, height 12.1 mm; sapphire crystal; transparent case back; water-resistant to 10 atm
Band: calf leather, folding clasp
Price: $2,150
Variations: stainless steel bracelet ($2,350)

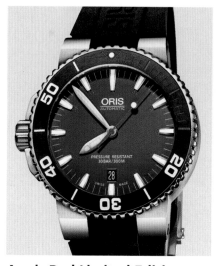

Aquis Red Limited Edition

Reference number: 733 7653 4183
Movement: automatic, Oris Caliber 733 (base Sellita SW200-1); ø 25.6 mm, height 4.6 mm; 26 jewels; 28,800 A/h; 38-hour power reserve
Functions: hours, minutes, sweep seconds; date
Case: stainless steel, ø 43 mm, height 12.6 mm; ceramic bezel, sapphire crystal; screw-in crown; water-resistant to 30 atm
Band: rubber, folding clasp with safety lock
Remarks: limited to 2,000 pieces
Price: $1,990
Variations: stainless steel bracelet ($2,190)

Aquis Chronograph

Reference number: 774 7655 4154
Movement: automatic, Oris Caliber 774 (base Sellita SW500); ø 30 mm, height 7.9 mm; 25 jewels; 28,800 vph; 48-hour power reserve
Functions: hours, minutes, subsidiary seconds; chronograph; date
Case: stainless steel, ø 46 mm, height 18.2 mm; unidirectional ceramic bezel, 60-minute divisions, sapphire crystal; screw-in crown; water-resistant to 50 atm
Band: rubber, folding clasp with extension link
Price: $3,700
Variations: stainless steel bracelet ($3,850)

Darryl O'Young Limited Edition

Reference number: 774 7611 7784
Movement: automatic, Oris Caliber 774 (base Sellita SW500); ø 30 mm, height 7.9 mm; 25 jewels; 28,800 vph; 48-hour power reserve
Functions: hours, minutes, subsidiary seconds; chronograph; date
Case: titanium with black PVD coating, ø 44.5 mm, height 16.1 mm; sapphire crystal; transparent case back; water-resistant to 10 atm
Band: rubber, folding clasp
Remarks: special edition with WTCC driver number "10"
Price: $3,800; limited to 500 pieces

Aquis Depth Gauge

Reference number: 733 7675 4154
Movement: automatic, Oris Caliber 733 (base Sellita SW200-1); ø 25.6 mm, height 4.6 mm; 26 jewels; 28,800 vph; 38-hour power reserve
Functions: hours, minutes, sweep seconds; depth gauge; date
Case: stainless steel, ø 46 mm, height 15 mm; unidirectional bezel with ceramic insert, 60-minute divisions, sapphire crystal; screw-in crown; water-resistant to 50 atm
Band: rubber, folding clasp with extension link
Remarks: physical depth gauge as water canal etched into crystal; additional stainless steel band
Price: $3,500

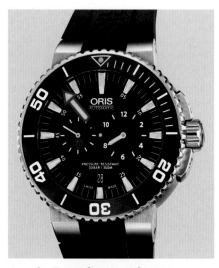

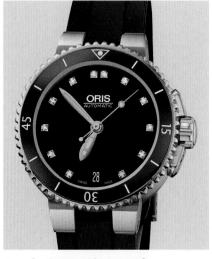

Aquis Regulator "the Master Diver"

Reference number: 749 7677 7154
Movement: automatic, Oris Caliber 749 (base Sellita SW220); ø 25.6 mm, height 5.05 mm; 28 jewels; 28,800 vph; 38-hour power reserve
Functions: hours (off-center), minutes, subsidiary seconds; date
Case: titanium, ø 43 mm, height 13.1 mm; unidirectional bezel with ceramic inlay, 60-minute divisions, sapphire crystal; transparent case back; screw-in crown; automatic helium valve; water-resistant to 30 atm
Band: rubber, folding clasp with extension link
Remarks: additional titanium bracelet

Aquis Date Diamonds

Reference number: 733 7652 4192
Movement: automatic, Oris Caliber 733 (base Sellita SW200); ø 25.6 mm, height 4.6 mm; 26 jewels; 28,800 vph; 38-hour power reserve
Functions: hours, minutes, sweep seconds; date
Case: stainless steel, ø 36 mm, height 11.9 mm; unidirectional bezel with ceramic inlay, with 60-second divisions, sapphire crystal; transparent case back; water-resistant to 30 atm
Band: textile, folding clasp
Remarks: dial set with 12 diamonds
Price: $2,000
Variations: stainless steel bracelet ($2,200)

Artelier Translucent Skeleton

Reference number: 734 7684 4051
Movement: automatic, Oris Caliber 734 (base Sellita SW200-1); ø 25.6 mm, height 4,6 mm; 26 jewels; 28,800 vph; 38-hour power reserve
Functions: hours, minutes, sweep seconds
Case: stainless steel, ø 40.5 mm, height 11.1 mm; sapphire crystal; transparent case back; water-resistant to 3 atm
Band: calf leather, folding clasp
Price: $2,700
Variations: reptile band ($3,000); stainless steel bracelet ($2,900)

MILUS

SWISS MADE SINCE 1919

A watch that saved lives

In the 1940s, US Navy pilots used to take a collection of precious items along on their missions to help them in case of need. One of the items was a Milus Snow Star watch. In homage to this flagship model from its history – and history in general – Milus is releasing the Snow Star in two limited editions, one in steel, the other in red gold. Each model comes along with a very original set of cufflinks and a military identification tag showing the number of the limited edition.

TOTALLY • WORTH • IT

info@totallyworthit.com
+1 724 263 2286
www.TotallyWorthIt.com

The original kit contained two rings, a chain and a gold pendant, as well as a Milus Snow Star "Instant Date" – an impressive accolade for the outstanding technical and aesthetic reputation of the Swiss brand.

Officine Panerai

Rue de la Balance 4
CH-2000 Neuchâtel
Switzerland

Tel.:
01139-02-363-138

Fax:
01139-02-363-13-297

E-Mail:
officinepanerai@panerai.com

Website:
www.panerai.com

Founded:
1860 in Florence, Italy

Number of employees:
approx. 250

U.S. distributor:
Panerai
645 Fifth Avenue
New York, NY 10022
877-PANERAI
www.panerai.com

Most important collections/price range:
Historic / approx. $5,000 to $35,000;
Contemporary / approx. $7,000 to $25,000;
Special Editions / approx. $5,000 to
$125,000; Specialties / approx. $20,000 to
$250,000

Panerai

Officine Panerai (in English: Panerai Workshops) joined the Richemont Group in 1997. Since then, it has made an unprecedented rise from an insider niche brand to a lifestyle phenomenon. The company, founded in 1860 by Giovanni Panerai, supplied the Italian navy with precision instruments. In the 1930s, the Florentine engineers developed a series of waterproof wristwatches that could be used by commandos under especially extreme and risky conditions. After 1997, under the leadership of Angelo Bonati, the company came out with a collection of oversize wristwatches, both stylistically and technically based on these historical models.

In 2006, Panerai headquarters was moved to Neuchâtel, Switzerland. A year later, the brand produced its first in-house *manufacture* movements (caliber family P.2000). In 2009, the new "little" Panerai *manufacture* movements (caliber family P.9000) were released. From the start, the idea behind them was to provide a competitive alternative to the base movements available until a couple of years ago.

Panerai movements are produced at the Manufacture Horlogère ValFleurier in Buttes, a facility that services other watch brands in the Richemont Group (Montblanc, for instance). The ValFleurier design office, to a certain extent the think tank of the whole concern, is on the top floor of Panerai headquarters in Neuchâtel.

The most recent calibers round off the *manufacture's* portfolio well, among them the first automatic chronograph with flyback function, the P.9100. In 2013 came the new P.5000 with an eight-day power reserve and manual winding, two features that the brand has supported ever since it received its first commissions from the Italian navy.

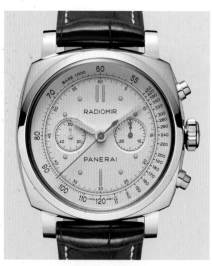

Radiomir 1940 Chronograph Platino

Reference number: PAM00518
Movement: manually wound, Panerai Caliber OP XXV (base Minerva 13-22); ø 28.76 mm, height 6.4 mm; 22 jewels; 18,000 vph; swan-neck fine adjustment, column wheel control of chronograph functions, côtes de Genève on bridges; 55-hour power reserve
Functions: hours, minutes, subsidiary seconds; chronograph
Case: platinum, ø 45 mm, height 15.55 mm; plexiglass; transparent case back; screw-in crown; water-resistant to 5 atm
Band: reptile skin, folding clasp
Price: $78,000; limited to 50 pieces

Radiomir 1940 Chronograph Oro Rosso

Reference number: PAM00519
Movement: manually wound, Panerai Caliber OP XXV (base Minerva 13-22); ø 28.76 mm, height 6.4 mm; 22 jewels; 18,000 vph; swan-neck fine adjustment, column wheel control of chronograph functions, côtes de Genève on bridges; 55-hour power reserve
Functions: hours, minutes, subsidiary seconds; chronograph
Case: red gold, ø 45 mm, height 15.55 mm; plexiglass; transparent back; screw-in crown; water-resistant to 5 atm
Band: reptile skin, folding clasp
Price: $58,500; limited to 100 pieces

Radiomir 1940 3 Days

Reference number: PAM00514
Movement: manually wound, Panerai Caliber P.3000; ø 37.2 mm, height 5.4 mm; 21 jewels; 21,600 vph; 2 spring barrels; 72-hour power reserve
Functions: hours, minutes, subsidiary seconds; date
Case: stainless steel, ø 47 mm, height 13.6 mm; sapphire crystal; transparent case back; screw-in crown; water-resistant to 10 atm
Band: leather, buckle
Price: $8,800
Variations: pink gold ($24,600)

Radiomir 10 Days GMT

Reference number: PAM00323
Movement: automatic, Panerai Caliber P.2003/6; ø 31 mm, height 8 mm; 25 jewels; 28,800 vph; 3 spring barrels; 240-hour power reserve
Functions: hours, minutes, subsidiary seconds; additional 12-hour display (2nd time zone), day/night indicator; power reserve indicator; date
Case: stainless steel, ø 47 mm, height 16.8 mm; sapphire crystal; transparent case back; screw-in crown; water-resistant to 10 atm
Band: reptile skin, buckle
Price: $13,800

Luminor Base 8 Days Acciaio

Reference number: PAM00560
Movement: manually wound, Panerai Caliber P.5000; ø 35.53 mm; height 4.5 mm; 21 jewels; 21,600 vph; 2 spring barrels, 192-hour power reserve
Functions: hours, minutes
Case: stainless steel, ø 44 mm, height 13.7 mm; sapphire crystal; transparent case back; hinged-lever crown protector; water-resistant to 30 atm
Band: calf leather, buckle
Remarks: additional bracelet
Price: $7,500
Variations: white dial ($7,500); titanium ($8,000)

Luminor Marina 8 Days Titanio

Reference number: PAM00564
Movement: manually wound, Panerai Caliber P.5000; ø 35.53 mm, height 4.5 mm; 21 jewels; 21,600 vph; 2 spring barrels; 192-hour power reserve
Functions: hours, minutes, subsidiary seconds
Case: titanium, ø 44 mm, height 13.7 mm; sapphire crystal; transparent case back; hinged-lever crown protector; water-resistant to 30 atm
Band: reptile skin, buckle
Remarks: additional bracelet
Price: $8,400
Variations: stainless steel with white dial ($7,900)

Luminor 1950 3 Days GMT Automatic Acciaio

Reference number: PAM00535
Movement: automatic, Panerai Caliber P.9001; ø 31.02 mm, height 7.9 mm; 29 jewels; 28,800 vph; 2 spring barrels; 72-hour power reserve
Functions: hours, minutes, subsidiary seconds; additional 12-hour display (2nd time zone); power reserve display (on case back); date
Case: stainless steel, ø 42 mm, height 16.35 mm; sapphire crystal; transparent case back; hinged-lever crown protector; water-resistant to 10 atm
Band: calf leather, buckle
Price: $9,700
Variations: power reserve indicator on dial ($9,900)

Luminor Marina 1950 3 Days Automatic Acciaio

Reference number: PAM00499
Movement: automatic, Panerai Caliber P.9000; ø 31.02 mm, height 7.9 mm; 28 jewels; 28,800 vph; 2 spring barrels; 72-hour power reserve
Functions: hours, minutes, subsidiary seconds; date
Case: stainless steel, ø 44 mm, height 17.95 mm; sapphire crystal; transparent case back; hinged-lever crown protector; water-resistant to 30 atm
Band: calf leather, buckle
Price: $8,500

Luminor 1950 3 Days Chrono Flyback

Reference number: PAM00524
Movement: automatic, Panerai Caliber P.9100; ø 31 mm, height 8.15 mm; 37 jewels; 28,800 vph; 2 spring barrels; 72-hour power reserve
Functions: hours, minutes, subsidiary seconds; flyback chronograph; date
Case: stainless steel, ø 44 mm, height 17 mm; sapphire crystal; transparent case back; crown protector with hinged lever; water-resistant to 10 atm
Band: leather, buckle
Price: $12,800
Variations: red gold ($30,900)

Luminor 1950 Regatta 3 Days Chrono Flyback Titanio

Reference number: PAM00526
Movement: automatic, Panerai Caliber P.9100/R; ø 31 mm, height 9.55 mm; 37 jewels; 28,800 vph; 2 spring barrels; 72-hour power reserve
Functions: hours, minutes, subsidiary seconds; flyback chronograph with preprogrammed countdown function precise to the minute
Case: titanium, ø 47 mm, height 19.06 mm; sapphire crystal; transparent case back; crown protector with hinged lever; water-resistant to 10 atm
Band: rubber, buckle
Price: $19,700

Luminor 1950 Left-Handed 3 Days

Reference number: PAM00557
Movement: manually wound, Panerai Caliber P.3000; ø 37.20 mm, height 5.3 mm; 21 jewels; 21,600 vph; 2 spring barrels; 72-hour power reserve
Functions: hours, minutes
Case: stainless steel, ø 47 mm, height 16.4 mm, sapphire crystal; transparent case back; hinged-lever crown protector; water-resistant to 10 atm
Band: calf leather, buckle
Remarks: additional bracelet
Price: $10,600

Luminor Submersible 1950 Amagnetic 3 Days Automatic Titanio

Reference number: PAM00389
Movement: automatic, Panerai Caliber P.9000; ø 31 mm, height 7.9 mm; 28 jewels; 28,800 vph; 2 spring barrels; 72-hour power reserve
Functions: hours, minutes, subsidiary seconds; date
Case: titanium, ø 47 mm, height 18.3 mm; unidirectional bezel with 60-minute division, sapphire crystal; crown protector with hinged lever; water-resistant to 30 atm
Band: rubber, buckle
Price: $12,500

Luminor 1950 3 Days Power Reserve

Reference number: PAM00423
Movement: manually wound, Panerai Caliber P.3002; ø 37.2 mm, height 6.3 mm; 21 jewels; 21,600 vph; 2 spring barrels; 72-hour power reserve
Functions: hours, minutes, subsidiary seconds; power reserve indicator
Case: stainless steel, ø 47 mm, height 17.2 mm; sapphire crystal; transparent case back; crown protector with hinged lever; water-resistant to 10 atm
Band: leather, buckle
Price: $10,900

Tuttonero Luminor 1950 3 Days GMT Automatic Ceramica

Reference number: PAM00438
Movement: automatic, Panerai Caliber 9001/B; ø 31.02 mm, height 7.9 mm; 29 jewels; 28,800 vph; 2 spring barrels, zero-position function for second hand; 72-hour power reserve
Functions: hours, minutes, subsidiary seconds; added 12-hour display; power reserve indicator on back; date
Case: ceramic, ø 44 mm, height 12 mm; sapphire crystal; transparent case back; hinged-lever crown protector; water-resistant to 10 atm
Band: ceramic, folding clasp
Price: $16,300

Luminor 1950 Chrono Monopulsante Left-Handed 8 Days Titanio

Reference number: PAM00579
Movement: manually wound, Panerai Caliber P.2004/9; ø 31.02 mm, height 8.2 mm; 31 jewels; 28,800 vph; 3 spring barrels, column-wheel control of chronograph functions with 1 button; zero-position function for second hand; 192-hour power reserve
Functions: hours, minutes, subsidiary seconds; power reserve indicator on case back; chronograph
Case: titanium, ø 47 mm, height 19.3 mm; sapphire crystal; transparent back; water-resistant to 10 atm
Band: calf leather, buckle
Price: $22,500; limited to 300 pieces

Caliber P.9100

Automatic; twin spring barrels, serially connected, 72-hour power reserve
Functions: hours, minutes, subsidiary seconds; flyback chronograph; date
Diameter: 31.1 mm
Height: 8.15 mm
Jewels: 37
Balance: glucydur
Frequency: 28,800 vph
Balance spring: flat hairspring
Shock protection: Kif
Remarks: reset second hand to zero by pulling crown ("zero reset"); 302 components

Caliber P.9100/R

Automatic; twin serially connected spring barrels; 72-hour power reserve
Functions: hours, minutes, subsidiary seconds; flyback chronograph with preprogrammed countdown function, precise to the minute
Diameter: 31.1 mm
Height: 9.55 mm
Jewels: 37
Balance: glucydur
Frequency: 28,800 vph
Balance spring: flat hairspring
Shock protection: Kif
Remarks: reset second hand to zero by pulling crown ("zero reset"); 328 components

Caliber P.5000

Manually wound; 2 serially connected spring barrels; 192-hour power reserve
Functions: hours, minutes, subsidiary seconds
Diameter: 37.2 mm
Height: 4.5 mm
Jewels: 21
Balance: glucydur with weighted screws
Frequency: 21,600 vph
Balance spring: flat hairspring
Remarks: 127 components

Caliber P.2006

Manually wound; 2 control wheels to control chronograph and flyback mechanism; 3 serially connected spring barrels, 192-hour power reserve
Functions: hours, minutes, subsidiary seconds; power reserve indicator; split-seconds chronograph
Diameter: 31 mm; **Height:** 9.6 mm
Jewels: 34
Balance: glucydur
Frequency: 28,800 vph
Balance spring: flat hairspring
Shock protection: Kif
Remarks: reset second hand to zero by pulling crown ("zero reset")

Caliber P.3000

Manually wound; 8-day power reserve
Functions: hours, minutes
Diameter: 37.2 mm
Height: 5.3 mm
Jewels: 21
Balance: glucydur
Frequency: 21,600 vph
Remarks: 160 components

Caliber P.9000

Automatic; 2 serially connected spring barrels, 72-hour power reserve
Functions: hours, minutes, subsidiary seconds; date
Diameter: 31 mm
Height: 7.9 mm
Jewels: 28
Balance: glucydur
Frequency: 28,800 vph
Remarks: 197 components

Parmigiani Fleurier SA
Rue du Temple 11
CH-2114 Fleurier
Switzerland

Tel.:
01141-32-862-6630

Fax:
01141-32-862-6631

E-Mail:
info@parmigiani.ch

Website:
www.parmigiani.ch

Founded:
1996

Number of employees:
600

Annual production:
approx. 6,000 watches

U.S. distributor:
Parmigiani Fleurier
Distribution Americas LLC
999 Brickell Avenue, Suite 740
Miami, FL 33131
305-260-7770; 305-269-7770
info@parmigiani.ch

Most important collections/price range:
Kalpa, Tonda, Pershing, Toric, Bugatti / approx.
$7,800 to $500,000 for *haute horlogerie*
pieces, no limit for unique pieces

Parmigiani

What began as the undertaking of a single man—a gifted watchmaker and reputable restorer of complicated vintage timepieces—in the small town of Fleurier in Switzerland's Val de Travers has now grown into an empire of sorts comprising several factories and more than 400 employees.

Michel Parmigiani is in fact just doing what he has done since 1976 when he began restoring vintage works. An exceptional talent, his output soon attracted the attention of the Sandoz Family Foundation, an organization established by a member of one of Switzerland's most famous families in 1964. The foundation bought 51 percent of Parmigiani Mesure et Art du Temps SA in 1996, turning what was practically a one-man show into a full-fledged and fully financed watch *manufacture*.

Four short years after the merger, three Swiss suppliers were acquired by the partners, furthering the quest for horological autonomy. Atokalpa SA in Alle (Canton of Jura) manufactures parts such as pinions, wheels, and micro components. Bruno Affolter SA in La Chaux-de-Fonds produces precious metal cases, dials, and other specialty parts. Elwin SA in Moutier specializes in turned parts. In 2003, the movement development and production department officially separated from the rest as Vaucher Manufacture, now an autonomous entity.

Parmigiani has enjoyed strong growth, notably in the United States. And having put its finger to the wind, it decided also to set its sights on Latin America, notably Brazil, where it signed a partnership with the Confederação Brasileira de Futebol. In addition to making watches and unique pieces, like his famed Islamic clock based on a lunar calendar, Parmigiani also devotes a part of the premises to restoring ancient timepieces.

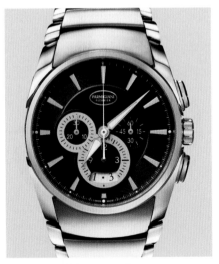

Tonda Métrographe

Reference number: PFC274-0001401-B33002
Movement: automatic, Parmigiani Caliber PF315;
ø 28 mm, height 6 mm; 46 jewels; 28,800 vph;
double spring barrel; finely finished with côtes de
Genève; 42-hour power reserve
Functions: hours, minutes, subsidiary seconds;
chronograph; date
Case: stainless steel, ø 40 mm, height 12.2 mm;
sapphire crystal, transparent case back; water-
resistant to 3 atm
Band: stainless steel, folding clasp
Price: $12,900
Variations: various dials

Tonda Métrographe

Reference number: PFC274-0001401-HE1442
Movement: automatic, Parmigiani Caliber PF315;
ø 28 mm, height 6 mm; 46 jewels; 28,800 vph;
double spring barrel; finely finished with côtes de
Genève; 42-hour power reserve
Functions: hours, minutes, subsidiary seconds;
chronograph; date
Case: stainless steel, ø 40 mm, height 12.2 mm;
sapphire crystal; transparent case back; water-
resistant to 3 atm
Band: calf leather, folding clasp
Price: $12,200
Variations: various dials

Tonda Métrographe

Reference number: PFC274-0002400-HE6042
Movement: automatic, Parmigiani Caliber PF315;
ø 28 mm, height 6 mm; 46 jewels; 28,800 vph;
double spring barrel; finely finished with côtes de
Genève; 42-hour power reserve
Functions: hours, minutes, subsidiary seconds;
chronograph; date
Case: stainless steel, ø 40 mm, height 12.2 mm;
sapphire crystal, transparent case back; water-
resistant to 3 atm
Band: calf leather, folding clasp
Price: $12,200
Variations: various dials

Tonda Hemispheres

Reference number: PFC231-0001800-HA3142
Movement: automatic, Parmigiani Caliber PF337;
ø 35.6 mm, height 5.1 mm; 38 jewels; 28,800 vph;
double spring barrel; côtes de Genève; 50-hour
power reserve
Functions: hours, minutes, subsidiary seconds;
additional 12-hour display (2nd time zone); double
day/night indicator; date
Case: stainless steel, ø 42 mm, height 11.15 mm;
sapphire crystal, transparent case back; water-
resistant to 3 atm
Band: reptile skin, buckle
Price: $24,900
Variations: white gold ($40,300); rose gold
($37,900)

Tonda Centum

Reference number: PFH227-1200300-HA1441
Movement: automatic, Parmigiani Caliber PF333; ø 27
mm, height 5.5 mm; 32 jewels; 28,800 vph; module
for perpetual calendar; double spring barrel; 50-hour
power reserve
Functions: hours, minutes, sweep seconds; perpetual
calendar with retrograde date, weekday, month,
double moon phase, leap year
Case: white gold, ø 42 mm, height 11.15 mm; sapphire
crystal; transparent case back; water-resistant to 3 atm
Band: reptile skin, folding clasp
Remarks: open-worked graphite dial
Price: $74,000
Variations: rose gold without open-worked dial
($64,800)

Tonda 1950

Reference number: PFC267-1000300-HA1441
Movement: automatic, Parmigiani Caliber PF701;
ø 30 mm, height 2.6 mm; 29 jewels; 21,600 vph;
42-hour power reserve
Functions: hours, minutes, subsidiary seconds
Case: rose gold, ø 39 mm, height 7.8 mm; sapphire
crystal; transparent case back; water-resistant to
3 atm
Band: reptile skin, buckle
Price: $17,900
Variations: white gold ($17,900)

Tonda Métropolitaine

Reference number: PFC273-0003300-HC6121
Movement: automatic, Parmigiani Caliber PF310; ø
23.9 mm, height 3.9 mm; 28 jewels; 28,800 vph;
double spring barrel; finely finished with côtes de
Genève; 50-hour power reserve
Functions: hours, minutes, subsidiary seconds;
date
Case: stainless steel, ø 34 mm, height 8.65 mm;
sapphire crystal, transparent case back; water-
resistant to 3 atm
Band: calf leather, folding clasp
Remarks: mother-of-pearl dial
Price: $8,900
Variations: stainless steel bracelet ($9,500);
diamonds ($11,500); various dials

Tonda Pomellato

Reference number: PFC267-1035500-HC2421
Movement: automatic, Parmigiani Caliber PF701;
ø 30 mm, height 2.6 mm; 29 jewels; 21,600 vph;
platinum microrotor; 42-hour power reserve
Functions: hours, minutes
Case: rose gold, ø 39 mm, height 7.8 mm; bezel
set with 112 diamonds; sapphire crystal; sapphire
cabochon on crown
Band: calf leather, buckle
Remarks: turquoise dial in cooperation with the
jeweller Pomellato
Price: $27,000

Toric Resonance 3

Reference number: PFH478-1200100-HA1441
Movement: manually wound, Parmigiani Caliber
PF359; ø 33.8 mm, height 8.89 mm; 33 jewels;
18,000 vph; hand-beveled mainplate and bridges;
40-hour power reserve
Functions: hours, minutes; minute repeater; large
date (jumping)
Case: white gold, ø 45 mm, height 14.1 mm;
sapphire crystal; transparent case back
Band: reptile skin, buckle
Remarks: guilloché gold dial
Price: on request

Pershing Tourbillon

Reference number: PFH552-2510100-X01402
Movement: manually wound, Parmigiani Caliber PF511; ø 33.84 mm, height 5.55 mm; 30 jewels; 21,600 vph; 30-second tourbillon; double spring barrel; skeletonized; 168-hour power reserve
Functions: hours, minutes, sweep seconds; power reserve display
Case: palladium, ø 45 mm, height 14.2 mm; unidirectional bezel with 60-minute divisions, sapphire crystal; transparent case back; water-resistant to 20 atm
Band: rubber, buckle
Price: on request

Pershing Tourbillon Abyss

Reference number: PFH551-3100600-HA3142
Movement: manually wound, Parmigiani Caliber PF511; ø 33.84 mm, height 5.55 mm; 30 jewels; 21,600 vph; 30-second tourbillon; double spring barrel; 168-hour power reserve
Functions: hours, minutes, sweep seconds; power reserve display
Case: titanium, ø 45 mm, height 14.2 mm; rose gold bezel; unidirectional bezel, with 60-minute divisions, sapphire crystal; transparent case back; water-resistant to 20 atm
Band: reptile skin, folding clasp
Price: on request; limited to 30 pieces

Bugatti Aerolithe

Reference number: PFC329-3400600-HE3132
Movement: automatic, Parmigiani Caliber PF335; ø 30.3 mm, height 6.81 mm; 68 jewels; 28,800 vph; double spring barrel; bridges with côtes de Genève; 50-hour power reserve
Functions: hours, minutes, subsidiary seconds; flyback chronograph; date
Case: titanium, ø 41 mm, height 12.55 mm; white gold bezel, sapphire crystal; transparent case back; water-resistant to 3 atm
Band: calf leather, folding clasp
Price: $27,000

Kalparisma Agenda

Reference number: PFC123-1000700-HE2421
Movement: automatic, Parmigiani Caliber PF331; ø 25.6 mm, height 3.5 mm; 32 jewels; 28,800 vph; 2 spring barrels; 55-hour power reserve
Functions: hours, minutes, sweep seconds; date
Case: rose gold, 31.2 x 37.5 mm, height 8.4 mm; sapphire crystal; transparent case back; water-resistant to 3 atm
Band: calf leather, buckle
Price: $20,000
Variations: brilliant-cut diamonds ($23,700)

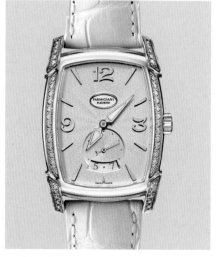

Kalparisma Agenda Steel

Reference number: PFC124-0000700-XA2422
Movement: automatic, Parmigiani Caliber PF331; ø 25.6 mm, height 3.5 mm; 32 jewels; 28,800 vph; côtes de Genève; 55-hour power reserve
Functions: hours, minutes, subsidiary seconds; date
Case: stainless steel, 31.2 x 37.5 mm, height 8.4 mm; bezel and lugs set with 46 diamonds, sapphire crystal; transparent case back; water-resistant to 3 atm
Band: reptile skin, folding clasp
Price: $10,600
Variations: w/o diamonds ($13,900)

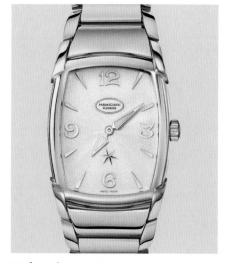

Kalparisma Nova

Reference number: PFC125-1000700-HE2421
Movement: automatic, Parmigiani Caliber PF332; ø 25.6 mm, height 3.5 mm; 32 jewels; 28,800 vph; 55-hour power reserve
Functions: hours, minutes
Case: rose gold, 31.2 x 37.5 mm, height 8.4 mm; sapphire crystal; transparent case back; water-resistant to 3 atm
Band: rose gold, double folding clasp
Price: $34,700
Variations: calf leather ($19,900); diamonds with rose gold bracelet ($37,300); diamonds on calf leather band ($23,700)

Caliber PF333

Automatic; module for perpetual calendar with retrograde date and precision moon phase; double spring barrel; 55-hour power reserve
Functions: hours, minutes, sweep seconds; perpetual calendar with month, moon phase, leap year, weekday, date
Diameter: 27 mm
Height: 5.5 mm
Jewels: 32
Frequency: 28,800 vph
Balance spring: flat hairspring

Caliber PF511

Manually wound; 30-second tourbillon; skeletonized mainplate and bridges; double spring barrel; 7-day power reserve
Functions: hours, minutes, sweep seconds; power reserve indicator
Diameter: 33.9 mm
Height: 5.55 mm
Jewels: 30
Frequency: 21,600 vph
Balance spring: flat hairspring

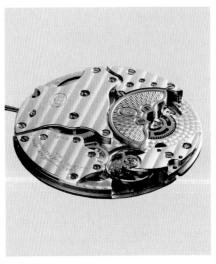

Caliber PF701

Automatic; platinum microrotor; single spring barrel; 42-hour power reserve
Functions: hours, minutes, subsidiary seconds
Diameter: 30 mm
Height: 2.6 mm
Jewels: 29
Frequency: 21,600 vph

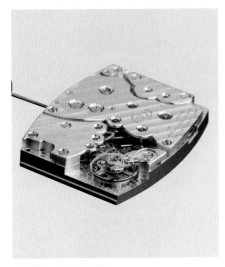

Caliber PF110

Manually wound; double spring barrel; 8-day power reserve
Functions: hours, minutes, subsidiary seconds; date; power reserve indicator
Measurements: 29.3 x 23.6 mm
Height: 4.9 mm
Jewels: 28
Frequency: 21,600 vph

Caliber PF334

Automatic; double spring barrel; 50-hour power reserve
Functions: hours, minutes, subsidiary seconds; chronograph; date
Diameter: 30.3 mm
Height: 6.8 mm
Jewels: 68
Frequency: 28,800 vph

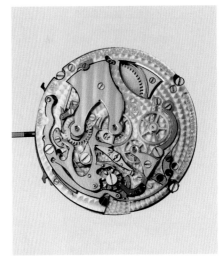

Caliber PF354

Manually wound; Dubois Dépraz chronograph module; double spring barrel; 72-hour power reserve
Functions: hours, minutes, subsidiary seconds; chronograph; power reserve indicator
Diameter: 29.9 mm
Height: 7.6 mm
Jewels: 29
Frequency: 21,600 vph

Patek Philippe

Patek Philippe SA
Chemin du pont-du-centenaire 141
CH-1228 Plan-les-Ouates
Switzerland

Tel.:
01141-22-884-20-20

Fax:
01141-22-884-20-40

Website:
www.patek.com

Founded:
1839

Number of employees:
approx. 2,000 (estimated)

Annual production:
approx. 45,000 watches worldwide per year

U.S. distributor:
Patek Philippe USA
45 Rockefeller Center, Suite 401
New York, NY 10111
212-218-1272; 212-218-1283 (fax)

Most important collections/price range:
Calatrava, Nautilus, Gondolo, Ellipse, Aquanaut / ladies' timepieces begin at $13,000 (Twenty~4) and men's at $20,800 (basic Calatrava)

Not many companies can boast a 175th anniversary. In the Swiss watchmaking landscape, Patek Philippe has a special status as the last independent family-owned business. The company was founded by Count Norbert Antoine de Patek in 1839, and in 1845, master watchmaker Jean Adrien Philippe came on board. Literally since then, Patek Philippe has been known for creating high-quality mechanical watches, some with extremely sophisticated complications. Even among its competition, the *manufacture* enjoys the greatest respect.

In 1932, Charles-Henri Stern took over the *manufacture*. His son Henri and grandson Philippe continued the tradition of solid leadership, steering the company through the notorious quartz crisis without ever compromising quality. The next in line, also Henri, heads the enterprise these days.

In 1997, Patek Philippe moved into new quarters, based on the most modern standards. The facility boasts the world's largest assembly of watchmakers under one roof, and yet production figures are comparatively modest. Approximately 20,000 mechanical watches leave the *manufacture* in Plan-les-Ouates—the rest of the offerings are women's quartz watches. A small section of the building is reserved for restoring old watches using either parts from a large and valuable collection of components or rebuilding them from scratch.

The company recently opened a highly industrialized second branch between La Chaux-de-Fonds and Le Locle, where case components are manufactured, cases are polished, and gem setting is done. Patek Philippe's main headquarters remain in Geneva, but the *manufacture* no longer has a need for that city's famed seal: All of the company's mechanical watches now feature the "Patek Philippe Seal," the criteria for which far exceed the requirements of the *Poinçon de Genève* and include specifications for the entire watch, not just the movement.

Nautilus Travel Time Chronograph

Reference number: 5990/1A
Movement: automatic, Patek Philippe Caliber 28-520 S C FUS; ø 31 mm, height 6.95 mm; 34 jewels; 28,800 vph; 45-hour power reserve
Functions: hours, minutes, subsidiary seconds; additional 12-hour display (2nd time zone), day/night indicator; flyback chronograph; date
Case: stainless steel, ø 40.5 mm, height 12.53 mm; sapphire crystal; transparent case back; screw-in crown, water-resistant to 12 atm
Band: stainless steel, folding clasp
Price: $57,300

Annual Calendar Chronograph

Reference number: 5960/1A
Movement: automatic, Patek Philippe Caliber CH 28 520 IRM QA 24H; ø 33 mm, height 7.68 mm; 40 jewels; 28,800 vph
Functions: hours, minutes, sweep seconds; flyback chronograph; annual calendar with date, weekday, month; power reserve indicator
Case: stainless steel, ø 40.5 mm, height 13.5 mm; sapphire crystal; transparent case back; water-resistant to 3 atm
Band: stainless steel, folding clasp
Price: $54,800

Chronograph Perpetual Calendar

Reference number: 5270G
Movement: manually wound, Patek Philippe Caliber CH 29 535 PS Q; ø 32 mm, height 7 mm; 33 jewels; 28,800 vph; 55-hour power reserve
Functions: hours, minutes, subsidiary seconds; day/night indicator; chronograph; perpetual calendar with date, weekday, month, moon phase, leap year
Case: white gold, ø 41 mm, height 12.4 mm; sapphire crystal; transparent case back; water-resistant to 3 atm
Band: reptile skin, folding clasp
Price: $176,300
Variations: blue dial

Perpetual Calendar

Reference number: 5140R
Movement: automatic, Patek Philippe Caliber
240 Q; ø 27.5 mm, height 3.88 mm; 27 jewels;
21,600 vph; 38-hour power reserve
Functions: hours, minutes; additional 24-hour
display; perpetual calendar with date, weekday,
month, moon phase, leap year
Case: rose gold, ø 37.2 mm, height 8.8 mm;
sapphire crystal; transparent case back; water-
resistant to 3 atm
Band: reptile skin, folding clasp
Price: $91,000

Perpetual Calendar

Reference number: 5496P
Movement: automatic, Patek Philippe Caliber
324 S QR; ø 28 mm, height 5.35 mm; 30 jewels;
28,800 vph; 35-hour power reserve
Functions: hours, minutes, sweep seconds;
perpetual calendar with retrograde date, weekday,
month, moon phase, leap year
Case: platinum, ø 39.5 mm, height 11.19 mm;
sapphire crystal; transparent case back; water-
resistant to 3 atm
Band: reptile skin, folding clasp
Remarks: diamond in case body between lower lugs
Price: $115,700

Perpetual Calendar

Reference number: 5940G
Movement: automatic, Patek Philippe Caliber
240 Q; ø 27.5 mm, height 3.88 mm; 27 jewels;
21,600 vph; 38-hour power reserve
Functions: hours, minutes; additional 24-hour
display; perpetual calendar with date, weekday,
month, moon phase, leap year
Case: white gold, 37 x 44.6 mm, height 8.48 mm;
sapphire crystal; transparent case back; water-
resistant to 3 atm
Band: reptile skin, buckle
Remarks: additional case back
Price: $93,800

Split-Seconds Chronograph with Perpetual Calendar

Reference number: 5204P
Movement: manually wound, Patek Philippe Caliber
CH 29-535 PS Q; ø 32 mm, height 8.7 mm; 34
jewels; 28,800 vph; 55-hour power reserve
Functions: hours, minutes, subsidiary seconds;
day/night indicator; split-seconds chronograph;
perpetual calendar with date, weekday, month,
moon phase, leap year
Case: platinum, ø 40 mm, height 14.3 mm;
transparent case back; water-resistant to 3 atm
Band: reptile skin, folding clasp
Price: $317,500

Rattrapante Chronograph

Reference number: 5950/1A
Movement: manually wound, Patek Philippe Caliber
CH 27-525 PS; ø 27.3 mm, height 5.25 mm; 27
jewels; 21,600 vph; single pusher for chronograph
functions; 48-hour power reserve
Functions: hours, minutes, subsidiary seconds;
rattrapante chronograph
Case: stainless steel, 37 x 44.6 mm, height 10.13
mm; sapphire crystal; transparent case back; water-
resistant to 3 atm
Band: stainless steel, folding clasp
Price: on request
Variations: opaline silver-gray or rose gold dial

Split-Seconds Chronograph with Perpetual Calendar

Reference number: 5951P
Movement: manually wound, Patek Philippe Caliber
CHR 27-535 PS Q; ø 27.3 mm, height 7.3 mm; 27
jewels; 21,600 vph; single pusher for chronograph
functions; 38-hour power reserve
Functions: hours, minutes, subsidiary seconds;
day/night indicator; split-seconds chronograph;
perpetual calendar with date, weekday, month,
moon phase, leap year
Case: platinum, 37 x 45 mm, height 12.33 mm;
transparent back; water-resistant to 3 atm
Price: on request

Minute Repeater

Reference number: 5078R
Movement: automatic, Patek Philippe Caliber R 27 PS; ø 28 mm, height 5.05 mm; 39 jewels; 21,600 vph; 43-hour power reserve
Functions: hours, minutes, subsidiary seconds; minute repeater
Case: rose gold, ø 38 mm, height 12.9 mm; sapphire crystal
Band: reptile skin, buckle
Remarks: enamel dial
Price: on request

Perpetual Calendar with Minute Repeater

Reference number: 5304R
Movement: automatic, Patek Philippe Caliber R 27 PS QR LU; ø 28 mm, height 7.23 mm; 41 jewels; 21,600 vph; 38-hour power reserve
Functions: hours, minutes, subsidiary seconds; minute repeater; perpetual calendar with date (retrograde), weekday, month, moon phase, leap year
Case: rose gold, ø 43 mm, height 12.9 mm; sapphire crystal; transparent case back
Band: reptile skin, folding clasp
Remarks: skeletonized dial
Price: on request

Annual Calendar

Reference number: 5396/1G
Movement: automatic, Patek Philippe Caliber 324 S QA LU 24H/303; ø 33.3 mm, height 5.78 mm; 34 jewels; 28,800 vph
Functions: hours, minutes, sweep seconds; additional 24-hour display; annual calendar with date, weekday, month, moon phase
Case: white gold, ø 38.5 mm, height 11.2 mm; sapphire crystal; transparent case back; water-resistant to 3 atm
Band: white gold, folding clasp
Price: $76,900
Variations: rose gold ($76,900)

Annual Calendar

Reference number: 5146/1R
Movement: automatic, Patek Philippe Caliber 324 S IRM QA LU; ø 30 mm, height 5.32 mm; 36 jewels; 28,800 vph
Functions: hours, minutes, sweep seconds; perpetual calendar with date, weekday, month, moon phase; power reserve indicator
Case: rose gold, ø 39 mm, height 11.23 mm; sapphire crystal; transparent case back; water-resistant to 3 atm
Band: rose gold, folding clasp
Price: $71,000
Variations: yellow gold ($68,500); white gold ($71,000)

Calatrava

Reference number: 5153G
Movement: automatic, Patek Philippe Caliber 324 S C; ø 27 mm, height 3.3 mm; 29 jewels; 28,800 vph; Spiromax silicon spring; 35-hour power reserve
Functions: hours, minutes, sweep seconds; date
Case: white gold, ø 38 mm, height 9.7 mm; sapphire crystal; transparent case back; water-resistant to 3 atm
Band: reptile skin, buckle
Remarks: hinged case back cover
Price: $37,000
Variations: black dial; yellow gold

Calatrava

Reference number: 5227G
Movement: automatic, Patek Philippe Caliber 324 S C; ø 27 mm, height 3.3 mm; 29 jewels; 28,800 vph; Spiromax silicon spring
Functions: hours, minutes, sweep seconds; date
Case: white gold, ø 39 mm, height 9.24 mm; sapphire crystal; transparent case back; water-resistant to 3 atm
Band: reptile skin, buckle
Remarks: hinged case back cover
Price: $37,300
Variations: yellow gold ($35,400); rose gold ($37,300)

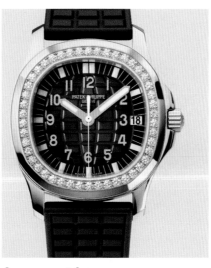

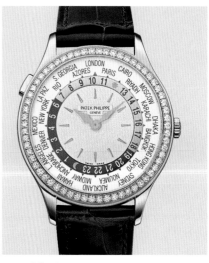

Nautilus

Reference number: 7018/1A
Movement: automatic, Patek Philippe Caliber 324 S C; ø 27 mm, height 3.57 mm; 29 jewels; 28,800 vph
Functions: hours, minutes, sweep seconds; date
Case: stainless steel, ø 33.6 mm, height 8.7 mm; bezel set with 50 diamonds, sapphire crystal; transparent case back; screw-in crown; water-resistant to 6 atm
Band: stainless steel, folding clasp
Price: $37,800

Aquanaut Luce

Reference number: 5068R
Movement: automatic, Patek Philippe Caliber 324 S C; ø 27 mm, height 3.57 mm; 29 jewels; 28,800 vph; 35-hour power reserve
Functions: hours, minutes, sweep seconds; date
Case: rose gold, ø 35.6 mm, height 8.5 mm; bezel set with 46 diamonds, sapphire crystal; transparent case back; screw-in crown; water-resistant to 12 atm
Band: rubber, folding clasp
Price: $47,600

World Time

Reference number: 7130R
Movement: automatic, Patek Philippe Caliber 240 HU; ø 27.5 mm, height 3.88 mm; 33 jewels; 21,600 vph
Functions: hours, minutes; world-time display (2nd time zone)
Case: rose gold, ø 36 mm, height 8.83 mm; bezel set with 62 diamonds, pusher-activated inner ring with 24 world-time zone reference cities, sapphire crystal; transparent back; water-resistant to 3 atm
Band: reptile skin, buckle
Price: $54,900
Variations: white gold

Calatrava

Reference number: 7200R
Movement: automatic, Patek Philippe Caliber 240; ø 27.5 mm, height 2.53 mm; 27 jewels; 21,600 vph
Functions: hours, minutes
Case: rose gold, ø 34.6 mm, height 7.37 mm; sapphire crystal; transparent case back; water-resistant to 3 atm
Band: reptile skin, buckle
Price: $29,300

Complication

Reference number: 4968G
Movement: manually wound, Patek Philippe Caliber 215 PS LU; ø 21.9 mm, height 3 mm; 18 jewels; 28,800 vph; 39-hour power reserve
Functions: hours, minutes, subsidiary seconds; moon phase
Case: white gold, ø 33.3 mm, height 7.98 mm; bezel set with 273 diamonds, sapphire crystal; transparent case back; water-resistant to 3 atm
Band: reptile skin, buckle set with 32 diamonds
Remarks: mother-of-pearl dial
Price: $58,600

Complication

Reference number: 7121/1J
Movement: manually wound, Patek Philippe Caliber 215 PS LU; ø 21.9 mm, height 3 mm; 18 jewels; 28,800 vph; 39-hour power reserve
Functions: hours, minutes, subsidiary seconds; moon phase
Case: yellow gold, ø 33 mm, height 8.35 mm; bezel set with 66 diamonds, sapphire crystal; transparent case back; screw-in crown; water-resistant to 3 atm
Band: yellow gold; folding clasp
Price: $53,600

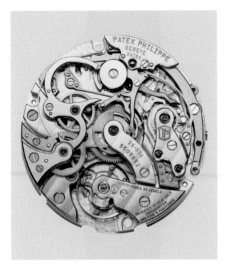

Caliber CH 29-535 PS

Manually wound; column-wheel control of chronograph functions; precisely jumping 30-minute counter; single barrel spring; 65-hour power reserve
Functions: hours, minutes, subsidiary seconds; chronograph
Diameter: 29.6 mm
Height: 5.35 mm
Jewels: 33
Balance: Gyromax, 4-armed, with 4 regulating weights
Frequency: 28,800 vph
Balance spring: Breguet
Shock protection: Incabloc
Remarks: 269 components, patent pending for 6 detail solutions

Caliber CHR 29-535 PS Q

Manually wound; 2 column wheels to control chronograph functions, split-second hand mechanism with isolator; single barrel spring; 65-hour power reserve
Functions: hours, minutes, subsidiary seconds; day/night indicator; split-second chronograph; perpetual calendar with date, weekday, month, moon phase, leap year
Diameter: 32 mm; **Height:** 8.7 mm; **Jewels:** 34
Balance: Gyromax, 4-armed, with 4 regulating weights; **Frequency:** 28,800 vph
Balance spring: Breguet
Remarks: 496 components, 182 alone for perpetual calendar and 42 for split-seconds mechanism with isolator

Caliber CHR 27-525 PS

Ultra-flat mechanical movement with manual winding; 48-hour power reserve; double column wheel control of chronograph functions with crown pusher (start-stop-reset) and separate split-seconds hand pusher
Functions: hours, minutes, subsidiary seconds; split-seconds chronograph
Diameter: 27.3 mm; **Height:** 5.25 mm; **Jewels:** 27
Balance: Gyromax, 2-armed, with 8 regulating weights
Frequency: 21,600 vph
Balance spring: Breguet
Shock protection: Kif
Remarks: 252 individual components; outstandingly high-quality finishing

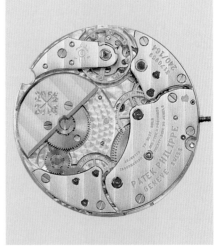

Caliber 28-20 REC 8J PS IRM C J

Manually wound; double spring barrel; 192-hour power reserve
Functions: hours, minutes, subsidiary seconds; power reserve indicator; weekday, date
Measurements: 20 x 28 mm
Height: 5.05 mm
Jewels: 28
Balance: Gyromax
Frequency: 28,800 vph
Balance spring: Spiromax silicon spring

Caliber 240 HU

Automatic; unidirectional winding off-center ball-bearing rotor in 22 kt gold; 48-hour power reserve
Functions: hours, minutes, world-time display (2nd time zone)
Diameter: 27.5 mm
Height: 3.88 mm
Jewels: 33
Balance: Gyromax
Frequency: 21,600 vph
Remarks: 239 individual parts

Caliber 240 PS IRM C LU

Automatic; unidirectional winding off-center ball-bearing rotor in 22 kt gold; 48-hour power reserve
Functions: hours, minutes, subsidiary seconds; power reserve display; date; moon phase
Diameter: 31 mm
Height: 3.98 mm
Jewels: 29
Balance: Gyromax
Frequency: 21,600 vph
Remarks: 265 individual parts

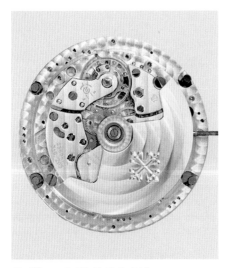

Caliber 315 S QA LU

Automatic; central rotor in 21 kt gold; single spring barrel; 48-hour power reserve
Functions: hours, minutes, sweep seconds; annual calendar with date, day, month, moon phase
Diameter: 30 mm
Height: 5.22 mm
Jewels: 34
Balance: Gyromax
Frequency: 21,600 vph
Remarks: 328 individual parts

Caliber 315 SC

Automatic; central rotor in 21 kt gold; single spring barrel; 48-hour power reserve
Functions: hours, minutes, sweep seconds; date
Diameter: 27 mm
Height: 3.22 mm
Jewels: 29
Balance: Gyromax
Frequency: 21,600 vph
Remarks: 213 individual parts

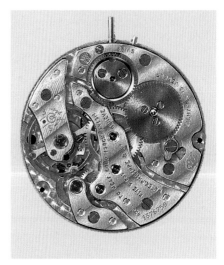

Caliber 215

Manually wound; single spring barrel; 44-hour power reserve
Functions: hours, minutes, subsidiary seconds
Diameter: 21.9 mm
Height: 2.55 mm
Jewels: 18
Balance: Gyromax with 8 masselotte regulating weights
Frequency: 28,800 vph
Balance spring: flat hairspring
Shock protection: Kif
Remarks: base plate with perlage, beveled bridges with côtes de Genève, 130 individual parts

Caliber 315 S IRM QA LU

Manually wound; central rotor in 21 kt gold; single spring barrel; 48-hour power reserve
Functions: hours, minutes, sweep seconds, calendar with date, weekday, month, moon phase; power reserve display
Diameter: 30 mm
Height: 5.22 mm
Jewels: 36
Balance: Gyromax
Frequency: 21,600 vph
Remarks: 355 individual parts

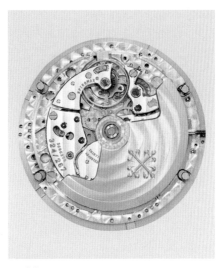

Caliber 324 S IRM QA LU

Automatic; central rotor in 21 kt gold; single spring barrel; 45-hour power reserve
Functions: hours, minutes, sweep seconds; calendar with date, day, month, moon phase; power reserve display
Diameter: 32 mm
Height: 5.3 mm
Jewels: 36
Balance: Gyromax
Frequency: 28,800 vph
Balance spring: Spiromax (silicon)
Remarks: silicon escape wheel; 355 individual parts

Caliber 324 S QA LU 24H/303

Automatic; central rotor in 21 kt gold; single spring barrel; 45-hour power reserve
Functions: hours, minutes, sweep seconds; calendar with date, day, month (programmed for 1 year), moon phase; 24-hour display
Diameter: 32.6 mm
Height: 5.78 mm
Jewels: 34
Balance: Gyromax
Frequency: 28,800 vph
Balance spring: Spiromax (silicon)
Remarks: silicon escape wheel; 347 individual parts

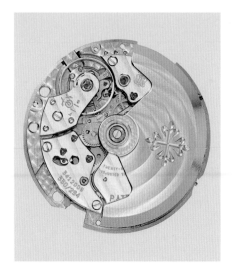

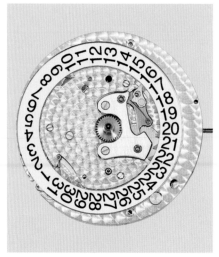

Caliber 330 SC

Automatic; central rotor in 21 kt gold; single spring barrel; 48-hour power reserve
Functions: hours, minutes, sweep seconds; date
Diameter: 27 mm
Height: 3.5 mm
Jewels: 29
Balance: Gyromax
Frequency: 21,600 vph
Balance spring: Breguet
Remarks: 217 individual parts

Caliber CH 28-520 C

Automatic, column-wheel control of chronograph functions; central rotor in 21 kt gold; single spring barrel; 55-hour power reserve
Functions: hours, minutes, sweep seconds; chronograph with combined hour and minute counter; date
Diameter: 30 mm
Height: 6.63 mm
Jewels: 35
Balance: Gyromax
Frequency: 28,800 vph
Balance spring: Breguet
Remarks: 327 individual parts

Caliber CH 28-520 IRM QA 24H

Manually wound; column-wheel control of chronograph functions; central rotor in 21 kt gold; single spring barrel; 55-hour power reserve
Functions: hours, minutes, sweep seconds; chronograph with combined hour and minute counter; calendar with date, day, month, moon phase; day/night indication; power reserve display
Diameter: 33 mm
Height: 7.68 mm
Jewels: 40
Balance: Gyromax
Frequency: 28,800 vph
Balance spring: Breguet
Remarks: 456 individual parts

Caliber RTO 27 QR SID LU CL

Manually wound; minute repeater; striking mechanism with 2 cathedral gongs, release mechanism integrated in watch movement; single spring barrel; 48-hour power reserve; COSC-certified chronometer
Functions: hours, minutes; perpetual calendar with date (retrograde), day, month, moon phase; leap year (front), sidereal time, celestial map with moon phase and moon age (on back)
Diameter: 38 mm; **Height:** 12.61 mm
Jewels: 55
Balance: Gyromax
Frequency: 21,600 vph
Remarks: 686 individual parts

Caliber RTO 27 PS

Manually wound, 1-minute tourbillon; single spring barrel; 48-hour power reserve; COSC-certified chronometer
Functions: hours, minutes, subsidiary seconds, minute repeater
Diameter: 28 mm
Height: 6.58 mm
Jewels: 28
Balance: Gyromax
Frequency: 21,600 vph
Balance spring: Breguet
Remarks: 336 individual parts

Caliber CH 28-520 C FUS

Automatic; column wheel control of chronograph functions, 21 kt gold central rotor; single spring barrel; 45-hour power reserve
Functions: hours, minutes; additional 12-hour indicator (2nd time zone); double day/night indicator; flyback chronograph; date
Diameter: 31 mm
Height: 6.95 mm
Jewels: 34
Balance: Gyromax
Frequency: 28,800 vph
Balance spring: Spiromax
Remarks: 370 components

Société des Montres Paul Picot SA

Rue du Doubs 6
CH-2340 Le Noirmont
Switzerland

Tel.:
01141-32-911-1818

Fax:
01141-32-911-1819

E-Mail:
info@paulpicot.ch

Website:
www.paulpicot.ch

Founded:
1976

U.S. distributor:
Time Innovations LLC
After Sales Services
444 Madison Avenue, Ste. 601
New York, NY 10022
718-725-7509
info@timeinnovationsllc.com

Most important collections:
Atelier, C-Type, Gentleman, Technicum, Firshire, unique pieces

Paul Picot

The 1976 establishment of the Société des Montres Paul Picot required a large dose of pioneering spirit on the part of its initiators. The new brand was born of the will to save the rich history of the Swiss watch industry and let its true values once again come to light. The age-old tradition of watchmaking was threatening to collapse; qualified masters of the craft were disappearing from the workplace, and the once-fascinating atmosphere of watchmakers' workshops had given way to the industrial hustle and bustle of anonymous brand names. For company founder and president Mario Boiocchi, the only chance for the survival of European watch culture was to rediscover quality and precision. While Japanese and American competitors were forcing the Swiss watch industry to make compromises in order to meet the demands of mass consumption, Paul Picot chose to walk a different path.

The market—that vague, undefinable, yet despotic entity—was calling for futuristic design and electronic technology. However, Paul Picot went in the exact opposite direction and produced fine gold cases and mechanical watch movements. In the years to follow, the collections attracted the attention of watch buyers the world over with their good balance of elegance and sportiness. This company located in Le Noirmont in the heart of watchmaking country is writing its own history. For a relatively small concern, it has managed to produce a very wide range of models each with a unique look. The Firshire series comes in sober round cases or as the 1937 or 3000 Regulateur in a comfortable tonneau with a dial tightly packed with displays. And while many brands are having to drop their prices to attract a coveted target group, Paul Picot has already staked out this territory.

Firshire Megarotor

Reference number: P0451.SG
Movement: automatic, ETA Caliber 2892A2; ø 25.6 mm, height 3.6 mm; 21 jewels; 28,800 vph; winding rotor with tungsten oscillating weight; 42-hour power reserve
Functions: hours, minutes, sweep seconds; date
Case: stainless steel, ø 42 mm, height 12 mm; sapphire crystal; transparent case back; water-resistant to 5 atm
Band: reptile skin, folding clasp
Price: $3,804
Variations: stainless steel links bracelet ($4,139)

Firshire Megarotor Big Date

Reference number: P0475.SG
Movement: automatic, ETA Caliber 2892A2 with module; ø 25.6 mm, height 5 mm; 31 jewels; 28,800 vph; winding rotor with tungsten oscillating weight; 42-hour power reserve
Functions: hours, minutes, subsidiary seconds; large date
Case: stainless steel, ø 42 mm, height 12 mm; sapphire crystal; transparent case back; water-resistant to 5 atm
Band: reptile skin, folding clasp
Price: $5,370
Variations: rose gold bezel ($8,725)

Firshire Megarotor Day & Date

Reference number: P453.SRG.5604
Movement: automatic, ETA Caliber 2892A2 with Dubois-Dépraz module; ø 25.6 mm, height 6 mm; 31 jewels; 28,800 vph; winding rotor with tungsten oscillating weight; 42-hour power reserve
Functions: hours, minutes, sweep seconds; date, weekday
Case: stainless steel, ø 42 mm, height 11 mm; rose gold bezel; sapphire crystal; transparent case back; water-resistant to 5 atm
Band: reptile skin, folding clasp
Price: $8,502
Variations: rose gold ($19,913)

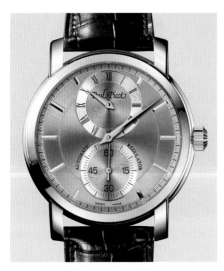

Firshire Megarotor Regulator

Reference number: P481.SG.1021
Movement: automatic, ETA Caliber 2892A2 with Dubois-Dépraz module; ø 25.6 mm, height 6 mm; 28 jewels; 28,800 vph; winding rotor with tungsten oscillating weight; 42-hour power reserve
Functions: hours (off-center), minutes, subsidiary seconds
Case: stainless steel, ø 42 mm, height 11 mm; sapphire crystal; transparent case back; water-resistant to 5 atm
Band: reptile skin, folding clasp
Price: $4,922
Variations: rose gold bezel ($8,055); rose gold ($19,578)

New Technicum Chronograph

Reference number: P3813.RG.8604
Movement: manually wound, Lemania Caliber 1872; ø 27 mm, height 6.9 mm; 18 jewels; 21,600 vph; 38-hour power reserve
Functions: hours, minutes, subsidiary seconds; chronograph
Case: rose gold, ø 42 mm, height 14 mm; sapphire crystal; transparent case back; water-resistant to 5 atm
Band: reptile skin, buckle
Price: $21,144
Variations: stainless steel ($5,482)

Minoia Chronograph Limited Edition

Reference number: P2127.SG.1022.3201.MINOIA
Movement: automatic, ETA Caliber 7750; ø 30 mm, height 7.9 mm; 28,800 vph; 42-hour power reserve
Functions: hours, minutes, subsidiary seconds; chronograph
Case: stainless steel, ø 43 mm, height 15 mm; sapphire crystal; screw-in crown; water-resistant to 5 atm
Band: calf leather, folding clasp
Remarks: special edition commemorating 1st Mille Miglia in 1927
Price: $4,419

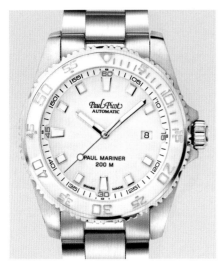

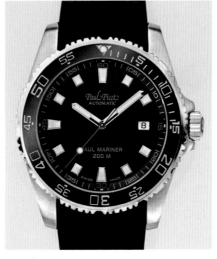

Paul Mariner

Reference number: P4352.SRG.CBL
Movement: automatic, ETA Caliber 2824; ø 25.6 mm, height 4.6 mm; 25 jewels; 28,800 vph; 42-hour power reserve
Functions: hours, minutes, sweep seconds; date
Case: stainless steel, ø 42 mm, height 14 mm; unidirectional rose gold bezel with 60-minute divisions, sapphire crystal; screw-in crown; water-resistant to 20 atm
Band: stainless steel, folding clasp
Price: $3,412
Variations: rubber band ($3,132)

Paul Mariner

Reference number: P4352.SRG.CNIC
Movement: automatic, ETA Caliber 2824; ø 25.6 mm, height 4.6 mm; 25 jewels; 28,800 vph; 42-hour power reserve
Functions: hours, minutes, sweep seconds; date
Case: stainless steel, ø 42 mm, height 14 mm; unidirectional rose gold bezel with 60-minute divisions, sapphire crystal; screw-in crown; water-resistant to 20 atm
Band: rubber, folding clasp
Price: $3,132
Variations: stainless steel bracelet ($3,412)

Atelier Tourbillon 42 mm

Reference number: P3389.WG
Movement: manually wound, TT Caliber 791; ø 30.4 mm, height 4.85 mm; 27 jewels; 28,800 vph; 1-minute tourbillon; 2 spring barrels; 120-hour power reserve
Functions: hours, minutes, subsidiary seconds (on tourbillon cage); power reserve indicator; date (retrograde)
Case: white gold, ø 42 mm, height 14 mm; sapphire crystal; transparent back; water-resistant to 5 atm
Band: reptile skin, folding clasp
Price: $154,383
Variations: rose gold ($147,671)

Perrelet SA

Rue Bubenberg 7
CH-2502 Biel/Bienne
Switzerland

Tel.:
01141-32-346-2626

Fax:
01141-32-346-2647

E-Mail:
perrelet@perrelet.com

Website:
www.perrelet.com

Founded:
1995

Number of employees:
12

U.S. distributor:
H5 Group Corp.
3230 West Commercial Blvd., Suite 160
Fort Lauderdale, FL 33309

Most important collections:
Turbine, Turbine XL, Turbine XS, Turbine
Chrono, Classic Double Rotor, First Class

Perrelet

The Perrelet story will sound familiar to anyone who has read about Swiss watchmaking: Abraham-Louis Perrelet (1729–1826) was the son of a middle-class farmer from Le Locle who developed an interest in watchmaking early on in life. He was the first watchmaker in Le Locle to work on cylinder and duplex escapements, and there is a persistent rumor that he was responsible for a repeater that could be heard echoing in the mountains.

Many watchmakers later to become famous were at one time Perrelet's apprentices, and some historians even suggest that Abraham-Louis Breguet was in this illustrious group. Suffice to say, Perrelet invented a great deal, including the "perpetual" watch from around 1770, a pocket watch that wound itself utilizing the motion of the wearer.

The brand has kept up with the times, combining modern design with solid technique. One of its outstanding models is the Turbine, which includes an element of wit and has made quite a splash, in particular in the U.S. market. The "turbo" appearance of the Turbine is achieved using Perrelet's own double rotor caliber, the P-331 (which is still something of a mystery to the watch world), which also powers the Diamond Flower and Double Rotor models. For a while, it looked as if Perrelet were going to branch out into more traditional watches. But the times demand adherence to DNA. Of late, the designers have even been getting bolder with a 48 mm pilot's watch and an attractive watch for sailors.

Turbillon

Reference number: A3037/1
Movement: automatic, P-371 in-house caliber;
ø 31.6 mm, height 3.85 mm; 25 jewels;
28,800 vph; 40-hour power reserve; exclusive patented Perrelet oscillating weight; 2nd sapphire crystal Perrelet rotor acts as "turbine" on dial side
Functions: hours, minutes, seconds on tourbillon carriage
Case: stainless steel with DLC coating, ø 46 mm, height 13.4 mm; rose gold bezel and back; sapphire crystal; water-resistant to 5 atm
Band: rubber, buckle
Price: $78,000

Turbine Yacht

Reference number: A1089/1
Movement: automatic, P-331 in-house caliber;
ø 31.6 mm, height 3.85 mm; 25 jewels;
28,800 vph; 42-hour power reserve; exclusive patented Perrelet double rotor; 2nd black titanium rotor acts as "turbine" on dial side
Functions: hours, minutes, sweep seconds
Case: stainless steel with bronze PVD coating, ø 47 mm, height 15.45 mm; crown activated rotating wind rose ring; sapphire crystal; transparent case back; water-resistant to 30 atm
Band: blue rubber, buckle
Price: $7,200
Variations: case with black PVD coating

Turbine Pilote

Reference number: A1085/1
Movement: automatic, P-331 in-house caliber;
ø 31.6 mm, height 3.85 mm; 25 jewels;
28,800 vph; 42-hour power reserve; exclusive patented Perrelet double rotor; 2nd black titanium rotor acts as "turbine" on dial side, with yellow stripes under dial
Functions: hours, minutes, sweep seconds; bidirectional rotating dial ring; aviation slide rule
Case: stainless steel, ø 48 mm, height 13.65 mm; sapphire crystal; screwed-down sapphire crystal case back; water-resistant to 5 atm
Band: rubber, buckle
Price: $6,550

Turbine Chrono

Reference number: A1074/2
Movement: automatic, Perrelet Caliber P-361;
28,800 vph; 42-hour power reserve
Functions: hours, minutes; sweep chronograph
hand, 60-minute counter on central sapphire disk;
date
Case: stainless steel with DLC coating, ø 47 mm,
height 16 mm; bezel with tachymeter scale; sapphire
crystal; screwed-down sapphire crystal case back;
water-resistant to 5 atm
Band: rubber, buckle
Price: $7,950

Turbine Black & Gold

Reference number: A8080/1
Movement: automatic, Perrelet Caliber P-331;
28,800 vph; 40-hour power reserve; exclusive
patented Perrelet double rotor; 2nd Perrelet rotor
acts as "turbine" on dial side
Functions: hours, minutes, sweep seconds
Case: pink gold, steel bezel and back with DLC
coating, ø 44 mm, height 13.88 mm; sapphire
crystal; antireflective sapphire crystal; transparent
case back; water-resistant to 5 atm
Band: reptile skin, DLC-treated folding clasp
Remarks: 12 black turbine blades produce flashing
by rotating over gold subdial
Price: $19,250; limited to 77 pieces

First Class Lady Open Heart

Reference number: A2067/1
Movement: automatic, Perrelet Caliber P-391;
25 jewels; 28,800 vph; 42-hour power reserve
Functions: hours, minutes, sweep seconds
Case: stainless steel, ø 35 mm, height 10 mm;
sapphire crystal; transparent case back; water-
resistant to 5 atm
Band: reptile skin, folding clasp
Remarks: dial with opening onto movement
Price: $2,700

New Diamond Flower

Reference number: A 3032/C
Movement: automatic, Perrelet Caliber P-181
(ETA 2892 with Perrelet module); ø 31.6 mm, height
4.75 mm; 21 jewels; 28,800 vph; 42-hour power
reserve
Functions: hours, minutes, sweep seconds
Case: rose gold, with stainless steel bezel and case
back; ø 36.5 mm; sapphire crystal; transparent case
back; water-resistant to 5 atm
Band: reptile skin, folding clasp
Remarks: dial set with 24 diamonds
Price: $17,500

Turbine Squelette

Reference number: A1082/1
Movement: automatic, Perrelet Caliber P-381;
25 jewels; 28,800 vph; 42-hour power reserve;
decorated Perrelet rotor; exclusive patented Perrelet
double rotor; 2nd silver rotor in dial center
Functions: hours, minutes, sweep seconds
Case: stainless steel/steel bezel and back with
PVD coating, ø 44 mm, height 13.3 mm; sapphire
crystal; sapphire crystal case back; water-resistant
to 5 atm
Band: rubber, pin buckle
Price: $7,250

Classic Double Rotor

Reference number: A1006/11
Movement: automatic, Perrelet Caliber P-181;
ø 31.6 mm, height 4.75 mm; 21 jewels; 28,800 vph;
42-hour power reserve; open-worked dial; Perrelet
exclusive double rotor, 2nd rotor on dial side
Functions: hours, minutes, sweep seconds; date
Case: stainless steel, ø 40 mm, height 10.9 mm;
sapphire crystal; transparent case back; water-
resistant to 5 atm
Band: reptile skin, stainless steel buckle
Remarks: black dial with gold-plated markers
Price: $4,300

Speake-Marin
Chemin en-Baffa 2
CH-1183 Bursins
Switzerland

Tel.:
01141-21-825-5069

E-Mail:
info@speake-marin.com

Website:
www.speake-marin.com

Founded:
2002

Number of employees:
5

Annual production:
500 watches

U.S. distributor:
Martin Pulli, Inc.
4337 Main Street
Philadelphia, PA 19127
215-508-4610
martinpulli@aol.com
www.martinpulli.com

Most important collections:
HMS, Spirit Mark 2, Triad, Resilience, Serpent
Calendar, Renaissance, Marin-1, Marin-2

Peter Speake-Marin

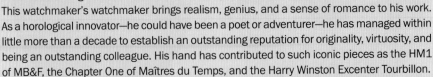

"*Genius* does what it must, and *talent* does what it can," said statesman Edward Bulwer-Lytton. The quote comes to mind when considering the life and career of Peter Speake-Marin. This watchmaker's watchmaker brings realism, genius, and a sense of romance to his work. As a horological innovator—he could have been a poet or adventurer—he has managed within little more than a decade to establish an outstanding reputation for originality, virtuosity, and being an outstanding colleague. His hand has contributed to such iconic pieces as the HM1 of MB&F, the Chapter One of Maîtres du Temps, and the Harry Winston Excenter Tourbillon.

Born in Essex in 1968, Speake-Marin attended Hackney College, London, and WOSTEP in Switzerland, before earning his first spurs restoring antique watches at a Somlo in Piccadilly. In 1996, he moved to Le Locle, Switzerland, to work with Renaud et Papi, at which point he set about making his own pieces. A dual-train tourbillon (the Foundation Watch) opened the door to the prestigious AHCI.

Speake-Marin has never stopped reflecting on, creating, recreating, and questioning his pieces. His first independent product, the Piccadilly, features a cylinder case with a narrow bezel and a frank dial. The Serpent Calendar saw a twisted sweep date hand in blued metal, a modern "surprise" perfectly in tune with the essentially eighteenth-century marine look of the pieces. The Spirit Mark 2 paid homage to the hardiness of his fellow watchmakers and bears the inscription "Fight, Love & Persevere."

The recession taught him something crucial: "I was a watchmaker, not an entrepreneur," he shares. "I had to become entrepreneurial to become a watchmaker again." And so he reorganized himself as a brand with three watch families: the Spirit, with a military, adventurous feel; the J-Class recalling the discreet elegance of J-Class yachts; and for his flashes of creative madness, the grab-bag Cabinet des Mystères.

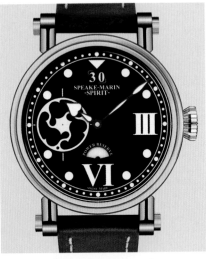

Spirit Wing Commander

Reference number: PIC.20002
Movement: automatic, Caliber 1024 S SPM; ø 30.4 mm, height 7.9 mm; 25 jewels; 28,800 vph; 48-hour power reserve
Functions: hours, minutes, "topping tool" seconds; power reserve indicator; large date
Case: stainless steel, ø 42 mm, height 12 mm; sapphire crystal; water-resistant to 3 atm
Band: calf leather, buckle
Price: $8,800

Spirit Seafire

Reference number: PIC.20003
Movement: automatic, Caliber C99001-D; ø 30.4 mm, height 7.9 mm; 25 jewels; 28,800 vph; 48-hour power reserve
Functions: hours, minutes, "topping tool" seconds; chronograph; date
Case: stainless steel, ø 42 mm, height 14 mm; sapphire crystal, water-resistant to 3 atm
Band: calf leather, buckle
Price: $9,300

Serpent Calendar

Reference number: PIC.10006
Movement: automatic, Caliber Eros; ø 30 mm, height 4.25 mm; 35 jewels; 28,800 vph; 2 spring barrels; 120-hour power reserve
Functions: hours, minutes, sweep seconds, "topping tool" seconds; date
Case: stainless steel, ø 42 mm, height 12 mm; sapphire crystal; water-resistant to 3 atm
Band: reptile skin, buckle
Price: $11,700
Variations: rose gold ($28,200); 38 mm stainless steel ($11,400); 38 mm rose gold ($22,600)

Piaget SA
CH-1228 Plan-les-Ouates
Switzerland

E-Mail:
info@piaget.com

Website:
www.piaget.com

Founded:
1874

Number of employees:
900

Annual production:
watches not specified; plus about 20,000
movements for Richemont Group

U.S. distributor:
Piaget North America
645 5th Avenue, 6th Floor
New York, NY 10022
212-909-4362; 212-909-4332 (fax)
www.piaget.com

Most important collections/price range:
Altiplano / approx. $13,500 to $22,000

Piaget

One of the oldest watch manufacturers in Switzerland, Piaget began making watch movements in the secluded Jura village of La Côte-aux-Fées in 1874. For decades, those movements were delivered to other watch brands. The *manufacture* itself, strangely enough, remained in the background. Until the middle of its fifth decade in business, Piaget provided movements to almost every renowned Swiss watchmaker. It wasn't until the 1940s that the Piaget family began to offer complete watches under their own name.

Even today, Piaget, which long ago moved the business side of things to Geneva, still makes its watch movements at its main facility high in the Jura mountains. Among its specialties in the 1960s were the ultra-thin calibers 9P and 12P (automatic), which were 2 mm and 2.3 mm thin, respectively. The production of movements for other brands has been largely discontinued. Only associated brands within the Richemont Group are supplied with special movements.

Because the brand came a little late in the day to the manufacturing of its own timepieces, it has often gotten less attention than it deserved. The brand's strategy to focus stubbornly on outstandingly thin movements has been working out, however. It lends these watches the kind of understated elegance that is the hallmark of the new post-recession times. Even high-tech watch fans have been impressed by the minute repeater on the new Emperador. And on the new 900P Altiplano, the caliber was inverted to enable repairs, and the case back is now used as a mainplate, thus removing an entire layer inside the watch. The Limelight's case, with the playfully dynamic single lug on each side, testifies to the creative acumen at Piaget. Besides, in the natural fashion cycle, the sixties are due for a revival.

Altiplano 38 mm 900P

Reference number: G0A39111
Movement: manually wound, Piaget Caliber 900P; ø 38 mm; 20 jewels; 21,600 vph; case back serves as mainplate; fine finishing; 48-hour power reserve; Geneva Seal
Functions: hours and minutes (off-center)
Case: white gold, ø 38 mm, height 3.65 mm; sapphire crystal; reptile skin, buckle
Band: reptile skin, buckle
Remarks: currently world's thinnest mechanical watch
Price: $27,800
Variations: with diamonds ($32,700)

Altiplano 38 mm 900P

Reference number: G0A39110
Movement: manually wound, Piaget Caliber 900P; ø 38 mm; 20 jewels; 21,600 vph; case back serves as mainplate; finely finishing; 48-hour power reserve; Geneva Seal
Functions: hours and minutes (off-center)
Case: rose gold, ø 38 mm, height 3.65 mm; sapphire crystal
Band: reptile skin, buckle
Remarks: currently world's thinnest mechanical watch
Price: $26,200
Variations: white gold with diamonds ($32,700)

Altiplano

Reference number: G0A35130
Movement: automatic, Piaget Caliber 1208P; ø 29.9 mm, height 2.35 mm; 27 jewels; 21,600 vph; rose gold microrotor; côtes de Genève; 42-hour power reserve
Functions: hours, minutes, subsidiary seconds
Case: white gold, ø 43 mm, height 5.25 mm; sapphire crystal; transparent case back
Band: reptile skin, folding clasp
Price: $24,000
Variations: rose gold ($23,000)

Altiplano Date

Reference number: G0A38131
Movement: automatic, Piaget Caliber 1205P; ø 29.9 mm, height 3 mm; 27 jewels; 21,600 vph; rose gold microrotor; côtes de Genève; 44-hour power reserve
Functions: hours, minutes, subsidiary seconds; date
Case: rose gold, ø 40 mm, height 6.36 mm; sapphire crystal; transparent case back
Band: reptile skin, buckle
Price: $25,000
Variations: white gold ($26,000)

Altiplano Skeleton

Movement: automatic, Piaget Caliber 1200S; ø 31.9 mm, height 2.4 mm; 26 jewels; 21,600 vph; black platinum microrotor; fully skeletonized; 44-hour power reserve; Geneva Seal
Functions: hours, minutes
Case: rose gold, ø 38 mm, height 5.34 mm; sapphire crystal; transparent case back; water-resistant to 3 atm
Band: reptile skin, buckle
Price: $60,000
Variations: white gold

Altiplano

Reference number: G0A34114
Movement: manually wound, Piaget Caliber 838P; ø 26.8 mm, height 2.5 mm; 19 jewels; 21,600 vph; 60-hour power reserve; Geneva Seal
Functions: hours, minutes, subsidiary seconds
Case: white gold, ø 40 mm, height 6.6 mm; sapphire crystal; transparent case back; water-resistant to 3 atm
Band: reptile skin, buckle
Price: $20,000
Variations: rose gold ($19,000); white or rose gold set with diamonds (on request)

Emperador Coussin Minutenrepetition XL

Reference number: G0A38019
Movement: automatic, Piaget Caliber 1290P; 34.9 x 34.9 mm, height 4.8 mm; 44 jewels; 21,600 vph; partially skeletonized, platinum microrotor; 40-hour power reserve; Geneva Seal
Functions: hours, minutes; minute repeater
Case: rose gold, ø 48 mm, height 9.4 mm; sapphire crystal; transparent back; water-resistant to 3 atm
Band: reptile skin, folding clasp
Remarks: currently world's thinnest automatic movement
Price: on request

Emperador Coussin XL Tourbillon

Reference number: G0A36041
Movement: automatic, Piaget Caliber 1270P; ø 34.9 mm, height 5.5 mm; 35 jewels; 21,600 vph; flying 1-minute tourbillon; dial-side white gold microrotor; 42-hour power reserve; Geneva Seal
Functions: hours and minutes (off-center), subsidiary seconds (on tourbillon cage); power reserve indicator on case back
Case: white gold, ø 46.5 mm, height 10.4 mm; sapphire crystal; water-resistant to 3 atm
Band: reptile skin, folding clasp
Price: on request
Variations: rose gold

Emperador Coussin XL Perpetual Calendar

Reference number: G0A33019
Movement: automatic, Piaget Caliber 855P; ø 28.4 mm, height 5.6 mm; 38 jewels; 21,600 vph
Functions: hours, minutes, subsidiary seconds; additional 12-hour display (2nd time zone), day/night indication; perpetual calendar with retrograde date and weekday, month, leap year
Case: pink gold, ø 46.5 mm, height 10.4 mm; sapphire crystal; transparent case back; water-resistant to 3 atm
Band: reptile skin, folding clasp
Price: $86,000
Variations: set with diamonds (on request)

Gouverneur

Reference number: GOA37110
Movement: automatic, Piaget Caliber 800P;
ø 26.8 mm, height 4 mm; 25 jewels; 21,600 vph;
twin spring barrels; 85-hour power reserve; Geneva
Seal
Functions: hours, minutes, sweep seconds; date
Case: rose gold, ø 43 mm, height 9 mm; sapphire
crystal; transparent case back; water-resistant to
3 atm
Band: reptile skin, buckle
Price: $26,000
Variations: white gold with diamonds ($45,000)

Gouverneur Chronograph

Reference number: GOA38112
Movement: automatic, Piaget Caliber 882P;
ø 27 mm, height 5.6 mm; 33 jewels; 28,800 vph;
50-hour power reserve; Geneva Seal
Functions: hours, minutes; flyback chronograph;
date
Case: white gold, ø 43 mm, height 10.4 mm;
sapphire crystal; transparent case back; water-
resistant to 3 atm
Band: reptile skin, folding clasp
Price: $37,000
Variations: pink gold ($36,000)

Gouverneur Moonphase Tourbillon

Reference number: GOA37114
Movement: manually wound, Piaget Caliber 642P;
22.4 x 28.6 mm, height 4 mm; 21,600 vph; flying
1-minute tourbillon; 40-hour power reserve; Geneva
Seal
Functions: hours, minutes, small seconds (on
tourbillon cage); moon phase
Case: rose gold, ø 43 mm, height 9.2 mm; sapphire
crystal; transparent case back; water-resistant to
3 atm
Band: reptile skin, folding clasp
Price: on request
Variations: white gold (price on request)

Altiplano 34 mm

Reference number: GOA39105
Movement: manually wound, Piaget Caliber 450P;
ø 20.5 mm, height 2.1 mm; 18 jewels; 21,600 vph;
40-hour power reserve
Functions: hours, minutes, subsidiary seconds
Case: rose gold, ø 34 mm, height 6.3 mm; sapphire
crystal; transparent case back; water-resistant to
3 atm
Band: reptile skin, buckle
Price: $15,300
Variations: white gold with diamonds ($28,000)

Limelight Gala

Reference number: GOA38160
Movement: quartz, Piaget Caliber 690P
Functions: hours, minutes
Case: white gold, ø 32 mm, height 7.4 mm; bezel set
with 62 diamonds, sapphire crystal; water-resistant
to 3 atm
Band: satin, buckle (set with diamonds)
Price: $35,000
Variations: pink gold ($34,000)

Limelight Tonneau

Reference number: GOA39197
Movement: manually wound, Piaget Caliber
438P20; 3 x 23.7 mm, height 2.1 mm; 19 jewels;
21,600 vph
Functions: hours, minutes
Case: pink gold, 27 x 38 mm, height 7.5 mm;
sapphire crystal; transparent case back; water-
resistant to 3 atm
Band: satin, buckle
Remarks: case set with 86 brilliants
Price: $37,600

Caliber 1270P

Automatic; flying 1-minute tourbillon with titanium cage; platinum microrotor visible through dial; single spring barrel; 44-hour power reserve; Geneva Seal
Functions: hours, minutes, subsidiary seconds (on tourbillon cage at "1")
Measurements: 34.9 x 34.9 mm
Height: 5.5 mm
Jewels: 35
Balance: glucydur
Frequency: 21,600 vph

Caliber 1208P

Automatic; 42-hour power reserve
Functions: hours, minutes, subsidiary seconds
Diameter: 29.9 mm
Height: 2.35 mm
Jewels: 27
Balance: glucydur
Frequency: 21,600 vph
Balance spring: flat hairspring
Shock protection: Incabloc
Remarks: world's thinnest automatic movement currently produced

Caliber 838P

Manually wound; stop-seconds; Geneva Seal; 62-hour power reserve
Functions: hours, minutes, subsidiary seconds
Diameter: 26.8 mm
Height: 2.7 mm
Jewels: 19
Balance: glucydur with weighted screws
Frequency: 21,600 vph
Balance spring: flat hairspring with fine adjustment over regulator
Shock protection: Incabloc

Caliber 882P

Automatic; stop-seconds, full gold rotor; single spring barrel, 50-hour power reserve; Geneva Seal
Functions: hours, minutes, subsidiary seconds; second time zone (additional 24-hour display); flyback chronograph; date
Diameter: 27 mm
Height: 5.6 mm
Jewels: 33
Balance: glucydur with weighted screws
Frequency: 21,600 vph
Balance spring: flat hairspring with fine adjustment regulator
Shock protection: Kif

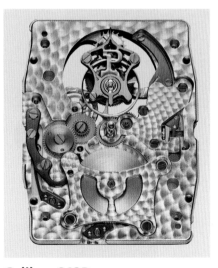

Caliber 642P

Manually wound; flying 1-minute tourbillon with titanium cage; platinum microrotor visible on dial; single spring barrel; 40-hour power reserve; Geneva Seal
Functions: hours, minutes, subsidiary seconds (on tourbillon cage); moon phase
Measurements: 22.4 x 28.6 mm
Height: 4 mm
Jewels: 23
Balance: glucydur
Frequency: 21,600 vph

Caliber 1200S

Automatic; platinum microrotor; single spring barrel; 44-hour power reserve; Geneva Seal
Functions: hours, minutes
Diameter: 31.9 mm
Height: 2.4 mm
Jewels: 26
Balance: glucydur
Frequency: 21,600 vph
Balance spring: flat hairspring
Remarks: fully skeletonized movement

Porsche Design

Porsche Design Group
Groenerstrasse 5
D-71636 Ludwigsburg
Germany

Tel.:
01149-711-911-0

E-Mail:
contact@porsche-design.com

Website:
www.porsche-design.com/timepieces

Founded:
1972

U.S. distributor:
Chartpak, Inc.
19683 Boca Greens Drive
Boca Raton, FL 33498
561-470-6925
www.porsche-design.com

Most important collections:
Heritage Series, Performance Series, Flat Six
Series

The Schaffhausen-based brand IWC produced watches under the name Porsche Design through a license agreement with the F.A. Porsche design firm starting in 1976. But when the Porsche family purchased Eterna in 1995, a new era began—for both brands. When the IWC license expired in 1998, Eterna took over manufacturing responsibilities for the designer brand.

Although Porsche Design has benefitted from Eterna's manufacturing expertise, the traditional Swiss watch brand also receives very welcome support when developing its own new models from the design office founded by Professor Ferdinand Alexander Porsche in 1972—the fountainhead of numerous objects in daily use beyond just watches. The Professor—a title bestowed by the Austrian government—who died in April 2012, created a string of classic objects at his "Studio," but sports car fans will always remember him for the Porsche 911.The brand is proud not only of its unusual designs, but also of its use of light metals: It was the first to apply titanium in watch cases, for instance. And it also constructed a watch with an integrated compass.

Eterna and Porsche Design were sold to the Chinese company International Volant Ltd., a 100-percent subsidiary of China Haidian. This concern operates two of the largest watch companies in the People's Republic as well as a chain of stores. It also has import rights for various Japanese watch brands. But in March 2014, Porsche Design Group, headquartered in Bietigheim-Bissingen, officially announced it would be going its separate way and repositioning the brand. It intends to continue producing luxury timepieces, but equipped with the company's own technology. In the meantime, Eterna will continue to service Porsche Design watches.

P'6510 Heritage Black Chronograph 1972

Reference number: 6510.43.41.0272
Movement: automatic, ETA Caliber 7750; ø 30 mm, height 7.9 mm; 25 jewels; 28,800 vph; personalized rotor; 48-hour power reserve
Functions: hours, minutes, subsidiary seconds; chronograph; date, weekday
Case: stainless steel with black PVD coating, ø 44 mm, height 14.25 mm; sapphire crystal; screw-in crown
Band: stainless steel with black PVD coating, folding clasp
Remarks: limited to 911 pieces
Price: $5,850

P'6520 Compass Watch 1978

Reference number: 6520.13.41.0270
Movement: automatic, Sellita Caliber SW 300; ø 25.6 mm, height 3.6 mm; 25 jewels; 28,800 vph; 42-hour power reserve
Functions: hours, minutes, sweep seconds; compass; date
Case: titanium with black PVD coating, ø 42 mm, height 14.6 mm; sapphire crystal; water-resistant to 5 atm
Band: titanium, black PVD coating, folding clasp
Remarks: compass in lower section, back with mirror
Price: $6,500; limited to 911 pieces

P'6530 Titanium Chronograph 1980

Reference number: 6530.11.41.1219
Movement: automatic, ETA Caliber 7750; ø 30 mm, height 7.9 mm; 25 jewels; 28,800 vph; personalized rotor; 48-hour power reserve; COSC-certified chronometer
Functions: hours, minutes, subsidiary seconds; chronograph; date, weekday
Case: titanium, ø 44 mm, height 14.3 mm; sapphire crystal; water-resistant to 6 atm
Band: titanium, folding clasp
Remarks: limited to 911 pieces
Price: $5,850

P'6750 Worldtimer

Reference number: 6750.13.44.1180
Movement: automatic, Eterna Caliber 6037;
ø 36.6 mm, height 10.23 mm; 59 jewels; 28,800
vph; 48-hour power reserve
Functions: hours, minutes, sweep seconds; world-
time display (digital)
Case: titanium with black PVD coating, ø 45 mm,
height 16.8 mm; sapphire crystal; screw-in crown;
second crown with integrated pusher; water-
resistant to 10 atm
Band: rubber, folding clasp
Price: $175,000
Variations: titanium w/o PVD coating ($175,000)

P'6780 Diver

Reference number: 6780.44.53.1218
Movement: automatic, ETA Caliber 2892-A2;
ø 25.6 mm, height 3.6 mm; 25 jewels; 28,800 vph;
personalized rotor; 42-hour power reserve
Functions: hours, minutes, sweep seconds; date
Case: stainless steel, titanium, stainless steel
movement container in titanium frame, opened
activating lateral buttons; ø 46.8 mm, height 17.05
mm; crown-adjustable inner bezel with 60-minute
divisions, sapphire crystal; water-resistant to 100 atm
Band: stainless steel, folding clasp with extension link
Price: $9,800
Variations: stainless steel and titanium with PVD
coating ($10,500)

P'6910 The Indicator

Reference number: 6910.12.41.1149
Movement: automatic, Eterna Caliber 6036;
ø 36 mm, height 11.81 mm; 101 jewels; 28,800
vph; digital chronograph display; 4 spring barrels;
46-hour power reserve
Functions: hours, minutes, subsidiary seconds;
power reserve display with 2 concentric circles;
chronograph
Case: titanium with black PVD coating, ø 49 mm,
height 19.9 mm; bezel affixed with 4 special screws;
sapphire crystal; water-resistant to 5 atm
Band: rubber, buckle
Price: $175,000
Variations: titanium w/o PVD coating ($,175,000)

P'6620 Dashboard

Reference number: 6620.11.46.0268
Movement: automatic, ETA Caliber 7753;
ø 30.4 mm, height 7.9 mm; 25 jewels; 28,800 vph;
personalized rotor; 48-hour power reserve
Functions: hours, minutes, subsidiary seconds;
chronograph; date
Case: titanium, ø 44 mm, height 14.5 mm; sapphire
crystal; transparent case back; screw-in crown;
water-resistant to 10 atm
Band: titanium, folding clasp
Price: $5,600
Variations: various bands and dials (from $5,200)

P'6360 Flat Six Automatic Chronograph

Reference number: 6360.43.04.0275
Movement: automatic, ETA Caliber 7750; ø 30 mm,
height 7.9 mm; 25 jewels; 28,800 vph; personalized
rotor
Functions: hours, minutes, subsidiary seconds;
chronograph; date, weekday
Case: stainless steel with black PVD coating, ø 44
mm, height 15 mm; sapphire crystal; transparent
case back; screw-in crown; water-resistant to 10 atm
Band: stainless steel with black PVD coating, folding
clasp
Price: $5,200
Variations: various dials and bands ($4,550)

P'6351 Flat Six Automatic

Reference number: 6351.47.64.1256
Movement: automatic, Sellita Caliber SW 200;
ø 25.6 mm, height 4.6 mm; 26 jewels; 28,800 vph;
38-hour power reserve
Functions: hours, minutes, sweep seconds; date
Case: stainless steel, ø 40 mm, height 11.25 mm;
rose gold bezel, sapphire crystal; transparent case
back ; screw-in crown with rose gold coating
Band: rubber, buckle
Price: $9,100
Variations: various bands and dials (from $2,950);
44 mm case (from $2,950)

Rado Uhren AG

Bielstrasse 45
CH-2543 Lengnau
Switzerland

Tel.:
01141-32-655-6111

Fax:
01141-32-655-6112

E-Mail:
info@rado.com

Website:
www.rado.com

Founded:
1957

Number of employees:
approx. 470

U.S. distributor:
Rado
The Swatch Group (U.S.), Inc.
1200 Harbor Boulevard
Weehawken, NJ 07086
201-271-1400

Most important collections/price range:
Centrix / from approx. $900; Diamaster / from approx. $1,350; D-Star / from approx. $1,700; Integral / from approx. $2,000; Sintra / from approx. $3,000; True / from approx. $1,400; Hyperchrome / from approx $1,600

Rado

Rado is a relatively young brand, especially for a Swiss one. The company, which grew out of the Schlup clockwork factory, launched its first watches in 1957, but it achieved international fame only five years later, in 1962, when it surprised the world with a revolutionary invention. Rado's oval DiaStar was the first truly scratch-resistant watch ever, sporting a case made of the impervious alloy hardmetal. In 1985, its parent company, the Swatch Group, decided to put Rado's know-how and extensive experience in developing materials to good use, and from then on the brand intensified its research activities at its home in Lengnau, Switzerland, and continued to produce only watches with extremely hard cases. A record of sorts was even set in 2004, when they managed to create a 10,000-Vickers material, which is as hard as natural diamonds.

Within the Swatch Group, Rado was the most successful individual brand in the upper price segment for a long time. But at some point, the brand's image became a little blurred, and it began suffering from the almost unbridgeable gap that had suddenly opened up between its jeweled watches and high-tech line. However, the pioneering spirit of the brand's ceramic researchers and engineers has won out. The company already holds more than thirty patents arising from research and production of new case materials. Nowadays, the cases begin as powders, already premixed with binding agents and additives to later achieve the desired color. They are then pressed into molds and fired. The final touch is polishing with diamond powder to make the outside of Rado timepieces even more robust and scratchproof. And the techno inside is reflected in an unabashed techno look outside.

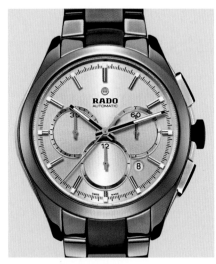

HyperChrome Automatic Chronograph

Reference number: R32276112
Movement: automatic, ETA Caliber 2894-2; ø 28.6 mm, height 6.2 mm; 37 jewels; 28,800 vph; finely decorated; 42-hour power reserve
Functions: hours, minutes, subsidiary seconds; chronograph; date
Case: ceramic, 45 x 51 mm, height 13 mm; sapphire crystal, transparent case back; water-resistant to 10 atm
Band: ceramic, double folding clasp
Price: $4,400

HyperChrome Small Second

Reference number: R32025115
Movement: automatic, ETA Caliber 2895-2; ø 25.6 mm, height 4.35 mm; 27 jewels; 28,800 vph; 42-hour power reserve
Functions: hours, minutes, subsidiary seconds; date
Case: ceramic, 42 x 48.4 mm, height 10.8 mm; sapphire crystal; transparent case back; water-resistant to 10 atm
Band: calf leather, folding clasp
Price: $3,200

HyperChrome UTC

Reference number: R32165102
Movement: automatic, ETA 2893-2; ø 25.6 mm, height 4.1 mm; 21 jewels; 28,800 vph; finely decorated; 42-hour power reserve
Functions: hours, minutes, sweep seconds; additional 24-hour display (2nd time zone); date
Case: ceramic, 42 x 48.4 mm, height 10.8 mm; sapphire crystal, transparent case back; water-resistant to 10 atm
Band: ceramic, double folding clasp
Price: $3,500

HyperChrome Touch Dual Timer

Reference number: R32114152
Movement: quartz, ETA Caliber F11.001; case touch setting of hands and changing time zones
Functions: hours, minutes; additional 12-hour display (2nd time zone)
Case: ceramic, 42 x 48.3 mm, height 10.2 mm; sapphire crystal, water-resistant to 5 atm
Band: ceramic, double folding clasp
Price: $2,800

HyperChrome Automatic

Reference number: R32109152
Movement: automatic, ETA Caliber 2824-2; ø 25.6 mm, height 4.6 mm; 25 jewels; 28,800 vph; finely decorated; 38-hour power reserve
Functions: hours, minutes, sweep seconds; date
Case: stainless steel, 38.7 x 47.5 mm, height 11.3 mm; ceramic bezel; sapphire crystal; water-resistant to 5 atm
Band: stainless steel with ceramic parts, double folding clasp, titanium
Price: $2,150

Diamaster Chronograph

Reference number: R14090192
Movement: automatic, ETA Caliber 2894-2; ø 28.6 mm, height 6.2 mm; 37 jewels; 28,800 vph; finely decorated; 42-hour power reserve
Functions: hours, minutes, subsidiary seconds; chronograph; date
Case: ceramic, ø 45 mm, height 12.6 mm; sapphire crystal; transparent case back; water-resistant to 10 atm
Band: ceramic, double folding clasp, titanium
Price: $4,700

Diamaster Automatic

Reference number: R14074106
Movement: automatic, ETA Caliber 2892-2; ø 25.6 mm, height 3.6 mm; 21 jewels; 28,800 vph; 42-hour power reserve
Functions: hours, minutes, sweep seconds; date
Case: ceramic, ø 41 mm, height 9.9 mm; sapphire crystal; transparent case back; water-resistant to 10 atm
Band: calf leather, double folding clasp, titanium
Price: $2,500

Centrix Automatic

Reference number: R30939132
Movement: automatic, ETA Caliber 2824-2; ø 25.6 mm, height 4.6 mm; 25 jewels; 28,800 vph; 38-hour power reserve
Functions: hours, minutes, sweep seconds; date
Case: stainless steel, ø 38 mm, height 9.7 mm; sapphire crystal; transparent case back; water-resistant to 3 atm
Band: ceramic with stainless steel parts, double folding clasp, titanium
Price: $1,700

D-Star Automatic Chronograph

Reference number: R15556155
Movement: automatic, ETA Caliber 7750; ø 30 mm, height 7.9 mm; 25 jewels; 28,800 vph; 48-hour power reserve
Functions: hours, minutes, subsidiary seconds; chronograph; date
Case: ceramic, 44 x 48.2 mm, height 14.5 mm; sapphire crystal; transparent case back; water-resistant to 10 atm
Band: calf leather, double folding clasp, titanium
Remarks: limited to 1,962 pieces
Price: $3,295

RGM Watch Company
801 W. Main Street
Mount Joy, PA 17552

Tel.:
717-653-9799

Fax:
717-653-9770

E-Mail:
RGMdesigns@aol.com

Website:
www.rgmwatches.com

Founded:
1992

Number of employees:
12

Annual production:
200–300 watches

Distribution:
RGM deals directly with customers.

Most important collections/price range:
Pennsylvania Series (completely made in the U.S.) / $2,500 to $125,000 range

RGM

If there is any part of the United States that can somehow be considered its "watch valley," it may be the state of Pennsylvania. And one of the big players there is no doubt Roland Murphy, founder of RGM. Murphy, born in Maryland, went through the watchmaker's drill, studying at the Bowman Technical School, then in Switzerland, and finally working with Swatch before launching his own business in 1992.

His first series, Signature, paid homage to local horological genius. It was powered by vintage pocket watch movements developed by Hamilton, a company that also hails from PA. His second big project was the Caliber 801, the first "high-grade mechanical movement made in series in America since Hamilton stopped production of the 992 B in 1969," Murphy grins. The next goal was to manufacture an all-American-made watch, which turned out to be the Pennsylvania Tourbillon.

And so, model by model, Murphy continues to expand his "Made in U.S.A." portfolio. In 2012, the twentieth anniversary of the brand, RGM went retro with the 801 Aircraft. The current pinnacle is the brand-new Caliber "20," which revives an old invention once in favor for railroad watches. The motor barrel is a complex but robust system in which the watch is wound by the barrel and the barrel arbor then drives the gear train. Less friction and wear and a slimmer chance of damage to the watch if the mainspring breaks are the two main advantages. And for the real engineering enthusiasts, it is a movement with a unique look, now in a proud tonneau case with a few complications to boot, like a moon phase and a seconds display on a disc recessed into an aperture in the dial.

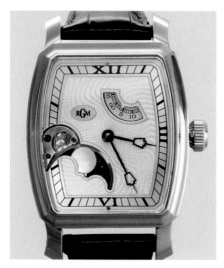

Caliber 20

Reference number: Caliber 20
Movement: manually wound, RGM motor barrel movement; 34.4 x 30.4 mm; 19 jewels; 18,000 vph; perlage and côtes de Genève; 42-hour power reserve
Functions: hours, minutes, subsidiary seconds on disk; moon phase
Case: stainless steel, 42 x 38.5 mm, height 9.7 mm; hands of blued steel; sapphire crystal; transparent case back
Band: reptile skin, buckle
Price: $27,500
Variations: rose gold ($42,500)

Pennsylvania Tourbillon

Reference number: MM2
Movement: manual winding, American-made; ø 37.22; 19 jewels; 18,000 vph; German silver and rose gold finish with perlage and côtes de Genève; 42-hour power reserve
Functions: hours, minutes; 1-minute tourbillon
Case: stainless steel, ø 43.5 mm, height 13.5 mm; blued-steel minute and hour hands; guilloché dial; sapphire crystal; transparent case back
Band: reptile skin, buckle
Price: $95,000
Variations: rose gold ($125,000); platinum (price on request)

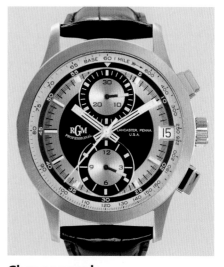

Chronograph

Reference number: 400
Movement: automatic, RGM-modified Valgranges; 25 jewels; 28,800 vph; 46-hour power reserve
Functions: hours, minutes; date; chronograph; 30-minute and 12-hour counters
Case: brushed and polished stainless steel, ø 42 mm, height 15.3 mm
Band: reptile skin, buckle
Remarks: rhodium markers and hands with Superluminova
Price: $3,500
Variations: various dials and hands; ostrich or carbon fiber band

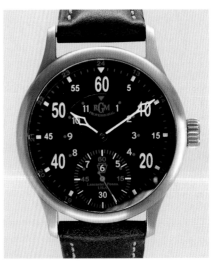

Professional Diver

Reference number: 300-3 Series 3
Movement: automatic, modified ETA Caliber 2892;
ø 25.6 mm, height 3.6 mm; 21 jewels; 28,800 vph;
bridges and plates with perlage and côtes de Genève;
42-hour power reserve
Functions: hours, minutes, sweep seconds; date
Case: brushed stainless steel, ø 43.5 mm, height 17 mm;
sapphire crystal (5 mm thick); unidirectional bezel with
60-minute divisions (240 clicks); screwed-down back;
screwed-in crown; water-resistant to more than 70 atm
Band: rubber strap, buckle
Remarks: comes with no date as well
Price: $3,700; limited to 75 pieces
Variations: stainless steel bracelet ($4,450)

Pennsylvania Series 801

Reference number: PS 801 ES
Movement: manually wound, RGM Caliber 801;
ø 37 mm; 19 jewels; lever escapement; screw balance;
U.S. components: bridges, main plate, settings, 7-tooth
winding click; circular côtes de Genève, silver guilloche;
partially skeletonized dial; 42-hour power reserve
Functions: hours, minutes, subsidiary seconds
Case: stainless steel, ø 43.3 mm, height 12.3 mm;
sapphire crystal; sapphire crystal transparent case
back; water-resistant to 5 atm
Band: reptile or ostrich skin, folding clasp
Price: $9,700
Variations: rose gold ($22,500); white gold ($24,500)

801 Aircraft

Reference number: 801 A_R
Movement: manually wound, RGM Caliber 801;
ø 37 mm; 19 jewels; lever escapement; screw balance;
U.S. components: bridges, main plate, settings, 7-tooth
winding click; circular côtes de Genève, silver guilloché;
partially skeletonized dial; 42-hour power reserve
Functions: hours, minutes, subsidiary seconds
Case: stainless steel, ø 42 mm, height 10.5 mm;
sapphire crystal; transparent case back; water-
resistant to 5 atm
Band: distressed leather, folding clasp
Price: $7,400
Variations: green or red dials; stainless steel bracelet
($7,950)

Vintage Chronograph

Reference number: 455
Movement: automatic, RGM/ETA Caliber 7750;
30 mm; 25 jewels; 28,800 vph; rhodium finish
with perlage and côtes de Genève; 46-hour power
reserve
Functions: hours, minutes, sweep seconds;
chronograph, 30-minute/12-hour timers
Case: polished stainless steel, ø 38.5 mm, height
13.9 mm; sapphire crystal
Band: calfskin, buckle
Remarks: features telemeter and tachymeter in blue
or black
Price: $3,900; limited to 100 pieces

Pilot Professional

Reference number: 151 P
Movement: automatic, RGM/ETA Caliber 2892-A2;
ø 25.6 mm; 21 jewels; 28,800 vph; rhodium finish
with perlage and côtes de Genève; 42-hour power
reserve
Functions: hours, minutes, sweep seconds; date
Case: brushed or polished stainless steel, ø 38.5
mm, height 9.9 mm; sapphire crystal; transparent
case back
Band: rubber or reptile skin, buckle
Remarks: date at 3, 6, or no date
Price: $2,850
Variations: brushed stainless steel ($2,850);
titanium ($3,950); stainless steel bracelet

Vintage

Reference number: 250 V
Movement: automatic, modified ETA Valgranges
Caliber A07.111; ø 36.6 mm, height 7.9 mm; 25
jewels; 28,800 vph; bridges and plates finished
with perlage and côtes de Genève; 46-hour power
reserve
Functions: hours, minutes, sweep seconds; date
Case: stainless steel, ø 42 mm, height 15 mm;
sapphire crystal; exhibition case back; water-
resistant to 5 atm
Remarks: brushed silver dial
Band: reptile skin, buckle
Price: $3,500; limited edition of 50 pieces
Variations: folding clasp; special request guilloché
patterns for custom dials available

Richard Mille

**Richard Mille Watches
c/o Horométrie SA**

11, rue du Jura
CH-2345 Les Breuleux
Switzerland

Tel.:
01141-32-959-4353

Fax:
01141-32-959-4354

E-Mail:
info@richardmille.ch

Website:
www.richardmille.com

Founded:
2000

Annual production:
over 2,600 watches

U.S. distributor:
Richard Mille Americas
132 South Rodeo Drive, 4th Floor
Beverly Hills, CA 90212
310-205-5555

Spain's hottest tennis star, Rafael Nadal, has been confident enough to wear a fully functional mechanical timepiece weighing less than 20 grams including the strap. That equals three quarters and a dime, but the watch, utilizing special materials, retails for over half a million dollars. It's a Richard Mille, of course. Now Jamaican sprinter Yohan Blake gets to put on a super-light, ultra-high-tech timepiece, one that will make no difference to his 9.69-second record sprint, in spite of featuring a tourbillon.

Mille never stops delivering the wow to the watch world with what he calls his "race cars for the wrist." His timepieces are usually built of exotic high-tech materials borrowed from automobile racing or even space travel. Mille is not an engineer by profession, but rather a marketing expert who earned his first paychecks in the watch division of the French defense, automobile, and aerospace concern Matra in the early 1980s. This was a time of fundamental changes in technology, and the European watch industry was being confronted with gigantic challenges.

"I have no historical relationship with watchmaking whatsoever," says Mille, "and so I have no obligations either. The mechanics of my watches are geared towards technical feasibility."

In the 1990s, Mille had to go to the expert workshop of Audemars Piguet Renaud & Papi (APRP) in Le Locle to find a group of watchmakers and engineers who would take on the Mille challenge. Audemars Piguet even succumbed to the temptation of testing those scandalous innovations—materials, technologies, functions—in a Richard Mille watch before daring to use them in its own collections (Tradition d'Excellence). Since 2007, Audemars Piguet has also become a shareholder in Richard Mille, and so the three firms are now closely bound. The assembly of the watches is done in the Franches-Montagnes region in the Jura, where Richard Mille opened the firm Horométrie.

RM 27-01 Nadal

Reference number: RM 27-01
Movement: manually wound, Caliber RM 27-0121; 27.2 x 21.72 mm, height mm; 19 jewels; 21,600 vph; 1-minute tourbillon; suspended in case on cable with pulleys, tensioners at 3 and 9; 45-hour power reserve
Functions: hours, minutes
Case: carbon fiber, 45.98 x 38.9 mm, height 10.05 mm; sapphire crystal; water-resistant to 3 atm
Band: textile, buckle
Remarks: monoblock case, weight including movement under 20 g
Price: $740,000

RM 35-01 Rafael Nadal

Reference number: RM 35-01
Movement: manually wound, Caliber RM RMUL3; 28.45 x 30.25 mm, height 3.15 mm; 24 jewels; 28,800 vph; skeletonized; titanium bridges and mainplate; 4 g weight; 2 spring barrels; 55-hour power reserve
Functions: hours, minutes, sweep seconds
Case: carbon fiber (NTPT multilayer carbon); 49.94 x 42 mm, height 14.05 mm; sapphire crystal; water-resistant to 3 atm
Band: rubber, buckle
Remarks: ultralight case material used for high-performance masts on sailboats
Price: $120,000

RM 36-01 Competition G-Force

Reference number: RM 36-01
Movement: manually wound, Caliber RM36-01; ø 36.6 mm, height 3.96 mm; 37 jewels; 21,600 vph; 1-minute tourbillon; affixed module (ø 17 mm, height 10 mm) for rotation accelerometer (G-sensor), consisting of 50 components; 70-hour power reserve
Functions: hours, minutes; power reserve display; acceleration sensor
Case: titanium, ø 47.7 mm, height 17.4 mm; bidirectional carbon nanofiber bezel for G-force; sapphire crystal; transparent case back; water-resistant to 5 atm
Remarks: Sébastien Loeb edition
Price: $625,000; limited to 30 pieces

RM 037 Automatic

Reference number: RM 037
Movement: automatic, Caliber CRMA1;
22.9 x 28 mm, height 4.82 mm; 25 jewels;
28,800 vph; function selector; skeletonized; winding
rotor with variable geometry; 50-hour power reserve
Functions: hours, minutes; large date
Case: titanium, 34.4 x 52.2 mm, height 12.5 mm;
sapphire crystal; transparent case back
Band: rubber, folding clasp
Price: $85,000
Variations: pink gold ($100,000); white gold
($110,000)

RM 039 Tourbillon Flyback Chronograph "Aviation"

Reference number: RM 039-01
Movement: manually wound, Caliber RM 039;
ø 38.95 mm, height 7.95 mm; 58 jewels;
21,600 vph; 1-minute tourbillon, selection button
for winding (W), null (N), hands (H), fast adjustment
(S); 70-hour power reserve
Functions: hours, minutes; power reserve/function
display; flyback chronograph; weekday, date
Case: titanium, ø 50 mm, height 19.4 mm;
bidirectional bezel with 60-minute divisions/
conversion tables; sapphire crystal; transparent
back
Price: $999,000

RM 50-01 Tourbillon Chrono G-Sensor

Reference number: RM 50-01
Movement: manually wound, Caliber RM RM50-01; 32
x 36.7 mm, height 7.53 mm; 35 jewels; 21,600 vph;
1-minute tourbillon, function switch for winding, hand
setting, rapid adjustment; 70-hour power reserve
Functions: hours, minutes, subsidiary seconds;
accelerometer (G-sensor); chronograph
Case: rose gold, 42.7 x 50 mm, height 16.4 mm; bezel
and case back of NTPT carbon fiber; sapphire crystal;
transparent back; water-resistant to 5 atm
Remarks: mechanical accelerometer; special edition
Lotus F1 Team (driver Romain Grosjean)
Price: $940,000

RM 60-01 Flyback Chrono Regatta

Reference number: RM 60-01
Movement: automatic, Richard Mille Caliber
RMAC2; ø 39.15 mm, height 9 mm; 62 jewels;
28,800 vph; titanium mainplate; adjustable rotor
geometry; 50-hour power reserve
Functions: hours, minutes, subsidiary seconds;
additional 24-hour display (2nd time zone); flyback
chronograph with countdown function; full calendar
with large date, month
Case: titanium, ø 50 mm, height 16.33 mm;
bidirectional bezel with 360º division, sapphire
crystal; transparent back; water-resistant to 3 atm
Band: rubber, folding clasp
Price: $150,000; limited to 35 pieces

RM 61-01 Yohan Blake

Reference number: RM 61-01
Movement: manually wound, Caliber RMUL2
(base Caliber RMUL1); 28.45 x 30.25 mm, height
3.15 mm; 24 jewels; 28,800 vph; skeletonized;
titanium bridges and plate; weight 4.3 g; 2 spring
barrels; 55-hour power reserve
Functions: hours, minutes, sweep seconds
Case: carbon fiber (NTPT); 42.7 x 50.24 mm, height
15.84 mm; ceramic bezel and case back, sapphire
crystal; transparent back; water-resistant to 3 atm
Band: rubber, folding clasp
Price: $120,000

RM 63-01 Dizzy Hands

Reference number: RM 63-01
Movement: automatic, Caliber CRMA3; ø 31 mm,
height 6.7 mm; 35 jewels; 28,800 vph; 50-hour
power reserve
Functions: hours, minutes
Case: titanium, ø 42.7 mm, height 11.7 mm;
rose gold bezel and case back; sapphire crystal;
transparent case back
Band: rubber, folding clasp
Remarks: "dizzy hands" function: pressing crown
launches anticlockwise rotation of hour disc, hour
hand turns clockwise; pressing again resets time
Price: $120,000

Manufacture ROGER DUBUIS

2, rue André-De-Garrini - CP 149
CH-1217 Meyrin 2 (Geneva)
Switzerland

Tel.:
01141-22-783-2828

Fax:
01141-22-783-2882

E-Mail:
info@rogerdubuis.com

Website:
www.rogerdubuis.com

Founded:
1995

Annual production:
over 5,000 watches (estimated)

U.S. distributor:
Roger Dubuis N.A.
645 Fifth Avenue
New York, NY 10022
888-RDUBUIS
info@rogerdubuis.com

Most important collections:
Hommage, Excalibur, La Monégasque,
Pulsion, Velvet

Roger Dubuis

Roger Dubuis, a *manufacture* fully committed to luxury and *"très haute horlogerie,"* was taken over by the Richemont Group in the late fall of 2007. The centerpiece of the deal was without a doubt the company's state-of-the-art workshops, where the finest movement components are made—parts that, because of their quality and geographical origins, bear the coveted Seal of Geneva. These credentials are interesting to other brands in the Richemont Group as well, especially to Cartier, which gets its new skeletonized movements from the Roger Dubuis *manufacture*.

This Geneva-based company was founded in 1995 as SOGEM SA (Société Genevoise des Montres) by name-giver Roger Dubuis and financier Carlos Dias. These two exceptional men created a complete collection of unusual watches in no time flat—timepieces with unheard-of dimensions and incomparable complications. The meteoric development of this *manufacture* and the incredible frequency of its new introductions—even technical ones—continue to astound the traditional, rather conservative watch industry. Today, Roger Dubuis develops all of its own movements, currently numbering more than thirty different mechanical calibers. In addition, it produces just about all of its individual components in-house, from base plates to escapements and balance springs. With this heavy-duty technological know-how in its quiver, the brand has been able to build some remarkable movements, like the massive RD101, with four balance springs and all manner of differentials and gear works to drive the Excalibur Quatuor, the equivalent in horology to a monster truck.

Hommage Automatic

Reference number: RDDBHO0565
Movement: automatic, Caliber RD 620; ø 31 mm, height 4.5 mm; 35 jewels; 28,800 vph; microrotor; 52 hours power reserve; Geneva Seal
Functions: hours, minutes, subsidiary seconds
Case: rose gold, ø 42 mm, height 11.12 mm; sapphire crystal; transparent case back; water-resistant to 3 atm
Band: reptile skin, buckle
Remarks: Roger Dubuis signature on case back
Price: $30,800
Variations: white gold ($31,900)

Hommage Chronographe

Reference number: RDDBHO0569
Movement: automatic, Caliber RD 680; ø 31 mm, height 6.3 mm; 44 jewels; 28,800 vph; microrotor; column wheel control of chronograph; 52 hours power reserve; Geneva Seal
Functions: hours, minutes, subsidiary seconds; chronograph
Case: rose gold, ø 42 mm, height 12.12 mm; sapphire crystal; transparent case back; water-resistant 3 atm
Band: reptile skin, buckle
Remarks: Roger Dubuis signature on case back
Price: $46,700
Variations: white gold ($48,500)

Hommage Flying Double Tourbillon

Reference number: RDDBHO0563
Movement: manually wound, Caliber RD 100; ø 36.1 mm, height 8.8 mm; 52 jewels; 21,600 vph; 2 flying 1-minute tourbillons with differential; 50 hours power reserve; Geneva Seal
Functions: hours, minutes
Case: rose gold, ø 45 mm, height 16.31 mm; sapphire crystal; transparent case back; water-resistant to 3 atm
Band: reptile skin, folding clasp
Remarks: Roger Dubuis signature on case back
Price: $328,500
Variations: white gold ($338,000)

Hommage
"Tribute to Roger Dubuis"
Reference number: RDDBH00568
Movement: manually wound, Caliber RD 540;
ø 33.8 mm, height 5.7 mm; 28 jewels; 21,600 vph;
flying 1-minute tourbillon; 60 hours power reserve;
Geneva Seal
Functions: hours, minutes, subsidiary seconds;
power reserve indicator; large date
Case: rose gold, ø 45 mm, height 14.56 mm;
sapphire crystal; transparent case back; water-
resistant to 3 atm
Band: reptile skin, folding clasp
Remarks: Roger Dubuis signature on case back
Price: $177,500; limited to 208 pieces
Variations: white gold, limited to 88 pieces

La Monegasque Automatic
Reference number: RDDBMG0000
Movement: automatic, Caliber RD 821;
ø 25.93 mm, height 3.43 mm; 33 jewels;
28,800 vph; 48 hours power reserve; Geneva Seal
Functions: hours, minutes, subsidiary seconds
Case: rose gold, ø 42 mm, height 9.51; sapphire
crystal; transparent case back; water-resistant to
5 atm
Band: reptile skin, folding clasp
Price: $27,400
Variations: stainless steel ($16,000)

La Monegasque Chronograph
Reference number: RDDBMG0009
Movement: automatic, Caliber RD 680; ø 30.6 mm,
height 6.3 mm; 42 jewels; 28,800 vph; microrotor;
column wheel control of chronograph; COSC-
certified chronometer; Geneva Seal
Functions: hours, minutes, subsidiary seconds;
chronograph
Case: stainless steel, ø 44 mm, height 13.15;
sapphire crystal; transparent case back; water-
resistant to 5 atm
Band: reptile skin, folding clasp
Price: $26,300
Variations: pink gold ($41,700)

Velvet
Reference number: RDDBVE0007
Movement: automatic, Caliber RD 821;
ø 25.93 mm, height 3.43 mm; 33 jewels;
28,800 vph; 48 hours power reserve; Geneva Seal
Functions: hours, minutes
Case: rose gold, ø 36 mm, height 8.77 mm; bezel
set with diamonds; sapphire crystal; water-resistant
to 3 atm
Band: white gold, folding clasp
Price: $43,800

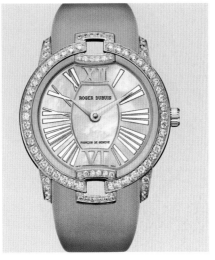

Velvet
Reference number: RDDBVE0006
Movement: automatic, Caliber RD 821;
ø 25.93 mm, height 3.43 mm; 33 jewels;
28,800 vph; 48 hours power reserve; Geneva Seal
Functions: hours, minutes
Case: rose gold, ø 36 mm, height 8.77 mm; bezel
set with diamonds; sapphire crystal, water-resistant
to 3 atm
Band: pink gold, folding clasp
Price: $42,600

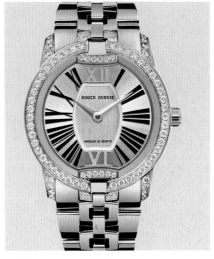

Velvet
Reference number: RDDBVE0008
Movement: automatic, Caliber RD 821;
ø 25.93 mm, height 3.43 mm; 33 jewels;
28,800 vph; 48 hours power reserve; Geneva Seal
Functions: hours, minutes
Case: pink gold, ø 36 mm, height 8.77 mm; bezel
set with diamonds; sapphire crystal; water-resistant
to 3 atm
Band: pink gold, folding clasp
Price: $57,400
Variations: white gold ($73,900)

Excalibur 36 Automatic

Reference number: RDDBEX0460
Movement: automatic, Caliber RD 821; ø
25.93 mm, height 3.43 mm; 33 jewels; 28,800 vph;
48 hours power reserve; Geneva Seal
Functions: hours, minutes, subsidiary seconds
Case: stainless steel, ø 36 mm, height 9 mm;
sapphire crystal; transparent case back; water-
resistant to 3 atm
Band: reptile skin, folding clasp
Price: $14,200

Excalibur 36 Automatic

Reference number: RDDBEX0275
Movement: automatic, Caliber RD 821;
ø 25.93 mm, height 3.43 mm; 33 jewels; 28,800
vph; 48 hours power reserve; Geneva Seal
Functions: hours, minutes, subsidiary seconds
Case: stainless steel, ø 36 mm, height 9 mm; bezel
set with diamonds; sapphire crystal; transparent
case back; water-resistant to 3 atm
Band: satin, folding clasp
Price: $23,700
Variations: rose gold bracelet ($50,300); rose gold
($31,900)

Excalibur 42 Chronograph

Reference number: RDDBEX0390
Movement: automatic, Caliber RD 681; ø 30.6 mm,
height 6.3 mm; 44 jewels; 28,800 vph; microrotor;
column wheel control of chronograph functions;
52 hours power reserve; Geneva Seal
Functions: hours, minutes, subsidiary seconds;
chronograph
Case: rose gold, ø 42 mm; sapphire crystal;
transparent case back; water-resistant to 3 atm
Band: reptile skin, folding clasp
Price: $45,900
Variations: stainless steel ($28,400)

Excalibur 42 Skeleton Tourbillon

Reference number: RDDBEX0392
Movement: automatic, Caliber RD 505SQ;
ø 33.8 mm, height 5.7 mm; 19 jewels; 21,600 vph;
flying 1-minute tourbillon; skeletonized; 60 hours
power reserve; Geneva Seal
Functions: hours, minutes
Case: rose gold, ø 42 mm; sapphire crystal;
transparent case back; water-resistant to 3 atm
Band: reptile skin, folding clasp
Price: $169,000
Variations: white gold ($175,000)

Excalibur Double Tourbillon Skeleton

Reference number: RDDBEX0395
Movement: manually wound, Caliber RD 01SQ;
ø 37.8 mm; height 7.67 mm; 28 jewels; 21,600 vph;
flying double tourbillon with differential; skeleton
design; galvanic blackening, beveling, perlage; 48
hours power reserve; Geneva Seal
Functions: hours, minutes
Case: pink gold with black coating; ø 45 mm,
sapphire crystal; transparent case back; water-
resistant to 5 atm
Band: reptile skin, folding clasp
Price: $328,500
Variations: white gold ($338,000); titanium
($286,500)

Excalibur Quatuor

Reference number: RDDBEX0425
Movement: manually wound, Caliber RD
101; ø 37.9 mm, height 10.6 mm; 113 jewels;
28,800 vph; 4 coupled escapement systems,
4-Hz frequency each; power transmission/
synchronization via 3 satellite differentials; 40 hours
power reserve; Geneva Seal
Functions: hours, minutes; power reserve indicator
Case: titanium, ø 48 mm; sapphire crystal;
transparent case back; water-resistant to 3 atm
Band: reptile skin, folding clasp
Price: $447,500
Variations: silicon ($1,000,000; limited to
3 pieces); rose gold ($489,500)

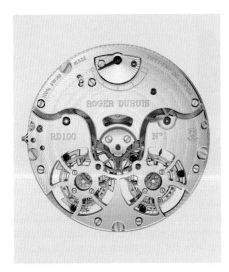

Caliber RD100

Manually wound, 2 flying tourbillons with differential; single spring barrel; 50-hour power reserve; Geneva Seal, COSC-certified chronometer
Functions: hours, minutes; power reserve indicator (on case back)
Diameter: 36.1 mm
Height: 8.8 mm
Jewels: 52
Balance: screw balance
Frequency: 21,600 vph

Caliber RD 101

Manually wound; 4 radially mounted and inclined lever escapements, synchronized with 3 balancing differentials; planetary gears for winding and power reserve; skeletonized movement; double spring barrel, 40-hour power reserve; Geneva Seal
Functions: hours, minutes; power reserve indicator
Diameter: 37.9 mm
Height: 10.6 mm
Jewels: 113
Balance: glucydur (4x)
Frequency: 28,800 vph (4x)
Balance spring: flat hairspring
Remarks: galvanic blackening and beveling of frame parts, perlage, 590 components

Caliber RD 01SQ

Manually wound; 2 flying tourbillons with differential; skeletonized movement
Functions: hours, minutes
Diameter: 37.8 mm
Height: 7.67 mm
Jewels: 28
Frequency: 21,600 vph
Remarks: galvanic blackening and beveling of frame parts, perlage, Geneva Seal, 319 components

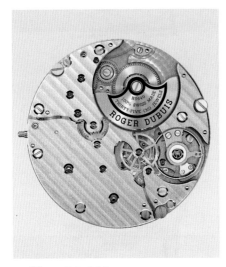

Caliber RD640

Automatic, microrotor; single spring barrel, 52-hour power reserve; Geneva Seal
Functions: hours, minutes, subsidiary seconds; date
Diameter: 31.1 mm
Height: 4.5 mm
Jewels: 35
Balance: glucydur, with a smooth rim
Frequency: 28,800 vph
Balance spring: flat hairspring
Shock protection: Incabloc
Remarks: finely finished with côtes de Genève, 198 components

Caliber RD 681

Automatic, column wheel control of chronograph functions, microrotor; single spring barrel, 52-hour power reserve; Geneva Seal
Functions: hours, minutes, subsidiary seconds; chronograph
Diameter: 30.6 mm
Height: 6.3 mm
Jewels: 44
Balance: glucydur
Frequency: 28,800 vph
Balance spring: flat hairspring
Remarks: finely worked with côtes de Genève, 280 components

Caliber RD 821

Automatic; single barrel spring, 48-hour power reserve; Geneva Seal, COSC-certified chronometer
Functions: hours, minutes, subsidiary seconds
Diameter: 25.95 mm
Height: 3.43 mm
Jewels: 33
Frequency: 28,800 vph
Remarks: finely finished with côtes de Genève, 168 components

Rolex

Rolex SA
Rue François-Dussaud 3
CH-1211 Geneva 26
Switzerland

Website:
www.rolex.com

Founded:
1908

Number of employees:
over 2,000 (estimated)

Annual production:
approx. 1,000,000 watches (estimated)

U.S. distributor:
Rolex Watch U.S.A., Inc.
Rolex Building
665 Fifth Avenue
New York, NY 10022-5358
212-758-7700; 212-980-2166 (fax)
www.rolex.com

Essentially, the Rolex formula for success has always been "what you see is what you get"—and plenty of it. For over a century now, the company has made wristwatch history without a need for *grandes complications*, perpetual calendars, tourbillons, or exotic materials. And its output in sheer quantity is phenomenal, at not quite a million watches per year. But make no mistake about it: The quality of these timepieces is legendary.

For as long as anyone can remember, this brand has held the top spot in the COSC's statistics, and year after year Rolex delivers just about half of all of the official institute's successfully tested mechanical chronometer movements. The brand has also pioneered several fundamental innovations: Rolex founder Hans Wilsdorf invented the hermetically sealed Oyster case in the 1920s, which he later outfitted with a screwed-in crown and an automatic movement wound by rotor. Shock protection, water resistance, the antimagnetic Parachrom hairspring, and automatic winding are some of the virtues that make wearing a Rolex timepiece much more comfortable and reliable. Because Wilsdorf patented his inventions for thirty years, Rolex had a head start on the competition.

Rolex watches and movements were produced for a long time in two different companies at two different sites. Only in 2004 did the Geneva-based Rolex buy and integrate the Rolex movement factory in Biel. Then, in 2008, for its 100th birthday, the company built itself three gigantic new buildings with loads of steel and dark glass in the industrial suburb of Plan-les-Ouates. For all its stability, since 2008, top management has changed quite a few times. In 2014, Jean-Frédéric Dufour moved from Zenith to the top rung at Rolex. He could bring the fresh energy the brand was looking for.

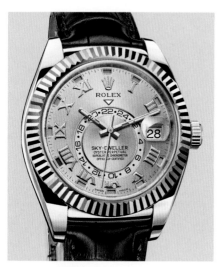

Sky-Dweller

Reference number: 326138
Movement: automatic, Rolex Caliber 9001; ø 33 mm, height 8 mm; 40 jewels; 28,800 vph; Parachrom Breguet spring; glucydur balance with microstella regulating screws; 72-hour power reserve; COSC-certified chronometer
Functions: hours, minutes, sweep seconds; 2nd time zone (additional 24-hour indicator); annual calendar with date, month
Case: yellow gold, ø 42 mm, height 14.1 mm; bidirectional bezel controls functions, sapphire crystal; screw-in crown; water-resistant to 10 atm
Band: reptile skin, folding clasp
Price: $38,150
Variations: rose gold bracelet ($46,150)

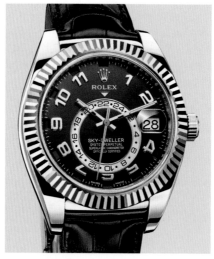

Sky-Dweller

Reference number: 326139
Movement: automatic, Rolex Caliber 9001; ø 33 mm, height 8 mm; 40 jewels; 28,800 vph; Parachrom Breguet spring; glucydur balance with microstella regulating screws; 72-hour power reserve; COSC-certified chronometer
Functions: hours, minutes, sweep seconds; 2nd time zone (additional 24-hour indicator); annual calendar with date, month
Case: white gold, ø 42 mm, height 14.1 mm; bidirectional bezel controls functions; sapphire crystal; screw-in crown; water-resistant to 10 atm
Band: reptile skin, folding clasp
Price: $39,550
Variations: white gold bracelet ($48,850)

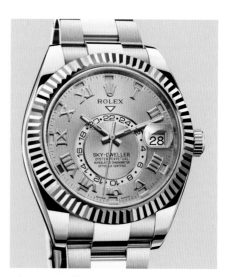

Sky-Dweller

Reference number: 326935
Movement: automatic, Rolex Caliber 9001; ø 33 mm, height 8 mm; 40 jewels; 28,800 vph; Parachrom Breguet spring; glucydur balance with microstella regulating screws; 72-hour power reserve; COSC-certified chronometer
Functions: hours, minutes, sweep seconds; 2nd time zone (additional 24-hour indicator); annual calendar with date, month
Case: rose gold, ø 42 mm, height 14.1 mm; bidirectional bezel controls functions, sapphire crystal; screw-in crown; water-resistant to 10 atm
Band: Oyster rose gold, folding clasp
Price: $48,850
Variations: reptile skin band ($39,550)

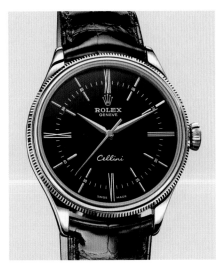

Cellini Time

Reference number: 50509
Movement: automatic, Rolex Caliber 3132 (base Caliber 3100); ø 28.5 mm; 31 jewels; 28,800 vph; Parachrom Breguet spring; 48-hour power reserve; COSC-tested chronometer
Functions: hours, minutes, sweep seconds
Case: white gold, ø 39 mm; sapphire crystal; screw-in crown; water-resistant to 5 atm
Band: reptile skin, buckle
Price: $15,200
Variations: various dials

Cellini Time

Reference number: 50505
Movement: automatic, Rolex Caliber 3132 (base Caliber 3100); ø 28.5 mm; 31 jewels; 28,800 vph; Parachrom Breguet spring; 48-hour power reserve; COSC-tested chronometer
Functions: hours, minutes, sweep seconds
Case: rose gold, ø 39 mm; sapphire crystal; screw-in crown; water-resistant to 5 atm
Band: reptile skin, buckle
Price: $15,200
Variations: various dials

Cellini Date

Reference number: 50519
Movement: automatic, Rolex Caliber 3165 (base Caliber 3187); 31 jewels; 28,800 vph; Parachrom Breguet spring; 48-hour power reserve; COSC-tested chronometer
Functions: hours, minutes, sweep seconds; date
Case: white gold, ø 39 mm; sapphire crystal; screw-in crown; water-resistant to 5 atm
Band: reptile skin, buckle
Price: $17,200
Variations: various dials

Cellini Date

Reference number: 50515
Movement: automatic, Rolex Caliber 3165 (base Caliber 3187); ø 31 jewels; 28,800 vph; Parachrom Breguet spring; 48-hour power reserve; COSC-tested chronometer
Functions: hours, minutes, sweep seconds; date
Case: rose gold, ø 39 mm; sapphire crystal; screw-in crown; water-resistant to 5 atm
Band: reptile skin, buckle
Price: $17,800
Variations: various dials

Cellini Dual Time

Reference number: 50529
Movement: automatic, Rolex Caliber 3180 (base Caliber 3187); 28,800 vph; Parachrom Breguet spring; 48-hour power reserve; COSC-tested chronometer
Functions: hours, minutes, sweep seconds; additional 12-hour display (2nd time zone), day/night indicator
Case: white gold, ø 39 mm; sapphire crystal; screw-in crown; water-resistant to 5 atm
Band: reptile skin, buckle
Price: $19,400
Variations: various dials

Cellini Dual Time

Reference number: 50525
Movement: automatic, Rolex Caliber 3180 (base Caliber 3187); 28,800 vph; Parachrom Breguet spring; 48-hour power reserve; COSC-tested chronometer
Functions: hours, minutes, sweep seconds; additional 12-hour display (2nd time zone), day/night indicator
Case: rose gold, ø 39 mm; sapphire crystal; screw-in crown; water-resistant to 5 atm
Band: reptile skin, buckle
Price: $19,400
Variations: various dials

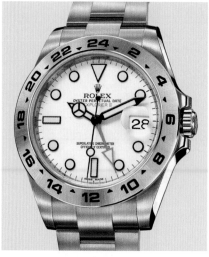

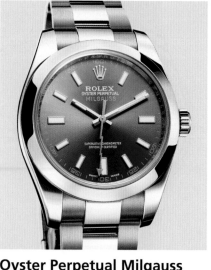

Oyster Perpetual GMT Master II

Reference number: 116719BLRO
Movement: automatic, Rolex Caliber 3186 (base Caliber 3135); ø 28.5 mm, height 6.4 mm; 31 jewels; 28,800 vph; Parachrom Breguet spring; 48-hour power reserve; COSC-tested chronometer
Functions: hours, minutes, sweep seconds; additional 24-hour display (2nd time zone); date
Case: white gold, ø 40 mm; bidirectional bezel with ceramic inlay, 24-hour division, sapphire crystal; screw-in crown; water-resistant to 10 atm
Band: Oyster white gold, folding clasp with safety lock and extension link
Price: $38,250
Variations: yellow gold with black ceramic bezel ($33,250)

Oyster Perpetual Explorer II

Reference number: 216570
Movement: automatic, Rolex Caliber 3187 (base Caliber 3135); ø 28.5 mm, height 6.4 mm; 31 jewels; 28,800 vph; Parachrom Breguet spring; Paraflex shock absorber; 48-hour power reserve; COSC-tested chronometer
Functions: hours, minutes, sweep seconds; additional 24-hour display (2nd time zone); date
Case: stainless steel, ø 42 mm, height 12.3 mm; bezel with 24-hour divisions; sapphire crystal; screw-in crown; water-resistant to 10 atm
Band: Oyster stainless steel, folding clasp with safety lock and extension link
Price: $8,100
Variations: various dials

Oyster Perpetual Milgauss

Reference number: 116400GV
Movement: automatic, Rolex Caliber 3131 (base Caliber 3135); ø 28.5 mm, height 5.37 mm; 31 jewels; 28,800 vph; Parachrom Breguet spring; Paraflex shock absorbers; antimagnetic protection via soft iron inner case and dial; 48-hour power reserve; COSC-tested chronometer
Functions: hours, minutes, sweep seconds
Case: stainless steel, ø 40 mm, height 13.2 mm; sapphire crystal; screw-in crown; water-resistant to 10 atm
Band: Oyster stainless steel, folding clasp with extension link
Price: $8,200
Variations: various dials

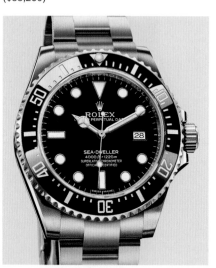

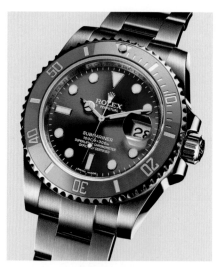

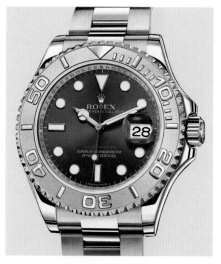

Oyster Perpetual Sea-Dweller 4000

Reference number: 116600
Movement: automatic, Rolex Caliber 3135; ø 28.5 mm, height 6 mm; 31 jewels; 28,800 vph; Parachrom Breguet spring; 48-hour power reserve; COSC-tested chronometer
Functions: hours, minutes, sweep seconds; date
Case: stainless steel, ø 40 mm, unidirectional bezel with ceramic inlay and 60-minute divisions; sapphire crystal; screw-in crown; helium valve; water-resistant to 122 atm
Band: Oyster stainless steel, folding clasp with safety lock and extension link
Price: $10,400

Oyster Perpetual Submariner Date

Reference number: 116610LV
Movement: automatic, Rolex Caliber 3135; ø 28.5 mm, height 6 mm; 31 jewels; 28,800 vph; Parachrom Breguet spring; 48-hour power reserve; COSC-tested chronometer
Functions: hours, minutes, sweep seconds; date
Case: stainless steel, ø 40 mm, height 12.5 mm; unidirectional bezel with ceramic inlay, with 60-second divisions; sapphire crystal; screw-in crown; water-resistant to 30 atm
Band: Oyster stainless steel, folding clasp with safety lock and extension link
Price: $9,040

Oyster Perpetual Yacht-Master

Reference number: 116622
Movement: automatic, Rolex Caliber 3135; ø 28.5 mm, height 6 mm; 31 jewels; 28,800 vph; Parachrom Breguet spring; glucydur balance with microstella regulating screws; COSC-certified chronometer
Functions: hours, minutes, sweep seconds; date
Case: stainless steel, ø 40 mm, height 11.7 mm; bidirectional platinum bezel with 60-minute divisions, sapphire crystal; screw-in crown; water-resistant to 10 atm
Band: Oysterlock stainless steel, folding clasp with flip-lock and extension link
Price: $11,550
Variations: platinum dial ($12,350)

LAURENT FERRIER
GENEVE

C R E A T I V E L Y   C L A S S I C

Grand Prix d'Horlogerie de Genève

Favourite Men's Watch • 2010

GALET CLASSIC TOURBILLON DOUBLE SPIRAL
18K/750 5N RED GOLD CASE | WHITE GRAND FEU ENAMEL DIAL |
EXCLUSIVE MANUFACTURE-MADE MANUAL WINDING MOVEMENT |
TOURBILLON DOUBLE HAIRSPRING | CHRONOMETER CERTIFIED

TWi
TOTALLY • WORTH • IT

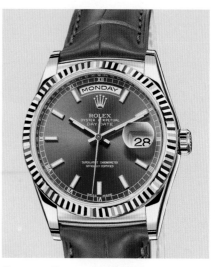

Oyster Perpetual

Reference number: 116000
Movement: automatic, Rolex Caliber 3130 (base Caliber 3135); ø 28.5 mm, height 5.85 mm; 31 jewels; 28,800 vph; Parachrome Breguet spring; 80-hour power reserve; COSC-certified chronometer
Functions: hours, minutes, sweep seconds
Case: stainless steel, ø 36 mm; sapphire crystal; screw-in crown; water-resistant to 10 atm
Band: Oyster stainless steel, folding clasp
Price: $5,400
Variations: various dial colors

Oyster Perpetual

Reference number: 177200
Movement: automatic, Rolex Caliber 2231 (base Caliber 2230); ø 20 mm, height 5.95 mm; 31 jewels; 28,800 vph; 48-hour power reserve; COSC-tested chronometer
Functions: hours, minutes, sweep seconds
Case: stainless steel, ø 31 mm; sapphire crystal; screw-in crown; water-resistant to 10 atm
Band: Oyster stainless steel, folding clasp
Price: $4,950
Variations: various dials

Oyster Perpetual Day-Date

Reference number: 118138
Movement: automatic, Rolex Caliber 3155 (base Caliber 3135); ø 28.5 mm, height 6.45 mm; 31 jewels; 28,800 vph; glucydur balance with microstella regulating screws; COSC-certified chronometer
Functions: hours, minutes, sweep seconds; date, weekday
Case: yellow gold, ø 36 mm; sapphire crystal; screw-in crown; water-resistant to 10 atm
Band: reptile skin, folding clasp
Price: $22,150
Variations: various dials and straps

Caliber 3135

Automatic; single barrel spring, 42-hour power reserve; COSC-tested chronometer
Functions: hours, minutes, sweep seconds; date
Diameter: 28.5 mm
Height: 8.05 mm
Jewels: 42
Balance: glucydur balance with microstella regulating screws
Frequency: 28,800 vph
Balance spring: Parachrom with Breguet overcoil
Shock protection: KIF

Caliber 4130

Automatic; single barrel spring, 42-hour power reserve; COSC-tested chronometer
Functions: hours, minutes, subsidiary seconds; chronograph
Diameter: 30.5 mm
Height: 6.5 mm
Jewels: 44
Balance: glucydur balance with microstella regulating screws
Frequency: 28,800 vph
Balance spring: Parachrom with Breguet overcoil
Shock protection: KIF
Remarks: used in Daytona

Caliber 3156

Automatic; single barrel spring, 42-hour power reserve; COSC-tested chronometer
Functions: hours, minutes, sweep seconds; date, weekday
Diameter: 28.5 mm
Height: 6.45 mm
Jewels: 31
Balance: glucydur balance with microstella regulating screws
Frequency: 28,800 vph
Balance spring: Parachrom spring
Remarks: used in Day-Date II

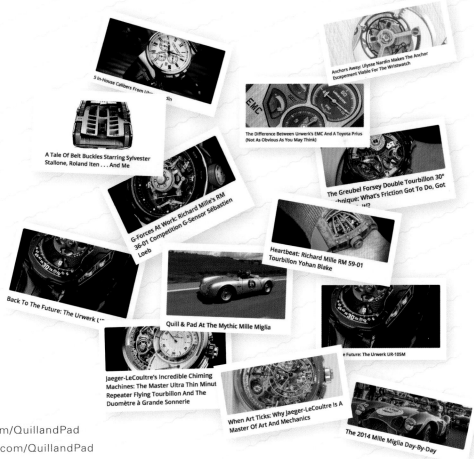

RJ WATCHES SA

11 Rue du Marché
CH-1204 Geneva
Switzerland

Tel.:
0041-22-319-29-39

Fax:
0041-22-319-29-30

E-Mail:
info@romainjerome.ch

Website:
www.romainjerome.ch

Founded:
2004

Number of employees:
approx. 20

Annual production:
3,000 watches and accessories

Distribution:
Please contact RJ-Romain Jerome
headquarters in Switzerland for any enquiries.

Most important collections/price range:
Titanic-DNA, Moon-DNA, Capsules / from
$10,000 to approx. $300,000 for highly
complicated watches

Romain Jerome

Tchaikovsky once said that he always put his best ideas into his work—and took them out again when editing. This singular approach to creativity makes its own kind of sense, but in a world where the hypest is the hippest, it may not be the most successful. When the fiery Yvan Arpa took hold of the barely known Romain Jerome in 2006, he quickly transformed its products, digging up unique and strange materials that caused the kind of chatter that means business—because there is no such thing as negative feedback. Quality and design, however, followed strict rules. The watches came in historical materials that connect the wearer to the bigger picture: bits of *Apollo 11*, moon dust, fibers from the space suits worn during the *International Space Station* mission.

Under new CEO Manuel Emch the oversize Moon Invader saw a shift toward a cooler techno-design using the company's stock of lunar module shreds. The Steampunk Chrono won the "Couture Time Award for Watch Architecture" in Las Vegas in 2012. Sticking with the historic theme, Romain Jerome has also combined the Steampunk models with *Titanic's* oxidized and stabilized metals, and in sharp contrast, some verdigris scraps from the Statue of Liberty are integrated into a clever, minimalist watch. Out of character almost was the Spacecraft, a seventies-style sci-fi time-telling trapezoidal object with a linear hour line on the side and a minute disc on top, a bit of a slap at the vintage crowd. No one is surprised to find that Emch collaborated with Eric Giroud and Jean-Marc Wiederrecht. Something new in 2014: Instead of more twisted rusted metal and dense dials, RJ has come out with an almost transparent watch, driven by a minimalistic movement, the Skylab.

Eyjafjallajökull-EVO

Reference number: RJ.V.AU.003.01
Movement: automatic, Caliber RJ002-A;
ø 26.2 mm, height 5.05 mm; 30 jewels; 28,800 vph; 40-hour power reserve
Functions: hours, minutes
Case: steel, PVD-coated; ø 43mm, height 12 mm; sapphire crystal; water-resistant to 3 atm
Remarks: crafted from lava from Eyjafjallajökull
Band: reptile skin, buckle
Price: $16,950; limited to 99 pieces

Spacecraft Black

Reference number: RJ.M.AU.SC.002.01
Movement: automatic; Caliber RJ2000-A; ø 36.4 x 33.26 mm, height 5.9 mm; 54 jewels; 28,800 vph; 38-hour power reserve
Functions: linear, retrograde, and jumping hour indicated by orange-lacquered cursor; dragging minutes on black disc with white numerals
Case: trapezoidal, titanium with black PVD, 50 x 44.5 x 32.85 mm; height 18.5 mm; metallized sapphire crystal; water-resistant to 3 atm
Band: buffalo, titanium buckle
Price: $29,500; limited to 25 pieces

Skylab Heavy Metal

Skylab Heavy Metal
Reference number: RJ.M.AU.023.01
Movement: automatic, Caliber RJ004-M;
ø 34.4 mm, height 5.6 mm; 21 jewels; 28,800 vph; skeletonized and ruthenium finished; 48-hour power reserve
Functions: hours, minutes, subsidiary seconds
Case: steel, ø 44 mm, height 12 mm; sapphire case back; water-resistant to 3 atm
Band: calf leather, buckle
Price: $19,500; limited to 99 pieces

PinUp-DNA Red

Reference number: RJ.P.CH.003.01
Movement: automatic, Caliber RJ001-CH;
ø 30.4 mm, height 7.9 mm; 27 jewels; 28,800 vph;
42-hour power reserve
Functions: hours, minutes, subsidiary seconds;
chronograph, 30-minute and 12-hour counter at 6
Case: black PVD-coated steel and pink gold,
ø 46 mm, height 14.1 mm; pink gold bezel, black
inner bezel; sapphire glass; water-resistant to 3 atm
Band: calf-leather NATO-style, buckle
Remarks: 1940s pinup on case back
Price: $15,950; limited to 99 unique pieces

New Moon Orbiter Speed Metal

Reference number: RJ.M.TO.MO.002.01
Movement: automatic, Caliber RJ3000; ø 42.2 x
29.8 mm, height 13.2 mm; 32 jewels; 28,800 vph;
1-minute flying tourbillon; 42-hour power reserve
Functions: hours, minutes; power reserve indicator
Case: black PVD-coated steel, 44.5 x 48.5 mm,
height 20.3 mm; 5 shaped antireflective sapphire
crystals; sapphire crystal back; water-resistant to
3 atm
Band: reptile skin, buckle
Remarks: moon dust with laser engraved "stellar
pattern" on dial, elements from *Apollo 11* spacecraft
Price: $133,500; limited to 25 pieces

Steampunk Chrono Red

Reference number: RJ.T.CH.SP.003.01
Movement: automatic; Caliber RJ001-CS;
ø 30.4 mm, height 6.6 mm; 39 jewels; 28,800 vph;
42-hour power reserve
Functions: hours, minutes, subsidiary seconds;
chronograph, 30-minute totalizer at 3
Case: steel; ø 50 mm, height 16.6 mm;
antireflective sapphire crystal; water-resistant to 3
atm
Band: black rubber, pink folding clasp
Remarks: bezel stabilized steel from *Titanic;*
integrated dial; bead-blasted, satin-brushed
ruthenium-colored bridge; mobile propeller at 6
Price: $32,950; limited to 2,012 pieces

Games-DNA – Space Invaders

Reference number: RJ.M.AU.IN.006.07
Movement: automatic; Caliber RJ001-A;
ø 30.4 mm, height 7.9 mm; 23 jewels; 28,800 vph;
42-hour power reserve
Functions: hours, minutes
Case: black PVD-coated steel; ø 46 mm; height
16 mm; sapphire crystal; case back with *Apollo 11*
parts and medallion in Moon Silver alloy; water-
resistant to 3 atm
Band: vulcanized rubber, black PVD-coated steel
folding clasp
Remarks: black 3D bead-blasted, satin-brushed
dial; lacquered Space Invaders
Price: $20,500; limited edition of 78 pieces

1969 Heavy Metal Brown Silicium

Reference number: RJ.M.AU.020.06
Movement: automatic; Caliber RJ003-A;
ø 26.2 mm, height 5.05 mm; 30 jewels; 28,800
vph; 40-hour power reserve
Functions: hours, minutes, subsidiary seconds
Case: black PVD-coated steel, ø 43 mm, height
12 mm; screwed-down case back with grainy stellar
pattern and Moon Silver medallion; water-resistant
to 3 atm
Band: reptile skin, steel buckle
Remarks: PVD-treated silicium dial
Price: $10,950; limited edition of 99 pieces

MOON-DNA – Moon Dust Red Mood Set Chrono

Reference number: RJ.M.CH.003.02
Movement: automatic, Caliber RJ001-CH1; ø 30.4 mm,
height 7.9 mm; 25 jewels; 28,800 vph; 42-hour power
reserve
Functions: hours, minutes; subsidiary seconds;
chronograph, 12-hour/30-minute counters at 6 and 3
Case: pink gold; ø 46 mm, height 17.2 mm; antireflective
sapphire crystal; pink gold screw-in crown; 4 paws set
with diamonds; carbon fiber and pink gold bezel; water-
resistant to 3 atm
Band: fabric, pink gold and black steel folding clasp
Remarks: dial containing moon dust
Price: $40,300; limited to 1,969 pieces
Variations: band with *ISS* spacesuit fibers

Schaumburg Watch

Lindburgh & Benson
Kirchplatz 5 and 6
D-31737 Rinteln
Germany

Tel.:
01149-5751-923-351

E-Mail:
info@lindburgh-benson.com

Website:
www.schaumburgwatch.com

Founded:
1998

Number of employees:
7

Distribution:
retail

U.S. distributor:
Schaumburg Watch
About Time Luxury Group
210 Bellevue Avenue
Newport, RI 02840
401-846-0598
nicewatch@aol.com

Most important collections/price range:
mechanical wristwatches / approx. $1,500
to $13,000

Schaumburg Watch

Frank Dilbakowski is the owner of this small watchmaking business in Rinteln, Westphalia, which has been producing very unusual, yet affordable timepieces since 1998. The name Schaumburg comes from the surrounding region. The firm has gained a reputation for high-performance timepieces for rugged sports and professional use. The chronometer line Aquamatic with water resistance to 1,000 m and the Aquatitan models, secure to 2,000 m, confirm the company's maxim that form, function, and performance are inseparable from one another.

By the same token, traditional watchmaking is also high on the agenda. The Rinteln workbenches produce the plates and bridges and provide all the finishing as well (perlage, engraving, skeletonizing). Some of the bracelets, cases, and dials are even manufactured here, but the base movements come from Switzerland. The current portfolio includes such outstanding creations as a special moon phase, which, rather than simply showing a moon, has a "shadow" crossing over an immobile photo-like reproduction of the moon. The Bullfrog is a simpler watch with a modern dial. Thanks to the tapered case, the bulky piece does not look daunting. If you examine the profile, it is reminiscent of a frog.

AQM 4 Carbon

Movement: automatic, SW Caliber 20a (base ETA 2824-2); ø 25.6 mm, height 4.6 mm; 25 jewels; 28,800 vph; 38-hour power reserve
Functions: hours, minutes, sweep seconds; date
Case: stainless steel, ø 45 mm, height 14.8 mm; sapphire crystal; screw-in crown; water-resistant to 50 atm
Band: calf leather, buckle
Remarks: carbon fiber dial; comes with automatic watch winder
Price: $1,900
Variations: black PVD coating ($2,050); stainless steel band ($2,120)

Rétrolateur 2

Movement: manually wound, SW Caliber 07.9, ø 36.6 mm, height 64 mm; 17 jewels; 18,000 vph; guilloché three-quarter plate ("Schaumburg bridge"), hand-engraved balance cock; 38-hour power reserve
Functions: hours (off-center), minutes, subsidiary seconds (30 seconds, retrograde)
Case: stainless steel, ø 42 mm, height 11 mm; sapphire crystal, transparent case back; water-resistant to 5 atm
Band: calf leather, folding clasp
Price: $3,250
Variations: silver-plated dial; blue or gold hands

AQM Bullfrog Chronovision

Movement: automatic, SW Caliber 50ac (base ETA 7750); ø 30 mm, height 7.9 mm; 26 jewels; 28,800 vph; 38-hour power reserve
Functions: hours, minutes, subsidiary seconds; chronograph; date
Case: titanium, ø 42 mm, height 12–15 mm; sapphire crystal, water-resistant to 20 atm
Band: calf leather, buckle
Remarks: comes with automatic watch winder
Price: $3,190
Variations: 3-hand ($1,845); 3-hand with 24-hour display ($2,025)

Seiko

Seiko Holdings
Ginza, Chuo, Tokyo
Japan

Website:
www.seikowatches.com

Founded:
1881

U.S. distributor:
Seiko Corporation of America
1111 Macarthur Boulevard
Mahwah, NJ 07430
201-529-5730
custserv@seikousa.com
www.seikousa.com

Most important collections/price range:
Grand Seiko / approx. $5,000 to $14,500;
Ananta / approx. $2,400 to $8,500; Astron
/ approx. $1,850 to $3,400; Seiko Elite
(Sportura, Premier, Velatura, Arctura) /
approx. $430 to $1,500

The Japanese watch giant is a part of the Seiko Holding Company, but as far as the development and production of its watches are concerned, the brand is fully self-sufficient. Seiko makes every variety of portable timepiece, and in its vast collection it offers mechanical watches with both manual and automatic winding, quartz watches with battery and solar power or with the brand's own mechanical "Kinetic" power generation, as well as the groundbreaking "Spring Drive" hybrid technology. This intelligent mix of mechanical energy generation and electronic regulation is reserved for Seiko's top models.

Also in the top segment of the brand is the Grand Seiko line, a group of watches that enjoys cult status among international collectors. For the Grand Seiko's fiftieth anniversary, the Tokyo-based company put together an extensive collection comprising numerous new models and, for the first time, officially offered them on the global market. Today, among the new GS models are several watches with the interesting Spring Drive technology, but most new Grand Seikos are conventional, mechanical hand-wound and automatic watches.

Classic Seikos are designed for tradition-conscious buyers. The Astron, however, with its automatic GPS-controlled time setting, suggests the watch of the future. In its second incarnation, the Astron is 30 percent more compact, and the energy required by the GPS system inside is supplied by a high-tech solar cell on the dial.

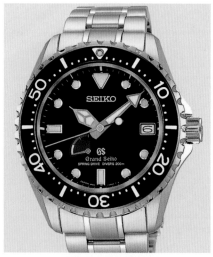

Grand Seiko Spring Drive Chronograph

Reference number: SBGC001
Movement: manually wound, Seiko Spring Drive Caliber 9R86; ø 30 mm, height 7.6 mm; 50 jewels; electromagnetic Tri-Synchro Regulator escapement system with sliding wheel; column wheel control of chronograph functions/vertical clutch
Functions: hours, minutes, subsidiary seconds; 12-hour display (2nd time zone); chronograph; date; power reserve indicator
Case: stainless steel, ø 43.5 mm, height 16.1 mm; sapphire crystal; transparent case back
Band: stainless steel, folding clasp
Price: $8,600

Grand Seiko Automatic Hi-Beat 36.000 GMT

Reference number: SBGJ001
Movement: automatic, Seiko Caliber 9S86; ø 28.4 mm, height 5.9 mm; 37 jewels; 36,000 vph; antimagnetic up to 4,800 A/m; 55-hour power reserve
Functions: hours, minutes, sweep seconds; additional 12-hour display (2nd time zone); date
Case: stainless steel, ø 40 mm, height 14 mm; sapphire crystal; transparent case back; screw-in crown; water-resistant to 10 atm
Band: stainless steel, safety folding clasp
Price: $7,000
Variations: black dial

Grand Seiko Spring Drive Diver's Watch

Reference number: SBGA031
Movement: manually wound, Seiko Spring Drive Caliber 9R65; ø 30 mm, height 5.1 mm; 30 jewels; electromagnetic Tri-Synchro Regulator escapement system with sliding wheel; 72-hour power reserve
Functions: hours, minutes, sweep seconds; date; power reserve indicator
Case: titanium, ø 44.2 mm, height 14 mm; unidirectional bezel with 60-minute divisions, sapphire crystal; screw-in crown; water-resistant to 20 atm
Band: titanium, folding clasp
Price: $7,700
Variations: stainless steel ($5,700)

Astron GPS Solar Chronograph

Reference number: SSE003J1
Movement: quartz, Seiko Caliber 8X82; solar energy-saving function
Functions: hours, minutes, sweep seconds; additional 24-hour display; world-time display (GPS in 39 time zones), flight mode, signal reception indicator; power reserve display, DST indicator; chronograph; date
Case: titanium with titanium carbide coating; ø 45 mm, height 14 mm; ceramic bezel, sapphire crystal; screw-in crown; water-resistant to 10 atm
Band: titanium, folding clasp
Price: $2,450

Astron GPS Solar

Reference number: SAST009G
Movement: quartz, Seiko Caliber 7X52; solar energy-saving function
Functions: hours, minutes, sweep seconds; additional 24-hour display; world-time display (GPS in 39 time zones), flight mode, signal reception indicator; power reserve display, DST indicator; date
Case: stainless steel, ø 47 mm, height 17 mm; ceramic bezel, sapphire crystal; screw-in crown; water-resistant to 10 atm
Band: silicon, folding clasp
Price: $1,750

Prospex Kinetic GMT Diver's

Reference number: SUN019P1
Movement: quartz, Seiko kinetic Caliber 5M85; own energy supply from rotor-driven micro-generator; up to 6-month darkness power reserve
Functions: hours, minutes, sweep seconds; additional 24-hour display (2nd time zone); date
Case: stainless steel, ø 47.5 mm, height 14 mm; unidirectional bezel with 60-minute divisions, sapphire crystal; screw-in crown and pusher; water-resistant to 20 atm
Band: stainless steel, safety folding clasp
Price: $575
Variations: textile band

Premier Automatic

Reference number: SSA213J2
Movement: automatic, Seiko Caliber 4R39; ø 25.6 mm; 24 jewels; 41-hour power reserve
Functions: hours, minutes; additional 24-hour display (2nd time zone)
Case: stainless steel, ø 41.5 mm, height 12 mm; sapphire crystal, transparent case back; water-resistant to 10 atm
Band: calf leather, folding clasp
Price: €529 (not available in the USA)
Variations: white dial and stainless steel bracelet (€549, not available in the USA)

Sportura Kinetic Direct Drive

Reference number: SRG017P1
Movement: quartz, Seiko Kinetic Caliber 5D22; own energy supply from rotor-driven micro-generator, hand winding; 1-month power reserve
Functions: hours, minutes, sweep seconds; power reserve display, energy indicator; date
Case: stainless steel, ø 44.5 mm, height 12 mm; unidirectional bezel with 60-minute divisions, sapphire crystal, water-resistant to 10 atm
Band: stainless steel, folding clasp
Price: $695
Variations: black dial and calf-leather band

Marinemaster Automatic

Reference number: SBDX001
Movement: automatic, Seiko Caliber 8L35; ø 25.6 mm; 26 jewels; 28,800 vph; 50-hour power reserve
Functions: hours, minutes, sweep seconds; date
Case: stainless steel, ø 43 mm, height 15 mm; unidirectional bezel with 60-minute divisions, sapphire crystal; screw-in crown; water-resistant to 30 atm
Band: stainless steel, safety folding clasp with extension link
Price: $2,500

Sinn Spezialuhren GmbH

Im Füldchen 5-7
D-60489 Frankfurt / Main
Germany

Tel.:
01149-69-9784-14-200

Fax:
01149-69-9784-14-201

E-Mail:
info@sinn.de

Website:
www.sinn.de

Founded:
1961

Number of employees:
approx. 100

Annual production:
approx. 12,500 watches

U.S. distributor:
WatchBuys
888-333-4895
www.watchbuys.com

Most important collections/price range:
Financial District, U-Models, Diapal / from
approx. $700 to $27,500

Sinn

Pilot and flight instructor Helmut Sinn began manufacturing watches in Frankfurt because he thought the pilot's watches on the market were too expensive. The resulting combination of top quality, functionality, and a good price-performance ratio turned out to be an excellent sales argument. Sinn Spezialuhren zu Frankfurt am Main is a brand with origins in technology. There is hardly another source that offers watch lovers such a sophisticated and reasonable collection of sporty watches, many conceived to take extreme pressure.

In 1994, Lothar Schmidt took over the brand, and his product developers began looking for inspiration in other industries and the sciences. They did so out of a practical technical impulse without any plan for launching a trend. "Products need to speak for themselves," Schmidt explains. That is why he continues to invest in research and development, with the aim of improving the everyday functionality of his watches. This includes application of special Sinn technology like the moisture-proof technology by which an inert gas, like argon, is pumped into the case. Other Sinn innovations include the Diapal (a lubricant-free lever escapement), the Hydro (an oil-filled diver's watch), and tegiment processing (for hardened steel and titanium surfaces).

Having noticed a lack of norms for aviator watches, Schmidt negotiated a partnership with the Aachen Technical University to create the Technischer Standard Fliegeruhren (TESTAF, or Technical Standards for Aviator Watches), which is housed at the Eurocopter headquarters.

In 2014, Sinn celebrated the fifteenth anniversary of the Financial District collection, which honors Frankfurt, with its banks and stock exchange. The new SZ03 features a function that shows the week number, a standard in European business planning.

6052

Reference number: 6052.010
Movement: automatic, Sinn Caliber SZ 03 (base ETA 7750); ø 30 mm, height 7.9 mm; 26 jewels; 28,800 vph; shockproof and antimagnetic (DIN norm); 42-hour power reserve
Functions: hours, minutes, subsidiary seconds; chronograph; annual calendar with date, weekday, calendar, month and weeks
Case: stainless steel, ø 41.5 mm, height 14.5 mm; sapphire crystal; transparent case back; water-resistant to 10 atm
Band: calf leather, buckle
Remarks: with extra stainless steel bracelet and changing tool
Price: $5,450

Financial District Watch

Reference number: 6099.010
Movement: automatic, modified Sellita Caliber SW SW500; ø 30 mm, height 7.9 mm; 26 jewels; 28,800 vph; shockproof and antimagnetic (DIN norm); 42-hour power reserve
Functions: hours, minutes, subsidiary seconds; additional 12-hour display; chronograph; date
Case: stainless steel, ø 41.5 mm, height 15 mm; crown-adjustable inner bezel with 12-hour divisions, sapphire crystal; transparent case back; water-resistant to 10 atm
Band: stainless steel, folding clasp
Remarks: extra stainless steel bracelet/changing tool
Price: $4,900
Variations: 6000 model in 38.5 mm case ($4,550); 6030 model in 34 mm case ($3,950)

6000 Rose Gold

Reference number: 6000.040
Movement: automatic, modified ETA Caliber 7750; ø 30.4 mm, height 7.9 mm; 28 jewels; 28,800 vph; fine finishing; shockproof and antimagnetic (DIN norm); 42-hour power reserve
Functions: hours, minutes, subsidiary seconds; additional 12-hour display (2nd time zone); chronograph; date
Case: rose gold, ø 38.5 mm, height 16.5 mm; crown-adjustable inner bezel with 12-hour divisions; sapphire crystal; transparent case back; water-resistant to 10 atm
Band: reptile skin, buckle
Price: $16,800
Variations: stainless steel ($4,550)

EZM 10 TESTAF

Reference number: 950.011
Movement: automatic, Sinn Caliber SZ 01 (base ETA 7750); ø 30 mm, height 8.5 mm; 33 jewels; 28,800 vph; shockproof, antimagnetic (DIN norm); sweep minute counter
Functions: hours, minutes, subsidiary seconds; additional 24-hour display; date
Case: tegimented/pearl-blasted titanium, ø 46.5 mm, height 15.6 mm; bidirectional bezel with 60-minute division, sapphire crystal; screw-in crown; hard-coated pushers; water-resistant to 20 atm
Band: calf leather, buckle
Remarks: TESTAF certified; Ar-dehumidifying technology
Price: $6,800
Variations: titanium bracelet ($7,150)

EZM 9 TESTAF

Reference number: 949.010
Movement: automatic, Sellita Caliber SW200-1; ø 25.6 mm, height 4.6 mm; 26 jewels; 28,800 vph; shockproof and antimagnetic (DIN norm); 38-hour power reserve
Functions: hours, minutes, sweep seconds; date
Case: tegimented titanium; ø 44 mm, height 12 mm; unidirectional bezel with 60-minute divisions, sapphire crystal; water-resistant to 20 atm
Band: tegimented titanium, folding clasp with safety lock and extension link
Remarks: TESTAF certified; Ar-dehumidifying technology
Price: $4,800
Variations: leather strap ($4,550)

103 Ti UTC TESTAF

Reference number: 103.0791
Movement: automatic, modified ETA Caliber 7750; ø 30.4 mm, height 7.9 mm; 25 jewels; 28,800 vph; shockproof and antimagnetic (DIN norm); 42-hour power reserve
Functions: hours, minutes, subsidiary seconds; additional 12-hour display; chronograph; date
Case: pearl-blasted titanium, ø 41 mm, height 17 mm; bidirectional bezel with 60-minute divisions, sapphire crystal; transparent case back; water-resistant to 20 atm
Band: calf leather, buckle
Remarks: TESTAF certified; Ar-dehumidifying technology
Price: $4,250
Variations: titanium bracelet ($4,600)

EZM 13 Diver's Chronograph

Reference number: 613.010
Movement: automatic, Sinn Caliber SZ 02 (base ETA 7750); ø 30.4 mm, height 7.9 mm; 25 jewels; 28,800 vph; 60-minute counter; shockproof and antimagnetic (DIN norm); 42-hour power reserve
Functions: hours, minutes, subsidiary seconds; chronograph; date
Case: stainless steel, ø 41.5 mm, height 15 mm; unidirectional bezel with 60-minute divisions, sapphire crystal; water-resistant to 50 atm
Band: silicon, buckle
Remarks: EU diving certified; Ar-dehumidifying tech; magnetic field protection to 80,000 A/m
Price: $3,575
Variations: stainless steel band ($2,275); 3-hand EZM ($3,700)

U1000 S

Reference number: 1011.020
Movement: automatic, Sinn Caliber SZ 02 (base ETA 7750); ø 30.4 mm, height 7.9 mm; 25 jewels; 28,800 vph; shockproof/antimagnetic (DIN); 60-minute totalizer; lubrication; 42-hour power reserve
Functions: hours, minutes, subsidiary seconds; chronograph; date
Case: tegimented submarine steel with black PVD coating; ø 44 mm, height 18 mm; unidirectional bezel with 60-minute division, sapphire crystal; screw-in crown and pushers (D-3 seal); water-resistant to 100 atm
Band: rubber, folding clasp
Remarkds: EU diving certified; Ar-dehumidifying technology
Price: $5,950

T1 (EZM 14)

Reference number: 1014.010
Movement: automatic, SOP A10-2A (base Soprod A10); ø 25.6 mm, height 3.6 mm; 25 jewels; 28,800 vph; shockproof/antimagnetic (DIN norm); 42-hour power reserve
Functions: hours, minutes, sweep seconds; date
Case: pearl-blasted titanium, ø 45 mm, height 12.5 mm; unidirectional bezel with 60-minute division, sapphire crystal; screw-in crown; water-resistant to 100 atm
Band: rubber, folding clasp with safety lock/extension link
Remarks: EU diving certified; Ar-dehumidifying technology
Price: $4,350
Variations: titanium bracelet ($4,500); "T2" model ($3,975)

757 DIAPAL

Reference number: 757. 030
Movement: automatic, ETA Caliber 7750; ø 30.4 mm, height 7.9 mm; 25 jewels; 28,8000 vph; lubricant-free escapement (Diapal)
Functions: hours, minutes; additional 12-hour display; chronograph; date
Case: tegimented stainless steel, ø 43 mm, height 15 mm; bidirectional bezel with 60-minute division, sapphire crystal; screw-in crown; water-resistant to 20 atm
Band: tegimented stainless steel, double folding clasp
Remarks: Ar-dehumidifying technology; magnetic field protection to 80,000 A/m
Price: $5,100

EZM 7

Reference number: 857.030
Movement: automatic, ETA Caliber 2893-2; ø 26.2 mm, height 4.1 mm; 21 jewels; 28,800 vph; shockproof and antimagnetic (DIN norm)
Functions: hours, minutes, sweep seconds; additional 24-hour display; date
Case: tegimented stainless steel, ø 43 mm, height 12 mm; unidirectional bezel with 60-minute divisions, sapphire crystal; screw-in crown; water-resistant to 20 atm
Band: silicon, buckle
Remarks: Ar-dehumidifying technology; magnetic field protection to 80,000 A/m
Price: $3,080
Variations: leather strap ($2,950)

856 UTC

Reference number: 856.010
Movement: automatic, ETA Caliber 2893-2; ø 25.6 mm, height 4.1 mm; 21 jewels; 28,800 vph; shockproof and antimagnetic (DIN norm); 42-hour power reserve
Functions: hours, minutes, sweep seconds; additional 24-hour display; date
Case: tegimented stainless steel, ø 40 mm, height 11 mm; sapphire crystal; rubber, folding clasp
Remarks: Ar-dehumidifying technology
Price: $2,500
Variations: w/o 2nd time zone ($2,350); rotating bezel (model 857; $2,850)

140 St S

Reference number: 140.010
Movement: automatic, Sinn Caliber SZ 01 (base ETA 7750); ø 30 mm, height 8.5 mm; 28 jewels, 28,800 vph; sweep minute counter; lubricant-free escapement (Diapal); shockproof and antimagnetic (DIN norm); 42-hour power reserve
Functions: hours, minutes, subsidiary seconds; chronograph; date
Case: tegimented stainless steel with black PVD coating; ø 44 mm, height 15 mm; crown-adjustable inner bezel with 60-minute divisions, sapphire crystal, screw-in crown; water-resistant to 10 atm
Remarks: dehumidifying technology
Price: $5,650

104 St Sa

Reference number: 104.010
Movement: automatic, Sellita Caliber SW220-1; ø 25.6 mm, height 5.05 mm; 26 jewels; 28,800 vph; shockproof and antimagnetic (DIN norm); 38-hour power reserve
Functions: hours, minutes, sweep seconds; weekday, date
Case: stainless steel, ø 41 mm, height 11.5 mm; bidirectional bezel with 60-minute division, sapphire crystal; transparent case back; screw-in crown; water-resistant to 20 atm
Band: calf leather, buckle
Price: $1,500
Variations: stainless steel bracelet ($1,800)

900 Diapal

Reference number: 900.013
Movement: automatic, Sellita Caliber SW500; ø 30 mm, height 7.9 mm; 25 jewels; 28,800 vph; shockproof and antimagnetic (DIN norm); Diapal escapement; 48-hour power reserve
Functions: hours, minutes, subsidiary seconds; additional 24-hour display; chronograph; date
Case: tegimented stainless steel, ø 44 mm, height 15.5 mm; crown-adjustable inner bezel with 60-minute division, sapphire crystal; screw-in crown; water-resistant to 20 atm
Band: stainless steel, folding clasp
Remarks: Ar-dehumidifying technology; magnetic field protection to 80,000 A/m
Price: $5,600

556 I

Reference number: 556.010
Movement: automatic, ETA Caliber 2824-2;
ø 25.6 mm, height 4.6 mm; 25 jewels; 28,800 vph;
shockproof and antimagnetic (DIN norm); 38-hour
power reserve
Functions: hours, minutes, sweep seconds; date
Case: stainless steel, ø 38.5 mm, height 11 mm;
sapphire crystal, transparent case back; water-
resistant to 20 atm
Band: calf leather, buckle
Price: $1,300

358 Flieger

Reference number: 358.010
Movement: automatic, ETA Caliber 7750;
ø 30.4 mm, height 7.9 mm; 25 jewels; 28,800 vph;
shockproof and antimagnetic (DIN norm)
Functions: hours, minutes, subsidiary seconds;
chronograph; weekday, date
Case: stainless steel, ø 42 mm, height 16 mm;
plexiglass; screw-in crown; water-resistant to 10 atm
Band: stainless steel, folding clasp with safety lock
Price: $2,550
Variations: sapphire crystal ($3,550); Diapal
technology ($4,800)

243 TW66 WG
Mother-of-Pearl W

Reference number: 243050
Movement: automatic, ETA Caliber 2671;
ø 17.2 mm, height 4.8 mm; 25 jewels; 28,800 vph;
shockproof and antimagnetic (DIN norm)
Functions: hours, minutes, sweep seconds; date
Case: titanium, 22.5 x 29.5 mm, height 9 mm;
white gold bezel set with 66 brilliant-cut diamonds;
sapphire crystal; water-resistant to 10 atm
Band: titanium, double folding clasp
Price: $7,450
Variations: w/o diamonds (from $3,300)

917 GR

Reference number: 917.010
Movement: automatic, ETA Caliber 7750; ø 30.4 mm,
height 7.9 mm; 25 jewels; 28,800 vph; shockproof
and antimagnetic (DIN norm); 42-hour power reserve
Functions: hours, minutes, subsidiary seconds;
chronograph; power reserve indicator
Case: stainless steel, ø 44 mm, height 15.5 mm;
crown-adjustable inner bezel with 60-minute
divisions; sapphire crystal; transparent case back;
screw-in crown; water-resistant to 10 atm
Band: calf leather, buckle
Remarks: Ar-dehumidifying technology
Price: $4,200
Variations: stainless steel band ($4,450); date
indicator (model 917; $3,550)

6110 Classik B

Reference number: 6110.010
Movement: manually wound, ETA Caliber 6498-1;
ø 36.6 mm, height 4.5 mm; 17 jewels; 18,000 vph;
shockproof and antimagnetic (DIN norm); 38-hour
power reserve
Functions: hours, minutes, subsidiary seconds
Case: stainless steel, ø 44 mm, height 10.6 mm;
sapphire crystal; transparent case back; water-
resistant to 10 atm
Band: reptile skin, buckle
Price: $2,975

1746 Classic

Reference number: 1746.011
Movement: automatic, ETA Caliber 2892-A2;
ø 26.2 mm, height 3.6 mm; 21 jewels; 28,800 vph;
shockproof and antimagnetic (DIN norm)
Functions: hours, minutes; date
Case: stainless steel, ø 42 mm, height 9.5 mm;
sapphire crystal; transparent case back; water-
resistant to 10 atm
Band: calf leather, buckle
Remarks: enamel dial
Price: $2,675
Variations: smaller 1736 Classic model ($2,450)

Stowa GmbH & Co. KG
Gewerbepark 16
D-75331 Engelsbrand
Germany

Tel.:
01149-7082-9306-0

Fax:
01149-7082-9306-2

E-Mail:
info@stowa.com

Website:
www.stowa.com

Founded:
1990

Number of employees:
15

Annual production:
maximum 4,000 watches

Distribution:
direct sales; please contact the company in Germany; orders are taken by phone Monday-Friday 9 a.m. to 5 p.m. European time with prices determined according to the daily exchange rate

Stowa

When a watch brand organizes a museum for itself, it is usually with good reason. The German firm Stowa may not be the biggest fish in the horological pond, but it has been around for more than eighty years, and its products are well worth taking a look at as expressions of German watchmaking culture. Stowa began in Pforzheim, then moved to the little industrial town of Rheinfelden, and now operates in Engelsbrand, a "suburb" of Pforzheim. After a history as a family-owned company, today the brand is headed by Jörg Schauer, who has maintained the goal and vision of original founder Walter Storz: delivering quality watches at a reasonable price.

Stowa is one of the few German brands to have operated without interruption since the beginning of the twentieth century, albeit with a new owner as of 1990. Besides all the political upheavals, it also survived the quartz crisis of the 1970s, during which the European market was flooded with cheap watches from Asia and many traditional German watchmakers were put out of business. Storz managed to keep Stowa going, but even a quality fanatic has to pay a price during times of trouble: With huge input from his son, Werner, Storz restructured the company so that it was able to begin encasing reasonably priced quartz movements rather than being strictly an assembler of mechanical movements.

Schauer bought the brand in 1996. Spurred on by the success of his eponymous line, he also steered Stowa back toward mechanical watches. His new Stowa timepieces are for the most part interpretations of successful old models now powered by Swiss ETA movements. For the last six years, Schauer has sold Stowa watches almost exclusively online or factory-direct, keeping its retail prices more than reasonable.

Marine Chronograph

Reference number: MarineChronograph
Movement: automatic, ETA Caliber 7753; ø 30.4 mm, height 7.9 mm; 27 jewels; 28,800 vph; 42-hour power reserve
Functions: hours, minutes, subsidiary seconds; chronograph
Case: stainless steel, ø 41 mm, height 14.7 mm; sapphire crystal
Band: reptile skin, buckle
Price: $2,450
Variations: calf leather band ($2,325); stainless steel band ($2,450)

Flieger Chronograph

Reference number: FliegerChrono
Movement: automatic, ETA Caliber 7753; ø 30.4 mm, height 7.9 mm; 27 jewels; 28,800 vph; 42-hour power reserve
Functions: hours, minutes; chronograph
Case: stainless steel, ø 41 mm, height 14.7 mm; sapphire crystal; water-resistant to 5 atm
Band: calf leather, buckle
Price: $2,370
Variations: retro leather band ($2,325); stainless steel bracelet ($2,475)

Marine Silver Date A10

Reference number: MarineSilbDatA10
Movement: automatic, Soprod Caliber A10; ø 25 6 mm, height 3.6 mm; 25 jewels; 28,800 vph; blued screws; 42-hour power reserve
Functions: hours, minutes, sweep seconds; date
Case: stainless steel, ø 40 mm, height 9.2 mm; sapphire crystal; transparent case back; water-resistant to 5 atm
Band: calf leather, buckle
Price: $975
Variations: reptile skin band ($1,300); stainless steel band ($1,300)

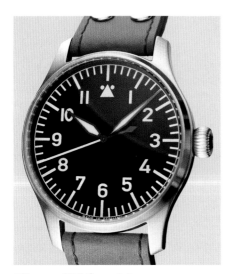

Flieger Without Logo

Reference number: FliegerohneLogo
Movement: automatic, ETA Caliber 2824-2;
ø 25.6 mm, height 4.6 mm; 25 jewels; 28,800 vph;
blued screws; handmade German silver rotor
Functions: hours, minutes, sweep seconds
Case: stainless steel, ø 40 mm, height 10.2 mm;
sapphire crystal; water-resistant to 5 atm
Band: calf leather, buckle (optionally folding clasp)
Price: $975
Variations: reptile band ($1,150); stainless steel
bracelet ($1,150), various movements

Antea Kleine Sekunde

Reference number: AnteaKS
Movement: automatic, ETA Caliber 7001; ø 23.3
mm, height 2.5 mm; 17 jewels, 21,600 vph; finely
finished with côtes de Genéve and blued screws;
42-hour power reserve
Functions: hours, minutes, subsidiary seconds
Case: stainless steel, ø 35.5 mm, height 6.9 mm;
sapphire crystal; transparent case back; water-
resistant to 3 atm
Band: deerskin, buckle
Price: $1,075
Variations: reptile skin band ($1,250); stainless
steel band ($1,250)

Marine Original

Reference number: MarineOriginalpolweissarabisch
Movement: manually wound, ETA Caliber 6498-1;
ø 36.6 mm, height 4.5 mm; 17 jewels; 18,000 vph;
screw balance, swan-neck fine adjustment; côtes de
Genéve, blued screws; 46-hour power reserve
Functions: hours, minutes, subsidiary seconds
Case: stainless steel, ø 41 mm, height 12 mm;
sapphire crystal; transparent case back; water-
resistant to 5 atm
Band: calf leather, buckle
Price: $1,270
Variations: reptile skin band ($1,365); stainless
steel band ($1,360)

Antea 390 A10

Reference number: Antea390A10
Movement: automatic, Soprod Caliber A10;
ø 25.6 mm, height 3.6 mm; 25 jewels; 28,800 vph;
blued screws, 42-hour power reserve
Functions: hours, minutes, sweep seconds; date
Case: stainless steel, ø 39 mm, height 8.1 mm;
sapphire crystal; transparent case back; water-
resistant to 5 atm
Band: calf leather, buckle
Price: $1,150
Variations: reptile skin band ($1,300); stainless
steel band ($1,250)

Seatime Black

Reference number: SeatimeSchwarz
Movement: automatic, ETA Caliber 2824-2;
ø 25.6 mm, height 4.6 mm; 25 jewels; 28,800 vph;
38-hour power reserve
Functions: hours, minutes, sweep seconds; date
Case: stainless steel, ø 42 mm, height 13.5 mm;
unidirectional bezel with reference marker; screw-in
crown; sapphire crystal; water-resistant to 30 atm
Band: rubber, double safety folding clasp with
extension link
Price: $1,075
Variations: calf leather band ($1,075); stainless
steel band ($1,195); various bezel colors

GMT Worldtime

Reference number: GMTWorldtime
Movement: automatic, ETA Caliber 07.171;
ø 36.6 mm, height 7.9 mm; 24 jewels; 28,800 vph;
46-hour power reserve
Functions: hours, minutes, sweep seconds;
additional 24-hour display (2nd time zone)
Case: titanium, ø 45 mm, height 12.9 mm;
bidirectional bezel with 24-hour division, sapphire
crystal; transparent case back; water-resistant to
20 atm
Band: buffalo skin, buckle
Price: $2,440
Variations: rubber strap ($2,400)

TAG Heuer

Branch of LVMH SA
6a, rue L.-J.-Chevrolet
CH-2300 La Chaux-de-Fonds
Switzerland

Tel.:
01141-32-919-8164

Fax:
01141-32-919-9000

E-Mail:
info@tagheuer.com

Website:
www.tagheuer.com

Founded:
1860

Number of employees:
approx. 1,000

U.S. distributor:
TAG Heuer/LVMH Watch & Jewelry USA
966 South Springfield Avenue
Springfield, NJ 07081
973-467-1890

Most important collections/price range:
TAG Heuer Formula 1, Aquaracer, Link, Carrera, Grand Carrera, Monaco / from approx. $1,000 to $20,000

TAG Heuer

Measuring speed accurately in ever greater detail has been the ultimate goal of TAG Heuer. The brand has also established numerous technical milestones including the first automatic chronograph caliber with a microrotor (created in 1969 in cooperation with Hamilton-Büren, Breitling, and Dubois Dépraz). Of more recent vintage is the fascinating mechanical movement V4 with its belt-driven transmission, unveiled in a limited edition for the brand's 150th anniversary. At the same time TAG Heuer released its first chronograph with an in-house movement, Caliber 1887, the basis of which was an existing chronograph movement by the Japanese company Seiko. Some of the components are made by the company itself in Switzerland, while assembly is done entirely in-house.

Lately, TAG Heuer has increased its manufacturing capacities to meet the strong and growing demand and to maintain its independence. It also serves as an extended workbench for companion brands Zenith and Hublot, also part of the LVMH Group.

TAG Heuer continues to conceive some spectacular concept watches and to break world speed records for mechanical escapements. In 2005, the outstanding Caliber 360 combined a standard movement with a 360,000 vph (50 Hz) chronograph mechanism able to measure 100ths of a second. In 2011, the Micrograph 1/100th housed a time display and measurement mounted on a single plate. Shortly after, the development department under Guy Sémon broke the 1,000th of a second barrier with the Mikrotimer Flying 1000. And in 2012, the frequency was doubled with the Mikrogirder 2000, featuring a vibrating metal strip instead of a balance wheel. The latest development is the MikrotourbillonS with a chronograph built on the dual-chain, start- and stopwatch principle. It has two escapements, each with a tourbillon. The chronograph one revolves in five seconds, driven at a record-breaking 360,000 vph, ten times that of the Zenith El Primero.

TAG Heuer Formula 1 Calibre 16

Reference number: CAZ2011.FT8024
Movement: automatic, TAG Heuer Caliber 16 (base ETA 7750); ø 30.4 mm, height 7.9 mm; 25 jewels; 28,800 vph
Functions: hours, minutes, subsidiary seconds; chronograph; date
Case: stainless steel with black titanium carbide coating; ø 44 mm; sapphire crystal; screw-in crown; water-resistant to 20 atm
Band: calf leather, buckle
Price: $3,400
Variations: stainless steel w/o coating ($2,900)

Aquaracer 300M Calibre 5

Reference number: WAY2110.BA0910
Movement: automatic, TAG Heuer Caliber 5 (base ETA 2824-2); ø 26 mm, height 4.6 mm; 25 jewels; 28,800 vph
Functions: hours, minutes, sweep seconds; date
Case: stainless steel, ø 40.5 mm, unidirectional bezel with 60-minute divisions, sapphire crystal; screw-in crown; water-resistant to 30 atm
Band: stainless steel, folding clasp with safety lock and extension link
Price: $2,500
Variations: rubber strap ($2,500); various dial colors

Aquaracer 500M Calibre 16

Reference number: CAK2110.BA0833
Movement: automatic, TAG Heuer Caliber 16 (base ETA 7750); ø 30.4 mm, height 7.9 mm; 25 jewels; 28,800 vph
Functions: hours, minutes, subsidiary seconds; chronograph; date
Case: stainless steel, ø 43 mm, height 16 mm; unidirectional bezel with ceramic inlay and 60-minute divisions, sapphire crystal; screw-in crown; automatic helium valve; water-resistant to 50 atm
Band: stainless steel, folding clasp with safety pushers
Price: $4,300

Aquaracer Calibre 5 Lady

Reference number: WAP2351.BD0838
Movement: automatic, TAG Heuer Caliber 5 (base ETA 2824-2); ø 26 mm, height 4.6 mm; 25 jewels; 28,800 vph
Functions: hours, minutes, sweep seconds; date
Case: stainless steel, ø 34 mm, rose gold bezel, sapphire crystal; transparent case back; screw-in crown; water-resistant to 20 atm
Band: stainless steel with rose gold inlays, folding clasp with safety pushers
Remarks: dial set with 11 diamonds
Price: $5,500
Variations: w/o diamonds ($4,700)

Carrera Calibre 9 Lady

Reference number: WAR2410.BA0770
Movement: automatic, TAG Heuer Caliber 9 (base Sellita SW1000); ø 20 mm; 18 jewels; 28,800 vph
Functions: hours, minutes, sweep seconds; date
Case: stainless steel, ø 28 mm; sapphire crystal; transparent case back; water-resistant to 10 atm
Band: stainless steel, folding clasp with safety lock
Price: $2,900
Variations: white mother-of-pearl dial

Carrera Calibre 5 Lady

Reference number: WAR211A.FC6180
Movement: automatic, TAG Heuer Caliber 5 (base ETA 2824-2); ø 26 mm, height 4.6 mm; 25 jewels; 28,800 vph
Functions: hours, minutes, sweep seconds; date
Case: stainless steel, ø 39 mm, height 12 mm; sapphire crystal; transparent case back; water-resistant to 10 atm
Band: reptile skin, folding clasp with safety lock
Price: $2,900
Variations: various dial and strap colors ($2,900); stainless steel bracelet ($2,900)

Carrera Calibre 5 Day-Date

Reference number: WAR201A.BA0723
Movement: automatic, TAG Heuer Caliber 5 (base ETA 2834-2); ø 29 mm, height 5.05 mm; 25 jewels; 28,800 vph
Functions: hours, minutes, sweep seconds; weekday, date
Case: stainless steel, ø 41 mm, height 13 mm; sapphire crystal; transparent case back; water-resistant to 10 atm
Band: stainless steel, folding clasp with safety lock
Price: $3,300
Variations: silver-colored dial

Carrera Calibre 1887

Reference number: CAR2A10.BA0799
Movement: automatic, TAG Heuer Caliber 1887; ø 29.3 mm, height 7.13 mm; 39 jewels; 28,800 vph
Functions: hours, minutes, subsidiary seconds; chronograph; date
Case: stainless steel, ø 43 mm, height 14.8 mm; ceramic bezel; sapphire crystal; transparent case back; water-resistant to 10 atm
Band: stainless steel, folding clasp with safety pushers
Price: $5,500
Variations: reptile skin band ($5,500)

Carrera Calibre 1887

Reference number: CAR2110.BA0720
Movement: automatic, TAG Heuer Caliber 1887; ø 29.3 mm, height 7.13 mm; 39 jewels; 28,800 vph
Functions: hours, minutes, subsidiary seconds; chronograph; date
Case: stainless steel, ø 41 mm, height 16 mm; sapphire crystal; transparent case back; water-resistant to 10 atm
Band: stainless steel, folding clasp with safety pushers
Price: $5,400
Variations: various dial colors; reptile skin band ($5,400)

Carrera Calibre 1887 Elegance

Reference number: CAR2012.FC6235
Movement: automatic, TAG Heuer Caliber 1887;
ø 29.3 mm, height 7.13 mm; 39 jewels; 28,800 vph
Functions: hours, minutes, subsidiary seconds;
chronograph; date
Case: stainless steel, ø 43 mm, height 16 mm;
sapphire crystal; transparent case back; water-
resistant to 10 atm
Band: reptile skin, folding clasp
Price: $6,400
Variations: black dial; stainless steel bracelet
($6,400)

Carrera Calibre 1887 Bullhead

Reference number: CAR2C12.FC6327
Movement: automatic, TAG Heuer Caliber 1887;
ø 29.3 mm, height 7.13 mm; 39 jewels; 28,800 vph
Functions: hours, minutes, subsidiary seconds;
chronograph; date
Case: titanium, ø 45 mm, height 14.5 mm; stainless
steel bezel with black titanium carbide coating,
sapphire crystal; transparent case back; water-
resistant to 10 atm
Band: reptile skin, folding clasp, with safety pushers
Remarks: bullhead case: crown and pushers over
upper lugs
Price: $7,800

Carrera Calibre 1887 Bullhead Carbon Matrix Composite

Reference number: CAR2C90.FC6341
Movement: automatic, TAG Heuer Caliber 1887;
ø 29.3 mm, height 7.13 mm; 39 jewels; 28,800 vph
Functions: hours, minutes, subsidiary seconds;
chronograph; date
Case: titanium, ø 45 mm, height 17 mm; stainless
steel bezel with black titanium carbide coating,
sapphire crystal; transparent case back; water-
resistant to 10 atm
Band: reptile skin, folding clasp, with safety pushers
Remarks: bullhead case: crown and pushers over
upper lugs
Price: $11,300

Carrera Calibre CH 80

Reference number: CBA2111.BA0723
Movement: automatic, TAG Heuer Caliber 80;
ø 31 mm, height 6.5 mm; 33 jewels; 28,800 vph
Functions: hours, minutes, subsidiary seconds;
chronograph; date
Case: stainless steel, ø 41 mm; sapphire crystal;
transparent case back; water-resistant to 10 atm
Band: stainless steel, folding clasp with safety lock
Price: $5,500
Variations: calf leather band ($5,500)

Carrera Calibre 8 Grande Date GMT

Reference number: WAR5012.FC6326
Movement: automatic, TAG Heuer Caliber 8 (base
ETA 2892-A2); ø 26.2 mm, height 3.6 mm; 21
jewels; 28,800 vph; COSC-certified chronometer
Functions: hours, minutes, sweep seconds;
additional 12-hour display (2nd time zone); large
date
Case: stainless steel, ø 41 mm, height 13 mm;
sapphire crystal; transparent case back; water-
resistant to 10 atm
Band: reptile skin, folding clasp, with safety pushers
Price: $4,000
Variations: black or anthracite dial, reptile skin
strap ($4,000)

Carrera Calibre 36 Flyback

Reference number: CAR2B10.BA0799
Movement: automatic, TAG Heuer Caliber 36 (base
Zenith El Primero 400); ø 30 mm, height 6.6 mm; 31
jewels; 36,000 vph; mounted in shockproof cage
Functions: hours, minutes, sweep seconds; flyback
chronograph; date
Case: stainless steel, ø 43 mm, height 15 mm;
sapphire crystal; transparent case back; water-
resistant to 10 atm
Band: stainless steel, folding clasp, with safety
pushers
Price: $7,900
Variations: reptile skin band ($7,900); titanium with
black coating and calf leather band ($7,900)

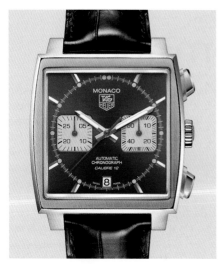

Monaco Calibre 12
Steve McQueen Edition

Reference number: CAW2111.FC6383
Movement: automatic, TAG Heuer Caliber 12 (base Sellita SW300 with Dubois Dépraz module 2008); ø 30 mm, height 7.3 mm; 59 jewels; 28,800 vph
Functions: hours, minutes, subsidiary seconds; chronograph; date
Case: stainless steel, 39 x 39 mm, height 13.5 mm; sapphire crystal; transparent case back; water-resistant to 10 atm
Band: calf leather, folding clasp
Price: $6,300
Variations: black dial and reptile leather band ($6,300)

Carrera Mikrograph 100
Avantgarde

Reference number: CAR5A50.FC6319
Movement: automatic, TAG Heuer Calibre Mikrograph; ø 35.8 mm; 62 jewels; 28,800 vph; 2 escapements for movement and chronograph; display of 1/100th seconds
Functions: hours, minutes, subsidiary seconds; power reserve indicator; chronograph; date
Case: titanium with black titanium carbide coating; rose gold lugs; ø 45 mm, height 17 mm; sapphire crystal; transparent back; water-resistant to 10 atm
Band: reptile skin, folding clasp
Price: $39,900; limited to 50 pieces
Variations: rose gold ($39,900; limited to 150)

Carrera Mikropendulum 100

Reference number: CAR2B83.FC6339
Movement: automatic, Calibre Mikrograph; ø 35.8 mm; 58 jewels; 28,800 vph; pendulum system (permanent magnet instead of hairspring) with own high-frequency escapement for chronograph functions, display of 1/100th seconds; 42-hour power reserve (watch), 90 minutes (chronograph); COSC-certified chronometer
Functions: hours, minutes; chronograph
Case: titanium, ø 45 mm, height 17 mm; sapphire crystal; transparent back; water-resistant to 10 atm
Band: reptile skin, folding clasp, with safety pushers
Price: $42,000

Carrera Mikrotourbillon S 100

Reference number: CAR5A51.FC6323
Movement: automatic, TAG Heuer Caliber Mikrotourbillon S; ø 35.8 mm; 75 jewels; 28,800 vph; 2 balance wheels with tourbillon; display of 1/100th seconds; 45-hour power reserve (watch), 60 minutes (chronograph)
Functions: hours, minutes; power reserve indicator; chronograph
Case: rose gold, ø 45 mm, height 17 mm; sand-blasted titanium bezel, sapphire crystal; transparent case back; water-resistant to 10 atm
Band: reptile skin, folding clasp, with safety pushers
Price: $240,000

Monaco V4 Titanium

Reference number: WAW2080.FC6288
Movement: automatic, TAG Heuer Caliber V4; 35 x 31.5 mm; 48 jewels; 18,000 vph; tungsten carbide linear winding mass, 4 spring barrels; 13 miniature belts transmit power; 39 micro ball bearings; 742 components in all
Functions: hours, minutes, subsidiary seconds
Case: titanium coated with silicon nitride ceramic, 41 x 41 mm; faceted sapphire crystal; transparent case back; water-resistant to 10 atm
Band: reptile skin, folding clasp, with safety pushers
Price: $70,000; limited to 200 pieces

Monaco V4 Tourbillon

Reference number: WAW2081.FC6348
Movement: automatic, TAG Heuer Caliber V4; 35 x 31.5 mm, height 9.13 mm; 46 jewels; 4 spring barrels, 13 miniature belts transmit power; 39 micro ball-bearings; belt-driven 1-minute tourbillon
Functions: hours, minutes
Case: titanium with black titanium carbide coating; 41 x 41 mm; sapphire crystal; transparent case back; water-resistant to 5 atm
Band: reptile skin, folding clasp
Price: $165,000

Temption GmbH
Raistinger Str. 46
D-71083 Herrenberg
Germany

Tel.:
01149-7032-977-954

Fax:
01149-7032-977-955

E-Mail:
ftemption@aol.com

Website:
www.temption.info

Founded:
1997

Number of employees:
4

Annual production:
700 watches

U.S. distributor:
TemptionUSA
Debby Gordon
2053 North Bridgeport Drive
Fayetteville, AR 72704
888-400-4293
temptionusa@sbcglobal.net

Most important collections/price range:
automatics (three-hand), GMT, chronographs,
and chronographs with complications /
approx. $1,900 to $4,200

Temption

Temption has been operating under the leadership of Klaus Ulbrich since 1997. Ulbrich is an engineer with special training in the construction of watches and movements, and right from the start, he intended to develop timekeepers that were modern in their aesthetics but not subject to the whims of zeitgeist. Retro watches would have no place in his collections. The design behind all Temption models is inspired more by the Bauhaus or the Japanese concept of wabi sabi. Reduction to what is absolutely necessary is the golden rule here. Beauty emerges from clarity, or in other words, less is more.

Ulbrich sketches all the watches himself. Some of the components are even made in-house, but all the pieces are assembled in the company facility in Herrenberg, a town just to the east of the Black Forest. The primary functions are always easy to read, even in low light. The company logo is discreetly included on the dial.

Ulbrich works according to a model he calls the "information pyramid." Hours and minutes are at the tip, with all other functions subordinated. To maintain this hierarchy, the dials are dark, the date windows are in the same hue, and all subdials are not framed in any way.

The Cameo rectangular model is a perfect example of Ulbrich's aesthetic ideas and his consistent technological approach: Because rectangular sapphire crystals can hardly be made water-resistant, the Cameo's crystal is chemically bonded to the case and water-resistant to 10 atm. The frame for the sapphire was metalized inside to hide the bonded edge. The overall look is one of stunning simplicity and elegance.

CM05

Reference number: 16
Movement: automatic, Temption Caliber T15.1 (base ETA 2892-A2); ø 25.6 mm, height 3.6 mm; 21 jewels; 28,800 vph; 42-hour power reserve
Functions: hours, minutes, sweep seconds; date
Case: stainless steel, ø 42 mm, height 11 mm; unidirectional bezel, 12-hour division, sapphire crystal; transparent case back; screw-in crown; water-resistant to 10 atm
Band: stainless steel, double folding clasp
Price: $2,400

CM01

Reference number: CM01
Movement: automatic, Temption Caliber T15.2; ø 25.6 mm, height 3.6 mm; 25 jewels, 28,800 vph; finely finished; 42-hour power reserve
Functions: hours, minutes, sweep seconds; date
Case: ø 43 mm, height 9.8 mm; sapphire crystal, transparent case back; screw-in crown; water-resistant to 10 atm
Band: calf leather, folding clasp
Price: $2,150

Chronograph CGK205

Reference number: 205
Movement: automatic, Temption Caliber T18.1 (base ETA 7751); ø 30 mm, height 7.8 mm; 25 jewels; 28,800 vph; finely decorated; 42-hour power reserve
Functions: hours, minutes, additional 24-hour display; chronograph; full calendar with date, weekday, month, moon phase
Case: stainless steel, ø 43 mm, height 14 mm; sapphire crystal; transparent case back; screw-in crown and pusher; with onyx cabochons; water-resistant to 10 atm
Band: stainless steel, double folding clasp
Remarks: additional leather or rubber bracelet
Price: $3,950

Thomas Ninchritz

In 1520, the locksmith Peter Henlein of Nuremberg was the first craftsman in Europe who could create "portable clocks." About half a millennium later, a trip to Nuremberg is still well worth the effort for watch aficionados: In his atelier, watchmaker Thomas Ninchritz produces a small collection of fascinating wristwatches.

The core of Ninchritz's watches is the extremely robust ETA Unitas caliber—though when he adds his own well-proportioned three-quarter plate, it is hardly recognizable. The master's meticulous work lends the classic manually wound movement a finish that does not need to shy away from comparisons even to expensive *manufacture* movements. Screw-mounted gold chatons, hand-engraved balance cocks, and swan-neck fine adjustments are among the elements that make a watch enthusiast's heart beat faster.

The creative watchmaker came up with a very interesting idea for his Vice Versa model: Using a relatively simple method, he routes the dial train of ETA Caliber 6498 (the hunter version featuring subsidiary seconds at 6 o'clock) across two transmission wheels and a long stem through to the back of the movement. There is enough room to poke it through between the spring barrel and the balance, with the hand arbors now appearing in a small dial on the gear train bridge, which Ninchritz has extended to become a true three-quarter plate decorated with a stripe pattern, engraving, and chatons secured by little blued screws. Additionally, the index is accompanied by a beautiful swan-neck spring, to ensure that no one will mistake this work of art for the "back" of the movement.

Thomas Ninchritz
Niebüller Strasse 7
D-90425 Nuremberg
Germany

Tel.:
01149-911-552-363

Fax:
01149-911-581-7622

E-Mail:
th.ninchritz@t-online.de

Website:
www.ninchritz-uhren.de

Founded:
2005

Number of employees:
1

Distribution:
WatchBuys
888-333-4895
www.watchbuys.com

Most important collections/price range:
Black & Diamonds, Fliegeruhr, Grande Seconde, Kathedral, Ornatis / $2,400 to $23,250

Vice Versa

Reference number: TN 2000.62
Movement: manually wound, TN Caliber 203 (base ETA 6498-1); ø 36.6 mm, height 4.03 mm; 18 jewels; 18,000 vph; three-quarter plate with gold chatons; swan-neck fine adjustment; back inverted by relocating hand gears; finely finished with blued screws and côtes de Genève; 38-hour power reserve
Functions: hours, minutes (off-center), subsidiary seconds (on back)
Case: rose gold, ø 42 mm, height 10.5 mm; sapphire crystal; transparent case back; water-resistant to 3 atm
Band: calf leather, buckle
Price: on request
Variations: stainless steel ($6,700)

Régulateur

Reference number: NI 2000.5
Movement: manually wound, TN Caliber 201 (base ETA 6498-1); ø 36.6 mm, height 4.6 mm; 17 jewels; 18,000 vph; three-quarter plate with screwed-in gold chatons, hand-engraved balance cock; swan-neck fine adjustment; finely finished; 38-hour power reserve
Functions: hours (off-center), minutes, subsidiary seconds
Case: stainless steel, ø 42 mm, height 10.5 mm; sapphire crystal, water-resistant to 3 atm
Band: calf leather, buckle
Price: $4,650
Variations: gold (on request)

Ornatis

Reference number: NI 2000.8
Movement: manually wound, TN Caliber 200 (base ETA 6498-1); ø 36.6 mm, height 4.03 mm; 17 jewels; 18,000 vph; base plate skeletonized and engraved, three-quarter plate with screwed-in gold chatons, hand-engraved balance cock; swan-neck fine adjustment; finely finished, 38-hour power reserve
Functions: hours, minutes, subsidiary seconds
Case: stainless steel, ø 42 mm, height 10.5 mm; sapphire crystal; water-resistant to 3 atm
Band: calf leather, buckle
Remarks: skeletonized dial
Price: $9,700
Variations: gold (on request)

Tissot

Tissot SA
Chemin des Tourelles, 17
CH-2400 Le Locle
Switzerland

Tel.:
01141-32-933-3111

Fax:
01141-32-933-3311

E-Mail:
info@tissot.ch

Website:
www.tissot.ch

Founded:
1853

U.S. distributor:
Tissot
The Swatch Group (U.S.), Inc.
1200 Harbor Boulevard
Weehawken, NJ 07087
201-271-1400
www.us.tissotshop.com

Most important collection/price range:
T-Touch / from $575

The Swiss watchmaker Tissot was founded in 1853 in the town of Le Locle in the Jura mountains. In the century that followed, it gained international recognition for its Savonnette pocket watch. And even when the wristwatch became popular in the early twentieth century, time and again Tissot managed to attract attention to its products. To this day, the Banana Watch of 1916 and its first watches in the art deco style

(1919) remain design icons of that epoch. The watchmaker has always been at the top of its technical game as well: The first antimagnetic watch (1930), the first mechanical plastic watch (Astrolon, 1971), and its touch-screen T-Touch (1999) all bear witness to Tissot's remarkable capacity for finding unusual and modern solutions.

Today, Tissot belongs to the Swatch Group and, with its wide selection of quartz and inexpensive mechanical watches, serves as the group's entry-level brand. Within this price segment, Tissot offers something special for the buyer who values traditional watchmaking, but is not of limitless financial means. The brand, which celebrated its 160th anniversary in style in 2013 with a comprehensive retrospective in Geneva, has gravitated toward the sports crowd. Tissot is timing everything from basketball to superbike racing, from ice hockey to fencing—and water sports, of course. The Sailing Touch, a watch that provides sailors with a vast array of needed information, came out in 2010. The chronograph Couturier line is outfitted with the new ETA chronograph caliber C01.211. This caliber features a number of plastic parts: another step in simplifying, and lowering the cost of, mechanical movements.

T-Touch Expert Solar

Reference number: T091.420.46.051.01
Movement: quartz, ETA Caliber E84.301; multifunctional with LCD display and solar cell
Functions: hours, minutes; additional 12-hour indicator (2nd time zone); weather report, altimeter and altitude difference meter, compass, regatta function; 2 alarms; chronograph with countdown timer; perpetual calendar with date, weekday, week
Case: titanium with black PVD coating, ø 45 mm, height 13 mm; sapphire crystal; water-resistant to 10 atm
Band: calf leather and textile, folding clasp
Price: $1,150

Chemin des Tourelles Squelette

Reference number: T099.405.16.418.00
Movement: manually wound, ETA Caliber 6497-1; ø 36.6 mm, height 4.5 mm; 17 jewels; 18,000 vph; partially skeletonized; 46-hour power reserve
Functions: hours, minutes, subsidiary seconds
Case: stainless steel, ø 42 mm, height 11.1 mm; sapphire crystal; transparent case back; water-resistant to 5 atm
Band: calf leather, double folding clasp
Price: $2,050

T-Complication Chronometer

Reference number: T070.406.16.057.00
Movement: manually wound, ETA Caliber 6498-2; ø 36.6 mm, height 4.5 mm; 17 jewels; 21,600 vph; 53-hour power reserve; COSC-certified chronometer
Functions: hours, minutes, subsidiary seconds
Case: stainless steel, ø 43 mm, height 11 mm; sapphire crystal; transparent case back; water-resistant to 5 atm
Band: calf leather, double folding clasp
Price: $1,950

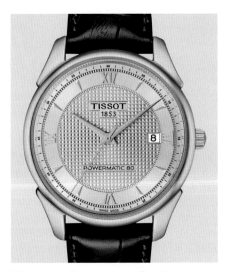

Vintage Powermatic 80

Reference number: T920.407.76.038.00
Movement: automatic, Tissot Powermatic 80 (base ETA 2824-2); ø 25.6 mm, height 4.6 mm; 23 jewels; 21,600 vph; variable inertia balance; 80-hour power reserve; COSC-certified chronometer
Functions: hours, minutes, sweep seconds; date
Case: stainless steel with rose gold-colored PVD coating, ø 40 mm, height 9.3 mm; sapphire crystal; transparent case back; water-resistant to 3 atm
Band: calf leather, double folding clasp
Price: $2,750

Bridgeport Automatic

Reference number: T097.407.26.033.00
Movement: automatic, Tissot Powermatic 80 (base ETA 2824-2); ø 25.6 mm, height 4.6 mm; 23 jewels; 21,600 vph; variable inertia balance; 80-hour power reserve
Functions: hours, minutes, sweep seconds; date
Case: stainless steel, ø 40 mm, height 9.44 mm; bezel and crown with rose gold PVD coating; sapphire crystal; transparent case back; water-resistant to 5 atm
Band: calf leather, double folding clasp
Price: $850

Titanium Automatic

Reference number: 407.44.037.00
Movement: automatic, Tissot Powermatic 80 (base ETA 2824-2); ø 25.6 mm, height 4.6 mm; 23 jewels; 21,600 vph; variable inertia balance; 80-hour power reserve
Functions: hours, minutes, sweep seconds; date
Case: titanium, ø 40 mm, height 9.75 mm; sapphire crystal; transparent case back; water-resistant to 5 atm
Band: titanium, double folding clasp
Price: $825

Quickster

Reference number: T095.417.36.057.00
Movement: quartz, ETA Caliber G10.211
Functions: hours, minutes, subsidiary seconds; chronograph; date
Case: stainless steel with black PVD coating, ø 42 mm, height 10.72 mm; sapphire crystal; water-resistant to 10 atm
Band: calf leather, buckle
Price: $495

T-Race Touch Aluminum

Reference number: T081.420.97.057.00
Movement: quartz, ETA Caliber E49.301; multifunctional with LCD display
Functions: hours, minutes; additional 12-hour indicator (2nd time zone); compass, tides calculator; 2 alarms; chronograph with 2 countdown timers; perpetual calendar with date, month
Case: aluminum, ø 42.15 mm, height 13.46 mm; sapphire crystal; water-resistant to 10 atm
Band: plexiglass; buckle
Price: $575

T-Race MotoGP Automatic Chronograph Limited Edition 2014

Reference number: T048.427.27.061.00
Movement: automatic, ETA Caliber C01.211; ø 30 mm, height 8.44 mm; 15 jewels; 21,600 vph; 45-hour power reserve
Functions: hours, minutes, subsidiary seconds; chronograph; date
Case: stainless steel, ø 45.3 mm, height 16.09 mm; bezel with black PVD coating; sapphire crystal; transparent case back; water-resistant to 10 atm
Band: rubber, folding clasp
Price: $1,425

Towson Watch Co.
502 Dogwood Lane
Towson, MD 21286

Tel.:
410-823-1823

Fax:
410-823-8581

E-Mail:
towsonwatchco@aol.com

Website:
www.twcwatches.com

Founded:
2000

Number of employees:
4

Annual production:
200 watches

Distribution:
retail

Most important collections/price range:
Skipjack GMT / approx. $2,950; Mission /
approx. $2,500; Potomac / approx. $2,000;
Choptank / approx. $4,500; custom design /
$10,000 to $35,000

Towson Watch Company

"The old charm, in truth, still survives in the town, despite the frantic efforts of boosters and boomers who, in late years, have replaced all its ancient cobblestones with asphalt," commented H. L. Mencken on his native Baltimore back in the 1920s. No doubt he would have sprayed his caustic ink at some of the more recent urban renewal projects, but he would still have welcomed the Towson Watch Company, founded in 2000 by two men with a deep-seated passion for mechanical timepieces. After forty years repairing high-grade watches, repeaters, and chronographs and making his own tourbillons, George Thomas, a master watchmaker, met Hartwig Balke, a graduate in mechanical engineering and also a talented watchmaker, by chance.

To create something special, mechanical instruments of beauty and precision, was always each man's dream. Thomas built his first tourbillon pocket watches, now displayed at the National Watch and Clock Museum in Columbia, Pennsylvania, in 1985 when he was fifty-three years old. In 1999, Balke made his first wrist chronograph, the STS-99 Mission, for a NASA astronaut and mission specialist, and it was worn during the first space mission in the new millennium.

With Towson these two men's passion has gone into timepieces named for local sites and sights, like the Choptank or Potomac rivers, or the skipjack sailboats. The timepieces emerging from their workshop are very imaginative, a touch retro, a bit nostalgic perhaps, and very personal—not to mention affordable. Their latest project is a return to the past, a pilot chronograph inspired by gauges on the Lockheed Martin China Clipper flying boats from the 1930s.

Skipjack GMT

Reference number: SKJ100-S
Movement: automatic ETA Caliber 2893-2;
ø 25.6 mm, height 4.1 mm; 21 jewels; 28,800 vph;
regulated in 5 positions; 42-hour power reserve; fine
finishing with côtes de Genève
Functions: hours, minutes, sweep seconds; 2nd
time zone, 24-hour hand individually adjustable
Case: stainless steel, ø 40.5 mm, height 10.5 mm;
sapphire crystal; transparent back; water resistant
to 5 atm
Band: calf leather, folding clasp
Price: $2,950; limited to 100 pieces
Variations: black dial

Choptank

Reference number: CT250-R
Movement: automatic, ETA Caliber 7751
("Valjoux"); ø 30 mm, height 7.9 mm; 25 jewels;
28,800 vph; fine finishing with côtes de Genève
Functions: hours, minutes, subsidiary seconds;
24-hour display; chronograph; weekday, month,
date, moon phase
Case: stainless steel, 40 x 44 mm, height 13.5 mm;
sapphire crystal, screwed-down back secured with
8 screws; transparent case back; water-resistant to
5 atm
Band: reptile skin, folding clasp
Price: $4,375
Variations: stainless steel bracelet ($4,750)

Potomac

Reference number: PO250-S
Movement: manually wound, Soprod Unitas Caliber
6498; ø 37.2 mm, height 7.9 mm; 17 jewels;
18,000 vph; swan-neck fine adjustment; fine
finishing with côtes de Genève
Functions: hours; minutes, subsidiary second
Case: stainless steel, ø 42 mm, height 13.5 mm;
domed sapphire crystal; screwed-down back;
sapphire crystal exhibition window; water resistant
to 5 atm
Band: reptile skin, folding clasp
Price: $1,995
Variations: stainless steel bracelet ($2,350)

1888

Montres Tudor SA
Rue François-Dussaud 3-7
Case postale 1755
CH-1211 Geneva
Switzerland

Tel.:
01141-22-302-2200

Fax:
01141-22-300-2255

E-Mail:
info@tudorwatch.com

Website:
www.tudorwatch.com

Founded:
1946

U.S. distributor:
Tudor Watch U.S.A., LLC
665 Fifth Avenue
New York, NY 10022
212-897-9900; 212-371-0371(fax)
www.tudorwatch.com

Most important collections/price range:
Heritage / $3,100 to $6,075; Pelagos /
$4,125; Grantour / $2,475 to $8,000;
Fastrider / $3,675 to $4,925

Tudor

The Tudor brand came out of the shadow cast by its "big sister" Rolex in 2007 and worked hard to develop a personality of its own. The strategy is to focus on distinctive models that draw inspiration from the brand's rich past and to remain in the "affordable quality watch segment," which derives from its close connection with its parent company.

Rolex founder Hans Wilsdorf started Tudor in 1946 as a second brand in order to offer the legendary reliability of his watches to a broader public at a more affordable price. To this day, Tudor still benefits from the same industrial platform as Rolex, especially in the area of cases and bracelets, assembly and quality assurance, not to mention distribution and after-sales. However, the movements themselves are not in-house. They are delivered by ETA and "tudorized" according to the company's own aesthetic and technical criteria.

In the era of vintage and retro, it's no wonder that the brand has started tapping into its own treasure trove of icons. Following the success of the Heritage Black Bay diver's watch, based on a 1954 model, came the turn of the blue-highlighted 1973 Chronograph Montecarlo. In 2014, Tudor completed the Heritage collection with the Ranger, a sports watch with an urban-adventurer feel, inspired by the same "tool watch" from the 1960s. In those days, the Ranger was part of the basic equipment for expeditions to, say, the icy stretches of the Arctic or the dizzying heights of the Himalayas.

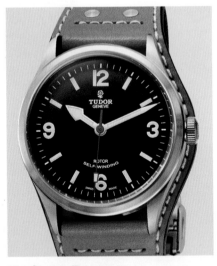

Heritage Ranger

Reference number: 79910
Movement: automatic, Tudor Caliber 2824 (base ETA 2824-2); ø 26 mm, height 4.6 mm; 25 jewels; 28,800 vph; 38-hour power reserve
Functions: hours, minutes, sweep seconds
Case: stainless steel, ø 41 mm, height 12.15 mm; sapphire crystal; screw-in crown; water-resistant to 15 atm
Band: calf leather, folding clasp with safety lock
Remarks: comes with extra fabric band
Price: $2,825
Variations: stainless steel bracelet ($2,950)

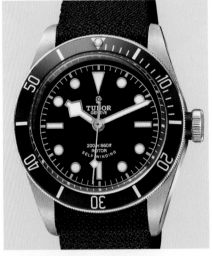

Heritage Black Bay

Reference number: 79220B
Movement: automatic, Tudor Caliber 2824 (base ETA 2824-2); ø 26 mm, height 4.6 mm; 25 jewels; 28,800 vph; 38-hour power reserve
Functions: hours, minutes, sweep seconds
Case: stainless steel, ø 41 mm, height 12.7 mm; unidirectional bezel with 60-minute divisions, sapphire crystal; screw-in crown; water-resistant to 20 atm
Band: textile, buckle
Remarks: comes with extra leather band
Price: $3,100
Variations: stainless steel bracelet ($3,425)

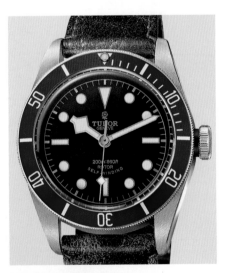

Heritage Black Bay

Reference number: 79220R
Movement: automatic, Tudor Caliber 2824 (base ETA 2824-2); ø 26 mm, height 4.6 mm; 25 jewels; 28,800 vph; 38-hour power reserve
Functions: hours, minutes, sweep seconds
Case: stainless steel, ø 41 mm, height 12.95 mm; unidirectional bezel with 60-minute divisions, sapphire crystal; screw-in crown; water-resistant to 20 atm
Band: calf leather, folding clasp
Remarks: comes with extra fabric band
Price: $3,100
Variations: stainless steel bracelet ($3,425)

Heritage Chrono Blue

Reference number: 70330B
Movement: automatic, Tudor Caliber 2892 (base ETA 2892-A2 with chronograph module); ø 30 mm, height 6.9 mm; 55 jewels; 28,800 vph; 42-hour power reserve
Functions: hours, minutes, subsidiary seconds; chronograph; date
Case: stainless steel, ø 42 mm, height 13.38 mm; bidirectional bezel with 12-hour divisions, sapphire crystal; screw-in crown and pushers; water-resistant to 15 atm
Band: fabric, buckle
Remarks: with additional stainless steel bracelet
Price: $4,425

Heritage Advisor

Reference number: 79620TN
Movement: automatic, Tudor Caliber 2892-901 (base ETA 2892-A2); ø 30.4 mm, height 6.3 mm; 31 jewels; 28,800 vph; additional module for mechanical alarm
Functions: hours, minutes, sweep seconds; alarm clock; date
Case: stainless steel, titanium, ø 42 mm, height 14 mm; sapphire crystal; water-resistant to 10 atm
Band: fabric, buckle
Remarks: with extra stainless steel bracelet
Price: $6,075
Variations: reptile skin strap ($5,850)

Fastrider Black Shield

Reference number: 42000CN
Movement: automatic, Tudor Caliber 7753 (base ETA 2892-A2); ø 30.4 mm, height 7.9 mm; 27 jewels; 28,800 vph; 46-hour power reserve
Functions: hours, minutes, subsidiary seconds; chronograph; date
Case: ceramic, ø 42 mm, height 14.48 mm; ceramic bezel with tachymeter scale, sapphire crystal; water-resistant to 15 atm
Band: alcantara, buckle
Price: $4,925
Variations: rubber or leather band

Fastrider

Reference number: 42000D
Movement: automatic, Tudor Caliber 7753 (base ETA 7750-1); ø 30.4 mm, height 7.9 mm; 27 jewels; 28,800 vph; 46-hour power reserve
Functions: hours, minutes, subsidiary seconds; chronograph; date
Case: stainless steel, ø 42 mm, height 14.3 mm; sapphire crystal; water-resistant to 15 atm
Band: calf leather, folding clasp
Remarks: comes with additional textile band
Price: $3,875

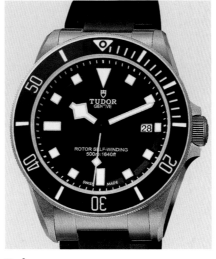

Pelagos

Reference number: 25500TN
Movement: automatic, Tudor Caliber 2824 (base ETA 2824-2); ø 26 mm, height 4.6 mm; 25 jewels; 28,800 vph; 38-hour power reserve
Functions: hours, minutes, sweep seconds; date
Case: stainless steel, titanium, ø 42 mm, height 14.25 mm; unidirectional bezel with 60-minute division, sapphire crystal; screw-in crown; water-resistant to 50 atm
Band: rubber, buckle
Price: $4,125

Grantour Chrono Fly-Back

Reference number: 20550N
Movement: automatic, Tudor Caliber 2892-A20 (base ETA 2892-A2); ø 30 mm, height 6.9 mm; 55 jewels; 28,800 vph; 42-hour power reserve
Functions: hours, minutes, subsidiary seconds; flyback chronograph; date
Case: stainless steel, ø 42 mm, height 12.6 mm; black lacquered bezel with 12-hour divisions, sapphire crystal; screw-in crown and lockable pushers; water-resistant to 15 atm
Band: leather strap, folding clasp
Price: $4,400
Variations: stainless steel bracelet ($4,725)

Tutima Uhrenfabrik GmbH Ndl. Glashütte
Altenberger Straße 6
D-01768 Glashütte
Germany

Tel.:
01149-35053-320-20

Fax:
01149-35053-320 222

E-Mail:
info@tutima.com

Website:
www.tutima.com

Founded:
1927

Number of employees:
approx. 60

U.S. distributor:
Tutima USA, Inc.
P.O. Box 983
Torrance, CA 90508
1-TUTIMA-1927
info@tutimausa.com
www.tutima.com

Most important collections/price range:
Patria, Saxon One, M2, Grand Flieger,
Hommage / approx. $2,600 to 22,000

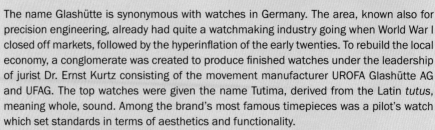

Tutima

The name Glashütte is synonymous with watches in Germany. The area, known also for precision engineering, already had quite a watchmaking industry going when World War I closed off markets, followed by the hyperinflation of the early twenties. To rebuild the local economy, a conglomerate was created to produce finished watches under the leadership of jurist Dr. Ernst Kurtz consisting of the movement manufacturer UROFA Glashütte AG and UFAG. The top watches were given the name Tutima, derived from the Latin *tutus*, meaning whole, sound. Among the brand's most famous timepieces was a pilot's watch which set standards in terms of aesthetics and functionality.

A few days before World War II ended, Kurtz left Glashütte and founded Uhrenfabrik Kurtz in southern Germany. A young businessman and former employee of Kurtz by the name of Dieter Delecate is credited with keeping the manufacturing facilities and the name Tutima going even as the company sailed through troubled waters. In founding Tutima Uhrenfabrik GmbH in Ganderkesee, this young, resolute entrepreneur prepared the company's strategy for the coming decades.

Delecate has had the joy of seeing Tutima return to its old home and vertically integrated operations, meaning it is once again a genuine *manufacture*. Under renowned designer Rolf Lang, it has developed an in-house minute repeater. In 2013, Tutima proudly announced a genuine made-in-Glashütte movement (at least 50 percent must be produced in the town), Caliber 617. With characteristic restraint, the brand has placed this fine piece of engineering inside the new Patria, which comes with a subsidiary second display or a second time zone. Another recent sign-off is a modern interpretation of a classic older pilot's watch for the Grand Flieger collection. The look is fresh, the hands longer, and the functionality outstanding.

Patria

Reference number: 6600-02
Movement: manually wound, Tutima Caliber 617; ø 31 mm, height 4.78 mm; 20 jewels; 21,600 vph; screw balance with weight screws and Breguet spring; Glashütte three-quarter plate; winding wheels with click; gold-plated and finely finished; 65-hour power reserve
Functions: hours, minutes, subsidiary seconds
Case: rose gold, ø 43 mm, height 9.7 mm; sapphire crystal; transparent case back; water-resistant to 5 atm
Band: reptile skin, buckle
Price: $19,900
Variations: Arabic numerals

Patria Dual Time

Reference number: 6601-01
Movement: manually wound, Tutima Caliber 619; ø 31 mm, height 4.78 mm; 20 jewels; 21,600 vph; screw balance with weight screws; Glashütte three-quarter plate; winding wheels with click; gold-plated and finely finished; 65-hour power reserve
Functions: hours, minutes, subsidiary seconds; additional 12-hour display (2nd time zone)
Case: rose gold, ø 43 mm, height 9.7 mm; sapphire crystal; transparent case back; water-resistant to 5 atm
Band: reptile skin, buckle
Price: $21,500
Variations: indices on dial

Hommage Minute Repeater

Movement: manually wound, Tutima Caliber 800; ø 32 mm, height 7.2 mm; 42 jewels; 21,600 vph; screw balance with 14 gold weight screws; Glashütte three-quarter plate; Breguet spring; winding wheels with click; finely finished; 65-hour power reserve
Functions: hours, minutes, subsidiary seconds; hour, quarter-hour, and minute repeater
Case: rose gold, ø 43 mm, height 14.4 mm; sapphire crystal
Band: reptile skin, buckle
Price: on request

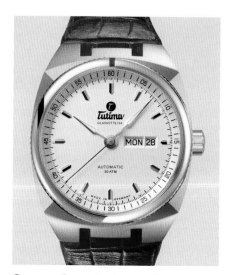

Saxon One Automatic

Reference number: 6120-04
Movement: automatic, Tutima Caliber 330 (base ETA 2836-2); ø 25.6 mm, height 5.05 mm; 25 jewels; 28,800 vph; 38-hour power reserve
Functions: hours, minutes, sweep seconds; date and weekday
Case: stainless steel, ø 42 mm, height 12.4 mm; sapphire crystal; transparent case back; screw-in crown; water-resistant to 20 atm
Band: reptile skin, folding clasp
Price: $3,800
Variations: stainless steel bracelet ($4,200)

Saxon One Chronograph

Reference number: 6420-03
Movement: automatic, Tutima Caliber 521 (base ETA 7750); ø 30 mm, height 7.9 mm; 25 jewels; 28,800 vph; sweep minute counter; 48-hour power reserve
Functions: hours, minutes, subsidiary seconds; additional 24-hour display; chronograph; date
Case: stainless steel, ø 43 mm, height 15.3 mm; sapphire crystal; transparent case back; screw-in crown; water-resistant to 20 atm
Band: reptile skin, folding clasp
Price: $6,700
Variations: stainless steel bracelet ($7,100)

M2

Reference number: 6450-01
Movement: automatic, Tutima Caliber 521 (base ETA 7750); ø 30 mm, height 7.9 mm; 25 jewels; 28,800 vph; sweep minute counter; 48-hour power reserve
Functions: hours, minutes, subsidiary seconds; additional 24-hour display; chronograph; date
Case: titanium, ø 46 mm, height 15.85 mm; sapphire crystal; screw-in crown; water-resistant to 30 atm
Band: calf leather, folding clasp
Remarks: soft iron cage for antimagnetic protection
Price: $6,500
Variations: titanium band ($7,100)

Grand Flieger Airport Chronograph

Reference number: 6401-01
Movement: automatic, Tutima Caliber 320 (base ETA 7750); ø 30 mm, height 7.9 mm; 25 jewels; 28,800 vph; 42-hour power reserve; COSC-certified chronometer
Functions: hours, minutes, subsidiary seconds; chronograph; date
Case: titanium, ø 43 mm, height 16.4 mm; bidirectional bezel with 60-minute division, sapphire crystal; transparent case back; screw-in crown; water-resistant to 20 atm
Band: calf leather, folding clasp
Price: $5,600
Variations: stainless steel bracelet ($6,100)

Grand Flieger Airport Automatic

Reference number: 6101-01
Movement: automatic, Tutima Caliber 330; ø 25.6 mm, height 5.05 mm; 25 jewels; 28,800 vph; 38-hour power reserve
Functions: hours, minutes, sweep seconds; weekday, date
Case: stainless steel, ø 43 mm, height 13 mm; bidirectional bezel with reference marker, sapphire crystal; transparent case back; screw-in crown; water-resistant to 20 atm
Band: calf leather, buckle
Price: $2,800
Variations: stainless steel bracelet ($3,200)

Grand Flieger Classic Automatic

Reference number: 6102-01
Movement: automatic, Tutima Caliber 330 (base ETA 2836-2); ø 25.6 mm, height 5.05 mm; 25 jewels; 28,800 vph; 38-hour power reserve
Functions: hours, minutes, sweep seconds; date and weekday
Case: stainless steel, ø 43 mm, height 13 mm; bidirectional bezel with reference marker, sapphire crystal; transparent case back; screw-in crown; water-resistant to 20 atm
Band: calf leather, buckle
Price: $2,800
Variations: stainless steel bracelet ($3,200)

Ulysse Nardin

Ulysse Nardin SA
3, rue du Jardin
CH-2400 Le Locle
Switzerland

Tel.:
01141-32-930-7400

Fax:
01141-32-930-7419

Website:
www.ulysse-nardin.ch

Founded:
1846

U.S. distributor:
Ulysse Nardin Inc.
7900 Glades Rd., Suite 200
Boca Raton, FL 33434
561-988-8600; 561-988-0123 (fax)
usa@ulysse-nardin.com

Most important collections:
Marine chronometers and diver's watches;
Dual Time (also ladies' watches);
complications (alarm clocks, perpetual
calendar, tourbillons, minute repeaters,
jacquemarts, astronomical watches)

At the beginning of the 1980s, following the quartz crisis that devastated the Swiss watch industry, Rolf Schnyder revived the venerable Ulysse Nardin brand, which once upon a time had a reputation for marine chronometers and precision watches. But those days were long gone when Schnyder bought what was essentially just a vague memory of a big name in the business.

He had the luck to meet the multitalented Dr. Ludwig Oechslin, who realized Schnyder's vision of astronomical wristwatches in the Trilogy of Time. Overnight, Ulysse Nardin became a name to be reckoned with in the world of fine watchmaking. Oechslin developed a host of innovations for Ulysse Nardin, from intelligent calendar movements to escapement systems. He was the first to use silicon and synthetic diamonds and thus gave the entire industry a great deal of food for thought. Just about every Ulysse Nardin has become famous for some spectacular technical innovation, be it the Moonstruck with its stunning moon phase accuracy or the outlandish Freak series that more or less does away with the dial.

Following Schnyder's sudden death in 2011, his wife Chai Schnyder was named president of the board of directors, and Patrik Hoffmann was appointed CEO. Ulysse Nardin continues exploring new paths to outstanding horology, quietly focusing on building new movements while cutting back on new models. To allow aesthetic explorations, a venture was launched with a company specializing in lithography, electroplating, and molding. Acquisition of the enameler Donzé Cadrans SA has already produced the Marine Chronometer Manufacture, powered by UN-118. The brand is pressing ahead with technological development by previewing for a group of select experts the first prototypes of a new anchor escapement at Baselworld 2014. It features a suspended silicon frame holding the two fork arms, which are blade driven. No pivot means no bridge, hence a slimmer movement.

Skeleton Tourbillon Manufacture

Reference number: 1702-129
Movement: manually wound, Caliber UN-170;
ø 37 mm, height 5.86 mm; 23 jewels; 18,000
vph; 1-minute tourbillon; skeletonized; twin spring
barrels; 170-hour power reserve
Functions: hours, minutes
Case: rose gold, ø 44 mm; sapphire crystal;
transparent case back
Band: reptile skin, buckle
Remarks: skeletonized dial
Price: $75,000
Variations: white gold ($85,000)

"Tiger" Hourstriker

Reference number: 6106-130/E2-TIGER
Movement: automatic, Caliber UN-610;
28,800 vph; hour and half-hour repeater; 42-hour
power reserve
Functions: hours, minutes; hour and half-hour
repeater with chime and jacquemart (automated
figure)
Case: rose gold, ø 42 mm; sapphire crystal;
transparent case back
Band: reptile skin, double folding clasp
Price: $107,800
Variations: platinum ($130,000)

"Jazz" Minute Repeater

Reference number: 749-88
Movement: manually wound, Caliber UN-74;
ø 27.6 mm, height 8.5 mm; 36 jewels; 28,800 vph;
hour, quarter-hour, and minute repeater on 2 gongs
with synchronously moving jacquemarts
Functions: hours, minutes; minute repeater with
jacquemarts (automated figures)
Case: platinum, ø 42 mm, height 14 mm; sapphire
crystal; transparent case back
Band: reptile skin, double folding clasp
Price: $455,000; limited to 18 pieces

"Stranger" Musical Watch

Reference number: 6902-125
Movement: automatic, Caliber UN-690; ø 37 mm, height 10.06 mm; 64 jewels; 28,800 vph; silicon escapement, pallet lever, and hairspring; music box on dial with visible peg disc, 10 gongs
Functions: hours and minutes (off-center), subsidiary seconds; date; music box (plays "Strangers in the Night" hourly or on demand)
Case: platinum, ø 45 mm; sapphire crystal
Band: reptile skin, double folding clasp
Price: $120,000; limited to 99 pieces
Variations: pink gold ($112,000; limited to 99 pieces)

Imperial Blue

Reference number: 9700-125
Movement: manually wound, Caliber UN-970; ø 37 mm; 84 jewels; 18,000 vph; flying 1-minute tourbillon; partly of sapphire
Functions: hours, minutes; large date; minute repeater (Westminster chime)
Case: white gold, ø 46 mm; sapphire crystal; transparent case back
Band: reptile skin, double folding clasp
Price: $750,000; limited to 20 pieces

Freak Phantom

Reference number: 2080-115/02
Movement: manually wound, Caliber UN-208; ø 35 mm; 28 jewels; 28,800 vph; flying 1-minute tourbillon on orbital carousel; silicon escapement and hairspring; components used as hands; time-setting with bezel, winding by turning case back; approx. 170-hour power reserve
Functions: hours, minutes, subsidiary seconds
Case: white gold, ø 45 mm, height 12.5 mm; bidirectional bezel sets hands, sapphire crystal; transparent case back
Band: reptile skin, double folding clasp
Price: $153,500
Variations: rose gold ($137,000; limited to 99 pieces)

Freak Blue Cruiser

Reference number: 2050-131/03
Movement: manually wound, Caliber UN-205; ø 35 mm; 28 jewels, 28,800 vph; silicon escapement and hairspring; components used as hands; time-setting via bezel, winding by turning case back; 170-hour power reserve
Functions: hours, minutes, subsidiary seconds
Case: white gold, ø 45 mm, height 13.5 mm; bidirectional bezel sets hands, sapphire crystal; transparent case back
Band: reptile skin, double folding clasp
Price: $95,000
Variations: rose gold ($87,500)

GMT Perpetual

Reference number: 322-10
Movement: automatic, Caliber UN-32; ø 31 mm, height 6.95 mm; 34 jewels; 28,800 vph; perpetual calendar mechanism crown-adjustable back and forth; COSC-certified chronometer
Functions: hours, minutes, subsidiary seconds; additional 24-hour display (2nd time zone); perpetual calendar with large date, weekday, month, year
Case: rose gold, ø 43 mm, height 12.5 mm; sapphire crystal; transparent case back
Band: reptile skin, double folding clasp
Price: $52,500; limited to 250 pieces
Variations: platinum ($69,500; limited to 250 pieces)

Classico Amerigo Vespucci

Reference number: 8156-111-2/AV
Movement: automatic, Caliber UN-815; 28,800 vph; 42-hour power reserve
Functions: hours, minutes, sweep seconds
Case: rose gold, ø 40 mm, sapphire crystal
Band: reptile skin, buckle
Remarks: handpainted mother-of-pearl dial
Price: $42,300; limited to 30 pieces
Variations: white gold ($45,600; limited to 30 pieces)

Dual Time Manufacture

Reference number: 3346-126/92
Movement: automatic, Caliber UN-334; 49 jewels; 28,800 vph; silicon escapement and hairspring
Functions: hours, minutes, subsidiary seconds; additional 24-hour display (2nd time zone); large date
Case: rose gold, ø 42 mm; sapphire crystal
Band: reptile skin, double folding clasp
Price: $26,500
Variations: stainless steel ($10,500)

Dual Time Manufacture

Reference number: 3343-126/92
Movement: automatic, Caliber UN-334; 49 jewels; 28,800 vph; silicon escapement and hairspring
Functions: hours, minutes, subsidiary seconds; additional 24-hour display (2nd time zone); large date
Case: stainless steel, ø 42 mm; sapphire crystal
Band: reptile skin, double folding clasp
Price: $10,500
Variations: rose gold ($26,500)

Marine Chronograph Manufacture

Reference number: 1506-150-3/63
Movement: automatic, Caliber UN-150; ø 31 mm, height 6.4 mm; 27 jewels; 28,800 vph; silicon escapement
Functions: hours, minutes, subsidiary seconds; chronograph; date
Case: rose gold, ø 43 mm, height 15 mm; sapphire crystal; transparent case back; screw-in crown
Band: reptile skin, double folding clasp
Price: $34,900
Variations: stainless steel ($12,700)

Marine Chronograph Manufacture

Reference number: 1503-150-3/62
Movement: automatic, Caliber UN-150; ø 31 mm, height 6.4 mm; 27 jewels; 28,800 vph; silicon escapement
Functions: hours, minutes, subsidiary seconds; chronograph; date
Case: stainless steel, ø 43 mm, height 15 mm; sapphire crystal; transparent case back; screw-in crown
Band: rubber with titanium elements, folding clasp
Price: $12,700
Variations: rose gold ($34,900)

Marine Chronometer Manufacture

Reference number: 1186-126/E0
Movement: automatic, Caliber UN-118; ø 31.6 mm, height 6.45 mm; 50 jewels; 28,800 vph; silicon hairspring, diamond-coated silicon escapement (DiamOnSil); 60-hour power reserve
Functions: hours, minutes, subsidiary seconds; power reserve indicator; date
Case: rose gold, ø 43 mm, height 13 mm; sapphire crystal; transparent case back; screw-in crown
Band: reptile skin, double folding clasp
Remarks: enamel dial
Price: $31,900; limited to 888 pieces
Variations: on rubber strap with gold element ($33,300)

Marine Chronometer Manufacture

Reference number: 1186-126-3/43
Movement: automatic, Caliber UN-118; ø 31.6 mm, height 6.45 mm; 50 jewels; 28,800 vph; silicon hairspring, diamond-coated silicon escapement (DiamOnSil); 60-hour power reserve
Functions: hours, minutes, subsidiary seconds; power reserve indicator; date
Case: rose gold, ø 43 mm, height 13 mm; sapphire crystal; transparent case back; screw-in crown
Band: rubber, folding clasp
Price: $31,800
Variations: stainless steel ($10,300)

Maxi Marine Diver Black Sea

Reference number: 263-92LE-3C/928-RG
Movement: automatic, Caliber UN-26; ø 25.6 mm, height 5.1 mm; 28 jewels; 28,800 vph; 42-hour power reserve; COSC-certified chronometer
Functions: hours, minutes, subsidiary seconds; power reserve indicator; date
Case: stainless steel with rubber coating, ø 45.8 mm, height 14 mm; unidirectional rose gold bezel with 60-second divisions, sapphire crystal; transparent case back; screw-in crown; water-resistant to 20 atm
Band: rubber with ceramic elements, folding clasp
Price: $13,500; limited to 250 pieces
Variations: stainless steel bezel ($10,700)

Marine Diver

Reference number: 263-10-3/93
Movement: automatic, Caliber UN-26; ø 25.6 mm, height 5.1 mm; 28 jewels; 28,800 vph; 42-hour power reserve
Functions: hours, minutes, subsidiary seconds; power reserve indicator; date
Case: stainless steel, ø 44 mm, height 13 mm; unidirectional bezel with 60-minute divisions, sapphire crystal; transparent case back; screw-in crown; water-resistant to 30 atm
Band: rubber with titanium elements, folding clasp
Price: $8,500
Variations: stainless steel bracelet ($9,700)

Executive Dual Time

Reference number: 246-00-3/43
Movement: automatic, Caliber UN-24, ø 25.6 mm, height 5.35 mm; 23 jewels; 28,800 vph
Functions: hours, minutes, subsidiary seconds; additional 24-hour display; large date
Case: stainless steel, ø 43 mm, height 12 mm; ceramic bezel, sapphire crystal; transparent case back; screw-in crown
Band: reptile skin, double folding clasp
Price: $22,200
Variations: stainless steel ($8,700)

Caliber UN-334

Automatic, silicon escapement, single spring barrel, 48-hour power reserve
Functions: hours, minutes, subsidiary seconds; additional 24-hour display (2nd time zone); large date
Jewels: 49
Balance: variable inertia balance
Frequency: 28,800 vph
Balance spring: silicon
Shock protection: Incabloc
Remarks: patented quick adjustment for 2nd time zone; perlage on plate, bridges with concentric côtes de Genève ("côtes circulaires")

Caliber UN-118

Automatic; patented DiamOnSil escapement; single spring barrel, power reserve approx. 60 hours
Functions: hours, minutes, subsidiary seconds; date; power reserve indicator
Diameter: 31.6 mm
Height: 6.45 mm
Jewels: 50
Balance: silicon balance with variable inertia
Frequency: 28,800 vph
Balance spring: silicon
Shock protection: Incabloc
Remarks: perlage on plate, bridges with concentric côtes de Genève ("côtes circulaires")

Caliber UN-32

Automatic; single spring barrel, power reserve approx. 45 hours
Functions: hours, minutes, subsidiary seconds; 24-hour display; perpetual calendar with month, weekday, date
Diameter: 31 mm
Height: 6.95 mm
Jewels: 34
Balance: glucydur
Frequency: 28,800 vph
Remarks: perpetual calendar mechanism can be set forward or backward using a single crown; patented quick setting of 2nd time zone

Urban Jürgensen & Sønner

P.O. Box 7170
CH-2500 Biel/Bienne 7
Switzerland

Tel.:
01141-32-365-1526

Fax:
01141-32-365-2266

E-Mail:
info@ujs-chronometry.ch

Website:
www.ujs-chronometry.ch

Founded:
1773/1980

Annual production:
max. 200 watches

U.S. distributor:
John McBarron
312-643-0148
usa@ujs-chronometry.ch

Most important collections:
High-end references with in-house movements

Urban Jürgensen & Sønner

For all aficionados and collectors of fine timekeepers, the name Urban Jürgensen & Sønner is synonymous with outstanding watches. The company was founded in 1773 and has always strived for the highest rungs of the horological art. Technical perfection consistently combines with imaginative cases. A lot of attention is given to dials and hands.

Today, Urban Jürgensen & Sønner—originally a Danish firm—manufactures watches in Switzerland where a team of eight superbly qualified watchmakers do the work in three ateliers. For over a quarter century now, they have been making highly complicated unique pieces and very upmarket wristwatches in small editions of 50 to 300 pieces. The series were based mostly on *ébauches* by Frédéric Piguet. Like all keen watchmakers, those at Urban Jürgensen & Sønner have also sought to make their own movements, which would meet the highest standards of precision and reliability and not require too much servicing.

In 2003, a team began collaborating with a well-known external design engineer to construct a base movement. The new UJS-P8 was conceived with both a traditional Swiss lever escapement and in a special variation featuring a pivoting chronometer escapement, available for the first time in a wristwatch. The initial watch containing the new movement was the Reference 11, which is visibly an Urban Jürgensen. It comes in platinum and rose gold cases. The Reference 11 with pivoting chronometer escapement typically has a hand-guilloché silver dial with three hands and a power reserve indicator. The latter is controlled by a newly developed and patented differential. The version with the lever escapement does not feature a power reserve indicator.

Chronometer Escapement Sweep Seconds

Reference number: 11C SC PT
Movement: manually wound, Urban Jürgensen Caliber UJS-P8; ø 32 mm, height 5.25 mm; 25 jewels; 21,600 vph; patented chronometer escapement with UJS pivoted detent; twin spring barrels; 72-hour power reserve
Functions: hours, minutes, sweep seconds; power reserve indicator
Case: platinum, ø 42 mm, height 12.3 mm; sapphire crystal
Band: reptile skin, buckle
Remarks: guilloché silver dial
Price: $65,000
Variations: pink gold ($54,000)

Minute Repeater Tourbillon

Reference number: Limited Edition 1/1
Movement: manually wound, Urban Jürgensen Caliber UJS-Cla92; ø 27.6 mm, height 6.89 mm; 28 jewels; 18,000 vph; 1-minute tourbillon; 40-hour power reserve
Functions: hours (off-center), minutes, subsidiary seconds; quarter-hour repeater, minute repeater
Case: platinum, ø 42.5 mm, height 13 mm; sapphire crystal; transparent case back
Band: reptile skin, buckle
Remarks: enamel dial; unique piece
Price: $425,000

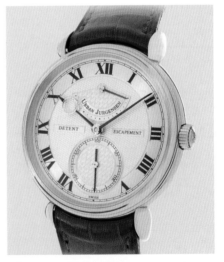

Chronometer Escapement Subsidiary Seconds

Reference number: 11C R
Movement: manually wound, Urban Jürgensen Caliber UJS-P8; ø 32 mm; height 5.25 mm; 25 jewels; 21,600 vph; patented chronometer escapement with UJS pivoted detent; twin spring barrels; 88-hour power reserve
Functions: hours, minutes, subsidiary seconds; power reserve indicator
Case: rose gold, ø 42 mm, height 12.3 mm; sapphire crystal
Band: reptile skin, buckle
Remarks: guilloché silver dial
Price: $54,000
Variations: platinum ($65,000)

Urwerk

Felix Baumgartner and designer Martin Frei count among the living legends of innovative horology. They founded their company Urwerk in 1997 with a name that is a play on the words *Uhrwerk*, for movement, and *Urwerk*, meaning a sort of primal mechanism. Their specialty is inventing surprising time indicators featuring digital numerals that rotate like satellites and display the time in a relatively linear depiction on a small "dial" at the front of the flattened case, which could almost—but not quite—be described as oval. Their inspiration goes back to the so-called night clock of the eighteenth-century Campanus brothers, but the realization is purely *2001: A Space Odyssey*.

Among their great achievements is the Black Cobra, which displays time using cylinders and other clever ways to recoup energy for driving rather heavy components. The Torpedo is another example of high-tech watchmaking, again based on the satellite system of revolving and turning hands. These pieces remind one of the frenetic engineering that has transformed the planet since the eighteenth century. And with each return to the drawing board, Baumgartner and Frei find new ways to explore what has now become an unmistakable form, using high-tech materials, like aluminum titanium nitride (AlTiN), or finding new functions for the owner to play with.

Urwerk SA
114, rue du Rhône
CH-1204 Geneva
Switzerland

Tel:
01141-22-900-2027

Fax:
01141-22-900-2026

E-Mail:
info@urwerk.com

Website:
www.urwerk.com

Founded:
1995

Annual production:
150 watches

U.S. distributor:
Urwerk
132 South Rodeo Drive, Fourth Floor
Beverly Hills, CA 90212
310-205-5555

UR-105M

Movement: manually wound, UR 5.10; 38 jewels; 28,800 vph; revolving hour satellites on planetary gear drive with Maltese Cross control; 42-hour power reserve
Functions: hours (digital, rotating), minutes, seconds (digital, on case side); power reserve indicator (on case side)
Case: titanium, 43.8 x 53.6 mm, height 17.8 mm; stainless steel bezel, sapphire crystal; water-resistant to 3 atm
Band: reptile skin, folding clasp
Remarks: tips of 4 hour satellites indicate minutes counterclockwise on semicircular scale
Price: $66,000

UR-105M AlTiN

Movement: manually wound, UR 5.10; 38 jewels; 28,800 vph; revolving hour satellites on planetary gear drive with Maltese Cross control; 42-hour power reserve
Functions: hours (digital, rotating), minutes, seconds (digital, on case side); power reserve indicator (on case side)
Case: titanium, 43.8 x 53.6 mm, height 17.8 mm; bezel with AlTiN coating, sapphire crystal; water-resistant to 3 atm
Band: reptile skin, folding clasp
Remarks: tips of 4 hour satellites indicate minutes counterclockwise on semicircular scale
Price: $72,000

UR-210Y "Black Hawk"

Movement: automatic, UR 7.10; 51 jewels; 28,800 vph; Arcap P40 mainplate; revolving hour satellites on planetary gear drive, telescopic minute hand; winding system regulated by fluid dynamics decoupling and adjustable efficiency; 39-hour power reserve
Functions: hours (digital, rotating), minutes (retrograde); power reserve display, winding efficiency indication
Case: titanium with AlTiN coating; 43.8 x 53.6 mm, height 17.8 mm; water-resistant to 3 atm
Remarks: hour satellites travel across semicircular minute scale, skeletonized minute hand jumps back at end of scale to "pick up" next satellite
Price: $170,000

UTS Watches, Inc.
630 Quintana Road, Suite 194
Morro Bay, CA 93442

Tel.:
877-887-0123 or 805-528-9800

E-Mail:
info@utswatches.com

Website:
www.utswatches.com

Founded:
1999

Number of employees:
2

Annual production:
fewer than 500

Distribution:
direct sales only

Most important collections/price range:
sports and diver's watches, chronographs /
from $2,500 to $7,000

UTS

UTS, or "Uhren Technik Spinner," was the natural outgrowth of a company based in Munich and manufacturing CNC tools and machines for the watch industry. Nicolaus Spinner, a mechanical engineer and aficionado in his own right, learned the nitty-gritty of watchmaking by the age-old system of taking watches apart. From there to making robust diver's watches was just a short step. The collection has grown considerably since he started production in 1999. The watches are built mainly around ETA calibers. Some, like the new 4000M, feature a unique locking bezel using a stem, a bolt, and a ceramic ball bearing system invented by Spinner. Another specialty is the 6 mm sapphire crystal, which guarantees significant water resistance. Spinner's longtime friend and business partner, Stephen Newman, is also the owner of the UTS trademark in the United States. He has not only worked on product development, but has also contributed his own design ideas and handles sales and marketing for the small brand. A new watch released last year, the 4000M Diver, boasts an extreme depth rating even without the need for a helium escape valve and is available in a GMT version. The collection is small, but UTS has a faithful following in Germany and the United States. The key for the fan club is a unique appearance coupled with mastery of the technology. These are a pure muscle watches with no steroids.

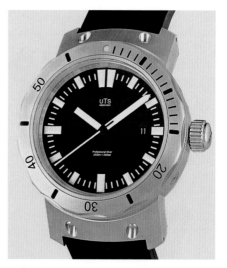

Diver 4000M

Movement: automatic, ETA Caliber 2824-2; ø 25.6 mm, height 4.6 mm; 25 jewels; 28,800 vph; 42 hours power reserve
Functions: hours, minutes, sweep seconds; date
Case: stainless steel, ø 45 mm, height 17.5 mm; bidirectional bezel with 60-minute scale; 6-mm sapphire crystal; antireflective on back; screwed-down case back; screw-in crown; locking bezel; screw-in buttons; water-resistant to 400 atm
Band: stainless steel with diver's extension folding clasp or rubber or leather strap
Price: $6,300

Diver 4000M GMT

Movement: automatic, ETA Caliber 2893-2; ø 25.6 mm, height 4.6 mm; 25 jewels; 28,800 vph; 42 hours power reserve
Functions: hours, minutes, sweep seconds; date, second time zone
Case: stainless steel, ø 45 mm, height 17.5 mm; bidirectional bezel with 60-minute scale; 6-mm sapphire crystal; antireflective on back; screwed-down case back; screw-in crown; locking bezel; screw-in buttons; water-resistant to 400 atm
Band: stainless steel with diver's extension folding clasp or rubber or leather strap
Price: $7,000

2000M

Movement: automatic, ETA Caliber 2824-2; ø 25.6 mm, height 4.6 mm; 25 jewels; 28,800 vph; 42 hours power reserve
Functions: hours, minutes, sweep seconds; date
Case: stainless steel, ø 44 mm, height 16.5 mm; unidirectional bezel with 60-minute scale; automatic helium escape valve; sapphire crystal; antireflective on back; screwed-down case back; screw-in crown; screwed-in buttons; water-resistant to 200 atm
Band: stainless steel with diver's extension folding clasp, comes with rubber leather strap
Price: $3,750

1000M V2

Movement: automatic, ETA Caliber 2824-2; ø 25.6 mm, height 4.6 mm; 25 jewels; 28,800 vph; 42 hours power reserve

Functions: hours, minutes, sweep seconds; date

Case: stainless steel, ø 43 mm, height 14 mm; unidirectional bezel with 60-minute scale; sapphire crystal; antireflective on back; screwed-down sapphire (optional) crystal case back; screw-in crown; screw-in buttons; water-resistant to 10 atm

Band: stainless steel with diver's extension folding clasp or rubber or leather strap

Price: $3,000

1000M GMT

Movement: automatic, ETA Caliber ETA 2893-2; ø 25.6 mm, height 4.1 mm; 21 jewels; 28,800 vph; 42 hours power reserve

Functions: hours, minutes, sweep seconds; second time zone; date; quickset GMT hand

Case: stainless steel, ø 43 mm, height 14 mm; unidirectional bezel with 60-minute scale; sapphire crystal; antireflective on back; screwed-down case back with optional transparent back (sapphire crystal); screw-in crown; screw-in buttons; water-resistant to 100 atm

Band: stainless steel with diver's extension folding clasp or rubber or leather strap

Price: $3,750

Adventure Automatic

Movement: automatic, ETA Valgranges Caliber A07.111; ø 36.6 mm, height 7.9 mm; 24 jewels; 28,800 vph; 46 hours power reserve

Functions: hours, minutes, sweep seconds; date

Case: stainless steel, ø 46 mm, height 15.5 mm; screw-in crown; antireflective sapphire crystal; screwed-down sapphire crystal case back; water-resistant to 50 atm

Band: rubber, buckle

Price: $4,000

Variations: leather strap; stainless steel bracelet with folding clasp and diver's extension

Adventure Automatic GMT

Movement: automatic, ETA Valgranges Caliber A07.171; ø 36.6 mm, height 7.9 mm; 24 jewels; 28,800 vph; 46 hours power reserve

Functions: hours, minutes, sweep seconds; date; second time zone

Case: stainless steel, ø 46 mm, height 15.5 mm; screw-in crown; antireflective sapphire crystal; screwed-down sapphire crystal case back; water-resistant to 50 atm

Band: rubber, buckle

Price: $4,550

Variations: leather strap; stainless steel bracelet with folding clasp and diver's extension

Chrono Diver

Movement: automatic, ETA Valjoux Caliber 7750; ø 30 mm, height 7.9 mm; 25 jewels; 28,800 vph; 45-hour power reserve

Functions: hours, minutes, subsidiary seconds; date; chronograph

Case: stainless steel, ø 46 mm, height 16.5 mm; unidirectional bezel with 60-minute scale; screw-in crown and buttons; antireflective sapphire crystal; screwed-down case back; water-resistant to 600 m

Band: stainless steel, folding clasp

Price: $5,000

Variations: leather strap

Adventure Manual Wind

Movement: manually wound, ETA Unitas Caliber 6497; ø 36.6 mm, height 5.4 mm; 18 jewels; 18,000 vph; 48 hours power reserve

Functions: hours, minutes, subsidiary seconds

Case: stainless steel, ø 46 mm, height 14 mm; screw-in crown; antireflective sapphire crystal; screwed-down sapphire crystal case back; water-resistant to 50 atm

Band: leather, buckle

Price: $3,000

Variations: rubber strap

Vacheron Constantin

Chemin du Tourbillon
CH-1228 Plan-les-Ouates
Switzerland

Tel.:
01141-22-930-2005

E-Mail:
info@vacheron-constantin.com

Website:
www.vacheron-constantin.com

Founded:
1755

Number of employees:
approx. 800

Annual production:
over 20,000 watches (estimated)

U.S. distributor:
Vacheron Constantin
Richemont North America
645 Fifth Avenue
New York, NY 10022
877-701-1755

Most important collections:
Patrimony, Malte, Quai de l'Ile, Overseas,
Historiques, Metiers d'Art

Vacheron Constantin

The origins of this oldest continuously operating watch *manufacture* can be traced back to 1755 when Jean-Marc Vacheron opened his workshop in Geneva. His highly complex watches were particularly appreciated by clients in Paris. The development of such an important outlet for horological works there had a lot to do with the emergence of a wealthy class around the powerful French court. The Revolution put an end to all the financial excesses of that market, however, and the Vacheron company suffered as well . . . until the arrival of marketing wizard François Constantin in 1819.

Fast-forward to the late twentieth century: The brand with the Maltese cross logo had lost some of its pizzazz but evolved into a tradition-conscious keeper of *haute horlogerie* under the aegis, starting in the mid-1990s, of the Vendôme Luxury Group (today's Richemont SA). In the last few years, a new collection has come to light that combines modern shapes with traditional patterns. The company has been expanding steadily. In 2013 it opened new boutiques in the United States as well as China, and it has become a leading sponsor of the New York City Ballet.

Vacheron Constantin is one of the last luxury brands to have abandoned the traditional way of dividing up labor. Today, most of its basic movements are made in-house at the production facilities and headquarters in Plan-les-Ouates (opened in 2005 for the company's 250th anniversary) and the workshops in Le Brassus in Switzerland's Jura region, which were expanded in the summer of 2013. Finally, there is the *maison* housing a museum and boutique in the heart of Geneva's old town.

Malte Small Second

Reference number: 82230-000G-9962
Movement: manually wound, Caliber 4400 AS; ø 28.6 mm, height 2.8 mm; 21 jewels; 28,800 vph; Geneva Seal
Functions: hours, minutes, subsidiary seconds
Case: white gold, 36.7 x 47.61 mm, height 9.1 mm; sapphire crystal; water-resistant to 3 atm
Band: reptile skin, folding clasp
Price: $26,800
Variations: rose gold ($26,800)

Malte Tourbillon Skeleton

Reference number: 30135-000P-9842
Movement: manually wound, Caliber 2795; 27.37 x 29.3 mm, height 6.1 mm; 27 jewels; 18,000 vph; formed movement with 1-minute tourbillon; Geneva Seal
Functions: hours, minutes, subsidiary seconds (on tourbillon cage)
Case: platinum, 38 x 48.24 mm, height 12.73 mm; sapphire crystal; transparent case back; water-resistant to 3 atm
Band: reptile skin, double folding clasp
Price: $264,700

Malte Tourbillon Collection Excellence Platinum

Reference number: 30130/000P-9876
Movement: manually wound, Caliber 2795; 27.37 x 29.3 mm, height 6.1 mm; 27 jewels; 18,000 vph; formed, with 1-minute tourbillon; Geneva Seal
Functions: hours, minutes, subsidiary seconds (on tourbillon cage)
Case: platinum, 38 x 48.24 mm, height 12.73 mm; sapphire crystal; transparent case back; water-resistant to 3 atm
Band: reptile skin, double folding clasp
Remarks: platinum dial
Price: $235,200
Variations: rose gold ($192,500)

Patrimony Contemporaine Calibre 1731

Reference number: 30110-000R-9793
Movement: manually wound, Caliber 1731;
ø 32.8 mm, height 3.9 mm; 36 jewels, 21,600 vph;
65-hour power reserve; Geneva Seal
Functions: hours, minutes, subsidiary seconds;
minute repeater
Case: rose gold, ø 41 mm, height 8.09 mm;
sapphire crystal; transparent case back
Band: reptile skin, folding clasp with safety lock
Remarks: comes with "La Musique du Temps"
resonance body
Price: $409,900

Patrimony Traditionnelle Tourbillon 14 Days Skeleton

Reference number: 89010-000P-9935
Movement: manually wound, Caliber 2260 SQ;
ø 29.1 mm, height 6.8 mm; 31 jewels; 18,000 vph;
1-minute tourbillon; fully skeletonized; 336-hour
power reserve; Geneva Seal
Functions: hours, minutes, subsidiary seconds (on
tourbillon cage); power reserve indicator
Case: platinum, ø 42 mm, height 12.22 mm;
sapphire crystal; transparent case back; water-
resistant to 3 atm
Band: reptile skin, double folding clasp
Price: $380,000

Patrimony Traditionnelle 14 Days Tourbillon

Reference number: 89000/000R-9655
Movement: manually wound, Caliber 2260;
ø 29.9 mm, height 6.8 mm; 31 jewels; 18,000 vph;
1-minute tourbillon; 336-hour power reserve;
Geneva Seal
Functions: hours, minutes, subsidiary seconds (on
tourbillon cage); power reserve indicator
Case: rose gold, ø 42 mm, height 12.2 mm;
sapphire crystal; transparent case back; water-
resistant to 3 atm
Band: reptile skin, folding clasp
Price: $292,700

Patrimony Contemporaine Perpetual Calendar

Reference number: 43175/000R-9687
Movement: automatic, Caliber 1120 QP;
ø 29.6 mm, height 4.05 mm; 36 jewels;
19,800 vph; Geneva Seal
Functions: hours, minutes; perpetual calendar with
date, weekday, month, moon phase, leap year
Case: rose gold, ø 41 mm, height 8.9 mm; sapphire
crystal; transparent case back; water-resistant to
3 atm
Band: reptile skin, folding clasp
Price: $83,000

Patrimony Traditionnelle World Time

Reference number: 86060/000R-9640
Movement: automatic, Caliber 2460 WT;
ø 36.6 mm, height 8.1 mm; 27 jewels; 28,800 vph
Functions: hours, minutes, sweep seconds; world-
time display with 37 zones
Case: rose gold, ø 42.5 mm, height 11.5 mm;
sapphire crystal; transparent case back; water-
resistant to 3 atm
Band: reptile skin, folding clasp
Price: $52,600

Patrimony Contemporaine Bi-Retro Day Date

Reference number: 86020/000R-9239
Movement: automatic, Caliber 2460 R31 R7;
ø 32.8 mm, height 6.75 mm; 27 jewels; 28,800 vph
Functions: hours, minutes; weekday, date
Case: rose gold, ø 42.5 mm, height 10.07 mm;
sapphire crystal; transparent case back; water-
resistant to 3 atm
Band: reptile skin, double folding clasp
Price: $49,600
Variations: white gold ($49,600)

Patrimony Traditionnelle Chronograph

Reference number: 47192/000R-9352
Movement: manually wound, Caliber 1141;
ø 31.5 mm, height 5.6 mm; 21 jewels; 18,000 vph;
column wheel control of chronograph functions;
Geneva Seal
Functions: hours, minutes, subsidiary seconds;
chronograph
Case: rose gold, ø 42 mm, height 10.94 mm;
sapphire crystal; transparent case back; water-
resistant to 3 atm reptile skin, folding clasp
Band: reptile skin, buckle
Price: $58,700
Variations: white gold ($58,700)

Patrimony Traditionnelle Manual Winding

Reference number: 82172/000P-9811
Movement: manually wound, Caliber 4400;
ø 28.6 mm, height 2.8 mm; 21 jewels; 28,800 vph;
65-hour power reserve; Geneva Seal
Functions: hours, minutes, subsidiary seconds
Case: platinum, ø 38 mm, height 7.77 mm;
sapphire crystal; transparent case back; water-
resistant to 3 atm
Band: reptile skin, buckle
Price: $35,700
Variations: white gold ($20,900); pink gold
($20,900)

Patrimony Contemporaine Date Automatic

Reference number: 85180/000R-9248
Movement: automatic, Caliber 2450 VC;
ø 26.2 mm, height 3.6 mm; 27 jewels; 28,800 vph;
Geneva Seal
Functions: hours, minutes, sweep seconds; date
Case: rose gold, ø 40 mm, height 8.31 mm;
sapphire crystal; transparent case back; water-
resistant to 3 atm
Band: reptile skin, buckle
Price: $27,800
Variations: yellow gold ($27,800); white gold
($27,800)

Patrimony Contemporaine

Reference number: 81180/000R-9159
Movement: manually wound, Caliber 1400; ø
20.35 mm, height 2.6 mm; 20 jewels; 28,800 vph;
Geneva Seal
Functions: hours, minutes
Case: rose gold, ø 40 mm; sapphire crystal;
transparent case back
Band: reptile skin, buckle
Price: $19,600
Variations: white gold ($19,600); yellow gold
($19,600)

Métiers d'Art Mécaniques Ajourées

Reference number: 82020-000G-9924
Movement: manually wound, Caliber 4400 SQ;
ø 28.6 mm, height 2.8 mm; 21 jewels; 28,800 vph;
fully skeletonized; 65-hour power reserve; Geneva Seal
Functions: hours, minutes
Case: white gold, ø 40 mm, height 7.5 mm; sapphire
crystal; transparent case back; water-resistant to 3
atm
Band: reptile skin, buckle
Remarks: inserted enamel ring, in blue, gray, or black
optionally
Price: $78,900
Variations: with diamonds ($126,700)

Historiques Ultra-Fine 1955

Reference number: 33155/000R-9588
Movement: manually wound, Caliber 1003;
ø 21.1 mm, height 1.64 mm; 18 jewels; 18,000 vph;
thinnest currently manufactured; Geneva Seal
Functions: hours, minutes
Case: rose gold, ø 36 mm, height 4.1 mm; sapphire
crystal; transparent case back; water-resistant to
3 atm
Band: reptile skin, buckle
Price: $32,200

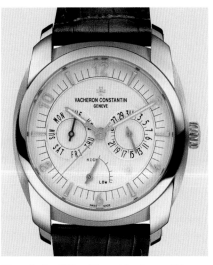

Quai de l'Ile Retrograde Annual Calendar

Reference number: 86040/000R-I0P29
Movement: automatic, Caliber 2460 QRA;
ø 26.2 mm, height 5.4 mm; 27 jewels; 28,800 vph;
Geneva Seal
Functions: hours, minutes, subsidiary seconds;
annual calendar with date, month, moon phase
Case: rose gold, 43 x 53.8 mm, height 13.5 mm;
sapphire crystal; transparent case back; water-
resistant to 3 atm
Band: reptile skin, folding clasp
Price: $71,200
Variations: many options for personalization

Quai de l'Ile Day Date with Power Reserve

Reference number: 85050/000D-9341
Movement: automatic, Caliber 2475 SC1; ø
26.2 mm, height 2.8 mm; 27 jewels; 28,000 vph;
Geneva Seal
Functions: hours, minutes, sweep seconds; power
reserve indicator; weekday, date
Case: palladium, 41 x 50.5 mm, height 12.9 mm;
sapphire crystal; transparent case back; water-
resistant to 3 atm
Band: reptile skin, folding clasp
Price: $49,600
Variations: many options for personalization

Quai de l'Ile Date Automatic

Reference number: 86050/000R-I0P29
Movement: automatic, Caliber 2460 QH;
ø 26.2 mm, height 5.7 mm; 27 jewels; 28,800 vph;
Geneva Seal
Functions: hours, minutes, sweep seconds; date
Case: rose gold, 41 x 50.5 mm, height 12.9 mm;
sapphire crystal; transparent case back; water-
resistant to 3 atm
Band: reptile skin, folding clasp
Price: $43,400
Variations: many options for personalization

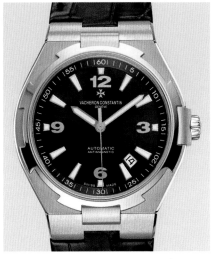

Overseas Date Automatic

Reference number: 47040/000R-9666
Movement: automatic, Caliber 1226; ø 26.6 mm,
height 3.25 mm; 36 jewels; 28,800 vph; Geneva
Seal
Functions: hours, minutes, sweep seconds; date
Case: rose gold, ø 42 mm, height 9.7 mm; sapphire
crystal; water-resistant to 15 atm
Band: reptile skin, folding clasp
Price: $34,500

Overseas Dual Time

Reference number: 47450/000W-9511
Movement: automatic, Caliber 1222 SC;
ø 26 mm, height 4.95 mm; 34 jewels; 28,800 vph;
antimagnetic protection with soft iron cap
Functions: hours, minutes, sweep seconds;
additional 12-hour display (2nd time zone); day/
night indicator; power reserve indicator; date
Case: titanium, ø 42 mm, height 12.45 mm;
sapphire crystal; screw-in crown and pusher; water-
resistant to 15 atm
Band: reptile skin, folding clasp
Price: $19,300
Variations: rose gold ($45,500)

Overseas Chronograph

Reference number: 49150/B01A-9745
Movement: automatic, Caliber 1137; ø 26 mm,
height 6.6 mm; 37 jewels; 21,600 vph; Geneva Seal
Functions: hours, minutes, subsidiary seconds;
chronograph; large date
Case: stainless steel, ø 42 mm, height 12.4 mm;
sapphire crystal; screw-in crown; water-resistant to
15 atm
Band: blue rubber strap, stainless steel, folding
clasp
Price: $21,500
Variations: stainless steel bracelet ($23,000)

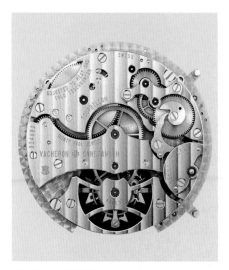

Caliber 2755

Automatic; 1-minute tourbillon; single spring barrel, 55-hour power reserve
Functions: hours, minutes, subsidiary seconds; perpetual calendar with month, leap year, weekday, date; hour, quarter-hour, and minute repeater
Diameter: 33.3 mm
Height: 7.9 mm
Jewels: 40
Balance: glucydur
Frequency: 18,000 vph
Remarks: 602 components; Geneva Seal

Caliber 1731

Manually wound; single spring barrel, 65-hour power reserve
Functions: hours, minutes, subsidiary seconds; hour, quarter-hour, and minute repeater
Diameter: 32.8 mm
Height: 3.9 mm
Jewels: 36
Balance: glucydur
Frequency: 21,600 vph
Remarks: perlage on plate, beveled edges, bridges with côtes de Genève; Geneva Seal

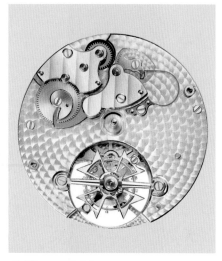

Caliber 2260

Manually wound, 1-minute tourbillon; single spring barrel, 336-hour power reserve; Geneva Seal
Functions: hours, minutes, subsidiary seconds (on tourbillon cage)
Diameter: 29.1 mm
Height: 6.8 mm
Jewels: 31
Balance: glucydur
Frequency: 18,000 vph

Caliber 1136 QP

Automatic; column wheel control of chronograph functions; single spring barrel, 40-hour power reserve
Functions: hours, minutes, subsidiary seconds; perpetual calendar with month, moon phase, leap year, weekday, date
Diameter: 28 mm
Height: 7.9 mm
Jewels: 38
Balance: glucydur
Frequency: 21,600 vph
Remarks: 228 components

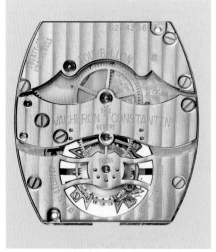

Caliber 2795

Automatic, 1-minute tourbillon; single spring barrel, 45-hour power reserve
Functions: hours, minutes, subsidiary seconds (on tourbillon cage)
Measurements: 27.37 x 29.3 mm
Height: 6.1 mm
Jewels: 27
Balance: glucydur
Frequency: 18,000 vph
Remarks: tonneau-shaped; Geneva Seal

Caliber 2460 QRA

Automatic; single spring barrel, 40-hour power reserve
Functions: hours, minutes, subsidiary seconds; annual calendar with date (retrograde) month, moon phase
Diameter: 26.2 mm
Height: 5.4 mm
Jewels: 27
Balance: glucydur
Frequency: 28,800 vph
Remarks: Geneva Seal

Caliber 2460 WT

Automatic; single spring barrel, 40-hour power
reserve
Functions: hours, minutes, sweep seconds; world-
time display; day/night indicator
Diameter: 36.6 mm
Height: 8.1 mm
Jewels: 27
Balance: glucydur
Frequency: 28,800 vph
Remarks: Geneva Seal

Caliber 1120 SQ

Automatic; single spring barrel, 40-hour power
reserve
Functions: hours, minutes
Diameter: 28.4 mm
Height: 2.45 mm
Jewels: 36
Balance: glucydur
Frequency: 19,800 vph
Remarks: entirely skeletonized and hand-engraved;
Geneva Seal

Caliber 4400SQ

Manually wound; single spring barrel, 65-hour
power reserve
Functions: hours, minutes
Diameter: 28.6 mm
Height: 2.8 mm
Jewels: 21
Balance: glucydur
Frequency: 28,800 vph
Remarks: entirely skeletonized and engraved by
hand; Geneva Seal

Caliber 2460 SCC

Automatic; stop-second system; single spring
barrel, 43-hour power reserve
Functions: hours, minutes, sweep seconds
Diameter: 26.2 mm
Height: 3.6 mm
Jewels: 27
Balance: glucydur
Frequency: 28,800 vph
Remarks: perlage on plate, beveled edges, bridges
with côtes de Genève; polished steel parts; gold
rotor of "Chronomètre Royale" type, Geneva Seal;
COSC-certified chronometer

Caliber 1003

Mechanical with manual winding; single spring
barrel, 31-hour power reserve
Functions: hours, minutes
Diameter: 21.1 mm
Height: 1.64 mm
Jewels: 18
Balance: glucydur
Frequency: 18,000 vph
Remarks: currently thinnest movement being
produced; Geneva Seal

Caliber 4400

Mechanical with manual winding; single spring
barrel, 65-hour power reserve
Functions: hours, minutes, subsidiary seconds
Diameter: 28.5 mm
Height: 2.8 mm
Jewels: 21
Balance: glucydur
Frequency: 28,800 vph
Remarks: perlage on plate, beveled edges, bridges
with côtes de Genève; Geneva Seal

Victorinox Swiss Army Watch S.A.

Chemin des Grillons 4
CH-2501 Biel/Bienne
Switzerland

Tel.:
01141-32-344-9933

Fax:
01141-32-344-9936

E-Mail:
info@victorinoxswissarmy.com

Website:
www.victorinoxswissarmy.com

Founded:
1884 / watches since 1989

Number of employees:
1,700

U.S. distributor:
Victorinox Swiss Army
7 Victoria Drive
Monroe, CT 06468
800-422-2706
www.swissarmy.com

Most important collections/price range:
Active, Classic, Professional / $325 to
$3,695

Victorinox Swiss Army

This brand with the Swiss cross in its logo is a real child of the years of rapid industrial expansion in central Europe. Today, it is as much a symbol for Switzerland as cheese and chocolate are. In 1884, the brand was founded as the cutler to the Swiss army, and in the over 125 years of its existence, the practical and versatile officer's knife known as the Swiss Army Knife has become a legend, especially in what has grown to be its main market: the United States. The Victorinox concern, which is a family enterprise, owns a handful of divisions, though, whose products all epitomize the principle of functionality coupled with style.

Perfect quality, high reliability, and consistent functionality also characterize this brand's watches and its business practices as well. Faced with a massive recession, CEO Karl Elsener saw to it that redundant employees had alternative sources of income till after the storm, while he opened new markets and developed new products, such as a line of suitcases and perfumes.

Since the purchase of its American branch, Swiss Army Brands, Inc. in 2002, the Victorinox concern has gone by the name Victorinox Swiss Army and has successfully begun to transfer the proverbial versatility and robustness of the practical pocketknives to its affordable watch line. The evidence can be found in the Infantry, Airboss, and Alpnach watches, which have emerged over the past several years and established themselves in the market. The Chrono Classic cleverly converts the watch's hour and minute hands into a chronograph with 100ths of a second displayed in the large-date window.

Chrono Classic

Reference number: 241656
Movement: quartz, ETA Caliber G10.211
Functions: hours, minutes, subsidiary seconds; chronograph; date
Case: stainless steel, ø 41 mm; sapphire crystal; water-resistant to 10 atm
Band: stainless steel, folding clasp
Price: $695

Infantry Mechanical

Reference number: 241646
Movement: automatic, ETA Caliber 2824-2; ø 25.6 mm, height 4.6 mm; 25 jewels; 28,800 vph; 38-hour power reserve
Functions: hours, minutes, sweep seconds; date
Case: stainless steel with golden PVD coating, ø 40 mm; sapphire crystal; water-resistant to 10 atm
Band: calf leather, buckle
Price: $750
Variations: quartz movement ($450)

Dive Master 500

Reference number: 241660
Movement: automatic, ETA Caliber 2894-2; ø 28.6 mm, height 6.1 mm; 37 jewels; 28,800 vph; 42-hour power reserve
Functions: hours, minutes, subsidiary seconds; chronograph; date
Case: titanium, ø 43 mm; unidirectional bezel with 60-minute divisions, sapphire crystal; transparent case back; screw-in crown and pusher; water-resistant to 50 atm
Band: titanium, folding clasp
Remarks: limited to 500 pieces
Price: $3,295

"*The History of Watches* . . . is a colorful and enlightening tour of the superb British Museum collection of rare timepieces . . . Illustrations as precise as the inner workings of the watchworks themselves offer a dazzling display of gold repousse cases, exquisite enameling, engraving and fretwork, as well as presenting the various technical innovations and variations."
—*Copley News Service*

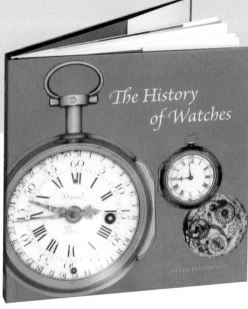

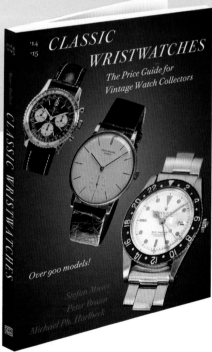

The History of Watches
Text by David Thompson
Photographs by Saul Peckham
Hardcover · $45.00
ISBN 978-0-7892-0918-4

Classic Wristwatches 2014–2015
By Stefan Muser and Michael Ph. Horlbeck
Paperback · $35.00
ISBN 978-0-7892-1143-9

ABBEVILLE PRESS
137 Varick Street, New York, NY 10013
1-800-Artbook (in U.S. only)
Also available wherever fine books are sold

Visit us at www.abbeville.com

Vogard SA
Oberer Kanalweg 12
CH-2560 Nidau/BE
Switzerland

Tel.:
01141-32-931-9000

Fax:
01141-32-931-9003

E-Mail:
discover@vogard.com

Website:
www.vogard.com

Founded:
2002

Number of employees:
5

Annual production:
approx. 500 watches

Distribution:
Please contact the company directly.

Most important collections/price range:
Timezoner / $7,250 to $31,000; Chronozoner / $13,500 to $17,500; Datezoner / $15,000 to $19,000

Vogard

In 2002, Michael Vogt founded his brand to create the "best travel watch there is." With the Timezoner, he turned his vision into reality. The brand quickly became a specialist in the design and production of mechanical world-time wristwatches.

According to Vogt, luxury objects must satisfy both emotional and functional needs. Accordingly, these objects must also offer real value in daily life—and they must be absolutely reliable when it comes down to the wire. Thus the time-measuring functions of the Chronozoner are simpler to operate than those of conventional chronographs thanks to a new arrangement of the control elements: The crown is positioned at 6 o'clock, while the start and stop buttons are found at 4 and 8, respectively. The Chronozoner also utilizes the ingeniously simple Vogard time zone setting mechanism: By opening a lever on the left side of the case and turning the bezel to the desired city, the time for that destination can be read; when the lever is closed, the watch is automatically set to the new zone. The skeletonized 24-hour hand identifies day and night. This system is not only exceptionally practical on trips; it can also be used to see the time in other parts of the world—for example, if the wearer wanted to make a phone call. The bidirectional bezel can be manipulated as much as the wearer likes without ever losing a second. The new Datezoner collection features a large date coupled to each time zone, so the correct date is displayed for each city.

Licensed Pilot

Reference number: LP 2634
Movement: automatic, Caliber Timezoner 01 (base ETA 2892-A2); ø 33 mm, height 5 mm; 21 jewels; 28,800 vph; patented bezel mechanism to adjust time zones
Functions: hours, minutes, sweep seconds; world-time display; date; day/night indicator
Case: stainless steel, ø 43 mm, height 14 mm; aluminum bezel with IATA airport codes, sapphire crystal; transparent case back; lateral activation and locking lever; water-resistant to 10 atm
Band: reptile skin, double folding clasp
Price: $8,250
Variations: rubber ($7,990) or stainless steel band ($8,750)

Chronozoner F1 Limited Edition

Reference number: CZ F161
Movement: automatic, Caliber Chronozoner CZ 1 (base ETA 7750); ø 36 mm, height 8.7 mm; 25 jewels; 28,800 vph; patented bezel mechanism to adjust time zones
Functions: hours, minutes, subsidiary seconds; world-time display; chronograph
Case: titanium, black carbide-coated, ø 48 mm, height 18 mm; stainless steel bezel with engraved racetracks, bidirectional time zone setting, sapphire crystal; transparent case back; activation/locking lever on case side; water-resistant to 5 atm
Band: alcantara, double folding clasp
Price: $15,500; limited to 99 pieces

Datezoner

Reference number: DZ 6131
Movement: automatic, Caliber Datezoner 01 (base ETA 7750); ø 36 mm, height 8.7 mm; 25 jewels; 28,800 vph; patented bezel mechanism to adjust time zone and date
Functions: hours, minutes, subsidiary seconds; world-time display; day/night indicator; chronograph; date
Case: titanium, ø 48 mm, height 18 mm; bidirectional stainless steel bezel sets time zone and date, sapphire crystal; transparent case back; activation and safety lever at edge of case; water-resistant to 5 atm
Band: reptile skin, double folding clasp
Price: $16,000

Vostok-Europe

Vostok-Europe is a young brand with old roots. In 2014, it celebrated its tenth anniversary.

What started as a joint venture between the original Vostok company—a wholly separate entity—deep in the heart of Russia and a start-up in the newly minted European Union member nation of Lithuania, has grown into something altogether different over the years. Originally, every Vostok-Europe model had a proprietary Russian engine, a 32-jewel automatic built by Vostok in Russia. Over the years, demand and the need for alternative complications expanded the portfolio of movements to include Swiss and Japanese ones. While the heritage of the eighty-year Russian watch industry is still evident in the inspirations and designs of Vostok-Europe, the watches built today have become favorites of extreme athletes the world over.

"Real people doing real things," is the mantra that Igor Zubovskij, managing director of the company, often repeats. "We don't use models to market our watches. Only real people test our watches in many different conditions."

That community of "real people" includes cross-country drivers on the Dakar Rally, one of the most famous aerobatic pilots in the world, a team of spelunkers who literally went to the bottom of the world in the Krubera Cave, and world free-diving champions. Much of the Vostok-Europe line is of professional dive quality. For illumination, some models incorporate tritium tube technology, which offers about twenty-five years of constant lighting. The Lunokhod 2, the current flagship of the brand, incorporates vertical tubes in a "candleholder" design for full 360-degree illumination.

The watches are assembled in Vilnius, Lithuania, and Zubvoskij still personally oversees quality control operations. The Mriya, named after the world's largest airplane, will be the first watch in the world to carry the new Seiko NE88 column wheel chronograph movement.

Koliz Vostok Co. Ltd.
Naugarduko 41
LT-03227 Vilnius
Lithuania

Tel.:
011370-5-210-6342

Fax:
011370-4-213-0777

E-Mail:
info@vostok-europe.com

Website:
www.vostok-europe.com

Founded:
2003

Number of employees:
24

Annual production:
30,000 watches

U.S. distributor:
Vostok-Europe
Détente Watch Group
244 Upton Road, Suite 4
Colchester, CT 06415
877-486-7865
www.detentewatches.com

Most important collections/price range:
Anchar collection / starting at $759; Mriya / starting at $649

Lunokhod 2 Automatic "Tritium Gaslight"

Reference number: NH35A-625210
Movement: automatic, Seiko Caliber NR35; ø 26.6 mm, height 5.32 mm; 24 jewels, 21,600 vph
Functions: hours, minutes, sweep seconds; date
Case: stainless steel, ø 49 mm, height 15.5 mm; unidirectional bezel with 60-minute divisions, mineral glass; water-resistant to 30 atm, helium release valve
Band: silicon, buckle
Remarks: with 2nd calf-leather band
Price: $899

Ekranoplan

Reference number: 2432.01-5455107
Movement: automatic, Vostok Caliber 2432.01 (base Vostok 2416/B); ø 24 mm, height 6.3 mm; 31 jewels; 18,000 vph; 31-hour power reserve
Functions: hours, minutes, sweep seconds; date; day/night display; 24-hour display
Case: black PVD-coated stainless steel, ø 47 mm, height 15.5 mm; unidirectional bezel with 60-minute divisions, K1 mineral crystal; transparent case back; screw-in crown; water-resistant to 20 atm
Band: silicon, buckle
Price: $749

Anchar "Tritium Gas Light"

Reference number: NH35/5105141
Movement: automatic, Seiko Caliber 35A; ø 27.4 mm, height 5.32 mm; 24 jewels, 21,600 vph; 45-hour power reserve
Functions: hours, minutes, sweep seconds; date
Case: stainless steel, ø 48 mm, height 15.5 mm; unidirectional bezel with 60-minute divisions, K1 mineral glass; screw-in crown; water-resistant to 30 atm
Band: rubber, buckle
Remarks: with calf-leather band
Price: $759

Expedition North Pole – 1

Reference number: 2432-5955192
Movement: automatic, Vostok Caliber 2432;
ø 24 mm, height 4.14 mm; 32 jewels; 19,800 vph;
38-hour power reserve
Functions: hours, minutes, sweep seconds; date;
24-hour disc and day/night indicator
Case: stainless steel, ø 48 mm, height 18 mm;
K1 mineral glass; transparent case back; water-
resistant to 20 atm
Band: leather, buckle
Remarks: with calf-leather band
Price: $499

GAZ Limo Watch

Reference number: NH35A-5654140B
Movement: automatic, Seiko Caliber NH25A;
ø 27.4 mm, height 5.32 mm; 21 jewels; 21,600 vph;
41-hour power reserve
Functions: hours, minutes, sweep seconds; date
Case: black PVD-coated stainless steel, ø 45 mm,
height 15 mm; K1 mineral glass; screw-in crown;
water-resistant to 5 atm
Band: black PVD-coated stainless steel, double
folding clasp
Remarks: "Trigalight" constant tritium illumination
Price: $749; limited and numbered edition

N1 Rocket Watch

Reference number: NH35A-2255149
Movement: automatic, Seiko Caliber NH35;
ø 27.4 mm, height 5.32 mm; 21 jewels; 21,600 vph;
41-hour power reserve
Functions: hours, minutes, sweep seconds; date
Case: stainless steel, ø 46 mm, height 15 mm;
unidirectional bezel with 60-minute divisions, K1
mineral glass; screw-in crown; water-resistant to
20 atm
Band: silicon strap, buckle
Remarks: "Trigalight" constant tritium illumination
Price: $549

Big Z Lunokhod 2 "For the World's Strongest Man"

Reference number: NH35A/6205344
Movement: automatic, Seiko Caliber NR35;
ø 26.6 mm, height 5.32 mm; 24 jewels, 21,600 vph
Functions: hours, minutes, sweep seconds; date
Case: stainless steel, ø 49 mm, height 15.5 mm;
unidirectional bezel with 60-minute divisions, K1
mineral glass; water-resistant to 30 atm
Band: silicon, buckle
Remarks: comes with 2nd calf-leather band
Price: $1,179

Mriya Column Wheel Chronograph

Reference number: NH35A/6205344
Movement: automatic, Seiko Caliber NE88;
ø 28.8 mm, height 5.32 mm; 24 jewels, 21,600 vph
Functions: hours, minutes, sweep seconds; date;
30-minute summing; 12-hour summing
Case: stainless steel, ø 50 mm, height 17.5 mm;
unidirectional bezel with 60-minute divisions, K1
mineral glass; water-resistant to 20 atm
Band: silicon, buckle
Remarks: comes with 2nd calf-leather band
Price: $2,249

Jurgis Kairys Pilot Signature Watch

Reference number: NH35A/5955334
Movement: automatic, Seiko Caliber NR35;
ø 26.6 mm, height 5.32 mm; 24 jewels, 21,600 vph
Functions: hours, minutes, sweep seconds; date
Case: stainless steel, ø 48 mm, height 18 mm; K1
mineral glass; etched case back with signature of
pilot; water-resistant to 20 atm
Band: leather, buckle
Remarks: comes with calf-leather band
Price: $539

Vulcain

In 1858, Maurice Ditisheim opened his own, high-quality pocket watch business in La Chaux-de-Fonds. Among the timepieces he produced were chronographs, a perpetual calendar, and a minute repeater. It was not until 1894 that Ditisheim gave his wares a brand name, Vulcain. After various name changes in the late 1800s and early 1900s, the company became Vulcain & Volta in 1911, Vulcain and Studio in the 1950s, and finally, simply Vulcain.

Ditisheim saw the potential of the wristwatch early on and soon began making various models with in-house calibers. The company's major turning point came at the 1947 World's Fair, where it presented its Cricket wristwatch. The aptly named timepiece with alarm, with its double soundboard that produced a loud, cricket-like chirp, was a huge sensation. The modern Cricket line banks on retro appeal—the love affair people have with the Western world of the 1940s and '50s, when work and money were plentiful after World War II. But Vulcain is also giving itself a face-lift under new CEO Renato Vanotti. Models like the cushion-cased, a touch gaudy, reedited Nautical Seventies are a reminder that the decade of disco wasn't too bad either. The Cloisonné series represents a bit of a break from the past, with bright enamel motifs in the middle of the dial.

Still, Vulcain's greatest claim to fame will always be that it became the unofficial brand of the U.S. Presidency—every commander in chief since Harry Truman has received his own engraved Cricket, with the exception of George W. Bush—earning the watch its nickname of "The Time Minister."

Manufacture des montres Vulcain S.A.
Chemin des Tourelles 4
CH-2400 Le Locle
Switzerland

Tel.:
01141-32-930-8010

Fax:
01141-32-930-8019

E-Mail:
info@vulcain-watches.ch

Website:
www.vulcain-watches.com

Founded:
1858

Number of employees:
20

Annual production:
5,500 watches

Distribution:
For sales information, contact Vulcain directly.

Most important collections/price range:
50s Presidents / from $3,450; Aviator / from $4,350; Nautical / from $5,400 ; Anniversary Heart / from $6,750

Aviator Instrument Chronograph

Reference number: 590163A17.BFC006
Movement: automatic, Vulcain Caliber V-59 (base Valjoux 7753); ø 30 mm; 27 jewels, 28,800 vph; skeletonized rotor; 48-hour power reserve
Functions: hours, minutes; chronograph; date
Case: stainless steel, ø 44.6 mm, height 15.4 mm; sapphire crystal; transparent case back; screw-in crown, water-resistant to 10 atm
Band: calf leather, folding clasp
Price: $4,350

50s Presidents' Moonphase

Reference number: 580158.328L
Movement: automatic, Vulcain Caliber V-58; ø 25.6 mm; 25 jewels; 28,800 vph; rhodium-plated; blued screws, côtes de Genève; 42-hour power reserve
Functions: hours, minutes, sweep seconds; full calendar with date, weekday, month, moon phase
Case: stainless steel, ø 42 mm, height 11 mm; sapphire crystal; transparent case back; water-resistant to 5 atm
Band: reptile skin, buckle
Price: $6,150
Variations: rose gold ($21,750)

50s President's Watch

Reference number: 110651.286L
Movement: manually wound, Vulcain Caliber V-11 (base Vulcain V-10); ø 28 mm, height 6.3 mm; 22 jewels, 18,000 vph; 2 spring barrels
Functions: hours, minutes, sweep seconds; alarm clock; date
Case: stainless steel, ø 42 mm, height 12.4 mm; rose gold bezel, sapphire crystal; transparent case back; rose gold crown and pusher; water-resistant to 5 atm
Band: reptile skin, buckle
Price: $10,400
Variations: stainless steel ($6,560)

Gerhard D. Wempe KG

Steinstrasse 23
D-20095 Hamburg
Germany

Tel.:
01149-40-334-480

Fax:
01149-40-331-840

E-Mail:
info@wempe.de

Website:
www.wempe.de

Founded:
1878

Number of employees:
500 worldwide; 35 at Wempe Glashütte i/SA

Annual production:
4,000 watches

U.S. distributor:
Wempe Timepieces
700 Fifth Avenue
New York, NY 10019
212-397-9000
www.wempe.com

Most important collections/price range:
Wempe Zeitmeister / approx. $1,000 to $4,500; Wempe Chronometerwerke / approx. $5,000 to $95,000

Wempe

Ever since 2005, the global jewelry chain Gerhard D. Wempe KG has been putting out watches under its own name again. It was probably inevitable: Gerhard D. Wempe, who founded the company in the late nineteenth century in Oldenburg, was himself a watchmaker. And in the 1930s, the company also owned the Hamburg chronometer works that made watches for seafarers and pilots.

Today, while Wempe remains formally in Hamburg, the manufacturing is done in Glashütte—a natural, since the company has long entertained a close relationship with the Saxon hub of horology. The workshops have been set up in the former Urania observatory and a factory in the Altenburgerstrasse.

But this does mean that the coveted Swiss COSC seal of approval is not an option, since the watches are of German provenance. So Wempe built its own chronometer testing site, which operates under the German Industrial Norm (DIN 8319) with the official blessings from the Saxon and Thuringian offices for measurement and calibration and accreditation from the German Calibration Service.

The Zeitmeister collection meets all the requirements of the high art of watchmaking and, thanks to its accessible pricing, is attractive for budding collectors. As for the production under the Wempe Chronometer logo (*Chronometerwerke*), this is the result of a partnership of ideas at the highest level. Both models were designed on the basis of an exclusive agreement with Nomos in Glashütte, where they are also built.

Chronometerwerke Tonneau Tourbillon

Reference number: WG 740001
Movement: manually wound, Wempe Caliber CW 2; 22.6 x 32.6 mm, height 6.5 mm; 19 jewels; 21,600 vph; 1-minute tourbillon; Breguet balance spring; sunburst pattern on bridges; rhodium-plated; DIN-certified chronometer
Functions: hours, minutes, subsidiary seconds
Case: platinum, 40.9 x 51 mm, height 13.7 mm; sapphire crystal; transparent case back
Band: reptile skin, buckle
Remarks: limited to 25 pieces
Price: $110,500

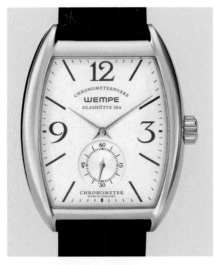

Chronometerwerke Manually Wound Tonneau

Reference number: WG 040008
Movement: manually wound, Wempe Caliber CW 1; 22.6 x 32.6 mm, height 3.6 mm; 23 jewels; 21,600 vph; 80 hours power reserve; DIN-tested chronometer
Functions: hours, minutes, subsidiary seconds
Case: yellow gold, 37 x 45.6 mm, height 10.2 mm; sapphire crystal; transparent case back; water-resistant to 5 atm
Band: reptile skin, buckle
Price: $12,100
Variations: stainless steel

Chronometerwerke Power Reserve

Reference number: WG 080005
Movement: manually wound, Wempe Caliber CW 3; ø 32 mm, height 6.1 mm; 42 jewels; 28,800 vph; three-quarter plate, 3 screwed-in gold chatons, hand-engraved balance cock, Glashütte stopwork; 80 hours power reserve; DIN-tested chronometer
Functions: hours, minutes, subsidiary seconds; power reserve indicator
Case: yellow gold, ø 43 mm, height 12.5 mm; sapphire crystal; transparent case back; water-resistant to 3 atm
Band: reptile skin, buckle
Price: $19,950
Variations: stainless steel ($8,500)

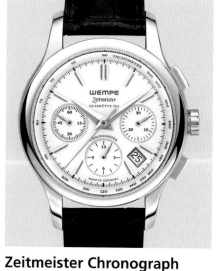

Chronometerwerke Power Reserve

Reference number: WG 080007
Movement: manually wound, Wempe Caliber CW 3; ø 32 mm, height 6.1 mm; 42 jewels; 28,800 vph; three-quarter plate, 3 screwed-in gold chatons, hand-engraved balance cock, Glashütte stopwork; 46 hours power reserve; DIN-tested chronometer
Functions: hours, minutes, subsidiary seconds; power reserve indicator
Case: stainless steel, ø 43 mm, height 12.5 mm; sapphire crystal, transparent case back; water-resistant to 3 atm
Band: reptile skin, buckle
Price: $8,500
Variations: yellow gold ($20,400)

Zeitmeister Chronograph

Reference number: WM 540001
Movement: automatic, ETA Caliber 7753; ø 30 mm, height 7.9 mm; 27 jewels; 28,800 vph; 42 hours power reserve; DIN-tested chronometer
Functions: hours, minutes, subsidiary seconds; chronograph; date
Case: stainless steel, ø 42 mm, height 15 mm; sapphire crystal, water-resistant to 5 atm
Band: reptile skin, folding clasp
Price: $3,110

Zeitmeister Moon Phase with Complete Calendar

Reference number: WM 350001
Movement: automatic, ETA Caliber 2892 with module; ø 25.6 mm, height 5.35 mm; 21 jewels; 28,800 vph; 42 hours power reserve; DIN-tested chronometer
Functions: hours, minutes, sweep seconds; full calendar with date, weekday, month, moon phase
Case: stainless steel, ø 42 mm, height 14.1 mm; sapphire crystal
Band: reptile skin, folding clasp
Price: $3,580

Zeitmeister Sport Diver's Chronograph

Reference number: WM 650009
Movement: automatic, Sellita Caliber SW500; ø 30 mm, height 7.9 mm; 25 jewels; 28,800 vph; 48 hours power reserve; DIN-tested chronometer
Functions: hours, minutes, subsidiary seconds; chronograph; date
Case: stainless steel, ø 45 mm, height 16.5 mm; unidirectional bezel with 60-minute divisions; sapphire crystal; screw-in crown; water-resistant to 30 atm
Band: stainless steel, folding clasp with safety lock and extension link
Price: $4,825

Zeitmeister Sport Diver's Automatic

Reference number: WM 650006
Movement: automatic, Sellita Caliber SW300; ø 25.6 mm, height 3.6 mm; 23 jewels; 28,800 vph; 42 hours power reserve; DIN-tested chronometer
Functions: hours, minutes, sweep seconds; date
Case: stainless steel, ø 42 mm, height 14.5 mm; unidirectional bezel with 60-minute divisions; sapphire crystal; screw-in crown; water-resistant to 30 atm
Band: stainless steel, folding clasp with safety lock and extension link
Price: $3,540

Zeitmeister Aviator Watch Chronograph XL

Reference number: WM 600005
Movement: automatic, ETA Caliber A07.211; ø 36.6 mm, height 7.9 mm; 25 jewels; 28,800 vph; 46 hours power reserve; DIN-tested chronometer
Functions: hours, minutes, subsidiary seconds; chronograph; date
Case: stainless steel, ø 45 mm, height 15.45 mm; sapphire crystal; water-resistant to 5 atm
Band: horse leather, folding clasp
Price: $3,580

Zeitwinkel Montres SA
Rue Pierre-Jolissaint 35
CH-2610 Saint-Imier
Switzerland

Tel.:
01141-32-914-17-71

Fax:
01141-32-914-17-81

E-Mail:
info@zeitwinkel.ch

Website:
www.zeitwinkel.ch

Founded:
2006

Annual production:
approx. 800 watches

U.S. distributor:
Tourneau
510 Madison Avenue
New York, NY 10022
212-758-5830
Also in Dallas, Costa Mesa, Las Vegas, and
Denver

Most important collections/price range:
mechanical wristwatches / starting at around
$5,500

Zeitwinkel

Timeless, simple, and sustainable—three attributes every watch manufacturer aspires to endow its creations with. Zeitwinkel models hew tightly to this perspective: The simplest of the company's offerings is a two-hand watch and the most complicated is a three-hand watch with power reserve display and large date. The dials are completely flat and marked with the company logo, a stylized "W." With their relatively heavy, steel cases designed by Jean-François Ruchonnet (TAG Heuer V4, Cabestan, among others), the watches look fairly "German," which comes as no surprise, because Zeitwinkel's founders, Ivica Maksimovic and Peter Nikolaus, hail from there.

The most valuable part of the watches is somewhat hidden, though. Behind the sapphire crystal backs tick veritable *manufacture* movements the likes of which are very rare in the business. The calibers were developed by Laurent Besse and his *artisans horlogers*, or watchmaking craftspeople. All components come courtesy of independent suppliers—Zeitwinkel balance wheels, pallets, escape wheels, and Straumann spirals, for example, are produced by Precision Engineering, a company associated with watch brand H. Moser & Cie.

In keeping with the company's ideals, you won't find any alligator in Zeitwinkel watch bands. Choices here are exclusively rubber, calfskin, or calfskin with an alligator-like pattern. "Gold cases are also taboo with us," says Nikolaus, "until we find a supplier who can guarantee that the gold comes from fair trade sources."

273° Galvano-black

Reference number: 273-41-0121
Movement: automatic, Caliber ZW0103;
ø 30.4 mm, height 8 mm; 49 jewels; 28,800 vph;
German silver three-quarter plate and bridges, côtes de Genève, beveled and polished screws and edges;
72-hour power reserve
Functions: hours, minutes, subsidiary seconds;
large date; power reserve indicator
Case: stainless steel, ø 42.5 mm, height 13.8 mm;
sapphire crystal; transparent case back; water-resistant to 5 atm
Band: calf leather, folding clasp
Price: $11,490
Variations: blue or silver dial; various strap options

181° Galvano-silver

Reference number: 181-22-01-21
Movement: automatic, Caliber ZW0102;
ø 30.4 mm, height 5.7 mm; 28 jewels; 28,800 vph;
three-quarter plate and bridges of German silver, côtes de Genève, beveled and polished screws and edges; 72-hour power reserve
Functions: hours, minutes, subsidiary seconds;
date
Case: stainless steel, ø 42.5 mm, height 11.7 mm;
sapphire crystal; transparent case back; water-resistant to 5 atm
Band: calf leather, folding clasp
Price: $7,490
Variations: black and blue dial; various bands

083° Galvano-blue

Reference number: 083-33-0123
Movement: automatic, Caliber ZW0102;
ø 30.4 mm, height 5.7 mm; 28 jewels; 28,800 vph;
three-quarter plate and bridges of German silver, côtes de Genève, beveled and polished screws and edges; 72-hour power reserve
Functions: hours, minutes, sweep seconds; date
Case: stainless steel, ø 39 mm, height 11.6 mm;
sapphire crystal; transparent case back; water-resistant to 5 atm
Band: calf leather, folding clasp
Price: $7,490
Variations: black, silver, and rhodium dials, various bands

Zenith

The tall narrow building in Le Locle, with its closely spaced high windows to let in daylight, is a testimony to Zenith's history as a self-sufficient *manufacture* of movements and watches in the entrepreneurial spirit of the Industrial Revolution. The company, founded in 1865 by Georges Favre-Jacot as a small watch reassembly workshop, has produced and distributed every possible type of watch over seven generations, from the simple pocket watch to the most complicated calendar. But it remains primarily associated with the El Primero caliber, the first wristwatch chronograph movement boasting automatic winding and a frequency of 36,000 vph. Only a few watch manufacturers had risked such a high oscillation frequency—and none of them in association with such complexity as the integrated chronograph mechanism and the bilaterally winding rotor of the El Primero.

That the movement even celebrated its fortieth anniversary, though, was thanks to the revival of the mechanical watch. After Zenith was sold to the LVMH Group in 1999, the label was fully dusted off and modernized perhaps a little too much. Eccentric creations catapulted the dutiful watchmaker's watchmaker into the world of *haute horlogerie*.

In 2009, Jean-Frédéric Dufour was made CEO. In the post-recession era, he placed his trust in tradition, reason, core horological values, and a real price-performance ratio—age-old virtues of Zenith. The leader of the comeback was the El–Primero-based Striking 10th. In 2014, Dufour moved to Rolex, leaving Zenith, now a healthy company again, in the hands of Aldo Magada.

Zenith SA
34, rue des Billodes
CH-2400 Le Locle
Switzerland

Tel.:
01141-32-930-6262

Fax:
01141-32-930-6363

Website:
www.zenith-watches.com

Founded:
1865

Number of employees:
over 330 employees worldwide

U.S. distributor:
Zenith Watches
966 South Springfield Avenue
Springfield, NJ 07081
866-675-2079
contact.zenith@lvmhwatchjewelry.com

Most important collections/price range:
Academy / from $82,700; Captain / from $3,200; El Primero / from $6,000; Pilot / from $5,400; Star / from $5,200

El Primero Chronomaster Power Reserve

Reference number: 03.2080.4021/01.C494
Movement: automatic, Zenith Caliber 4021 "El Primero"; ø 30 mm, height 7.85 mm; 39 jewels; 36,000 vph; partially skeletonized below regulator; 50-hour power reserve
Functions: hours, minutes, subsidiary seconds; power reserve indicator; chronograph
Case: stainless steel, ø 42 mm, height 14.05 mm; sapphire crystal; transparent case back; water-resistant to 10 atm
Band: reptile skin, folding clasp
Price: $9,800
Variations: black dial ($9,800); stainless steel bracelet ($10,300)

El Primero Chronomaster Power Reserve – Tribute to Charles Vermot

Reference number: 03.2085.4021/51.C700
Movement: automatic, Zenith Caliber 4021 "El Primero"; ø 30 mm, height 7.85 mm; 39 jewels; 36,000 vph; partially skeletonized under regulator; 50-hour power reserve
Functions: hours, minutes; power reserve indicator; chronograph
Case: stainless steel, ø 42 mm, height 14.05 mm; sapphire crystal; transparent case back; water-resistant to 10 atm
Band: reptile skin, folding clasp
Price: $9,800; limited to 1,975 pieces

El Primero Chronomaster 1969

Reference number: 03.2040.4061/69.C496
Movement: automatic, Zenith Caliber 4061 "El Primero"; ø 30 mm, height 6.6 mm; 31 jewels; 36,000 vph; 50-hour power reserve
Functions: hours, minutes; chronograph
Case: stainless steel (special alloy), ø 42 mm, height 13 mm; sapphire crystal; transparent case back; water-resistant to 10 atm
Band: reptile skin, folding clasp
Price: $9,800
Variations: rose gold ($21,600)

El Primero Chronomaster Open Grande Date

Reference number: 03.2160.4047/01.C713
Movement: automatic, Zenith Caliber 4047 "El Primero"; ø 30.5 mm, height 9.05 mm; 32 jewels; 36,000 vph; 50-hour power reserve
Functions: hours, minutes, subsidiary seconds; chronograph; large date; sun and moon phase displays (integrated day/night indication)
Case: stainless steel, ø 45 mm, height 15.6 mm; sapphire crystal; transparent case back; water-resistant to 5 atm
Band: reptile skin, folding clasp
Price: $13,100
Variations: black dial; rose gold ($28,500)

El Primero 36,000 VpH 1969

Reference number: 03.2040.400/69.C494
Movement: automatic, Zenith Caliber 400B "El Primero"; ø 30 mm, height 6.6 mm; 31 jewels; 36,000 vph; 50-hour power reserve
Functions: hours, minutes, subsidiary seconds; chronograph; date
Case: stainless steel, ø 42 mm, height 12.75 mm; sapphire crystal; transparent case back; water-resistant to 10 atm
Band: reptile skin, folding clasp
Price: $8,800

El Primero 36,000 1969 VpH

Reference number: 03.2040.400/69.M2040
Movement: automatic, Zenith Caliber 400B "El Primero"; ø 30 mm, height 6.6 mm; 31 jewels; 36,000 vph; 50-hour power reserve
Functions: hours, minutes, subsidiary seconds; chronograph; date
Case: stainless steel, ø 42 mm, height 12.75 mm; sapphire crystal; transparent case back; water-resistant to 10 atm
Band: stainless steel, folding clasp
Price: $9,000

El Primero 410

Reference number: 03.2091.410/01.C494
Movement: automatic, Zenith Caliber 410 "El Primero"; ø 30 mm, height 7.7 mm; 31 jewels, 36,000 vph; 50-hour power reserve
Functions: hours, minutes, subsidiary seconds; chronograph; full calendar with date, weekday, month, moon phase
Case: stainless steel, ø 42 mm, height 12.75 mm; sapphire crystal; transparent case back; water-resistant to 5 atm
Band: reptile skin, folding clasp
Price: $10,900
Variations: rose gold ($22,100)

El Primero Synopsis

Reference number: 03.2170.4613/01.C713
Movement: automatic, Zenith Caliber 4613 "El Primero"; ø 30 mm, height 5.58 mm; 19 jewels; 36,000 vph; partially skeletonized below regulator; 50-hour power reserve
Functions: hours, minutes, subsidiary seconds
Case: stainless steel, ø 40 mm, height 11.7 mm; sapphire crystal; transparent case back; water-resistant to 10 atm
Band: reptile skin, double folding clasp
Price: $6,000
Variations: stainless steel bracelet ($6,600); rose gold ($15,300)

El Primero Synopsis

Reference number: 03.2170.4613/01.M2170
Movement: automatic, Zenith Caliber 4613 "El Primero"; ø 30 mm, height 5.58 mm; 19 jewels, 36,000 vph; partially skeletonized under regulator; 50-hour power reserve
Functions: hours, minutes, subsidiary seconds
Case: stainless steel, ø 40 mm, height 11.7 mm; sapphire crystal; transparent case back; water-resistant to 10 atm
Band: stainless steel, double folding clasp
Price: $6,600
Variations: reptile skin band ($6,000)

El Primero Lightweight

Reference number: 10.2260.400/69.R573
Movement: automatic, Zenith Caliber 400B "El Primero" Titanium; ø 30 mm, height 6.6 mm; 31 jewels; 36,000 vph; titanium plate and bridges, only 15.9 g; 50-hour power reserve
Functions: hours, minutes, subsidiary seconds; chronograph; date
Case: aluminum/carbon composite; ø 45 mm, height 13.2 mm; sapphire crystal; transparent case back; titanium crown and pushers; water-resistant to 10 atm
Band: rubber with textile covering, double folding clasp
Price: $19,200; limited to 250 pieces

Captain Moonphase

Reference number: 03.2143.691/02.C498
Movement: automatic, Zenith Caliber 691 "Elite"; ø 25.6 mm, height 5.67 mm; 27 jewels; 28,800 vph; 50-hour power reserve
Functions: hours, minutes, subsidiary seconds; moon phase
Case: stainless steel, ø 40 mm, height 8.9 mm; sapphire crystal; transparent case back; water-resistant to 5 atm
Band: reptile skin, buckle
Remarks: rhodium-plated indices and hands
Price: $7,800
Variations: rose gold ($15,400)

Captain Power Reserve

Reference number: 03.2122.685/21.C493
Movement: automatic, Zenith Caliber 685 "Elite"; ø 25.6 mm, height 4.67 mm; 38 jewels; 28,800 vph; 50-hour power reserve
Functions: hours, minutes, subsidiary seconds; power reserve indicator; date
Case: stainless steel, ø 40 mm, height 9.25 mm; sapphire crystal; transparent case back; water-resistant to 5 atm
Band: reptile skin, buckle
Price: $6,500
Variations: rose gold ($14,100); white gold ($14,100)

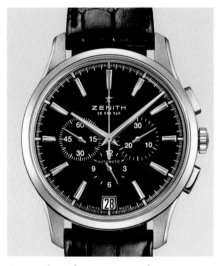

Captain Chronograph

Reference number: 03.2110.400/22.C493
Movement: automatic, Zenith Caliber 400B "El Primero"; ø 30 mm, height 6.6 mm; 31 jewels; 36,000 vph; 50-hour power reserve
Functions: hours, minutes, subsidiary seconds; chronograph; date
Case: stainless steel, ø 42 mm, height 12 mm; sapphire crystal; transparent case back; water-resistant to 5 atm
Band: reptile skin, folding clasp
Price: $8,500
Variations: rose gold ($17,800)

Captain Central Second

Reference number: 03.2020.670/22.C498
Movement: automatic, Zenith Caliber 670 "Elite"; ø 25.6 mm, height 3.47 mm; 27 jewels; 28,800 vph; 50-hour power reserve
Functions: hours, minutes, sweep seconds; date
Case: stainless steel, ø 40 mm, height 8.15 mm; sapphire crystal; transparent case back; water-resistant to 5 atm
Band: reptile skin, folding clasp
Price: $5,800

Captain Winsor Annual Calendar

Reference number: 18.2070.4054/02.C711
Movement: automatic, Zenith Caliber 4054 "El Primero"; ø 30 mm, height 8.3 mm; 29 jewels; 36,000 vph; 50-hour power reserve
Functions: hours, minutes, subsidiary seconds; chronograph; annual calendar with date, weekday, month
Case: rose gold, ø 42 mm, height 13.85 mm; sapphire crystal; transparent case back; water-resistant to 5 atm
Band: reptile skin, buckle
Price: $22,200
Variations: stainless steel ($10,700)

Heritage Ultra Thin

Reference number: 03.2010.681/01.C493
Movement: automatic, Zenith Caliber 681 "Elite";
ø 25.6 mm, height 3.47 mm; 27 jewels; 28,800 vph
Functions: hours, minutes, subsidiary seconds
Case: stainless steel, ø 40 mm, height 8.3 mm;
sapphire crystal; transparent case back; water-
resistant to 5 atm
Band: reptile skin, buckle
Price: $5,300
Variations: silver, black, or white lacquered dial
($5,300)

Pilot Doublematic

Reference number: 03.2400.4046/21.C721
Movement: automatic, Zenith Caliber 4046 "El
Primero"; ø 30 mm, height 9.05 mm; 41 jewels;
36,000 vph; 50-hour power reserve
Functions: hours, minutes; world-time display (2nd
time zone); alarm clock with display of functions and
power reserve; chronograph; large date
Case: stainless steel, ø 45 mm, height 15.6 mm;
crown rotates inner bezel with reference city names;
sapphire crystal; transparent case back; water-
resistant to 5 atm
Band: reptile skin, folding clasp
Price: $16,400
Variations: rose gold ($31,900)

Pilot Big Date Special

Reference number: 03.2410.4010/21.M2410
Movement: automatic, Zenith Caliber 4010 "El
Primero"; ø 30 mm, height 7.65 mm; 31 jewels;
36,000 vph; 50-hour power reserve
Functions: hours, minutes, subsidiary seconds;
chronograph; large date
Case: stainless steel, ø 42 mm, height 13.5 mm;
sapphire crystal; transparent case back; water-
resistant to 5 atm
Band: stainless steel Milanese mesh, folding clasp
Price: $7,900
Variations: calf leather band ($7,600)

Montre d'Aéronef Type 20 GMT 1903

Reference number: 96.2431.693/21.C738
Movement: automatic, Zenith Caliber 693 "Elite";
ø 25.6 mm, height 3.94 mm; 26 jewels; 28,800
vph; 50-hour power reserve
Functions: hours, minutes, subsidiary seconds;
additional 24-hour display (2nd time zone)
Case: titanium with black DLC, ø 48 mm, height
15.8 mm; sapphire crystal; water-resistant to
10 atm
Band: calf leather, buckle
Price: $7,900; limited to 1,903 pieces

Montre d'Aéronef Type 20 Annual Calendar

Reference number: 03.2430.4054/21.C721
Movement: automatic, Zenith Caliber 4054 "El
Primero"; ø 30 mm, height 8.3 mm; 29 jewels;
36,000 vph; 50-hour power reserve
Functions: hours, minutes, subsidiary seconds;
chronograph; full calendar with date, weekday,
month
Case: stainless steel, ø 48 mm, height 15.8 mm;
sapphire crystal; water-resistant to 10 atm
Band: calf leather, buckle
Price: $11,300
Variations: rose gold/titanium ($19,700)

Montre d'Aéronef Type 20 40 mm

Reference number: 03.1930.681/21.C723
Movement: automatic, Zenith Caliber 681
"Elite"; ø 25.6 mm, height 3.47 mm; 27 jewels;
28,800 vph; 50-hour power reserve
Functions: hours, minutes, subsidiary seconds
Case: stainless steel, ø 40 mm, height 11.8 mm;
sapphire crystal; water-resistant to 10 atm
Band: calf leather, buckle
Price: $6,600

Caliber El Primero 410

Automatic; single spring barrel, 50-hour power reserve

Functions: hours, minutes, subsidiary seconds; chronograph; full calendar with date, weekday, month, moon phase

Diameter: 30 mm

Height: 6.6 mm

Jewels: 31

Balance: glucydur

Frequency: 36,000 vph

Balance spring: self-compensating flat spring

Shock protection: Kif

Caliber El Primero 4054

Automatic; single spring barrel, 50-hour power reserve

Functions: hours, minutes; chronograph; annual calendar with date, weekday, month

Diameter: 30 mm

Height: 8.3 mm

Jewels: 29

Balance: glucydur

Frequency: 36,000 vph

Balance spring: self-compensating flat spring

Shock protection: Kif

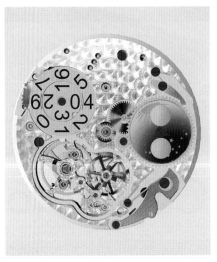

Caliber El Primero 4047

Automatic; single spring barrel, 50-hour power reserve

Functions: hours, minutes; chronograph; large date; display of sun and moon phases (integrated day/night indication)

Diameter: 30.5 mm

Height: 9.05 mm

Jewels: 41

Balance: glucydur

Frequency: 36,000 vph

Balance spring: self-compensating flat spring

Shock protection: Kif

Caliber El Primero 4057B

Automatic; single spring barrel, 50-hour power reserve

Functions: hours, minutes, subsidiary seconds; chronograph shows 1/10th of a second thanks to fast drive of chronograph hands (1 revolution every 10 seconds), totalizer for 6 revolutions; date

Diameter: 30.5 mm

Height: 6.6 mm

Jewels: 31

Balance: glucydur

Frequency: 36,000 vph

Balance spring: self-compensating flat spring

Shock protection: Kif

Caliber El Primero 400B

Automatic; single spring barrel, 50-hour power reserve

Functions: hours, minutes, subsidiary seconds; chronograph; date

Diameter: 30 mm

Height: 6.6 mm

Jewels: 31

Balance: glucydur

Frequency: 36,000 vph

Balance spring: self-compensating flat spring

Shock protection: Kif

Caliber Elite 681

Automatic; single spring barrel, 50-hour power reserve

Functions: hours, minutes, subsidiary seconds

Diameter: 25.6 mm

Height: 3.81 mm

Jewels: 27

Balance: glucydur

Frequency: 28,800 vph

Balance spring: self-compensating flat spring

Shock protection: Kif

Concepto

The Concepto Watch Factory, founded in 2006 in La Chaux-de-Fonds, is the successor to the family-run company Jaquet SA, which changed its name to La Joux-Perret a little while ago and then moved to a different location on the other side of the hub of watchmaking. In 2008, Valérien Jaquet, son of the company founder Pierre Jaquet, began systematically building up a modern movement and watch component factory on an empty floor of the building. Today, the Concepto Watch Factory employs eighty people in various departments, such as Development/Prototyping, Decoparts (partial manufacturing using lathes, machining, or wire erosion), Artisia (production of movements and complications in large series), as well as Optimo (escapements). In addition to the standard family of calibers, the C2000 (based on the Valjoux), and the vintage chronograph movement C7000 (the evolution of the Venus Caliber), the company's product portfolio includes various tourbillon movements (Caliber C8000) and several modules for adding onto ETA movements (Caliber C1000). A brand-new caliber series, the C3000, features a retrograde calendar and seconds, a power reserve indicator, and a chronograph. The C4000 chronograph caliber with automatic winding is currently in pre-series testing.

These movements are designed according to the requirements of about forty customers and at times heavily modified. Complicated movements are assembled entirely, while others are sold as kits for assembly by the watchmakers. Annual production is somewhere between 30,000 and 40,000 units, with additional hundreds of thousands of components made for contract manufacturing.

Caliber 2000

Automatic; column wheel control of chronograph functions; single spring barrel, 48-hour power reserve
Functions: hours, minutes, subsidiary seconds; chronograph; date
Diameter: 30.4 mm; **Height:** 8.4 mm
Jewels: 27
Balance: screw balance
Frequency: 28,800 vph
Balance spring: flat hairspring
Shock protection: Incabloc
Remarks: plate and bridges with perlage or côtes de Genève, polished steel parts and screw heads

Caliber 8000

Manually wound; 1-minute tourbillon; single spring barrel, 72-hour power reserve
Functions: hours, minutes
Diameter: 32.6 mm
Height: 5.7 mm
Jewels: 19
Balance: screw balance
Frequency: 21,600 vph
Balance spring: flat hairspring
Remarks: extensive personalization options for finishing, fittings, and functions

Caliber 8050

Automatic; 1-minute tourbillon; bidirectional off-center winding rotor; single spring barrel, 72-hour power reserve
Functions: hours, minutes
Diameter: 32.6 mm
Height: 7.9 mm
Jewels: 19
Balance: screw balance
Frequency: 21,600 vph
Balance spring: flat hairspring
Remarks: extensive personalization options for finishing, fittings, and functions

ETA

This Swatch Group movement manufacturer produces more than five million movements a year. And after the withdrawal of Richemont's Jaeger-LeCoultre as well as Swatch Group sisters Nouvelle Lémania and Frédéric Piguet from the business of selling movements on the free market, most watch brands can hardly help but beat down the door of this full service manufacturer.

ETA offers a broad spectrum of automatic movements in various dimensions with different functions, chronograph mechanisms in varying configurations, pocket watch classics (Calibers 6497 and 98), and manually wound calibers of days gone by (Calibers 1727 and 7001). This company truly offers everything that a manufacturer's heart could desire—not to mention the sheer variety of quartz technology from inexpensive three-hand mechanisms to highly complicated multifunctional movements and futuristic Etaquartz featuring autonomous energy creation using a rotor and generator.

The almost stereotypical accusation of ETA being "mass goods" is not justified, however, for it is a real art to manufacture filigreed micromechanical technology in consistently high quality,

illustrated by the long lead times needed to develop new calibers. This is certainly one of the reasons why there have been very few movement factories in Europe that can compete with ETA, or that would want to. Since the success of Swatch—a pure ETA product—millions of Swiss francs have been invested in new development and manufacturing technologies. ETA today owns more than twenty production locales in Switzerland, France, Germany, Malaysia, and Thailand.

In 2002, ETA's management announced it would discontinue providing half-completed component kits for reassembly and/or embellishment to specialized workshops, and from 2010 only offer completely assembled and finished movements for sale. The Swiss Competition Commission, however, studied the issue, and a new deal was struck in 2013 phasing out sales to customers over a period of six years. ETA is already somewhat of a competitor to independent reassemblers such as Soprod, Sellita, La Joux-Perret, Dubois Dépraz, and others thanks to its diversification of available calibers, which has led the rest to counter by creating their own base movements.

Caliber A07.111 Valgranges

Mechanical with automatic winding, ball bearing rotor, stop-seconds, power reserve 42 hours
Functions: hours, minutes, sweep seconds; quick-set date window at 3 o'clock
Diameter: 36.6 mm (16 3/4''')
Height: 7.9 mm
Jewels: 24
Frequency: 28,800 vph
Index system: Etachron with index correction
Related calibers: A07.161 (power reserve display)

Caliber A07.171 Valgranges

Mechanical with automatic winding, ball bearing rotor, stop-seconds, power reserve 42 hours
Functions: hours, minutes, sweep seconds; separately settable 24-hour hand (2nd time zone); quick-set date window at 3 o'clock
Diameter: 36.6 mm (16 3/4''')
Height: 7.9 mm
Jewels: 24
Frequency: 28,800 vph
Index system: Etachron with index correction

Caliber A07.211 Valgranges

Mechanical with automatic winding, ball bearing rotor, stop-seconds, power reserve 42 hours
Functions: hours, minutes, subsidiary seconds at 9 o'clock; chronograph (30-minute counter at 12 o'clock, 12-hour counter at 6 o'clock, sweep chronograph seconds); quick-set day and date window
Diameter: 36.6 mm (16 3/4''')
Height: 7.9 mm
Jewels: 25
Frequency: 28,800 vph
Index system: Etachron with index correction

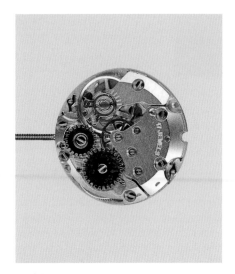

Caliber 2660

Mechanical with manual winding, power reserve 42 hours

Functions: hours, minutes, sweep seconds
Diameter: 17.2 mm (7 3/4''')
Height: 3.5 mm
Jewels: 17
Frequency: 28,800 vph
Fine adjustment system: Etachron

Caliber 1727

Mechanical with manual winding, power reserve 50 hours

Functions: hours, minutes, subsidiary seconds at 6 o'clock
Diameter: 19.4 mm
Height: 3.5 mm
Jewels: 19
Frequency: 21,600 vph
Fine adjustment system: Etachron
Remarks: based on design of AS 1727

Caliber 7001

Mechanical with manual winding, ultra-flat, power reserve 42 hours

Functions: hours, minutes, subsidiary seconds at 6 o'clock
Diameter: 23.3 mm (10 1/2''')
Height: 2.5 mm
Jewels: 17
Frequency: 21,600 vph

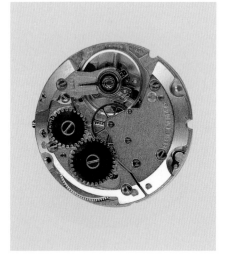

Caliber 2801-2

Mechanical with manual winding, power reserve 42 hours

Functions: hours, minutes, sweep seconds
Diameter: 25.6 mm (11 1/2''')
Height: 3.35 mm
Jewels: 17
Frequency: 28,800 vph
Fine adjustment system: Etachron
Related caliber: 2804-2 (with date window and quick set)

Caliber 6497

Only a few watch fans know that ETA still manufactures 2 pure pocket watch movements. Caliber 6497 (the so-called Lépine version with subsidiary seconds extending from the winding stem) and Caliber 6498 (the so-called hunter with subsidiary seconds at a right angle to the winding stem) are available in 2 qualities: as 6497-1 and 6498-1 (rather sober, undecorated version); and 6497-2 and 6498-2 (with off-center striped decoration on bridges and cocks as well as beveled and striped crown and ratchet wheels). The photograph shows Lépine Caliber 6497-2.

Caliber 6498

Mechanical with manual winding, power reserve 38 hours

Functions: hours, minutes, subsidiary seconds
Diameter: 36.6 mm (16 3/4''')
Height: 4.5 mm
Jewels: 17
Frequency: 21,600 vph
Fine adjustment system: ETACHRON with index
Remarks: the illustration shows a finely decorated hunter version like Nuremberg-based watchmaker Thomas Ninchritz uses

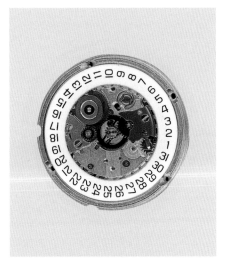

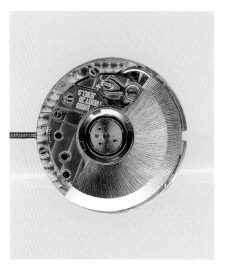

Caliber 2671

Mechanical with automatic winding, ball bearing rotor, stop-seconds, power reserve 38 hours
Functions: hours, minutes, sweep seconds; quick-set date window at 3 o'clock
Diameter: 17.2 mm (7 3/4''')
Height: 4.8 mm
Jewels: 25
Frequency: 28,800 vph
Fine adjustment system: Etachron with index
Related caliber: 2678 (additional day window at 3 o'clock, height 5.35 mm)

Caliber 2681 (dial side)

Mechanical with automatic winding, ball bearing rotor, stop-seconds, power reserve 38 hours
Functions: hours, minutes, sweep seconds; quick-set date and day window at 3 o'clock
Diameter: 19.4 mm (8 3/4''')
Height: 4.8 mm
Jewels: 25
Frequency: 28,800 vph
Fine adjustment system: Etachron with index
Related caliber: 2685 (sweep date hand and moon phase 6 o'clock)

Caliber 2000

Mechanical with automatic winding, ball bearing rotor, stop-seconds, power reserve 40 hours
Functions: hours, minutes, sweep seconds; quick-set date window at 3 o'clock
Diameter: 19.4 mm (8 3/4''')
Height: 3.6 mm
Jewels: 20
Frequency: 28,800 vph
Fine adjustment system: Etachron with index

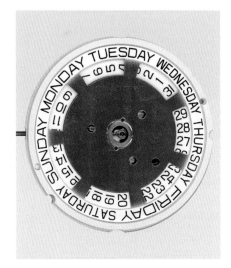

Caliber 2004

Mechanical with automatic winding, ball bearing rotor, stop-seconds, power reserve 40 hours
Functions: hours, minutes, sweep seconds; quick-set date window at 3 o'clock
Diameter: 23.3 mm (10 1/2''')
Height: 3.6 mm
Jewels: 20
Frequency: 28,800 vph
Fine adjustment system: Etachron with index

Caliber 2824-2

Mechanical with automatic winding, ball bearing rotor, stop-seconds, power reserve 38 hours
Functions: hours, minutes, sweep seconds; quick-set date window at 3 o'clock
Diameter: 25.6 mm (11 1/2''')
Height: 4.6 mm
Jewels: 25
Frequency: 28,800 vph
Fine adjustment system: Etachron with index
Related calibers: 2836-2 (additional day window at 3 o'clock, height 5.05 mm); 2826-2 (with large date, height 6.2 mm)

Caliber 2834-2 (dial side)

Mechanical with automatic winding, ball bearing rotor, stop-seconds, power reserve 38 hours
Functions: hours, minutes, sweep seconds; quick-set date window at 3 o'clock and day
Diameter: 29 mm (13''')
Height: 5.05 mm
Jewels: 25
Frequency: 28,800 vph
Fine adjustment system: Etachron with index

Caliber 2891-A9

Mechanical with automatic winding (base caliber ETA 2892-A2), ball bearing rotor, stop-seconds, power reserve 42 hours
Functions: hours, minutes, sweep seconds; perpetual calendar (hand displays for date, day, and month), moon phase disk, leap year indication
Diameter: 25.6 mm (11 1/2''')
Height: 5.2 mm
Jewels: 21
Frequency: 28,800 vph
Fine adjustment system: Etachron with index
Related calibers: 2890-A9 (without second hand and stop-seconds)

Caliber 2892-A2

Mechanical with automatic winding, ball bearing rotor, stop-seconds, power reserve 42 hours
Functions: hours, minutes, sweep seconds; quick-set date window at 3 o'clock
Diameter: 25.6 mm (11 1/2''')
Height: 3.6 mm
Jewels: 21
Frequency: 28,800 vph
Fine adjustment system: Etachron with index

Caliber 2893-1

Mechanical with automatic winding, ball bearing rotor, stop-seconds, power reserve 42 hours
Functions: hours, minutes, sweep seconds; quick-set date window at 3 o'clock; world time display via central disk
Diameter: 25.6 mm (11 1/2''')
Height: 4.1 mm
Jewels: 21
Frequency: 28,800 vph
Fine adjustment system: Etachron with index
Related calibers: 2893-2 (24-hour hand; second time zone instead of world time disk); 2893-3 (only world time disk without date window)

Caliber 2895-1

Mechanical with automatic winding, ball bearing rotor, stop-seconds, power reserve 42 hours
Functions: hours, minutes, subsidiary seconds at 6 o'clock; quick-set date window at 3 o'clock; world time display via central disk
Diameter: 25.6 mm (11 1/2''')
Height: 4.35 mm
Jewels: 30
Frequency: 28,800 vph
Fine adjustment system: Etachron with index

Caliber 2896 (dial side)

Mechanical with automatic winding, ball bearing rotor, stop-seconds, power reserve 42 hours
Functions: hours, minutes, sweep seconds; power reserve display at 3 o'clock
Diameter: 25.6 mm (11 1/2''')
Height: 4.85 mm
Jewels: 21
Frequency: 28,800 vph
Fine adjustment system: Etachron with index

Caliber 2897

Mechanical with automatic winding, ball bearing rotor, stop-seconds, power reserve 42 hours
Functions: hours, minutes, sweep seconds; power reserve display at 7 o'clock
Diameter: 25.6 mm (11 1/2''')
Height: 4.85 mm
Jewels: 21
Frequency: 28,800 vph
Fine adjustment system: Etachron with index

Caliber 2094

Mechanical with automatic winding, ball bearing rotor, stop-seconds, power reserve 40 hours
Functions: hours, minutes, subsidiary seconds at 9 o'clock; chronograph (30-minute counter at 3 o'clock, 12-hour counter at 6 o'clock, sweep chronograph seconds); date window at 3 o'clock
Diameter: 23.3 mm (10 1/2''')
Height: 5.5 mm
Jewels: 33
Frequency: 28,800 vph
Fine adjustment system: Etachron with index

Caliber 2894-2

Mechanical with automatic winding, ball bearing rotor, stop-seconds, power reserve 42 hours
Functions: hours, minutes, subsidiary seconds at 3 o'clock; chronograph (30-minute counter at 9 o'clock, 12-hour counter at 6 o'clock, sweep chronograph seconds); quick-set date window at 4 o'clock
Diameter: 28.6 mm (12 1/2''')
Height: 6.1 mm
Jewels: 37
Frequency: 28,800 vph
Fine adjustment system: Etachron with index
Related caliber: 2894 S2 (skeletonized)

Caliber 7750

Mechanical with automatic winding, ball bearing rotor, stop-seconds, power reserve 42 hours
Functions: hours, minutes, subsidiary seconds at 9 o'clock; chronograph (30-minute counter at 12 o'clock, 12-hour counter at 6 o'clock, sweep chronograph seconds); quick-set date and day window at 3 o'clock
Diameter: 30 mm (13 1/4''')
Height: 7.9 mm
Jewels: 25
Frequency: 28,800 vph
Fine adjustment system: Etachron with index
Related caliber: 7753 (tricompax arrangement of counters)

Caliber 7751 (dial side)

Based on chronograph Caliber 7750, Caliber 7751 differs in having 24-hour hand, moon phase indication, sweep date hand, and windows for day and month placed prominently below the 12. All calendar functions, including moon phase, can be quick set.

Caliber 7754 (dial side)

Mechanical with automatic winding, ball bearing rotor, stop-seconds, power reserve 42 hours
Functions: hours, minutes, subsidiary seconds at 9 o'clock; chronograph (30-minute counter at 12 o'clock, 12-hour counter at 6 o'clock, sweep chronograph seconds); quick-set date window at 3 o'clock; settable sweep 24-hour hand (2nd time zone)
Diameter: 30 mm (13 1/4''')
Height: 7.9 mm
Jewels: 25
Frequency: 28,800 vph
Fine adjustment system: Etachron with index

Caliber 7765

Mechanical with manual winding, stop-seconds, power reserve 42 hours
Functions: hours, minutes, subsidiary seconds at 9 o'clock; chronograph (30-minute counter at 12 o'clock, sweep chronograph seconds); quick-set date window at 3 o'clock; settable sweep 24-hour hand (2nd time zone)
Diameter: 30 mm (13 1/4''')
Height: 6.35 mm
Jewels: 17
Frequency: 28,800 vph
Fine adjustment system: Etachron with index
Related caliber: 7760 (with additional 12-hour counter at 6 o'clock and day window at 3)

Sellita

Sellita, founded in 1950 by Pierre Grandjean in La Chaux-de-Fonds, is one of the biggest reassemblers and embellishers in the mechanical watch industry. On average, Sellita embellishes and finishes about one million automatic and hand-wound movements annually—a figure that represents about 25 percent of Switzerland's mechanical movement production according to Miguel García, Sellita's president.

Reassembly can be defined as the assembly and regulation of components to make a functioning movement. This is the type of work that ETA loved to give to outside companies back in the day in order to concentrate on manufacturing complete quartz movements and individual components for them.

Reassembly workshops like Sellita refine and embellish components purchased from ETA according to their customers' wishes and can even successfully fulfill smaller orders made by the company's estimated 350 clients.

When ETA announced that it would only sell *ébauches* to companies outside the Swatch Group until the end of 2010, García,

who has owned Sellita since 2003, reacted immediately, deciding that his company should develop its own products.

García planned and implemented a new line of movements based on the dimensions of the most popular ETA calibers, whose patents had expired. Having expanded within a new factory on the outskirts of La Chaux-de-Fonds with 3,500 square meters of space, Sellita offers a number of movements—such as SW 200, which corresponds in all of its important dimensions to ETA Caliber 2824, and Caliber SW 300, equivalent to ETA Caliber 2892.

Another expansion project began as a joint venture with Mühle Glashütte: Gurofa in Glashütte currently makes some components for Calibers SW 220 and 240.

Caliber SW 200

Mechanical lever movement with automatic winding, ball bearing rotor, stop-seconds, power reserve 38 hours
Functions: hours, minutes, sweep seconds, date window with quick-set function
Diameter: 25.6 mm (11 1/2'''); **Height:** 4.60 mm
Jewels: 26; **Frequency:** 28,800 vph
Fine adjustment system: eccentric screw
Balance: nickel-plated for standard movement, glucydur on request
Balance spring: Nivaflex II for standard movements, Nivaflex on request
Shock protection: Novodiac
Remarks: base plate and rotor with perlage

Caliber SW 220

Mechanical lever movement with automatic winding, ball bearing rotor, stop-seconds, power reserve 38 hours
Functions: hours, minutes, sweep seconds, day/date window with quick-set function
Diameter: 25.6 mm (11 1/2'''); **Height:** 5.05 mm
Jewels: 26; **Frequency:** 28,800 vph
Fine adjustment system: eccentric screw
Balance: nickel-plated for standard movement, glucydur on request
Balance spring: Nivaflex II for standard movements, Nivaflex on request
Shock protection: Novodiac
Remarks: base plate and rotor with perlage

Caliber SW 300

Mechanical lever movement with automatic winding, ball bearing rotor, stop-seconds, power reserve 42 hours
Functions: hours, minutes, sweep seconds, date window with quick-set function
Diameter: 25.6 mm (11 1/2'''); **Height:** 3.60 mm
Jewels: 25; **Frequency:** 28,800 vph
Fine adjustment system: eccentric screw
Balance: nickel-plated for standard movement, glucydur on request
Balance spring: Nivaflex II for standard movements, Nivaflex on request
Shock protection: Novodiac

Rudis  Sylva

Harmonious Oscillator
THE TOURBILLON KILLER

Two complete toothed balances are interlinked.

This combination ensures the same amplitude.

The symmetry and energy of the balance springs are constantly opposed,
enabling instantaneous average correction in vertical position

WHICH ELIMINATES THE EFFECT OF GRAVITY!

www.rudissylva.com

Cadness

+1 646 416 1353

Soprod

Soprod, at home in Reussilles, Switzerland, has made a name for itself in the era of the mechanical renaissance by reassembling mechanical movements from ETA *ébauches*. Now the company also manufactures interesting display and function modules that can be added to a standard ETA caliber. Power reserve displays, dial train modifications for subsidiary seconds and regulators, calendar modules, and many other variations have given numerous small watch brands the possibility of adding value to their collections with somewhat more exclusive dials, thus setting themselves apart from other manufacturers.

ETA's announcement of no longer offering individual components or *ébauche* kits for reassembly after 2010 has thus hit Soprod especially hard.

In 2005, this company was purchased by a group of Swiss investors —and so came into direct contact with SFT (quartz movements) and Indtec (micromechanics and component production) in Sion, which also belonged to the same concern and already had automatic and chronograph movements developed to the serial production stage.

The Peace Mark Group, headquartered in Hong Kong, purchased all three companies in 2007 and began adding capacity, especially to the reassembly departments. At the same time, business with universally usable automatic calibers in the popular eleven-and-a-half-line format (such as ETA 2824 and 2892) is slated for expansion.

Surprisingly, at the end of 2008, the Festina Lotus Group, whose president also owns the H5 Group (Perrelet, Le Roy), formerly a minority shareholder, acquired Soprod's entire capital stock. Thus, Festina and the other companies belonging to that group have now also received a new platform base for Swiss-made mechanical watches. Soprod will continue to supply third-party brands.

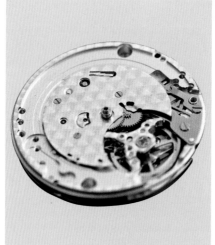

Caliber A10

Mechanical with automatic winding, stop-seconds, regulated in 4 positions, power reserve 42 hours
Functions: hours, minutes, sweep seconds, date window with quick-set function
Diameter: 25.6 mm (11 1/2''')
Height: 3.60 mm
Jewels: 25
Frequency: 28,800 vph
Fine adjustment system: index system with pinion
Balance spring: flat hairspring
Shock protection: Incabloc
Remarks: base plate available with various fine finishings

Caliber A10 Visible Balance

Mechanical with automatic winding, stop-seconds, regulated in 4 positions, power reserve 42 hours
Functions: hours, minutes, sweep seconds
Diameter: 25.6 mm (11 1/2''')
Height: 3.60 mm
Jewels: 25
Frequency: 28,800 vph
Fine adjustment system: index system with pinion
Balance spring: flat hairspring
Shock protection: Incabloc
Remarks: cutaway in base plate to make balance visible, base plate available with various fine finishings

Caliber A10 Red Gold

Mechanical with automatic winding, stop-seconds, regulated in 4 positions, power reserve 42 hours
Functions: hours, minutes, sweep seconds, date window with quick-set function
Diameter: 25.6 mm (11 1/2''')
Height: 3.60 mm
Jewels: 25
Frequency: 28,800 vph
Fine adjustment system: index system with pinion
Balance spring: flat hairspring
Shock protection: Incabloc
Remarks: red gold, base plate available with perlage, côtes de Genève or côtes circulaire; bridges with côtes de Genève

Tempting Timekeepers From Around The World

If you love the art and engineering of a fine timepiece, WristWatch Magazine is a must-read.

$49.00 (6-issues) for a one year subscription

From the rarest masterpieces, to popular trends, **WristWatch Magazine** will fan the flames of your watch passion. Famous brands will be joined by deserving up-and-comers on the pages of **WristWatch Magazine**. Education, collecting, watch news and events from around the world will come together on our pages to sharpen your watch knowledge and immerse you in the world of micro machines that are mechanical wristwatches.

ISOCHRON Media Llc

Publishers of: **WristWatch Magazine** and **AboutTime Magazine**
Office **(203) 485-6276** • E-mail **info@isochronmedia.com**

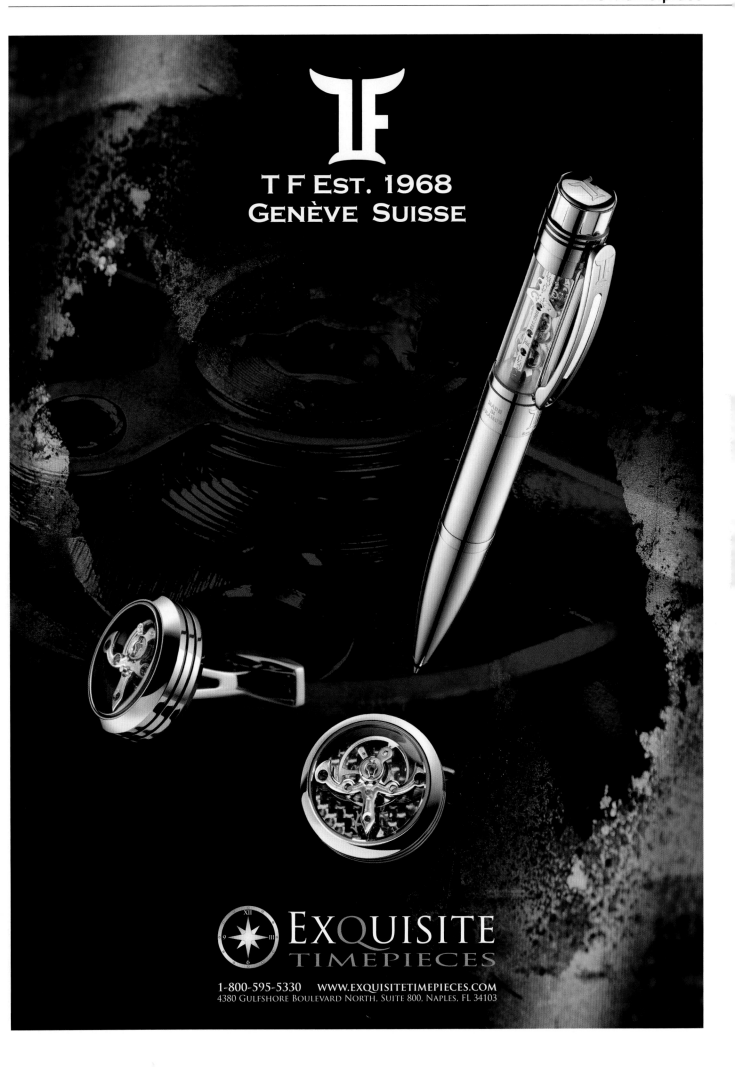

TF EST. 1968
GENÈVE SUISSE

EXQUISITE
TIMEPIECES

1-800-595-5330   WWW.EXQUISITETIMEPIECES.COM
4380 GULFSHORE BOULEVARD NORTH, SUITE 800, NAPLES, FL 34103

RITUALS OF TIME

Paleograph
The new mono-pusher
column wheel chronograph
from MeisterSinger

—

www.meistersinger.net

MEISTERSINGER

EXQUISITE
TIMEPIECES

Watch Your Watch

Mechanical watches are not only by and large more expensive and complex than quartzes, they are also a little high-maintenance, as it were. The mechanism within does need servicing occasionally—perhaps a touch of oil and an adjustment. Worse yet, the complexity of all those wheels and pinions engaged in reproducing the galaxy means that a user will occasionally do something perfectly harmless like wind his or her watch up only to find everything grinding to a halt. Here are some tips for dealing with these mechanical beauties for new watch owners and reminders for the old hands.

1. DATE CHANGES

Do not change the date manually (via the crown or pusher) on any mechanical watch—whether manual wind or automatic—when the time indicated on the dial reads between 10 and 2 o'clock. Although some better watches are protected against this horological quirk, most mechanical watches with a date indicator are engaged in the process of automatically changing the date between the hours of 10 p.m. and 2 a.m. Intervening with a forced manual change while the automatic date shift is engaged can damage the movement. Of course, you can make the adjustment between 10 a.m. and 2 p.m. in most cases—but this is just not a good habit to get into. When in doubt, roll the time past 12 o'clock and look for an automatic date change before you set the time and date. The Ulysse Nardin brand is nota-

Bovet's barrier to pressing the wrong pusher.

ble, among a very few others, for in-house mechanical movements immune to this effect.

2. CHRONOGRAPH USE

On a simple chronograph start and stop are almost always the same button. Normally located above the crown, the start/stop actuator can be pressed at will to initiate and end the interval timing. The reset button, normally below the crown, is only used for resetting the chronograph to zero, but only when the chronograph is stopped—never while engaged. Only a "flyback" chronograph allows safe resetting to zero while running. With the chronograph engaged, you simply hit the reset button and all the chronograph indicators (seconds, minutes, and hours) snap back to zero and the chronograph begins to accumulate the interval time once again. In the early days of air travel this was a valuable complication as pilots would reset their chronographs when taking on a new heading—without having to fumble about with a three-step procedure with gloved hands.

Nota bene: Don't actuate or reset your chronograph while your watch is submerged—even if you have one of those that are built for such usage, like Omega, IWC, and a few other brands. Feel free to hit the buttons before submersion and jump in and swim while they run; just don't push anything while in the water.

3. CHANGING TIME BACKWARD

Don't adjust the time on your watch in a counterclockwise direction—especially if the watch has calendar functions. A few watches can tolerate the abuse, but it's better to avoid the possibility of damage altogether. Change the dates as needed (remembering the 10 and 2 rule above).

4. SHOCKS

Almost all modern watches are equipped with some level of shock protection. Best practices for the Swiss brands allow for a three-foot fall onto a hard wood surface. But if your watch is running poorly—or even worse has stopped entirely after an impact—do not shake, wind, or bang it again to get it running; take it to an expert for service as you may do even more damage. Sports like tennis, squash, or golf can have a deleterious effect on your watch, including flattening the pivots, overbanking, or even bending or breaking a pivot.

5. OVERWINDING

Most modern watches are fitted with a mechanism that allows the mainspring to slide inside the barrel—or stops it completely once the spring is fully wound—for protection against overwinding. The best advice here is just don't force it. Over the years a winding crown may start to get "stickier" and more difficult to turn even when unwound. That's a sure sign it is due for service.

6. JACUZZI TEMPERATURE

Don't jump into the Jacuzzi—or even a steaming hot shower—with your watch on. Better-built watches with a deeper water-resistance rating typically have no problem with this scenario. However, take a 3 or 5 atm water-resistant watch into the Jacuzzi, and there's a chance the different rates of expansion and contraction of the metals and sapphire or mineral crystals may allow moisture into the case.

Panerai makes sure you think before touching the crown.

Do it yourself at your own risk.

7. SCREW THAT CROWN DOWN (AND THOSE PUSHERS)!

Always check and double-check to ensure a watch fitted with a screwed-down crown is closed tightly. Screwed-down pushers for a chronograph—or any other functions—deserve the same attention. This one oversight has cost quite a few owners their watches. If a screwed-down crown is not secured, water will likely get into the case and start oxidizing the metal. In time, the problem can destroy the watch.

8. MAGNETISM

If your watch is acting up, running faster or slower, it may have become magnetized. This can happen if you leave your timepiece near a computer, cell phone, or some other electronic device. Many service points have a so-called degausser to take care of the problem. A number of brands also make watches with a soft iron core to deflect magnetic fields, though this might not work with the stronger ones.

9. TRIBOLOGY

Keeping a mechanical timepiece hidden away in a box for extended lengths of time is not the best way to care for it. Even if you don't wear a watch every day, it is a good idea to run your watch at regular intervals to keep its lubricating oils and greases viscous. Think about a can of house paint: Keep it stirred and it stays liquid almost indefinitely; leave it still for too long and a skin develops. On a smaller level the same thing can happen to the lubricants inside a mechanical watch.

10. SERVICE

Most mechanical watches call for a three- to five-year service cycle for cleaning, oiling, and maintenance. Some mechanical watches can run twice that long and have functioned within acceptable parameters, but if you're not going to have your watch serviced at regular intervals, you do take the chance of having timing issues. Always have your watch serviced by qualified watchmaker (see box), not at the kiosk in the local mall. The best you can expect there is a quick battery change.

Gary Girdvainis is the founder of Isochron Media Llc., publishers of WristWatch and AboutTime magazines

Glossary

ANNUAL CALENDAR

The automatic allowances for the different lengths of each month of a year in the calendar module of a watch. This type of watch usually shows the month and date, and sometimes the day of the week (like this one by Patek Philippe) and the phases of the moon.

ANTIMAGNETIC

Magnetic fields found in common everyday places affect mechanical movements, hence the use of anti- or non-magnetic components in the movement. Some companies encase movements in antimagnetic cores such as Sinn's Model 756, the Duograph, shown here.

ANTIREFLECTION

A film created by steaming the crystal to eliminate light reflection and improve legibility. Antireflection functions best when applied to both sides of the crystal, but because it scratches, some manufacturers prefer to have it only on the interior of the crystal. It is mainly used on synthetic sapphire crystals. Dubey & Schaldenbrand applies antireflection on both sides for all of the company's wristwatches such as this Aquadyn model.

AUTOMATIC WINDING

A rotating weight set into motion by moving the wrist winds the spring barrel via the gear train of a mechanical watch movement. Automatic winding was invented during the pocket watch era in 1770, but the breakthrough automatic winding movement via rotor began with the ball bearing Eterna-Matic in the late 1940s. Today we speak of unidirectional winding and bidirectionally winding rotors, depending on the type of gear train used. Shown is IWC's automatic Caliber 50611.

BALANCE

The beating heart of a mechanical watch movement is the balance. Fed by the energy of the mainspring, a tirelessly oscillating little wheel, just a few millimeters in diameter and possessing a spiral-shaped balance spring, sets the rhythm for the escape wheel and pallets with its vibration frequency. Today the balance is usually made of one piece of antimagnetic glucydur, an alloy that expands very little when exposed to heat.

BAR OR COCK

A metal plate fastened to the base plate at one point, leaving room for a gear wheel or pinion. The balance is usually attached to a bar called the balance cock. Glashütte tradition dictates that the balance cock be decoratively engraved by hand like this one by Glashütte Original.

BEVELING

To uniformly file down the sharp edges of a plate, bridge, or bar and give it a high polish. The process is also called *anglage*. Edges are usually beveled at a 45° angle. As the picture shows, this is painstaking work that needs the skilled hands and eyes of an experienced watchmaker or *angleur*.

BRIDGE

A metal plate fastened to the base plate at two points leaving room for a gear wheel or pinion. This vintage Favre-Leuba movement illustrates the point with three individual bridges.

CALIBER

A term, similar to type or model, that refers to different watch movements. Pictured here is Heuer's Caliber 11, the legendary automatic chronograph caliber from 1969. This movement was a coproduction jointly researched and developed for four years by Heuer-Leonidas, Breitling, and Hamilton-Büren. Each company gave the movement a different name after serial production began.

CARBON FIBER

A very light, tough composite material, carbon fiber is composed of filaments comprised of several thousand seven-micron carbon fibers held together by resin. The arrangement of the filaments determines the quality of a component, making each unique. Carbon fiber is currently being used for dials, cases, and even movement components.

CHAMPLEVÉ

A dial decoration technique, whereby the metal is engraved, filled with enamel, and baked as in this cockatoo on a Cartier Tortue, enhanced with mother-of-pearl slivers.

CERAMIC

An inorganic, nonmetallic material formed by the action of heat and practically unscratchable. Pioneered by Rado, ceramic is a high-tech material generally made from aluminum and zirconia oxide. Today, it is used generally for cases and bezels and now comes in many colors.

CHRONOGRAPH

From the Greek *chronos* (time) and *graphein* (to write). Originally a chronograph literally wrote, inscribing the time elapsed on a piece of paper with the help of a pencil attached kind of hand. Today this term is used for watches that show not only the time of day, but also certain time intervals via independent hands that may be started or stopped at will. Stopwatches differ from chronographs because they do not show the time of day. This exploded illustration shows the complexity of a Breitling chronograph.

CHRONOMETER

Literally, "measurer of time." As the term is used today, a chronometer denotes an especially accurate watch (one with a deviation of no more than 5 seconds a day for mechanical movements). Chronometers are usually supplied with an official certificate from an independent testing office such as the COSC. The largest producer of chronometers in 2008 was Rolex with 769,850 officially certified movements. Chopard came in sixth with more than 22,000 certified L.U.C mechanisms like the 4.96 in the Pro One model shown here.

COLUMN WHEEL

The component used to control chronograph functions within a true chronograph movement. The presence of a column wheel indicates that the chronograph is fully integrated into the movement. In the modern era, modules are generally used that are attached to a base caliber movement. This particular column wheel is made of blued steel.

CONSTANT FORCE MECHANISM

Sometimes called a constant force escapement, it isn't really: in most cases this mechanism is "simply" an initial tension spring. It is also known in English by part of its French name, the *remontoir*, which actually means "winding mechanism." This mechanism regulates and portions the energy that is passed on through the escapement, making the rate as even and precise as possible. Shown here is the constant force escapement from A. Lange & Söhne's Lange 31—a mechanism that gets as close to its name as possible.

COSC

The Contrôle Officiel Suisse de Chronométrage, the official Swiss testing office for chronometers. The COSC is the world's largest issuer of so-called chronometer certificates, which are only otherwise given out individually by certain observatories (such as the one in Neuchâtel, Switzerland). For a fee, the COSC tests the rate of movements that have been adjusted by watchmakers. These are usually mechanical movements, but the office also tests some high-precision quartz movements. Those that meet the specifications for being a chronometer are awarded an official certificate as shown here.

CÔTES DE GENÈVE

Also called *vagues de Genève* and Geneva stripes. This is a traditional Swiss surface decoration comprising an even pattern of parallel stripes, applied to flat movement components with a quickly rotating plastic or wooden peg. Glashütte watchmakers have devised their own version of *côtes de Genève* that is applied at a slightly different angle called Glashütte ribbing.

CROWN

The crown is used to wind and set a watch. A few simple turns of the crown will get an automatic movement started, while a manually wound watch is completely wound by the crown. The crown is also used for the setting of various functions, almost always including at least the hours, minutes, seconds, and date. A screwed-down crown like the one on the TAG Heuer Aquagraph pictured here can be tightened to prevent water entering the case or any mishaps while performing extreme sports such as diving.

EQUATION OF TIME

The mean time that we use to keep track of the passing of the day (24 hours evenly divided into minutes and seconds) is not equal to true solar time. The equation of time is a complication devised to show the difference between the mean time shown on one's wristwatch and the time the sun dictates. The Équation Marchante by Blancpain very legibly indicates this difference via the golden sun-tipped hand that also rotates around the dial in a manner known to watch connoisseurs as *marchant*. Other wristwatch models such as the Boreas by Martin Braun display the difference on an extra scale on the dial.

ESCAPEMENT

The combination of the balance, balance spring, pallets, and escape wheel, a subgroup which divides the impulses coming from the spring barrel into small, accurately portioned doses. It guarantees that the gear train runs smoothly and efficiently. The pictured escapement is one newly invented by Parmigiani containing pallet stones of varying color, though they are generally red synthetic rubies. Here one of them is a colorless sapphire or corundum, the same geological material that ruby is made of.

FLINQUÉ

A dial decoration in which a guilloché design is given a coat of enamel, softening the pattern and creating special effects, as shown here on a unique Bovet.

FLYBACK CHRONOGRAPH

A chronograph with a special dial train switch that makes the immediate reuse of the chronograph movement possible after resetting the hands. It was developed for special timekeeping duties such as those found in aviation, which require the measurement of time intervals in quick succession. A flyback may also be called a *retour en vol*. An elegant example of this type of chronograph is Corum's Classical Flyback Large Date shown here.

GEAR TRAIN

A mechanical watch's gear train transmits energy from the mainspring to the escapement. The gear train comprises the minute wheel, the third wheel, the fourth wheel, and the escape wheel.

GLUCYDUR

Glucydur is a functional alloy of copper, beryllium, and iron that has been used to make balances in watches since the 1930s. Its hardness and stability allow watchmakers to use balances that were poised at the factory and no longer required adjustment screws.

GUILLOCHÉ

A surface decoration usually applied to the dial and the rotor using a grooving tool with a sharp tip, such as a rose engine, to cut an even pattern onto a level surface. The exact adjustment of the tool for each new path is controlled by a device similar to a pantograph, and the movement of the tool can be controlled either manually or mechanically. Real *guillochis* (the correct term used by a master of guilloché) are very intricate and expensive to produce, which is why most dials decorated in this fashion are produced by stamping machines. Breguet is one of the very few companies to use real guilloché on every one of its dials.

INDEX

A regulating mechanism found on the balance cock and used by the watchmaker to adjust the movement's rate. The index changes the effective length of the balance spring, thus making it move more quickly or slowly. This is the standard index found on an ETA Valjoux 7750.

JEWEL

To minimize friction, the hardened steel tips of a movement's rotating gear wheels (called pinions) are lodged in synthetic rubies (fashioned as polished stones with a hole) and lubricated with a very thin layer of special oil. These synthetic rubies are produced in exactly the same way as

sapphire crystal using the same material. During the pocket watch era, real rubies with hand-drilled holes were still used, but because of the high costs involved, they were only used in movements with especially quickly rotating gears. The jewel shown here on a bridge from A. Lange & Söhne's Double Split is additionally embedded in a gold chaton secured with three blued screws.

LIGA

The word LIGA is actually a German acronym that stands for lithography (*Lithografie*), electroplating (*Galvanisierung*), and plastic molding (*Abformung*). It is a lithographic process exposed by UV or X-ray light that literally "grows" perfect micro components made of nickel, nickel-phosphorus, or 23.5-karat gold atom by atom in a plating bath. The components need no finishing or trimming after manufacture.

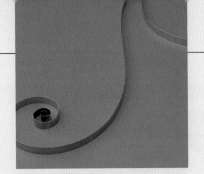

LUMINOUS SUBSTANCE

Tritium paint is a slightly radioactive substance that replaced radium as luminous coating for hands, numerals, and hour markers on watch dials. Watches bearing tritium must be marked as such, with the letter T on the dial near 6 o'clock. It has now for the most part been replaced by nonradioactive materials such as Superluminova. Traser technology (as seen on these Ball timepieces) uses tritium gas enclosed in tiny silicate glass tubes coated on the inside with a phosphorescing substance. The luminescence is constant and will hold around twenty-five years.

MAINSPRING

The mainspring, located in the spring barrel, stores energy when tensioned and passes it on to the escapement via the gear train as the tension relaxes. Today, mainsprings are generally made of Nivaflex, an alloy invented by Swiss engineer Max Straumann at the beginning of the 1950s. This alloy basically comprises iron, nickel, chrome, cobalt, and beryllium.

MINUTE REPEATER

A striking mechanism with hammers and gongs for acoustically signaling the hours, quarter hours, and minutes elapsed since noon or midnight. The wearer pushes a slide, which winds the spring. Normally a repeater uses two different gongs to signal hours (low tone), quarter hours (high and low tones in succession), and minutes (high tone). Some watches have three gongs, called a carillon. The Chronoswiss Répétition à Quarts is a prominent repeating introduction of recent years.

PERPETUAL CALENDAR

The calendar module for this type of timepiece automatically makes allowances for the different lengths of each month as well as leap years until the next secular year, which will occur in 2100. A perpetual calendar usually shows the date, month, and four-year cycle, and may show the day of the week and moon phase as well, as does this one introduced by George J von Burg at Baselworld 2005. Perpetual calendars need much skill to complete.

PERLAGE

Surface decoration comprising an even pattern of partially overlapping dots, applied with a quickly rotating plastic or wooden peg. (Here on the plates of Frédérique Constant's *manufacture* Caliber FC 910-1.)

PLATE

A metal platform having several tiers for the gear train. The base plate of a movement usually incorporates the dial and carries the bearings for the primary pinions of the "first floor" of a gear train. The gear wheels are made complete by tightly fitting screwed-in bridges and bars on the back side of the plate. A specialty of the so-called Glashütte school, as opposed to the Swiss school, is the reverse completion of a movement not via different bridges and bars, but rather with a three-quarter plate. Glashütte Original's Caliber 65 (shown) displays a beautifully decorated three-quarter plate.

POWER RESERVE DISPLAY

A mechanical watch contains only a certain amount of power reserve. A fully wound modern automatic watch usually possesses between 36 and 42 hours of energy before it needs to be wound again. The power reserve display keeps the wearer informed about how much energy his or her watch still has in reserve, a function that is especially practical on manually wound watches with several days of possible reserve. The Nomos Tangente Power Reserve pictured here represents an especially creative way to illustrate the state of the mainspring's tension. On some German watches the power reserve is also displayed with the words "auf" and "ab."

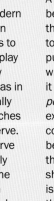

PULSOMETER

A scale on the dial, flange, or bezel that, in conjunction with the second hand, may be used to measure a pulse rate. A pulsometer is always marked with a reference number—if it is marked with *gradué pour 15 pulsations*, for example, then the wearer counts fifteen pulse beats. At the last beat, the second hand will show what the pulse rate is in beats per minute on the pulsometer scale. The scale on Sinn's World Time Chronograph (shown) is marked simply with the German world *Puls* ("pulse"), but the function remains the same.

QUALITÉ FLEURIER

This certification of quality was established by Chopard, Parmigiani Fleurier, Vaucher, and Bovet Fleurier in 2004. Watches bearing the seal must fulfill five criteria, including COSC certification, passing several tests for robustness and precision, top-notch finishing, and being 100 percent Swiss made (except for the raw materials). The seal appears here on the dial of the Parmigiani Fleurier Tonda 39.

RETROGRADE DISPLAY

A retrograde display shows the time linearly instead of circularly. The hand continues along an arc until it reaches the end of its scale, at which precise moment it jumps back to the beginning instantaneously. This Nienaber model not only shows the minutes in retrograde form, it is also a regulator display.

ROTOR

The rotor is the component that keeps an automatic watch wound. The kinetic motion of this part, which contains a heavy metal weight around its outer edge, winds the mainspring. It can either wind unilaterally or bilaterally (to one or both sides) depending on the caliber. The rotor from this Temption timepiece belongs to an ETA Valjoux 7750.

SCREW BALANCE

Before the invention of the perfectly weighted balance using a smooth ring, balances were fitted with weighted screws to get the exact impetus desired. Today a screw balance is a subtle sign of quality in a movement due to its costly construction and assembly utilizing minuscule weighted screws.

SAPPHIRE CRYSTAL

Synthetic sapphire crystal is known to gemologists as aluminum oxide (Al_2O_3) or corundum. It can be colorless (corundum), red (ruby), blue (sapphire), or green (emerald). It is virtually scratchproof; only a diamond is harder. The innovative Royal Blue Tourbillon by Ulysse Nardin pictured here not only features sapphire crystals on the front and back of the watch, but also actual plates made of both colorless and blue corundum within the movement.

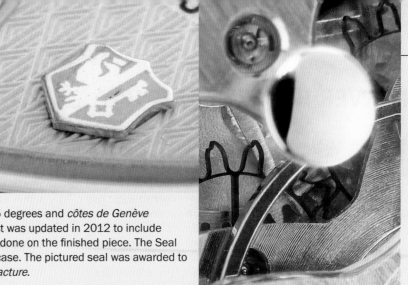

SEAL OF GENEVA

Since 1886 the official seal of this canton has been awarded to Genevan watch *manufactures* who must follow a defined set of high-quality criteria that include the following: polished jewel bed drillings, jewels with olive drillings, polished winding wheels, quality balances and balance springs, steel levers and springs with beveling of 45 degrees and *côtes de Genève* decoration, and polished stems and pinions. The list was updated in 2012 to include the entire watch and newer components. Testing is done on the finished piece. The Seal consists of two, one on the movement, one on the case. The pictured seal was awarded to Vacheron Constantin, a traditional Genevan *manufacture*.

SILICIUM/SILICON

Silicon is an element relatively new to mechanical watches. It is currently being used in the manufacture of precision escapements. Ulysse Nardin's Freak has lubrication-free silicon wheels, and Breguet has successfully used flat silicon balance springs.

SKELETONIZATION

The technique of cutting a movement's components down to their weight-bearing basic substance. This is generally done by hand in painstaking hours of microscopic work with a mini handheld saw, though machines can skeletonize parts to a certain degree, such as the version of the Valjoux 7750 that was created for Chronoswiss's Opus and Pathos models. This tourbillon created by Christophe Schaffo is additionally—and masterfully—hand-engraved.

SONNERIE

A variety of minute repeater that—like a tower clock—sounds the time not at the will of the wearer, but rather automatically (*en passant*) every hour (*petite sonnerie*) or quarter hour (*grande sonnerie*). Gérald Genta designed the most complicated sonnerie back in the early nineties. Shown is a recent model from the front and back.

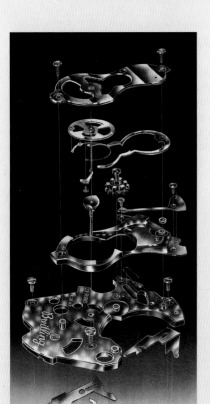

SPLIT-SECONDS CHRONOGRAPH

Also known in the watch industry by its French name, the *rattrapante* (exploded view at left). A watch with two second hands, one of which can be blocked with a special dial train lever to indicate an intermediate time while the other continues to run. When released, the split-seconds hand jumps ahead to the position of the other second hand. The PTC by Porsche Design illustrates this nicely.

SPRING BARREL

The spring barrel contains the mainspring. It turns freely on an arbor, pulled along by the toothed wheel generally doubling as its lid. This wheel interacts with the first pinion of the movement's gear train. Some movements contain two or more spring barrels for added power reserve.

SWAN-NECK FINE ADJUSTMENT

A regulating instrument used by the watchmaker to adjust the movement's rate in place of an index. The swan neck is especially prevalent in fine Swiss and Glashütte watchmaking (here Lang & Heyne's Moritz model). Mühle Glashütte has varied the theme with its woodpecker's neck.

TACHYMETER

A scale on the dial, flange, or bezel of a chronograph that, in conjunction with the second hand, gives the speed of a moving object. A tachymeter takes a value determined in less than a minute and converts it into miles or kilometers per hour. For example, a wearer could measure the time it takes a car to pass between two mile markers on the highway. When the car passes the marker, the second hand will be pointing to the car's speed in miles per hour on the tachymetric scale.

TOURBILLON

A technical device invented by Abraham-Louis Breguet in 1801 to compensate for the influence of gravity on the balance of a pocket watch. The entire escapement is mounted on an epicyclic train in a "cage" and rotated completely on its axis over regular periods of time. This superb horological highlight is seen as a sign of technological know-how in the modern era. Harry Winston's Histoire de Tourbillon 4 is a spectacular example.

VIBRATION FREQUENCY (VPH)

The spring causes the balance to oscillate at a certain frequency measured in hertz (Hz) or vibrations per hour (vph). Most of today's wristwatches tick at 28,800 vph (4 Hz) or 21,600 vph (3 Hz). Less usual is 18,000 vph (2.5 Hz). Zenith's El Primero was the first serial movement to beat at 36,000 vph (5 Hz), and the Breguet Type XXII runs at 72,000 vph.

WATER RESISTANCE

Water resistance is an important feature of any timepiece and is usually measured in increments of one atmosphere (atm or bar, equal to 10 meters of water pressure) or meters and is often noted on the dial or case back. Watches resistant to 100 meters are best for swimming and snorkeling. Timepieces resistant to 200 meters are good for scuba diving. To deep-sea dive there are various professional timepieces available for use in depths of 200 meters or more. The Hydromax by Bell & Ross (shown) is water-resistant to a record 11,000 meters.

Copyright © 2014 HEEL Verlag GmbH, Königswinter, Germany

English-language translation copyright © 2014 Abbeville Press,
137 Varick Street, New York, NY 10013

Editor-in-Chief: Peter Braun
Editor: Marton Radkai
Copy Editor: Ashley Benning
Layout: Muser Medien GmbH
Composition: Paul Aljian

For more information about advertising, please contact:
Gary Girdvainis
Isochron Media, LLC
25 Gay Bower Road, Monroe, CT 06468
203-485-6276, garygeorgeg@gmail.com

For more information about book sales, please contact:
Abbeville Press, 137 Varick Street, New York, NY 10013, 1-800-Artbook, or www.abbeville.com.

ISBN 978-0-7892-1202-3

Seventeenth edition
10 9 8 7 6 5 4 3 2 1

Library of Congress Cataloging-in-Publication Data available upon request.

For bulk and premium sales and for text adoption procedures, write to Customer Service Manager,
Abbeville Press, 137 Varick Street, New York, NY 10013 or call 1-800-Artbook.

Visit Abbeville Press online at www.abbeville.com.

ISBN 978-0-7892-1202-3 U.S. $37.50
5 3 7 5 0
EAN
9 780789 212023